Sandakan

A Conspiracy of Silence

Lynette Ramsay Silver

SALLY MILNER PUBLISHING

Dedication

*For the six who came home,
and the 2428 who did not.*

Acknowledgements

The author gratefully acknowledges all those who provided assistance, information, memorabilia and photographs, particularly the late Keith Botterill, Owen Campbell, Eric Davis, Frank Murray, the late Nelson Short, Jack Sue, Rod Wells and Billy Young; the Directors and staff at Australian Archives, The Office of Australian War Graves and the Australian War Memorial and especially Yoshi Tosa, who translated Japanese records. The author particularly recognises the generosity of Billy Young for his drawings, Jeff Harris and the ABC Archives, the encouragement of Maureen Devereaux and Frank Murray, the faith and support of publisher Sally Milner and the forbearance of her husband Neil Silver, who understood the importance of the project and whose unstinting and unselfish support made the researching and writing of this book possible.

Note: For place names, the spelling which appears on wartime maps has been used; for local people, that which is the most consistent.

First published in August 1998
Second edition November 1998

Sally Milner Publishing Pty Ltd
1423 Burra Road
Burra Creek 2620
New South Wales
Australia

© Lynette Ramsay Silver, 1998

Cover and text design by Anna Warren, Warren Ventures, Sydney
Maps by Anna Warren, Warren Ventures, Sydney
Printed and bound by Australian Print Group, Maryborough, Victoria, Australia

National Library of Australia, Cataloguing-in-Publication data:

Silver, Lynette Ramsay, 1945-
Sandakan. A conspiracy of silence.

Bibliography.
Includes index.
ISBN 1 86351 223 3.

1. Sandakan (Sabah : Concentration camp). 2. Prisoners of war — Malaysia — Sandakan (Sabah). 3. World War, 1939-1945 — Prisoners and prisons, Japanese. 4. Prisoners of war — Australia. I. Title.

940.547252

All rights reserved. No part of this publication may be reproduced, stored in a retrieval system or transmitted in any form or by any means, electronic, mechanical, photocopying, recording or otherwise, without prior written permission of the copyright holders.

Table of Contents

Prologue		4
Chapter 1:	Last Hope, Last Bastion	7
Chapter 2:	Selarang	20
Chapter 3:	To Sandakan	36
Chapter 4:	White Coolies	60
Chapter 5:	Living Dangerously	86
Chapter 6:	Comings and Goings	99
Chapter 7:	Disaster	118
Chapter 8:	Japanese Justice	136
Chapter 9:	'For The Duration'	155
Chapter 10:	A Plan Evolves	172
Chapter 11:	To Ranau	186
Chapter 12:	'Annihilate Them All'	208
Chapter 13:	'As The Situation Dictates'	229
Chapter 14:	And Then There Were Six	243
Chapter 15:	'And Not Leave Any Traces'?	258
Chapter 16:	'A Most Regrettable Business'	283
Epilogue		308
Chronological Sequence of Events		313
Appendix 1:	Nominal Rolls	317
Appendix 2:	Burial Table	357
Appendix 3:	Recovery of Relics	361
Appendix 4:	Corrupted Names	364
Appendix 5:	Wanted or Convicted War Criminals	365
Appendix 6:	Bibliography and Subject References	368
Endnotes		376
Index		380

PROLOGUE
Australian Archives, Melbourne
August 1995

I close the door and sit down. It is very quiet. Although the morning peak hour is not yet over, no sound penetrates here. Hermetically-sealed by the building's outer double-glazed windows, and further cocooned by the glass walls of the cubicle, my immediate world is far removed from the hustle and bustle of Lonsdale Street, only a few metres away.

I am quite alone. The sole archives officer on duty is occupied elsewhere, cut off from the main research room by a sliding glass screen, and there is no one else in sight. The feeling of isolation is heightened by the clean, uncluttered lines of my surroundings and the almost imperceptible whisper of cool, dehumidified air drifting down from the ceiling duct just above my head.

I have made the trip from Sydney to check details of the stories of several ex-prisoners of war. During World War 2 they were held at a camp at Sandakan, formerly British North Borneo, now known as Sabah. I do not doubt the integrity of these witnesses, but five decades have passed and time can play strange tricks with the memory — minimising or magnifying events and telescoping one into another. Although I have already isolated scores of investigation files, I have yet to locate a contemporary account of prison life, which may have been hidden by a prisoner during captivity and recovered from the camp after the war. I doubt that much of value has survived, but even a few cryptic notes will do — anything which might verify some of the events described by my eye-witnesses.

I turn my attention to the bundles of documents stacked randomly upon the desk. There are perhaps 30 or 40 in all, bringing the total I have examined so far to about 300. Some are very thick, their contents threatening to spill from dog-eared folders, the original labels now so faded as to be almost illegible. The contents of others, enshrouded in similarly-faded covers, are quite thin. I run my eyes more closely over the piles. While it is obvious that some of the papers have been examined previously, it is equally obvious that others have not. They have been untouched for more than 50 years and are in pristine condition, the outer covers immaculate and the inner sheets crisp and uncreased.

An envelope is perched on top of the stack closest to me. It is nothing special, just an ordinary, large, manila envelope of the type to be found at any stationers. I check the label and feel a pang of disappointment as I had hoped for something far more substantial than this. I undo the seal and retrieve the meagre contents. They are uninspiring — some small tatty pieces of paper, a few larger sheets covered in faded pencil scrawl, and a cheap, school exercise book.

Putting the papers to one side for the moment, I study the book. It's not much to look at. The cover, once a rich, glossy black, is now a lifeless, dull charcoal; the once-proud words, proclaiming it to be a Golden Eagle Series, 120-page and single-lined, the product of Peter Chong and Company, printers and booksellers, of Singapore, Malacca, Serembang, Kuala Lumpur, Ipoh, Penang and Branches, so faded they are barely discernible.

Carefully, I open the pages. They are filled with neat, well-formed and rounded handwriting, but the words are very difficult to read as the ink, although indelible, has faded. Great chunks of script are indecipherable on some pages, owing to damage by what appears to be a mixture of water and mud, while on others the words have disappeared altogether.

I begin reading and am immediately catapulted half a century back in time to enter the world of Private Tom Burns, NX72757, World War 2 infantry soldier. I follow Tom, a member of the Australian 8th Division's 2/20th Battalion, through the ill-fated Malayan campaign to the ignominious surrender of all Allied forces to the Japanese Imperial Army, following the fall of Singapore on 15 February 1942. He writes that he had not intended to continue his narrative any further but, as his captives have failed to find his diary despite numerous searches, has decided to take up his pen again, to record his experiences as a prisoner of war.

The voice of Tom Burns, now a prisoner of the Japanese, cuts across the void of 50 years and chills me to the bone. He has no next of kin. After expressing the hope that anyone who may happen one day to read his words will not be bored by them, Tom reveals the story of his life in captivity in the POW camp at Sandakan, British North Borneo, the same camp as my eyewitnesses. Even though some of his handwriting is no longer legible, his is not a tale for the faint-hearted, chronicling as it does the suffering, the desperation and the feeling of utter hopelessness which at times threatens to overwhelm him and his companions. And then, quite abruptly, on page 82, the narrative stops.

I flick through the remaining pages — notes on the Malayan Campaign, a dictionary of Malay words, much of it too faint to read — but there is nothing more. It is not until I discover a loose piece of scrap paper in the pile taken from the envelope that I find the last entry, written on Australia Day, 26 January 1945, many months later. Partly obliterated by mud stains, it has been inscribed on the back of two old pre-war bank cheques, which Tom had evidently scrounged when his paper ran out. The cheques themselves provide no clue as to how they came to be in his possession. The first, made out to an Asian firm, is signed by the Superintendent of Prisons, while the other, dated 1 December 1941, is that of the Minister for Customs and Excise, Government of North Borneo. The payee is a local European firm, trading as Harrisons and Crosfield Limited.

Tom, writing smaller than normal to fit his words into the precious, confined space, records:

> *We are only having two meals a day now. Dinner consists of a very small ladle of slurry and a ladle of tapioca stem. Tea is very poor also ... before long we will lose hundreds of men as they are now dying of starvation. Tea is at 5.30 and we have to wait until 12.30 the next day for our next meal. No hope...*

I replace the loose sheets and return to the diary, still lying open on the desk. The place where the scraps of paper containing Tom's entry had been inserted are clearly delineated by muddy water stains. But it is no longer just a diary, no longer simply corroborative evidence. It is my link to Tom Burns, an Australian soldier who went off to war long before I was born; a man full of life and vitality who, like many others, endured so much for so long; a man who, even in his darkest hours, managed to find the strength to leave a written record in the hope that someone, one day, would read it. Impulsively, I lift the mud-spattered pages to my face and inhale deeply.

I am totally unprepared for the assault upon my nostrils. Impregnated into the very essence of the paper, where it has lain for five decades waiting to be released, is that over-ripe smell of the jungle, that sickly, sweet aroma of decaying leaves, of damp and dank earth, of mould and rotting vegetation.

It is the smell of death. It is the smell of Borneo.

Chapter One
LAST HOPE, LAST BASTION

It was mid-afternoon. The bombardment which had begun at dawn had not let up and, to make matters worse, it was still raining heavily. Crouched in their flooded slit trenches, or behind totally inadequate breast works dug among mangroves and rubber trees, the Australians watched and waited, eyes red-rimmed and bloodshot from lack of sleep, watering with the strain of peering through the driving rain. The enemy too was watching and waiting, all 20 000 of them, on the other side of the narrow Straits of Johore. Described by military boffins in England as a splendid moat, this waterway was, in reality, a hopelessly inadequate barrier. The Australians were well aware, however, that it was the only thing separating them, and Singapore Island, from Japanese-occupied Malaya.

All, from the Australian Imperial Forces' (AIF) rawest recruit to the most battle-hardened soldier, knew this would be the decisive battle. The Japanese had steam-rollered their way down Malaya in a matter of weeks, overrunning battalions of poorly-trained British and Indian troops, some of whom had offered little or no resistance. Finally, after cutting a swathe through their opposing ranks with alarming speed, the invaders had come face to face with the Australians. Although the AIF, well-trained in jungle warfare, had put up a fierce and determined attack, stopping the enemy in its tracks, it had proved ultimately to be a lopsided contest. After days of nonstop bitter fighting the Japanese, in total command of the air and the sea, emerged victorious. Battered and bleeding, but nevertheless uncowed, the AIF had joined the exodus to the south.

On the last day of January 1942, only seven weeks after the initial landings hundreds of kilometres to the north, Japanese domination of Malaya was complete. The Allied armies could retreat no more. Protected by a rear guard composed of the Australians and what remained of a battalion of jungle-toughened Argyll and Sutherland Highlanders, they had trudged across the causeway linking the Malay peninsula to Singapore Island, their last hope, and the British Empire's last bastion.

The Australians, spread thinly across almost 20 kilometres of coastal terrain on the western side of the island, harboured no illusions about the job they now faced. The area assigned to them was a defensive nightmare — a mixture of tidal mud flats, swampy marshes, rubber plantations and heavily-vegetated hillocks — all fragmented and dissected by countless streams and inlets. Although they had been given the most difficult sector, it would not have been so daunting had there been proper coastal and beachhead defences. The Australians, who had heard about the invincibility of Singapore, had eagerly reconnoitred their positions on arrival, expecting to see massive concrete fortifications, anti-tank traps, weapons' pits, pill boxes and all the other paraphernalia so essential to defence. To their horror they found nothing — not even a strand of barbed wire.

The British military hierarchy and the inept local civil administration had ignored all evidence to the contrary, and clung, ostrich-like, to the fantastic myth that any assault on Singapore must come from the sea. With the island protected by an impressive array of gigantic guns ranged along the southern shoreline, and the mighty British navy standing by to sail to their assistance, Singapore was deemed impregnable to attack.

The destruction, by enemy aircraft, of the two great British naval ships, *Repulse* and *Prince of Wales*, off the coast of Malaya in early December, showed the fallacy of that theory. So too had the lightning-fast, land-born invasion by the Japanese over mountainous, jungle-clad terrain in the height of the rainy season — a time of year when such an attack was considered out of the question.

All but the most obtuse realised by early February that the enemy, having achieved the seemingly impossible, was in a winning position. Not only did the Japanese have vastly superior numbers of well-trained men, absolute control of Malaya, its airfields, its waterways, its resources and its people, they also controlled Singapore's water supply, piped across the causeway from Johore Bahru. Although there was a supply of fresh water stored at three reservoirs in the centre of the island, it would not last for long, even with careful rationing. Singapore's already substantial indigenous population was now well over 1 000 000, swelled by the hordes of homeless Indian, Malay and Chinese refugees who had streamed across the causeway, barely one step ahead of the rapidly-advancing Japanese. Frightened and bewildered, they now cowered in Singapore city, seeking shelter in bombed-out buildings, in the flimsy shanties of Chinatown or, for a lucky few, in bungalows hastily vacated by fleeing British residents.

It was now the eighth day of February. Scattered throughout the mangroves

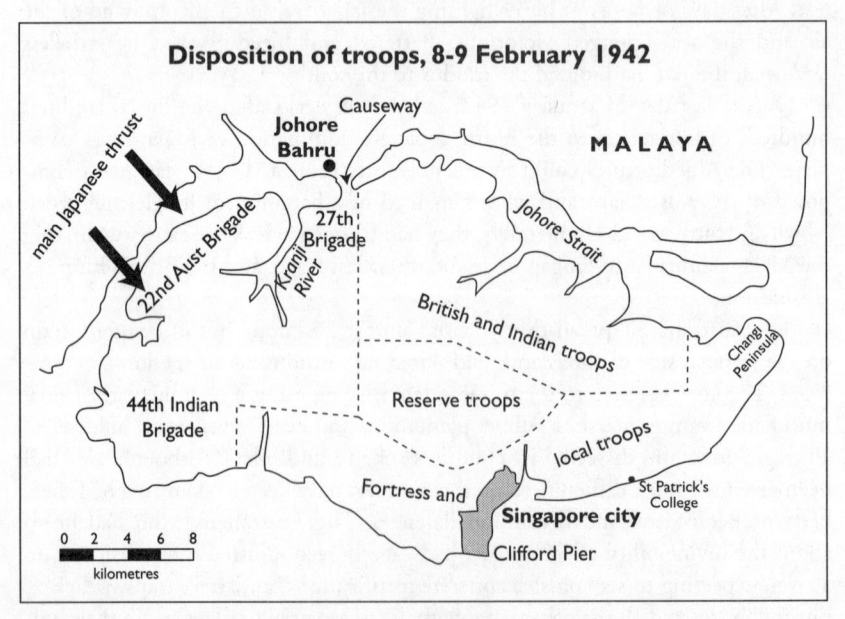

Map of Singapore Island, showing troop dispositions and key points.

on the north-west tip of the island, 23 kilometres away from the relative safety of Singapore city, 35-year-old Tom Burns and the rest of his 2/20th Battalion were dug in as best the swampy conditions would allow. So too were the 22nd Brigade's other battalions, the 2/18th and 2/19th, positioned further round to the south, on Tom's left. These three infantry units, along with a portion of the 2/4th Machine-Gun Battalion stationed in the most forward positions, were to bear the brunt of the attack.

Those occupying the foremost defensive positions of Tom's battalion were surrounded by mud and mangroves, virtually isolating Eric 'Mo' Davis and his company from the rest of the unit. Although only seventeen, Mo, who had seen action with the battalion at Mersing on Malaya's east coast, was a veteran compared to the recently arrived reinforcements. He was also experienced far beyond his years, having left home at the age of thirteen, ridden the rattlers around the back-blocks of New South Wales in search of work, and then joined the merchant marine. It was in February of 1941, while working on the troopship *Queen Mary* as a boilerman, that Mo had first come into contact with the 8th Division's 22nd Brigade, then en route for Malaya. When his next voyage took his ship to Suez with troops bound for the Middle East, Mo decided the army was the place to be. Signing off, he had headed straight for the recruiting office in Sydney's Martin Place, raised his age to eighteen and joined the AIF. Although army regulations decreed that the fuzzy beard he had grown while at sea had to come off, he was able to retain his moustache — which, because of his youth, made him stand out from the mob, prompting fellow infantryman Joe Kenny to dub him Mo.

To the right of Tom and Mo, on the far side of the Kranji River, were the three battalions of the other Australian brigade, the 27th. Adjacent to the all-important, but unfortunately only partially-demolished causeway, were the 2/30th and 2/26th Battalions and behind them, in reserve, was the 2/29th. This unit, which had sustained severe losses in Malaya after a horrendous battle, had been hastily and heavily reinforced, as had the 2/19th Battalion.

To the rear of the 22nd Brigade, not far from Tengah airfield, was Brigade Headquarters, over which Brigadier Harold Taylor presided. Here Mo Davis's boyhood friend, seventeen-year-old Private Keith Botterill, waited with fellow infantryman Private Richard Murray. Officially, Botterill was nineteen. He had put up his age by two years to enlist, following an ANZAC Day visit by a recruiting train to the resort town of Katoomba, in the Blue Mountains of New South Wales, where he was staying with his family at the time.

This pair, posted originally to the 2/19th Battalion, formed an odd alliance. The teenage Botterill, whose longish, somewhat serious face was enlivened by bushy eyebrows beneath which danced a pair of very blue eyes, was of average height and of a lean, wiry build. Although quite strong he was a mere stripling compared to the well-built Murray, whose darkly curling hair and strong, ruggedly-handsome features betrayed his Scottish Celtic roots. Moreover Murray was ten years older and had a wife and small son.

Yet, despite the age gap and physical disparity, they had much in common. Both were rebels at heart, although Murray was more overtly so. In Malaya, his habit of over-extending his leave without permission had landed him in trouble more than once, resulting in some heavy fines and temporary transfer to the Mobile Laundry Unit — the army's subtle way of dealing with persistent transgressors. Both men were also exceedingly tough, having been raised in working class Sydney suburbs. Botterill, quick-witted and fearless, was so game that his playmates had called him Ned Kelly — a title he had undoubtedly earned, and which had far more appeal than the one with which he was currently stuck — Sad Sack — after the rather morose looking comic-strip character of the same name. His slight stature was no handicap. A veteran street fighter from an early age, he was fast on his feet and handy with his fists.

While bullies, looking for an easy mark, might have been misguided enough to pick a fight with Botterill, only the foolhardy or brave would knowingly have taken on Murray, a talented welterweight boxer whose success in the ring was no secret.

Botterill, growing up in a neighbourhood where gangs were the norm and territories fiercely defended, had never been short of friends on whom he could rely in a crisis. Murray, although raised in a less hostile urban environment, also appreciated the value of mateship, and his many friendships were nurtured by his amiability and warm, ready smile. Popular with everyone, Murray had always been surrounded by a posse of loyal and steadfast friends.

Murray and his friends in Sydney had enlisted, almost *en masse*, in July 1940. Unfortunately, when they arrived at Martin Place to sign up, Murray had been classified as temporarily unfit because of a boil on his foot. By the time the aspiring recruit had been passed medically fit a month later, his mates had already been dispersed to various units. He had, therefore, linked up with the much younger Botterill when they had been posted to brigade headquarters. Although neither had any inkling at this stage, the tentative friendship which was being forged under such unlikely conditions would one day prove to be beyond measure.

Supporting the various infantry battalions were the artillerymen. Bombardier Dick Braithwaite and Gunner Wal Blatch, of the 2/15th Field Regiment, were not only good mates, they were manning the same gun. The strongly-built Blatch came from Yeoval, New South Wales. He was only 21 but had a maturity about him which, along with a luxurious black moustache, made him appear much older. Married the previous year, he had volunteered for active service after the fall of Greece and Crete, a decision which did not particularly please The Union Bank, which employed him as a clerk at its Barellan branch, in western New South Wales. Blatch had teamed up with 25-year-old Dick Braithwaite, a very dapper-looking photo engraver from Brisbane, who had never been known to have a hair out of place, not even when in action. Arriving in Malaya in mid-1941, the pair had been assigned to the same gun crew and had been together ever since.

Gunner Eric Tomkyns, attached to headquarters battery, also belonged to their regiment. Born and raised in India he was no stranger to military life, having served with the University Regiment at Agra. After graduating as a Bachelor of Arts at Agra, Tomkyns had emigrated to Sydney where, while undergoing teacher training, he had pursued his love of the outdoors at every opportunity, spending almost every weekend bushwalking and camping in the foothills of the Blue Mountains to the west of the city. On obtaining his qualifications, he had moved to the northwest of the state to accept a post at a primary school in the country town of

Warialda. At the age of 28 the good-looking, chestnut-haired Tomkyns, now married with two small children, had forsaken his teaching career to take up arms in the belief that it was his personal responsibility to protect his wife and family.

His sense of duty was matched by that of 21-year-old John Barnier, who hailed from the rich dairy country near Grafton on the lush north coast of New South Wales. He had joined up at the same time as two other local boys — John 'Jacky' Jackson, who was of Aboriginal-Torres Strait Islander descent, and Johnny O'Donohue who, like John Barnier, had been raised on a dairy farm. After their final home leave, the local community, in typical country style, had assembled at the tiny, weatherboard Alumny Creek Hall to give them a send-off they would never forget. During the proceedings, by way of appreciation, Jacky, who had a magnificent singing voice, had entertained the crowd with a beautiful rendition of 'One Day When We Were Young', while John Barnier had recited a moving poem by M. L. Haskins. The following morning, when all three had boarded the North Coast Mail to much good-natured banter and shouts of 'Good Luck', John's younger sister, Maureen, turned her head against the picket fence running along the rear of the platform and sobbed as if her heart would break.

A qualified agricultural scientist who had relinquished a place at New South Wales' prestigious Armidale Teacher Training College in order to volunteer, Barnier was a religious young man whose abhorrence of killing had been overridden by his deep sense of patriotism. Although both he and Tomkyns were well-educated and highly intelligent, they rejected the idea of Officer Training School, preferring to be simply 'one of the boys'. In an effort to be sent overseas, having failed to be posted to an infantry battalion destined for the Middle East, Barnier had opted for the Australian Army Service Corps (AASC), a unit whose diverse duties ranged from maintaining ammunition supplies to the front line to ferrying stores wherever they were needed. However, in early 1941, much to Barnier's disgust and disappointment, he had found himself not on the battlefields of North Africa but in the backwaters of jungle-clad Malaya. Chaffing with frustration, he had volunteered to ride 'shot-gun' on the truck and eventually came to terms with the prospect of spending the war far from the action, fulfilling a role as a rifleman destined never to fire a shot in anger, with a unit servicing a non-existent front line. To his immense satisfaction, Barnier's garrison duties had come to an abrupt end with the invasion of Malaya.

Quiet and compassionate by nature, his perpetual look of youthful innocence heightened rather than diminished by the severity of his army uniform, John Barnier was much tougher than he appeared. Determined to carry on after complications following abdominal surgery, he had defied all attempts to ship him home, preferring instead to take up a temporary post in the orderly room until he was pronounced 100 per cent fit.

Billy Young was a different type, a street-wise orphan raised in the inner Sydney suburb of Ultimo who, though by no means lacking in intelligence, loathed and detested school, so much so that he had quit at the earliest opportunity. Only fifteen years old at the time, but well developed physically, this underaged tearaway had raised his age to nineteen, falsified the necessary 'consent' from a fictitious aunt and then enlisted.

Billy's sights, like John Barnier's, had been set on an overseas posting with the infantry and he was overjoyed to find he was being sent as a reinforcement for the 2/29th Battalion, the ranks of which had been depleted after protracted fighting in Malaya. Here, at the base depot at Johore Bahru, he met and forged a lasting friendship with nineteen-year-old Harry Longley, who came from the New South Wales country town of Yass. A couple of larrikins, Young and Longley were fortunate to find themselves taken in hand by Paddy O'Toole (who, being quintessentially Irish, was universally described as 'mad') and the older, far more sane, sensible and steady Corporal Bob Shipsides, a practical bushman from Victoria. These self-appointed guardians had managed so far, with varying degrees of success, to keep Young and Company from getting into too much trouble.

Waiting just behind the infantry was Private Albert Anderson who, at 42, was old enough to be Billy Young's father. Like so many others who had been out of work during the Depression, Anderson, who came from the inner Sydney suburb of Glebe, had volunteered because of the financial security the armed services provided. Father of six young children, he was a caring man with a well-developed sense of humour — handy attributes for his job as driver with the 2/3 Motor Ambulance Convoy (MAC). This outfit, which had been attached originally to the 11th Indian Division, had been thrown into action when the Japanese attacked the north coast of Malaya on 8 December 1941. Since then it had never left the front line and had seen more action than any other Australian unit. Always the 'tail-end Charlies', two ambulances belonging to the 2/3 MAC were the very last vehicles to leave Malaya, roaring across the causeway to safety at the last minute. Now the unit's job was to ferry the wounded to one of the casualty clearing stations or hospitals which, along with the combat, service and administrative groups, formed the 8th Australian Division under the command of General H. Gordon Bennett.

Further to the rear, also waiting for the action to begin, were the equally mature Private Ray Carlson and the slightly younger Corporal Neil Christie. Carlson, a cook with the 4th Reserve Motor Transport, came from Victoria and was the father of eleven children ranging in age from late teens to a few months. Devoted to his wife and family, to whom he sent a constant stream of presents, Ray had managed to find time the previous day to write one more letter. Although it was covered in blobs and blots where globules of sweat had trickled down his arm and smudged the ink, the letter was cheerful enough, telling of a visit by three small Chinese children who had dropped by the field kitchen for a treat of bread and jam. It had ended with the assurance that, although the Japanese numbers were enormous, 'we will beat them here'. Aware that, with the artillery barrage increasing by the minute, this missive might be the last for some time, Ray had signed off with 'so long, not good-bye'.

Queensland-based Neil Christie, also married and father of three, had been working as an accountant at a large sugar mill in tropical Mackay at the start of the war. Believing that all able-bodied men would soon be conscripted anyway, he, and a number of other employees, had decided to take the plunge and join up. Born into a family which had extensive farming interests, Christie was as much at home in the bush as in the city, despite his sedentary occupation. Throughout his formative years he had spent a great deal of time on the land, much of it on a merino sheep property near Inverell, New South Wales, where his grandfather was a well known grazier. While his experience of country life had made him self-reliant and resourceful, it was his flair for figures that made him well-suited for his posting to army ordnance stores, where part of his job was to keep track of weapons, explosives and ammunition supplies. Quite tall, but of slender build, the dark, curly-headed Christie was a quietly cheerful soul who always had time for a friendly word or two.

While a number of these 'old blokes' had jobs which kept them back from the front line, this was not the case for 41-year-old Staff-Sergeant William Baird McDonald. A tailor by trade, Bill McDonald, the 18th Battalion's clothing quartermaster, had been posted to headquarters company, now sited only slightly to the rear of the rifle companies. If nothing else, McDonald had the satisfaction of knowing the battalion was going into battle properly clad. When his nose had told him that most of the combat troops had not had close contact with soap and water for the best part of a fortnight, he had made it a priority to replace their sweaty, smelly field-dress with brand new gear. However, making sure that the troops were adequately clothed was not as dull, nor as safe, as it sounded. McDonald's clothing depot had ceased to exist as a result of one bombing attack while his chest still showed evidence of severe gravel rash, caused by diving headlong into monsoon drains. For someone who was 183 centimetres tall, strongly built and weighed just on 90 kilograms, these acrobatic manoeuvres were no mean feat. Married and the father of three children, Bill McDonald came from the prosperous New South Wales town of Armidale, famous as much for its rich grazing country as for John Barnier's alma mater, the Armidale Teachers' College.

The rain had stopped now and it was quite dark. The tropical night had fallen with its usual suddenness, taking those still accustomed to a lingering twilight by surprise. As the blackness increased, the shelling reached crescendo pitch, with 60 to 80 shells a minute falling on some areas. The older soldiers, who had lived through similarly terrifying experiences in the Great War, told the younger men it would eventually stop. And when it did, it was almost certain that the enemy would make its move.

As predicted, the barrage finally ceased. The deafening roar of artillery and mortar explosions and the rat-a-tat-tat of heavy calibre weapons were now replaced by something far more unnerving. Silence. Those at the forward posts, aware of the perilousness of their situation, focussed their entire energies on the black strip of water in front of them, ears now strained for the faintest sound, eyes peeled for the slightest movement. As they watched, they became aware of an almost imperceptible shifting of shadows, as dark, indeterminate shapes detached themselves from the even darker shoreline. Before long, they detected the faint splash of oars and the shadows were shadows no longer but hundreds of barges and boats, filled with thousands upon thousands of enemy troops. As they moved closer, protected by a covering mortar barrage, Tom Burns steadied himself. This was it. This time, he vowed, there would be no retreat. This time they would all hold their ground or die in the attempt.

While Tom, and many more like him, were unflinching in their resolve to stay at their posts no matter what the cost, the intensity of the mortar barrage undermined the resolve of some who had not been in battle before. Unaware that the mortars were being fired at a fixed elevation and not creeping towards them, some troops withdrew to new positions. This premature movement, while understandable, unfortunately created even bigger gaps in the already over-extended line.

When the landing craft reached the shore, the Australian machine gunners opened up. Thousands of rounds of ammunition spewed forth in murderous cross-fire, felling the enemy like wheat stalks before the scythe, but still they came. The infantry now joined in, their grenades and rifle fire adding to the carnage. But it was not enough. Scrambling over the bodies of their fallen comrades, the Japanese poured ashore, wave after fanatical wave, infiltrating the gaps between the forward posts and overwhelming the Australian positions. In some places the advance was so rapid that many of the forward posts found themselves completely isolated. Private Ron Moran and a small band of fellow machine gunners, realising they had been cut off from the rest, had no option but to destroy their faithful Vickers and fight their way back through enemy-held territory in the hope of linking up with the infantry.

With communication lines cut by the shelling, the artillery remained silent, unable to fire for fear of hitting their own men. However, after word was received to 'bring down fire everywhere' Blatch, Braithwaite, Tomkyns and the rest of the gunners fired off a total of 4800 rounds. But despite the efforts of the artillerymen, the situation worsened. When the machine guns, barrels now red-hot, eventually ran out of ammunition, the gunners, bayonets fixed, joined the infantry who were now fighting hand-to-hand. All were in a desperate position. As the situation deteriorated, some were able to withdraw to previously assigned positions to regroup. Others, completely cut off and isolated in the dark, could do nothing but try to fight their way out, metre by bloody metre.

By morning, it was all over. The Japanese, outnumbering the Australians eight to one, had gained the foothold they needed and, once having gained it, proved impossible to move, in spite of the reserve battalion being brought into the fray. Forced back to the other side of the Tengah Airfield, the survivors of the badly mauled Australian units re-formed. It was a pitifully small force. For the second time in a month the 2/19th Battalion had ceased to exist as a fighting force, the majority of its men killed, cut off or wandering around in the rear areas completely disoriented. The two other battalions, the 2/20th and 2/18th, suffered similar casualties.

The death rate would have been higher had it not been for individual acts of heroism, such as that displayed by the 2/19th's Padre Harold Wardale-Greenwood. With scant regard for his personal safety, and in the face of unrelenting heavy mortar and automatic weapon fire, he had moved among the wounded, applying field dressings where possible and keeping up the men's spirits. Others in the battalion, finding themselves entirely surrounded and with no hope of getting out alive, owed their lives to the self-sacrifice of some of their mates. The gunners manned the machine guns until the ammunition was spent, keeping the enemy at bay until the others had escaped.

As the small bands of survivors straggled in, some to brigade headquarters, some to collection posts, each had a tale to tell. Captain Rod Richardson, with the remnants of a company from Mo's battalion and some machine gunners, had defied impossible odds to get out alive. Occupying one of the most forward posts, they had maintained their position through sustained hand-to-hand fighting, unaware that a withdrawal to battalion headquarters had been ordered. At dawn, finding themselves quite alone, they had moved to a small knoll, where they soon bore the full force of an attack by Japanese who had advanced into the surrounding area. Somehow, they managed to cling on until 10.30am, when they eventually received the much-delayed order to withdraw.

Finally reaching the place where he had expected to find battalion headquarters, Richardson had found only dead men. He and his troops then pushed on through country completely over-run by the enemy, only to be ambushed. Ditching most of their clothes and equipment, the survivors split into two groups and took to the swamps and rivers where a number were killed by sniper and automatic fire. It was not until afternoon that the remainder, utterly exhausted and without their weapons, staggered past Tengah Airfield and down the track to Bulim village, where Richardson reported to Brigadier Taylor, as ordered.

Throughout this terrible night it had been relatively quiet in the 27th Brigade's sector. However, their turn came the next evening when the Japanese, having routed the 22nd Brigade, crossed the Straits and attacked the coastline immediately west of the causeway. Although there were some incursions along the left flank, the tenacious Australians, supported by the artillery, managed to hold their own. However, the brigade commander, believing his men to be in danger of being cut off, ordered them to withdraw to a new position about 5 kilometres back. Before doing so, they were instructed to destroy all oil and fuel stocks by opening the cocks of nearby storage tanks. As thousands of litres of highly volatile aviation spirit flowed down the nearby waterways, the defenders set it alight, incinerating a battalion of enemy troops attempting an outflanking manoeuvre. General Nishimura, Japanese commander of the elite Guards Regiment, was seeking permission to call off his attack when, by the light of the burning fuel, he saw that the Australians were leaving. Scarcely able to believe his good luck, Nishimura took the initiative and pressed home his attack. Once the territory had been lost it proved impossible to regain. Despite a planned counter-attack, the Australians were once more in retreat.

Although the 2/29th Battalion had been held in reserve initially, it had not been for long, and Billy Young was called into action. He soon realised that being an infantry soldier on active service was not nearly as glamorous as he had imagined. Furthermore, a fighting retreat was not on his agenda, especially since it was his job to lug heavy ammunition for the section's Lewis gun.

Billy and his mates, still fortunately under the care of Paddy O'Toole and Bob Shipsides, had been taking up a new position when they were caught in the open. Under intense mortar and machine-gun fire they reached the shelter of some trees and took cover in what Billy, under the circumstances, considered to be more of a rabbit scrape and less of a foxhole. Suddenly, a shell slammed into a tree, immediately above his head, cutting the trunk in two and showering earth over those hugging the ground beneath it. Temporarily deafened by the explosion and gagging from the smell of cordite, Billy also realised that there was a pain in the region of his thigh. He felt tentatively for the spot with his hand, only to discover warm, sticky blood. Horrible images, prompted by childhood memories of a World War 1 soldier, a neighbour who had lost his leg while fighting on the Western Front, immediately flashed through his mind. It was with great relief that, upon further examination, he discovered he had sustained a shrapnel wound in the groin and his leg was not, as he had imagined, hanging by a thread and in imminent danger of falling off. He received no sympathy at all from Paddy O'Toole who, on ascertaining that the shrapnel had missed Billy's vital organs, quickly applied a field dressing to the wound and pulled him to his feet. Shipsides' orders were to withdraw and, as they were now more or less surrounded by enemy troops, Billy either moved or he would be left to the ministrations of the Japanese.

Despite a harrowing journey which lasted throughout the night, with one man dying and another wounded, Billy's group eventually reached Australian lines and an aid post. Now an official war casualty, Billy, a borderline stretcher case, was given the choice of joining one queue of men, bound for Alexandra Military Hospital, or joining the walking wounded. While it was tempting to be carried off on a stretcher to the Military Hospital, he resisted and chose the other queue. He was sent to the 13th Australian General Hospital (AGH), which had taken over St Patrick's Roman Catholic College at Katong, on the coast road leading to Changi. Although he was unaware of it at the time, Billy Young's choice was the difference between living and dying. Alexandra Hospital would shortly be over-run by the enemy and almost every person bayonetted to death.

Meanwhile, 200 soldiers from the 22nd Brigade's newly formed X Battalion had been having an even worse time. With the infantry units so fragmented, a nucleus of survivors from the first day's fighting and some non-combatants, including a number from Albert Anderson's ambulance convoy, had formed a scratch battalion. Towards dusk on the afternoon of 10 February, their commanding officer, Colonel Boyes, received an order to advance to high ground near Bukit Timah, into an area which none of them knew and which would soon be in darkness. As they passed through Bukit Timah village, now a mass of flames, they learned that the enemy was just ahead.

One of those attached to X Battalion was 23-year old Private George Plunkett, a likeable character who usually worked in the 2/18th's quartermaster's store. Over 190 centimetres tall and in superb physical condition, Plunkett, who came from the northern Sydney suburb of Hornsby, was as well-known to the local Chinese as to the men of the 8th Division. While stationed in Malaya, Plunkett, gregarious by nature and a highly-gifted tennis player, had entered the Malayan Open Tennis Championships, along with the similarly talented Private Sid Breakspear of the 2/19th. Dubbed 'giant killers' by the local and Singaporean press, the pair had become celebrities overnight when they had beaten all-comers, including the hot favourites and two-times local champions, to take out the men's doubles title in straight sets.

Despite Plunkett's fitness, he and the rest of X Battalion were now extremely tired, having had no sleep for the past three days. After passing through terrain littered with the bodies of hundreds of dead Indian troops, they eventually reached their designated positions, a map reference known as Jurong I. The Japanese were not far away and the men felt very uneasy but, by 1.00am, almost all had fallen asleep from exhaustion. A couple of hours later the Japanese launched a sudden assault. Aided by the flames from a petrol dump they had set alight with hand grenades, the enemy swarmed from a road and attacked the sleeping Australians. Taken by surprise, the pickets who were still awake had little time to raise the alarm. Troops not bayonetted in their sleep were soon overwhelmed and, despite desperate hand-to-hand fighting, there were few survivors. While Captain Richardson, who had led his men to safety in the swamps two days before, managed to extricate a handful of troops, others who had not been killed outright were not so fortunate. About 20 of those captured alive were trussed and made to kneel beside a monsoon drain on nearby Jurong Road. Before long, most were sprawled in pools of blood in the bottom of the ditch, either beheaded or bayonetted by officers and men of the advancing Japanese 18th Division.

Some time later, after the enemy had passed on, the 2/18th's Private 'Titch' H. Burgess, regained consciousness and realised that one of the bayonet thrusts meant to kill him had severed his bonds. Although severely wounded he managed to free three others, all from his battalion and the only men still alive — George Plunkett, John 'Jacky' Ings and Ron Marshall. Although Plunkett and Ings were suffering from multiple stab wounds and deep sword cuts to the neck, and Marshall had been bayonetted twice in the back, the men managed to drag themselves out of the ditch to the safety of a house, where a Chinese family took them in. Despite their horrific injuries, Plunkett, Ings and Marshall lived. Titch Burgess, who had lost far too much blood, did not.

Richie Murray and Keith Botterill first became aware that a terrible calamity had overtaken X Battalion when a few terrified survivors arrived at brigade headquarters. In the wake of this ambush, fierce fighting had also broken out along the Reformatory Road ridge, near Bukit Timah village, where Taylor's much depleted infantry brigade was battling to contain the Japanese advance. Flush with success, the enemy began to drive home the attack from a nearby ridge. As they increased the pressure on brigade headquarters all able-bodied men — staff and attached officers, signallers, machine gunners, support staff and infantry — were ordered to counter-attack across Reformatory Road and push the enemy back.

Murray and Botterill were involved in the charge which, under mortar bomb attack, managed to drive back the Japanese with grenade and bayonet, at a cost of one officer killed and two officers and two men (Corporal Tommy Graham and their fatally injured cook, Cobbie) wounded. One of the wounded officers taken to Alexandra Hospital with Cobbie and Graham was brigade headquarter's Major Beale, who had led the bayonet charge.

While both Murray and Botterill had narrowly escaped injury on that occasion, Botterill's luck ran out at about 6.00pm the following day. Brigade headquarters had retreated down Holland Road where the Australians had set up two machine-gun posts to cover the golf links, the direction from which the enemy was expected to attack. When a Japanese ammunition truck, which had become lost, unexpectedly appeared from the opposite direction, the gunners swung their weapons towards it and opened up. Unfortunately, the rear-most gunner was unaware that the front gunner was now directly in his line of fire. Botterill, who was on the other side of the road, watched in horror as the bullets ripped through the first gunner's body, riddling his back, buttocks and legs. He shouted a warning to stop shooting but it was useless against the din and, in any case, the Japanese gunner on top of the truck was returning the fire. During the exchange, which accounted for all the Japanese in and on the truck, Botterill was hit in the lower abdomen by a ricocheting bullet. Enemy action ceased when Murray lobbed a well-aimed grenade at the truck, setting fire to both it and the ammunition. By the time the Australians recovered their wits, Botterill had disappeared.

Under the direction of Captain J. N. Hordern (a member of the family which owned the huge Sydney emporium known as Anthony Hordern's), Botterill and the critically-wounded gunner had been loaded into the back of the ration truck, which had just delivered the evening meal. Knowing that several evacuation ships had been embarking nurses, civilians and military personnel, Hordern raced his improvised ambulance to the harbour. Discovering that all vessels had left the wharf he took his patients instead to St Patrick's College. He and the patients were unaware that, as it was outside the line chosen as Singapore's final defensive perimeter, it would soon fall into the hands of enemy troops who had landed on the east coast near Changi. The following day Botterill, and Billy Young, along with all the other patients and the medical staff, were surrendered to the Japanese.

Meanwhile the battle raged on. The Allies, forced back into an ever-diminishing circle, were now fighting on the outskirts of the city itself. Owing to the soaring number of casualties in the infantry units, the 22nd brigade could scarcely find enough men to form a battalion, some battalions being down to company strength. As survivors regrouped and stragglers found their way back to their own lines, more composite 'battalions', numbering only 200 or 300, were formed from a handful of front line troops, greatly reinforced by non-combatant transport, supply and service personnel.

With St Patrick's College in enemy hands, makeshift hospitals were established at St Andrew's Cathedral and the Cathay Building, Singapore's tallest and most prominent structure. It was here that Tom Burns, admitted for treatment, was relieved to find alive and well his best friend, Sergeant Colin Smyth, a member of the 10th AGH, which had taken over the lower floors. With the enemy artillery homing in on such an obvious target, neither the building nor the convalescent depot, set up in the adjacent Cathay Theatre, provided a secure refuge. It was not long before shells hit both the building and the theatre, killing a number of the wounded. Although Tom escaped further injury he was not spared the horror of witnessing the effect of the shelling on the civilian population, now jammed into a very small area. As the attack on the city centre increased, the results were devastating, with an estimated 70 000 civilians killed in a two-day period.

Although by this stage blood and gore were no stranger to him, Tom was sickened by the carnage. Bodies, or rather parts of bodies were everywhere. They lay on pock-marked streets, in the bottom of monsoon drains, on shattered sidewalks and the front lawns of what were once immaculately tended gardens. Here and there pools of rapidly congealing blood oozed from beneath piles of rubble, all that remained of a row of shops or houses, while elsewhere severed limbs were draped like bits of steaming flotsam among the ruins. In some places where the shelling had been particularly intense, the ground was so slick with blood and remains it was difficult to keep a footing. Although in the sauna-like heat the sickly stench of blood and rapidly decomposing corpses was stomach-churning, there was no hope of burying the dead. The able-bodied were too busy looking after the wounded, and each other, to do anything about those who were now beyond all earthly help.

With fires raging unchecked, and neither water nor anyone available to fight them, the situation could not possibly continue — and it didn't. After consultation with his most senior Allied officers, Britain's General Percival unconditionally surrendered all British, Australian and Indian troops to the Imperial Japanese Army. At 8.30pm on 15 February 1942, the guns stopped and all hostilities ceased. As an eerie silence, punctuated only by the occasional cries of the wounded, descended over the smouldering ruins of the city, the soldiers and civilians were confronted by the reality of what had occurred. To the consternation of Private Tom Burns and all those for whom the very thought of either defeat or surrender was an absolute anathema, the unthinkable had happened.

Singapore, the impregnable fortress, had fallen.

Chapter Two
SELARANG

The order to cease fire was met with a mixture of disbelief, outrage and shock by the Australians. While some wept openly with shame and frustration and others fumed at the injustice of it all, most simply felt cheated. If only they hadn't been constantly withdrawing. If only they had been given the chance to show what they could really do. For the 2nd AIF, who had wanted so very much to prove themselves in battle in the way their fathers had done before them, defeat was a bitter pill.

They found just how bitter the following morning. Under the terms of the surrender signed by General Percival, all must lay down their arms. The final collection point for the AIF was the square at Tanglin Barracks, formerly Divisional Headquarters and the site from where General Bennett had directed their last, futile stand. For those who had fought so hard, it was almost too much to bear. While all knew the battle was lost, the Allied capitulation until now had been an abstract thing, something in the control of generals, something quite out of the control of the ordinary soldier. This laying down of arms, this stripping away of the last vestiges of pride was such an intensely personal gesture. It was, for each and every one of them, the ultimate act of surrender. And for Mo Davis, who turned eighteen years old that day, it was a rotten way to celebrate a birthday.

Now unarmed and vulnerable, bitterness and anger gave way to apprehension. That very morning the 2/18th Battalion had received a visit from the Japanese who demanded that all Bren-gun carrier drivers step forward. For Private Nelson Short, who had been at the base depot during the Japanese assault, it was his first encounter with the Japanese. Aware that the Bren gunners had inflicted heavy casualties on the enemy, he had watched in trepidation as Mick Simmons and five others obeyed the order. As nothing had been heard of them since, grave fears were held for their safety. Word had also spread among the Australians of the massacre at the Alexandra Hospital the day before, of the wounded being murdered when aid posts were over-run, and of captured soldiers being beheaded or used for bayonet practice. With a track record like that there was no telling what the Japanese might do next.

For the military captives at least, the fears of imminent mass murder and mayhem were unwarranted. Few Japanese were seen at first and, apart from the incident with the Bren-gun carriers, those encountered within the Australian perimeter seemed friendly enough, with many offering cigarettes and striking up a conversation in surprisingly good English. While it was galling to witness triumphant enemy troops parading down the streets and to step aside for the stream of cars, trucks, bicycles, lorries and tanks, all bedecked with the odious Japanese flag and with horns tooting madly, the only thing hurt was the Australians' sense of pride.

The Chinese lost far more than their self-esteem. As had been the case in the

Chinese city of Nankin, the victorious armies of the Emperor of Japan gave no quarter to their long-time and bitter enemies. An appalled Tom Burns, still at the Cathay Building with the wounded, watched helplessly as the Japanese moved into his area, torturing the able-bodied Chinese citizens and rounding up the weak, the frail and the elderly, the mothers with babies and children. To the taunts and curses of the soldiers, who appeared to delight in their misery, the Chinese were hunted from the ruins of their homes and then prodded down the street at bayonet point, many of them to meet their death within a day or two.

Others were also killed. Sure that future comforts would be few, AIF officers encouraged their men to scout about for provisions and anything else they thought might be of use, before the main Japanese forces arrived. With bombed shops and warehouses overflowing with all manner of goods, and homes, abandoned by the wealthy, stocked with the most delectable imported and potentially useful items, the Australians had no qualms about appropriating things which did not belong to them, particularly since the alternative was to leave them for the enemy. The local Indians and Malays, evidently employing the same logic, also joined in the free-for-all with even more enthusiasm than the troops.

While the Australians referred to acquiring goods in this manner as 'scrounging', the Imperial Japanese Army deemed it to be looting, and a capital offence. Before long some English soldiers and one Australian were hanged for this crime, and a number of local people shot dead. When the Japanese found that shooting was not a deterrent, all locals found looting were decapitated. While such drastic punishment made no difference to the Australian resolve to scrounge wherever and whenever possible, the sight of severed heads on display at street corners made even the most daring among them more selective and less overt.

Following a conference between the Japanese and senior Allied commanders on 16 February, all troops were ordered to move east to the Changi area the next day, taking rations for at least ten days. Fortunately, since all but essential personal kit had been placed in storage, the Australians were able to access a stockpile of food and clothing at the Tanglin Barracks. This, along with the scrounged items, were piled onto the few trucks provided as transport, with baggage filling any spare space.

After an all-day wait in the hot sun, it was late afternoon by the time the bulk of the AIF joined the long procession of Allied prisoners on the 25-kilometre march to Changi. Determined to show a brave face to enemy troops stationed along the route, as well as the local residents, they marched with a carefree swagger, cracking jokes and calling out rude remarks to staff officers riding by in the comfort of a motor car. Although to onlookers they all seemed cheerful enough, they presented a rather motley appearance. While the majority, particularly those who had raided clothing stores, were smart and well-outfitted, others had turned out in an assortment of battle-stained and tattered clothing as well as an amazing array of headgear, including rakish pork-pie hats and topees more suited to a trek across Africa than a forced march to a Japanese prison camp. There was even the odd turban or two. While those lucky enough to have personal possessions toted them in some kind of pack, one well-endowed and very enterprising individual, determined to begin prison life with maximum comforts, merrily wheeled all his worldy goods along the road in a high-wheeled baby carriage.

The route chosen by the Japanese passed through the most populous sections of the town, evidently to inflict as much humiliation as possible. As the prisoners tramped along Napier, Tanglin and Scott Roads to Newtons Circus, and then Kampong Java, Norfolk and Serengoon Roads to Changi Road, it became obvious, from the number of Japanese flags displayed on shops and houses, that the Indians and Malays in particular had realised the inevitable. The Chinese, fiercely anti-Japanese, were not nearly as acquiescent. They risked punishment, pressing small gifts of food and cigarettes onto the troops and offering them water at every opportunity.

It was a long and tiring march. Even those who had started out bright enough were flagging by the time night fell. Apart from a short meal break, there was no respite until, tired, hungry and footsore, the head of the Australian column reached its destination at around 4.00am. Under normal conditions, their new billets would have been voted most desirable. In peacetime the barracks on the Changi peninsula, surrounded by the sea on three sides and home to Britain's garrison troops, was a showplace. Consisting of four separate barracks areas, it spread across hectares of lushly green, manicured parkland, dotted with tropical trees and brilliantly-coloured ornamental shrubs.

The 14 860 Australians were to occupy the first of these — Selarang Barracks, pre-war home to a regiment of Gordon Highlanders. The British, numbering around 37 000, along with Indian and some Dutch prisoners, were billeted further down the road at Roberts, India and Kitchener Barracks, the latter on the most easterly end of the peninsula and not far from Changi village. The high-security, recently built Changi Gaol, where British civilians would soon be interned, was diagonally opposite Selarang, while the buildings set aside for the yet-to-be-established POW hospital were adjacent to Roberts Barracks.

When day broke the Australians, feeling a little better after a couple of hours sleep, took a look at their new surroundings. The battle-scarred walls, covered in black camouflage paint, of previously airy, smartly painted, cream and yellow three-storeyed buildings, came as something of a shock to those who had seen them in peacetime. Huge shell craters in the formerly immaculate parade ground were enough to make the most hardened regimental sergeant-major weep, while the seven main barrack buildings surrounding it, although structurally intact, had been completely stripped and all power, water and sewerage services rendered inoperable. The six Australian infantry battalions, along with the medical units and artillery regiments (temporarily housed across the road in the old Birdwood Camp site with the 4th Anti-Tank Regiment) were allocated these buildings, while the rest were assigned to numerous administrative, officers' and married quarters scattered about the place. The principal buildings boasted a flat roof as well as covered balconies on all three floors, and a large number of men were forced to build makeshift humpies from whatever materials they could find in these additional spaces.

As the Japanese had not provided anything in the way of equipment or facilities, the first few days were spent making the camp habitable — setting up kitchen areas, transforming scrap metal into cooking equipment, digging latrines, trying to restore essential services and scrounging material suitable for bedding, the alternative being the concrete floor. Although most settled down to the various tasks, morale was not good. Food and water were severely rationed and once the place had been tidied up and organised there was little to occupy the men, despondent and listless from the shock of their defeat and the subsequent surrender.

Discipline among the Australians, which had always been rather relaxed compared to the spit-and-polish image demanded by the class-conscious British Army, now fell to an all-time low. With the consensus being that those at the top, staff officers in particular, were responsible for their predicament, the general feeling around the camp was one of simmering resentment. As prisoners of war many could see no valid reason why they should act as if they were on a parade ground 24 hours a day or even continue to obey all orders without question.

Restoring discipline would not have been so difficult had it not been for a small minority who, perhaps, should never have left Australia. Described as typical of the 'black sheep' to be found in any army, some were reinforcement depot troops who General Bennett described as 'the worst disciplined Australians I have ever seen'. Under normal circumstances they would not have been there, for the policy of the AIF was for neither the untrained nor the poorly disciplined to go into battle. Nor, if at all possible, were they to be led by sub-standard or indifferent officers. In the early days all troops being sent to Malaya had been put through a rigorous training programme to eliminate those not suited to active service. While the odd few had slipped through the net, this system had worked well enough until December 1941 when, in response to an urgent call for more men, Army authorities in Australia began to send raw reinforcements. While most of the new recruits simply lacked proper military training and a sense of cohesion, others had no concept of discipline at any level, nor any inclination to accept it. With no time to instil any kind of responsibility into these newcomers before Singapore fell, the 8th Division found itself lumbered with a higher percentage of sub-standard officers and men than would otherwise have been the case. Among these were a number found to be 'lacking in moral fibre' — the AIF's polite way of describing all those who had not stood up to the rigours of battle.

Believing, rightly, that law and order must not be allowed to break down, Selarang's senior officers decided the most expedient way to handle the situation was not by promoting discipline from within but by imposing it ruthlessly. Consequently, there was an immediate crackdown. Sloppiness in either personal appearance or behaviour would not be tolerated. Early morning parade ground drills, fastidious attention to personal grooming, and meticulous adherence to recognising and maintaining differences in rank, were rigidly enforced. On the assumption that idle hands made mischief, repetitious fatigue duties were also introduced.

While the maintenance of discipline was essential to long-term survival, the enforcement of such a strict code, particularly by very junior, inexperienced, or over-zealous officers, was not generally welcomed by the rank and file. Many thought that saluting officers was inappropriate and also an unnecessary and outdated anachronism, because, as prisoners, they were all in the same situation. Even those accustomed to army regimentation thought the discipline excessive, especially when punishment for infringing regulations resulted in being placed under guard on reduced rations. And, while such privileges had always been part and parcel of military life, the insistence on maintaining strictly separate officers' messes complete with facilities and accoutrements befitting their status, along with the assigning of a batman to even the most junior officers, did not help matters.

It was not only the naturally rebellious or the green, untrained reinforcements who had trouble accepting the tightening up of discipline. Experienced soldiers, who appreciated the importance of unquestioning obedience and the need to improve morale, found the petty drills, the constant orders, endless saluting and pointless, time-filling tasks both irksome and unnecessary. However, with the Japanese handing full responsibility for the internal running of the camp to the Australian commanders, the men had no option but to obey orders, or face the consequences. Many did so with very bad grace. Covert as well as overt insubordination and rumblings of discontent were rife, resulting in punishments which in turn further fuelled the resentment, widening the gulf between the officers and men.

Despite the united front presented by officers in regard to camp discipline, petty jealousies flourished between individuals at all levels of seniority. Furthermore, bitterness and recrimination over the handling of the campaign and the subsequent capitulation were not confined to the rank and file. Junior officers blamed senior officers, combatant commanders blamed staff officers, junior staff blamed senior staff and senior staff blamed Malaya Command, General Percival in particular. The only thing about which everyone agreed was that Malaya Command and the local British administration had a great deal to answer.

About three weeks after the POWs' arrival at Selarang, their captors issued orders to isolate each area from its neighbour with a double apron of barbed wire. Anyone found outside the wire would be shot. To the AIF the delivery to Selarang of hundreds of coils of this wire was the ultimate irony. The Australians, whose pleas to Malaya Command for barbed wire prior to the Japanese attack had fallen on deaf ears, discovered that now they were in captivity they were detailed to imprison themselves with the very same wire.

Within a few days of the able-bodied settling in at Selarang, the wounded began to trickle in from the various hospitals and convalescent depots. While some made the trip in vehicles, others, including amputees on crutches from the Cathay Theatre, were on foot. Among those sent by ambulance from St Patrick's a week or two after the surrender were Keith Botterill and Billy Young, now recovered from their wounds. Although Botterill's reappearance was greeted with pleasure by Murray, who had given him up for dead, some of his other mates, who had put his sudden disappearance at the height of the battle down to desertion, took some convincing that he had indeed been wounded. Also among the injured was Corporal Tommy Graham, who had more than just a bullet wound as a reminder of the battle for Singapore. He also had a pistol belonging to Major Beale, wounded in the same charge but later massacred at the Alexandra Hospital.

Young, while pleased enough to be reunited with his mates, was even more pleased to be out of the clutches of the Japanese. Although the patients at St Patrick's had not been subjected to any acts of barbarity, Billy was among those who had heard the screams as some captured Australian soldiers were bayonetted and hacked to death outside the college gates. When it had been safe to do so, the doctors had ventured outside to find alive only one of seven men who had been attacked. Shortly after, the Japanese had entered the hospital itself.

Ron Marshall, George Plunkett and Jacky Ings also arrived at about this time, Plunkett and Ings wearing scarves around their necks to hide the tell-tale sword cuts which would have told the Japanese that witnesses to the X Battalion massacre were still alive. Plunkett, who had also been stabbed thirteen times in the body, was the worst of the three and thought to have little chance of surviving. Despite the doctor's gloomy prognosis, he defied the odds, his super-fitness undoubtedly as big a factor in his ultimate recovery as the determination to live to see his wife and baby daughter, born a few months before.

Like Plunkett, Ings and Marshall, the other sick and convalescent arriving at Selarang were helped to some extent by the fit who bought, scrounged or bartered for drugs, food and other commodities at every opportunity. Although at first the main source of supply was trading on the black market with the local population, this took a back seat when the Japanese realised they had a great, untapped labour force at their disposal. Within days of their arrival 500 POW 'volunteers' were back in Singapore, cleaning up the rubble and mess left by the shelling, burying bodies and generally restoring order. This group was soon followed by another, which was put to work in the warehouses or godowns by the docks. Accommodation for some groups was poor and the guards could be unpredictable but, as the POWs soon discovered, the possibilities for scrounging were endless. The workers took full advantage, assisted by the laxity of many of the guards, some of whom were active participants.

When working parties began to send medical supplies, food and tobacco back to the main camp, it didn't take long for the word to spread that life was better outside Selarang than in it. This forced camp administration to rethink the criteria for the selection process. With camp discipline a major problem, quite a number of the 'volunteers' sent out so far had been those who had demonstrated a rather cavalier attitude towards camp rules and regulations. Now there was no shortage of eager volunteers for the subsequent drafts. The demand increased even more when a medical officer, sent out to check on conditions, reported that in addition to a meat ration of four ounces (about 115 grams) a day, prisoners on outside working parties were paid — 25 cents a day for sergeants, fifteen for other non-commissioned officers (NCOs) and ten for privates. By May, with the Japanese finding plenty of outlets for labour and the prisoners only too happy to provide it, there were more POWs outside the Changi area than in it.

By far the largest working parties, numbering into the thousands, were sent to the MacRitchie Reservoir-Bukit Timah area where two ambitious projects, under the supervision of an Hawaiian-born Japanese engineer, Lieutenant Nekemoto Toshiyuki, were in full swing. The first of these, on a heavily forested hill overlooking the reservoir, was a large Shinto temple, consisting of several open-sided, colonnaded buildings roofed in traditional style with material especially brought in from Japan. The approach to the complex, named Shonan Jinjya after an old Japanese shrine built in Singapore before the war, was via an ornamental bridge spanning an arm of the reservoir and a flight of granite-hewn steps.

The other, equally ambitious undertaking was the Shonan Chureto War Memorial at Bukit Batok, a hill just behind the Ford Motor Works at Bukit Timah, where the surrender documents had been signed. Here the Japanese war dead were to be commemorated by a slender wooden obelisk rising more than 20 metres into the air and the Allied by a 4-metre, far less obtrusive, wooden cross. Although the prisoners were quite taken aback by the decision to allow them to erect their memorial, they were unaware that the reasons for doing so were not as altruistic as they appeared. While Lieutenant Nekemoto had given the idea his enthusiastic support, his commanding officer had only given the project his approval when its propaganda value, to be captured on Japanese newsreels, was pointed out. Although some Australians were not too keen on building monuments to honour the enemy war dead, others, who had placed termites beneath the foundations, were not troubled in the slightest. Their confidence, however, was misplaced. While quite a large number of the voracious, timber-eating insects had been successfully relocated it appears that the termite queen, the colony's sole egg layer, did not survive the move.

Mo Davis, for one, was against the project. As far as he was concerned, if the Japanese wanted a memorial they could build it themselves. Consequently, instead of reporting for work he, along with the similarly intractable Dobie James and Jacky Sullivan, spent the day at a Chinese cemetery near their Lornie Road Camp — a move which did not go unnoticed by the camp's commanding officer, Colonel Robertson, who sent them back to Selarang as punishment.

As roads and footways, as well as the bridge, had to be constructed to access both the temple and obelisk sites, which in turn had to be cleared and levelled to create a large enough building area, the required labour force was considerable. Billy Young and Harry Longley, who had already had a taste of the good life at the godowns, were members of one of the road construction parties. Housed as they were in luxurious mansions from which wealthy civilians had been ousted, they found living at the Thomson Road camp very agreeable. It was even better when, owing to an administrative error, the prisoners were left without guards for four or five days, allowing them to roam all over Singapore at will.

While Billy and Harry were living it up at Thomson Road, Keith Botterill and his mate Richie Murray, having managed to get on a working party, were also enjoying themselves. In late May they were sent to Pulau Bukum, a small island off Singapore city where 3.15 billion litres of oil were stored in huge concrete tanks. For oil-starved Japan these fuel reserves, which had only been partially destroyed by the British, were a godsend. Although prisoners who were at Bukum later were not well treated, Murray and Botterill were more than satisfied. The POWs were housed in quite comfortable pre-war huts about halfway up the hill and while rolling and stacking full drums of oil to be loaded onto the tankers arriving every few days was hard work, the food was good and there was plenty of it. They were also allowed to go fishing after work every day, had the whole of Sunday off and the guards were quite friendly. Indeed, one guard even came around with a torch after the prisoners were all in bed to make sure their mosquito nets were well tucked in, under the mattress.

There was even sick leave! One of the jobs was to scrape burnt debris onto a sheet of galvanised iron which was then carried away to be dumped. The only way to handle the sheet was for the man in front to grasp the edge of the iron in his hands, which he held behind his back, while his partner held the other end. The downside of this stretcher-type arrangement was that the person in the rear could not see where he was putting his feet. One day Botterill's partner, the rear-carrier, tripped. The iron shot forward, slicing Botterill's middle finger almost in half. Although the Australian doctor who had been sent with the working party stitched it neatly and bandaged the wound, the Japanese declared that the injury warranted no less than two weeks off work — on full pay. Botterill, who had no argument with this decision, spent the next fortnight fishing, much to the envy of his mates. During this time he also had the opportunity to wander around the old British-built quarters which the Japanese did not use, preferring their specially constructed barracks at the top of the hill. In one of the recreation rooms, Botterill found a full-sized billiard table, covered in beautiful, finely-woven, green woollen cloth. As he did not have a blanket, his kit being in storage, he could not resist the temptation. A few quick slashes and the soft green baize was his.

Tom Burns, who had been confined to Roberts Hospital with severe dysentery, was pleasantly surprised too when he arrived at Bukum, especially after he discovered that prisoners engaged in heavy work were given a break every half-hour, so as to not over-tax themselves. With the improved and plentiful diet, which included a 700 gram daily rice ration, bread, lashings of condensed milk and fresh meat stew for breakfast every day, Tom began to put on condition.

There was also the opportunity to obtain extra food whenever a cargo ship was unloaded. These additional rations were not always obtained by the time-honoured method of scrounging, but often as a reward for working hard. Tom, who weighed about 72 kilograms, was very strong and, being accustomed to lumping heavy loads, found handling 100-kilogram rice sacks relatively easy. The nonchalant way in which he hefted the bags onto his shoulders certainly impressed the Japanese, who rewarded his prowess with a full packet of Australian-made army biscuits and a pack of cigarettes — by now a hard-to-come-by commodity. After their hard work, he and the other workers were allowed a swim to cool off. Sunday brought a respite from both manual labour and the Japanese. The guards, anxious to partake of the various attractions on offer in Singapore city, left the prisoners in the care of their own officers, with instructions to spend the day as they wished. Some of the men rested, some fished off the wharf while others simply swam in the warm waters of the outer harbour.

Unfortunately, about three weeks after his arrival at this workers' paradise, Tom came down with an attack of dengue fever and had to be sent back to Selarang. Although he had not been anxious to leave Pulau Bukum, at Selarang things had improved since those first unhappy weeks. All prisoners now received the same rates of pay as those outside, while the officers had negotiated with the Japanese to receive a reasonable monthly 'allowance', debited against their pay books. In addition, there were now many ways to fill spare time constructively. A 'university', offering a wide range of courses from basic primary education through to legal studies and cordon bleu cookery, was now well established. There was a well-stocked library and concerts were organised. Although Nelson Short, who was quite musical and had a pleasant voice, had joined the first concert group, he had since gone off to work at Blakang Mati [Sentosa] Island, where conditions at that stage were even better than Bukum.

The food situation had also improved. The vegetable gardens, planted in response to an order from the Japanese that the camp must be self-sufficient in all but rice by the end of April, were thriving. Many of the 1000 men employed on the 35-hectare plot were so taken with the job they had enrolled in the university's agricultural course with the intention of taking up farming after the war. The cooks, after an abysmal start, had also mastered the art of cooking rice. The glutinously inedible messes of the first weeks had been replaced by reasonably tasty, if somewhat repetitious, rice-based meals.

In an attempt to improve the vitamin intake for the sick, a fishing party had been formed and in May the AIF Poultry Farm was established under the direction of a Captain McGregor. His civilian occupation as a bank officer might have seemed a little out of step with poultry farming, but McGregor's interest in 'chooks', as the Australians called them, was by no means unusual. Corporal Neil Christie, the sugar-mill accountant turned ordnance storeman, was absolutely mad about them. A bird fancier and breeder who had won a number of trophies at agricultural shows, Christie intended to buy a large poultry farm and go into business after the war. Whether he was part of the AIF's Selarang enterprise is unknown, but it is highly likely he would have jumped at the opportunity to share his expertise and indulge in his hobby.

Thanks to an enthusiastic construction team, Anglican and Catholic chapels were close to completion at Selarang by April and, for those who wished to express their creative talents on a more individual level, there had been a recent Art and Craft Show. This event, staged at the Education Centre on 19 April, presented works of high quality and innovation. Black and white sketches, topical cartoons, clay sculptures and wood carvings were on show in the art section, while among the crafts were exquisitely carved chess sets, ornate walking sticks, elegant smokers' stands, ashtrays carved from polished coconut shells, woven rugs, bamboo artifacts and, for the purely practical, brooms.

As the numbers inside Selarang dwindled, it had became increasingly difficult to find enough man-power to take care of the day-to-day running of the camp, particularly the hum-drum, menial and energy-sapping tasks. The shortage of willing volunteers for less popular chores was solved in typical army fashion. As there was no Mobile Laundry Unit here, Selarang's less tractable found themselves hauling heavy carts or digging six-metre deep latrines, the latter requiring a labour force of 200 men, working in shifts. Murray who, judging from his past form, should have been a prime candidate, was never on the punishment list. As soon as the Australians had been placed on a battle footing, Murray had become a model soldier and, now they were in captivity, he was a model prisoner. The same could not be said for 30-year-old Bill Moxham, of the 2/15th Field Regiment. He was on punishment detail more often than not.

Moxham had been born with a wild, almost reckless streak which had never been tamed, despite his having attended very expensive private schools. He enjoyed sport, was a good mixer, and, although averse to discipline, was better-than-average on academic performance. After leaving school at the age of seventeen, Moxham had spent the next eleven years, until his enlistment in 1940, overseeing or managing three of his family's rural properties. He was fiercely patriotic, the reason why he and his two equally wild brothers had joined up, but army life was not to his liking [1]. Self-reliant after years of working on the land, where every day was a challenge, Moxham was easily bored and objected to taking orders.

Moxham had discovered that one way to relieve the monotony of army life was simply to absent himself — without leave. This, evidently, was no hindrance to promotion. A week after being 'admonished' for absenting himself from Tattoo Roll at Nee Soon, shortly after arriving in Singapore, Moxham had been promoted to Lance-Bombardier. Five days later he failed to appear at parade, which saw him cooling his heels in camp for a week, but keeping his stripe. He was caught again within two months, this time charged with 'neglect to the prejudice of good order and military discipline' for not only allowing Gunner Phoenix to undergo driving instruction while wearing heavy army boots, but for letting him do so at an excessive speed. This misdemeanor attracted nothing more than a reprimand — delivered by the unit's Major Workman — while failing to appear at parade, earned him a seven-day stretch confined to barracks.

Moxham was, nevertheless, a capable soldier once he was on exercise, or in battle, so he was not censured unduly, nor demoted or sent home. Indeed, in some units, unless a soldier's physical or mental health broke down or he committed some heinous crime, the chances of being sent back to Australia had been very remote.

When this was realised during the early days in Malaya, some of those who were physically fit but fed up with the boredom of army life had tried to feign mental illness in order to escape. The most well-known and possibly only successful attempt to do so originated in the actions of Nelson Short, who had joined the army hoping to be a cook but had wound up in the infantry. Not content with simply going absent-without leave (AWL), which had resulted in either a hefty fine or fourteen days' detention, Short's next stunt had been to invent an imaginary dog. He had taken his 'dog' everywhere, patting and grooming it and talking to it as it walked along on the end of an equally imaginary piece of rope. Then Nelson's 'wife' (whom he had married the day before he left Australia) began to accompany him on his walks and sat down to dinner beside him. This bizarre behaviour was taken up by others who, not content to simply walk dogs, began riding imaginary horses around the camp. One group carried it to the extreme by organising sheep musters, complete with imaginary sheep, sheep dogs and sound effects, much to the bemusement of level-headed individuals like George Plunkett and the amazement of the local press. Before long, Singapore-based journalists were writing that the heat had addled the brains of some members of the AIF, who had 'gone troppo'.

At least one army medical officer thought so too. On 21 July 1941 Short had been admitted to hospital suffering from 'neurasthenia' (neurotic maladjustment) but was released a fortnight or so later when his antics were realised. Consigned to kitchen detail, he was soon in strife again, this time for refusing to clean dixie lids as ordered by Sergeant Jobbins — another misdemeanour deemed to be 'conduct to the prejudice of good order and military discipline' and one which had earned him a 10 shilling fine and confinement to the General Base Depot (GBD) at Johore Bahru.

One of Short's contemporaries, however, succeeded in persuading his senior officers he was mentally ill. Bluey Haydon, a private in Short's battalion, had tried everything in his power to obtain a discharge, without success, until he punched a major who he had accused of 'kicking' his 'dog'. Placed under guard in a detention centre, the outraged 'dog owner' kept up the pretence until declared unfit for further military service. Bluey wrote a letter to Short, still languishing at the GBD, crowing, 'You invented the dog Shorty, but I am riding the bastard home'.

While Bill Moxham's behaviour was never sufficiently outrageous to land him in a detention centre, his arrival back in Selarang from the Bukit Timah work party was not unexpected. The tedium of POW life did not suit rebels like Moxham. Strong, nuggety and tough, both mentally and physically, Moxham appears to have been unmoved by being on constant report — a situation which often resulted in relegation to 'the cart'. Far more than a cart, it was a stripped-down vehicle chassis, one of a number of 'Changi trailers' used to haul wood, water, supplies and even the sick around the camp. They were propelled, or rather dragged along, by a number of POWs who were harnessed to the front by traces attached to strong ropes or wire hawsers. The chassis, even without the engine, was no mean weight, and it was back-breaking work.

It was work for which Bob Shipsides and Harry Longley were also destined. It came as no surprise that Harry, being in and out of scrapes, would eventually blot his copybook sufficiently at Thompson Road to be sent back to Selarang for disciplinary reasons, but Corporal Bob Shipsides' appearance on the punishment list was a shock. Ironically, he owed his unexpected return and his subsequent temporary demotion to the rank of private, to both the laxity and vigilance of the Japanese, as well as the wrath of Thomson Road's commanding officer.

When it had been discovered that, owing to an administrative bungle, hundreds of prisoners working on the Bukit Timah and MacRichie Reservoir projects were on the loose in Singapore, the Japanese had taken immediate steps to rectify the situation. Posting guards every few metres around the perimeter of the camp, they had simply waited for the missing prisoners to turn up. Shipsides, who had been well outside the perimeter when the pickets were posted, was caught in the trap. However, it was not just the Japanese who were displeased by the large numbers of prisoners taking unauthorised recreational leave. In charge at Thomson Road was Lieutenant-Colonel Frederick 'Black Jack' Galleghan, the 2/30th Battalion's senior officer and an absolute stickler for discipline. Galleghan, who had taken steps to prevent his men going walkabout, was not at all impressed to learn that among those rounded up were NCOs who, in his opinion, should have known better. Consequently, after a week's detention on the orders of the Japanese, Bob Shipsides found himself back in Selarang, minus his stripes, on the orders of the Australian commander.

Billy Young and Harry Longley, through good timing, had not been among those caught outside the wire. After gorging themselves at a gargantuan dinner with an affluent and very friendly Chinese businessman and his family, they were on their way back to Thomson Road when they spotted a large contingent of guards, running at the double. The pair scampered over the single strand of wire marking the camp boundary just in time. However, by the latter half of June, both Billy and Harry were back at Selarang with Shipsides — Harry for some minor transgression, and Billy with an attack of dysentery. Billy had only just recovered when, on 4 July, the Japanese announced 2000 AIF were needed for an overseas draft in three days' time.

The announcement was not entirely unexpected. At the end of April Lieutenant-General 'Boots' Callaghan, now the AIF's senior commander following General Bennett's escape from Singapore, had been ordered to supply 3000 men for a working party. When it was learned they were to be transferred somewhere up north, where there were better facilities and abundant food supplies, Callaghan had no trouble finding volunteers to fill the quota. Although he was suspicious of the rosy picture painted by the Japanese, many of those fed up with working on the wharves or the monotonous, rice-based diet at Selarang took it at face value.

Mindful that a time might come when it could be possible to stage a revolt, the senior officers compiled the draft, known as A Force, carefully. By ensuring that there was adequate representation of various combat units and a balanced command structure, they were able to form a mini 'brigade', composed of three 'battalions' (A, B and C) and a headquarters, under the command of the 2/18th's Varley, now a brigadier. It was hoped that if the opportunity presented itself this group would be able to function as a composite fighting unit.

With the departure of A Force in the middle of May the number of Australians remaining in Selarang had been reduced to 3800. This included the sick, the convalescent, those on light duties, the less-well disciplined, the older men, those engaged in the running of the camp, senior NCOs not needed to supervise working parties and quite a large group of officers and warrant officers who were not required to work. When it was realised that the quota of 2000 required in three days' time could not be filled, the Japanese set a target of 1500 instead. Even then, to find 1500 eligible and able-bodied workers from this meagre pool would have been a problem had the Japanese not insisted they were destined for a convalescent camp overseas, where any work the prisoners might be required to do would be very light and where there was plenty of nourishing food and more than enough medical supplies. Captain (Dr) Rod Jeffrey who, on hearing about the draft, had swapped places with colleague Captain Catchlove, was ordered to conduct a medical inspection to choose 1500 men fit to travel.

This group, known as B Force, was also divided into three 'battalions' (D, E and F), but its ability to function as a fighting unit is very questionable. Only 40 per cent of the force was drawn from combat units — artillery and anti-tank included. And while a proportion of the infantry was relatively young and able, there was a large number of 'old blokes', mostly from non-combatant and service units, as well as those recuperating from battle wounds or illness. Ray Carlson, aged 42, Neil Christie, 37, and his equally 'elderly' mates Ronald McDonald, Harry Tanzer and John Davis were among the older men. These men, protected from working parties by being kept at Selarang, made up a whopping one third of the party. Corporal Tommy Graham, Privates John Barnier, Tom Burns, George Plunkett, Jacky Ings, and Cornelius Anzac 'Vic' Johnston (a mate of Botterill and Murray who had been suffering from shell shock since the day of the bayonet charge), were among the convalescents. So too was Dick Braithwaite, still in camp after being hospitalised for the removal of his appendix.

Others, neither old nor convalescent, were nominated by officers in charge of the various units for quite different reasons. Some, including Private Eddie McAppion of the Royal Australian Engineers, possessed skills which might be useful. McAppion, who lived in Fremantle within sight and smell of the sea, was an avid sailor and volunteer naval reservist who had also spent quite a lot of time on a family farm. His passion for sailing was so great he would have enlisted in the navy had it not been for his wife, pregnant at the time with his son, who thought the army far safer. A good cricketer, swimmer and footballer, McAppion's all-round sporting skill, coupled with a well-developed musical talent and easy-going personality, made him a popular figure.

Commanders also included in B Force the so-called larrikin element, the poorly-disciplined, late reinforcements (who, not having the opportunity to prove themselves or forge bonds with their units, were an unknown quantity), senior NCOs and an excessive number of surplus officers whose quality, to coin a phrase in use at the time, went 'from cream to sour milk'. As a result, the proportion of officers to men was extraordinarily high. In the 4th Anti-Tank Regiment, there were no less than twelve — two majors, one captain and nine lieutenants — to oversee 33 men, nine of whom were NCOs. Of the 1494 soldiers on the B Force draft, 143 were officers — one for every ten men. If the 312 NCOs were taken into account, the overall ratio decreased to one in three.

All those who had found themselves in trouble at some time or other were chosen. Harry Longley, Bob Shipsides, Bill Moxham and Mo Davis, in camp for disciplinary reasons, were on the list. Billy Young who, having recovered from dysentery, had just graduated from light duties to trailer hauling, was named, along with his friend, Joey Crome. They were joined by a number of others, including Privates Annear, Bowe (who had enlisted as Anderson), Buckley, Beer, Brett, Donohue, Longbottom and Lytton. All were from the 2/30th Battalion and all had made two mistakes: first, having a casual attitude to discipline and, second, having been brought to Black Jack Galleghan's attention.

Not all of those on Black Jack's hit list were young men. Private James Stuart Smith, aged 42, was such a renegade that he had spent more time in detention than out of it. Nothing, not even hefty fines or long periods of confinement had made the slightest bit of difference. Arrested for forging leave passes and taking himself off on extended periods of unauthorised leave, he had even tried to escape before the surrender by hitching a ride in a 'borrowed' Bren-gun carrier, which had managed to travel all the way from Mandai Road to Singapore Harbour without any awkward questions being asked. There, however, the escape attempt had faltered. Smith, learning that the Japanese navy was lying in wait to blast all vessels fleeing Singapore out of the water, realised that the chances of reaching Sumatra by motor launch were practically nil and had given himself up.

There were some volunteers for B Force, and some of them battle-hardened soldiers. Lieutenant Ron Ollis, an instructor at a special training school until he was 'head-hunted' by Black Jack for the 2/30th, was there, along with his elder brother, John. Although Ron had been hospitalised with malaria during the battle for Singapore, both he and John had seen action in Malaya, where the 2/30th Battalion had covered itself in glory with a particularly well-planned and well-executed ambush near Gemas. Another officer with extensive combat experience was the 2/18th's Captain Ken Mosher, a stern disciplinarian and university graduate who had earned the respect of his men the hard way — by example. On learning that doctors and paramedics were needed, Lieutenant-Colonel Sheppard and 130-odd members of the 2/10th Field Ambulance — all those still at Selarang and about half the entire unit — had also stepped forward. Three of them were close friends — Don Brack, from the New South Wales Central Coast and two men from the bush, Robert Bruce of Byangum, a tiny hamlet near the New South Wales-Queensland border and Bill Ney, who hailed from Gollan, in the rich wheat/sheep belt of Central New South Wales. Had Singapore not fallen with such rapidity, Ney, aged 25, would have by now been in the Middle East, claimed by his elder brother Ivan, whose enlistment into the AIF had inspired Bill to do the same in April 1941. Quite tall and very fit from working outdoors and indulging his passion for cricket and tennis, Ney, like so many young men raised in the country, could turn his hand to just about anything. That such an enormous number of men from his unit was permitted to volunteer for B Force was most likely owing to the high proportion of convalescents and older men placed on the draft — a consideration which also saw Albert Anderson and about 50 of his mates from the 2/3 MAC also added to the list. Although, like Anderson, most were 'old blokes', all had considerable medical experience.

Two volunteers were civilians — Mr Ronald Hamilton Wilson, an Australian Red Cross Representative, and Mr H. J. Fleming, of the Salvation Army who, for administrative purposes, were attached to the 2/10th Field Ambulance. Other volunteers included 22-year-old signaller Lieutenant Rod Wells, a wireless and communications expert from country Victoria who had been lecturing at Selarang 'university', and Botterill and Murray, who had just arrived back in camp. It had been Murray's idea to go back. Although they had no real complaints about Pulau Bukum, Murray thought it 'a bit rich' having to work on Saturdays when at Selarang you didn't have to work at all and still received your pay. Botterill had agreed. Their minds made up, the pair told the doctor they were suffering from dysentery, a sure way to get back to the main camp.

As soon as they stepped off the boat and saw severed heads on display at just about every street corner in Singapore, Botterill realised what a mistake it had been to leave Bukum. If the Japanese were doing this to the locals, it might be only a matter of time before the POWs in Singapore suffered the same fate. When he and Murray arrived at Selarang and learned that there was a group leaving for 'somewhere overseas' the next day, they grabbed some kit from the piles of gear which had been released from storage and got themselves on the list, believing the further away from Singapore with its sword-happy Japanese they were, the better.

Brigadier Taylor was due to be moved from Singapore with other senior officers on 16 August, so command of B Force was given to Lieutenant-Colonel Alf Walsh, a graduate from Duntroon Military College and the 2/10th Field Regiment's senior officer. Unfortunately it was an appointment that was not greeted with particular joy by B Force. He was short and a little overweight, both of which tended to make him appear somewhat unprepossessing, but also word had circulated that Walsh was not popular with his own men and not reliable under pressure. While this assessment appears to have had some foundation, the colonel's lack of popularity was not entirely of his own making.

Shortly before the Japanese had invaded Malaya, the 2/10th's charismatic and very popular commanding officer, Lieutenant-Colonel Gordon Kirwood, who had raised the wholly Queensland-based unit and moulded it into a fiercely loyal outfit, was relieved of his command following an incident of an embarrassing personal nature in Malaya. The gunners, seething with bitterness and indignation over his removal, had not been placated in the slightest to find his successor was the recently promoted Walsh who, apart from not being a Queenslander, was a 'staff wallah' — a member of the much derided staff corps, deemed to be long on text book tactics but short on practical experience. His appointment was particularly unpopular with the infantry rank and file — although this seems to have more to do with the infantry's traditional dislike of non-infantrymen than anything else. Consequently, Walsh had no hope of forging any kind of working relationship, let alone a close one, with his men. He responded by withdrawing into himself, which did nothing to enhance his image.

Fifty-three NCOs and gunners from Walsh's regiment were also drafted, along with 20 officers, making the ratio between officers and men as disproportionate as that of the anti-tank regiment. Why Walsh included so many officers is not clear, neither is it possible to establish why he was selected over other more senior officers to lead the force. It is possible that General 'Boots' Callaghan, previously Commander of Artillery and Walsh's immediate superior, may have considered him to be better suited to oversee a convalescent, rather than a working, camp.

While the families of the prisoners assigned to B Force had no way of knowing they were leaving Singapore they would, in time, receive post cards confirming that the men had been taken prisoner there. On 20 June, four months after the surrender, the Japanese had at last permitted all POWs in Singapore to send a message home. Restricted to a measly 25 words written in block capitals, the messages were brief and impersonal. Albert Anderson told Dot, his wife, 'I AM A PRISONER OF WAR. I AM FIT AND WELL. LOVE TO YOU AND THE CHILDREN.' Ray Carlson and John Barnier wrote almost identical messages: 'I AM A PRISONER OF WAR. I WAS NOT WOUNDED. I AM WELL.' After signing off with 'FONDEST LOVE TO' Barnier had enough spare words to mention the names of his siblings, Maureen, Margaret and Brian, while Carlson, with his eleven off-spring, had to settle for the all-encompassing 'LOVE TO YOU AND THE CHILDREN'.

The card would not be delivered to the Barnier farm in Grafton until 6 October the following year, but its arrival would bring great relief to Barnier's family — not simply because there was a chance that John was still alive and well but because his message did not contain the words 'TELL ROY THAT...'. Had it

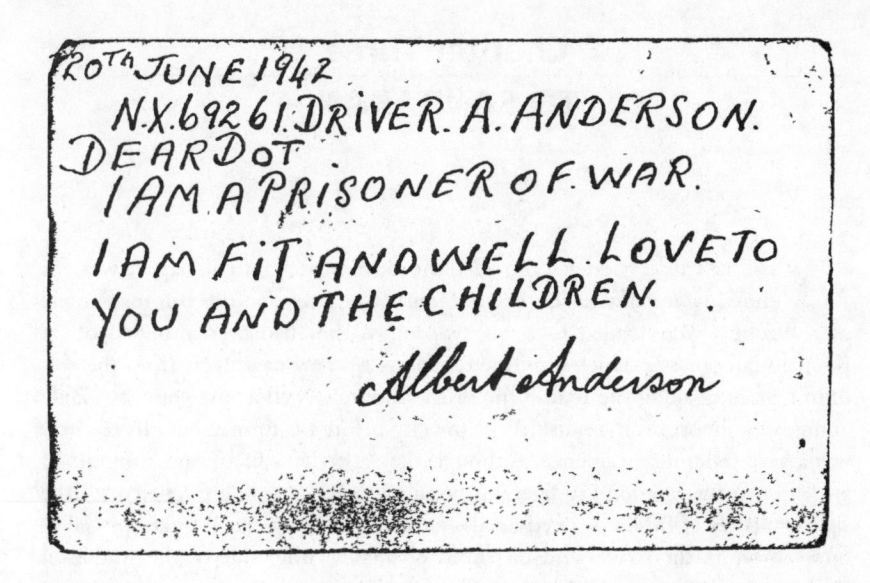

> 20TH JUNE 1942
> N.X.69261. DRIVER. A. ANDERSON.
> DEAR DOT
> I AM A PRISONER OF WAR.
> I AM FIT AND WELL. LOVE TO
> YOU AND THE CHILDREN.
> Albert Anderson

Albert Anderson's first postcard home, written two weeks before B Force left Singapore for Borneo.

done so, the Barniers would have known immediately that the exact opposite to anything written on the card about his well-being or conditions was true. This clever but simple code had been devised months before by John who, although never voicing any doubt the Australians would drive the Japanese back, nevertheless had faced the possibility that he could, at some time in the future, be captured.

On the morning of 7 July the men of B Force woke at 5.00am to pack their gear and wolf down a breakfast of rice porridge with milk and sugar, half a slice of bread and a mug of tea. At 7.30am, following a touching farewell speech by Brigadier Taylor, they were ready to leave. Confident that a better future was in store, they formed orderly ranks and, with a dollar note and a cigarette ration to help see them on their way, marched out of Selarang Barracks.

Chapter Three
TO SANDAKAN

As some trucks had been provided the journey back into Singapore was, for most, a good deal easier than the journey out, five months before. The less robust were loaded first, but as soon as they had been dropped off at Keppel Harbour the vehicles returned, picking up new passengers from the column marching along the road. One of the fittest, as well as the youngest, Billy Young was almost on the outskirts of the city before his turn came. His re-entry was a very sobering experience. Although the Australians had heard rumours of atrocities against the local indigenous population, most were unprepared for the sight of scores of freshly severed heads, rammed on sharp metal stakes placed at intervals along the streets and displayed on tables either side of the Anderson Bridge.

The men had hoped to board a hospital ship and morale plummeted when they realised the vessel, rumoured to be taking them to a place called Sandakan in Borneo, was Yubi Maru. Although her name (pronounced 'yoo-bi') meant grace or elegance, a less elegant ship would have been hard to find[1]. The small, decrepit, rusty tramp-steamer of about 2000 tonnes looked scarcely capable of sailing across the harbour, let alone across the open sea. Evidently built for the Australian wheat trade, she was one of the many obsolete cargo ships sold before the war to the Japanese as scrap metal — ostensibly for their domestic market. When it became known that most of the vessels had been melted down and recycled into Japanese munitions, an outraged Australian public had dubbed Prime Minister Robert Gordon Menzies, who had urged the sale, 'Pig-Iron Bob'.

Yubi Maru had three holds — for'ard, aft and amidships — all accessed by rickety vertical iron ladders and with a machine gun mounted at each corner. The ship had previously been used as a collier and the centre hold, divided into two iron decks, was covered with coal dust about 15 centimetres deep. There were no portholes. The only ventilation was through a canvas air-scoop and tube funnelled into each hold, but this worked only when the ship was moving.

It was mid-afternoon before the men began filing up the gangplank and into the bowels of the vessel, her iron plates now super-heated in the fierce tropical sun. Major Errol Maffey, one of the 2/10th Field Ambulance doctors, estimated the space per person in the centre hold, into which 760 men, luggage and rations were jammed, was roughly 165 centimetres by 45 centimetres. In the for'ard hold were 340 officers and men while the remaining 400, squeezed on top of the cargo in an after-hold measuring about 20 metres by 10 metres, were so cramped they were forced to sit with their knees under their chins. Tom Burns, who was as squashed for space as anyone, was reminded of the stories he had heard of the nineteenth century slave traders, who had stacked their living cargo head-to-toe to maximise profits.

Sanitation facilities, Yubi Maru. *Drawing by Billy Young.*

Although the ship left the wharf that afternoon, she sailed only as far as the Straits to anchor overnight. All those who could fit (about half at any one time) were allowed up on deck until after the evening meal, but they were herded down the ladders as soon as it was dark, to the accompaniment of much yelling and shoving from the Japanese guards. Some shoddy straw mats, which soon disintegrated into chaff and disappeared into the coal dust, were issued to the occupants of the centre hold. Other than that, bedding was non-existent.

Sleep was almost impossible. The sweltering heat and severe overcrowding allowed only fitful rest, and there was always a long queue of men waiting to use the latrines, attached to the railings either side of the upper deck. The ladders leading topside could only be reached by stepping on dozens of tightly packed bodies, and these nocturnal excursions provoked much cursing and the odd blow or two. The stalwarts who succeeded in reaching their goal found it a makeshift affair. Billy Young discovered that the latrines allocated to his section of the ship were nothing more than four open-fronted booths constructed from old packing cases and connected at 'seat' height by two horizontal planks, placed a few centimetres apart. As the whole contraption dangled out over the sea, those enthroned made sure they kept a secure grip on the railings at all times.

The first night was hard going, but it was nothing compared to the rest of the voyage, which lasted a hideously long ten days. There were sundry beatings and bashings and the rations supplied by the Japanese were abysmal — heavily limed, weevilly rice, some green strands of what appeared to be chopped up grass and an occasional 'whiff' of meat, washed down with about half a litre of warm, brownish fluid masquerading as tea. The Australian cooks tried to wash out some of the lime residue from the rice by lowering the bags into the sea on a rope, but the result was always the same — an almost inedible, putrid, worm-riddled mess, smelling and tasting revoltingly of rotten eggs.

The men had no salt and only 1.5 litres of fluid a day, and even the fittest began to suffer from dehydration. The water, stored in a 2.4-metre, square tank for'ard and a slightly smaller one aft, was severely rationed, yet the supply in the small tank ran dry after only three days. The Japanese, depending on the mood of their senior officer, Lieutenant Okahara, occasionally allowed Major Maffey to give extra fluid to the sick, but the rest had to make do as best they could. At the risk of a beating, some fell back on that wonderfully Australian stand-by — scrounging — and appropriated Japanese supplies.

A few of the sick were taken on deck by their mates, to lie beneath the steam-driven winches, mouths open to catch the drops of condensation that fell every few seconds. However, no one was allowed to remain on deck except during specially designated periods, a regulation strictly enforced by Australian officers. Botterill, desperate for a drink and dehydrated from dengue fever, was helped from the hold and positioned beneath one of the winches by Murray and Vic Johnston who was 26 and the proud wearer of a well-clipped moustache, which made him far more impressive-looking than the average private soldier. Keith had scarcely had time to moisten his lips when along came an officer to hunt them below. Richie Murray, who when drawn to his full height was quite an imposing figure, said it was all right as they were with an officer — Johnston. Although the patrolling officer was suspicious as Johnston was not wearing his shirt (not something an officer would normally do) he let it go at that, allowing the fever-ridden patient to slake his thirst.

It was not long before most of the men were suffering from some form of diarrhoea or vomiting. As many were unable to reach the upper deck in time, the holds, ladders and decks were soon awash with foul smelling filth. Dysentery broke out, adding to the misery of everyone on board. It was impossible to do anything about the smell, for while the decks and latrine areas were hosed down early each morning and in the evening, the holds and ladders were not. The only positive aspect of being below decks was that the stench was so overpowering the Japanese kept their distance. So little fresh air reached the holds, despite the ventilation tubes, that Tom Burns and Dick Braithwaite, who was one of those crushed into the after-hold, were sure there would be a number of deaths before long.

Why no one died on that nightmare voyage will forever remain a mystery, but perhaps the rumour that they were to be repatriated, along with the determination not to let the Japanese 'grind them down', had some bearing. Although crammed cheek-by-jowl in the sweaty, fetid holds, they maintained morale by playing cards, yarning and joining in community singing, organised by ex-Boy Scout types who taught them the words of simple rounds and campfire songs. Gunner Johnny Moule-Probert, squashed beside Braithwaite in the rear hold, kept those around him spellbound with the story of his World War 1 experiences. A '39 liar', who was really aged 45 but had put his age back to 39 to enlist the second time around, Johnny had served in the Great War with the Royal Flying Corps until he was shot down over German lines. He had polished up his schoolboy German while recovering, so that by the time he was discharged from hospital he was fluent. A very likable and affable bloke, he was a great hit with his captors, who appointed him a Red Cross liaison officer and set him up in a flat in Berlin. He escaped to Switzerland after living it up as a privileged civilian for some months, and was repatriated to Britain, a feat which automatically earned him a Military Cross.

Moule-Probert rose to the rank of flying officer with the Royal Australian Air Force (RAAF) between the wars but, after two years acting as a courier between Sydney and Melbourne, decided he wanted to see some real action. Somehow or other he obtained a discharge from the RAAF, went to Melbourne and joined the AIF. He was sent to the Middle East as a Warrant Officer, contracted sand-fly fever and was sent home, where he was discharged as medically unfit. He joined up again as soon as he recovered, this time in Sydney, and was sent to Malaya with the 2/15th Field Artillery. His position as a lowly gunner was viewed with some consternation by one British general, unable to fathom the strange ways of 'colonials' who put an ex-Royal Flying Corps *officer* in the *ranks*. Johnny Moule-Probert was evidently a supreme scrounger as well as a capable gunner. Somewhere along the way he had managed to souvenir the Bukit Timah Post Office clock, which he still had in his kit bag.

There was not a single man on board *Yubi Maru* who was not relieved when the ship stopped to refuel at the first and only port of call — the oil-producing depot at Miri, on the northern tip of Sarawak. The relief, however, was short lived. The ship anchored off-shore for two-and-a-half days, during which time the prisoners were rarely allowed on deck. It was while sitting crouched in the after hold, knees tucked under his chin and eyes lowered, that Mo Davis noticed light from a naked electric globe shining through a gap in the timber decking. Botterill and Sid Outram helped him prise up the boards to see what was down below. They discovered that they were sitting on cases of meat and vegetables, plundered from the Singapore godowns and now destined for the Japanese market. It was just as well Mo had discovered the cache for, although the Japanese returned from their furlough ashore loaded down with pineapples and bananas, not one morsel of the succulent fruit went to the prisoners.

The unexpected tinned rations did as much to lift the morale of those aft, but the men could do nothing about the stifling conditions. The first night at Miri, Billy Young and Joey Crome, desperate for a respite from the heat and stench, stayed on deck after the evening meal and secreted themselves in a space between the latrines and a storage locker. As they took deep breaths of blessedly fresh air the pair weighed up the possibility of swimming to Miri which, from their elevated vantage point, appeared tantalisingly close. They were still arguing the possibilities when the galley door flew open and a bucket of swill was tossed over the side. Almost immediately the placid waters became a seething, boiling mass of phosphorescence as hundreds of fish fought for the spoils. Billy and Joey watched as a malevolent shadow shot without warning from the depths, scattering the fish with one terrifying snap of its massive jaws before disappearing below the inky surface. Abandoning all thoughts of swimming ashore, the pair retreated to the safety of the hold to help Mo Davis and the others finish off the tinned meat and vegetables before the Japanese saw the empty tins floating away on the tide and realised that a considerable part of the cargo had disappeared.

It was a great relief when the ship was finally underway again. As she stuttered along at a pace of six knots Mo, the merchant-sailor, raised the idea of taking over the ship — a notion quickly quashed by the officers who thought such a move would be premature. Caution was well-advised, as it turned out. The following morning, gazing out to sea while at the topside sanitation facilities, Mo caught sight of what looked like the conning tower of a submarine. Unable to discern whether it was friend or foe, he decided to stay where he was and keep an eye on it. A Japanese submarine surfaced and semaphored the ship. Mo was forced to concede that even if the prisoners had mutinied they would not have got very far.

The Japanese became very edgy as they neared the Balabac Straits. This narrow waterway, separating the northern-most tip of Borneo from the south-western Philippine Island of Balabac, was a well-known hunting ground for American submarines. The ship hugged the north-western coastline, treating those fortunate enough to be on deck at the time to the magnificent sight of Mt Kinabalu, at 4000 metres the highest mountain in Borneo, thrusting its majestic, mist-enshrouded volcanic peak into the sky.

On 18 July *Yubi Maru* rounded the north-eastern coast of Borneo and set a course for the short run south to Sandakan, peace-time capital of British North Borneo. Sandakan no longer existed officially, as, following the arrival of Japanese occupation forces on 19 January, the town had been renamed Elopura and the East Coast Residency, the geographical subdivision in which it was located, Tokai Shui. Kudat, on the north-west tip, along with the West Coast and Interior Residencies, had been joined together to create a western governorate called Seikai Shui, while the principal town, Jesselton, was now known as Api.

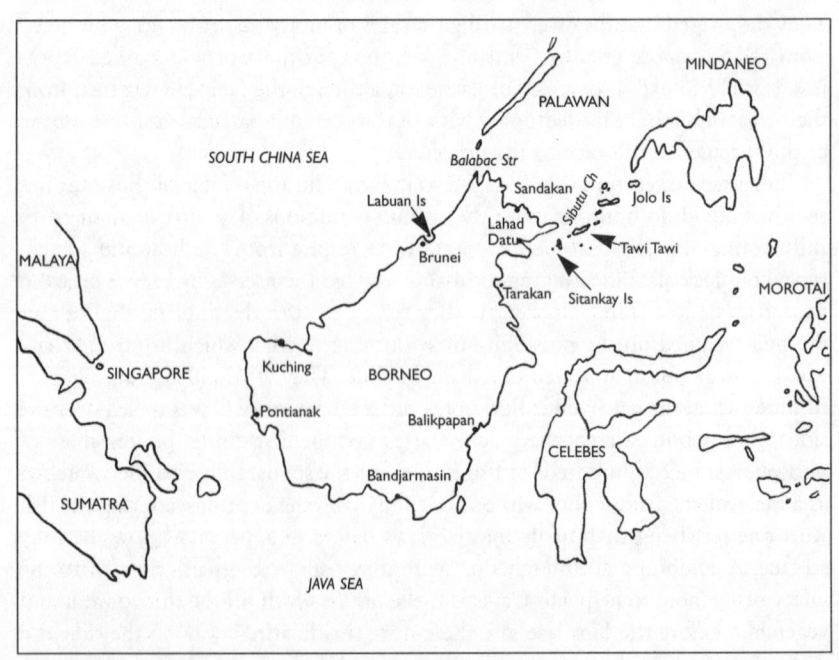

Locality map of Singapore, Borneo and the Philippines.

The Japanese had also altered both the time and the date and introduced a new currency. The clocks in Borneo, usually eight hours ahead of Greenwich, were put forward another hour to coincide with Tokyo time and the year 1942 became 2602, Japanese reckoning. To further complicate matters, the years also acknowledged the reign of the current emperor, so that 1942 was also referred to as Showa 17, the seventeenth year of the reign of Emperor Hirohito. The occupation paper currency, issued in dollar denominations, featured an engraving of bananas as part of the design and was supposedly on a par with the local British currency. However, they devalued at such a rate that they were virtually worthless within six months, giving rise to the derisive term 'duit pasang' or 'banana money'.

It was just dawn, after ten tedious days at sea, when *Yubi Maru* eased towards her berth, giving the Australians on deck their first glimpse of the settlement. They could not fail to appreciate that Sandakan, the name still defiantly used by pro-British locals, was stunningly beautiful. The town spread along the narrow foreshores of a magnificent harbour, backed by lush green hills dotted with spacious and opulent homes belonging to wealthy European residents. From the most north-easterly point at Tanjung Papat, rugged coastal cliffs continued on as the 100-metre-high Bukit Sim Sim Ridge before dropping away to the west where they merged into the hill behind the township. Guarded on its northern entrance by the spectacular, towering red-chalk cliffs of Berhala Island, the harbour's most southern extremity was marked by Tanjung Aru, a small island about 2 kilometres across open water from Tanjung Papat.

Most of the harbour's upper reaches were as yet uncharted, fed by numerous rivers and fringed by mangroves and nipah palms which gave way to thickly-timbered country further inland. The water, which opened out considerably once inside the entrance, varied in width from 4 to 9 kilometres and extended for about 25 kilometres inland, providing an excellent anchorage for any number of medium-draught ships. The main commercial and business district, on land sloping gently back from a stone sea-wall and roughly 1.5 kilometres from Tanjung Papat, centred around the wooden Government Wharf and consisted of neat rows of mainly single-storeyed, red-roofed buildings. Further to the left, the stone wall gave way to a sandy beach, at the end of which was a fishing village, its palm-thatch and bamboo huts jutting out into the water on spindly stilts. About half a kilometre beyond was a large sawmill, currently lying idle following the destruction of its machinery by the British residents, and beyond that again was Bokara village, where the coastal road ended. Immediately to the left of the Government Wharf and extending right down to the sea wall was a large swathe of unbelievably green grass — the town's padang or playing field, on which the civilians played soccer at night. Stretching into the distance beyond the town were the vast rubber, timber, palm-oil and coconut estates, the source of the country's wealth, and beyond that, the virtually unexplored interior — a remote and alien region of rugged, jungle-clad mountains, criss-crossed by wild, turbulent rivers and populated only by small isolated pockets of self-sufficient tribespeople, some of whom were as yet untouched by western civilisation. And keeping watch over it all was Mt Kinabalu.

There was only one thing to spoil the tranquillity of this idyllic, picture-postcard scene, a scene which could have come straight from the pages of a Somerset Maugham novel or the brush of Paul Gauguin. The one jarring note was the blood-red sun upon white — the unmistakable design of the Japanese flag, fluttering triumphantly aloft from every official building in town.

It was not until the afternoon that an order was given for the prisoners to disembark and line up on the padang. About half, including those in the after-hold, were left on board for the time being, there being no place to billet them. As the men filed down the gangplank, their feet and legs were sprayed with a carbolic acid solution which, according to the Japanese, would kill all dangerous germs and so put an end to the dysentery that had broken out.

On the wharf they were counted and recounted under the watchful eye of Lieutenant Hoshijima Susumi, a tall, arrogant-looking army officer who, the prisoners learned, was to be the camp commandant. A graduate of Osaka University, he had been appointed to the post at the request of General (Marquis) Maeda, Commander-in-Chief of all Japanese forces in Borneo. When Hoshijima was satisfied that the tally was correct, they were escorted under heavy guard to the padang. Roughly triangular in shape, it was bordered on the western side by shops, dwellings, a cinema and the main administration building (occupied by 30 Japanese soldiers), and on the north by more shops and houses. The local residents, informed of the prisoners' arrival in advance, had turned out in force to take a look. Those who had resented living under British administration waved their Japanese flags and looked smugly satisfied at seeing the white 'tuans' humbled, but others, especially the Chinese, were visibly distressed.

Hoshijima had given strict orders prohibiting any contact between civilians and prisoners, but some of the men, including Artillery Sergeant Walter Wallace, managed to make their way to the edge of the padang to exchange a few words with some of the less intimidated onlookers. Using a mixture of Malay and English, they learned that the Sandakan residents, whose radios had been confiscated to prevent them following the progress of the war, had been told the prisoners had been brought from Australia, now under Japanese occupation. Before the Japanese guards put an end to further fraternisation, the Australians told them the truth.

The prisoners had only just assembled for the evening meal — dirty, battered buckets of the same disgusting limed rice that had been on the menu for the last ten days — when there was a brief rain shower. As no one had bathed since they left Singapore, some stripped off and removed the worst of the grime, much to the amusement of the locals who were not accustomed to seeing white men behave in this fashion. At about half-past five, after washing down the cupful of rice with the usual cup of watery tea, the Australians were formed up into batches of 44 and marched, under heavy guard, towards a hill at the south-west of the town.

They laboured up the winding road, watched by local residents clustered along the route at various vantage points. The sick and crippled, including Wallace, who had recently had his appendix removed, brought up the rear, accompanied by a small, plump Japanese guard. Wallace, realising from the guard's attempts to converse that he was trying to be friendly, made signs that he was thirsty. While the guard waited, Wallace disappeared inside a dwelling. He emerged not only with information about the local topography, the climate, the flora, the fauna and endemic diseases in his head but a map of Borneo and Sandakan in his pocket.

It was quite dark by the time they reached the top of the hill, where the road ended abruptly in the grounds of a large stone church and convent. The men tried to make themselves comfortable inside the church buildings, using the light of hurricane lamps which cast gloomy shadows across the pillared nave. At about 4.00am they were roused, counted and recounted, before being marched back down the hill to join those left on the ship, many of whom had been allowed ashore to sleep on the padang. All were hungry, yet few had any stomach for the breakfast — the previous night's leftovers, reheated and even more unpalatable than before. As their destination was a camp 14 kilometres along Kabon China Road, about 20 of the sick were ordered to wait for a truck to transport them and the heavier baggage. The rest moved off, shouldering whatever gear they could carry, the strong encouraging the weak, to the rousing strains of 'Waltzing Matilda'.

The all-weather road they were following, prominently marked with mile posts along its length, ran in a north-westerly direction for about the first 10.5 kilometres, and then due west for another 12 kilometres. The metalled surface then gave way to dirt for another 6.5 kilometres, eventually dwindling into a dry-weather bridle track leading to the fishing village of Beluran on the Labuk River estuary. The prisoners had started out well enough but most found the march difficult. Their route wound partly through fern-banked cuttings with trees forming a green arbor overhead, but it was all uphill to the 3 mile peg, where they were allowed to have a short rest and a smoke. However, by the time the column reached more open terrain marking the beginning of the rubber estates, the sun was high in the sky and the men, after days at sea sustained only by a minimum rice ration, exhausted. As the pace slackened the guards moved in on the stragglers, hurrying them along with kicks, sticks and well-aimed jabs from rifle butts — if a man left the column for any reason he jeopardised his life. One prisoner, who stepped away from the road to take some fruit that was being offered, found himself being shot at.

At the 8 mile peg, where a small police post had been recently established, the weary marchers turned off to the right to follow a dusty track, cutting through a rubber plantation belonging to the pre-war government's Experimental Agricultural Farm. About 400 metres from the turn-off, on the left, was the farm's administration building and a further 400 metres on, at the foot of a small hill, a boiler house and small power plant. A galvanised-iron pipe ran from the boiler house in a direct line to large concrete water tanks on the crest of the hill, about 100 metres away. A small cottage belonging to the farm stood beyond the tanks, over to the left, while on the right was a grove of mature palms.

The track degenerated beyond the boiler, swinging away to the right past a good-sized buffalo wallow and then up the hill. It skirted the palms, then veered left and petered out in front of two large, timber-framed gates, criss-crossed with barbed-wire and with additional strands splayed out from the top at an angle of about 45 degrees. Opening inwards for greater security, they were fastened with a length of chain and a large padlock. A wooden sign hung in the middle, identifying the establishment as 'No 1 Prisoner-of-War Camp, British North Borneo', and also advising that POW Administrative Headquarters was at Kuching — the capital of Sarawak, hundreds of kilometres away on the west coast.

This was obviously their destination and some of the newcomers, with an eye to a possible escape, began to take greater interest in their surroundings. The chances did not look good. The interlaced barbed wire continued in both directions from the gate in the form of a fence. Another outer fence, of about the same height but composed of single strands of horizontal wire, ran parallel to it. A few metres back from the fence and to the right of the gate, were two guardhouses. These elevated wooden buildings could have been mistaken for residences were it not for the machine gun mounted on the open-sided verandah of the house closest to the gate.

There was no mistaking that the two-hectare site, roughly square in shape, had been set out according to military regulations. The area was small and the terrain irregular, yet the layout was precise and orderly and the use of space efficient. Three neat rows of thatched wooden huts and a few other assorted buildings, all mounted on substantial square-shaped timber stilts, were placed parallel to the front fence, either side of the gate. The six huts on the right and another six or so on the left, measuring roughly 13 metres by 6 metres and split into three distinct rooms, had been constructed from milled hardwood planks. The rooms opened onto a common verandah, where individual sets of steps provided access to ground level. There was no glass in the windows, only hopper-style wooden shutters.

It was obvious, from the quality of the buildings, the small, louvred weather station to the right of the gate, the access road and the substantial nature of the water and power plant, that No 1 Borneo POW Camp had been constructed originally as some kind of permanent barracks buildings. Evidently, it had been occupied first by Indian Army troops and then, when war broke out in Europe, by German and Italian internees. The site is a good 12 kilometres from town, so it is unlikely it was erected purely as a garrison. It is far more likely that, with the Royal Air Force (RAF) planning to construct an airfield nearby, it was built to accommodate engineers, skilled construction workers and/or defending troops. Whatever the camp's origins, for the six weeks following the outbreak of war with Japan it had apparently been used as a detention centre for about 40 Japanese civilian internees.

On the right-hand side of the large open space separating the two sets of wooden huts was a huge Belian tree, identified by Captain Mosher as a type of fig but thought by others to be a maple. Soon to be dubbed 'The Big Tree', as it towered 70 metres into the air, its immense height and massive buttress roots were a reminder that this ancient giant was all that was left of a lush rainforest. Its crown, ravaged from repeated lightning strikes, was now a distinctive landmark which stood out for kilometres. The ground dropped away beyond the tree to both the rear and the left to form a muddy pond and swamp, once an elephant watering hole but latterly the domain of several water-buffalo, now relocated outside the wire on the left. Two dozen closely-spaced, palm-leaf huts straddled the slope to the right of the pond. They were arranged in four rows of five and one of four (which were slightly larger), running at right angles to those at the gate, and they helped to define an area around the tree large enough for all the prisoners to assemble. The huts in this block were also perched on stilts but, because of the gradient, those at the far end, especially on the eastern side, were a considerable height above the ground.

It was quite apparent that these 24 huts were not part of the original plan. They were constructed in typical native style, with walls of nipah palm, otherwise known as atap, tied in overlapping horizontal layers to a rough-sawn timber framework. There is nothing wrong with this type of general construction. Atap which has been dried and shrunk before use makes an excellent building material, quite waterproof and capable of withstanding all but the most violent storms. Green atap does not. The gaps in the walls and roof and the use of logs, rather than sawn timber, for the supporting piers, suggested to Billy Young that these particular huts had been put up in something of a hurry. One, immediately in front of where Dick Braithwaite was billeted, was so poorly constructed it collapsed, giving the occupants and onlookers a fright but causing no serious injuries.

A flattish, open area suitable as a parade ground lay between the atap huts and the right-hand camp boundary, and beyond that, just outside the perimeter wire, was a small grove of aromatic cinnamon trees. The ground separating the cinnamon trees from a small rubber plantation visible on a distant rise was quite open, apart from two lone trees, a few coffee bushes and occasional patches of tapioca. A clump of overgrown rubber trees and some nondescript scrub were to the south-east, while a small plantation of kapok trees was beyond the wire on the left, or western, side. There were patches of various types of vegetation on three sides of the compound, but the land to the north, beyond the rear boundary, had been cleared of all trees for the RAF's intended airstrip, leaving an open stretch of ground about 1.5 kilometres long and 800 metres wide.

The men could see that whoever was responsible for security (said to be the Sandakan Public Works Department) had done a good job. The interlaced inner-wire, which ran two-thirds of the way around the perimeter, was stretched tightly between timber poles and reinforced by heavy-gauge horizontal, vertical and diagonal wires. The lower edge was hard up against the ground while from the top sprouted rows of barbed wire angled out in the same way as those on the gate. In the swamp area the interlaced wire gave way to horizontal strands, but security was maintained by filling the space between the two fences with tangled loops of concertina wire. Several electric light standards were spaced fairly evenly around the inner fence while beyond the outer wire were seven elevated sentry boxes, linked in the upper section by a foot track and in the swamp area by an elevated wooden walkway, supported on posts about a metre above the water. The one and only entrance was the gate, guarded day and night and in a direct line of fire from the machine gun.

It was about 2.30pm, two and a half hours after the head of the column arrived, that Tom Burns and the tail-enders reached the camp. They struggled through the gates, exhausted and wet through from the rain which was now falling in torrents. Sergeant Wallace and the sick, who had made the journey by truck, had been there for some time. Wallace, like Billy and Botterill, had given the place the once over and conceded that the prospects for an early escape did not look at all bright.

Colonel Walsh and his officers wasted no time in inspecting the camp and allocating the accommodation. The men were quartered in the atap huts, while the 143 officers and two civilians occupied the timber buildings near the gate which, although they had atap roofs, boasted proper wooden ceilings and woven straw mats on the sleeping platforms. The number in each hut varied but, as in peace-time, the allocation of space reflected the strict pecking order which separated each level of seniority from the next. The remainder of the buildings adjacent to the officers' quarters was assigned to the senior NCOs and hospital, with the quartermaster's-store and large kitchen in the far left corner. The latter exceeded all expectations having its own water storage tank and two large cast-iron woks set in properly constructed brick hearths, rather like the fuel coppers found at that time in many Australian laundries. Billy doubted the woks would ever be used. Army cooks, in his experience, had an arrogant disregard for anything even slightly foreign, and preferred to stick with their cauldrons, made from 44-gallon drums cut in half.

The malodorous latrines were far too close to Tom Burns' hut for his liking, but the huts assigned to the other ranks (ORs) were more or less habitable. The roofs leaked and the walls had gaps in the atap, enabling rats to enter at will, but all had verandahs and the floors — fifteen-centimetre-wide, sawn planks — were sturdy enough. The installation of waist-high, timber railings effectively split each hut into three or, in the case of the larger ones, four, stall-like rooms, each with its own doorway and set of steps. Two raised platforms ran across the rooms, either side of the doorway. They were constructed from planks, of the same type as the floor, and they provided a sleeping space measuring 60 centimetres by 183 centimetres for each of its human occupants, and a wonderful home for thousands of blood-sucking bed bugs, lice and other parasites — unwelcome legacies of previous tenants. There were no doors to the rooms, although atap shutters not purloined by the locals still swung in some window openings, while interior lighting was provided by a naked globe dangling from one of the roof trusses. The only other furniture was an open shelf above each platform in the four larger huts. This was supposed to be 'locker' space but, with sixteen men to each room (64 to a hut), the amount of storage space per person was strictly limited. There were no dining facilities as such, but a wide plank forming the topmost verandah railing and another below at seat height provided a makeshift refectory table and bench.

The ablution facilities, which were under, or at one end of, each hut, varied. Some had 'tongs' — large tubs and native-style dippers — while others had two or three western-style shower heads.

Hut allocation was more or less by unit, and Botterill and Murray were pleased to find that they were in the back row and amongst friends — Tommy Graham, Vic Johnston and Stan Andrews, all originally from the 2/19th Battalion and all survivors of Major Beale's bayonet charge. Tommy, who still had the major's pistol and ammunition, despite the various searches, now secreted them in a hiding space beneath the hut. Dick Braithwaite and Wal Blatch were also together, while Billy, Mo and their high-spirited mates were elated to find they had been given a hut at the very end of the block — handy to their other friends but far enough away from the officers to discourage casual visits. The youngsters occupying Billy's hut were dubbed 'The Dead End Kids'.

Later that afternoon after the baggage arrived, all of it soaking wet and some of it pilfered, the men did their best to settle into their new quarters. The rain continued to pelt down, giving those who were occupying huts which leaked badly a miserable time. Billy and his room mates huddled in a corner to avoid the worst of the drips, while others made for the sub-floor area where, although muddy underfoot, it was drier. The evening meal, when it arrived, did nothing to lift their spirits — a cup of rice, half a cup of unidentifiable green vegetable matter, and a cup of purple-coloured liquid, said to be tea.

The huts were stiflingly hot, despite the unremitting rain, making sleep almost impossible. Some tried to read but the lights were switched off at 10.00pm, plunging the rooms into suffocating darkness. The men had sweat dripping from every pore and the rain was dripping through the roof. It was a very long night. It was still pouring the next morning and, with no sign of a let-up, the rank and file set to work attending to maintenance and trying to get the camp into some kind of order. The latrines, all stinking and in a sad state of repair, were

The Number 1 POW Camp Sandakan, drawn by Private Norm Tully who placed it in a box and buried it beneath The Big Tree, where it was retrieved post-war. X marks The Dead End Kids' hut.

top priority. They were similar to the outback dunnies back home, of lean-to construction and with removable waste pans, but there were no doors and the seating arrangements were 'four at a time', separated only by small partitions. The ablution facilities for each hut were limited, but the constant downpour meant that bathing was not a problem for the time being. Drinking water, however, was a concern as the water in the large concrete tanks was polluted. Colonel Sheppard, the camp's senior medical officer, decreed that, until the water supply was fixed, rainwater would have to be collected and stored for drinking purposes.

The water tanks were sheltered by pyramid-style atap roofs but they had not stopped the contents, which had been standing there for five months, from becoming very contaminated. The water was normally quite potable. It came from the Sibuga River, about 2.5 kilometres away, and the way in which it was purified and delivered to the camp was ingenious. The secret lay in the large vertical boiler and steam-driven generator at the foot of the hill, both housed in buildings constructed specifically for the purpose and under the control of a middle-aged Chinese engineer named Chan (Ah) Ping.

The vertical iron boiler sat in the middle of a basic, dirt-floored hut, grandiosely termed the boiler room. The boiler, roughly 1.2 metres in diameter and 2.4 metres tall, just about filled all the available space, apart from its 3-metre exhaust flue which poked through a moth-eaten-looking atap roof. One side of the hut was completely open, two sides were of rough-sawn planks, while the other side was half-and-half. Billets of wood, about a metre in length, were stacked along the open side to feed the fire box under the boiler, while the opening in the side closest to the adjoining engine room was used as a doorway.

The engine room, set roughly at right-angles to the boiler house, was larger and much better constructed. It was made from milled weather boards but open for easy access at the end closest to the boiler. About 4 metres by 6 metres, it was big enough to comfortably accommodate the engine room staff, the 10.5 horsepower steam engine and a large, cylindrical alternator (more commonly called a generator). The machinery was bolted firmly to a concrete base. Above the alternator was a window opening, while the bank of switches controlling the electricity supply were on the wall behind the engine. Uninsulated copper wires, strung crudely between bush poles, conducted single phase electrical power to the camp and the boiler room.

It worked like this: steam from the boiler drove the engine which provided the power to turn the alternator which created electricity, in a form known as 110 volt alternating current (AC). At the same time, steam fed from the boiler was used to boil and sterilise 2500 litres of water stored beside the boiler house in a riveted steel 'steam reserve tank', painted a bright orange. Some of the piping-hot water from this tank was returned to the boiler to make more steam while the rest was pumped uphill by another electric motor to supply water for the camp. To make all this possible, there had to be a primary water supply. Snaking away to the river from the boiler house was a galvanised water pipe and attached to the underside was an insulated electricity cable connected to a small pump, set on a wooden platform at the edge of the river bank. From the other side of the pump, a galvanised pipe extended horizontally beyond the platform before dropping vertically to the river, about 3 metres below. Depending on the river level, at least a metre of the pipe was always underwater. Screwed to the end of the pipe was a filter, about the size of a small soccer ball and made of perforated stainless steel. Inside was a non-return valve.

The boiler went day and night as electricity had to be generated 24 hours a day, although water was only pumped from the river when the powerhouse engineer activated the various switches. The first pump, at the river bank, lifted the water from the river and pushed it into the smaller pipe. The second drew it across country to the orange tank while a third pumped hot, sterilised water up the hill to the large concrete storage tanks, to cool. From here, galvanised pipes carried the water to smaller tanks, near the guardhouse and the camp's kitchen area. Once the water was in the tanks, gravity did the rest.

Although the compound had running water, the accommodation would not have been passed as fit for human habitation by western standards. The atap huts in particular were so overrun with rats, snakes, lice and bedbugs that the men spent much of their time in the first few days trying to eliminate them. Those with sharp razors found that body shaving helped dispatch the lice, but the rats required more cunning methods. The Dead End Kids organised regular rat-catching competitions. After gathering an arsenal of boots, sticks, water bottles and anything else they could lay their hands on, they switched off the lights and waited. As soon as the tell-tale rustling in the atap announced that the rodents were emerging from their hiding places between the layers, the lights went on and the air was filled with flying missiles. Once the rats were ousted from the huts the snakes, which fed on them, ceased to be a problem.

The bedbugs were far more resistant. Lighted tapers sent some of them packing, but they were soon replaced by others who emerged from their hiding places at night, attacking with such ferocity that by morning their victims were covered from head to toe with itchy red marks. Some, unable to stand it any longer, retreated under the buildings at night, but Botterill, who was in one of the larger huts, had a much better idea. He managed to scrounge four lengths of heavy gauge wire and three wide timber planks, each about 2 metres long, which he fashioned into a crude hammock using nails obtained from one of the guards in exchange for cigarettes. Once he had fastened a length of wire to each corner of the hammock, he was able to secure the other end to a roof truss so that the contraption dangled 60 centimetres from the floor. An occasional persistent bedbug would drop from the roof, but most were thwarted, allowing Botterill and all who followed his example to get a good night's sleep.

Although the camp was in need of maintenance, not everyone was engaged on work inside the compound. Two days after their arrival, the young and fit, which included Botterill, Murray, Billy Young and most of The Dead End Kids, were roused from their beds at dawn and marched off to build a road. It was bucketing down rain but this made no difference to the Japanese — a road would be built, hail, rain or shine. While the rest sloshed along behind, those at the front followed the vestiges of an overgrown foot-track until it petered out. They were then told they must now cut their own trail with parangs (machetes). The leaders were making slow but steady progress when the heavens really opened up.

Inside an officers' hut. Sketched by Corporal Frank Woodley, 2/10th Field Company, who sold it to Lieutenant Hugh Waring.

Billy Young had never before witnessed such an awesome display of Nature's brute force. Within seconds, the newly-blazed track became a raging torrent of swirling water while overhead thunder and lightning fused together in an electrifying cacophony of sound and light. As the storm worked itself into a frenzy, great rain forest giants crashed to the ground, leaving behind shattered stumps of sizzling timber and the sharp smell of ozone.

The storm's aftermath was worse than the storm itself. As the rain eased a little and the water began to penetrate the earth instead of running straight off it, the trail became a black quagmire, sucking boots from feet and energy from bodies. After what seemed an eternity, but was only 3.5 kilometres, the Japanese sergeant called a halt. He told them, using a combination of fractured English and much arm waving, that they had reached the site of a yet-to-be-constructed airfield. Billy had a sinking feeling he might be one of those earmarked to build it.

It didn't look much of a place to build anything, in Billy's opinion, much less an airfield. The ground, which rose and fell like giant ocean waves, was composed of a coral-like substance — the legacy of some long-ago volcanic eruption which had covered the area with metres of ash. This had consolidated to form a startlingly white, porous rock known as 'tufa' which was obviously not nearly as sterile as it appeared. Most of the area had been previously cleared in anticipation of the RAF strip, but it was now covered with a tangled growth of scrubby secondary vegetation bordered by coconut and rubber trees. Billy figured that to clear this area, even with heavy machinery, would take months.

The sun had come out momentarily, sending columns of steam rising into the air, so the sergeant decided that instead of concentrating on improving the track they should begin working on the airport facilities, right there and then. Using a pick-handle as a pointer to indicate an area he wanted levelled, he positioned himself on a rise to issue the instructions. 'Hill here, go in valley over there. All men get chonkol [hoe] and basket. Ichie [one] metre, ichie man dig. When finish, all mens go back to camp.'

Billy soon found that being a substitute for an earth-moving machine, especially on an empty stomach and standing in centimetres of swirling water, was easier said than done. In its normal state tufa is easy to cut and handle, but the rain had transformed it into a jelly-like form, somewhat like a blancmange. A few hours of watching gobs of the stuff being scraped laboriously into a basket and then scraped out equally laboriously at the dump site, only to have the floodwaters wash it all away, persuaded even the Japanese of the futility of such an exercise. After handing out a few wallops with the pick-handles, brought along specifically for the purpose, the sergeant called it a day.

Some days later Lieutenant Hoshijima issued orders for all prisoners to assemble for 'tenko' (roll call) beneath The Big Tree. The commandant-elect presented a striking figure. He was more than 1.8 metres tall, of slender build and quite good-looking. This was his first address to the camp and he had decided the occasion warranted his wearing both his sword and his pride and joy — an Italian-made pistol with a wooden holster, which doubled as a stock, enabling the weapon to be converted into a rifle. Climbing onto a platform about 30 centimetres high, he turned to face the prisoners. Beside him stood an interpreter, a Formosan civilian named Ozawa who was about 50 years of age and as short as Hoshijima was tall. Hoshijima insisted on speaking through the interpreter, even though his English was superior and he interrupted constantly to either correct or improve on Ozawa's translation. After introducing himself as a graduate engineer of Osaka University and reminding them, in case they had forgotten, that they were 'prisoners of the Japanese' he launched into a motivational talk on the wonders of the Japanese Co-Prosperity Sphere. After winding up his speech with the pronouncement that 'Japan will be victorious even if it takes a hundred years', he dropped the bombshell. 'You are here to build an aerodrome.'

Lieutenant Boundy, of the Royal Australian Engineers, went to inspect the site. The men, worried that they could be required to work on a project which was intended for military use, waited for his return with some trepidation. Although no general parade was called, it did not take long for the word to circulate. Yes, the Japanese intended to build an airstrip, but no one should be too concerned. In Boundy's opinion, even if they worked on it for ten years it wouldn't be finished. By that time, the war would be over.

Days passed. Billy sometimes glimpsed gangs of Javanese coolies or locals toiling away in the distance, but no real work was done on the aerodrome site itself by the prisoners. However, various POW gangs were kept busy improving the track, constructing a log bridge across a creek and digging deep monsoon drains to cope with the run-off. Although the track-workers were required to put in a full day's labour and the guards, depending on their mood, not backward in handing out a few whacks here and there, it was not always unrelieved hard yakka. On one memorable occasion, much to Billy's joy, the guards allowed those game enough to try it to 'surf' to work on the torrent of water roaring down the drains after a heavy rainstorm.

Outside working parties were occasionally treated to a complete change of scenery when they were sent to town to collect bags of rice and other heavy goods. Although everyone enjoyed these jaunts in the large British army trucks appropriated by the Japanese, the job Botterill and Murray liked best of all was being assigned to Japanese-born Mrs Wong, wife of Wong Yun Siow, an agricultural farm employee who, although he was only aged 33, had been dubbed 'Pop' by the prisoners. The Wongs had a beautiful daughter and not only was the work, being mostly odd jobs, very light but there was always a good chance of getting something to eat. However, like most good things in life, there was a down-side to visiting Mrs Wong's house. The Japanese soldiers billeted there had a disgusting habit of standing on the elevated front verandah and using the garden below as a urinal. The overpowering smell, not to mention the possibility of having an unexpected shower, rather took the edge off the occasion.

Only a small proportion of the men were engaged in heavy manual labour or camp chores, and the others needed something to keep them occupied. The boiler, running non-stop, used huge amounts of fuel, so wood gathering parties were organised. The officers, however, were not required to work. Although the Japanese did not embrace as a whole the Geneva Convention (which, although Japan was a signatory to it, had not been ratified by its government), they had agreed to abide by some of the terms, including officers not being obliged to work. Idleness did nothing to improve morale in the upper ranks and the lack of cohesion so prevalent in Selarang was even more pronounced here. Petty bickering and jealousies over seniority had resulted in internal squabbles and cliques. A couple of senior officers, who should have been giving Colonel Walsh the support a commanding officer had every right to expect, allowed personal dislike of him to overtake good discipline. They committed acts of gross insubordination, which their batmen could not help but overhear. In next to no time word had circulated throughout the lower ranks, reinforcing the view that Walsh was ineffectual and that the officers, with a few exceptions, were not worthy of respect.

In an attempt to increase morale as well as the food supply, Walsh obtained permission for the officers to establish a vegetable patch out near the airfield in the grounds of the adjoining Agricultural Farm. Therefore a large number of unattended officers were outside the wire, and it did not take long for locals loyal to the British to make contact with the outside working parties. Within days the beginnings of an intelligence network was established, under the control of Lieutenant Norman Kenneth Sligo, who spoke Malay and English fluently. A New Zealander by birth, the 42-year-old Sligo had worked before the war as a river boat captain in Malaya. He had enlisted with the Royal Naval Reserve at the outbreak of hostilities but had been transferred to the Royal Australian Naval Reserve by the order of Malaya Command the day before B Force left Selarang.

Now 'attached' to the Australian Army Ordnance Corps, he had been appointed the camp's intelligence officer.

Captain Lionel Matthews, of 8th Division Signals and a 'company commander' of the force's 'E Battalion', had been the first to be approached by the locals. He was contacted by an agricultural employee, a Malay by the name of Dick Majinal. Majinal, Matthews learned, was a member of a local assistance group which had been smuggling food, medicines and news to 100 or so European civilians interned in the old quarantine station on Berhala Island, at the entrance to the harbour. The composition of the assistance group was very diverse. Its members included Filipino-born Lamberto Apostol, a radio mechanic and ex-forestry employee in his thirties, who was now supervising agricultural production at the Experimental Farm; the farm's night watchman, Matusup bin Gungau, who was also in charge of a cow shed where the officers collected dung for the garden; 'Pop' Wong, farm employee, husband of the popular Mrs Wong and father of the even more popular Miss Wong; Ah Ping from the boiler house; Sergeant Abin, a Dusan tribesman and resident policeman at the Eight Mile Police Post, and a Eurasian family of part-Australian descent named Funk, whose various members worked in town and on the family's nearby rubber plantation. Before long Matthews, using the cow shed as a rendezvous, had made contact with both Matusup and Pop Wong.

These locals were in constant contact with a much larger town-based group, headed by Australian-born Dr Jim Taylor, British North Borneo's senior medical officer, who had lived there for the best part of 20 years. Other prominent members were Taylor's right-hand man, Ernesto Lagan, a former employee of Harrisons and Crosfield and now, ostensibly, working as a 'detective' for the Japanese; Doctors Wands and Johann (Val) Stookes, a World War 1 fighter pilot who owned a rather battered but nevertheless still-functioning amphibian plane; Dr J. F. Laband, a Jewish dentist who had fled Hitler's Germany and now held the post of Government Dental Surgeon; Dr Laidlaw, a dentist from America; the Manager of the North Borneo Timber Company, Mr A. E. Phillips and his slipway apprentice, Alex Funk, one of three Funk brothers; Scottish-born Mr Gerald Mavor who, as superintendent of the Sandakan Light and Power Company, was also Ah Ping's boss; Felix Adzcona, a radio mechanic; and Palestinian-born Mrs Moselle Cohen, a wealthy Jewish refugee from Hungary who owned a department store and was the central figure in Sandakan society. Members of the British North Borneo Constabulary involved in the assistance group included Murut tribesman Corporal Koram bin Anduar and four Indian police officers — Inspector Guriaman and Jemadurs (Sergeant-Majors) Ojaga Singh (an immensely tall and well-built Sikh), Yusup, Guriaman and Yangsalang. All five policemen had remained fiercely loyal to Police Chief Major Dahlan Rice-Oxley, who was interned at Berhala with Governor Robert Smith, Harry Keith (Conservator of Forests and Director of Agriculture) and Keith's Assistant Conservator Mr G. Brown. In addition to these principal figures, many other civilians from all walks of life regularly contributed money to a comfort fund for the internees. Control of this fund was vested in the generous and irrepressibly cheerful Mrs Cohen, a many-chinned, lavishly-endowed lady whose passion for voluminously-flowing, flamboyant clothing enabled her to conceal enormous amounts of cash around her ample person.

Through Majinal, Matthews had also managed to set up a link with Sergeant Abin, the policeman at the Eight Mile Post, who offered to arrange for messages to be taken from the camp to Berhala Island internees and Doctor Taylor. The main courier for the Sandakan-Berhala link was Mohamet Salleh who had been watchman for the quarantine and adjoining leper stations before the war. The Japanese, who had kept him on, had no idea that Salleh was now carrying far more than officially-sanctioned goods on his daily trips to and from the mainland.

The Japanese had agreed to advance funds for the establishment of an officers' canteen, giving Sligo, in his cover-role as canteen officer, and Colonel (Dr) Sheppard, the opportunity to go to Sandakan to purchase goods. While there, they handed a letter to Taylor requesting medical supplies. This appears to have been a rather naive move, as the note was passed with the full knowledge of the Japanese guard, who reported the incident on his return to the camp. However, other than delaying the establishment of the canteen for two or three weeks, the commandant took no further action and, with the guards not bothering to accompany the wood or vegetable parties, Sligo was able to explore the possibility of meetings with the local assistance group members. He had been working on establishing this network when eleven prisoners escaped.

Despite the barbed wire, perimeter lighting, security gate and sentry boxes, camp surveillance was extremely lax, so lax that on the last day of July, a mere twelve days after their arrival, five men from Billy Young's battalion and six members of the AASC had absconded. While the infantrymen would manage to evade recapture for more than five months, the AASC men were not as lucky, even though they had been provided with rations, anti-malarial drugs and a compass by their unit's Warrant Officer, Bill Sticpewich. Taking advantage of a severe storm, Lance-Corporal Herb Trackson and Private Matt Carr left first, followed by Drivers J.N. Shelley, E.A. Allen, M.E. Jacka and T.I. Harrington a little later, at about 9.30pm. Sticpewich, who had undertaken to cover their absence at tenko, was able, with the assistance of the officer temporarily in charge of the camp, Major Lawler, to hide their absence from the Japanese for two days, giving them ample opportunity to get away.

The six headed in a north-westerly direction across relatively open ground and rubber estates for about 5 kilometres before intercepting the Sungei Batang Road, a dirt track linking the 11 mile peg on the tarred road with the Manila River. There were numerous native gardens running along the eastern side of this road and it was here, at about 7.00 one night, that they knocked on the door of a Chinese farmer named Chu Li Tsia. His house was a good 14 kilometres from the nearest road junction and almost 30 from Sandakan, so Chu was surprised to see anyone at that hour of night, let alone six hungry white soldiers. After giving them food and drink he followed them into the jungle to inspect their hiding place — a small hut recently vacated by coolie timber cutters. On Chu's advice the Australians continued to conceal themselves there by day, emerging only after dark to make their way to his house to have a meal. After three days the escapees moved back towards Sandakan where Trackson and Carr split from the others.

Apparently acting on information from Chu that Mr Phillips, manager of the North Borneo Timber Company and a member of the assistance group, might be able to help them, the remaining foursome headed for the sawmill situated at Leila Road, on the harbour foreshore.

If the AASC men had informed Sligo they intended to escape, they would have had a better idea of the degree of caution required when moving about inhabited areas. While most of the Chinese were intensely loyal to the British, many of the Malays and Indians were decidedly pro-Japanese. Unfortunately, although the four escapees found Mr Phillips, they were also seen entering his house. Phillips, whose wife was Malay, had not been interned as the senior Malay leaders had vouched for him and the Japanese wanted to have the sawmill, which had been sabotaged by the British, up and running again. Phillip's unexpected visitors had placed him in a most invidious position, especially since the headquarters of the dreaded military secret police, the Kempei-tai, were directly across the road, in the palatial former home of the Bacau and Kenya Extract Company's general manager. Once the Japanese learned he had been harbouring escapees, Phillips knew he was bound to be arrested and interrogated, something which would place the entire assistance organisation in jeopardy. Faced with the option of voluntarily turning in the men or waiting for the Kempei-tai to arrive on his doorstep, he did the only thing possible under the circumstances. On 8 August, a day considered by the Chinese to be particularly lucky, Harrington, Allen, Jacka and Shelley found themselves behind bars in Sandakan Gaol.

Seventeen days later they were joined by Trackson and Carr. As Tom Burns, on hearing of the escape had predicted, they had not really stood a chance, the land around Sandakan being 'very dense jungle and very marshy and full of swamps'. Although they had travelled more than 100 kilometres, they had not gone very far. After leaving the Chinese farmer they had reached a small island in a stolen boat, then stolen another which, when it proved unreliable, they abandoned. Skirting the southern shores of Sandakan Harbour, raiding fish traps and native gardens for food, they ended up at Tanjung Aru, a mere 2 kilometres across the water from the northern harbour garrison. Trackson, by this time, had come down with malaria and could go no further. However, before they had a chance to make arrangements with some friendly Chinese for a boat to take them to the Philippines, they were betrayed by one of the Malay villagers.

The escapes had, of course, caused repercussions back at the camp. Discovering that eleven men were missing, the Japanese had ordered a muster beneath The Big Tree. The prisoners were kept standing out in the sun all morning while the guards counted and recounted them. With the count finally completed Ozawa gave them all a 'pep talk' on the values of patience and good behaviour — an oration considered by Tom Burns to be 'a lot of bull'. Ozawa then announced that no one was permitted to leave the camp for the rest of the day and, in order to keep a closer watch on who was doing what, every prisoner was to be issued with a POW number. This number, allocated sequentially, hut by hut, and stamped onto on a piece of white fabric, had to be displayed on their hats at all times. Lieutenant Rod Wells, the radio expert, was POW 667 while Lieutenant Rus Ewin, who slept alongside him, was given the 'devil's number', 666.

The basic rice ration remained at a more than adequate 550 grams a day for general workers and 750 for those engaged in heavy manual labour, but as a further punishment the meagre supply of fish and meat was cut out altogether and the vegetable ration reduced. However, as this was to be for only one week it was not considered to be particularly onerous. The cigarette ration was also stopped, causing some distress to the nicotine addicts, and security was also smartened up a bit, both inside and outside the camp, making it no longer possible for the wood and gardening parties to roam at will but still giving them plenty of latitude, provided they were careful.

While these retaliatory measures were little more than annoying, for two senior camp personnel the escape had far more serious consequences. On 27 August, two days after Trackson and Carr were apprehended at Tanjung Aru, Major George Campbell and Captain Doug Scrivener, the two officers in charge of the AASC prisoners, were taken away for questioning by the Kempei-tai. Their arrest had been prompted by statements, made by all the recaptured escapees, that their senior officers had told them it was the duty of every Australian soldier to try to escape.

It looked very much as if the officers, as well as the escapees, would be executed. However, the intractable stance taken by Campbell and Scrivener led the Kempei-tai to transfer them all to Kuching for trial. On 30 August, after spending three days at the Sandakan Gaol, the Australians were placed on board the small coastal steamer, *Burong*. The vessel stopped off at Labuan Island on the way down the west coast and there, in an effort to inflict as much humiliation as possible, the Japanese tied all eight prisoners together and exhibited them through the streets of Victoria, the island's main town. This ordeal over, they boarded another vessel, *Margaret*, finally reaching Kuching on 6 September, where the two officers were reinterrogated. During this time they were paraded before Major Suga Tatsuji, the officer in charge of all Borneo POW camps. Ironically, having served on the same side in World War 1, when Japan was an ally of Britain, both Suga and George Campbell were wearing the same campaign ribbons.

On 13 October, unable to extract a confession from the officers that they had ordered the others to escape — an admission which would have resulted in dire punishment, probably death — the Kempei-tai sent them to join the others in Kuching Gaol. They remained there until 2 November, when they were transferred 6 or 7 kilometres away to a large POW camp, which included Lintang Barracks, the pre-war home of the 2/15th Indian Punjabi Regiment.

The six AASC men, after languishing in large wire cages at the gaol for almost two months, were brought before the court on 25 October. All were found guilty. Their sentence, under the circumstances, was exceptionally light — four years solitary confinement in Outram Road Gaol, Singapore.[2]

Even so, the very sound of the words 'Outram Road' was enough to instil dread and horror into anyone unfortunate enough to be aware what went on behind the walls of that terrible place. Built of impregnable stone by the British in the style of many nineteenth-century prisons, it was reserved for all those, Japanese and Allied alike, who had the misfortune to come to the notice of the Kempei-tai. A top security prison with a very large number of cells, Outram Road was perfect for the needs of the secret police, who had moved in as soon as the British had moved out. The Kempei-tai, or 'thought police', believed that a few years incarceration in solitary confinement in Outram Road would result in all transgressors thinking only 'good thoughts'.

Unfortunately for some of the prisoners, especially those of Asian background, the re-education process was so severe they did not survive long enough to ever think again. During 1942 and well into 1943, the constant beatings, hideous tortures, inadequate food and vermin-ridden cells took a heavy toll on the bodies of disease-racked prisoners. During this period, and indeed, up until the end of the war, some of the Allied inmates teetering on the fine line dividing life from death survived purely because of their transfer to Roberts Hospital, and later Changi Gaol, when death appeared imminent. It was a foolproof arrangement, as far as the Japanese were concerned. If the prisoners survived, they were sent back to Outram Road to finish their sentences. If they did not, the Kempei-tai simply blamed their demise on the incompetence of the POW medical staff.

Back at Sandakan, Lieutenant Sligo died, following an attack of dysentry. His death, on the last day of August, brought the number of deaths at the camp to four. When Sligo had become ill, his jobs had been subdivided into two distinct tasks, expanded and reallocated. First, the previously 'officers only' canteen (operating from beneath one of the officers' huts and stocked with a variety of goods either bartered from local natives or purchased from Goto, a Japanese shopkeeper in Sandakan town) had been taken over by Captain Jim Heaslop. Second, camp administration, evidently aware that the men, especially those on the 'drome, resented the fact that officers received camp rations, drew pay for doing nothing at all, and had exclusive use of a canteen, had decided to establish another canteen for the rank and file. Captain Fred Elliott, who had had created a good impression with the troops by supplying members of his unit with fish he had purchased from the officers' canteen, was placed in charge of it. Third, Lionel Matthews, who had been working closely with Sligo, had inherited the role of intelligence officer. Although he had no formal training in intelligence, his signals expertise and experience gained while acting as Sligo's assistant made him an obvious choice.

Matthews was known to some of his contemporaries as 'The Boy Scout' because of his life-long interest in the Scouting movement, or, more commonly, as 'The Duke' because of his uncanny resemblance to HRH The Duke of Gloucester, brother of King George VI. The 30-year-old Matthews had been in military service for the past twelve years. He had started in the militia, then joined the Royal Australian Volunteer Reserve as a signalman, before accepting a commission in the army with 8th Division Signals. Fearless, resourceful and highly respected, both as an officer and man, Matthews had shown conspicuous bravery during the Malayan Campaign by laying and maintaining vital signal communications under the most perilous conditions — a feat which had earned him a Military Cross.

Matthews had more than proved himself capable of undercover work. In mid-August, before Sligo had become ill, Captain Dominic (Don) Picone, known to his 2/10th Field Regiment gunners as 'Pills Pinocchio' and medical officer for 'E

Battalion', had become concerned about the number of men having trouble with their sight — a condition brought about by a deficiency of Vitamin A in the diet. As supplies of cod-liver oil or yellow vegetables, both a good source of Vitamin A, were unavailable, Picone, through Colonel Sheppard, gained permission from the Japanese to form a special working party to collect nuts from the palm-oil trees so oil could be extracted. The gardening party was now under stricter surveillance following the escapes, so Lionel Matthews volunteered to collect the nuts, nominating three other signallers — Lieutenants Foster, Esler and Wells' mate, Rus Ewin — to join him. The group was not accompanied by any guards and the officers wasted no time in heading for the nearest palm-oil grove, which happened to be right across the road from Sergeant Abin's police post. After establishing a 'post box' in a large tree in the jungle between the Funk's property and the police station, Matthews, with Abin's help, was able to open up a line of communication to both Dr Taylor and Governor Smith on Berhala Island. A small supply of drugs, mainly Vitamin B, so essential in the treatment of the debilitating, potentially-fatal disease known as beriberi, was soon on its way.

The nut party was also able to arrange meetings at the tree with members of the assistance group, including Abin and Alex Funk, who Matthews had already met at the cow shed, and Alex's younger brother, Johnny. During his meetings with Alex Funk, Matthews learned that members of the Chinese community in Sandakan were in contact with a Filipino guerrilla unit operating in the Sulu Islands, to the south-east of Sandakan. He also received forestry survey maps and data about inland tracks supplied by Apostol, who had worked for the forestry and was in contact with his former boss, Mr Brown, now interned at Berhala Island. Alex also gave Matthews a .38 calibre pistol and Rus Ewin a fountain pen, which was as good as hard currency when it came to trading. The officers had no trouble getting the gifts back into camp — Ewin slipped the pen into the fly of his shorts while The Duke, who had nerves of steel, simply walked through the gate with the pistol in his haversack, hidden under the palm-oil nuts.

Although Matthews had not been stopped or searched, he had an uneasy feeling he was being watched and decided to forego further nut-gathering excursions. For the next week, after which permission to collect nuts was withdrawn, contact with the outside was maintained by notes carried by Ewin and Foster.

At about the same time that the nut party had been formed, Rod Wells took command of the wood party, putting him in contact for the first time with Ah Ping. Believing that Ah Ping, who was fiercely loyal to his Scottish boss Gerald Mavor of the Sandakan Power Company, could help them secure enough parts to make a wireless, Wells received permission from Major Workman, B Force's 'brigade major' and Walsh's second-in-command, to stay with the wood party permanently. Wells soon learned that Ah Ping, appointed to the post by Mavor personally, was a close friend of Pop Wong, who also knew Majinal well. This information was given to Matthews by Wells who, up until this time, had no idea of the extent of the fledgling underground network since The Duke operated on a 'need to know' basis only. With Hoshijima happy to have Wells remain in charge of the wood party, Matthews decided to take the young lieutenant into his confidence and made him his deputy.

Meanwhile, the man who was to become the prisoners' greatest adversary, Lieutenant Hoshijima Susumi, had received written confirmation of his appointment as Camp Commandant and promotion to captain on 15 August. He wasted no time in exercising his new-found authority, especially since Colonel Walsh had been making himself tiresome by protesting that the use of POW labour to build a military installation was in direct contravention of the Geneva Convention. This was one part of the Convention which the Japanese government had chosen to ignore, and Hoshijima had no intention of abiding by this particular rule. A few days after his official appointment had come through, and just as the more naive were beginning to think that Sandakan might be not such a bad place after all, Hoshijima called another parade to show Walsh, and everyone else, exactly who was boss.

Hoshijima climbed onto his platform again, once more employing Ozawa as translator.

You have been brought here to Sandakan to have the honour to build for the Imperial Japanese Forces an aerodrome. For this you will be paid ten cents a day. You will work. You will build this aerodrome if it takes three years.

The very suggestion that the war would last another three years was too much for the Australians. Sniggers, accompanied by derisive remarks about the intelligence of Japanese in general, rumbled round the ranks, raising Hoshijima's ire to such an extent that by the time the noise had died down he had worked himself into a rage.

He bellowed angrily:

I tell you, I have the power of life and death over you. You will build this aerodrome if you stay here until your bones rot under the Borneo sun.

Chapter Four
WHITE COOLIES

An aerodrome was to be built and the prisoners, along with more than 4000 coolies imported from Java, and a large number of local people, would provide the necessary labour. Aircraft were unable to fly non-stop between Singapore and the Philippines or the more distant parts of the Dutch East Indies, so it had not taken long for the high command to realise that Jesselton and Labuan on the west, and Sandakan and Tawao on the east of Borneo, would provide ideal refuelling spots. Masahara Yamada, an ambitious young lieutenant attached to Japanese Army Headquarters, Borneo had developed the idea to construct an airstrip at Sandakan on ground already conveniently surveyed and cleared by the British. A suitable labour force was available. With tens of thousands of Allied prisoners in Singapore, all Yamada had to do was obtain permission to transfer 2000 young, fit and healthy POWs to Borneo. As soon as his plan had been sanctioned by his superiors, he had travelled to Singapore to collect them.

Yamada's plans had not altered, even though only 1500 POWs, whose state of health ranged from extremely ill to very fit, and whose ages ranged from sixteen to 54, had disembarked from the *Yubi Maru*. In the latter part of August, shortly after Hoshijima's announcement, two working parties of 300 men each were lined up and marched out the gate in groups of about 50, each under the control of a senior NCO.

There was not a single officer in either party. Officers could work if they wished, and Hoshijima considered all prisoners, being of equal status, should do so, but the very idea was fiercely resisted by all those above the rank of warrant officer. Indeed, the few officers who had volunteered to join the wood-collecting parties had been criticised by the others, who believed that if a precedent were set they would all be expected to work. This attitude by the officers was not viewed favourably by many of the rank and file, who resented the fact that they were doing all the work. While they happily donated 20 per cent of their pay to the hospital fund to buy rations for the sick, they could not abide able-bodied officers sitting around doing nothing, while men who were ill went out to work.

One working party headed for the aerodrome, while the other was ordered to begin constructing a road network capable of carrying vehicular traffic to service the airfield. Billy, Botterill, Murray and Mo were among those who followed the rough foot track to the 'drome site, clambering over fallen branches and wading through mud puddles with their eating utensils and water bottles slung over their shoulders. The cooks and kitchen detail followed, carrying rice for the midday meal, cooking equipment and buckets of water. It was a fair hike, but for men who had been cooped up at the camp for four or five weeks, it was a welcome change. It would have been very pleasant indeed if they had been allowed to pick any of the succulent paw-paws and thirst-quenching coconuts growing along the way.

Waiting for them at the site was a short, prominently-toothed, bespectacled Japanese army officer — Lieutenant Okahara. His physical attributes, or lack of them, were a cartoonist's delight, but Okahara was one of the most severe and least compassionate taskmasters any POW would ever have the misfortune to encounter. The prisoners were informed, through an interpreter, that a landing strip 850 metres long and 50 metres wide was required urgently and, as it was Okahara's responsibility to ensure it was completed in record time, they would work six days a week from dawn until dusk. The men were marched off immediately under guard to an atap store-house where they were handed either a chonkol or an axe.

The first task was to clear the entire area — runway site, taxi areas and aircraft bays. Billy, a city-slicker who had never had any cause to wield an axe other than splitting kindling for his grandmother's fire, was relieved when the NCOs delegated the cutting down of coconut and rubber trees to the country blokes. The plantations earmarked for removal were quite extensive, but the 'bushies' who were used to tree-felling, were not at all fazed. After all, this was soft wood in comparison to Australian native gums, and only a proportion of the trees would actually have to go. The Japanese decreed that, since all the cleared vegetation was going to be dumped in the hollows as fill, anything already growing there could stay.

The Australian engineers discovered that their Japanese counterparts had some other strange ideas. Drains, they were told, were entirely unnecessary — a very odd decision, considering the airstrip was to be built from fill on land a mere 2.4 metres above sea level and in a country where rainfall is measured in metres rather than centimetres.

It was an extremely long day. Hacking at scrubby undergrowth and grubbing out roots was back-breaking work, especially for those not used to such hard physical labour. Although there was a ten-minute break each hour and a fifteen-minute 'smoko' about mid-morning, the time until the noon break seemed an eternity to Billy. Lunch, eaten out in the open under the blazing sun, was the usual rice, stewed greens and weak, black tea. Although there was plenty of rice, it was a gelatinous mess, as the cooks, working out of a lean-to shed, had yet to master the art of dealing with 44-gallon drums of rice over an open fire. The afternoon was even worse than the morning as tired muscles protested at every strike of the chonkol and unprotected backs burned and blistered. By 6.00pm everyone was exhausted. As Billy lined up with all the other weary workers to return his chonkol, he looked around to see how much progress they had made. It was pitifully small — so small it did not seem possible that they could ever clear the site, far less turn it into an airstrip.

For the next ten days, one hour rolled monotonously into the next, the tedium broken only by a beating when the work went too slowly for Okahara's liking. Even then, the guards were not over-zealous, being mostly older soldiers who had been wounded in battle and taken out of the front line. Then, without warning, on the morning of 2 September, Billy was woken by a rifle butt jabbing into his ribs. The entire camp was in an uproar, with Japanese troops armed to the teeth running hither and thither, shouting orders and lashing out at any prisoner who did not have enough time or agility to get out of their way.

Stumbling about in the dark, the prisoners were ordered to produce all their kit for a special inspection. The search, which was relatively superficial, yielded nothing of interest as all forbidden items had been carefully hidden. All prisoners, officers included, were then herded at rifle point to The Big Tree, where they milled about like sheep as the Japanese troops screeched unintelligible commands. By the time the Australians had formed up in ranks all were completely on edge, their feelings of apprehension heightened dramatically by the realisation that mortars had been placed at strategic points around the entire compound and additional machine guns set up and manned. Bob Shipsides, still keeping an eye on Billy and The Dead End Kids, shepherded his charges to one side where he issued a fiercely whispered instruction to take cover inside the nearest hut at the first sign of trouble.

The sound of 'ki wo tsuke', the Japanese order for 'attention', reverberated across the ground and brought the prisoners to silence. Captain Hoshijima, accompanied by an escort of guards, strode into sight. The commandant informed them, through Ozawa, that they must listen to his statement very carefully. Speaking slowly, Ozawa explained that they had been assembled for the signing of 'ze oase', which he now picked up from a nearby table and read aloud.

1. We abide by the rules and regulations of the Imperial Japanese Army.
2. We agree not to attempt to escape.
3. Should any of our soldiers escape we request that you shoot him to death.

It was as if time had stopped. No one moved or uttered a sound. Then, to the amazement of every one of the Australians, Colonel Walsh, who had kept such a low profile Billy had almost forgotten he existed, walked purposefully from his position on the parade ground and climbed onto the table. After looking across the assembly he said, 'I will re-read this statement to you'.

Loudly and clearly, so that even those furthest away could hear every syllable, he repeated Ozawa's words, adding, 'the Japanese are demanding that I, on behalf of you all, sign this statement'. He paused a moment as if to gather his strength and then, in a remarkably strong voice declared, 'I for one, will not sign such a document'. To underline his utter and complete contempt, he threw the paper at Hoshijima's feet.

The effect was electric. Hoshijima, who had understood every word, ordered the colonel's immediate arrest. The Japanese troops closed in on the prisoners who, as if on cue, had turned to face the guard nearest them. Walsh was dragged from the table. Hands tied behind his back he was frog-marched outside the gate and tied to a newly-erected post, where an enraged Hoshijima slapped him across the face in full view of the horrified men. With great deliberation, a firing squad of four Japanese soldiers lined up in front of Walsh, pulled back the bolts on their rifles, and took aim. At the same time, machine gunners trained their weapons on the others, lest anyone make any untoward move. Shipsides, in a voice that was barely audible warned The Dead End Kids 'this could be it fellows, so be ready'.

No one moved. Walsh stood rigid and unwavering. Some of his officers, unable to bear the tension and convinced that they were about to be a party to cold-blooded murder, called for him to sign. The impasse was broken when Major Workman, being the 2 I/C, approached Hoshijima with a suggestion that, as it was not possible for a representative of a group to sign a contract on another's behalf, the document should be rephrased and everyone should sign. While Hoshijima and the two Australian officers were locked in lengthy negotiations, word was passed throughout the ranks to remind them that anything signed under duress was not binding. Finally a call for 'attention' signalled it was all over. The negotiators had come up with a statement acceptable to both sides — a statement which saved both Hoshijima's face and Walsh's life. The wording had been altered to make it clear that the contract was an individual matter and each person would have to sign. However, as the POWs soon discovered, they were not signing separate declarations. In order to save himself the bother of printing and distributing 1500 separate sheets of paper, Hoshijima merely amended 'ze oase' so that it read 'we individuals', and then supplied enough blank sheets to accommodate the signatures. Even then, he did not get quite what he wanted. Had he bothered to peruse the signatures he would have found an overwhelming number of men in the camp were named after colonial bushranger Ned Kelly, former Prime Minister Bob Menzies or some other Australian figure.

Walsh, who now stood more than 3 metres tall in the eyes of an awe-struck Billy and a frankly admiring Tom Burns, was set free, but the Japanese had not yet finished with the prisoners. They were kept standing in the sun for another six hours while the troops ransacked the huts from top to bottom, confiscating everything they could find in the way of paper, photos, pencils and pens and removing armloads of gear from the officers' quarters.

The next day it was back to business. Out at the 'drome, the prisoners were now working on three distinct tasks: clearing the remainder of the growth; hacking away at the tufa; and removing the spoil to the dump sites in woven wicker baskets, balanced on the head, native-style. As the amount of exposed tufa increased, so did the eye problems. It was not dust or grit causing the trouble, but the reflective qualities of the rock. Dazzlingly white in the tropical sun, it created the type of 'snow blindness' usually associated with polar exploration. As there was not a hope of the Japanese providing anti-glare goggles, the prisoners made their own. Like most ingenious devices, they were simple — two flattish sticks, about 5 millimetres apart, positioned across the bridge of the nose and fastened around the back of the head with a piece of string, fabric or plaited palm leaf. The makeshift goggles made working on the 'drome a lot easier, but Billy was always relieved when it was announced that his group was wanted elsewhere for the day.

Although the working parties, who were now under the control of an officer, were generally composed of the same men, there were some variations, depending on the fitness of the men and who was delegating the duties. Sometimes those expecting to go to the 'drome found they were assigned to road construction or, if they were lucky, to wood gathering or rice collecting.

These excursions away from the camp provided a wonderful opportunity to gather local intelligence for Lionel Matthews, whose underground system had grown steadily. Since early September, using a most efficient smuggling network set up by Police Chief Rice-Oxley, there had been a constant stream of messages and contraband between the camp, Dr Taylor and Berhala Island. As a security precaution the signatories to these messages did not use their real names, Matthews adopting the *nom de plume* 'Roslyn' and Dr Taylor opting for 'Geebung', after an Aborigine of that name who lived in his hometown of Yass, New South Wales. Matthews' messages, the more confidential of which were encoded, passed through a number of hands before they reached their destination. The first exchange took place at the power plant, where Ah Ping gave them to Apostol. He then left them at the jungle post box or handed them to Abin, who delivered them in Sandakan or redirected them to Berhala via Corporal Koram or some other trusted member of the constabulary. These policemen, who had been especially rostered for duty by Sergeant-Major Yangsalang, took the papers by boat to Berhala where they were delivered into the safe hands of the watchman, Mohamet Salleh. The Japanese still trusted Salleh implicitly, believing him to be anti-British.

There were further developments at the 'drome. In mid-September, about a fortnight after signing 'ze oase', Billy arrived for work to see a huge pile of light steel rails, fish plates and spikes, wooden sleepers and a small, four-wheeled skip — all of which had been trucked in via a rubber estate road linking the airfield to the main road at the 7 mile peg. They had been appropriated from one of the local timber companies. Although there were only two sealed roads in the whole of eastern North Borneo, an extensive private light-rail network, set up and maintained by the various logging concerns, criss-crossed the Sandakan hinterland. Light and easy to handle, the rails could be moved about at will, giving year-round access to even the most remote stands of timber.

Working on the airfield, November 1942. Drawing by Billy Young.

Once the rail was layed the tempo of the work increased, although, whenever possible, output was kept to a minimum. Mo Davis and a number of the The Dead End Kids, who had formed a 'special party' to dig ditches, were so adept that they managed to look busy digging the same ditch for days on end. As soon as they arrived they would get to work, throwing up the tufa at such a rate that their guard, pleased but bored to be overseeing such diligent prisoners, wandered off to pass the time of day with one of the other guards. As soon as this happened, the men 'downed tools' until such time as the 'cockatoo' on watch warned that the guard was on his way back. By the time he reached the ditch, the workers were hard at it once more.

All across the 'drome site the prisoners tried every trick to slow up the work: tools went missing, the skips turned over unexpectedly, fish plates and spikes became loose or disappeared, as did lengths of rail lines. While some of the iron and steel commodities were simply spirited away for recycling into useful gadgets or, in the case of a skip, into a camp oven, quite a few construction tools were swallowed up by fill.

One day Mo and his gang went too far. On discovering that a large number of chonkols, shovels, picks and steel rails had inexplicably disappeared, the Japanese overseer complained to the Australians' senior officer, who happened, on that occasion, to be Ken Mosher. Mosher, a qualified geologist before the war, was known throughout the ranks as a capable, experienced combat officer and a no-nonsense disciplinarian. He put himself between the men and the rice and informed them that, until the missing tools and equipment could be accounted for, there would be no meal. When no one stepped forward, Mosher repeated his demand but once again it fell on deaf ears.

After about five minutes Mo Davis could stand it no longer. Storming out, he broke the impasse by punching Mosher on the jaw and barking, 'Now give us the bloody rice'. Mosher threatened to court-martial Mo on their return to Australia, but looking Mosher in the eye, Mo said slowly and deliberately, 'And if you do, I'll tell every newspaper in the country that you aided and abetted the Japanese while we were trying to sabotage them'. Mosher, without another word, moved aside and allowed the men to have the rice. There were never any repercussions over the incident, which Mosher never reported. Had he done so, Mo, whose experience as a ship's boiler-man had placed him on the short list to work full-time at the power plant, would never have landed the job.

As Major Suga, in charge of all POWs,was due to inspect both The Eight Mile and Berhala Island Camps in early October, Okahara kept up the pressure. When he arrived, it was such an important occasion the prisoners were ordered to parade *en masse* beneath The Big Tree to hear a special address from the Major.

They formed up in orderly ranks to see a short, much bemedalled Japanese officer standing with his back to the guardhouse, a ridiculously long sword hanging by his side and a pith helmet on his head. Suga was a former school teacher who was proud of his grasp of the English language so he spoke without an interpreter. He climbed onto the platform and announced that his name was major Suga — S U G A. Unaware that he had just declared himself to be Major Sugar, he declared, 'I am The Commandants of all the Borneos. The Japanese government very good treat you well, so you must have impatience while we get inconveniences for you.'

The troops had suppressed their mirth over his name, but were unable to keep a straight face while listening to this fantastic mangling of their language. Ripples of barely suppressed laughter ran along the rows, greatly annoying Suga who, in an effort to regain control of the situation, reared up to his full height of 152 centimetres and bellowed, 'That is FACT'. His mispronunciation unfortunately rendered this into a crude Anglo-Saxon word, not generally used in polite society. With his audience laughing uncontrollably and Suga becoming more enraged, it was time for Ozawa to step in and restore the major's equilibrium by explaining the joke.

Bandy-legged Ozawa claimed to have been a jockey in Adelaide and was known to the prisoners as Jimmy Pike — a famous Australian jockey who had ridden the legendary Phar Lap to victory in the 1930 Melbourne Cup. He mollified his superior officer and Suga continued with his address. He finished his oration by declaring:

All Japanese officers — Samurai. All Japanese officers — honourable. You work hard, finish airfield, you be fine.'

Suga's visit certainly made an impact — for the worst. The length of the strip was to be increased to 1400 metres and discipline was tightened. At tenko everyone now had to count off in Japanese. Retribution for those who made a mistake was swift — a good whack on the back with a rifle butt, a slap across the face or a kick in the shins. They were also expected to be able to speak and understand Japanese, especially basic orders. The lessons, conducted by Ozawa and Warrant Officer Laurie Maddock, who knew some Japanese, involved the entire assembly repeating words parrot-fashion until they were mastered. The POWs looked forward to this 'community singing' each evening, once they discovered that, with a bit of imaginative mispronunciation, most of the Japanese phrases could be transformed into an English obscenity.

Overall, discipline became more rigid, especially out at the 'drome. Okahara had been ordered to increase output before the onset of the monsoon season, now only weeks away. More rails and skips arrived. The sick and convalescent were now hauled onto the parade ground but, when this proved insufficient, Hoshijima announced that all officers must also work. Walsh protested so vigorously over this proposal that a compromise was reached — only those holding the rank of lieutenant would be called upon to form a working party.

The quota of work per man per day was also lifted. To ensure that these goals were reached a roving, four-man 'basher gang' of Formosan conscripts, under the command of Lieutenant Moritake, was brought in. Moritake's gang members were thick-set and powerfully built. All had Japanese names and all claimed to have come from Japan but some of the POWs thought they were Manchurian — especially when Private Lance Maskey, who had picked up some Japanese, said that the insignia on their uniform indicated they were Chinese and spoke the Foo dialect.

Fifteen Borneo natives, bare-footed for the most part and all sporting tattooed necks and pierced body parts, were also recruited to act as guards at the 'drome. They were quiet and inoffensive, and did not cause the POWs any grief. This could not be said for Moritake and his henchmen. Moritake, swarthy of skin and with mean eyes peering from behind his thick-lensed glasses, exuded hostility. Not that he ever struck prisoners himself. That particular task was delegated to his Formosans. Like the notoriously cruel Korean conscripts at other POW camps, they had expected that once in the Japanese army they would be afforded the same status and privileges as their masters. They had not. Instead, they found themselves still treated as second-class citizens. The disillusioned guards took out their resentment on the prisoners, subjecting them to the same type of de-humanising behaviour as they suffered.

Moritake's bashers were led by a civilian military employee named Kada, known to the prisoners as 'Mad Mick' or 'Black Mick'. Armed with heavy pickhandles fashioned in the shape of swords, the gang members pursued their task with zeal, selecting groups in rotation to receive punishment, whether it was warranted or not. Any prisoner who failed to complete his quota in the allotted time, stopped for a breather, wiped his brow, had a sip of water or leaned momentarily on his chonkol was a target. At any sign of slacking, real or imagined, Mad Mick and his gang descended, lashing out not only at the alleged transgressor but also his entire crew.

Group punishments, quite unknown in western society but considered a normal part of training in the Japanese army, were also instituted. One form was to pair the prisoners off and order them to hit one another. It was useless to pull the punches, for as soon as the guards detected any half-heartedness in the blows they weighed in with their sticks, inflicting an even worse beating. Another favourite punishment was to force an entire squad to look directly into the sun with arms, supporting the weight of a heavy chonkol, extended horizontally to the sides. Any

Flying practice. Drawing by Billy Young.

prisoner who even looked like sagging would soon have his resolve stiffened by a hefty blow across the spine with a pick handle. This punishment, which strained the muscles to the point of collapse and left permanent solar scars on the retinas of the eyes, became known to the prisoners as 'flying practice', while the number of whacks, each of which left a livid mark across the bare back, were designated as various levels of rank. Anyone who had the misfortune to receive three such swipes in a day would report to his mates, 'I got my sergeant's stripes today at flying practice'.

Pleas to Okahara for the bashers to show some restraint were useless. He was soon to be transferred elsewhere and as the behaviour of the guards was not his responsibility, he 'could not help what happened to Australian soldiers'. The strip had to be made operational for a trial landing before Christmas and the work must be completed, no matter what. Those on the sick list were continually forced out to work and, despite fierce protests, so too were the other officers, who had been told that rations to the entire camp would be cut unless they were prepared to form a working party.

Rod Wells' wood party, usually away from the 'drome area, generally managed to avoid the worst of the guards' excesses, but was not entirely immune. If the regular guard, a Formosan by the name of Toyoda Kokishi, were in charge, being assigned to this detail was almost as good as going to Mrs Wong's. Toyoda showed great compassion for the prisoners in his care — at the noon break even cooking them rice, fish and chicken, all purchased with his own money — and allowing them to work at their own pace. He also shared a tot of whisky with one or two prisoners with whom he had become friendly and even lent another, who had lost heavily at gambling, money to cover his debts. However, one day, for no apparent reason, a replacement guard struck Warrant Officer Athol Osgood so severely across his ear with a wooden stick that his eardrum was ruptured. Even those prisoners who had managed to grab the easier jobs did not miss out. This included Warrant Officer Bill Sticpewich who, along with a number of his mates, had been canny enough to form what was called a technical party almost as soon as they had set foot in the camp. They spent most of their time working as Jacks-of-all-trades for the Japanese and had soon made themselves indispensable, avoiding hard physical labour. However, on one occasion during this period of heightened activity on the 'drome, Sticpewich himself was ordered to join a party destined for airfield construction. It had been a most unpleasant experience to learn what it was like to spend a day at the 'drome and to have a taste of flying practice. The midday meal had also been a shock, since one of the privileges extended to the technical party, apart from extremely relaxed working conditions, was an extra meal a day consisting of as much tapioca, sweet potato, greens, sugar and salt as they could eat, plus an occasional supply of meat and fish.

The iron wheels on the skips at the 'drome tended to seize up because of the high humidity. The first time this happened the Japanese delivered a 44-gallon drum of oil to the 'drome with instructions for the POWs to apply the contents liberally to the axles. To the delight of Botterill and his crowd, they discovered the drum contained coconut oil — a much sought-after commodity which was perfect for frying rice. Within hours there was not a drop left. To prevent a similar occurrence, the Japanese made sure the next drum was a 50/50 mix of coconut oil and kerosene. Undeterred and with their usual flair for improvisation, the POWs found the oil-kero combination perfect for removing grease and other stubborn stains from their skins.

In response to Colonel Walsh's recent defiance and his insistence that officers should not work, and on the assumption that without senior officers the prisoners could be better controlled, Hoshijima announced that Walsh and seven other officers were to be transferred to Kuching at the end of October. Colonel Sheppard, Majors Workman, Blanksby, Fraser and Lawler, Captain Owen, Red Cross representative Ronald Wilson, Corporal Sydney Field of the medical corps, Signaller F. Watson and two persistent troublemakers, Privates Constant and Bowe would accompany the colonel. The group, which was given a good send off by the camp, eventually left on 27 October. Since they spent three days of the seven-day voyage sustained only by raw cucumbers, which Chinese crewmen had the generosity to donate, they arrived at Kuching considerably thinner and weaker.

Meanwhile, the airstrip was growing at a rate which amazed even the prisoners. It did not seem possible that it had been only a little over three months since they had turned the first sod. Work had speeded up considerably with an increase in the number of skips transporting excavated material to the dump sites, some of which were now filled to a depth of ten or more metres. Still, the work was very laborious as only the commercially-made skips, called 'tumbling tommies' by the POWs, had the ability to tip the load to either side. The rest were nothing more than a bottomless wooden box set on top of a flat wooden base, mounted on four wheels. Two parallel wooden grips protruded from each end of the box, rather like stretcher handles. Once the prisoners, working at the face of the excavation, had filled the box to a certain height, a gang of pushers trundled it to the dump site where, after removing the box, they used their combined strength to tip the flatbed onto its side to discharge the contents.

It was probably the improvement in the speed of construction during October which prompted Hoshijima to allow the prisoners to listen to 'war news' on Radio Tokyo. Prior to this, they had only had one piece of news, when Signals' Lieutenant (Alexander) Gordon Weynton was sent to fix the plug on a Japanese short-wave wireless. While checking the reception he had tuned in long enough to hear of the death of King George VI's younger brother, The Duke of Kent, killed in an air accident in Scotland on 25 August.

Okahara also mellowed enough to permit some of the locals to sell or trade food from a roped-off section alongside the 'drome during the noon break. One of those who made his way to the trading area in the guise of a cake seller was Heng Joo Ming, a young Chinese who lived close to the airstrip. For the past six weeks he had been supplying food to Rus Ewin who had contacted Heng through his de facto wife, Siti binte Jakariah. Having heard that Ewin had been beaten after reporting back late to camp after one of their meetings, Heng was most anxious to discover whether or not he had been compromised. To his relief, he learned from Wallace that Ewin had managed to hide the food and that all was well. In the course of this conversation, Wallace discovered the Japanese had offered Heng, a geologist previously employed by British Petroleum, a job as mandor, to oversee coolie labourers at the aerodrome. Realising that his new-found friend might be a valuable contact, Wallace urged him to accept the post.

While Wallace and Heng had been exchanging confidences, the rest of the prisoners, Billy and Botterill among them, had been negotiating deals with legitimate traders, exchanging their rice ration for a variety of tasty foodstuffs ranging from dim-sims and meatballs to turtle eggs and, most popular of all, banana fritters. Until this time, the only way the men had been able to supplement their diet (apart from canteen purchases) was by raiding a bees' nest in The Big Tree or cutting hearts of palm from felled coconut trees. The tender green shoots, curled up and ready to emerge as the next season's growth, were called 'poor man's cabbage' and were highly prized.

Before the Red Cross's Ronald Wilson left for Kuching, he purchased some of these delicacies for the sick. Using funds provided by the Australian Red Cross Society which he had brought from Changi (supplemented with a 50-dollar profit from the canteen, money collected by the 'assistance group' and donations amounting to 150 dollars from the prisoners), Wilson had taken on the task of purchasing additional rations for the hospital. In the three months from the end of July until his departure, he managed to obtain a total of 5088 eggs, five fowls, 284 litres of fresh milk, 30 litres of coconut oil, roughly half a tonne of peanuts, potatoes, tapioca root, corn cobs and fresh fruit as well as a fair amount of tinned fish and soup, for a total cost of 530 occupation dollars. The most difficult commodity to obtain had been Marmite, rich in Vitamin B, without which they had no hope of curing beriberi. It was also extremely expensive, one jar costing the equivalent of twenty tins of soup or fifty coconuts.

The Japanese now decided it was time to remove a gigantic tree growing defiantly at the end of the runway, in the middle of the intended flight path. Billy Young, one of those assigned to the task, had been digging rather ineffectually around its base for some time when a truck pulled up. Several guards jumped out. They ordered the prisoners out of the way and announced, 'Nippon fix', before producing several bundles of gelignite which they proceeded to pack into the holes around the tree. The Australians noticed that the explosive was very old, very leaky and very unstable, and beat a hasty retreat. The Japanese, two of whom were members of the much reviled basher gang, unwound the fuse, took cover behind the truck and pressed the plunger. The resulting explosion was immense. The entire tree, along with a mass of earth, pulverised roots and rocks, rocketed skywards. As gravity took over, the trunk fell, disintegrating into large shards of timber which shot in all directions. For a few seconds it looked as if the truck, by some miracle, would be saved. But, to Billy's joy, it was not to be. As his tormentors scrambled beneath the rear tray in an effort to put something solid between them and a sizable chunk of the forest giant, the cabin took a direct hit. Much to Billy's disappointment the tray held firm.

Although the tree was down, the surface of the runway, running roughly east to west, was extremely unstable. The composition of the strip was suitable, built layer by layer from small gravelly river pebbles (an entire hill of which had been discovered nearby), and tufa. It was the drainage, or lack of it, that was the trouble. The same peculiarities which had made the tufa so difficult for the initial

A Ruston-Bucyrus ditcher of the type sabotaged by Sgt Stevens. All that remains of the ditcher today is the chassis and track machinery.

working party to handle way back in July had once more become apparent. The natural drainage of the entire area was now blocked by fill and there was nowhere for the rainwater to go. Before long, large lakes had formed, particularly on the northern side. The tufa soaked up the water like a giant sponge and the more moisture it absorbed, the more unstable it became. The skips, especially on a downhill slope, began to run off the rails without any assistance. However, it was not until a particularly boggy patch appeared in an area of very deep fill, that the Japanese engineers realised the extent of the problem.

They sent for the only two pieces of equipment available — an antique, ornate and extremely heavy iron steamroller, the property of the Sandakan Public Works Department, and a reasonably new Ruston-Bucyrus 10-RB Universal Excavator, imported from Lincoln, England. This was a very versatile track machine which had, among other things, a drag shovel capable of scooping up and dumping 375 cubic metres of any type of soil, from sandy loam to heavy clay. However, after only one day's work it broke down. Confident that someone in the camp would have the necessary technical know-how to fix whatever was wrong with it, the Japanese arranged to transport the excavator as far as the boiler house, where it was dumped on the verge, not far from the engine room.

A mechanically-minded corporal was sent down from the camp to tinker with the engine, but the Ruston-Bucyrus machine was destined never to go again. Realising that such a useful piece of equipment would vastly hasten the completion of the 'drome, Rod Wells, who was now engaged in full time undercover work with the help of Mo Davis and his engine-room pal, Sergeant Alf Stevens, had decided that Stevens should put sand in the engine sump. The wily mechanic, not at all anxious for the Japanese to discover that the excavator was beyond all repair, kept up the pretence that it was fixable, providing himself with a comfortable job for quite some time.

Wells extended the sabotage to a Fordson tractor, which he had spied parked in the grounds of the Experimental Farm, by arranging for some of the locals, with whom he had become increasingly involved, to also add a little something to its sump. However, while he was able to put both the excavator and the tractor out of commission, Wells could do nothing about the steamroller, and in the end, he didn't need to.

The Japanese had pinned all their hopes on the magnificent steamroller. It was so big and so heavy they felt sure it could squeeze enough moisture from the strip to make a dry, hard surface. After a bit of tinkering with the engine, this great relic from the glorious age of steam started up. The Japanese appointed an Australian driver, under the direction of a Japanese superintendent balanced alongside him in the narrow cabin. Although the roller bogged repeatedly, and 'all mens' had to take up ropes to pull it free, the Japanese did not give up. Slowly but surely the great iron monster trundled down the airstrip, each revolution of its enormous rollers bringing it closer to the boggy patch. The inevitable happened. The roller faltered, stopped and, still in the upright position, gracefully sank into the bog, forcing the driver and overseer to abandon it lest they too disappear into the quicksand-like morass.

The Australians clustered around the hole in delight but the Japanese were most unhappy. Major Suga was due to arrive within a day or two, expecting to see the strip almost ready to receive its first aeroplane. The engineers eventually extracted the roller from the bog, almost losing two trucks in the process, but it was too late to be of any use. By that time, Suga had arrived.

The prisoners were again mustered beneath the tree and again Suga had plenty to say. He began his oration by informing his audience that they were much better treated than Japanese prisoners in Australia — a claim which Tom Burns derisively dismissed as 'all bull', especially when Suga added that 4 cents per man per pay day was to be deducted for the meat ration. As none of the workers had seen any money, or for that matter, much meat, the reduction was, for the present, academic.

Suga then progressed to the main item on his agenda — the airfield construction. The aerodrome, he assured them, was not to be used by Nippon war planes. It was being built for civil administration, for the 'Enterprise of Greater South-Eastern Asia' — another statement rubbished by Burns, who had seen military-style barracks being erected near the 'drome by coolie labour. Suga finished his oration by reminding them that as they were all part of the 'Co-Prosperity Sphere', it was the duty of every prisoner to work hard and make the airstrip operational. The first stage had to be finished by the following month (early December), he warned, and no one would have a day off until the work was complete.

They didn't. The Japanese pulled out all stops to make sure that the deadline was met. With the excavator dead, teams of men were set to work digging a network of channels alongside and across the strip in an effort to drain the water away before the monsoon really set in. There were no pipes available, so box drains, measuring a metre square, were constructed from thick timber planks or the trunks of coconut palms. To replace the steamroller, the Japanese ordered the prisoners to stamp in unison in bare feet. This compacted the surface just as well as any mechanical device.

Meanwhile, the road workers were hard at it, constructing a new road. It started just past Mr Wong's house and was necessary, so they were told, because the log bridges on the old road had washed away. However, as the Japanese still used the original track, the workers had a suspicion that the detour was to keep POWs from discovering the purpose of an area recently deemed 'out of bounds'.

As prisoners were now working seven days a week, more and more were reporting sick each morning. Ailments included dysentery, malaria, beriberi, appendicitis, tropical ulcers, severe tinea and a very nasty scrotal itch (commonly called 'rice balls') caused by a fungal infection which left the skin raw and weeping. As the quota for the working parties had to be filled, doctors, medical orderlies and even those suffering from tropical ulcers so advanced that the lower leg bones were exposed, were forced out to work, leaving about 250 bedridden patients to fend for themselves.

The guards took no pity on the sick or the weak. If anything, the punishment inflicted on the ailing was even more severe. On one occasion Gunner Des Rooke who, although ill, had volunteered to take the place of another sick mate, failed to meet the standard of work required. His punishment — flying practice, out in the blazing sun with neither boots nor hat, for a good half hour. The sick bay was not pleasant either. When Tom Burns, who had already spent six weeks in hospital when he arrived, was readmitted with a severe ear infection and weeping tinea covering his entire body, he found the place overrun with bed bugs and scabies.

Considering the number of ill men, and the severe working conditions at the 'drome, the death toll was surprisingly low. By mid November there had been fourteen deaths, most of them due to dysentery. All were buried in the Civil Cemetery in Sandakan, giving Dr Taylor, who had appointed himself 'official grave digger', ample opportunity to hand out coffee and sandwiches to the burial party and pass on much-needed drugs, messages and information. But Dr Taylor was not the only one using his initiative to help the prisoners at every opportunity. While Mrs Agnes Keith, wife of the Forestry chief and author of *The Land Below the Wind*, a hugely successful book about life in Borneo, was subjected to the same living conditions as all other civilian internees, she took full advantage of her status as a 'famous author' amongst her Japanese fans to wheedle small concessions whenever she could. In late October, Mrs Keith had contracted malaria and was transferred to Sandakan Civil Hospital for treatment. When discharged six weeks later she left with far more than her health restored.

Sewn into her clothing for delivery to various Berhala internees was a total of $675, every cent of which had been surreptitiously smuggled in by her visitors, including the indefatigable Mrs Cohen. Cash was not the only thing they managed to bring in. Wrapped up in the spare clothing in Agnes Keith's suitcase were 4 kilograms of sugar, two tins of butter and two tins of powdered milk.

Smuggling this contraband past the guards and into the camp was hazardous enough, but it was nothing compared to the other risk she was taking. Secreted inside a panda bear belonging to her small son, George, was a letter for Lionel

Matthews' Berhala contacts. It seems that Mrs Keith's recruitment as a courier had been prompted by the arrest of Corporal Koram, who operated between The Eight Mile and Berhala Camps. Arrested twice and gaoled for a fortnight on suspicion of carrying messages for the POWs, he had been warned that next time he would be shot. Koram, consequently, had curtailed his activities for the time being.

There was, however, some small respite from the prisoners' harsh treatment. The Australian government had decided to return to Japan the ashes of four Japanese naval officers who had been killed during the midget submarine raid on Sydney Harbour on 31 May. There was not a Japanese soldier alive who had not heard of their daring attempt to penetrate the defences of the harbour, fire off a torpedo which took the lives of nineteen naval ratings and send all of eastern Australia into a panic. The Sandakan guards, quick to capitalise on the raid's propaganda value, taunted the prisoners constantly with details of bombings which were allegedly reducing the whole of Australia to a pile of rubble. It had not taken the POWs long to wake up that almost all the war news, to coin Tom Burns' favourite word, was 'bullo', especially when the Japanese declared that not only had Sydney and Melbourne gone 'boom, boom' but that 'HMAS *Garden Island*' [the RAN's shore depot] had also been sunk in Sydney Harbour.

That the Australian government had given the dead submariners a full military funeral had impressed the Japanese so much that Suga, who declared Australian Prime Minister John Curtin to be a 'good man' and waxed lyrical about the 'goodness' of the Australian people, arranged for the distribution of a small can of pineapple and a coconut to every prisoner. The Japanese were even more impressed when they learned that the sailors' cremated remains had been sent home to Japan. Indeed, Hoshijima was so overcome by this display of unexpected chivalry that when the ship carrying the ashes called into Sandakan en route, he marked the occasion by presenting a dugong, commonly known as a sea cow, to the camp. One appreciative recipient was Billy Young, who thought he had never tasted anything quite so delicious.

The dugong had scarcely been digested when the prisoners learned that their great benefactor, the Emperor of Japan (as well as all the Borneos) had agreed not only to pay them but to give them a pay rise. NCOs would receive 12 cents a day, the same as officers (who were paid whether they worked or not), while the pay of all other ranks would rise by 2 cents, to 10 cents a day. Furthermore, there would be a 'Best Worker Competition'. Each day the best workers would be rewarded with a special token which they could exchange, at lunchtime, for a cup of coffee.

The Emperor's promise of 10 cents a day did not mean much to the men. An undertaking to pay them for their labour had been made months before and so far they had seen hardly a cent. Billy Young was far more interested in the 'Best Worker Competition' and was determined to win the prize. As the 'judge', immediately dubbed 'The Coffee King', neared his group, Billy quickly doused his shirt with water, creating a large wet patch that looked just like sweat. The Coffee King was so impressed by the evidence of his physical effort that he awarded him one of the coveted tokens. Billy, his mouth watering at the thought of that aromatic

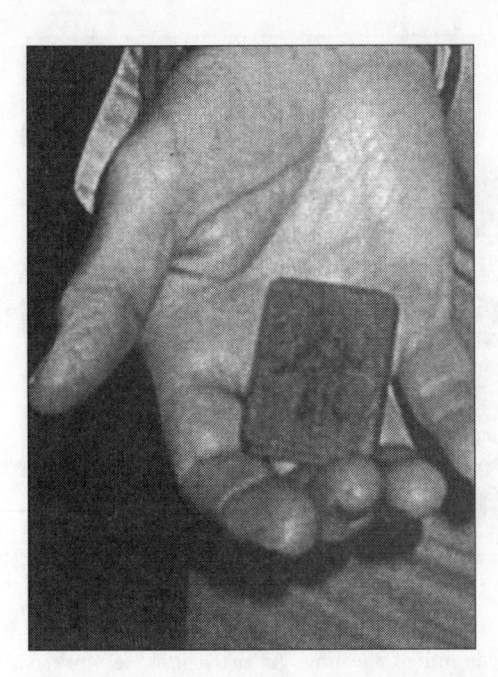

One of the Coffee King's coveted coffee tokens.

cup of coffee, could hardly wait until the lunch break. He strode to the coffee hut at the far end of the strip, presented his token and received his longed-for reward. It was a great disappointment. Without milk or sugar, it tasted terrible, and the walk to collect his prize had taken him so long that, by the time he returned, the lunch break was over and he had missed out on his bowl of rice.

Some thought the coffee quite delicious. However the largess of the Emperor through his servant, The Coffee King, did not last long. Some prisoners, realising that the tokens — merely pieces of flat bamboo with Japanese characters painted on them — were easily duplicated, flooded the market with counterfeits. The Coffee King shut up shop.

Almost as if to counter-balance these sweeteners, Hoshijima introduced a new form of punishment to the camp — a wooden cage. Perched on 60-centimetre-high stilts and with sides constructed entirely from 5-centimetre-wide wooden slats, the cage itself was roughly 1.5 metres long, 1.2 metres wide and 1.2 metres tall. Half of one of the smaller sides was hinged to form a door which was secured with a slip bolt and padlock. The floor was solid timber planking and although the atap roof was pitched, a slatted wooden ceiling had been installed, making it impossible for anyone of average height to stand up. The Japanese, who called the contraption 'Esau', placed it beside The Big Tree, right in front of the main guardhouse.

Among the first to experience Esau's cramped accommodation were Billy Young and fellow Dead Ender, Joey Crome. Eager to get outside the camp during daylight to do some serious food scrounging, the pair had hatched a plan they considered foolproof. Their chance came when they were allocated camp duties for the day. As the technical party left the compound to tip the waste buckets in the swampy area behind the camp, Billy and Joey, shouldering a clean, empty

Esau, the punishment cage. Drawing by Billy Young

bucket, tacked themselves onto the end of the line. As the legitimate workers headed for the dumping ground, the interlopers made a detour into the bushes. When they rejoined the party on its return they had coconuts and yams in their bucket and also a chicken, which foolishly had crossed their path.

All went well until the party reached the guardhouse. For the first time ever, there was a head count, supervised by Fukishima Maseo, otherwise known as 'The Black Bastard', the meanest and most vindictive guard in Sandakan. He surveyed the scene from his elevated position on the verandah stairs, and realised that not only were there two extra men, but they undoubtedly had contraband in their container. Storming down the steps, he upended the bucket and, without further ado, beat the culprits into unconsciousness. When they regained consciousness, they were forced to their feet and made to stand in front of the guardhouse for the entire night. The next morning both were sentenced to confinement in the cage.

When Billy and Joey were finally released from Esau's clutches two days later it was back to the 'drome, the first stage of which was nearing completion. To coincide with a trial landing in early December, an official opening would take place, the details of which were posted on a camp notice board erected by Hoshijima. Unlike a previous depressing announcement, disclosing the fate of the six escapees recently tried at Kuching, this latest communication was designed to 'improve the morale of the Australian prisoners'. All POWs would attend the official opening ceremony. The next day sporting events would be held on the airstrip where prizes, consisting of fruit, chickens and other longed-for commodities (all confiscated from local farmers), would be distributed by Hoshijima himself.[1]

Some of the Japanese army's most senior officers were to have the honour of being in the first plane to land and were to attend the opening. No effort was spared to mark the occasion. An enormous floral arch of jungle vines and bril-

A view of the main entrance to the camp, showing The Big Tree, the weather station, cage, guardhouses and gate. The trees in the background are kapok trees. Woodcut by J. R. Kilgour, from a sketch by Frank Woodley.

liantly coloured flowers, put together by the coolies, was erected at the entrance to the 'drome, with smaller ones positioned at strategic intervals. Japanese 'poached-egg' flags were handed to all and sundry and strict instructions given to the locals to wave them. The prisoners who, like the locals, were given no option other than to attend, were ordered to make themselves presentable — a difficult task as few owned any decent clothing and razor blades were scarce. Boots for the rank and file were a rarity, as the leather had long since rotted from the combined effects of rain and heat. Although the Japanese had supplied a type of wooden-soled scuff, hardly anyone wore them. The foot problems they created were so great that the men preferred to go bare-footed.

The great day arrived. The prisoners, all of whom were subjected to a security search as they went through the gate, were marched onto the 'drome. Looking anything but smart in their worn-out, ragged clothing and bare feet they lined up alongside some very smartly-dressed fellow spectators — Chinese and Malay coolies, clad from top to toe in kit purloined from AIF supplies. Hoshijima arrived in his huge black Buick sedan, formerly the property of Harry Keith, flanked on either side by motor-cycle outriders. Soon a monotonous drone heralded the arrival of the aircraft — two fighters escorting a light bomber. As the fighters pealed away, the lone bomber lined up for its landing. To the great disappointment of every Australian watching, it missed the bog and made a perfect touchdown.

The plane door opened and out stepped a Japanese officer, covered in ribbons and medals and in full ceremonial dress, including jack boots, gloves and an enormously long sword which threatened to trip him up at every step. The visitor was escorted to the flower-decked dais where all bowed before him. The prisoners, much to their disgust, were also forced to bow. Although most were ignorant of his identity, the object of their obeisance was none other than General Yamakawi Masataka, the most senior army officer in Borneo, following the death of Maeda in an air crash, two months before.

The speeches, presumably officially opening the 'Yasuo Air Port' were all delivered in unintelligible Japanese but cheered and clapped on cue at the appropriate places. The general and his entourage then retreated to a marquee for refreshments while the prisoners marched back to camp. Next day, watched by Hoshijima and the guards, they were back at the 'drome again, this time to participate in the long-awaited sports' day. One of the highlights was a marking competition, organised by Lieutenant Vern Rae, a well-known Australian Rules footballer from the North Hobart Football Club. He was so football mad that he had taken his ball with him to Malaya. Amazingly, he had managed to hold onto it throughout his captivity. The Japanese watched the proceedings with particular interest, taking special note of the miraculous improvement in health of those who had previously been pronounced unfit to work.

While the sports carnival was a definite morale booster, the spirits of those who had spent the last four months toiling on the 'drome or constructing roads had remained high for the simple reason that they had refused to allow the Japanese to break them. Just as all had joined in the community singing during the hideous voyage on *Yubi Maru*, and again on the trek from Sandakan, every evening they sang as they marched from the 'drome, to the astonishment of the Japanese and the admiration of their fellow Australians waiting back at the camp. Even at night, after a hard day's work, they managed to find ways to amuse themselves. While older prisoners settled for playing chess, with chessmen laboriously carved from scraps of wood, or indulging in a few hands of poker, or just yarning on the verandah with some special mates, one of Billy Young's favourite diversions was to persuade George Plunkett to show off his bayonet wounds. Understanding the fascination his scars held for the youngest member of the camp, the ever-amiable Plunkett always obliged, much to the delight of Billy who never tired of examining and counting them.

Impromptu sing-songs were always popular, especially with The Dead End Kids who were quite good singers. One of them, Miles Pierce 'M.P.' Brown, was an accomplished harmonica player. One of their favourite songs, The Ringle-Rangle Ram, was a nonsensical ditty, taught to them by Trevor Dobson whose farming ancestors had brought the song with them from England when they settled in Parattah, Tasmania.

A few of The Dead End Kids also indulged in another, far more dangerous pastime — going out under the wire at night. Despite repeated warnings from Murray, who realised the consequences of such behaviour could well be fatal, Keith Botterill regularly slipped away to scrounge for food. Billy Young, Harry Longley and Joey Crome, seemingly mindless of the enormous risks they were taking, were even more foolhardy, going out twice, sometimes three times a week. Sometimes these nocturnal excursions were in search of edible goods. Sometimes they simply wanted to get an idea of the lie of the land, as escape was always a possibility.

It was during one of their foraging trips that Billy discovered a perfect hide-out in a rocky outcrop not far from the Sibuga River. At one stage, when they were seriously considering making a break for it, Billy and his mates stockpiled some food there, only to discover that Sandakan's climate was not at all suited to long-term storage of either canned or dried commodities. However, they were not too upset to find their cache had deteriorated into a pile of rusty tins and mouldy rice. As life at the camp was relatively good, they had shelved plans to escape, at least for the time being.

The most dangerous part of any scrounging expedition was leaving and re-entering the camp. It had not taken Billy and his mates long to work out that only the top part of the camp was under constant surveillance (as the guards rarely, if ever, bothered to patrol as far as the ramp, let alone cross it). The best way in and out of the compound, therefore, was underwater, through the swamp. Negotiating the two fences and the concertina wire the first time had taken some doing, but once they had snipped back the lower strands and cut a path through the underside of the coils, subsequent trips had been easy. Even on the blackest nights they could see, for, threaded under the maze, was a length of coconut fibre.

On one occasion in November, Billy and Joey agreed to take one of Black Jack's black sheep, Jimmy 'Punchy' Donohue, with them. Donohue, a pugilist, was a game enough bloke but had indulged in one fight too many which had left him slightly punch-drunk. The trio had left the camp without any problem but once outside the perimeter wire had been spotted by the guards, who opened fire. Fortunately, these guards were poor shots.

When the noise died down, Billy and Joey discovered that Donohue was missing. Believing that he must have made his way back to the camp, they tried to do likewise, only to find the entire area crawling with Japanese. Luckily, the searchers were making so much racket that the fugitives reached the wire at the edge of the swamp undetected. The hard part, however, was yet to come. The wooden ramp was swarming with Japanese soldiers and Formosan guards, talking and laughing and puffing on cigarettes as they waited for their quarry to put in an appearance. Some even sat along the edge of the walkway, feet dangling just above the surface of the water. Shielding their faces with kit bags camouflaged with weeds, Billy and Joey slid silently into the swamp. As the bags were stuffed with coconuts and quite buoyant, the pair was able to keep an eye on the welcoming party as they edged towards the rope, their heads almost touching the dangling feet as they passed beneath the ramp.

About an hour later they reached the safety of their hut only to be confronted by a complete stranger — a young, fair-headed officer who, much to their amazement, announced he was their 'hut officer'. His message was as brief as his visit and very much to the point. He informed them that, unless they surrendered, Donohue, who had been caught outside the wire, would be executed. With that he turned on his heel and left, leaving Joey and Billy, barely seventeen and sixteen years of age, to face the consequences on their own.

The reception committee — interpreter Ozawa, flanked by a corporal and

Fukishima Masao, The Black Bastard —was waiting for them beside The Big Tree. Behind them stood Donohue, hands trussed behind his back and obviously badly beaten. Saluting smartly, Billy opened the dialogue by stating, 'We believe you were looking for us Sir'. Whatever Ozawa, who had been left in charge of the camp, was expecting, it was not this. It took some time to register that the two prisoners standing in front of him, inside the compound, were the very two men the guards were still searching for, outside the wire.

Finally, Ozawa spoke, his words reflecting the consternation he was feeling. 'You men got out of this camp, even though my men were here to stop you?' Before Billy could decide whether to answer or not, the interpreter continued, 'And you then got back in, even though I had trebled the guard to stop you?' As the pair nodded dumbly and steeled themselves for the bashing they knew must come, Ozawa, announced, 'You may go now'. The trio scuttled down the hill where, from a safe distance, they were treated to the sight of Ozawa removing his scabbard and beating The Black Bastard who then took reprisals against the corporal, and so on, down the line.

The Dead End Kids were not the only ones taking risks at night. Gambling of any kind was banned by the Japanese, but this had not stopped 30-year-old Corporal Henry John 'Gunboat' Simpson setting up an illicit gambling den. Gunboat, who occasionally travelled the agricultural show circuit with the Jimmy Sharman Boxing troupe, had arrived in Singapore with the reinforcements for Billy's battalion just in time to be captured. A man of great versatility, he now operated pontoon games in a cubby-hole built in a natural depression beneath his hut. Cunningly constructed from atap and other bits and pieces found about the place, the den was dead centre of the hut, well hidden from view by the unevenness of the ground and by blankets, washing and hammocks draped about the sub-floor area. It even had an electric light, thanks to the resourceful Mo Davis

Gunboat Simpson's gambling den, December 1942. Drawing by Billy Young.

who had scrounged bits of copper wire from the power station until he had enough to tap into the mains supply to the hut.

Only players who could show they had a 10-cent coin were allowed into the den. Entry was strictly controlled by Gunboat, who took up a position inside the first of two door-flaps — a clever device which ensured, first, that no light escaped to alert the Japanese and, second, that Gunboat had time to check whether his patrons had the entry fee before allowing them to proceed into the inner sanctum. Gunboat's patrons soon learned that not only was his word law, but that the penalty for entering the second door-flap before the first one closed was a good clip over the ear. Once they were inside, the game was straightforward enough. The tricky bit was making sure any winnings were paid up before 'lights out'. Gunboat's memory had a habit of failing at the same time as the electricity supply.

There were impromptu games of 'Two-up', which Billy Young often attended. Held in the space where four huts met, they were usually run by Keith 'Shearer' Gillett, with help from Shipsides. The pot had been lean at first as few players had funds, but once the workers began to receive their pay the games really picked up. The Two-up 'school' immediately following the first payday was particularly well patronised since, up until then, all betting had been in cents or, for the really impecunious, paper IOUs. This time the wagers were in dollars and Gunboat was taking bets on the side. Billy, helping Shipsides run the main game, listened with interest as one of Gunboat's wagers rose higher and higher, eventually peaking at an unprecedented 17 dollars, the equivalent of 170 days' pay. When the pennies came down Gunboat had lost, or so everyone thought, until the gambler came to collect his winnings. Looking at the handful of coins passed to him, he protested that he was owed 17 dollars, not 17 cents. To which Simpson, whose voice and demeanour made it quite clear he would brook no argument, replied, 'You may have been betting in dollars mate, but I was betting in cents!'

The most popular forms of entertainment were boxing matches and an occasional wrestling match, held about once a month in a makeshift ring on the parade ground near the cinnamon trees. Lining up contestants was not a problem. There was Gunboat, heavyweight champion of Victoria; Richie Murray, the talented semi-professional welterweight; and Jimmy Warren, reputed to be Queensland's lightweight boxing champion. There was also a number of others willing to have a go, including Billy's mates Jimmy Finn, John Bryant (also known as Snowy) and Keith Gillett, as well as Punchy Donohue and Clarrie Grinter, Hoshijima's driver. The best, however, was Jimmy Darlington, a strongly-built private in the 2/18th Battalion who was Ken Mosher's batman. Jimmy, part-Aboriginal and fiercely proud of his lineage, was a well-known member of the Sharman troupe. A tenacious fighter, he was the pride of the 8th Division following an excellent showing against a well-known American boxer, the Alabama Kid, during an exhibition match in Singapore.

All fights, whether exhibition bouts or grudge matches, always attracted a large crowd, but the most memorable fight of all was one promoted by Gunboat Simpson and Shearer Gillett in their capacity as trainer/managers of the 2/30th's Punchy Donohue and the 2/18th's Snowy Bryant, both of whom were lightweights. When word spread that a purse and trophy had been provided, the entire camp took an even greater interest than usual. The greatest buzz was in Billy's hut which, with the aid of a makeshift punching bag and skipping rope, had been turned into a training facility for Gillett's man, Bryant. The favoured few allowed to watch the training sessions agreed that Bryant, who was fast on his feet and snappy with his punches, certainly looked good — so good that Donohue had no chance of winning. Gillett was so confident he offered outrageous odds to attract wagers from those backing the opposition.

The match was a sell-out. Even the off-duty guards came down to watch. From the minute the protagonists entered the ring it was obvious that Donohue was clearly outclassed by his opponent. Round one was a walkover for Bryant, round two likewise. As far as his backers were concerned the money, great heaps of it, was in the bag. All Bryant had to do was to go through the motions until the end of the third and final round. Then the impossible happened. With only thirty seconds to go, Donohue knocked out Bryant with an uppercut to the jaw, forcing Gillett, who was ruined, to make himself scarce. When it was safe to show his face a couple of days later, the best The Shearer could do for his disgruntled creditors was to offer one cent in the dollar.

Educational pursuits were almost non-existent, even though Brigadier Taylor, when forming the B Force draft, had included Sergeant George 'Bill' Bundey, South Australian lawyer and 'Changi University' lecturer, so that the work of the Education Centre could continue. Bundey had held a couple of impromptu discussion groups down at the boxing ring but, to date, camp administration had made no move to implement Taylor's orders. Twenty-eight-year-old Bundey, a man of great intellect, was now labouring on the airstrip. However, the officers, who had a great deal of spare time, provided some cultural entertainment. A choir formed by Captain Claude Pickford, and a Sextet, under the leadership of former band-leader Lieutenant John Pool, was soon polished enough to give recitals on Sunday evenings. Hoshijima even came up with some instruments — a piano with ten strings missing, two well-used violins, and a set of drums, only one of which had a skin. Still, they were all fixable and on 8 December, which happened to be the first anniversary of the outbreak of hostilities with Japan, a group of officers presented *Radio Rubbish*. This very slick revue, consisting of musical items and a couple of sketches intriguingly entitled *Lecherous Loves of Laura* and *The Cricket Match*, was performed on the floor of the parade-ground boxing ring which, being at the foot of the slope, formed a rough amphitheatre. The concert was attended by everyone, including about 50 ill men who were carried on stretchers. The Japanese also turned out in force, bringing with them a special guest — the Japanese Governor of the East Coast Residency, Tanuki Kumabe, whose habit of appearing in public wearing all his campaign medals, baggy shorts and old-fashioned suspenders to keep up his socks, had made him a well-known identity.

Prior to the concert, Governor Tanuke had been taken on a tour of inspection of the new hospital hut, one end of which had been put aside for use as a small chapel. Built from sawn timber by a group of prisoners under the direction of Captain Lewis, Royal Australian Engineers, it was on the eastern side of the camp,

The infantry soldier carved by Sergeant Jack Gaven, 2/10th Field ambulance, for the Art and Craft Show to commemorate the opening of the hospital/chapel, December 1942.

near the officers' quarters. Although he had not been part of the construction team, Billy Young had indirectly had a hand in building it. With raw materials scarce, he and a few others had been taken off the airfield one day to reactivate dozens of bags of rock-hard cement — a process which involved smashing the cement to powder and then heating it on sheets of corrugated iron over a fire to remove the water content. Although the bulk of the cement was earmarked for the airfield, Hoshijima had made some of it available for the hospital. Billy was impressed with the workmanship of the new building, particularly the interior. Separating the ward from the chapel area was a stunningly beautiful wall, built from inlaid rainforest timbers.

To commemorate the opening of the new hospital/chapel an Art and Craft Show was held. Although on a much smaller scale than that held at Selarang the previous April, the quality was as good, if not better, with displays ranging from sketches and paintings to exquisite wood carvings. One outstanding exhibit was a beautifully crafted statue of an infantry soldier, standing about 20 centimetres high, whittled from a piece of teak by ambulanceman Sergeant Jack Gaven. Billy also admired a pack of playing cards made from Players' cigarette packets, ornately decorated with coloured inks, but the exhibit which he considered eclipsed all others was a magnificent wooden bird cage on a wooden chain. Carved from a single piece of teak by a patient suffering severe leg ulcers, it was complete in every detail, from its elegantly domed top to a door which opened on tiny hinges to reveal a little bird sitting on a perch. The bird cage was a masterpiece. Billy, and the judges who awarded it first prize, were not the only ones to think so.

Hoshijima was so impressed he not only provided another dugong for dinner but invited the Governor to come and look.

As Christmas approached, the wet weather arrived with a vengeance. It poured for three solid days and nights, bringing the rainfall reading for the week to a total of over 50 centimetres. The swamp overflowed and the camp was reduced to a series of quagmires connected by duck boards. Although most prisoners were getting about bare-footed, their boots having rotted, the wet weather could not dampen spirits, bolstered considerably by a great improvement in the food ration and the extras that the canteen had been able to obtain to brighten up Christmas dinner. Furthermore, although Christmas Day fell on a Friday, Hoshijima had announced they would not be required to go to the 'drome. As a special concession they could do jobs around the camp instead!

On Christmas Eve Claude Pickford gave everyone a special treat. As the men sat in groups filling in time until the midnight service, some eating fritters and drinking coffee, others joining in the occasional carol or thinking of their families at home, the choir suddenly appeared. The choristers, draped in various bits and pieces to represent the shepherds at the Nativity, moved through the camp singing 'Silent Night'. Everyone stopped. The sound of this melodious and much-loved carol was so moving that even the guards stood still and listened.

It was fortunate that the canteen had stocked up on a few delicacies for Christmas, for the only festive offerings the Japanese saw fit to provide were a small piece of fish for breakfast followed by a spoonful of watery yak stew, rice and an eighth of a paw-paw for dinner. Some, however, received a taste of succulent pork. Pop Wong, who had become a very adept thief and smuggler by this time, donated a pig, butchered and roasted by him, which he had appropriated from the Japanese piggery. When Sergeant Wallace opened a parcel left for him in the jungle by Heng the previous day, he found to his delight that it contained a veritable feast — two cooked chickens, fried fish, fried rice, some native-style cakes, six turtle eggs, fruit, cigarettes and matches, along with a note wishing him a Merry Christmas.

Some of the other prisoners had a very merry time by concocting a 'coconut Christmas toddy'. This highly illicit and potent tipple was brewed from whole coconuts. After puncturing a small hole in the outer skin of the unripened fruit, the bootleggers added molasses or some other fermenting agent to the milk, plugged up the hole, buried the coconut in the ground and waited for it to 'go off'. And go off it did! Some of the stills even blew up underground.

There was also the possibility of an after-dinner smoke, provided the smoker could squeeze into one of the four designated 'smoking places' and could hold out until whatever time the Japanese decreed smoking could begin that week. These areas, clearly marked by signs, were small pits about the size of a double bed and about 20 centimetres deep. They were the only places where smoking was permitted. Any prisoner who dared light up anywhere else, at the wrong time, or without a tin of water in his hand to catch the ash, risked an immediate bashing.

Despite all these draconian rules and the fact that cigarettes were all but impossible to obtain, many found it so difficult to give up the habit that they resorted to smoking either home-made pipe tobacco or cigars made from dried paw-paw leaves encased in a piece of atap (or, for the less devout, a page torn from a Bible). The pipe tobacco was very popular, with nine out of ten huts having their own special blend. The constantly-refined recipes were a jealously guarded secret. While the ingredients varied from hut to hut, the basic method involved compressing alternate layers of oily Javanese tobacco leaves and dried foliage from a paw-paw tree (or perhaps leaves from a tea or coffee bush) between two boards, roughly 30 centimetres square. Once the components had dried out to form a consolidated slab, plugs could be cut off and smoked in a pipe. While a lucky few owned a commercially-made pipe, most had to make do with a home-made corn cob or bamboo variety, although the latter often burst into flames itself long before the tobacco was finished.

On Christmas night, after the toddies had been drunk and the pipes smoked, Major Fleming called everyone together beneath The Big Tree and delivered a stirring Christmas oration. The men were left with the impression that the major's exhortations — for the quarrelsome and fractious to make an effort and pull together — was directed more towards the officers than to them.

As 1942 drew to a close, Billy and Keith Botterill considered that, apart from the behaviour of some of the higher ranks, the past few months had been as good as could be expected. The Japanese had eased off a bit at the 'drome, the food was adequate and morale, which had never been a problem among the rank and file, was high. Indeed, in the past few weeks it had been better. Rumour had it that, at long last, the camp had a radio.

Chapter Five
LIVING DANGEROUSLY

For once, the rumour-mongers were right. A wireless had been made, and its construction had been no mean feat. It had taken weeks to obtain some of the parts. With Ah Ping, and then Mo Davis and Stevens acting as go-betweens, Rod Wells had received a crystal detector and headphone from Dick Majinal, which Gordon Weynton had used to make a crystal set. It was only able to pick up local stations, so Wells had cast around for more sophisticated components with which to build a proper receiver. He obtained valves from Pop Wong and Lamberto Apostol and a telephone receiver from Sergeant Abin. The variable condensor, one of the most difficult parts to locate, had been provided by Gerald Mavor who entrusted its delivery to his chief engineer Ng Ho Kong who was also a friend of Ah Ping. Once the parts had been located, they were passed along the line until they reached the engine room staff. More often than not the final link in this very long chain was Mo Davis, whose job of checking and maintaining the water-intake valve at the Sibuga River enabled him to meet secretly, on a regular basis, with Apostol or some other appointed courier. If an item proved impossible to obtain it was made by the inventive Wells, the only person with sufficient technical know-how to tackle such a task. The ready-made components, along with any raw materials Wells might need, were smuggled into the camp by Mo when he made his daily trip from the engine room to the cookhouse to collect the rations.

The Japanese took little notice of Mo's comings and goings. They were accustomed to seeing him and Stevens roaming around, protected from harassment by a cloth patch attached to their hats — the horizontal red stripes and Japanese characters signifying at a glance that they were permitted to operate outside the camp perimeter. However, the conspirators had to exercise a great deal of caution at the power plant itself. Ali Asar, the Malay boiler-attendant who lived full-time at the boiler house, was a known Japanese informant and the loyalties of Chun Ah Teng, who worked at the engine room during the day, were highly suspect.

In October Wells had had to face the fact that, despite all their efforts, the radio was still a long way off. Unless other vital components were obtained, the construction of a receiver capable of picking up long-range broadcasts was simply not possible. The breakthrough had come a few days later but it was not due to either the intelligence organisation or the assistance group, but to Heng Joo Ming who, after his conversation with Wallace, had accepted the position of Mandor at the 'drome. Making full use of the lunch-time trading, Wallace had established such a rapport with Heng that he agreed to try and obtain a radio. The young Chinese was not at that stage a member of the Sandakan underground movement, yet he confided to Wallace that he might be able to obtain a set, or at least enough parts to make one.

Within a day or two Heng had broken into a locked shed where he knew radio components were stored and handed Wallace parts from a battery-operated set, minus the batteries. Everyone was desperate for news from the outside world, and Wallace realised that he had a highly valuable commodity. Capitalising on his windfall, Wallace sold the lot to Corporal J. Rickards, who had brought a very large amount of money with him from Singapore. Rickards then approached Signaller Bill Constable to try and assemble the parts. Constable deferred to Lionel Matthews, who in turn informed his superior, Major Fleming. Fleming made it quite clear that he wanted nothing to do with the exercise, so Matthews took control. With The Boy Scout at the helm, things moved quickly. Weynton and Wells, with some assistance from Rickards and Corporals Arnold Small and C. Mills, began work.

The penalty for listening to a radio, let alone owning or building one, was extremely severe, so security was of paramount importance. The small band worked in secrecy, sometimes in Matthews' or Wells' cubicle, sometimes in other huts while the occupants were engaged elsewhere. After each session the partly-built set was safely hidden, usually wrapped in a groundsheet and lowered on lengths of wire to the bottom of a disused latrine.

By late October, Wells and Weynton had succeeded in building a type of radio known as a regenerative receiver. It was capable of enormously powerful reception and was strong enough to pick up broadcasts from London, America and Australia. Wells knew that operating it carried an element of risk. If even slightly mistuned it emitted a high frequency whistle which could be picked up by any set in the area tuned to the same band. However, he believed that, as the Japanese usually listened to their own stations, and as they would not be likely to realise the significance of the interference, the risk of discovery was minimal.

At this stage, the question of discovery was academic anyway. Without batteries to provide DC (direct current) power, or an aerial, the radio was useless. When a determined search for fresh batteries proved fruitless, Wells demonstrated how inventive he could be. Using test tubes supplied by ambulanceman Sergeant W. 'Mac' McDonough, boracic acid and sodium borate brought in as medical supplies, along with pieces of metal foil from the lining of a tea chest in which the rice was delivered, he came up with an ingenious chemical rectifier which enabled him to convert the camp's electricity supply (alternating current or AC) to DC. The aerial, an integral part of the system, was more easily solved — a length of wire was attached to a clothes line strung between the huts.

Getting the radio to work required far more effort than simply flicking a switch. The trouble was that by the time the electricity generated at the powerhouse reached the camp the voltage had dropped from 110 to about 90 volts — far too low to operate the set. Obviously, it would have to be stepped up. The key lay with Ah Ping, down at the powerhouse, who agreed to co-operate provided he received some 'Chunking news', to him on a par with the revered BBC World Service. The wood party ensured there was an adequate fuel supply for the boiler, which would need an extra quarter of a tonne of timber a night. Wells found the first attempt to increase the voltage was rather nerve-wracking. In his eagerness to obtain access to his Chunking news, Ah Ping increased the supply so quickly that the intensity of the lights rose dramatically. The next day, terrified the Japanese would realise that something fishy was going on if there were a repeat performance, Wells explained to the engineer that the process must be very gradual. That evening at about 9:00 pm Ah Ping began to slowly raise the voltage — one volt at a time.

On 4 November, after much trial and error, Wells and Weynton were rewarded by the sound of Big Ben and an undeniably English voice coming through their one and only headphone announcing 'This is the BBC'. Unfortunately, as it was not time for the news, all they heard on this occasion was a 45 minute progamme on hop-growing in Kent. Nevertheless they shut down the set feeling most optimistic.

If security had been tight during the building of the set, it was even tighter now. The radio was operated only at night, in short bursts of 5 or 10 minutes timed to coincide with news transmissions. To enable the operator and his lookout to see what was happening in the floodlit compound outside, it was decided to use an atap hut near the kitchen. Should a guard be spotted skulking about, the radio would be turned off. All five men were rostered on a listening watch, but Rickards was given the lion's share during the first few weeks — as, having provided the funds for the originals parts, he had assumed a rather proprietorial attitude.

The radio was operated in complete darkness and the news was taken down in abbreviated note form on the backs of naval message pads, which had survived the paper purge. Small notches were cut into the left-hand side of the pad so the listeners could, by feel, keep their writing well-spaced and more or less straight. The notes were then re-written in a more journalistic style by Weynton before being given to Major Fleming, who had at last decided to take an interest, for censorship. The news, once cleared by him, was disseminated throughout the camp in the form of rumours so that only a few knew for sure that a radio was in operation. Special weekly news summaries were sent by Wells to Dr Taylor and the Berhala internees every Friday. Wells substituted letters for words wherever possible and eliminated all non-essential detail, but they could still be understood by anyone familar with idiomatic English. He then rolled them tightly and hid them in his spare pair of socks until it was time for the power house workers, through Ah Ping, or Rus Ewin, to pass them to Abin.

As Wells had given up the wood party to concentrate on the radio, the responsibility for passing or collecting 'mail' through Abin had also passed to Ewin, who managed to accomplish this task even when under guard. The 40-man wood party and their guard travelled in a truck which had an open-sided cabin. Whenever a drop-off was required, Ewin rolled Wells' notes tightly and secured them with wax. While the guard was busily returning Abin's salute at the police post, Ewin dropped the note on the ground for Abin to retrieve. This was then sent via the usual channels to Taylor. Mail collection was a little more risky. Using a broken axe or a saw that needed sharpening as a ploy to leave the wood party, Ewin made his way to the police post where Abin handed over a Players' cigarette tin containing whatever contraband Dr Taylor had managed to provide.

Wells and Matthews also spent a good deal of time compiling detailed camp reports and collating local information — nominal rolls, intelligence summaries and the like. Wells' contributions were passed to Abin, who secreted them behind a loose hearth rock in the kitchen of his house. Matthews, however, elected to hide his paperwork in the camp. Only he knew where.

While the radio was being built, the underground network had been expanding rapidly. The Finance Department, which Ernesto Lagan had begun by collecting funds for the POWs, was now exchanging substantial amounts of Australian currency for the local money, and at a very favourable rate, subsidised by Dr Taylor. Commission was deducted on each exchange, and this money was used to buy food for the camp hospital.

An increasing number of Chinese had joined the organisation, their traditional hatred of the Japanese multiplied a hundred-fold by atrocities perpetrated against the local community. POWs working at the 'drome had stood by helpless as a pregnant woman was beaten badly and left in the sun for six hours, while another Chinese had been stripped to the waist and tied to a post for an entire day for trying to sell food to the canteen. However, the most barbaric incident had taken place in Sandakan town when Japanese soldiers had cut open the abdomen of a pregnant Chinese woman for no other reason than to satisfy their curiosity as to the sex of the unborn child.

The most prominent civilian to offer his services to the underground was Wong Mu Sing, a Chinese-Filipino who had traded in sandalwood in Borneo before the war. When the Japanese had arrived he, and a number of other like-minded individuals, including 1000 Filipino troops under the command of Lieutenant-Colonel Saurez, son-in-law of the Sultan of the Sulus, had moved to the Philippine Islands to the east of Sandakan where they formed a guerrilla force. He traded from the Philippine Islands and unbeknown to Isumi, his Japanese trading partner in Sandakan, Mu Sing operated as an undercover agent, using his numerous kompits (ocean-going wooden craft) and two power boats to move much more than trading goods between his home base at Sitankay, the most southerly island in the Sulu group, and his store in Sandakan which his boats visited about every ten days.

In October, after Mu Sing had contacted Matthews through the police network, he had relayed the presence of B Force to his commander at Batu Batu, near Tawi Tawi Island, who in turn had passed on the information to American submarines supplying guerrilla forces in the area. By the end of December a full report of the POW situation in Sandakan was in Allied hands. In return Matthews received a map of Tawi Tawi and details of the guerrilla organisation. When Major Fleming decided to form a chain of command to cope with the possibility of the prisoners being mobiled to take part in an Allied landing or local uprising, Matthews was nominated as Chief of Police by Rice-Oxley. Jim Heaslop was appointed Quartermaster and Dr Rod Jeffrey, Chief Medical Officer. Ken Mosher, one of the most experienced combat officers in the camp, was to command four platoons made up of the most able men.

Now that the Filipino guerrillas were in regular contact with the Americans, it was possible to stockpile weapons to arm Mosher's platoons. Early in the new year the Tawi Tawi force had delivered two machine guns, 27 rifles and 2500 rounds of ammunition to the assistance group which had hidden them at a location near the 15 mile peg. During the delivery, Mu Sing's kompit had been challenged by a Japanese patrol boat, which indicated that a search of the vessel was in order. Mu Sing's response was to open fire from a concealed cannon and deck-mounted machine gun, blasting the patrol boat to smithereens and annihilating the crew. The underground organisation was no longer merely a collector of intelligence. It had moved into very dangerous territory indeed.

Meanwhile, the internal camp intelligence organisation had undergone a slight adjustment. Corporal Rickards had become so prickly to work with he had been given complete control of the radio, while Wells was now assigned permanently to the powerhouse during the day.

In Sandakan township the work of the assistance group went on. Two of the many Chinese who had volunteered their services were Peter Raymond Lai (also known as Lai Kiu Fook), a dresser at the Sandakan hospital and fellow employee Richard Low. Dr Taylor warned them of the risks, but welcomed them with open arms. Taylor had been making false entries in the hospital ledger, and had been sending to the camp a steady supply of atebrin, quinine and other drugs, ether, sterile bandages, iodine, disinfectants, surgical intruments for operations and chemicals for the rectifier. Whenever possible he had also tried to find nutritious food for the seriously ill. His new helpers, who also had access to drugs, took on the task of supplementing the supplies which Peter Lai, who had close links to Matusup, then delivered to The Eight Mile on his bicycle. These precious parcels were secreted in bushes near the camp for collection by the prisoners.

Chin Piang Syn, aged nineteen, had been recruited by Heng Joo Ming, the Mandor at the airstrip who had himself joined the ranks shortly after supplying the radio parts to Wallace. Chin, who spoke good English, was so anxious to help that he changed his name to Chin Chee Kong and took a job as a coolie at the aerodrome stores office in order to be closer to the prisoners. Dubbed 'Sini' by the Australians, Chin was a keen member of the Scouting movement, fiercely patriotic, and proud to live in a country which was part of the mighty British Empire. Because he was small, slightly built and looked far younger than he was, the Japanese regarded him with some affection. Sini exploited their benevolence. He moved freely between Sandakan and The Eight Mile, and was soon responsible for carrying the most important messages, including letters, maps and data from Apostol and Mr Brown of the Forestry Department, as well as money and cigarettes. Once the mail was safely in the jungle post box Sini left a sign at the aerodrome to indicate that a delivery was awaiting pick up.

Sini's involvement in the underground movement and his apparent extreme youth worried Captain Mosher. One day, after Sini had signalled that a delivery was ready for collection, Mosher asked if he realised the enormous risks he was taking. Sini had replied, 'Yes Sir, I know what will happen if the Japanese catch me, but I must do my duty. I am British and I am also a boy Scout.'

In January, with work on stage two of the airfield beginning, and the barracks, to house Japanese military personnel, underway, Wallace decided it was time to go. However, before Sini, who believed the way of escape lay with the sea, had a chance to initiate enquiries about a boat, the camp had some disappointing news.

On 27 January Private Allan Minty and the other four members of the 2/29th battalion, who had escaped the previous July, were re-captured.

They had started out with the right idea. After moving away from the camp precincts they had gone to the headwaters of the Sungei Batang, a tributary of the Gum Gum, not far from the 15 mile peg, where they had hidden in a tract of jungle adjoining a tobacco estate run by a wealthy Chinese named Sin Tshau. When Matthews learned through the underground that the escapees had made no effort to move on, Abin made contact with them through another policeman, Mandor Kassim. One of Kassim's relatives, Surat Min, took food to the POWs and, nine days after their escape, Sin Tshau made himself known to them. Quinine was sent out from the camp and, with money from a special POW escape fund organised by Dr Taylor and the Governor, two local storekeepers — the corpulent Go brothers, Tiek Soong and Tiek Tshi — kept the absconders supplied with food and ensured they had enough materials and utensils to build and furnish a rough hut.

For some inexplicable reason the escapees stayed where they were for almost six months. However, in January they became restless and told Sin Tshau that they wanted to try to sail to Australia. Although the Chinese pointed out that January, the height of the monsoon season, was not a good time to put to sea, the Australians would not be dissuaded, insisting that they were good navigators. Their benefactor then began negotiations to buy a boat moored in the nearby river. When it was discovered that this vessel was unseaworthy, the POWs took the initiative and, on Sin's advice, stole another boat. Sin gave them a map and rations for two months, and his son accompanied them out to sea before returning in his own kompit.

The Australians were blown ashore at Bongong Kechil, a small cape near Sandakan Harbour, where they were unlucky enough to be seen by Sin Kee Seng, a 50-year-old Cantonese and his friend Chong Mew Lee (also known as Kechil). They reported the sighting to Chong Fong, a prosperous gardener who, realising that 'POW hunting' was a potentially lucrative source of extra income, formed a gang with Sin, Chong and five other locals. They informed the Japanese and the Australians were captured. It was probably just as well because all five were in a shocking state, suffering from beriberi, malaria and assorted skin diseases. They were so ill they were incarcerated in the Sandakan Civil Gaol where Dr Stookes, the Dutch doctor-cum-pilot, and Damudaran, a member of the underground, were working. Once again the underground movement came to the Australians' aid. With the assistance of Warder 18, Mohamed Zamen, and Dr Taylor's helpers Richard Low and Peter Lai, Stookes was soon smuggling nourishing food in to them.

January 1943 was also eventful for a number of other POWs and civilian internees. Late in the afternoon of 12 January, the women and children were removed from the camp at Berhala and sent by ship to the large POW camp at Kuching. Accompanying them on the voyage were a contingent of guards and several Japanese officers, one of whom was Captain Takakuwa Takuo. Cold and calculating, Takakuwa had been commandant of all Sandakan's civilian internees — a role now taken over by Hoshijima. Takakuwa was a notorious womaniser whose extra-curricular activities had left him with a hefty dose of syphilis. The women internees, who generally regarded Japanese officers as figures of fun, loathed and detested him.

While the transfer of Takakuwa to Kuching brought a measure of relief to the civilians still in Sandakan, there was no such respite for the prisoners working out at the 'drome. Officers and men alike were subjected to the same mindless brutality that had set the standard during the 'speedo' before Christmas. There appeared to be no reason for many of the punishments. In the second week of January a working party of 68 officers was lined up by three guards who then marched smartly along the ranks flogging bare shoulders and backs with lengths of cane. The Australians were being subjected to flying practice when Major Fleming turned up and asked why they were being punished. He was told that all were 'bad men' and that he, being a 'bad man' also, could join them.

It was not only the punishment schedule which had been stepped up following the all too brief break at Christmas. With Hoshijima determined that stage two of the aerodrome should be completed as soon as possible, the working party quota was raised and the sick were again forced to make up the numbers. Fukishima, The Black Bastard, had a method of determining whether a hospital patient, claiming exemption because of a tropical ulcer, was malingering or not — he gave the bandaged limb a swift, hard kick with the toe of his army boot.

Two of the few who had no trouble convincing the Japanese they were unfit for work were Billy Young, bitten by a snake during a foraging expedition, and M.P. Brown, whose leg ulcers were huge. Billy still had a fantastically swollen leg and he was given light duties and confined to camp until the swelling went down — a slow process which took about two weeks. He was, however, no longer the slightest bit sick.

Until now it had been the custom to pool the rice ration, ensuring that the sick, who were on a much smaller allowance than the fit, received enough to eat. Hoshijima decided to put a stop to this egalitarian Australian practice and decreed that from now on the rice ration must be taken out and eaten at the 'drome. He also ordered Moritake to crack down on anyone trying to obtain extra food outside the prescribed trading hours. Beatings, bashings and cagings followed but they were not nearly as bad as being sentenced to a stretch in the humiliation cage, erected in Sandakan itself. Two of those who were subjected to the horror of the cage, plus the indignity of being on public view 24 hours a day were Vince Jeffrey and his mate Ron Tyrrell, both privates in the 2/3 Ordinance Corps. Officers were not let off either. If they crossed Hoshijima they could expect to spend the next day or two, or even three, standing at attention in the commandant's office.

A collaborator, Jackie Lo Ah Fock, a Chinese ex-gunner with the British North Borneo Constabulary, was infiltrated into the camp at about this time to spy on the prisoners. Lo, who spoke English, Japanese and Malay as well as Chinese, saw Matthews talking to Matusup's wife Halima, who was acting as go-between for her husband, arranging delivery of food he had purchased for the camp. Jackie Lo demanded they accompany him to the Japanese barracks and when they refused he returned with a guard, who escorted them to Hoshijima. Halima was certainly made of stern stuff. When questioned by Hoshijima she

The basher gang with Jimmy Darlington, February 1943. Drawing by Billy Young.

stuck to the same story she had already given to Lo — that they were not talking about anything in particular. Hoshijima, not satisfied with this reponse, hit her about the head with a stick. She and Matthews were then tied to a post and left in the sun for over an hour. When further interrogation failed Hoshijima let them go with a warning.

This punishment did not deter Jimmy Darlington from standing up to the guards. On 17 February, shortly after the noon meal, Mad Mick stopped off at the POWs' cookhouse at the 'drome where he proceeded to wash his dirty underpants in one of the 44-gallon cooking drums. One of the cooks, a 'nice old bloke', made the mistake of pointing out that washing one's smalls in the cooking pot was not acceptable. Mad Mick's answer to these protests was to knock the cook flying and to lay in the boot.

When Darlington, standing nearby, went to the cook's aid, Mad Mick lashed out at him. The Australian saw it coming, dodged and, with the instinct of a born fighter, came up with a solid right hook that sent the guard sprawling, his jaw and teeth shattered. Darlington was immediately set upon with rifle butts and sticks by other members of the basher gang, while the rest, weapons drawn, held the other prisoners at bay. By the time the bashers had finished with him, Darlington was more dead than alive. They then dragged him to a pile of split firewood by the cookhouse and, after making a platform composed of the sharpest pieces, one group forced Darlington, hands tied behind his back, into a kneeling position, while the rest wedged more firewood behind his knees and the crooks of his elbows. Lengths of wet, thin rope were then criss-crossed tightly around his body.

As the cords dried they began to shrink, biting deeply into Darlington's flesh and cutting off his circulation. His hands and feet began to turn black and it was obvious that unless someone did something he would surely die. The Dead End Kids noticed that 'Mac' McDonough, now in charge of first aid at the 'drome, was edging forward with his kit bag, waiting for an opportunity to go to Darlington's aid. Darlington's best mate Harry Longley, with the help of the rest of The Dead Enders, started a minor riot, yelling and shouting and throwing anything they could find. As the guards turned to quell this sudden disturbance, McDonough grabbed a knife from his bag, darted forward from his hiding place, cut the cords and relieved the pressure. Although the guards made a half-hearted attempt to re-tie the cords, Mac's action, which earned him a beating, undoubtedly saved Darlington's life.

Darlington, left kneeling out in the hot sun for the rest of the afternoon, fainted from time to time, but was revived when one of the guards tossed a bucket of water over him. At about 3.30pm he was thrown into the back of a truck and taken away.

When the working parties arrived back at camp that night they discovered that Darlington, who had been beaten up again, was lying delirious on the floor of the cage. He was still trussed and, as he had been allowed no medical attention, was in a shocking condition. He was bruised, battered and covered in blood from head to toe, both eyes were closed and his face was so swollen that his features were no longer recognisable. Each time Darlington regained consciousness throughout the night his screams reverberated from one end of the camp to the other — his agony so acute that he begged the guards to kill him. Eventually, they could stand it no longer and sent for Don Picone, who was able to give Darlington a drink of water laced with enough morphine to send him into a deep and merciful sleep.

Two days later, when Mo Davis came up from the boiler house to check on the water storage tanks, he saw that the prisoners were lined up under The Big Tree for tenko and that Darlington, now freed from his bonds, was outside the cage waiting to be loaded onto a truck. Having been trussed up for so long, the prisoner was bent almost double and, as the blood had been washed away, those nearest him could gauge some idea of his injuries. His forearms, the tendons exposed where the ropes had cut into into his muscle tissue, were so misshapen it appeared that one bone, at least, was broken. As Mo watched from his vantage point beside the tanks, he was puzzled to see Darlington make his way slowly and agonizingly towards the officers' lines. To Mo's utter amazement, Ken Mosher broke ranks, strode over to Darlington and shook his faithful batman by the hand.

Only three days after seeing Darlington bashed to within an inch of his life, Billy Young chose to absent himself from the 'drome at lunchtime. Ever since they had put foot in Sandakan The Dead End Kids had discussed the possibility of escape, only to procrastinate for some reason or other. During his fortnight off work recovering from his snake bite, Billy and M.P. had again examined the possibility of giving it a try. Billy had a map, albeit hand-drawn, which showed that Australia was only about 15 centimetres away from Borneo, while M.P. spoke fluent Malay, a smattering of Spanish and excellent Dutch, including the odd obscenity or two. As the hideout was still secure, Billy suggested that perhaps it was time to start stockpiling some more rations so that when the time came, they would be ready.

Although he was not keen, M.P., who had not been outside the camp perimeter except when on working parties, agreed to go with Billy at lunchtime on 20

February to pick up some supplies he had been promised. They slipped away undetected, but when they returned to the edge of the 'drome (empty handed as the rendezvous had failed) they saw the entire work force lined up and being counted. They decided their best option was to flee — permanently. They were heading for Billy's hideout when disaster struck. Straddling the track was a posse of half-a-dozen Formosan privates and three Japanese NCOs, led by bounty-hunting locals eager to cash in on the promise of 25 dollars per fugitive, the going rate at the time.

Subdued by rifle butts, boots and sticks, Billy and M.P. gave up any thought of resistance and surrendered. Hands tied behind their backs and roped together around the neck, they were pummelled along the track, where they found Moritake waiting beside a truck. They were not driven to the cage but were dumped unceremoniously outside the boiler house. While Moritake watched from an elevated position behind the engine room, each private chose a length of timber from the woodpile — metre-long, sharp-edged billets. As Moritake was only allowing them one hit each, the Formosans took their time over the selection process. A few practice swings, and the beating began.

The prisoners tried to fend off each blow but, still tethered together, they succeeded only in pulling one another over, much to the annoyance of the attackers, who kicked them to their feet. When the privates had finished, the more powerfully built NCOs and Moritake had their turn. The two men were then dragged, spluttering and choking on the end of the rope, up the hill to the front gates of the camp. As they collapsed onto the gravel, Moritake gave them both a well-aimed kick in the ribs before turning on his heel and retreating to the shade of the main guardhouse.

Billy and M.P. were still there when the working parties returned from the 'drome. Bob Shipsides managed to give Billy, who had regained consciousness, a drink, but the guards saw him and beat him off. M.P. had actually borne the brunt of the attack and was still unconscious, but Billy's injuries looked far worse. A blow to his forehead had flayed the skin in such a way that the flesh hung down over his eyes in raw, meaty chunks, giving the impression that he had been blinded.

Towards nightfall Billy was dragged into Hoshijima's office where the commandant, fired up with alcohol, was in a rage. Billy, his head spinning and his senses reeling, did his best to stay on his feet, while Hoshijima vented his spleen in a mangled stream of Japanese, English and Malay. Billy's last memory, before Hoshijima lashed out with his fists to send him hurtling down the steps and into merciful oblivion, was of a face distorted with fury yelling, 'Kura. You bad man, you no honour.'

When he came to, it was dark and he and M.P., tied together once more, were in the back of the truck. As it pulled away from the camp gates, Billy looked up and saw The Big Tree, its enormous crown clearly etched against the brilliance of the tropical, starlit night.

When the camp rose the following morning to discover that Billy and M.P. had disappeared, the general concensus was that, like Darlington, both were probably dead — as the result of a beating so brutal that Billy Young's eyes had been gouged out. But they had underestimated the trio's capacity for survival.

When Billy and M.P. arrived at Kempei-tai headquarters in Sandakan they had company — Jimmy Darlington. After giving them a couple of weeks to recover from their injuries, the Kempei-tai began their interrogations, concentrating on guns, submarines and civilian conspirators. The Kempei-tai could get no sense out of the prisoners, who had no idea of what they were talking about. Eventually, after about eight days of interrogation, the inquisitors realised that their prisoners had no information to give.

During the latter half of March, Billy, M.P., Jimmy Darlington, and Private Minty's escape group, were taken to Kuching on a small coastal vessel *Treasure*, formerly the luxury private yacht of Robert Brooke, Sarawak's White Rajah. They were held in the wire-mesh cages for three months and then the Australians, along with five Chinese arrested for alleged subversive activities, were taken before the court. There was no presumption of innocence, only guilt and there was no provision for a defence lawyer. Charges were read and evidence presented, but the judge did not sit in judgement as the very fact that a court had been convened meant that the accused were guilty as charged. After the prosecutor had finished presenting his 'evidence', all the judge had to do was to hand out the punishment.

On 26 June, after a mass 'trial' which was completely unintelligible to the accused as it was carried out entirely in Japanese, the sentences were handed down. A tremor ran along the line as the prisoners, handcuffed one to the other, awaited the announcement of their fate — death for the Chinese and Outram Road for the Australians. For attempted escape: Private Allan Minty — six years; Corporal W.F. Fairy, Private Bruce McWilliams and Private Norm Morris — five years; Lance Corporal Fred New — four years; Private Miles Pierce Brown — eight years; Private William Young (to whom the court had shown great leniency because of his youth) — four years. For striking a guard: Private James Darlington — six months.

The bashing incidents prompted senior officers at Sandakan to continue to advise caution to all those harbouring ideas of escape. Wallace, however, was not to be put off. Neither was Sini. Nothing the Japanese did appeared to intimidate him — not even the very public execution in early March of one of his countrymen. It was a slow and hideous death. Accused of looting, the victim had been hamstrung with lengths of wire and then suspended upside down from the crossbar of the padang goal posts. Shortly after, Sini returned with Mu Sing to Tawi Tawi to check out the work of the guerillas himself. The 240-kilometre voyage, in a small boat, had been hazardous. They were waylaid near Tawi Tawi by Moro pirates who robbed them of everything except the clothes they were wearing, but the pair reached Sitankay Island safely, only to be arrested by the Japanese. Fortunately Sini's story that they had only put into Sitankay for protection, following their encounter with the pirates, was believed, and the Japanese let them go. Sini returned to Sandakan at the end of March and reported to an incredulous Wallace that everything Mu Sing had told him was true. Furthermore, two letters written by Wallace, which Sini had hidden in his shoes, had been handed over to the guerrilla fighters for delivery to the Allied powers. Sini added that, although Mu Sing was keen to give assistance, Wallace must not attempt to flee until a proper escape route had been established.

Major Fleming gave Wallace a well-deserved dressing-down for doing something as dangerous as sending unauthorised letters out of the camp. All this did was stop Wallace confiding in senior officers. Consequently when Wallace's mate Frank Martin began to have second thoughts about joining him in an escape attempt, Wallace began to canvass the rank and file for someone willing to give it a go. He settled on two signallers — Howard Harvey, 21, of Townsville and Theodore 'Mac' MacKay, a 32-year-old Thursday Islander who, wanted for going AWOL under his real name, had re-enlisted as Daniel MacKenzie.

Another would-be escapee had Fleming's unqualified support. Sergeant Adair Macalister Blain was the current Northern Territory member of the Australian parliament. As it was planned to try and evacuate Sini to Australia through Tawi Tawi, Blain had written a personal letter to Mr Frank Forde, Minister for the Army, for Sini to deliver. It was, by necessity, brief:

Dear Frank: Things are very tough here, and we are badly in need of medicine and the sick are dying. The messenger will explain everything to you. Please recompense the messenger for what he has done on an arduous and perilous journey. Macalister.

With Fleming's blessing, Blain, who wanted to escape himself, gave his parliamentary gold pass to Driver Scott, a member of the wood party, who arranged its delivery to Dr Taylor, along with a note seeking assistance. Taylor's response was simply to return the pass and instruct Blain to wait. Blain then approached Staff Sergeant James, who worked with Frank Martin at the 'drome. Martin, while no longer interested in escaping himself, was willing to help and approached Sini, taking the gold pass with him. Blain received the same advice that Sini had given to Wallace — wait.

Although chaffing at the bit, Wallace was doing precisely that when an influx of 43 guards, under the command of a newly-arrived officer, Captain Nagai Hirawa, took up duties at the camp on 20 April. Unlike the previous guards, who were brought out in trucks from the central barracks in Sandakan, these were to live almost on site, in buildings under construction to the south-east and for which the camp's water pipes and electricity cables were being taken down and recycled. Armed with English, Dutch and Japanese rifles, they belonged to the Hong Regiment and had come from a POW camp at Jesselton. Immediately dubbed 'kitchi' soldiers because of their small size, the newcomers were not Japanese but Formosan conscripts aged between sixteen and 20 years who had been recruited into the Bushido Youth Corps.

The Bushido boys were very young and slightly built, but they made up for their lack of years and slight physique with a swaggering aggression that rivalled that of the basher gang. Drunk with unaccustomed and newly-acquired power and commanded by a Japanese officer who allowed them to do whatever they liked, the kitchi soldiers were infinitely worse than the old soldiers who had previously guarded the camp.

It was now that Padre Wardale-Greenwood proved he could be just as heroic in captivity as he had been in battle. Worried about the kitchi's violence at the 'drome, the padre secretly took the place of any ill men ordered out to work.

When his subterfuge was detected his punishment was confinement to Esau for 36 hours and confiscation of his ecclesiastical books.

The POWs wondered why Nagai and his juvenile thugs had been sent to Sandakan and it didn't take long for them to find out. The entire camp was soon abuzz with the news that more than 700 English prisoners had just been installed in huts out near the aerodrome. And that was not all. According to the locals, the male civilian internees at Berhala Island had been shipped off to Kuching and in their place were 500 Australian prisoners.

After nine months of virtual isolation, it looked as if the men of B Force were to have company.

Chapter Six
COMINGS AND GOINGS

While the men had not been informed, Wells and Matthews had heard through the underground that there were British prisoners housed at Jesselton on the west coast, two or three days' journey by boat from Sandakan. And that there were 1500 Australian prisoners at Sandakan was not news to Squadron Leader Ted Hardie at Jesselton. He and the other senior British officers had learned of their existence in early November, when a message containing details of B Force was received from Rod Wells through Chinese-born Mrs Wales, a member of the Sandakan underground. Mrs Wales, wife of an interned English planter, had volunteered her services and had delivered the message safely. Yet the British had not responded. Having witnessed the beheading of several airmen in Java, Ted Hardie was wary of Japanese reprisals and, despite several overtures from Jesselton agents, had resisted all invitations to become involved with any subversive activity. Consequently the Australians knew only what Mrs Wales had told them — that the British at Jesselton were army and air force personnel captured in Java.

The Australians had no idea that 776 POWs[1] had been transferred from Jesselton until the first batch, numbering about 200, were seen on a track near the airstrip gravel pit by an Australian party. Although the 50 or so workers had formed a guard of honour and saluted as the newcomers marched by, they knew nothing more until an Australian driver, sent in a truck to Sandakan harbour to pick up the sick, arrived back at The Eight Mile with a few more details. The driver confirmed that apart from three Australians — Andrew Sommerville and Albert Tyrrell of the 2/2nd Pioneers, and South African-born Sapper Aubrey Zinn — the POWs were Royal Army and Air Force personnel. Captured in Java they had been on the move ever since. Almost all of the 350 or so airmen, including two Australian Flight Lieutenants serving with the RAF — Queenslander Charlie 'Johnnie' Johnston and English-born Humphrey 'Harry' Burgess from Perth — had been in no fewer than six camps by the time they arrived in Sandakan. After spending six months in various compounds in and around Batavia they had been trans-shipped to Singapore, only to be uprooted three weeks later, this time to Borneo. The rest of the party were all soldiers, mostly gunners from anti-aircraft units.

When they had arrived at Keppel Harbour in Singapore to embark on the rusty, filthy cargo vessel tied up alongside the dock, they found that there were more than 1000 British POWs already on board who were bound for Kuching. They set sail on 9 October on a voyage uncannily like that experienced by the Australians three months previously — an almost complete lack of sanitation, appalling food, little water and severe overcrowding. Nine prisoners in Hardie's group died from illness during the voyage while another simply vanished, thought to have fallen overboard. The British, too, discovered they were sitting on crates of edible commodities — sugar, tinned fish and vegetables — enabling them to eke out the miserable Japanese rations.

After off-loading the Kuching party, the rest, now numbering 827, had arrived in Jesselton on 19 October to be incarcerated in Victoria Gaol, built to hold 40 native prisoners. The 40 officers were housed in pairs in comparatively roomy stone cells and the NCOs shared a wooden barracks, while the ORs were squashed into atap huts which had been squeezed between the main buildings and the three-metre-high outer wall. The remaining spare ground, on an incline to the rear of the buildings, was taken up by inadequate trench latrines which flooded the entire compound with raw sewage every time it rained. It was not until the Japanese stationed at the gatehouse became concerned about their own health that they had allowed new latrines, fully enclosed by barbed wire, to be built at the bottom of the slope beyond the entrance.

As at Sandakan, the rank and file were required to provide working parties each day for airfield construction. However, the Jesselton commandant, Lieutenant Nagata, was more humane than his Sandakan counterpart, and the prisoners under his command were not subjected to quite the brutality the Australians suffered. Despite the better treatment, morale was poor. While at Sandakan there was a certain amount of coolness between many of the officers and men, the situation at Jesselton was far worse.

Although the behaviour of some British officers was beyond reproach, the majority were concerned more with their own welfare than anything else. According to Flight-Lieutenant Peter Lee, Squadron Leader Hardie spent much of his time lazing around in his sarong and was so completely useless and ineffective that the men under his command thought he made 'a good latrine wall'. This lack of leadership, coupled with carping criticism and back-biting between the officers themselves, as well as schisms between army and air force senior ranks, discouraged respect from the men. The attitude of one army officer, Captain Larder, just about summed it up. 'He didn't give a damn about his men, as they didn't seem to care about him, and would not do anything he told them.'

On 23 November Major Suga, The Commandants of all the Borneos, inspected the camp. After delivering a speech, Suga invited the senior officers and the padre to lunch. All but one accepted the invitation. Over a meal of soup, rice and pork, followed by coffee and saki, the officers took the opportunity to complain about their own living quarters, not mentioning those of their men. Two days later, all, except the padre and the RAF medical officer, were moved to superior accommodation a kilometre or so from the overcrowded gaol. A total of 52 — 38 officers, four warrant officers, seven batmen and three cooks — made the move to roomy wooden barracks, empty following the transfer of the civilian internees to Kuching. The ill-will this relocation generated among the rank and file was fuelled by the discovery that the officers were receiving more than their share of sugar and that they had purloined extra meat rations for their mess from the delivery truck.

While their superiors spent their days sniping at one another, reading books, chatting, dozing and doing odd-jobs, conditions at the men's camp deteriorated rapidly. Complaints to Lieutenant Nagai, who took over from Nagata in December, were useless. Although Captain Daniels and Flight-Lieutenant Blackledge, the unit medical officers, did their best, deaths occurred daily from the effects of dysentery and malnutrition. In early April, with the death toll rising to an alarming 48 and three more dangerously ill, Nagai received orders to shut the camp down and transfer all prisoners to Sandakan.

Nagai and the 200 fittest prisoners, including almost all the RAF officers, left first. Arriving at Sandakan on 8 April after a two-day voyage, the POWs found that, if things were crook at Jesselton, they were worse here. The huts in their compound at the far end of the aerodrome, hurriedly erected by coolies on a dry, open patch of dusty ground, were long unpartitioned atap huts, with sleeping platforms running along either side and a door at the end. The latrines were not only inadequate but fly-blown, there was no electricity and the only water available had to be drawn from a small creek or a muddy, smelly well outside the camp. Even the perimeter fencing, which was still being erected, was sub-standard — a double run of barbed wire cannibalised from the multi-stranded Australian compound. By the time the rest of the party turned up ten days later, things were a little better. The locals had finished the fence, working parties had been organised to collect wood and water and new latrines had been dug.

The new arrivals were brought up the Sibuga River on barges to a jetty, where they remained in the hot sun for the entire day, each prisoner sustained only by two rissoles sent from the Australian camp at around noon. At about 4.30pm the entire party of 576, 240 of whom were very ill, were herded along one of the narrow gauge railway lines that the timber companies had cut through the jungle. By the time they reached the camp an hour later, most were near to collapse. The voyage from Jesselton to Sandakan in a 1000-tonne vessel had been horrendous, especially for the sick who had to be manhandled up sloping gang planks and then down vertical ladders into the hold. Even in that short space of time many of the 'fit' had been reduced to an almost skeletal state. They had brought very little with them and some were so poorly equipped that their only eating utensils were half-coconut shells. Although, after Jesselton's confining, corrugated-iron and stone perimeter walls, the openness of the new camp was a welcome change, the men soon discovered that with over 70 jammed into each hut they were just as crowded as before.

Meanwhile, the Australians were having difficulties with their radio. The valves and other vital components were so decrepit it had broken down. However, the word went out and before long Wells and Weynton had enough replacement parts to rebuild the set — the new valves, resistors and condensors coming through the ever-reliable Heng Joo Ming and two relatively new members of the underground, Samuel Aruliah, an Indian customs examiner, and Amigaw, a Malay employee of the Post and Telegraph Department.

The reconstruction of the receiver was held up when some of the laboriously-collected parts, hidden in a false-bottomed onion box in the vegetable shack, were stolen. This felony, coming on top of a previous incident when drugs stolen from the camp had been sold to the locals, so enraged Matthews that he instituted a Court of Inquiry under the 2/10th Field Regiment's Lieutenant Len Draney, who had legal training. While Draney, with the assistance of Ken Mosher, who was investigating the previous theft, concentrated on bringing the culprit to justice, Wells set about the difficult task of obtaining duplicate parts from his underground suppliers.

With the re-building of the wireless receiver came a change in its management. Rickards, who had become ill, insisted that no one else could operate the radio while he was in hospital, forcing Major Fleming to step in and relieve him of his 'ownership' rights. Wells then became more ambitious — he would build a transmitter. He opened up contact with Gerald Mavor who, prior to this, had maintained only indirect communication with the camp. In the ensuing weeks, Mo Davis and Stevens continued to smuggle into the camp power transformers (made by Mavor in his workshop), rectifier valves and condensors. At the same time Heng used his contacts at the 'drome to pass highly specialised valves to Lieutenant Pascoe-Pierce, one of Fleming's 4th Anti-tank officers. While most of the parts came via Mavor's chief engineer, Ah Kong, who gave them to Ah Ping, Mr Phillips delivered some directly to Abin. Although some things were quite unprocurable, this was no deterrent to Wells. He simply made the parts, improvising components whenever necessary. As had been the case with the radio receiver, the gridleak condensors were made from metal foil, paper and coconut oil. The resistors were from string, with burnt coconut husks or cinnamon bark providing the carbon. Wire stolen from Japanese beehives outside the compound and coated with baked-on coconut oil and flour provided the necessary insulated wire, while a pair of improvised chemical cells supplied the valve filament voltage. To remove some of the high-voltage 'hum', a choke coil was made from beehive wire wrapped around a small piece of fish plate, stolen from the airfield, and the filter condensor from an oiled sheet of newspaper, sandwiched between two pieces of foil and rolled together to form a tube 45 centimetres long. The transmitter, when completed, was, like the radio, testament to Wells' ingenuity and determination and, furthermore, it worked. However, as it was to be used only to contact invading Allied forces, once the test transmissions were successfully completed, it was wrapped in a waterproof cape and buried.

Weynton, meanwhile, had taken over the compiling and distribution of the news. Although he continued to send the town bulletins out by the usual channels, he embarked upon a different, and very risky, mode of delivery to the British. Australian prisoners, working at various places as truck drivers for the Japanese, were given the summaries, which they then crunched into a ball and threw to British working parties as the trucks drove past. Weynton, who continued distributing his news bulletins in this hit and miss method, was soon to have even more customers.

While the British had been settling in at their aerodrome camp, another 500 Australians had arrived at Berhala from Singapore. Officially designated E Force (C and D Force having gone to Japan and Thailand), this group had consisted originally of 1000 men, half of whom were British destined for Kuching. The 500-strong Australian contingent, under the command of the 2/20th Battalion's Major John Fairley and with Major Carter as his second in command, differed markedly from B Force. The vast majority had been drawn from combat and engineering units which had been employed on working parties around Singapore for months, the men were fitter and there were fewer 'old blokes'. The number of officers had also been cut to the minimum and, as there had been a rigid medical inspection, there were no ill men in the party.

There were, however, some former convalescents. Machine gunner Ron Moran had survived the carnage as the Japanese had over-run his isolated position on 8 February. Although fortunate enough to be assigned to a party working on the wharves in Singapore, his eyesight had begun to fail after a few months owing to the lack of Vitamin A in his diet. His mate Owen Doust covered for him to prevent him being beaten for being slow or inefficient, but Ron's eyesight deteriorated so badly that he went completely blind. However, once he was back at Selarang and given an enriched diet, he recovered his sight enough to be placed on the E Force draft.

There were also a few miscreants on the list. Like Boots Callegan, Black Jack Galleghan (now the AIF's commanding officer following Boots' departure to Formosa the previous August) had taken the opportunity to relieve himself of any able-bodied troublemakers still in Selarang. Nelson Short, whose well-publicised antics had made him very conspicuous, was chosen. So was Mo Davis' mate Fred 'Nutsy' Roberts, a 33-year-old infantryman who was known as much for his distinctive gravelly voice as his anti-establishment attitude, and W. 'Curly' Kent — a camp trader who had elevated scrounging to an art form. Kent, a member of the 6th Division, which had been sent to the Middle East, was being sent home for disciplinary reasons when hostilities broke out in the Far East. Off-loaded in Singapore from *Empress of Canada*, he had made his way to Endau on Malaya's east coast to find his brother Roy, commonly known as 'Slim'. Curly had stayed in Singapore after the capitulation, masquerading as an Irish cook. He was discovered by the Japanese and sent to Selarang where he could have remained as a camp cook, had he not drawn attention to himself by indulging in black-market activities.

Curly was joined by one of Nelson Short's mates, Private Howard 'The Turk' Hewitt, an even more notorious black marketeer. Also expelled from the 6th Division, The Turk had been taken prisoner in Singapore while awaiting further shipment to Australia. Hewitt saw prison life as an opportunity of increasing, rather than curtailing, his activities, and had converted his profits into gold and diamonds. His enterprise came to an end when Black Jack learned about it and sent him to Borneo.

As most of the men of E Force were fit, there was no need for large numbers of medical staff. There were only ten: two doctors, Major Howard Eddey and Captain John Oakeshott, from the 13th and 10th Australian General Hospitals respectively; Tom Burns' friend Sergeant Colin Smyth, also of the 10th AGH; and seven privates, all from the Australian Army Medical Corps (AAMC). There were also two chaplains, Father John Rogers and acting padre Corporal Alan Garland, and fourteen officers, all of whom were described by the hard-to-please Black Jack as 'competent'. In fact, this group was made up of seasoned campaigners of the calibre of Captain Richardson, who had extricated his men from a perilous position on at least two occasions. As unit war diaries would attest, many of these officers were in a class of their own.

So too was Father Rogers, ordained Roman Catholic priest and master scrounger. While on a working party at the Bukit Timah memorial, Rogers had managed to appropriate five gallons (22.5 litres) of petrol from a Japanese truck every day, while two guards dozed on the front seat. The highly marketable petrol, which Rogers siphoned into the Australians' now-empty communal tea can, was then sold to eagerly-waiting Chinese, giving the padre funds to buy medical supplies for the sick. According to a frankly-admiring Lieutenant Rex Blow (who was not a bad scrounger himself, having recently relieved a mosque's ornamental pool of almost its entire stock of Sacred Carp), God must definitely have been on the padre's side. The only consequence of this daring operation was the foul taste of the tea.

It was while working at Bukit Timah that Rex Blow and his mate Lieutenant Miles Gillon, also from the 2/10th Field Regiment, had first met fellow artilleryman Captain Ray Steele, of the 2/15th. All three had extensive battle experience and all three had one thing on their minds — escape. Blow had a compass, pistol, 45 rounds of ammunition and a map, and they formed an alliance dubbed the Dit Party ('dit' being Morse-code for 'E' and 'E' standing for 'Escape'). The trio bided their time until they learned that another working party was about to be sent overseas. Not only was the destination said to be Borneo, which they could see from their map was closer to home than any other place so far, it was, by coincidence, designated as 'E' Force.

The Dit Party, along with the other 497 Australians, left Selarang early on the morning of 28 March, each officer in the group carrying part of a dismantled radio set in his kit. Waiting for them at Keppel Harbour was *de Klerk*, a battered steamer, built in 1900, of about 3300 tonnes.

As he sat on his kit-box waiting to board, Rex Blow struck up a conversation with Private R. 'Jock' McLaren, a veterinary surgeon from Bundaberg. Born in Scotland, McLaren had served with a Scottish regiment in the Great War, emigrated to Queensland and then, at the age of 42, had lined up again, this time to serve in the field workshops with Neil Christie's unit, the AAOC. Although he had been taken prisoner with everyone else, he had not stayed long at Selarang. Four days after the fall of Singapore he and three workshop mates were gone, out of the camp and across the Straits of Johore, where they spent a couple of weeks with a Chinese guerrilla unit operating from a jungle hide-out in Southern Malaya. The four men, who had been on the run for six weeks, were making for Burma along the old opium trails when they were reported by Malays keen to claim a reward. After spending some time in various camps, McLaren and his mates, who were fortunate not to have been executed, arrived back in Selarang. He had been waiting for another chance to escape ever since, carrying in his pocket a 10-centimetre-square map of South East Asia. When Blow learned of McLaren's exploits, and that he had a pistol and 20 rounds of ammunition, which he had stolen from the Japanese and sewn into the collar of his gas cape, the Dit Party gained a new member.[2]

Once on board ship, the officers were left topside along with a few troops manning a first aid station. The rest were bundled below decks, where accommodation consisted of two very small, very hot holds alongside the engine room, double-decker cattle pens for'ard, or wooden planks balanced on top of leaky 44-gallon petrol drums aft. The trip on SS *de Klerk* was almost a re-enactment of the two preceeding voyages to Borneo — poor sanitation, cramped accommodation and monotonous rice rations, relieved on this occasion, following a tip-off from friendly Portuguese Timorese crewmen, by the tins of pork-and-baked beans in tomato sauce that formed part of the cargo. The remainder of the cargo was even better — cartons of Japanese cigarettes.

As they approached the Borneo coast, Ray Steele raised with Major Fairley the possibility of seizing the ship and sailing it to Australia — an idea enthusiastically supported by the force's intelligence officer, Lieutenant Charlie Wagner. Wagner, formerly the 2/18th's intelligence officer, spoke fluent Malay and had already tried to escape while working with a party sent to Mersing, in Malaya, to defuse mines and other explosives. Fairley thought obtaining an adequate fuel supply might be an insurmountable hurdle, and expressed grave reservations about the feasibility of such a plan. He nevertheless put the proposal to Britain's Lieutenant-Colonel Whimster, E Force's most senior officer. The audience was brief. Whimster turned on his heel and went below, eliminating the possibility of any further discussion.

When the ship docked at Kuching the next afternoon, 1 April, the Japanese discovered the shrinkage in the cargo. Then it became clear that every man, even a senior Japanese officer, has his price — in this case, 100 cartons of cigarettes. Although an immediate whip-round netted only 70, as the POWs had smoked their way through an estimated 30 000 cigarettes in three days, the Japanese officer was satisfied. The missing pork-and-beans, about which nothing could be done, was evidently not an issue.

To their surprise, the Australians as well as the British were disembarked at Kuching, loaded 40 at a time into motor lorries and taken to the POW camp. Crammed into two huts, one of which was an open-sided canteen, the first 400 Australian men were allocated buildings alongside the officers' quarters, while the rest were shunted off to the British area. Complaints about gross overcrowding were pointless.

As it turned out, the Australians were only in transit — disembarked to labour for a few days. A party of about 200, under the control of the 2/20th's Captain Frank Gaven and Charlie Wagner, were soon back at the wharf. For the next week they unloaded a cargo of oil drums, crockery and 700 tonnes of cement from *Taka Maru*, most of which they managed to either drop over the side or smash beyond repair.

On the second day, Major Suga ordered the recent arrivals to assemble for his customary exhortation and speech of welcome. After that, the troops were to sign a 'no escape' agreement. As most had already signed a similar document in Singapore, Major Fairley, worried about repercussions for refusing to comply, ordered everyone to do so. Then tragedy struck. It was raining and space was restricted. Jostling for a bit of room, Nelson Short's mate, Private Jimmy Picken, sought to steady himself by grabbing a stay-wire on one of the compound's security light poles. The Japanese had merely hooked the camp's electricity supply to the mains via the perimeter fence and, with no insulation, the stay-wire was 'live'.

Picken, who grasped the wire with both hands, died instantly. Miraculously a young soldier, knocked off balance, and who also touched the wire, and Short, who fell between him and Picken, escaped unscathed.

About 400 metres from the Australian huts was a compound holding Allied civilian women and children, some of whom had been transferred from Sandakan. The more daring soldiers were soon wriggling under the wire of their compound and across the civilian men's vegetable garden to the barbed wire barricade surrounding the women's camp. Some, with escape in mind, made the perilous journey to see the lie of the land, while others did it simply to have a chat with a woman. The Turk, who had attempted an escape from Selarang, was anxious to make use of a compass cunningly concealed in the false lower half of his water bottle, but he decided to combine business with pleasure. To the delight of Agnes Keith, who had responded to Hewitt's appeal for information, The Turk tossed her a tube of lipstick and a packet of cigarettes, both worth their weight in gold on the black market.

Sapper Don Marshall of Western Australia crawled in the direction of the men's camp. He, along with Sappers Ted Keating and C. Jensen, and signals' sergeant Joe Weston, wanted to make a break, so Marshall was anxious to collect as much useful information as possible. Luck was certainly with him. The Sandakan male civilian internees had just arrived from Berhala and Marshall was immediately taken to see senior members of the Sandakan Assistance Group — Harry Keith, his forestry off-sider Mr Brown and Police Chief Rice-Oxley. They were happy to help. When Marshall returned to his hut he carried with him maps of British North Borneo, a Forestry Department Survey chart and notes of introduction from Brown to Apostol and Paddy Funk (who also happened to be Brown's houseboy), as well as information on two possible escape routes — one through the Celebes and the other to the Philippines via Kudat and Job Island.

Jock McLaren had also managed to collect useful information. On arriving at Kuching, E Force had been met by Colonel Walsh and the eight officers who had been transferred from Sandakan the previous October. Recognising that one of them, the AAOC's Captain Owen, was from his unit, McLaren was able to gain an introduction to Governor Smith, who told him his best chance of escape was through Mata-mata (police agent) 142. Although McLaren didn't know it, Mata-mata 142 was none other than Corporal Koram.[3]

When the Australians marched out of Kuching camp at 6.00am on 9 April to the strains of 'Auld Lang Syne' floating from the women's camp, Majors Fairley and Carter and fifteen ORs were not with them. The two senior officers, combatants above the rank of major, had been ordered to remain behind so the Japanese could keep a closer eye on them. Fourteen of the others who stayed behind were ill, but, in the case of Curly Kent, at least, he may also have been detained so the officers could keep an eye on him. The only fit man in the group was Roy Kent who managed to persuade Major Fairley to allow him to remain behind with his brother.[4]

In their place were two men who had gone to Kuching with Walsh — Corporal Sydney Field of the AAMC and the recalcitrant, and now supposedly reformed, Jimmy Bowe (alias Anderson, originally 2/30th Battalion but latterly of the Mobile

Laundry Unit), along with eighteen other Australians captured in Java. Two, Bandsman Henry Kelly and Able Seaman G. Morriss, were survivors from HMAS *Perth*, sunk in the Sunda Straits between Java and Sumatra on 28 February 1942, a fortnight after Singapore's fall. The remainder of the group were either 8th Divison soldiers who had managed to escape to Java from Singapore at the time of the surrender, or members of the 7th Division who had arrived from the Middle East just in time to witness the collapse of the Netherlands East Indies.[5]

With the force restored to more than full strength (eighteen officers and 485 ORs), Captain Richardson, who had replaced Fairley as commanding officer, led his men onto the Kuching wharf. Tied up alongside was *Taka Maru*, the ship they had just spent a week unloading. A rusting iron vessel of about 1500 tonnes.[6] *Taka Maru*'s three holds, one with headroom of only 1.2 metres, were not only hot and uncomfortable, they were covered with a thick layer of cement dust. The highly alkaline cement, when mixed with sweat, burnt their skin, causing great discomfort. In other ways the voyage on *Taka Maru* was predictably miserable. Food was meagre (170 grams of rice a day, spread over two meals), water was scarce, seasickness was common and latrine visits were rarely granted. When they were, the contents of the tins leaked onto the troops below decks. Fortunately, when the ship berthed at Labuan to unload a steamroller and bunker coal, all were allowed to take a swim. A day or two later, as they turned south towards Sandakan, Ray Steele once more raised the question of hijacking the ship. Had Richardson known that the Filipino guerrillas were operating within 160 kilometres of their position, he might have been more receptive.

It was a relief when *Taka Maru*, after a five-day voyage, finally reached Sandakan. Rex Blow had just enough time to retrieve his pistol and ammunition, which he had hidden in an air vent, before boarding one of the large timberlighters waiting to ferry them to Berhala. There, waiting for them at the end of the wharf, was their new commandant, Captain Hoshijima.

They marched past the immaculately-dressed commandant to the small parade ground in front of the huts. A search was ordered and all prisoners had to display their kit for immediate inspection. McLaren, by holding his cape up by the collar, and shaking it vigorously, managed to conceal his pistol and ammunition. Blow, with the help of Frank Gaven, hurriedly scratched a hole in the soft sand for his pistol and ammunition, which he covered with his groundsheet, unobserved by a guard standing less than 2 metres away.[7] Gavan quickly rolled the wireless transformer he was carrying in the end of his mosquito net. While the search turned up a number of prohibited imports, including a Bofors shell, the guards were only interested in writing materials.

It was time for Hoshijima to deliver his mantra-like oration, translated as usual by Ozawa. They were prisoners of Japan; they were there to build an airstrip; they would work until their bones rotted under the tropical sun. He also warned that escape was futile — if he didn't capture them, the jungle would. Moreover, escape attempts would result in bloody reprisals, as would any move to communicate with any other POW camp. In conclusion, Hoshijima declared: 'The war, it will go 100 years. We will win.'

Although the former Quarantine Station, situated about 50 metres from the shoreline on the western side of Berhala, boasted excellent latrines and concrete plunge baths, it was far too small for a force of 500 men. Covering about half-a-hectare and surrounded by a 2-metre barbed-wire fence, it consisted of three elevated, two-storey wooden huts. Just outside the wire was a smaller building, set aside for a hospital and quartermaster's store, a cookhouse and a guard hut to cater for between six to eight guards. The three main huts were designed to accommodate a total of 150 inmates and space was so tight that many had to sleep either under the buildings or out in the open. The Japanese were not interested in hearing any complaints — as soon as the prisoners had felled enough timber to build a new camp, all would be shifted over to the mainland.

They had just settled into their new quarters when Charlie Wagner, as the force's intelligence officer, was approached by Ted Keating who had firmed up plans to escape with Marshall, Jensen and Weston. Wagner agreed and said he would not only join, but lead them. As Wagner was to arrange the finer details and date of departure, Weston gave him copies of all the material he had obtained from Harry Keith in Kuching.

Nelson Short and his friend, The Turk, heard about this plan. Short asked for them to be included and, in a gesture of good faith, The Turk handed over his compass. When Short pressed for further details, Wagner put him off by telling him that any escape attempt would have to be from the mainland. Wagner did not, however, return the compass.

Perhaps it was the impermanence of the camp, or the fact that Berhala was surrounded by water, that led the Japanese to be more lax than usual. Whatever the reason, they were so relaxed about Berhala's security that they ordered Corporal Koram, who had been disciplined only six months earlier for carrying messages to the internees, to take up guard duties. He was also ordered to spy on the prisoners. Koram agreed to do it, realising that this would give him the opportunity to come and go as he pleased. And he was not the only member of the assistance group working on the island. Salleh, who had played a key undercover role when the civilians were at Berhala, was still at his hut on the end of the wharf, keeping watch over not only the quarantine buildings, but also the nearby Leper Colony. His loyalty to the Rising Sun continued to remain unquestioned.

When it became clear to Blow and Wagner, through a series of cautious conversations, that Mata-mata 142, Corporal Koram, could be trusted, they expressed their desire to escape. He told them that the underground could make this a reality, and they immediately sent a message to Matthews seeking assistance. However, before Matthews had time to act, something most unexpected occurred.

Corporal Koram was fishing from his prahau when, without warning, an American submarine surfaced beside him. Corporal Abdul (Alberto) Quadra, who was working with the American Forces in the Philippines, emerged from the conning tower and handed the astonished Koram a letter with a request to deliver it to any white man he saw. Quadra also told Koram that if anyone wanted to escape and join the guerrillas, Mu Sing, whose trading vessels were still calling at Sandakan every ten days, could make arrangements for the submarine to pick them up and take them to Tawi Tawi. The letter, which contained similar information, was passed to Matthews through Taylor with instructions that messages to and from the camp were to be passed through Mu Sing, Felix Adzcona and Abin. However, tempting as the offer of escape was, it was rejected by Major Fleming who felt that, in view of the work being done by the camp's underground, all personnel should remain at Sandakan.

At the direction of Dr Taylor, Koram also relayed Quadra's offer to Wagner and the other officers in the Dit Party. They jumped at the chance, believing that their duty to escape was greater than their obligation to remain with their men. While Koram set about making arrangements for a pick-up, the Dit members concentrated on building up their fitness and stockpiling food. The guards, most of whom were loyal members of the constabulary hand-picked for the roster by Sergeant-Major Yangsalang, indirectly assisted in the former by allowing all POWs to play baseball and go swimming twice a day, while Koram took care of the latter by smuggling in dried fish and prawns, fruit and potatoes. However, before the Dit Party had a chance to formulate any escape plans, there was a great disturbance over on the mainland. Sergeant Wallace and two others had bolted from The Eight Mile Camp.

Although Wallace had told Frank Martin and Joo Ming, who supplied him with rations, that he was going, no one else had any idea he had escaped until the alarm was raised the next morning. Sini, stunned to learn from Frank Martin that the 'white tiger', as he called Wallace, had left before any outside support had been finalised, went immediately to Mu Sing and Ernesto Lagan. They had been coordinating Wallace's escape they were as astonished as Sini to learn he had already gone. Perhaps the only one not surprised by this sudden departure was Ken Mosher, who was about to arrest Wallace for stealing the drugs and transmitter parts.

On the night of 30 April, Wallace, MacKay and Harvey had hidden beneath the vegetable hut, slipping under the wire at about 9.30pm. Wallace, who had a pistol, a home-made dagger, maps, food and 200 dollars in cash, planned to head cross-country in a south-westerly direction to Seroi on the Locan River, then turn south-east towards the coastal town of Lahad Datu where he hoped to find a boat to take them to Tawi Tawi. The direct distance between Sandakan and Lahad Datu was more than 160 kilometres and there was a mountain range between Seroi and the coast, but Wallace was confident. Even if the Lahad Datu route proved impossible, he would return to the 'drome and make contact with Joo Meng in the hope that he could arrange a boat to take them to freedom.

Wallace had a compass and had read a book, lent to him by Joo Ming, on the geography of Borneo, yet he had seriously underestimated the difficult nature of the terrain. After days of heavy-going through snake-infested vegetation interspersed with slimy, miasmal swamps, the trio came across locals who told them they were at the 15 mile peg — only 7 miles from the camp and a long way from their intended destination. Abandoning any idea of trying to reach Lahad Datu, Wallace led the party to the north-east in an attempt to trace the course of the Sibuga River. After a few more days threshing through jungle, swamps and mangroves, and with no rations left, Wallace's companions became disgruntled. After a protracted argument, Harvey and MacKay elected to float downstream on the tide, leaving Wallace to battle the jungle and swamps alone.

Towards nightfall the next day, hungry and close to exhaustion, he too opted for the river route. Buoyed by logs, he drifted with the current for some distance, then ran aground on the opposite bank. He was alarmed to see a discarded cigarette packet on the ground — evidence that, during daylight hours at least, the Japanese had the river under surveillance. Avoiding the aerodrome and its sentries, he then struck out for Heng Joo Ming's house.

Wallace hid in the hen house at Heng's cottage. He managed to attract the attention of Heng's wife, Siti, who was astounded to find him holding a stout stick and dressed in nothing more than what appeared to be swimming trunks. The fugitive was given clothes and a meal before a discussion about his immediate future. An hour before dawn, after a night-long conference, Wallace was taken to a secure hideout in the jungle where Koram and two other policemen had built a small shelter. The entire area was swarming with search parties, and it was agreed that Wallace should stay in the shelter by day, only venturing to Heng's house after dark. Siti would keep him supplied with food. Meanwhile, Sini undertook to make arrangements with Lagan, Mu Sing and Dr Taylor to get him away to Tawi Tawi.

The following day when Heng returned home from his job at the 'drome, he had some very sobering news. Harvey and MacKay were both dead.

They had made it downstream without incident but, on coming ashore on the afternoon of 11 May, about 6 kilometres north-west of the camp, they were seen by five pro-Japanese Malays. Two feigned friendship and went off to 'arrange' for a boat while the others stayed with the Australians who busied themselves by gathering coconuts. When the Malays returned, they were accompanied by JackieLo and two truckloads of Japanese guards under the command of Moritake and Sergeant Shoji.

The escapees, who tried to repel the Japanese with stones, had no hope of survival. Under Japanese law anyone who tried to escape after signing the 'no escape' agreement could be gaoled for a minimum of one year, and guards were allowed to shoot anyone attempting to escape. However, many Japanese officers, including Moritake, thought that, as all POWs were members of the Japanese army, escape was tantamount to desertion — an act which was a capital offence.

Shortly before 4.30pm the men were tied up and taken to a secluded spot where Private Kurama and Munerichi Kamimura (a civilian employed by the army) fired a complete clip of cartridges into Howard Harvey, who died instantly, and then Theodore MacKay, who did not.[8] After finishing him off with their rifle butts, the search party blooded their bayonets on the bullet-riddled bodies.

Prisoners working at the 'drome, lined up at 4.30pm to witness the touchdown of a DC-3 (one of Japan's many spoils of war), heard the gunfire. However, it was not until half-an-hour later that they realised its significance. At about 5.00pm, after Frank Martin had been given the unenviable job of identifying his two friends, two Australian burial parties were sent to retrieve the bodies from the edge of the aerodrome where they had been dumped. Placed in simple wooden coffins, they were carried down the road leading to the new cemetery near the Eight Mile Police Post where they became the second and third Australians to be buried there.[9]

Hoshijima still allowed the officers to stage their new revue '*Let's Boong it On*' on Saturday 1 May, the night after the escape, but he was far less kindly disposed towards the prisoners 48 hours later. Gordon Weynton had dispatched a letter to the British on 2 May advising that medical supplies would be sent over from the Australian camp. The Japanese, who saw the crunched paper ball being thrown from the truck and intercepted the message, arrested Weynton at 7.30pm the following day. After a thorough beating, delivered by Hoshijima himself, he was forced to spend the night standing at attention outside the guard hut. Then he was lowered up to his neck in a water-filled pit — which would have resulted in drowning had he fallen asleep. At 10.00am, when Weynton was removed from the pit, he was sentenced to fourteen days' imprisonment in the cage. He did not want for company. There were already five others in residence, convicted on various charges.

It was only by the greatest stroke of luck that Mo Davis had not joined them. On the morning of 4 May he and Ali Asar had been involved in an altercation down at the boiler. Infuriated by the Malay's taunts that Australia was finished and Japan would win the war, Mo lost his temper and knocked him out cold, with a right hook to the jaw. When Ali recovered he rushed up the hill to Hoshijima's office.

Until this time Mo's dealings with Hoshijima and the other Japanese had been quite cordial. His ability to pick up languages had given him a working knowledge of camp Japanese, while his engine room skills had impressed Hoshijima, himself a qualified engineer. When the thread had been stripped on the globular intake-valve at the Sibuga River pump a few months earlier, the pair had spent an entire day together trying to obtain a second-hand replacement. The excursion in Hoshijima's huge black limousine, chauffeured by Harry Grinter, had also included a stop for lunch at his house which, like the car, had been 'acquired' from Harry Keith. As Mo sat on the lawn making the most of this unexpected repast prepared by Hoshijima's personal cook, the commandant drew 'Daveriso's' attention to the magnificent view of the harbour and confided his intention of having a house with a similarly magnificent view on the foreshores of Sydney Harbour.

Indeed, Mo had done such a good job of passing himself off as a model prisoner that, when the guards called at the boiler house to collect hot water from the orange tank, he was ordered to shave them each morning — with a cut-throat razor! This had not stopped the guards having a joke at their barber's expense. Their favourite, and oft-repeated antic, was to mount an 'attack' on the engine room in the dead of night by thrusting their bayonets through the open window just above Mo's head. Although Ah Ping, Mo and Stevens were never harmed, the sight of the glistening blades and the yells of 'bonzai' never failed to frighten all three.

Now Mo's heart sank as he saw Suga's car sweep past the boiler house. Shortly afterwards, he was summoned to Hoshijima's office, at the rear of the guardhouse. The sight of Weynton, still up to his neck in water, was not reassuring, and Mo entered Hoshijima's office with some trepidation. Waiting inside were not only Hoshijima and Suga, but also two members of the Sandakan Kempei-tai. As soon as the questioning began, Mo realised how big a mistake it had been to hit Ali Asar. His inquisitors were not the slightest bit interested in the fisticuffs — they were only interested in Mo's comings and goings at the boiler. Ali, out for revenge, had told Hoshijima he suspected Mo of having contact with locals outside the camp.

Fortunately, since Ali had no hard evidence, the interrogation was exploratory, focussing on whether or not Mo knew various people who the Kempei-tai and Hoshijima now named. Some, of course, were only too well known to him while others were not. Asked about his relationship with Apostol, Mo replied that he waved to him when he saw him and had once asked about a cure for dysentery. Pop Wong, Mo said, was also a 'waving' acquaintance and he had no idea who any of the others were. The Kempei-tai were evidently satisfied with these answers and Mo, for the time being at least, was dismissed.

The next day or two were agony. Mo had heard enough about Hoshijima's methods, let alone those of the secret police, to realise that if there were a second interrogation it would not be so benign. He was still fretting about the matter three days later when a truckload of guards rumbled past the engine room, evidently in response to a call to step up the hunt for the escapees. After the vehicle had passed, Mo spotted a leather wallet lying in the middle of the track. It contained a Japanese ID card and a condom, as well as wads of folding occupation money. Mo's first impulse was to keep it. However, realising that, in his present circumstances, it might be better if he handed it in, he gave it to Hoshijima. It was a very wise move.

The next day, Suga returned. Mo was called to Hoshijima's office, where Suga and the camp's liaison officer, Captain George Cook, were in attendance. Hoshijima and Suga carried on a rapid conversation which Mo, with his limited Japanese, could not follow. Suga then turned to Mo and said, 'I give to you, for honest man, the presento'. With that, he produced from the boot of his car an enormous stalk of bananas, 200 or more. The dumbfounded recipient passed them to Cook for the camp hospital. As the Australian walked towards the door of the office, Suga remarked that, 'I could have put you in gaol for a long time, perhaps seven or eight years'. By handing in the wallet, Mo Davis, aged nineteen, had received in return a gilt-edged life insurance policy.

Suga went back to his headquarters at Kuching, Hoshijima calmed down and the camp settled back into its normal routine. Hoshijima even sanctioned a distribution of mail. It was rather haphazard. Mo Davis, John Barnier and Ray Carlson were among those who received no letters at all while a delighted Dick Braithwaite received nine. Even more amazingly, Hoshijima decided that the prisoners could send a postcard to their families. These cards were merely standard printed messages, parts of which could be struck out or amended by specially designated scribes. When his turn came Ray Carlson lined up to tell his wife Alma that he had received 'no letter yet', that his health was 'excellent' and that he hoped everything was well and she was receiving her allotment. The final sentence asked her to please remember him to 'all the family'. Ray's only input, except for telling the scribe what to strike out or add, was to sign his name at the bottom. Young John Barniers' card to his mother, which struck out the reference to the marriage allotment, was virtually identical to Ray's. There was no opportunity for him to add 'tell Roy that', even if he had wanted to. The cards, written in May

1943, would not be received in Australia until December 1944.

Wallace, on the outside, was sending messages into the camp. Terrified, he begged Matthews to let him back in. This was impossible. Wallace was too well known and there were head counts and tenkos every day. In short, Wallace had become both a liability and a nuisance.

All attempts to smuggle the escapee onto a Tawi Tawi-bound kompit had failed. Sini had met with Mu Sing, Lagan and Taylor on 14 May and arranged to further discuss the details the next day. Unfortunately, he fell head-first out of a bus in an inebriated state before he had a chance to do so. By the time he was discharged from hospital another week had passed. A rendezvous was attempted without Sini on the night of 17 May. Accompanied by Heng, Wallace had made his way down jungle trails to the river, where Mu Sing and Lagan were waiting with a small, ocean-going sailing boat. They waited all night at the appointed place, hoping that the fishing lines they dangled over the side would fool enemy patrols, but there was no sign of the kompit. With dawn approaching, they had no option but to return Wallace to his former hiding place.

As each day passed, the situation had become more dangerous and Wallace demanded that Taylor hurry the proceedings. Eventually, following another lengthy conference at Heng's house, it was decided to move the fugitive to Berhala where he could be hidden by Koram and Salleh until the Dit Party made its break. Before Wallace left his hideout, Sini gave him Blain's letter, with instructions to deliver it to Frank Forde.

On the night of 26 May he was rowed down the Kaya River to Sandakan Harbour in a small boat manned by Siti's father, Jakariah, and his fisherman friend Sidek, and then taken out to sea. They waited for some time for Koram, Mu Sing and Police Constable Mohammed Tahir to pick up Wallace but this rendezvous also failed and Wallace was again returned to the mainland. It was then decided that Heng should take Wallace directly to the island. Four days later he was delivered safely into the capable hands of Corporal Koram on Berhala. Within hours of being installed in an excellent hideout erected by Koram, Wallace had made contact with the Dit Party, which brought him food to supplement that left by Koram. As there had been no firm arrangements made for his escape, the plan was for Wallace to stay hidden until the time came for the others to leave the compound. This was sooner rather than later.

In the early hours of 4 June, Koram told Wallace the E Force prisoners were about to be transferred to the mainland. The Dit Party would have to make its break that night.

The original five-man group had swelled to seven with the discovery that McLaren's mates, Sapper Jim Kennedy and Private Rex Butler, were also intending to flee. With Wallace, it now numbered eight — far too many, it was felt, to abscond together. The party was split in two. The four officers and Wallace were to remain on the island in hiding and wait for the kompit. The others were to leave by small canoe, make contact with a prahau at sea and sail south to rendezvous with a submarine. While a party led by Koram and Salleh dismantled and hid a large boat belonging to the leper colony, McLaren, Butler and Kennedy, with the help of Blow and Wagner, were to take the lepers' two canoes. Using paddles they had carved from planks, the three ORs were to quit the area immediately, leaving Blow and Wagner, who were very strong swimmers, to take the other canoe off-shore and sink it in the hope that, with all three boats missing, the Japanese would believe all seven had fled.

E Force's commanding officer, Rod Richardson, was very much against the officers' escape plan. So grave were his misgivings that he threatened to inform the Japanese but, after some effective counter-arguments, was finally dissuaded. Short and The Turk, meanwhile, knew nothing of the escape bid. Neither did Keating, Jensen, Marshall or Weston. Confident that Wagner, who had copies of all their escape data, would keep his part of the bargain, Keating's party waited patiently to be told it was time to move. Hearing that a transfer to the mainland was imminent, they went to Wagner and asked if he were ready to make the attempt. Wagner's response was to tell the men to wait until better conditions prevailed on the mainland. That night, he and the rest of the Dit Party escaped.

They had no trouble leaving the compound. At about 7.00pm, just as the main gate was due to be closed for the night, the group made its way to the camp latrines, built native-style out over the sea. It was a simple matter to drop through the seat and onto the tidal flats below. A quick dash across the mangroves to the jungle and they were free. As soon as it was completely dark, Blow and Wagner took care of one canoe by sinking it in the channel between Berhala and the mainland, while the other three made their get-away, as planned, in the other. There was a tense moment or two when the sound of the cumbersome, home-made metal anchor clanking around in the bottom of Blow's and Wagner's boat woke the lepers. They were extremely upset to discover they had lost their only means of transportation, but took no immediate action.

The Japanese did not realise the Dit Party was missing until morning muster. Even then it was not immediately apparent. When the guards, instead of conducting a head-count, ordered the assembled POWs to number off, the prisoners called out numbers at random, instead of in numerical order. However, eventually the guards realised they were seven men short, and search parties were dispatched to the mainland. As the irate lepers reported that the prisoners had made off with their boats, the Japanese did not suspect that four of the absconders, as well as Wallace, were still on the island. Salleh certainly gave no hint of it, not even when Hoshijima paid him a visit, offering a 1000-dollar reward, a sum of fabulous proportions to a man as poor as Salleh, for information leading to the arrest of the escapees. The old watchman pledged his full co-operation. Three times a day the search parties would call at the wharf to see if Salleh had anything to report and three times a day Salleh would reply, 'I am sorry that I have not seen the white men. I wish I could, I would love to have the reward.'

For the next 21 days, while they waited for the kompit to take them to Tawi Tawi, the Australians managed to remain undetected due to the steadfastness of Salleh, the assistance of Koram who brought in food and other supplies, and the generosity of Dr Taylor and Mrs Cohen, who donated the 60 dollars needed to buy them. Ernesto Lagan, with the help of Mr Chan Tian Joo, also opened an appeal for additional funds.

Koram was sent to Sandakan when E Force transferred to the mainland, but he soon contrived a way to return to the island with the full approval of the Japanese. They had agreed to him giving a blow-pipe demonstration at a forthcoming sports' day, and now allowed him to visit Berhala for a supply of the paralysing drug needed for the dart — the only place, so Koram said, it could be obtained.

It was just as well the Australians had the assistance of Koram and Salleh. Although Mu Sing's boats had been in port waiting for the signal to move to Berhala and pick up the fugitives, the Japanese, on discovering the prisoners were missing, had ordered all boats to leave Sandakan immediately. As it would be at least ten days, possibly longer, before they could return safely, the officer party was in for a long wait.

Meanwhile, Kennedy, McLaren and Butler had paddled out to sea and made a successful rendezvous at about 9.00pm with a small prahau which, as arranged, had taken them about 60 kilometres down the coast to Kuala Kinabatangan, where they were to meet an American submarine. Although the prahau arrived well before 3.00am, the appointed time for the rendezvous, the submarine was unable to surface because a Japanese motor torpedo boat was in the area. As dawn was only three hours away, the escape party had no alternative but to try and make it to Tawi Tawi. The following night, when the submarine was able to surface, Koram delivered a letter to the commander, along with the message that the escapees had gone on alone. It was unable to find them but the Australians, fortunately, arrived safely in Tawi Tawi on 14 June.

Twelve days later, the waiting was over for the rest of the Dit Party. For the past two nights the men had been keeping watch at the small beach below their hideout. Koram, Alberto Quadra and Mohammed Tahir had arrived with food, the money collected by Lagan and Chan and the news that Quadra, who was in Sandakan visiting his brother Bernard on a 'trading mission', would be returning to Tawi Tawi within a day or two. Shortly before 9.00pm on 26 June, as they waited in the dark with the ever-faithful Salleh, they heard a faint splash of oars and the sound of a sail slapping against a mast as Quadra's 7-metre kompit, crewed by four Moro tribesmen, neared the beach. Guided by the glow of the evil-smelling cigars on which the Australians were now puffing madly, Quadra steered the craft to the pick-up point. Within ten minutes, all five men were on board and on their way to Tawi Tawi.

The four-day journey was not without its dramas. The first, running aground on a sandbank, was a minor irritation and the craft was soon free. The second arose when Rex Blow discovered they were heading in the wrong direction. The navigator had fallen asleep, but Blow believed he was deliberately taking them back to Borneo. Rex, with the aid of his pistol, soon had the startled navigator back on course. The third incident was by far the most nerve-wracking. On the second day out from Berhala they were all but becalmed in the Sibutu Channel between Tawi Tawi and Tambisan Island, to the north of Lahad Datu, when Quadra spied smoke on the horizon to the south. He ordered his passengers to take refuge in a space formed by a false floor, installed precisely for such an emergency. Lying flat on their stomachs on the bottom of the boat and with heavy rice sacks stacked on top of them so that they could hardly breathe, the Australians, sweating profusely, were kept informed of the progress of two Japanese transports and a cruiser escort by Quadra, who kept up a running commentary.

Quadra remained calm, confident that with the sail lowered, the atap roof erected and the crew rowing along at a leisurely pace, the kompit looked for all the world like a native fishing vessel going about its normal business. The Japanese officer on board the cruiser, who had them under close surveillance through a pair of binoculars, was fooled. After returning the friendly waves from the Moros, he continued on his way.

Two days later, having made good progress running before a stiff westerly breeze, Quadra pointed out three small bumps on the horizon and announced — Tawi Tawi. The officers and Wallace were reunited with Kennedy, McLaren and Butler, who had given them up for dead, and the five Australians were taken to meet the guerrilla chief, Lieutenant-Colonel Suarez. The following day, 1 July, the entire Dit Party was formally inducted into the 125th Infantry Regiment of the United States Forces in the Philippines, known to the locals as the Filipino Guerrilla Army.

Meanwhile the rest of E Force had been taking up residence at the new camp. On leaving Berhala at about 6.00am on 5 June, the prisoners had not alighted at Sandakan as expected. Instead, the barges had headed directly up the Sibuga River, disgorging their passengers at the end of a narrow, rough track on the eastern bank, about 4 kilometres from the camp. Pushed along by irate guards, the

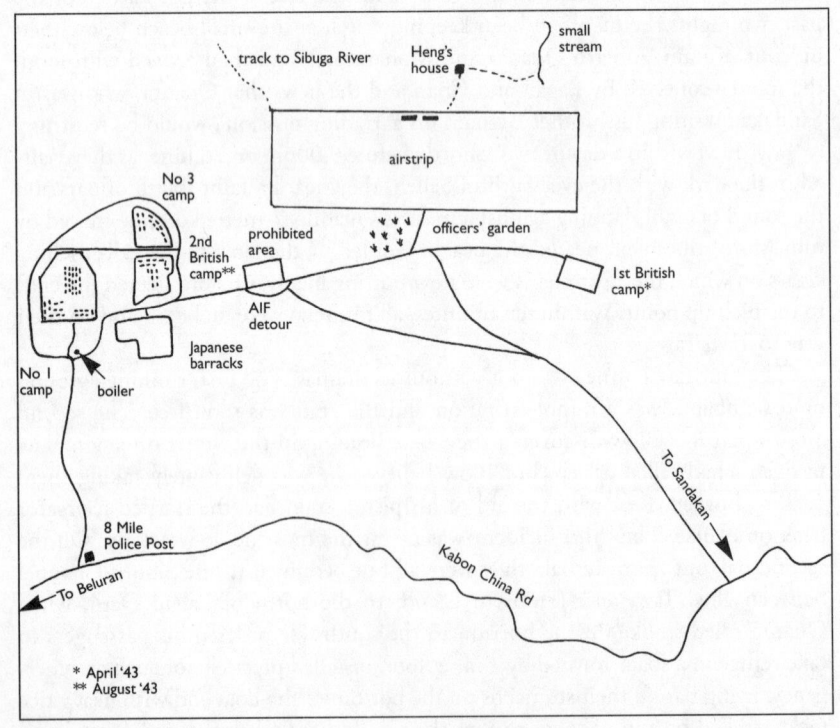

Map showing the positions of the three camps and the airstrip.

prisoners, fit and ill alike, made the rest of the journey on foot. They found that the new camp was situated on the side of a small gully about a kilometre to the north-east of the B Force camp. Hurriedly erected, its lack of amenities put it on a par with the British camp over at the airstrip. The fourteen central-aisle style atap huts, perched atop rubber tree-stump foundations, were supplied with neither electricity nor water, while the latrines were merely token pits. One hut was reserved as a hospital and another for the quartermaster's store and canteen. As the remaining twelve could not hope to accommodate everyone, many had to seek refuge beneath the buildings. Apart from rain water, the only water supply was a small creek or a muddy well, while the security fence, purloined from the now much-depleted B Force compound, was simply a double run of barbed wire strung between bush poles.

Some of the B Force men had been detailed to help bring up the gear from the river, and now all at Number 1 Camp (as B Camp was now called) knew of E Force's arrival. There was much excitement as almost every able-bodied person jostled for a position on the slope, trying to catch a glimpse of the new arrivals, but, although the camp was just on the other side of the gully, there was too much foliage to see them. However, they could hear one another perfectly. After securing a spot down by his old hut, which The Dead End Kids still occupied, Mo shouted out as loudly as he could. 'Any 2/20th blokes over there?' Almost immediately came a reply. 'Is that you, Mo?' To his great joy it was a voice that he, and almost every other member of the 8th Division's 22nd Brigade knew only too well — the gravelly, grating, raucously distinctive voice of Nutsy Roberts.

Although it was obvious that as little contact as possible would be permitted between the two camps, Mo was hopeful that he could, somehow, catch up with Nutsy and the others before too long. Unfortunately, Matthews and Hoshijima had other ideas. Two days later, Mo was on his way to Kuching.

Chapter Seven
DISASTER

The order that Mo was to move to Kuching came as a complete surprise. One minute he was exchanging pleasantries across the gully with Nutsy Roberts and the next hastily packing what was left of his meagre kit. Protesting to Captain Cook, the liaison officer, was a waste of breath. Cook informed Mo that it was out of his hands.

His travelling companions — Majors Fleming (the commanding officer), Maffey and Rayson (medical officers), Armstrong, Johnstone, Lewis and Owen, Captain Claude Pickford (the choir master), nine other junior officers and four Dead End Kids — were a most diverse group. According to Hoshijima, the officers were being transferred because of their seniority; The Kids — Hilton 'Terry' Risley, Sid Outram, Joey Crome and Wally 'Henry' Ford — for general larrikinism and ill-discipline. Mo was the odd man out. He was never told why he was on the list but was led to believe that Hoshijima, unsure whether Mo was a potential trouble-maker, wanted him out of the camp while Matthews, aware of how much Mo knew about the underground network, wanted to keep him out of the hands of the Kempei-tai.

They were given a memorable send off on 8 June when Hoshijima had the transport drivers divert to his house for refreshments — a good-sized chunk of mouth-watering watermelon. They were taken to the harbour where they boarded *Treasure,* the same vessel that had taken Billy Young, M.P., Jimmy Darlington and the recaptured escapees to Kuching almost three months before.

The trip back to Kuching was vastly different from the voyage on *Yubi Maru* — accommodation was under a permanent awning in the stern, the Japanese sergeant guarding them was most decent, and they were allowed to purchase food at every port of call. Mo, who had been taught to cook very tasty dishes by Ah Ping during his stint at the boiler house, volunteered for the job as head chef, and they all ate extremely well. Yet, it was a dispute over the catering that caused the only serious ruction. When they reached Labuan, Mo and his catering corps (Sid Outram, as assistant chef, and the other three Dead Enders as kitchen hands) had been given permission to go ashore to buy provisions. Returning with a few chickens and some fresh vegetables they soon had a fine meal underway which the cooks tasted first. When one of the officers accused Mo and Sid of 'stealing' the rations, the entire catering corps immediately went on strike. Although ordered back to work by Major Fleming, they refused to do so until they received an apology. The dispute was resolved when the accuser, driven more by hunger pangs than contrition, apologised.

This behaviour did not endear The Dead End Kids to their senior officer. Major Fleming's opinion of them was not high, and he informed interpreter Ozawa, who was travelling with them to Kuching (evidently in connection with the Billy Young/Minty trial), that 'they are criminals. I will not have them in the camp with us.' Indeed, at Kuching the two groups parted company — the officers to join their colleagues and the privates to the British Other Ranks' Camp where they, along with three American sailors shipwrecked in the Sunda Straits after the sinking of USS *Houston,* were in the minority. Unable to place them in separate accommodation, Ozawa drew an imaginary line across one end of a hut and deemed that part to be combined Australian/US territory.

About a fortnight later Mo was working down at the wharf when the guards ordered all prisoners to avert their eyes from the ship moored there. It was not until years afterwards that he learned that Billy Young and the others, fresh from their trial, were being swung aboard inside a horse-box, on their way to Outram Road Gaol.

Meanwhile, back at Sandakan, Hoshijima was taking no chances with the Australians under his control. To prevent contact between B and E forces out at the 'drome, every person in the E Force compound, now called Number 3 Camp, had his head shaved. As an added precaution, new POW numbers were also issued. They were now given according to rank, and then more or less alphabetical order within that rank. Captain Cook was number 20. Rod Wells, a Lieutenant but well down the alphabet, was number 124. Private John Barnier, a lowly-ranked private, was 424. Corporals Neil Christie and Bob Shipsides found that their new numbers were 163 and 338 respectively.

The Japanese allocated the numbers to the various camps in a very methodical fashion — below 1490 for B Force, between 1491-2100 for E Force and over 2100 for the English camp. Although Privates Bowe and Field, who had been sent back to Sandakan after their temporary sojourn to Kuching, were returned to their old compound, they were classified as B Force 'add-ons' and the numbering system reflected the differentiation — Bowe being 1484 and Field 1488, with the intervening numbers evidently reserved for Crome, Davis and Ford, in case they should return. The other eighteen 'extras' from Kuching were slotted into the numbers designated for E Force.

With the new numbering system also came a change in the method of display. The cloth badges were replaced with more durable wooden tags on which each prisoner's number was clearly marked.

Hoshijima also stepped up night surveillance, introducing guard dogs which were kept in a yard behind the main guardhouse during the day and tied beneath the sentry boxes at night. They looked fairly ferocious but, before long, several of the dogs had vanished. Braithwaite told one of the guards that the dogs must have fallen prey to crocodiles which, the Australian assured him, were often seen in the vicinity of the swamp at night. Never suspecting that the missing canines had fallen prey to the meat-starved prisoners, the guard spread the word. For weeks afterwards, he and his colleagues gave the swamp, and more especially the ramp which crossed it, a wide berth.

Although Hoshijima had no intention of allowing the three camps to mix he did allow E Force to line up opposite the other Australians on their first morning out at the 'drome. The men were not permitted to converse but as they gave silent salutes across the 50 metres that separated them, they had the opportunity to see who was there and who was not. Tom Burns' mate Colin Smyth was among E Force as was Tom Dorizzi, elder brother of Gordon and Herbert, and Ted Skinner, John's older brother. Much to his delight, Captain Frank Gaven spied his brother Jack — the 2/10th ambulanceman whose beautifully-crafted carving of the infantryman had caught the eye of Billy Young at the Art and Craft Show.

The Australians found ways to communicate with the British at the 'drome, using a combination of hand signals, crunched paper balls and clandestine meetings. Charlie Johnstone, one of the Australian Flight-Lieutenants serving with the RAF, was taking a drink of water from a bucket near the blacksmith's shed when a B Force sergeant, sharpening tools, attracted his attention. He whispered to Charlie, who was supervising drain digging nearby, that if he came to the shed once a week, the Australians could pass on the radio news. The arrangement worked very well for a month or so until Hoshijima spotted Charlie making his way to the water bucket. Although not sure anything was amiss, the commandant slapped Johnstone hard across the face four times and sent him off for flying practice.

With the exception of this incident, the only thing British officers had to complain about was boredom. Apart from taking a turn to supervise working parties out at the 'drome, which generally consisted of walking up and down, the officers spent most of their time thinking up ways to fill in the day. They would read one of the numerous books in the camp, write up a diary, or perhaps do 'a spot of Spanish revision' in the morning and have 'a sleep in the afternoon'.

Nagai's and Hoshijima's relationship with the British officers could be described as one of mutual goodwill. Nagai even lent the hospital for three days his portable gramophone and classical record collection, presented to him by a Dr MacArthur at Jesselton in January that year. Hoshijima also extended invitations to the officers to use the Japanese canteen facilities down at the main barracks. On Sunday 27 June, no less than 25 officers, led by Squadron Leader Hardie and Captain Mills, and including Doctors Daniels and Blackledge as well as Padre Wanless, marched out of the camp with polished boots and in their best khaki drill to eat at Hoshijima's canteen. When they returned more than four hours later, having consumed as many bananas, pineapples, donuts, toffee, coffee and other goods as they could, they reported to their disgusted colleagues who had not accepted Hoshijima's offer that the cost of this feast had been all of 75 cents each, plus a mass salute to a Japanese second-lieutenant. The displeasure generated throughout the rest of the camp by this excursion to Hoshijima's 'Friendship Garden' had no effect on the participants. Three weeks later they lined up to do it all again.

Although B Force's Captain Cook and Warrant Officer Laurie Maddock, who organised working parties, dined with the commandant, most of the Australians despised Hoshijima. However, despite this lack of congeniality, he did not exclude them from what he termed 'Amusing Hours', introduced to all camps on 26 May. In this two hour recreation period, generally held on Saturday evenings, prisoners were permitted to participate in a previously vetted programme provided 'no warsong or martial air' were included.

While British prisoners occasionally incurred the wrath of the guards at the 'drome, on the whole they fared far better than the Australian working parties. On

21 June, a week before the officers went off on the first of Hoshijima's 'Friendship Garden' outings, the British parties were withdrawn from the airstrip. The three crow's-nest type guard towers at their camp were also relocated to a spot near the main Japanese barracks, thought to be the site of a new compound. For the next three weeks the occupants of Number 2 Camp dismantled three huts ear-marked for the new camp, and spent their days cutting down rubber trees, a job generally regarded as 'light work'. On their return to the 'drome they were assigned to clearing tasks, work deemed as 'easy' by one of their supervising officers.

The Australians were certainly not having it 'easy'. Things were as bad as ever with the guards, riled by the recent escapes and their punishment, taking out their ill-humour on the prisoners. The situation was worse if Hoshijima or Nagai happened to be around as the guards, eager to demonstrate their efficiency, became even more brutal than usual. It was while Hoshijima was watching the 2/18th's tailor, Bill McDonald and a group of E Force prisoners excavating a 'swimming pool' out along the road to the airfield, that one of the guards decided to make an example of Corporal Peters of the AAMC. Lashing out with a heavy stick, the guard delivered a blow of such severity across Peters' face that he had to have one of his eyes removed. Major Eddey performed the surgery and lodged a protest over this unwarranted barbarity, but he was told by Nagai it was none of his business. The prisoners never did get their promised swimming pool. The men worked diligently enough, but they had only dug down a couple of feet when the Japanese called the whole thing off.

No one who crossed the guards was safe from retribution. Sergeant John 'Mort' Codlin, the paymaster for both Number 1 and Number 3 Camps, was asked to change money for two Formosan guards, unaware that the cash had been stolen by the guards from their own canteen funds. The following day he was ordered to identify the embezzlers and pointed out Goto Tsuneyoshi and Kiyoshima Tadeo who, because of his prominent gold tooth and habit of sneaking around to catch POWs unawares, was known as 'Panther Tooth' or 'The Black Panther'. The following afternoon, as Codlin took the pay to the Number 3 Camp, Kitamura Kotaro, a jujitsu expert, and Kawakami Kyoshi, better known as 'The Gold-Toothed-Shin-Kicking-Bastard' or 'The Gold-Toothed Runt', accused him of not saluting properly. The two guards, with the assistance of other willing hit-men, waylaid Codlin on both the inward and outward journey, punishing him for this 'betrayal' by attacking him about the head with a pick-handle and inflicting such severe injuries that he was dangerously ill for a week.

Despite a lighter work load and less brutal treatment, the British were dying at more than ten times the rate of the Australians. By 23 June, a mere ten weeks since their arrival, eight British soldiers and one airman had died of illness, one in 86. During the same period the Australians had lost only two men out of just under 2000: 40-year-old Driver Cyril Dalton-Godwin who had succumbed to cardiac beriberi on 1 May and Corporal Frank Burchnall, aged 52, who had died from malaria on 19 May, a week after Harvey and MacKay were shot. The British, initially, had been ordered to bury their dead at the 8 mile cemetery, near the road junction at the eight mile peg. However, this meant that burial parties, forced to go the long way round so as not to pass the Australian camp, had to trek about 5 kilometres there, carrying a coffin, and 5 kilometres back. After the burials of Gunner Bill Starmer and Air-Craftsman Thomas Smith, cremation was introduced. Bodies were cremated on open wood fires out near the airstrip and the ashes collected and stored until such time as there were sufficient remains to warrant the 90-minute hike to the burial ground. Although the Australian camps were only about a kilometre from the cemetery site, the ashes of their dead were also stored in boxes for multiple burials at a later date.

The Japanese, amazingly, revered the dead. On 3 June a British burial party of fifteen made the journey to the cemetery to inter the ashes of six of their men. They were joined by Moritake and Nagai who sent eight members of the party to collect baskets of fruit from a roadside stall. Once the remains had been buried with due solemnity in individual plots, and the graves marked, Nagai stepped forward, placed a basket of fruit on each grave and saluted. Of course, as soon as the funeral rites were over the burial detail collected the fruit and took it back to the hospital, where it would do far more for the living than for the dead.

The hospital at the Number 1 Camp was considered the best. Although it lacked all normal hospital facilities and the medical staff, by June, had been reduced from 136 to 74, it did have electric light and a reliable water supply, unlike the E Force and British camps where illumination was provided by crude coconut oil lamps. The dedicated B Force medical staff was remarkable. While there was no operating theatre as such, surgical procedures were carried out in a small room, cut off from the rest of the hut by a one-metre partition — just the right height to support the weight of interested spectators as they leaned over from the adjoining ward to watch the proceedings. Apart from the odd broken arm brought about by the severe bashings at the aerodrome, most of the operations were appendectomies. The mortality rate for this surgical procedure was zero, even though the doctors deferred operating until it was absolutely necessary.

One patient to go under the knife at the Number 3 Camp was Gunner Owen Campbell of the 2/10th Field Regiment, who, shortly after arriving from Berhala, had been carrying a heavy bucket of water when he suddenly felt something 'pop'. While the 'pop' was most likely a hernia, Dr Howard Eddey had no qualms about removing Campbell's appendix. The surgery was carried out under local anaesthetic and the patient, while not experiencing any pain, could feel everything that was going on. Dr Eddey did an excellent job. Despite the crudeness of the surroundings, infection did not set in and Campbell, after a period of convalescence, recovered fully. Of course, there were fringe benefits for patients who had undergone surgery — exemption from airfield construction. B Force convalescents were also given special treats such as eggs, smuggled in under the wire by Gunboat Simpson and other scroungers.

However, the Australians were once more heading for trouble. Ted Keating's party, still rankling over Charlie Wagner's duplicity, was more determined than ever to escape, as was the much-thwarted duo of Blain and James, who had now been joined by Driver Scott. Blain no longer had his gold pass. Realising that, if the Japanese found it, it might create more trouble than it was worth, he had wrapped it in a gas cape and buried it, along with a pistol, compass and revolver until such time as he might need them. There were also four other E Force men who were keen to escape — Privates Stan Davis and T. Rumble, both from ordinance workshop units, and two sergeants from the 2/18th battalion, Ray Holly and Colin Lander.

When E Force arrived to start work at the airstrip, Keating and Davis had been delegated to drive some recently-acquired road rollers. As he manoeuvred his machine past the area assigned to the locally-recruited labour force, Davis managed to make contact with Henry Chang Ting Kiang, one of Mu Sing's off-siders. However, as nothing had yet been heard of the fate of the Berhala escapees, Mu Sing told him to wait and on no account attempt to escape into the jungle. This was not what Keating, who still had Mr Brown's letters of introduction to Apostol and Paddy Funk, wanted to hear. After writing a note asking for assistance which he signed 'Carter' (possibly a form of code, since 'Carter Brown' was the name of a popular fiction writer) he gave the note and the letters from Brown to Henry Chang for delivery. While Apostol responded by sending money and cigarettes, Paddy's reply was very low-key. He simply proffered the same advice Mu Sing had already given Stan Davis — wait until a feasible plan could be worked out.

In early July, a month after the escapees had left Berhala, word was received that all eight had arrived in Tawi Tawi and were serving with the guerrillas — a message which gave Taylor the confidence to assist the Keating and Blain groups. Sini and Mu Sing now worked quickly, advancing the escape plans. All they needed was the final agreement from Taylor.

While they were doing their best to assist the POWs, Sini, Heng and Mu Sing were also involving themselves in a plot to overthrow the Japanese in a joint operation involving Saurez's guerrillas, the local civilian population, the British North Borneo constabulary and the Australian POWs. The uprising was part of a much larger movement to co-ordinate armed rebellions in Jesselton and Sandakan in the north with, possibly, Dutch-led insurrections in the south. The Jesselton group was under the direct command of Albert Qwok, a well-known Chinese medical practitioner who, while studying traditional medicine in China, had been made an intelligence officer by the Chinese government. Having returned to Borneo before the Japanese invasion, he was only too aware of the appalling atrocities and bloody massacres that accompanied occupation. He knew also that survival depended entirely upon the whim of the Japanese. Ten months before, in August 1942, a proclamation had informed the Chinese in Jesselton that, 'the power of seizing them and putting them all to death rests with [Borneo's] Japanese High Command'. This edict, delivered shortly after news of the massacre of the entire population of Long Nawan in Dutch Borneo, had convinced Qwok that the time had come for him to actively oppose the enemy.

Shortly afterwards he had met Jesselton businessman Lim Teng Fatt, an officer in Saurez's army, who introduced him to Imam Marajukim, a Muslim priest. The Imam, who was also a Filipino guerrilla agent and trader, worked in Jesselton as Mu Sing did in Sandakan. Following a trip to the Philippines in early 1943, Qwok had returned to Jesselton where he formed the Kinabalu Guerrilla Defence Force, based at Menggatal, just to the north of Jesselton. In June, accompanied by the Imam, he again visited Saurez, taking with him medical supplies and a donation of $11 000 to assist the Filipino guerrillas. When Qwok returned he was not only North Borneo Guerrilla Chief but also Lieutenant, United States Army.

Very few Australians in the Number 1 Camp knew of Sandakan's role in the planned uprising. However, Sini and Mu Sing were laying the ground work, travelling to Sunuyan Laut Island to organise hiding places for arms, as well as secreting rifles and machine guns brought in from the Philippines in strategic spots close to the POW camp and in the Satang River area. According to the locals, cooperation from the civilians had been ensured when Matthews, 'appointed' Sandakan Police Chief by Major Rice-Oxley, promised that if they took part in the uprising they could be assured of much better treatment. It was planned that, as soon as word arrived that an invasion was imminent, a whistle was to be blown to alert the POWs at the camp. It would not be long before Rod Wells' transmitter could be brought out of hiding.

Isolated as they were, on the north-eastern coast of Borneo, the Sandakan underground had no idea that a similar planned revolt in the south had ended in disaster. Dr B. J. Haga, the Dutch Governor, had formed a group committed to the overthrow of the occupying forces. However, in June the Kempei-tai discovered an arms cache and radio transmitter in the southern coastal town of Banjarmasin. Governor Haga and his wife were arrested at Pontianak, on the north-west coast. A further 257 people, accused of being implicated in the plan, were rounded up and tortured. Not one of them, the Hagas included, survived.

The Sandakan conspirators were, therefore, totally unprepared for what happened next. On the morning of Thursday 22 July, a search party swooped on the Sandakan Number 1 Camp. The lightning nature of the raid gave the prisoners little time to hide anything. The sick, and those on camp duties, were herded outside the wire and the searchers, led by Hoshijima, all but tore the place apart. They collected a mountain of prohibited material, including compasses, two pistols belonging to Corporal Tommy Graham and Sapper Roy Davis, two message forms containing the latest news summaries which Wells had left inside his socks, and a map of the South-West Pacific belonging to Vern Rae. Late that afternoon Matthews, Rae, Davis and Graham were placed under arrest.

They were discovered because of a falling out among friends. For some time Heng Joo Ming and his friend Dominic Koh had been operating a profitable business buying rice from small neighbouring islands for resale in Sandakan where, owing to a shortage, it fetched a good price. On one of these excursions there had been a disagreement which had left Koh feeling disgruntled. As he knew that Heng had harboured Wallace and was mixed up in some kind of assistance group, he decided to blackmail him. Koh put a proposition to an Indian friend, Bah Chik, who worked at the aerodrome with Heng. Offered a half-share in the payoff, Chik approached Heng and threatened to expose him unless he paid up. When Heng called their bluff, Chik and Koh told collaborator Jackie Lo, who was still spying for the Kempei-tai, everything they knew. On 17 July about 20 Japanese, together with Bah Chik and Lo, arrested Heng Joo Ming.

Taken to Kempei-tai headquarters in Sandakan, Heng was subjected to a long and painful interrogation. A jujitsu expert failed to extract anything of interest, so the Kempei-tai moved on to the water treatment — a hideous and highly-effective torture previously unknown in Sandakan. The victim was spread-eagled on the ground and as much water as possible was forced down his gullet through a length of hose. One of the interrogators would then jump from a chair onto the victim's distended stomach, forcing the water out through his nose and mouth. When Heng's father-in-law Jakariah, who had assisted in Wallace's escape, was also arrested and subjected to this treatment, it did not take long for names to be named.

In the early hours of 18 July, the Japanese descended on Sini's house. Sini and his friend, Lo En Wai, were arrested and taken to a building at the 'drome where they joined Heng's wife Siti, his mother-in-law, Mrs Jakariah, Apostol and Henry Chang Ting Kiang. Soon after, all were taken to Sandakan where the Kempei-tai, naively thinking the youthful, slight-statured Sini would be the weakest, decided to interrogate him first. For the next four days, he was subjected to no less than five forms of severe torture, including the water treatment and a local variation on the Darlington's excruciating log torture, where the log placed behind the knees was used as a see-saw.

At 7.00am on Monday 19 July, the morning after Sini's arrest, a car pulled up at the home of Ernesto Lagan. He was taken to the Sandakan Civil hospital where he was ordered, in his capacity as a detective, to arrest Doctors Taylor and Wands. Then Lagan himself was arrested. Taylor, suffering appalling beatings and prolonged torture, still managed to maintain his silence but Lagan was unable to hold out completely and gave up some information. Even then, it was not sufficient to satisfy the Kempei-tai. For the next fortnight they terrorised Mrs Lagan and her four children, but without result.

Meanwhile, Mu Sing and Dick Majinal had been taken into custody as had Gerald Mavor, Corporal Koram and Paddy Funk, all rounded up on the day of Lagan's arrest. Koram had been named by three collaborators — Guriaman, Wah Shing and Burong who, on learning from the Berhala lepers that Koram had been seen with the E Force escapees, had promptly passed their information to the Kempei-tai. Koram was badly beaten but denied everything. Lagan, however, revealed that Koram had helped the Australians escape. Koram took advantage of a break in the interrogation to climb out the lavatory window and escape. Sensibly, he did not flee, but hid close by — so close that he ate stores stolen from the Kempei-tai's own larder.

After about a week Koram moved to the reservoir, where he was supplied with food by fellow policemen Apuk and Gatua. A fortnight later, recovered from his injuries, he made his way to the jetty at Sandakan, where he set fire to the Japanese oil store and a fuel lighter. He then travelled to the Japanese office at Beluran on the Labuk River, where he told them he had been sent to take a census of local civilians. The Japanese gave him food and cigarettes and supplied him with three coolies to carry his belongings to his next destination, which he said was Keningau, hundreds of kilometres away in the south-west. Instead of going to his nominated destination Koram went to Kota Belud on the north-west coast, a journey which took almost three weeks. Here he met up with two old friends from the police force, Dado Siniong and Jemadur Gabudand, who invited him to join the Kinabalu Guerrillas.

The Funk family suffered at the hands of the Japanese, too. Alexander, along with a few others, had been taken in for routine questioning in early July and, although they had been released, Paddy knew it was only a matter of time before the Kempei-tai got to him. Paddy was just finishing off a meagre supper of ubi kayu (tapioca) chips at dusk on 19 July when there was a loud bang, followed by a kick, at his front door. A truckload of soldiers, bayonets drawn, waited by the side of the road and, as he unlocked his door, a Kempei-tai officer and two soldiers entered. Paddy was slapped across the face, kicked in the stomach, loaded onto the truck and taken to Kempei-tai headquarters. There he was beaten and subjected to the usual range of tortures, including two bouts of water treatment. Loss of consciousness brought no respite. The Japanese revived their victims by injecting a stimulant.

In solitary confinement for a week, Paddy was unaware that the number of people under arrest was growing rapidly. Bernard Quadra, customs official and brother of Alberto, was arrested on 20 July, along with Matusup who was lured into the arms of the Kempei-tai by a Chinese collaborator. On 22 July, the day the Australian camp was raided, the arrests began to escalate. Lagan, unable to resist the horrendous torture, had signed a statement which implicated many, while Heng had admitted passing wireless parts to Wallace. The arrest of the four Australians at the camp was followed within 24 hours with the arrest of Berhala's watchman Mohamet Salleh, Samuel Aruliah of the Customs Department and Sergeant Abin.

Most of the B Force officers had been working in the vegetable garden at the time of the search and were caught unawares. The Kempei-tai had yet to realise the significance of the news summaries (which, ever since Weynton's arrest for passing notes to the British, had been compiled by Wells), but anyone who had had contact with the underground was in danger. Matthews, who had been named by both Heng and Lagan, was arrested out in the vegetable garden. Tommy Graham turned himself in on his return from the 'drome when he learnt that his pistol and ammunition were now in Hoshijima's office.

Tommy's own carelessness had been his undoing. The previous evening he had taken the pistol from its hiding place beneath the hut to give it a clean, and check on its condition. Instead of putting it away again, as Botterill urged, he had left it lying on the shelf above his bunk space. On Lieutenant Frank Washington's advice, Graham went to Hoshijima and confessed that, while he had brought the pistol into the camp, he was not the owner. The real owner, he declared, was Major Beale who had been killed in 'an honourable battle', and he was taking the pistol home to Beale's relatives in Australia, in the same way that swords of Japanese officers killed in action were returned to their families. While this 'confession' did not save Graham from arrest, it would go some way towards mitigating his sentence.

Fortunately for Matthews, his pistol and the five rounds of ammunition were not discovered. One of Matthews' hut mates, Captain John Rowell, who had been confined to the camp with illness at the time of the raid, had the presence of mind to hide them in the bottom of a cupboard. As soon as was practicable, Rus Ewin arranged for them to be smuggled to Abin's house, where they were hidden in the chimney, along with Ewin's diary and some nominal rolls.

Although all of Wells' intelligence reports were with Abin, there was no doubt that the Japanese had found the news summaries, as his socks had been unrolled and discarded on his bunk. In another 24 hours they would have been gone from the camp as Friday was the day on which they were passed to Abin. The contents were in an abbreviated code-like form, but Wells knew it would not take the Kempei-tai long to work out what they were. As soon as they did so, they would be back.

On 24 July, while the able-bodied were out at work, there was another, more thorough, search of the camp. The Japanese did not find the radio in its hiding place at the bottom of the disused latrine, nor did they find the transmitter, wrapped and buried in the officers' lines. They did, however, find some other very incriminating evidence. Although Rus Ewin had managed to get rid of the pistol, he was evidently unaware that documents belonging to Matthews were still in the camp. There were three maps, collated and drawn for him by the locals — one of Sandakan township, another of the camp area showing secret military information and troop dispositions, and a third giving the numbers and locations of Japanese and local civilians. While searching for these documents the Japanese also discovered a small, black, pocket-sized notebook, ownership unknown.

That afternoon, when the working parties returned, they were stopped on the road outside the gate. When all were assembled, Hoshijima mounted the back of a vehicle and called for prisoner 124 to step forward. When Wells did so, Hoshijima feigned surprise before producing the news summaries from his pocket, which he referred to as a 'diary'. When Wells admitted ownership of the papers, an enraged Hoshijima yelled, 'You have radio', punched him about the head and face and attempted to throttle him with the sweat rag tied around his neck. Wells was then marched off to Hoshijima's office for questioning.

For the next two hours Wells repeatedly denied all knowledge of any radio until confronted with a list of wireless parts, obtained under duress from the civilians undergoing interrogation. He then took Hoshijima on a wild-goose chase throughout the camp looking for the radio, but soon accepted that he could not go on like this. Judging, quite rightly, that the Japanese would not know one piece of wireless equipment from another, he decided to sacrifice the transmitter in order to save the receiver. At about 6.00pm he handed it over. Hoshijima then ordered the camp to assemble beneath The Big Tree where Wells, his hands tied together, was paraded on the dais as a prize exhibit. 'Look at this man!', bellowed Hoshijima. 'You will not see him again.' On that sobering note, Wells was removed from the camp for transportation to Kempei-tai headquarters — in Hoshijima's black limousine.

With or without the news summaries Hoshijima had been certain there was a radio in the camp. Not only had he Lagan's signed statement, the list of components and the names of those who had supplied them, he also had a full confession from Ng Ho Kong whose name, along with that of Ah Ping, had been mentioned by Gerald Mavor. As a result, Ng had been taken into custody and beaten up on the morning of Wells' arrest. Shortly after noon the following day the Kempei-tai, accompanied by Ng, went to Ah Ping's house at The Eight Mile. By 3.30pm, Ah Ping was under interrogation. When he refused to confess, he was slapped across the face and head with the sole of a wooden sandal which had been rubbed in wet sand, thrown on the floor and kicked and then hit 30 times about the body with a heavy wooden stick. When this failed to weaken his resolve, he was taken to the Sandakan Civil Gaol, where he was given a cell next to Ng. On learning that Ng had admitted everything, Ah Ping decided the wisest course was for him to do the same.

The following morning, Monday 26th, when Ah Ping was returned to the Kempei-tai for reinterrogation, he made a full and signed confession. On the strength of it Moritake went immediately to the engine room and arrested Sergeant Stevens and 43-year-old Private Jim Pickering, who belonged to the same unit as Mo and had apparently inherited his job when Mo had been transferred to Kuching. Both were questioned by Moritake for about 10 minutes. Pickering, who pointed out he was new to the job and protested his innocence, was detained at the camp. Stevens, who evidently admitted his complicity, was bashed and kicked before being tied up by the Kempei-tai and taken to Sandakan where he was joined the next day by two other long-term engine room workers — Corporals Roffey and McMillan.

While Pickering and Stevens were being grilled, Warrant Officer Sticpewich and Sergeant Davidson had also been called up to the guardhouse. A false-bottomed cupboard in the carpentry shop, Sticpewich's domain, had been one of the places indicated as a possible hiding place for the radio during Wells' wild-goose chase, so Hoshijima had added him to his list of suspects. Although Sticpewich enjoyed a good working relationship with the Japanese and had played no part whatsoever in the building or working of the wireless, Hoshijima was unmoved by his declarations of innocence. Along with Davidson and Pickering, he was tied up and spent the next five or six hours either undergoing interrogation in the office or standing outside in the rain. At 1.30am, when all three were put into the cage, they found Matthews' hut mates Captains Bruce Waddell, John Rowell, Charles Filmer and Frank Mills, as well as Private Herman Reither, another member of Sticpewich's technical staff.

Hoshijima kept the officers on short rations and confined them to the cage for well over a week, but Sticpewich, Davidson, Pickering and Reither were not in the cage for long. Neither were they sent to the Kempei-tai for further questioning. While they were not allowed to bathe or wash for the four days they were in the cage, and their food alternated between normal rations and salt and water, they were not bashed or mistreated in any way. At about 5.00pm on 29 July they were taken out and paraded before Moritake. Pickering, obviously innocent, was released. The other three were informed, through an interpreter, that although they had been found guilty of certain crimes they were free to go. What these crimes were, Moritake refused to disclose.

In spite of this lenient treatment, the entire camp was in a state of high tension. Anyone who had been associated with Matthews or the underground waited in fear. Harold St John, now Acting Camp Commanding Officer, and Captain R. H. 'Pom' Brown, both of whom shared a cubicle with Matthews, had already been taken to Sandakan for questioning, while on 29 July Gordon Weynton, not yet recovered from the effects of his previous, lengthy incarceration, was removed from hospital and put back in the cage, just vacated by Sticpewich and the others. Lieutenant Carment, who had been with Matthews in the garden when he was arrested, was very nervous, but not nearly as nervous as Rus Ewin, who had not only been actively involved in the underground, but slept in the bunk next to Wells.

Ewin need not have worried. There was no way the Kempei-tai were going to get anything out of Wells. Questioned about the identity of POW 666, who one of the guards recalled on a wood-gathering party, Wells kept his wits about him. Gambling, quite correctly, that the Japanese would not have bothered to keep any record of the old numbers, he told the Kempei-tai that under the previous system number 666 (Ewin's number) was his own.

Meanwhile, Matthews and Taylor, who had been severely flogged, had been taken out of solitary confinement and placed in a large room, measuring about 8 metres by 11 metres, along with other members of the underground. Vern Rae, Corporal Graham and Sapper Davis, along with Harold St John and several other minor suspects, had been moved to the Sandakan Gaol. Staffed by members of the local constabulary, this was a holiday camp compared to Kempei-tai headquarters where all inmates, except when being interrogated, were required to sit cross-legged and at attention from 7.30am until 9.30pm. The only movement allowed was during a five-minute session of physical exercises, carried out each morning and afternoon. Anyone not performing these compulsory callisthenics to the satisfaction of the guards was beaten or made to 'freeze' in an awkward position for five or ten minutes. At night prisoners slept on the floor. They were under constant surveillance and the light was left burning. Food was the same as that served to those in solitary — a small teacup of rice, with a small amount of vegetable or a cubic centimetre of salt fish or rock salt twice a day. The native prisoners were a little better off as the Japanese allowed food to be sent to them by their families. Sometimes, if the guards were not vigilant, they managed to smuggle a few extra rations to the POWs. Ernesto Lagan was so distressed because he had been unable to withstand the torture that he sent food whenever possible and instructed his wife to sell his clothing to buy extra rations for the Australians.

Six other attempts to escape via the lavatory window, as Koram had done, failed. Messages, however, were smuggled in and out of the headquarters building, and from one prisoner to another, in the bottom of the food containers brought in by relatives. Matthews, who had not met Taylor face to face until they were imprisoned, also managed to communicate with him by using his fingers to spell out words on his thigh. Later, when Matthews' signallers joined him, they devised a method of using finger movements to send Morse code. Although they were seated and all facing the same way, with their arms folded, the rows were staggered, enabling those behind to see easily the finger movements of those in front. The reverse process was more difficult, but they managed it. The guards didn't suspect. Although they noticed Matthews' constant finger movements they put it down to some kind of mental instability. Unfortunately, while these channels of communication helped the prisoners to corroborate one another's stories, they did nothing to stem the arrests.

A civilian named Iwai, who was a university graduate and former manager of the Mitsubishi Company's Tawau Estates, had now translated the contents of the little black notebook, which were then passed to interpreter Isamu Miura for use during the interrogations. Miura, now aged 35, had left Japan at the age of sixteen to settle in Sandakan with his uncle. After graduating from St Michael's School, where he had learned to speak English, he went to work for the North Borneo Trading Company. The interrogations undoubtedly gave Miura, who had been interned by the British at the outbreak of war, a great deal of satisfaction.

The note book, said to have been found hidden at the base of The Big Tree, contained information which was known to a number of officers including Matthews. However, although the diarist was never identified, rumour quickly attributed ownership to Wells, apparently on the basis that he had been seen compiling reports and that papers, described by Hoshijima as a diary, had been found in his socks. His accusers were evidently unaware that Wells did not possess a black note book, and did not keep any incriminating material at the camp. In any case, the note book did not make a lot of difference to the investigation. It did, however, provide corroborative evidence which could be used as a lever against those who chose, even under torture, to deny everything.

It was certainly used in this way against Gordon Weynton who, although arrested on 29 July, was not sent down to Kempei-tai headquarters until 14 August. Those sixteen days had been spent in the cage. For the first fourteen he had not been interrogated. However, while the secret police were oblivious that the set handed over by Wells was a transmitter, by 12 August they knew from information extracted from locals during interrogations that there was definitely another wireless set in the camp and that Weynton had something to do with it. That day Hoshijima paraded Weynton in his office and demanded to know where the second radio was. When Weynton denied all knowledge he was returned to the cage for two days, during which time he was allowed no food or water and was not permitted to go to the latrines. On the morning of 14 August he was bound hand and foot, thrown into a lorry and taken to Sandakan.

The rest of the Australians had no idea what was happening. For a number of days after Weynton's arrest no work at all had been done at the 'drome, although some working parties had been engaged on road construction or sent to work in the gardens. However, the Australians knew more than the British, who were at a loss to explain why all work had stopped or why their camp had been searched not once, but twice. They were still none the wiser when, on the afternoon of 16 August all but ten of their 40 officers were removed without warning and transferred to Kuching. Two days later, the entire camp was uprooted and all remaining prisoners moved to a new compound, where the three watch towers and huts had been relocated a few weeks before. Situated between the E Force camp and the road leading to the airstrip it was even worse than the previous camp — not because the huts, built of atap on rubber tree stumps, were any less crude but because the site was, as had been rumoured, directly opposite the Japanese guard barracks. In keeping with the previous numbering system, the new camp was still known as Number 2 POW Camp Sandakan.

Stretched north-south along the crest of the gully opposite the Number 1 Compound, the camp comprised seventeen huts — fourteen for accommodation, one a combined officers' mess/medical inspection unit and two for the hospital

— built in the shape of an 'L'. As the shortest arm had been erected on sloping terrain, the westernmost huts were a considerable distance above the ground. Apart from rain showers, water was supplied from wells and a nondescript stream which the prisoners would soon widen to create a bathing pond at the bottom of the gully. As was the case in the adjoining Number 3 Camp, there was no electricity. The double barbed-wire fence which ringed the perimeter was broken by the main gate, facing the entrance to the Japanese barracks, and a smaller, rear access gate on the north-east corner, near the entrance to the Number 3 Camp.

While the Australian working parties had been having an unexpected holiday and the British had been moving camp, the Kempei-tai had been brutally interrogating Wells. He had proved to be particularly obdurate and had refused to admit a thing. When he first arrived at Kempei-tai headquarters he was housed in one of the cells downstairs, where he had been kept in solitary confinement for three weeks. Left only with his singlet and shorts and with no bedding, he was kept on starvation rations and permitted to wash only when the latrine bucket was emptied, which was anything from once a day to twice a week.

It was not until he was taken from his cell to one of the upstairs interrogation

The Number 2 Camp, Sandakan, occupied by the British from August 1943- April 1945. Artist unknown.

rooms that Wells realised just how effective the Kempei-tai's intelligence methods were. Attached to the wall was a large flow-chart of circles and lines, showing the progress of the investigations and linking one name to another. It was obvious that the secret police only needed outright confessions to close their case. To this end Wells, like Matthews and Taylor, was subjected to the most diabolical forms of torture. On 14 August, when the interrogators realised that the usual whippings, floggings and beatings would not produce results, Wells was passed over to Sergeant Major Ehara, otherwise known as 'The Bulldog', one of the Kempei-tai's torture specialists. He rapped Wells repeatedly on the head with a hammer, then tapped a thin bamboo skewer into his ear canal, perforating his ear-drum and destroying the nerves in his middle ear. When Wells regained consciousness after this excruciating torture and still refused to confess, Ehara forced him to eat three or four cups of raw rice, washed down with copious amounts of water. As the rice absorbed the water and swelled, Wells' stomach and intestines became so grossly distended that loops of his lower bowel extruded from his body. Instead of admitting anything, Wells pushed his intestines back.

Two days later, while trying to force Wells to confess that Major Fleming was involved in the planned insurrection, Ehara used a version of the rack — a torture not used in the Western world since the days of Elizabeth I and the Spanish Inquisition. Wells, handcuffed, was suspended by his wrists from one of the verandah rafters so that his knees were about 15 centimetres above the floor. A long plank of wood, about 10 centimetres square, was then placed behind his knees. Two men stood on either end of the plank and the upper body was effectively 'racked'. When the plank was placed across his heels, the flesh was torn from Wells' ankles, causing him to pass out. He called for his mother in his delirium, but never once did he tell his tormentors what they wanted to know.

Years later, Rod's mother, Mrs Wells, would recall that at the same time as this was happening, she knew something was horribly wrong. On 16 August, her birthday, she had woken from a terrifying dream, convinced that he had been calling to her for help. Two days before, her son's framed photograph had fallen inexplicably from its place on the mantelpiece and crashed to the floor.

The sight of Wells' ruptured bowel and his racking helped strengthen Weynton's resolve. He, too, would prove impossible to break. A former accountant with the Castlemaine Woollen Mills, Weynton was an absolute stickler for discipline. Now he put his strict code of conduct to good use. Like Wells, Matthews and Taylor, Gordon Weynton had no intention of caving in, no matter what the punishment. He had spent the first two days sitting cross-legged in the main holding room. At 9.00am on 16 August, the day of Wells' racking, he was taken to an interrogation room where Ehara, believing he could extract information about Matthews, Wells and the radio, beat him about the head and shoulders with a riding crop and pressed burning cigarettes into the flesh of his armpits. Weynton steadfastly refused to talk — even when Ehara put him through it all again three days later, with a jujitsu session thrown in for good measure.

On 28 August Weynton was removed from the main room, subjected to another round of torture and reinterrogated. When he still refused to admit anything, the Kempei-tai placed before him statements obtained by the locals which named Weynton as one of those who had gone outside the camp to obtain radio parts. They then produced Dick Majinal's updated list of components and the little black book. When Weynton realised it referred to activities in which he, Small and Mills had taken part, he had no option but to admit to the existence of the second radio, resulting in its recovery from the camp on 30 August and the arrest of its custodians, Rickards, Small and Mills.

With all those involved with the transmitter and receiver now identified, the Kempei-tai increased the pressure. For the next four-and-a-half days the suspects were interrogated and reinterrogated. Every time one of them differed on a detail, all would be beaten until agreement was reached. Once the issue of the second radio had been satisfactorily resolved, the Kempei concentrated their attention on Weynton in an attempt to gain more information on Wells and Matthews. When tacks hammered under Weynton's fingernails failed to break him he was racked. When that also failed, Ehara finally turned his attention to other, possibly less resilient, victims.

Sini had admitted nothing but Heng had mentioned Frank Martin's name, resulting in his arrest on 31 July. Flogged severely, Martin's face and body were so severely mutilated that he found it difficult to move for some time. Blain was picked up with James on 8 September, while Ted Keating, implicated by Henry Chang and also his note to Apostol, was arrested at the E Force camp on the 10th. The rest of his group followed — Weston, Rumble, Lander, Jensen, Marshall and Holly on 19 September, and Stan Davis on the 25th. Keating, suffering from amoebic dysentery and barely able to walk, was beaten unmercifully by Ehara, while the others were given yet another variation of the log treatment. Marshall, along with Sergeant Stevens, was considered to be a 'serious' case and was burned with cigarettes. Although Sergeant Bill McDonough was not involved in any escape plans, the Japanese discovered he had provided chemicals, for what they were unsure, resulting in his arrest on 15 September. Abin who, despite his stoicism, was unable to withstand the prolonged and brutal bouts of interrogation, had let other information slip, resulting in the arrests of Mrs Cohen, Dr Laband and Mr Phillips. As Abin had also confessed to carrying messages between The Eight Mile and E Force on Berhala, Matthews was forced to admit that Lieutenants Poole and Morrison were two of the recipients. Morrison's message had been to tell him he was the father of a baby girl, but this made no difference to the Kempei-tai. So zealous was their search for suspects they even rounded up Mrs Taylor and Mrs Mavor and placed them in cells under the house.

Abin definitely did not reveal the hiding place in the chimney. Had he done so, Wells would have been finished. The Kempei-tai, knowing that Abin was a key figure in the underground, set out one morning from their headquarters to search his house for evidence. Fortunately, this was one raid that did not go according to plan as the driver hit a large water buffalo, greatly delaying their arrival. Mrs Abin, who could not have known the Kempei-tai were on their way, was so overcome by a premonition of impending doom that she disposed of Matthews' pistol and burnt every scrap of paper. There was nothing left to find.

It was Pop Wong's quick thinking and talent as an actor that saved his life. At 10.00am on the morning of Friday 13 August, Pop had been roused by a voice calling his name from a paddy field near his house. He found Ehara waiting for him, accompanied by another member of the Kempei-tai and Lamberto Apostol, who had been severely tortured following his arrest almost a month before. At Kempei-tai headquarters, Ehara slapped Pop across the face and demanded to know where the radio valves were. Although Apostol confessed to giving them to him, Pop insisted that all he had obtained from Apostol were lamp globes for the experimental farm store and that when the two he had been given did not fit the sockets, he had thrown them away. Ehara did not believe him, so, for the next six days, Pop was subjected to the log treatment, water torture and wet sandal slap, beaten with a heavy stick, lacerated with a sword scabbard, had chilli rubbed into his genitals and threatened with decapitation. At the end of the interrogation period Ehara could only believe that Pop Wong was insane.

Pop knew that the Japanese treated the mentally-afflicted well, and put on the performance of his life. When Ehara beat him he laughed, when given food he threw it away, when ordered to sit at attention he threw himself down the stairs with a wild-eyed look, or he sang. He even drank his own urine — not to add to the impression that he was mad, but because he had heard that ingesting it would help heal internal injuries. The Japanese, quite convinced that he had gone completely mad, stopped the interrogations and confined him to Sandakan's Buli Sim Sim Mental Asylum.

Pop Wong kept up the pretence. At the end of three months, having convinced everyone, including the other inmates, that he was an 'orang gila', a madman, he was fined and released. Once outside, he continued his charade by taking off his trousers, urinating and then walking the length of the main street with his trousers in his hands, laughing and shouting all the while. It was all too much for the Japanese. They returned his fine and told him to go and buy some medicine with it. Once out of sight, Pop slipped quietly away and hid at a plantation near the 15 mile peg until the Japanese had forgotten all about him.

Unfortunately, the Kempei-tai had not forgotten about Pop's accomplices, whose screams and cries echoed around the building day and night. By early September just about anyone who had any connection with the Sandakan Assistance Group was behind bars — Felix Adzcona, the radio mechanic; Richard Low, the hospital dresser; the Goh brothers and other Chinese at the 15 mile who had helped Minty and his mates in their escape bid; contributors to Mrs Cohen's fund; Alex and Johnny Funk; Damudaran, the gaol clerk who had helped smuggle food and medicine to Minty's group after recapture; Sidek, the fisherman; and Inspector Guriaman and other loyal members of the British North Borneo constabulary, all of whom had pledged unswerving allegiance to Matthews. Two of these policemen, Jemadurs Ojaga Singh and Yangsalang, were especially targeted. Singh, who had his jaw and elbow broken, was denied medical treatment while Yangsalang only capitulated when statements by Lagan, Abin and two other members of the police force convinced him there was no point in his holding out. His statement did not, however, put an end to his suffering. The Kempei-tai punished him for not telling the truth to begin with, putting him through another round of torture.

At least two of the suspects had already been arrested and set free, only to be rearrested. Samuel Aruliah, released after Abin's initial interrogation in July, was apprehended on 11 August, while Alex Funk, who was questioned early and released, was arrested again on 8 August — a day generally considered by the Chinese to be particularly auspicious. The Kempei-tai travelled all the way to Kemansi, north-west of Beluran and on the other side of the Labuk River, to make the arrest, having been informed that Alex had a weapon. He was taken back to the family estate at Sandala, where his wife Maggie and other family members were questioned regarding the currency conversions and the whereabouts of the rifle. When torture forced Alex to reveal that he had buried his .303 at the 7½ mile, Johnny and Paddy were given a dose of the same treatment in an attempt to discover if they too had weapons secreted anywhere. After Johnny's final interrogation he was moved into the same room as Matthews who, like Taylor, had been flogged and racked repeatedly. By tapping out a message in Morse with his foot, the Australian was able to tell Johnny that he had not divulged anything and advised him to keep quiet as well. Matthews finished his message with a very personal plea: 'If anything happens to me Johnny, and if you ever happen to meet my wife, or any Australians, tell them I have died for my country.'

By mid-September the Kempei-tai had finished their investigation of what they called The Sandakan Incident. Not only had the principal ringleaders 'confessed', they had confessed most satisfactorily — largely because Ozawa, now back from Kuching, had 'translated' the confessions. All that remained was for the 52 civilians and 20 POWs to be shipped to Kuching to stand trial for crimes ranging from insurrection to money changing. While the key personnel would face the most serious charges, Lamberto Apostol had the longest and most diverse list. His crimes included supplying milk and eggs to the camp hospital, trafficking in chickens and salt, sending Christmas cakes to internees at Berhala, acting as a news courier, passing notes, procuring radio parts and helping POWs escape.

The apprehension of 72 criminals would have made Ehara and his gang feel smug, but they had even more reason to feel satisfied. Another uprising, even bigger than the last, had been thwarted in Dutch Borneo. During September, acting on a report that resistance fighters connected to Dr Haga's Banjarmasin group were planning to overthrow Pontianak, the Japanese had rounded up more than 1500 suspects, almost all of whom had been tortured and killed.

A fortnight later Hoshijima and the Sandakan Kempei-tai were still congratulating themselves when alarming news arrived — this time from Jesselton. Albert Qwok and the Kinabalu Guerrillas had staged a massive revolt.

Chapter Eight
JAPANESE JUSTICE

Qwok had returned from Tawi Tawi on 10 September and had immediately begun to reorganise his guerrilla organisation, which now included the Suluks and other islanders as well as former members of the disbanded North Borneo Volunteers and the police force. The Dusan farmers and Murut tribesmen of the interior, fearful of losing their land, were not ready to take up arms at this stage. However, Qwok had been making progress with his recruiting drive when the Japanese made an appalling announcement. To release regular army personnel for combat duties, 2000 young Chinese men were to be conscripted into the Japanese army as garrison troops. Chinese families reacted to this edict with dismay, but for Qwok, as resistance leader, the implications were extremely worrying. Enforced conscription would not only deprive him of a large number of potential recruits, it would free up large numbers of Japanese troops to hit back at his guerrillas. And there was worse. Local Chinese girls were to be sent to work as 'comfort women', forced into prostitution, while all former members of the Volunteers were to be called up for immediate military duty. Qwok, therefore, had to strike immediately, ready or not.

The opposition was formidable. Apart from the regular troops stationed in Jesselton, Ranau, Pensiagan and the coastal towns, there were numerous Kempei-tai detachments, Japanese-controlled police garrisons at Jesselton, Tuaran and Menggatal, as well as the Jikidans — paid informants who acted as spies in the villages. At this stage, Qwok's Jesselton force consisted of about 100 Kinabalu guerrillas and 250 other recruits, mainly islanders. Unfortunately, with the removal of all the British POWs to Sandakan in April, he and the locals were on their own. While some of the men had military training, the rest were raw recruits and Qwok seems to have been banking on a groundswell of resistance to help him hold off the Japanese until arms and assistance, promised by Saurez, arrived from the Philippines. Once outside aid arrived, Qwok evidently planned to carry out hit-and-run attacks until such time as the Allies could mount an invasion force and drive the Japanese out of Borneo.

After much deliberation, the date for a coordinated uprising at various centres around Jesselton was fixed for the night of 9 October — the eve of the Double Tenth festivities, held on the tenth day of the tenth month to mark the anniversary of the successful Chinese revolution in the 1930s, led by Dr Sun Yat Sen. Qwok believed that if the local Chinese could celebrate this day as free people it would boost their morale and motivate them to continue the fight against the Japanese.

Despite an efficient spy network, the Japanese in Jesselton had no inkling that an uprising was planned until a Formosan spy ran in from Menggatal. However, by that time the revolt was well underway. One group of guerrillas took on all police posts (apart from Victoria Barracks, which were too well-fortified), while another attacked the area near the customs house. Fortunately, as the Kempei-tai had not come to the aid of the local police but had hidden in the fortified barracks instead., after a short but fierce battle, Qwok's men gained the upper hand. Their objectives secured, the guerrillas sounded a bugle, the signal for the islanders, who had paddled in under cover of darkness, to swarm over the sea wall and invade the main part of town. Fleeing Japanese were either shot dead or beheaded.

The fight lasted a mere three hours. During this time the Suluks ignited the main customs warehouse and Corporal Koram and his two police friends set fire to the main jetty and the dockside godowns. These warehouses stored highly inflammable rubber and it was hoped that the conflagration would alert patrolling Allied submarines. Unfortunately, although the blaze lasted for more than a week, there was no response.

When dawn broke on the morning of the Double Tenth, the inhabitants of Jesselton rose to see the flags of British North Borneo, Great Britain, the United States of America and China fluttering atop every prominent building in town. It was the same in other centres, especially in Mansiang, near Menggatal, where Qwok had his headquarters and where the festivities were the most jubilant of all. Two days later, when Kota Belud fell to the guerrillas, they celebrated the occasion by executing every member of the Japanese police force.

It did not take long for the enemy to regroup. On 14 October they struck back, rushing troops into Jesselton and dispatching eight planes from Kuching to bomb and strafe the villages along the Tuaran road. Reprisals were swift and merciless. Despite the annihilation of entire villages, many more rebels joined the cause. More than 2400 took part in the revolt over the next two months, carrying out a series of strikes on Japanese stationed along the west coast and hinterland. The guerrillas lost 1300 men and the Japanese 1900 — calculated by counting the decapitated heads. But without outside help the momentum could not last. Qwok and his men kept up the fight but ammunition and supplies ran short, forcing them to pull back to new positions — not to the safety of the mountains, but along the coast where they could keep watch for the relief vessels which must surely come. They were confident that aid would arrive. Saurez had pledged his assistance, and Lim Teng Fatt had gone to the east coast to hurry things along.

Lim arrived at Tawi Tawi in early December to some very surprising news — Allied soldiers were at Labian Point, about 140 kilometres to the south-east of Sandakan. They were not an invasion force, as he had hoped, but a small group infiltrated on 6 October to collect intelligence on enemy movements along the east coast of Borneo. The party, code-named Python, comprised only six men, under the command of Captain F. Chester, British Army. More commonly known as Gort, because of his uncanny resemblance to Field Marshal, Viscount Gort, formerly Chief of the British General Staff and now Governor of Malta, Chester was a planter who had lived in British North Borneo for almost 20 years. Like Gort, he had a round head, a hairline receding to the point of baldness, bushy eyebrows and lush moustache.

Gort Chester was not just a planter turned soldier. Recruited by the British Secret Intelligence Service known as MI6, Gort, and a number of others, had been involved in pre-war activities in South-East Asia so irregular and secret that only a handful of highly-placed people, including their chief, Winston Churchill, knew about them. Forming an off-shoot of the clandestine organisation operating in Europe known as Special Operations Executive or SOE, the undercover agents of SOE (Far East) carried out various unusual missions. Some, such as killing Japanese agents in non-British territory, breached every rule of international law. The SOE men, trained in all facets of undercover work from silent assassination to sabotage, were resilient, resourceful and ruthless.

As Britain's Far Eastern Empire fell to the enemy at the beginning of 1942, SOE had made every attempt to remove its agents. Some took to the jungle-clad mountains in Malaya to lead 'stay behind parties', while others made their way to Australia, India or England. Those who reached Australia had regrouped in July 1942 as SOE (Australia), under the leadership of two Englishmen, Majors Edgerton Mott and Trappes-Lomax, previously the head of 101 Special School, SOE's secret training establishment in Singapore. Within weeks of Mott's appointment, SOE was backing its first Far Eastern mission behind the lines — to sabotage shipping and oil installations in Japanese-occupied Singapore. The plan was code-named Operation Jaywick. Gort Chester, a graduate of SOE's 101 school, had been sent out from London to take part.

He was not, however, destined to go on the Jaywick raid. The team left Sydney with high hopes in January 1943, but the ship's engine died off the coast of Queensland the mission was postponed. At about the same time, SOE's Australian operation folded following a decision to absorb it, along with other Allied undercover groups, into a combined Allied Intelligence Bureau (AIB). It was a merger doomed to failure. With AIB and military intelligence unable to accept that SOE indulged in activities about which no outsider, especially a government, should ever know, Major Mott was recalled to England and SOE (Australia) dissolved. With Jaywick on the back-burner and Special Operations in Australia dissolved, it looked very much as if Gort Chester was out of a job.

However, by April, General Thomas Blamey, now Australia's most senior army officer, came to the conclusion that, with America's General Douglas MacArthur playing such a prominent role in the Far Eastern war, some British and Australian 'flag-waving' behind enemy lines would be an astute move. Later that month, with the approval of British secret intelligence, he set up a completely new, and autonomous undercover group, answerable only to the general himself. Although officially classified as Special Operations Australia (SOA) it was known, for security reasons, as Services Reconnaissance Department or SRD. Now in direct competition with AIB's undercover groups for funding, supplies, personnel and transportation, SRD immediately set about consolidating its position by planning a number of missions.

Within a month, Operation Python was on the drawing board. The British were keen, once the war was over, to regain control of their Empire, with its extensive and valuable resources, and Borneo was seen as an excellent starting point. American submarines were already running a shuttle service to the guerrilla units scattered throughout the Philippines, so getting to Borneo would not be a problem, especially as Python's area of operation was to be at Labian Point, on the south-eastern tip of British North Borneo, just across the Sibutu Channel from Saurez's stronghold. And who better to lead a team than the newly-promoted Major Gort Chester, the ex-planter, SOE-trained graduate who had pre-war connections among Borneo's Chinese and indigenous population. Python's second-in-command, Captain Douglas Broadhurst, was an experienced agent who had been infiltrated into Timor the previous year on an SOE (Australia) mission. He was also British Army, but the other four members, handpicked by Gort — Captain E. 'Paddy' O'Keefe, Lieutenant Lloyd Woods and two signallers, Sergeants Leonard Cottee and Frank Olsen — were all Australian.

Python's tasks were to set up a local intelligence-gathering network and to prepare the way for a campaign of sabotage and underground resistance. The plan was approved by General MacArthur who, as the Supreme Allied Commander of the South-West Pacific Area, had to give his permission for special operations to enter his zone of responsibility and to travel in one of his submarines. After a short training period in Brisbane, Gort and his Python team left Garden Island, Western Australia, on 24 September 1943 on the US submarine *Kingfish*. They took with them 97 bundles of stores and equipment, weighing more than 3 tonnes and enough to last four months. Twelve days later Gort Chester was looking at Labian Point through the periscope.

The party ferried their stores from the submarine to shore in inflatable rubber boats. After a miserable night huddled out of the rain under an upturned boat, the men spent the next few days establishing a camp site about 3 kilometres further north on a small strip of sand, dubbed Python Beach. The site, at the mouth of the Tengian Kechil River, seemed ideal, but within hours their presence had been discovered by native fishermen who had noticed a pair of trousers hanging in a tree to dry. A furious Gort ordered the team to move up river to a new spot further inland. It took days to shift the gear. While the site was only 1.5 kilometres from the coast, the river twisted and turned back on itself in giant loops, so close together they were separated by only a few metres of impenetrable jungle. By the time they had paddled and dragged the boats up the switch-back waterway in the stifling heat, dodging snags and negotiating fallen trees, they were exhausted.

Olsen and Cottee scouted the area for a suitable site for the wireless transmission station. The pair chose a hill, about 3 kilometres inland, where they set about clearing the jungle of trees and undergrowth to erect their aerial which, being a horizontal variety, required open space. It was a back-breaking task, and one which had to be accomplished with nothing more than a native-style parang as no axes had been packed. The main wireless shack was constructed and made waterproof beneath an upturned five-man rubber boat, then an outstation, manned by Cottee, was set up at Labian Point, about 8 kilometres away.

By the time the signal stations and the base camp were established almost all of the men were ill or suffering from exhaustion. General morale and Gort's temper were not improved by another breach of security. Python had been requested to bring stores for Captain John Hamner, a United States Army officer, sent to Tawi Tawi to set up a wireless link for the guerrillas. On arriving in Borneo, Python had buried Hamner's heavy stores on the beach, where they were to be collected at a later date. However, on about 12 October, before any arrangement could be made, a kompit under the command of a Lieutenant Frank Young, United States Army, sailed over from Tawi Tawi, located the hiding place, dug up the supplies and decamped, without making contact with any of the Python team. The first the Australians knew about the visit was when they found a large piece of cardboard, tied to a tree for all to see, with a message written in plain English, signed by Young, that the stores had been retrieved.

It was not until 23 November, when Hamner paid them a visit, that the Australians met their American counterparts. Python had only small inflatable rubber craft, which were unsuitable for either coastal or ocean-going reconnaissance, so Hamner offered the use of his boat to take them to Sitankay Island, where they bought a native kompit and caught up with one of Gort's pre-war contacts, Lieutenant Valera. In early December, while Chester, Broadhurst and O'Keefe were visiting Saurez at the guerrilla base on Tawi Tawi, it was agreed that Valera, who had lived in British North Borneo for a number of years, and had worked in Harry Keith's Forestry Department, should become Python's liaison officer. An intelligence network, stretching from Tarakan in the south, to Sandakan in the north, was soon up and running.

Python's own observation post was high in a tree near the mouth of the Nyamok River, about 3 kilometres south of Labian Point. It overlooked the Sibutu Channel and the Australians had a clear view of every vessel moving to and from the oil ports of Tarakan and Balikpapan, in Dutch Borneo. Before long Python's reports, relayed by a signals hook-up to the transmission station, along with information collected from native coast watchers by special agents, were being transmitted in a steady stream back to Australia.

On returning from his visit to Tawi Tawi in December, Chester received information that a force of at least 2000 Chinese guerrillas was operating near Jesselton under the command of his old friend, Albert Qwok and that another old friend, Lim Teng Fatt, Qwok's deputy, was looking for him. Lim had certainly come to the right man. Gort pledged weapons, ammunition and medicine from Australia, as well as personnel to help Qwok's men set up an intelligence network in the west.

However, before either of these promises could be fulfilled, shattering news was received from Jesselton. Qwok was in enemy hands. With no sign of the promised assistance from the Philippines, resistance had faltered. On 19 December Qwok, in order to save the inhabitants of the valley in which his guerrilla group was sheltering, surrendered. With the collapse of the Jesselton resistance, Gort realised that any hope of revitalising the revolt, or rescuing Qwok and his men, rested entirely on the arms shipment promised from Australia, due to arrive with the next submarine sortie.

Back at The Eight Mile Camp Hoshijima, unable to break the major conspirators in the Sandakan Incident, was taking out his frustrations on the remaining prisoners. The rice ration had been cut and it had been the working parties, back at the airfield after the lay-off, which had born the brunt of his ill-humour. The slightest infringement was likely to result in a severe bashing. The officers were confined to camp or the vegetable garden on Hoshijima's orders, so it had been left to one or two stalwart NCOs to do their best for the rank and file, many of whom had been dragged from their beds to make up the numbers. As E Force's Corporal Gerald Fitzgerald discovered, punishment for transgressions was both swift and excessive.

On the morning of 16 October Hoshijima had arrived at the 'drome to hear that two cooks, one of whom was Fitzgerald, one of Albert Anderson's motor ambulance mates, had browned rice on a shovel held over the fire. Declaring that this act of 'desecration' would 'send the shovel bad', Hoshijima stood the cooks at attention, knocked them savagely to the ground three times and sentenced both to one week's confinement in the cage.

By 1.30pm on the same day Hoshijima had given all but eight of the Australian officers their marching orders. The first they knew of the impending move was when their names were read from a list, drawn up by Captain Cook. Cook, the liaison officer, was one of seven B Force officers not on the list. Captain Jim Millner of the AASC was astounded that Cook, whose apparent unwillingness and/or inability to stand up to the Japanese was viewed generally with contempt, was remaining behind, and as camp commanding officer. Captain Boscolo, Acting Commanding Officer following Harold St John's arrest, was furious. However, there was no time to argue. They had been given 30 minutes to report to the gate for transfer to Sandakan, where a small coastal vessel, *Tiensin*, was waiting to take them to Kuching.

The officers were unable to farewell the troops, which was difficult for those officers who had a good rapport with their men, but was worse for Ron Ollis, who had no opportunity to say good-bye either to his men, or his brother John, who had been with him throughout. As the handful of officers remaining behind were isolated from the rest, there was no chance either to hand over any records or give any last minute instructions. It was the same over at E Force. Prevented at bayonet point from having any contact with Dr John Oakeshott, the only officer not being transferred, Captain Rod Richardson could do nothing more than leave the camp cash, amounting to $540, near the doctor's quarters and hope for the best.

The first the working parties knew of the transfer was when they returned from the 'drome that evening. B Force marched into camp to discover the only officers in occupation were Cook, Captain Jim Heaslop (canteen officer), Lieutenant Gordon Good (quartermaster), Padres Harold Wardale-Greenwood and Albert Thompson and Doctors Picone and Jeffrey. While the departing officers viewed Cook's elevation to leader with a mixture of fury and disbelief, Keith Botterill was not the least surprised. Of all the officers in camp, Botterill figured that, for Hoshijima, Cook was the obvious choice. Short and rather plump, he was a 'voyage only' officer (an officer given a temporary elevation in rank for the duration of a voyage) and had not been in combat. Apart from having no battle experience, the yardstick by which the bulk of the AIF rank and file judged their superiors, Cook was an administrator, not a practical soldier. His cherubic features, still in evidence despite the recent paucity of the rations, and his apparent willingness to do whatever the Japanese wanted, reinforced the perception that his interests did not lie solely with the men.

The three chaplains left at Sandakan, Wardale-Greenwood and Thompson from B Force, and Acting Padre, Corporal Alan Garland from E Force, were all

Protestant. While all would administer to anyone who was in need of their services, the exclusion of Fathers Rogers and O'Donovan, despite their vehement protests, meant that Last Rites were not available to those of the Catholic faith requiring absolution.

The ratio of officers to men was now 1:250, but the purge had been far less severe in the British compound, where the transfers to Kuching eight weeks before had left one officer for every 70 men. Drawn from both the army and air force, the remaining officers were diverse in age and background: Captain Jim Mills, aged only 28, who had been appointed commanding officer; the even more youthful camp administrator, Lieutenant Ian Rolfe, aged 23; two medical officers, 26-year-old Captain Frank Daniels and Flight-Lieutenant R. Blackledge, aged 31; Squadron Leader John Wanless, the chaplain; three older men — 51-year-old Flying-Officer Alf Linge (a civil contractor from Malaya), 40-year-old Humphrey Burgess (Australian by adoption, tile and brick merchant by trade) and the camp's hospital administrator Flying-Officer Stan Cressey, aged 45 (an expatriate Australian from the Government Printer's Office, Hong Kong). Completing the list were two army lieutenants — Geoffrey Chopping, a 24-year-old former magistrate's clerk and Mills' right-hand man, Philip Young, who was a year older than Chopping.

All officers left in Sandakan, both British and Australian, were in for a busy time. On 17 October, the day after the removal of the Australian contingent, there had been another major upheaval. The number of Australian prisoners had been reduced by death, escape, arrest or transfer to roughly 1750 so Hoshijima had ordered E Force to amalgamate with B Force. E Force was not at all upset by this decision. While the Number 1 Camp could no longer boast piped water to every hut and electric light to every cubicle, it was infinitely better than the Number 3 Camp with its muddy well-water and complete lack of lighting. And there was plenty of room at the new camp. As soon as E Force moved out, all the sick were installed in its old compound, greatly decreasing the amount of accommodation required in the Number 1. The pressure was relieved even further when a task force of 200, including Murray and Botterill, dismantled and moved to the combined camp all huts surplus to the hospital's requirements. A number of other alterations also took place. The front gate and guardhouse were moved to the south-west corner of the compound near the old hospital/chapel building (now a store room) while Esau was relocated to a nearby and much more public position, on the far side of the track linking the boiler house to the main Japanese barracks. As part of the internal reorganisation process the NCOs moved into the empty officers' quarters while the rank and file rearranged themselves to leave ample room for the newcomers.

On the whole, the units stayed together. Owen Campbell and his 2/10th Field Regiment mates from E Force took the third hut in the row closest to the swamp while others, keen to be reunited with old friends or family members, moved in with some of the B men. The camp buzzed half the night as men sought news of the fate of old Selarang comrades, some of whom had died or moved to other camps. While B Force had 29 deaths to report, E Force had only two — Nelson Short's mate Jimmy Picken, electrocuted at Kuching, and Corporal Max Martin, struck by lightning during a violent electrical storm while urinating at the Number 3, only a fortnight or so before. Martin's death led the Japanese to urge the British prisoners to 'protect' themselves from any similar occurrence by constructing an atap roof over their facility.

While there had been only one death at the new British camp, that of Signalman James Taylor on 29 September, two other prisoners had been transferred to Kuching. When Air-Craftsman Wilson had developed appendicitis in about mid-October, Hoshijima, showing solicitude to his British prisoners, had him admitted to Sandakan Hospital, along with Air-Craftsman Mockeridge as his personal nursing orderly. The operation was successful. However, while they were there the pair had come into contact with some of the Australians involved in the Sandakan Incident. Unwilling to allow 'contaminated' prisoners, even if they were British, to re-enter the camp, Hoshijima had shipped them off to Kuching as well. Their appearance at the British officers' compound on November was most welcome. They brought with them all the camp gossip, which included details of the move to the new site, reports of a general improvement in health and news of civil contractor Alf Linge's engineering project to divert water from the stream to the camp, using a system of bamboo pipes.

With December rapidly approaching, thoughts at Sandakan turned again to Christmas. A canteen was still operating in the Number 1 Camp and, largely due to the efforts of Jim Heaslop, was well stocked with delicacies such as chickens, ducks and pork. To Richie Murray's disappointment, fresh milk was no longer procurable. Although one beer-bottle full had cost Murray $1 (the equivalent of ten days' pay), the pleasure it had given Botterill, who poured his share over his rice ration, had made the expense worth it. Even for those flush with funds, there was now not a drop of milk available. Matusup, the main supplier, was in custody, and recently-arrived Sergeant Watanabe had, without provocation, attacked with a shovel the Indian milk vendor at the 'drome, making it highly unlikely that he would appear again.

The Australians nevertheless still managed to prepare a three-course traditional Christmas dinner. Someone with access to a typewriter typed out the full menu, along with a small verse, written especially for the occasion. Tom Burns and his mates creatively turned their menus into small booklets, bordered with holly and bells, with a map of Australia (minus Tasmania) emblazoned on the cover in red pencil. Tom dined with twelve others — Tom's friend Colin Smyth, Nelson Short and Norm Channell from the 2/18th, Fred and Harold Roberts from the 2/19th, three of Black Jack's boys, David Gloag, Noel Brett and Ken Molde (masquerading as Leigh Dawson), Gunners Stan Duggan and Les Grosvenor, and Ivan Downes and Jack Raleigh, both of the 2/10th Field Workshops. They were in for a treat — chicken soup, followed by a main course of roast duck and pork pie smothered in onion gravy, with kang kong (native spinach), baked potatoes and pumpkin on the side and, to top it all off, steamed Christmas pudding and fruit salad for dessert.

The one stanza poem, by an unknown poet and entitled simply 'Borneo', encapsulated the staunchness of spirit that for so long had sustained the Australians but so antagonised the Japanese.

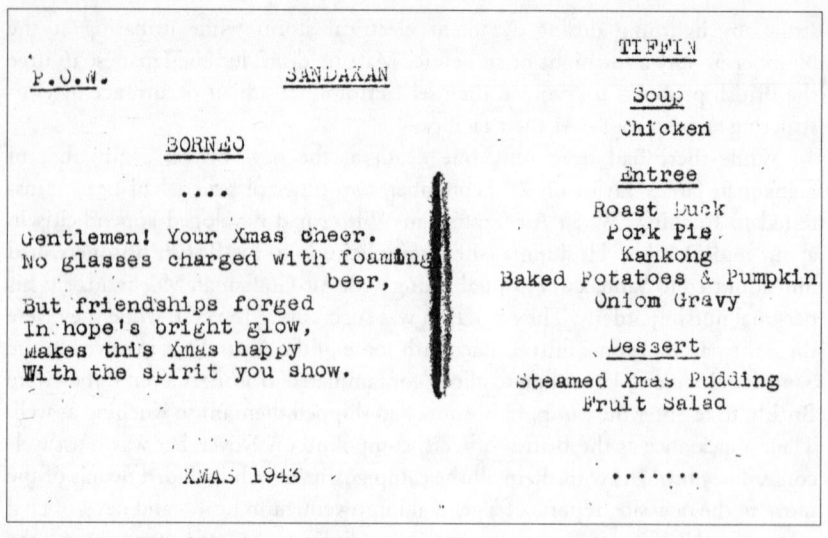

```
P.O.W.              SANDAKAN                    TIFFIN
                                                Soup
                                                Chicken
            BORNEO
                                                Entree
            ....
                                                Roast Duck
Gentlemen! Your Xmas Cheer.                     Pork Pie
No glasses charged with foaming                 Kankong
                         beer,         Baked Potatoes & Pumpkin
But friendships forged                          Onion Gravy
In hope's bright glow,
Makes this Xmas happy                           Dessert
With the spirit you show.
                                        Steamed Xmas Pudding
                                             Fruit Salad

            XMAS 1943                           ........
```

Tom Burns' Christmas menu, 1943.

For those involved in the Sandakan Incident and the Jesselton Revolt, it was a miserable Christmas. On 25 October all prisoners held by the Kempei-tai, along with the 'contaminated' Mockeridge and Wilson, had been taken down to Sandakan Harbour and embarked upon SS *Subuk* for transfer to Kuching. The voyage had been horrendous. The first night they ran into a storm of such ferocity that the prisoners, handcuffed to the ship's railings, thought they would surely drown. The ship stopped briefly at Miri but this brought no respite as the prisoners, confined to the open deck, were unable to seek any shelter from the fierce tropical sun. Matthews was encouraged to escape during the voyage, as he would be facing the most serious charges, but declared that the repercussions for the others would be too great and besides, where would he go?

The ship arrived in Kuching on Australia's 'unofficial' national day — Melbourne Cup Day, the first Tuesday in November. The two Englishmen were taken to the POW camp along with Harold St John, Pom Brown, Vern Rae, Lieutenants Poole and Morrison, Joe Weston and three ORs, against whom the Japanese had insufficient evidence to proceed. Matthews and the others were sent to the military's Penjarah Orang Sansarah Gaol where they sat in the vermin-infested wire cages, 25 to each cage, cross-legged and at attention, from 7.00am until 10.30pm.

Meanwhile, Qwok and his men, after being taken into custody on 19 December, had been marched to the Jesselton Hotel before being handed over to the Kempei-tai, now headquartered at the Jesselton Sports Club. Although Albert Qwok was put through every form of torture, he flatly refused to answer a single question, insisting that responsibility for the rebellion lay on his shoulders alone. His courage and stoicism did not spare his men, or anyone thought to be connected with the uprising. Those who were not tortured or bludgeoned to death during the interrogations were sent to Batu Tiga Gaol where, in early January, they were still awaiting their fate.

Eric 'Mo' Davis, who gave up his job as boiler-man on *Queen Mary* to join the AIF.

Keith Botterill, at Circular Quay Sydney, just prior to embarkation for Malaya, 1941.

Botterill's best mate, Richie Murray, welterweight fighter.

Dick Braithwaite, photo engraver from Queensland.

Braithwaite's mate, Wally Blatch, bank officer from Yeoval.

Eric Tomkyns, Indian-born school teacher from Warialda, who loved the Australian outdoors.

John Nicholson Barnier, patriotic school teacher from Grafton and one of the three Alumny Creek boys.

John 'Jacky' Jackson, the Alumny Creek boy with the fine singing voice and one of five soldiers of Aboriginal descent who went to Borneo.

Johnny O'Donohue, the third Alumny Creek boy.

Billy Young, under-age teenage recruit, Dead End Kid, and one of the youngest to enlist in the AIF.

Ray Carlson of Victoria, devoted father of eleven children.

Dot Anderson, with her husband Albert, one of the 'old blokes', who joined up to provide for his family.

Another 'old bloke', Neil Christie, accountant and 'chook' fancier, from Mackay, Queensland.

Bill McDonald, of Armidale, the 2/18th Battalion's dedicated tailor.

Rod Richardson, who twice extricated his men from danger during the battle for Singapore Island.

Soldiers from Billy Young's 2/29th Battalion. From this group, only Paddy O'Toole, left rear, survived the war. The rest were either killed in action or died while POWs. Harry Longley, Billy's mate and one of The Dead End Kids, is front right.

George Plunkett, champion tennis player, bayonetted 13 times during the X Battalion massacre.

John 'Jacky' Ings, Plunkett's mate and another survivor of the X Battalion massacre.

Eddie McAppion, the soldier from Fremantle who loved the sea.

Ken Mosher, of the 2/18th Battalion, who led his men by example.

Aerial photograph of The Eight Mile Camp, 6 March 1945. The numbers relate to the original key provided by Allied Aerial Reconnaissance. The large camp at the right is Number 1 Compound and the camp in the centre is Number 2. The buildings, left foreground, are all that remained of the Number 3 Compound. The 'unidentified buildings', far right, are the engine room and boiler house. The white-on-black 'POW', in the open area between the two larger camps, is the POW sign. 'Truck garden' is an American term meaning vegetable or kitchen garden.

The open area between the two smaller accommodation blocks in the Number 1 Compound was the assembly ground near The Big Tree which, along with its shadow, forms the dark lines in the centre of the area. The original gate was also here.

Key:

1. Japanese barracks and administration area. The oblong 'cultivated' area and the open square to the right of it form the L-shaped Japanese parade ground. Sticpewich's carpentry shop was to the right of it, across the road from the entrance to the Number 1 Compound (see 11).
2. Hoshijima's house, formerly the home of Pop Wong.
3. Parade grounds. The parade ground in Number 1 Compound is where the boxing matches and concerts were held.
4. Drainage canals. The large area identified as a truck garden in Number 1 Compound is the site of the swamp.
5. Guard towers.
6. Guard shacks.
7. A building thought by reconnaissance to be a 'mess hall', but which was simply one of the buildings brought across from the Number 3 Compound.
8. A depression outside the gate, incorrectly identified as a weapons' pit.
9. Pig sty.
10. Small bridge across the stream running into Number 2 Compound.
11. Gates to compounds. The buildings (not identified), near the Number 1 Compound gate are the main guardhouse, the guards' Q-store and the kitchen.

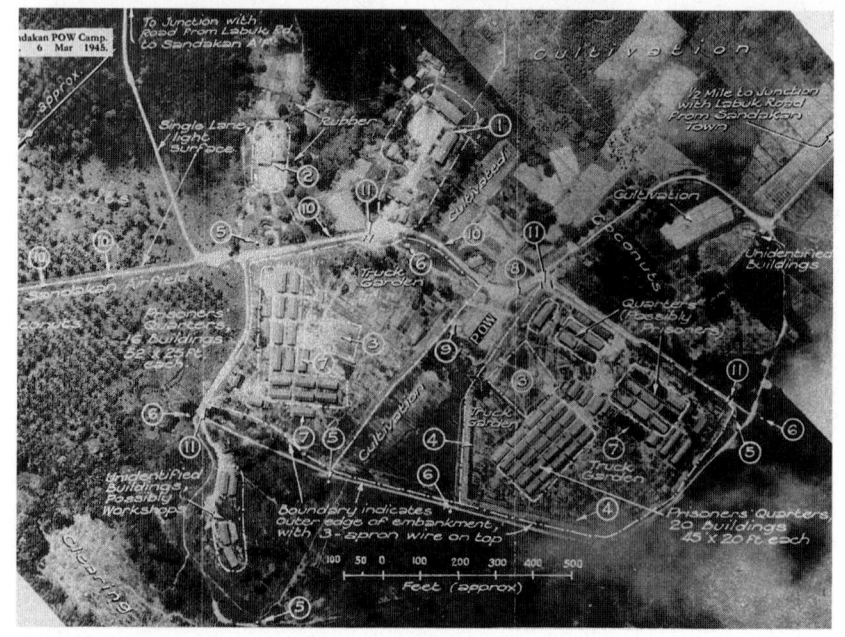

A sign indicating one of the designated 'smoking' pits. (AWM 120458)

Lionel Matthews, 'The Duke', who set up the camp underground. (AWM 059358)

Three boys from the bush (L to R), Bill Ney, Bob Bruce and Stan Brack.

Adelaide barrister George (Bill) Bundey, sent with B Force to establish an Education Centre, but thwarted by the apathy of the camp administrators.

Matthews' deputy and wireless genius Rod Wells, who made the camp radio and transmitter from scratch, including almost all the components.

Dr Jim Taylor, head of Sandakan's civilian underground movement.

Corporal Koram, British North Borneo constabulary and dedicated resistance fighter.

Ray Steele, a member of the Dit Party, who escaped to Tawi Tawi from Berhala Island.

Ron Ollis, who was moved to Kuching in October 1943.

John Ollis, brother of Ron, who arrived with E Force.

Nelson Short, song writer and camp entertainer.

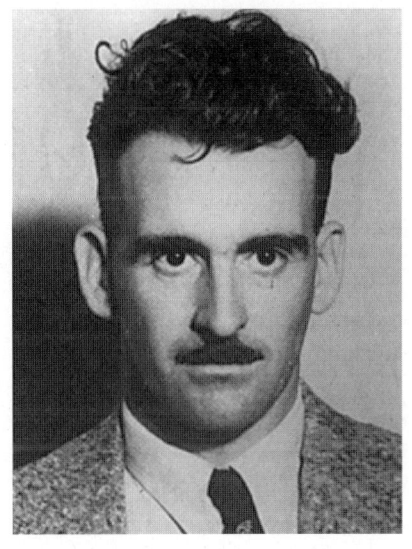

Owen Campbell, who arrived with E Force. (AWM 41489)

John (Mort) Codlin, the paymaster who was beaten up by guards.

Paul Muir, who monitored signals in New Guinea from the AIB agent in Borneo.

The Nicholson brothers — Gerard, left, who died at Sandakan and John, who went on the first march.

Able Seaman G Morriss, who died while being moved to the Number 2 Camp prior to the second march. (AWM P02149.001)

Members of the Agas team, dressed in sarongs made from parachute silk, who operated behind enemy lines in Borneo. (L to R) Ma'aruff bin Said, Jack Wong Sue, Gort Chester, Skeet Hywood, Mohammed Sariff.

Lance/Bombardier Tom Tadman, aged 25, 155th Field regiment, Royal Army. One of the 200 POWs sent to Labuan from Kuching. Died at Brunei 3/4/45.

Ron Sullivan, the corporal who accompanied Botterill on his scavenging expeditions and who was bayonetted to death while carrying rice, Easter Saturday 1945

Herb Lytton, buried with his wallet by Botterill, in the hope that he would be identified.

Lance Maskey, the camp interpreter, murdered at Ranau 1 August 1945.

Three of the four Ranau survivors. (L to R) Nelson Short, Bill Sticpewich, Keith Botterill, with an Auster pilot, prior to evacuation from Ranau.

Mo Davis' American hut mates from USS *Houston*, Harry McManus (L) and Harry Stone, inspect the body of Colonel Suga, shortly after his suicide.

The Number 1 Compound, following its destruction by fire on 29 May 1945. The rows of ashes in the foreground are the ORs' huts.

Looking from the swamp area towards The Big Tree and the ruins of the cookhouse wing, Number 1 Compound. (AWM 120461)

The remains of the huts near the cookhouse. Note that two of the Number 2 huts, in background, far left, are still standing. (AWM 120463)

Investigating officers search through the remains of the now overgrown first aid 'post', Number 2 Compound. (AWM 120439)

Exhuming the slit trenches, Number 2 Compound. (AWM 120448)

The author with Keith Botterill at the Sandakan Memorial, Burwood Park, Sydney, in 1994.

The new headstone of Ranau hero, Richie Murray, erected after his grave was located by the author in 1995.

All hope now rested on Python's submarine, due from Australia any day and bringing with it, not only the promised arms and ammunition, but also reinforcements. They were Major Bill Jinkins who, with Alec Chew, a warrant officer of Chinese descent, had escaped from a POW camp in Ambon, Lieutenant Alfred 'Jack' Rudwick, and three sergeants — Don McKenzie, Bill Brandis and Stan Neil. However, following a communication breakdown between SRD, AIB and the Americans, the submarine *Tinosa* did not leave Fremantle until 10 January. When they arrived in Borneo eight days later to unload the 2.2 tonnes of stores, Gort was enraged — not just because of the delay but because SRD administration had added to his stores list to such an extent that some had to be left behind. When the bundles were unpacked Gort discovered, to his horror that the arms, ammunition and medicines for Albert Qwok were still sitting on the dock at Fremantle. As there was no point going without the weapons, the trip to the west was postponed. Qwok and his men would have to wait until the next shipment.

The next shipment, however, would be too late. On 24 January 1944 time ran out for the Kinabalu guerrillas. Found guilty of mounting an insurrection, Qwok and his four most prominent leaders were beheaded at Pitigas. The rest were machine-gunned to death. A few days later, at the same place, 176 civilians found guilty of assisting the rebels were executed by firing squad.

Python, too, had experienced a calamity. On the afternoon following the arrival of the reinforcement party, Bill Brandis had disappeared. He, Neil, McKenzie and Hamner, who had come over from Tawi Tawi, had been on the beach when they noticed a sailing boat coming into the bay. Leaving Hamner on watch, the other three had set out for the main camp to report the sighting. They had gone only 100 metres when a major disagreement erupted on the direction they should take. The party split and then split again. The men were wandering in territory which was completely alien to them and although Mckenzie and Neil managed to locate the camp eventually, Brandis did not. No trace of him could be found. This was too much for Gort. He fumed at SRD.

It was obvious that SRD had taken no notice of Gort's criteria for selecting special agents, so he spelt them out again. SRD was reminded that it was imperative for all field operatives to be thoroughly conversant with local languages, jungle lore (especially the three 'golden rules' of survival — '…If lost, stay until found, [know the] direction of ther coast, [know that] most water in rivers runs to the sea…'), sailing, general handling of small arms and every weapon likely to be used in the field, explosives, and intelligence procedures. Last, all field agents must have sufficient signalling skills to enable all personnel — not just signallers — to transmit and receive at a minimum rate of eight to ten words per minute.

Gort had other problems, too. SRD staff, incapable of grasping the concept that unsolicited supplies created enormous logistical problems, was still amending Python's stores list. When the submarine arrived on sortie number three with over 7 tonnes of equipment instead of the 3.5 tonnes requested, and with vital pieces missing, Gort was livid. It was not merely the extra weight and bulk that was the trouble, it was transporting them from the drop-off point at Tawi Tawi to his base in Borneo — an exercise which involved three 225-kilometre round trips.

Despite the problems with stores, Python continued with its task of gathering and transmitting intelligence. Chester knew from Hamner that information from Sandakan was available from the Dit Party (whom he had not met as they had left Tawi Tawi in December for the main guerrilla headquarters at Mindaneo), but he also realised that their information was now at least eight months old. On 7 February Gort reported that, according to his agents, there were now only 150 B-class enemy troops, 40 POW guards, 11 military police, 1 governor general and 150 native police at Sandakan. The food position in the town was bad, with rationing in place and no provisions in the shops. Although an aerodrome under construction using labour supplied by an estimated 2800 POWs was not completed, it was in use. Gort finished his message by adding that he had a 'reliable man' going there in a few days' time who would contact his 'old friends'.

Eight days later, Gort's man had completed his mission, enabling SRD to confirm on 15 February that Berhala was no longer operating as a POW camp and that the aerodrome at the 8 mile peg was receiving flights and being extended.

The day after this report was made, Python was uncovered. The Japanese had arrested Brandis. On 9 February, after wandering along the coast to the north of Labian Point for three weeks, Brandis, naked and more dead than alive, had been found by Osman Panjang on a beach near Kampong (village) Atiam, Tambisan Island, less than a kilometre off the mainland. Indicating by sign language that he had been in the water for three days and needed food, the Australian had been taken to the kampong where his rescuer fed and looked after him. However when the village chief, Mandor Alam, heard a few days later that the soldier's presence had been betrayed by an informer named Jaria, he was forced to disclose Brandis' whereabouts to avoid serious repercussions to the local community. The Australian was arrested by a Japanese named Sawa Mura and assistants Pallsing and Muntin, who alerted the Sandakan Kempei-tai.

Python had developed a cover story — that the party had been sent to Borneo to obtain information on escaped POWs. However, it appears that, under torture, Brandis was unable to keep up the pretence. During an interrogation carried out by Sergeant-Major Masaji Nakao, he revealed that he was a member of a party commanded by Major Chester, which had come by submarine with orders to transmit information back to Australia. Although he was unable to remember the landing point, he recalled that there was a boat under construction nearby. On 16 February he had been taken by the Kempei-tai to join a party of about 100 Japanese from the Sandakan garrison, led by First-Lieutenant Okamura. They landed at a spot 1.5 kilometres south of the Python camp at the Nyamok River, where they carried out a two-hour reconnaissance. Early the following morning, while Gort was cooking breakfast over an open fire, Stan Neil and Len Cottee spotted from their tree-top look-out a small tug-boat with several troop-barges in tow. As a task force of at least 60 was heading for a landing point only 400 metres from their observation post, the Australians hurriedly doused the fire and shifted to a new location, about 6.5 kilometres further north.

Gort did not know what had happened to Brandis but he realised that the Japanese had picked up Python's scent — a conclusion confirmed by local agents who reported the Kempei-tai knew white soldiers were in the area. Since there had been no response from SRD to a request to evacuate Python to the west coast by submarine, Gort took the initiative. Without further ado, Lim Fatt, who had been given 2400 pounds sterling in gold sovereigns, was dispatched to Jesselton to make arrangements with Qwok's successor for their reception and to organise a boat to pick them up. It was the last the Python party ever saw of him.

The 17th of February was a busy day. That night, in keeping with prior arrangements, O'Keefe, Broadhurst, Jinkins and Valera left in the kompit for Tawi Tawi for a rendezvous with the United States super-submarine *Narwhal* — Valera to pick up the next load of stores and the other three to be evacuated to Australia, along with Hamner, and other American personnel. But the Americans were not informed that Mantabuan Island, 24 kilometres to the south of Tawi Tawi, was insecure and that a new pick-up point had been nominated. Not surprisingly, with the submarine at one place and the shore party at another, the two groups failed to meet. The Australians waited at the new rendezvous until 27 February but the position was becoming perilous with increased Japanese activity and they were forced to move on. They finally made contact on the night of 5 March, only to be interrupted during the unexpectedly protracted unloading of the stores when enemy destroyers were detected less than than 3000 metres away. *Narwhal* headed immediately for the open sea before she was forced to dive, giving Valera, who was below decks when the hatch was slammed shut, an unexpected trip to Australia. The stores already unloaded reached Tawi Tawi but, with search parties still looking for Python and Valera en route to Australia, they were unable to be moved any further.

The Python evacuees were unaware they were not the only Australians hitching a ride home. Also on board were Steele, Wallace and Kennedy, who had spent the last eight months serving with the guerrillas. Since December they had been based at Mindaneo where the overall guerrilla commander, the United States' Lieutenant-Colonel Wendell Fertig, had his headquarters. Wallace, suffering from a double hernia, and Kennedy, very ill with malaria, were being evacuated home for urgent medical attention while Steele, as senior officer, had been ordered to join them for a full debriefing. Of the eight Australians who had fled Berhala, only six were left alive. Rex Butler, promoted to sergeant instructor with the 1st Battalion of Saurez's 125th regiment, had been killed and beheaded by pro-Japanese, head-hunting Moros in an ambush near the Dugan River at Tawi Tawi on 18 August while Charlie Wagner had been shot by a Japanese sniper at 8.00am on 21 December at Liangan, Mindaneo.

Meanwhile, on the mainland, Gort and the other eight members of the Python party were only just managing to keep one jump ahead of the enemy. The Japanese discovered a rubber dinghy and empty storage containers in the vicinity of the Mera River, south of Labian Point, and had stepped up the search. Between 22 and 24 March no less than twelve patrols landed between the Mera and Tenagian Kechil Rivers. The food dumps were found and the wireless station, within an hour of Python's abandoning it, on 24 March. It did not take long for the Japanese to discover marked trees and a track leading to the new camp. When Alex Chew and Sam Neil, sent to relieve McKenzie and Rudwick (who were guarding the track while the others evacuated the wireless station) discovered there was no sign of them, the remainder of the party fled.

By 29 March the situation became critical. Forced to keep constantly on the move and unable to access their food dumps, Gort transmitted an urgent request for evacuation. Although Task Force 71, the United States submarine fleet operating out of Fremantle, arranged for a pick-up within 24 hours, it took four attempts before they were successful. The first, scheduled for 30 March, just to the north of Labian Point, failed because the submarine commander had been given the wrong time for the rendezvous. The second, at the mouth of the Mera River on 10 April, was aborted when Python, which had just survived an attempted ambush, was unable to make the rendezvous as they could not cross the river because of the close proximity of the enemy. Although USS *Haddo*'s captain, Chester Nimitz Jnr, waited for several hours, he was unaware that Python did not have a boat and had no way of reaching the submarine, lying well off-shore. A third attempt twelve days later near Dent Haven (about 16 kilometres north of Labian Point) was abandoned when the rubber boat manned by the rescue team from USS *Redfin* was carried by the tide to the north, where it ran into a Japanese patrol. Fortunately, the sailors escaped unscathed during the subsequent altercation. Captain McCollum, of United States Headquarters, was not impressed. Neither was SRD, which deleted all reference to these rescue attempts from the files of its official history.

On 26 May Captain Sam Dealey, commander of USS *Harder*, was ordered to sail for Exmouth Gulf, Western Australia. At a secret American base known as 'Potshot', he was instructed to conduct a dress rehearsal with Bill Jinkins and the level-headed Sergeant Stan Dodds, who were to perform the rescue. Then *Harder* headed north for the rendezvous, scheduled between the hours of 6.00pm and midnight on any night from 6 June to 13 June. The point of contact was at Tangusu Bay, about 160 kilometres north of Labian Point and a little to the west of Tambisan Island.

Shortly before midnight on 8 June the Python party, which had endured a forced march on hard tack for five days across difficult terrain to make the rendezvous, was rewarded by the sight of a lamp, flashing from Jinkins' folboat about 500 metres from the shore. As soon as recognition signals were exchanged, Jinkins and Dodds paddled as close to the shore as the tide would allow. Only when voice recognition had been established between Gort, Alec Chew and the rescue team, did Python emerge from the dense cover of the mosquito- and sandfly-infested mangroves. As the tide was well out, it was not exactly easy going. Within four or five steps they were up to their thighs in mud. With at least 100 metres of black, sticky goo between them and the rescue party's folboats, they did the only thing possible. With the exception of Stan Neil, who was determined to hang onto his weapons by hook or by crook, they threw away their guns and crawled the rest of the way on their stomachs.

The trip back to Australia was routed via the Philippines. *Harder*, which made attacks on destroyers and an aircraft carrier, was subjected to a depth-charge attack, creating excitement Sam Neil thought he could have done without. The evacuees disembarked on 21 June at Darwin to continue the journey to Melbourne by train, where they received an unexpectedly warm welcome. Waiting at Spencer Street Railway Station was a reception committee composed of colleagues, overjoyed by their safe return, and smug SRD chiefs who felt that Python had vindicated their faith in special operations.

Three men had been lost and much of Python's shipping intelligence simply duplicated information decoded from intercepted Japanese signals, but SRD hierarchy still proclaimed the mission an outstanding success. They even considered Python's discovery in a positive light. With Allied submarines homing in on enemy shipping with uncanny accuracy, they thought the Japanese would assume the information had come via Python and not realise that their codes had been compromised. Chester, however, felt the loss of his men keenly and, consequently, it was probably just as well that he had no knowledge of what had unfolded in Borneo.

The Japanese, in pursuit of Python, inevitably uncovered some of Gort's agents. Chin En Sung, also known as Michael Chan, was captured and imprisoned and took his own life at Lahad Datu Gaol on 20 April. His brother, En Fu, was beaten to death ten days later. Police boy Samudi who, like many of those forced to work for the Japanese had maintained his loyalty to the British, was shot dead on Tungku Mountain in the same month, while his colleague, Abok, after a lengthy period in Kempei-tai custody, was shot at Lahad Datu. Fortunately, other key agents in the area, Yan Chepong, Chong Fatt, Floranzia Fernandez, Ismail bin Andan and the Tungku village headman, Pangalima Buaya, managed to evade detection.

Lim Fatt did not have the same good fortune. After he left Gort on 15 February he reached the west coast safely on 2 March, confident of obtaining a boat for Python. With 300 rounds of ammunition and a .45 pistol, given to him by Saurez, he had also been confident of continuing the struggle until the arms, promised by Gort, arrived. On 28 March, unaware that Python was on the run, he had dispatched a message to the east, giving an up-to-date report. He asked for pistols to replace those surrendered to the Japanese, and reminded his Australian friends to bring plenty of side-arms, hand grenades and sub-machine guns, not only to re-arm the resistance fighters but also to bring the tribespeople on side. His exhortations for urgent assistance and for quinine, which was now costing $30 an ounce, were not received in time to save him, or any of his compatriots. As his money ran out, Lim was forced to retreat to Bayau, near Tuaran, where he was murdered and robbed of his remaining funds by the village headman on 6 April.

In their search for Lim Fatt, the Japanese had offered a reward of $5000 for his capture and, convinced that the Suluks were harbouring him, had systematically wiped out entire communities and burnt their villages to the ground. No one was spared, not mothers with babes in arms, not tiny children, not old people. On the mainland the civilians, fearing further retaliation, took to the hills but, betrayed by collaborators, they were hunted down and either massacred, beheaded or hanged.

The Sandakan Kempai-tai had meanwhile caught both McKenzie and Rudwick. They had moved away from their post guarding the track to the wireless station, evidently in search of food. McKenzie, armed with a sub-machine gun, and Rudwick, following behind with a pistol, had been spotted by collaborators and the search party set up a successful ambush. Rudwick, shot in the leg, and McKenzie were taken to Kempei-tai headquarters at Sandakan for interrogation. They were incarcerated with Brandis in the cells beneath the headquarters building and, as all three were suffering from dysentery and fever, they had no hope of resisting the finely-honed investigative techniques of the Kempei-tai. Using a combination of starvation and severe physical torture, carried out largely by a thug named Owara, chief interrogator Warrant Officer Kuroda Shintaro had gradually extracted the information. As he spoke no English, he was assisted in his work by interpreters Mizouchi Shinegobu, who had received only six weeks' English language instruction, and Miura and Ozawa, who had helped falsely incriminate Matthews, Taylor and Wells. The prisoners had no hope of talking their way out of their predicament for McKenzie had been found in possession of a black-covered note book. Measuring about 6 centimetres by 12 centimetres it contained details — tonnage, direction, speed, date and time — of all ships observed moving up and down the Sibutu Channel, many of which had been torpedoed subsequently by American submarines. Having already discovered Python's wireless transmission station and captured some of the equipment, the secret police did not need McKenzie's confession. There was no doubt whatsoever why the three men had entered Borneo — espionage.

McKenzie's book showed, too, that the local people had been cooperating. The Kempei-tai were now convinced that the Sandakan underground, and all those involved in the Sandakan Incident, were part of a highly-organised spy ring, so well advanced that it even involved the infiltration of special agents from Australia. Certain that, if plans were underway to invade the east coast, the POWs at the airfield would become involved, the Japanese High Command took immediate action. To ensure that the prisoners would not be able to take part in any invasion, they permanently cut back the rice ration.

The Kempei-tai were feeling extremely pleased with themselves. Brandis' capture, which coincided with the Kuching trials of those arrested over the Sandakan Incident, had been well timed. As soon as Brandis had confessed, the Kempei-tai knew they had been right about the guilt of those involved in the underground. Consequently, it had been with a great deal of satisfaction that at the end of February, three weeks after Brandis' confession, they had brought Matthews, Wells, Weynton and the major civilian conspirators to trial.

The re-interrogations of the Sandakan conspirators held in the Kuching Gaol had commenced about mid-November and continued, spasmodically, until February, by which time the chief prosecutor found either that there was no charge to answer (as in the case of Private Lander who was released on 23 January) or amassed sufficient evidence to guarantee a conviction. The trials, which had begun on 3 February, generally lasted less than one hour and were quite unlike those conducted in any Western court room. First, there was an automatic assumption of guilt, not innocence. Second, the charges were dove-tailed to suit the evidence by a senior legal officer, whose versatility was such he could double as a prosecutor or judge. Third, the penalty was decided upon well before the trial. Although there was a prosecutor to present the case, and a panel of judges to hand down the pre-ordained verdict, there was no defence counsel.

The venue for the Kuching hearings was the art room in the teaching block of the Roman Catholic Convent, a low brick building forming an annex to the main structure, chosen because it had a raised dais. The first of the Sandakan defendants to appear in this court were Doctor Taylor, Gerald Mavor, Mrs Cohen and some of those facing minor charges. Mrs Cohen, who had been kept in solitary confinement in Sandakan, was fined and sent home. Convicted because of the deliberate mistranslations of Ozawa, Taylor and Mavor were sentenced to fifteen years in Outram Road Gaol, while those accused of lesser crimes, including POWs Blain, James, Graham, Stan Davis and Martin, received sentences ranging from eighteen months to three years. Sapper Ted Keating, who was to be tried for passing letters and plotting to escape, did not reach the court room. Already severely crippled by the huge tropical ulcer on his leg, he had come down with dysentery on the way to Kuching. He received no treatment, other than two or three vitamin tablets, and died in gaol from the combined effects of dysentery, beriberi and general debilitation on 11 February.

As the hearings continued, each of the accused was found guilty, receiving prison terms ranging from one year (in the case of the Goh brothers, Dr Laband and others) to five years for Jakariah and his fisherman friend Sidek. Gordon Weynton, tried with Rickards, Small, Mills and McDonough on 26 February, was found guilty of spreading rumours and violating POW regulations. He received ten years. McDonough, saved from a much longer sentence by the insistence of Wells and Weynton that the chemicals he had obtained had nothing to do with the wireless, received six months, while Rickards, Mills and Small faced terms of six, two years and eighteen months respectively. No one brought to trial was acquitted, not even Major Rice-Oxley, who was not even in Sandakan at the time of the arrests. The Japanese had discovered he had been a major player prior to his removal to Kuching and he too was dragged before the court and sentenced to one year's gaol.

By 29 February, there were only five Australians and the most prominent members of the Sandakan assistance group left. The prisoners, like those who had been tried before them, were to face special and very severe forms of 'gunritsu kaigi' (a court martial reserved for POWs and civilians in occupied zones). The POWs were tried first and, as Matthews and Wells were by far the most important of the white prisoners, the gallery at the back of the room held a number of interested and high-ranking onlookers.

Seated at the bench were the same officers who had presided over the trials of Taylor and Weynton. Heading the tribunal was the Chief Judge, Lieutenant-Colonel Egami Sobei, from Borneo Headquarters. On either side of him were Major Nishihara Shuji and Captain Tsutsui Yoichi, also from Headquarters staff. Presenting the case on behalf of the 37th Army's Lieutenant-General Yamawaki Masataka, the same general who had been guest of honour at the opening of the aerodrome, was 33-year-old lawyer Watanabe Haruo who, on this occasion, had opted for the role of prosecutor. It had been Watanabe, in his capacity as a legal officer, who had assessed the evidence, framed the charges, prepared the case for trial and obtained the signed 'confessions' which would form the bulk of the prosecution's evidence. He had already advised the general of the charges and an appropriate punishment. One judge, at least, would not have to concentrate on the proceedings. Major Nishihara, who had been well briefed by Watanabe, had already seen all of the evidence. He had also selected the judges. During the hearing, the prosecutor was assisted by the court secretary, Ishikawa Takeo, who recorded the proceedings and presented documented evidence when required. The remaining officials were all Formosan civilians — Interpreter Sumaga and two guards named Ino and Kusata. Major Suga, being in Kuching and The Commandants of all the Borneos, was present as a spectator.

At about 9.00am the five accused, all handcuffed, were marched into court. While McMillan and Roffey were accused of violating POW regulations with their extra-curricular wood gathering activities, and Stevens, Mo Davis's mate, faced the additional charge of spreading rumours, Matthews and Wells were on trial for their lives. Although they had not been informed of the wording of the offences — espionage, rebellion, violation of prisoner of war regulations and the spreading of rumours — they had been made aware that they were facing capital charges and that the outlook was not at all bright.

Once the preliminaries were over — name, age, unit, rank and place of birth — the charges, in detail, were read out in Japanese by the prosecutor, who then tabled the evidence and formally demanded that the trial proceed. At this point the so-called Chief Judge handed over to the well-briefed Major Nishihara, who would ask all the questions. Matthews, on behalf of the defendants, now asked for legal representation. His request was denied, citing regulations. The prisoners were then asked, through the services of the almost unintelligible interpreter, whether the charges were correct. Wells, for one, indicated that they were not, but his answer was translated by Sumaga into the affirmative. The prisoners were asked how they pleaded. According to the court record, all five Australians pleaded guilty as charged. According to Wells, they did not.

The acting chief judge now assumed the role of prosecutor by presenting further evidence — the signed 'confessions', a pistol, ammunition, the maps, the note book and the transmitter, which the Japanese believed to be a receiver. Wells, realising that a wireless expert had been called to testify, felt he was doomed. He need not have worried — the expert witness did not realise the 'receiver' was actually a transmitter.

Once Major Nishihara, the acting chief judge, had presented the case for the prosecution he asked Watanabe, the prosecutor, for his opinion about the evidence submitted and whether the charges against the prisoners could be upheld. As Watanabe knew the evidence backwards, having prepared it himself, and as the prisoners had allegedly pleaded guilty, he had no problem in giving his opinion.

> *Matthews: Guilty*
> *Wells: Guilty*
> *Stevens: Guilty*
> *Roffey: Guilty*
> *McMillan: Guilty*

As the charges had been proven, Watanabe announced that all would be punished according to Japanese law. Furthermore, as the trial had been held under special wartime regulations, appeals were not permissible. It was now that The

Commandants of all the Borneos stepped forward. Apparently concerned that the trial should stand up to international scrutiny, he appealed to the court for lenient sentences and to abide by International Law which, as Japan had failed to ratify the Geneva Convention, was that according to the Hague Convention of 1907.

The proceedings, which had taken only 40 minutes, were over. The Australians had scarcely understood a word. All that remained was for the tribunal to decide upon the sentences. As the judges evidently wanted to leave this until after the civilians had been tried, the prisoners were taken back to the gaol for sentencing at a later date.

The following day, 1 March, the final batch of civilians appeared before the court. Unlike the POWs' court martial, which was the court's interpretation of Japanese Law, this hearing concerned itself with the interpretation of the regulations and orders made by the commanding general, in this case General Tarauchi Juichi of the South Seas Expeditionary Army, based in Saigon. Apart from this distinction, and the use of interpreter Hanad, who spoke Malay, rather than Sugama, the proceedings and the court members were virtually the same. The trial, which involved a large number of defendants, lasted about two hours. All but eight were given terms of imprisonment to be served in various detention centres throughout Borneo.

Sergeant-Major Yusup, who had been attending an instruction course in Kuching when arrested, was given fifteen years — the severity probably due to the discovery in his house of a pencil drawing of Matthews as well as pictures of Great Britain's King, Queen and Winston Churchill. Sergeant-Major Yangsalang and Damudaran, the gaol official, received fifteen years. Salleh the watchman and hospital dresser Peter Raymond were sentenced to twelve years, while Apostol and Ng Ho Kong received ten, Inspector Guriaman and Sini eight, Dick Majinal seven, Paddy Funk six and his brother Johnny and Chan (Ah) Ping, four. The other defendants, Jemadur Ojaga Singh, whose broken elbow was still unset, Sergeant Abin, Ernesto Lagan, Heng Joo Ming, Wong Mu Sing, Alex Funk, Felix Adzcona Junior and Matusup bin Gungau, were remanded until the next day.

Major Suga paid Matthews and Wells a visit in gaol that night and brought them each a banana as a gift, as well as a copy of *Tokyo Ichinichi*, Tokyo's daily newspaper, with their photographs featured on the front page. They knew then that they would be punished severely. The following morning, as they were marched along the street handcuffed together, Matthews turned to his young companion and said, 'Rod, you'll get home. Give my love to Lorna and to my son.' To which Wells quietly but firmly replied, 'I won't be going home. I'll be with you.'

As they entered the courtroom, they saw the eight civilians, remanded overnight and who had just been sentenced. Some were weeping bitterly. Those who were not drew their fingers across their throats to indicate that they were to be executed. As the five Australians entered the court, Wells noticed Suga in the gallery. He turned to face him but The Commandants of all the Borneos could not bring himself to look the young lieutenant in the eye.

It was now the turn of Lieutenant-Colonel Egami, who had reclaimed his role as Chief Judge, to take centre stage. Reading a long screed, which was later translated into reasonably clear English, he recounted the many sins of the accused, including 'having a hostile feeling against Japan and dislike for being a prisoner'. When Egami finally finished his dissertation, Wells steeled himself for the pronouncement.

> *Captain Lionel John Matthews: Death by firing squad.*
> *Lieutenant Roderick Graham Wells: Twelve years solitary confinement with hard labour.*
> *Sergeant Alfred Stevens: Six years penal servitude.*
> *Corporals McMillan and Roffey: Eighteen months penal servitude.*

Wells, who had been expecting the death sentence, was stunned. As they left the courtroom, Matthews had time or a few private words with Wells, who promised to deliver his messages to his family. Realising they were about to be parted, Stevens then turned to Matthews and asked, 'Do you mind if I shake hands with you?' In a clear voice that betrayed no hint of a tremor, Matthews enquired, 'Any particular reason, Steve?' 'Just in case we don't meet again', he replied. Displaying that calm, inner strength that would prompt Dr Taylor to describe him as 'Christ-like' and his King to confer upon him a posthumous George Cross for Gallantry, Matthews answered, 'Oh, we'll meet again, don't worry about that, and if we ever get back into action, Steve, the first man I'll have with me is you.'

As they took him away to his place of execution, bundled into the back of a prison van with the eight condemned civilians, Lionel Matthews showed that even in the face of death he had lost none of his courage or defiance. 'Keep your chins up boys', he shouted through the grill. 'What the Japs do to me doesn't matter. They can't win.'

That night, at the Kuching camp, a lone piper played *The Lament*.

Chapter Nine
'FOR THE DURATION'

Mo Davis knew something terrible was about to happen. A convoy of three Japanese staff cars, a van and a black prison vehicle had just passed, and the sight of the deathly white knuckles clutching at the wire mesh had been enough to send a shiver up his spine. They disappeared down the road, past the civilian cemetery where Mo was heading, to a small clearing in an isolated patch of jungle near the aerodrome. In the middle of the cleared area was a long pit along which, at roughly 3-metre intervals, were nine tall, stout, wooden posts, each surmounted by a horizontal beam to form a cross. While a nine-man firing squad, under the command of Sigimata Tadachi readied itself, the prisoners were tied securely to the posts and a mark placed in the centre of their foreheads.

Over to one side were Major Suga, Judge Nishihara, prosecutor Watanabe Haruo and Lieutenant Nagita Toru, the doctor. Watanabe watched Sigimata, the rifleman standing in front of Matthews, as he took aim. Just as he was about to fire, the Australian, who had refused a blindfold, shouted, 'My King and God forever. My King and God forever.' Sigimata's first shot hit Lionel Matthews between the eyes, killing him instantly. Other shots merely ensured he was dead, a fact that was confirmed by Nagita who examined the corpse and signed the death certificate. The other eight victims were proclaimed dead and taken down and buried in the pit, while Matthews' body, now wrapped in a blanket, was placed in a rough wooden coffin and taken immediately to the Kuching Civil Cemetery, near St Catherine's Church, for interment.

The Japanese had come mid-morning to the British ORs' camp looking for a grave-digging detail, a job usually performed by British prisoners. When Mo, who by this time was fairly fluent in Japanese, discovered that the grave was for an Australian, he asked the guards to allow him, Hilton Risley, Sid Outram and the Kent brothers, along with four Australian ORs captured in Java (Private Fraser, Dickie Rixon, Gil Gunning and Keith Simpson) to carry out the task. The burial detail had been escorted under guard to the cemetery where they were joined by Colonel Walsh, Matthews' commanding officer Major Johnstone, Captain Rowell, Lieutenant Tony White from Mo's battalion and two of Matthews' junior officers, Lieutenants Ewin and Esler. While the officers obviously guessed the identity of the deceased, it was some time before Mo and his mates, who had been in Kuching at the time of the Sandakan Incident, knew anything other than it was an Australian officer. When Mo asked Suga he refused to divulge the name, saying only that it was an officer and that he had been 'warui tomago' — a 'bad egg'.

After about thirty minutes or so the van drew up. Watched by the officers and the officiating chaplain, Padre Hawthorne from the civilian camp, Mo and Sid retrieved the coffin with the assistance of the Kent brothers, who scrambled into the back of the vehicle. As the pallbearers lifted the coffin up they all noticed that the planks on the underside were covered with congealing blood, leading them to believe that whoever it was had been beheaded. This assumption was given even more credence later when two Franciscan monks, neither of whom had been near the killing ground, circulated a story that Matthews and the others had been executed by the sword.

Rod Wells, now back in gaol awaiting transfer to Outram Road, had heard the shots. Although he knew he was fortunate to be alive, he did not know just how close he had come to joining Matthews. When the tribunal had adjourned to discuss his fate, they had all agreed the death penalty was the appropriate punishment. However, before an execution could be carried out it had to be approved by the Southern Army Chief in Saigon. General Yamawaki had dispatched a signal to his superiors requesting authorisation to execute two European soldiers and eight native civilians. The answer, a mere formality, was not long in coming. However, permission had been granted to execute only one European. The judges therefore agreed that Matthews, the senior officer, should be the one to die. Years later the reason for Wells' unexpected reprieve became known. Saigon had sanctioned the executions as requested, but the Japanese cipher clerk in Borneo had typed 1 in place of 2. Roderick Wells owed his life to a typographical error.

The prisoners back at the Sandakan camp knew nothing about the Kuching trials, Matthews' death, the failure of the Jesselton rebellion or the capture of the Python men, but they had felt the consequences — ration cuts every time there was an 'incident'. And every time there was a cut, the prisoners in each hut watched those distributing the food even more closely. It was nerve-wracking for those elected by their hut-mates to supervise the food distribution. Although they had a variety of different-sized tins, nailed to bits of wood, to use as scoops, they sometimes miscalculated, forcing a recall from those who had been served so that the tail-enders could receive their fair share. As this was never a popular move, the food handlers tried to give less, rather than more, to avoid a shortfall. Any surplus, known as 'lagi', the Malay word for 'more', was then distributed by means of a lagi board — a piece of wood on which the names of the huts' occupants had been burnt with a piece of hot wire. Beside each name was a small hole, into which a peg was inserted to keep track of who had last received the lagi. The method ensured that everyone, sooner or later, received a second helping.

In June a further rice cut was ordered by General Yamawaki, not as punishment, but because he assumed that as the Americans controlled the sea lanes, rice deliveries from Kuching would soon cease — which they did, the following month. Tapioca was substituted and, while the vegetable ration was still reasonable and there was an occasional dugong, meat and fish were a rarity, even though the POWs raised a small number of pigs in a sty outside the wire near Sticpewich's carpentry hut. The pigs could only be butchered if Hoshijima gave his approval — a favour restricted to Japanese holidays and festivals.

The ever-diminishing food supply may have encouraged another escape. Sometime in the first half of 1944 two more Australians left the camp. They made their way to Nonoyan, north of Sandakan Bay, where they were helped by Hadji Manso. Unfortunately, Ali bin Omar, a Kempei-tai agent, reported that Hadji was hiding them and while the Australians were able to flee, their benefactor had been taken into custody and had not been seen since. The British also lost some of their men, though not through escaping. In June Hoshijima received orders to transfer 99 rank and file and one British officer to Labuan Island on the west coast, where an airfield was being constructed to defend a fleet anchorage planned for Brunei Bay. The working party, accompanied by Captain Nagai, 57 regular soldiers and sixteen guards, arrived on 16 June. The POWs were accommodated in a compound in the grounds of the Victoria Golf Club, near the harbour. Two months later, on 15 August, they were joined by a party of 200 from Kuching, many of whom, including their commanding officer, Captain Campbell of the RAMC, had come from Dahan, about 32 kilometres to the south of the main camp. While most at Labuan were British, there were five Australians: Joey Crome and 'Henry' Ford, two of the four Dead Enders who had left Sandakan with Mo Davis in June 1943, E Force provost Bill Geelan, who had been off-loaded in Kuching, B Force's Alex Adams, who had enlisted as Alex White and, for some reason, had been sent back to Kuching, and Private Ken Radcliffe, of the 2/2 Pioneers, who had been captured in Java. Already at Labuan was another member of the AIF, Aubrey Zinn, who had made the transfer with the Sandakan group.

Back at Sandakan, where the Japanese expected work at the 'drome to continue at the same rate, the reduced rations were beginning to affect the prisoners' health, although the death rate did not rise above one death per month in the Australian camp and slowed in the British camp. However, conditions were deteriorating. As more and more cables and pipes were removed to the Japanese barracks, supplies of electricity and water to the Australian camp had finally ceased, forcing the men to collect rain water for drinking purposes or boil up buckets of water hauled from the creeks and the pond near the boiler house. Those who wanted to bathe had to do so in the swamp which was by now dangerously polluted. The latrine buckets had rotted away and the men were forced to dig pit latrines which, when full, had to be emptied by hand as the Japanese refused to allow any more pits to be dug. The sullage was ladled onto the tapioca patch or dumped on the swampy land at the bottom of the camp, leading to a dramatic upsurge in the number of dysentery cases and skin infections. The outbreak within the camp was controlled with hastily-issued sulphanilamide drugs, and the Japanese protected themselves from contamination by wearing masks and immersing their feet (boots and all) in a disinfectant bath at the camp gate. However, there was nothing much that could be done to prevent the bare-footed gardeners, most of whom had tropical ulcers, from being infected.

In an effort to keep the infection and the ulcers under control, some prisoners carved syringes from wood, which the medical orderlies used to remove the pus. The dead flesh was then cut away with nail scissors or scraped out with a sharpened spoon, and the wound painted with corrosive copper sulphate solution or, for the lucky few, acriflavin. When supplies of these ran out, Nelson Short and other sufferers had their ulcers dabbed with hydrochloric acid, which ate into both the dead and living tissues and was even more painful than the copper sulphate. Some of the ulcers were so large that entire leg bones were exposed, yet the acid swab was the only treatment available, other than amputation which, under the circumstances, generally proved fatal.

As the Japanese faced the unpalatable idea that they might lose the war, concessions at The Eight Mile Camp all but ceased. There were Red Cross medical supplies and drugs, which Sticpewich identified and labelled for the Japanese, but the only issues to the Australians were a few quinine tablets, for the most serious malaria cases, and some gauze bandages. The doctors had brought panniers of equipment and medical supplies from Selarang but most of it had been purloined by Sergeant Fujita, the kitchi guards' medical orderly who, over the protests of the Australian medical staff, helped himself to whatever he wanted, whenever he wanted. While there had been one issue of Red Cross comfort parcels on 7 May, the packages, weighing 20 kilograms when they left the United States, had shrunk considerably. As Tom Burns recorded, the Japanese had removed most of the soap, all the milk and a large number of cigarettes, so that each POW received half a tin of bully beef, half a tin of butter, one third of a tin of meat and vegetables (110 grams), one sixth of a tin of soup, one seventh of a packet of cheese (170 grams), six prunes, one third of a bar of soap, 22 Chesterfield cigarettes, 28 grams of chocolate and eleven cubes of sugar.

There had been three more inward mail deliveries, with one lucky POW receiving 45 items, but only two outward-going. Both were postcards. The first, written sometime after June 1943, would not be received in Australia until mid-1945, the other not until after the war. The initial batch consisted of four brief sentences, typed, plus the salutation and signature, which were written in ink. Once again, because of the standard format, John Barnier's message to his mother was identical to that of Ray Carlson to his wife and children. 'No letter or parcel yet. All are well. Am fit and longing to be with you. Fondest love to all.'

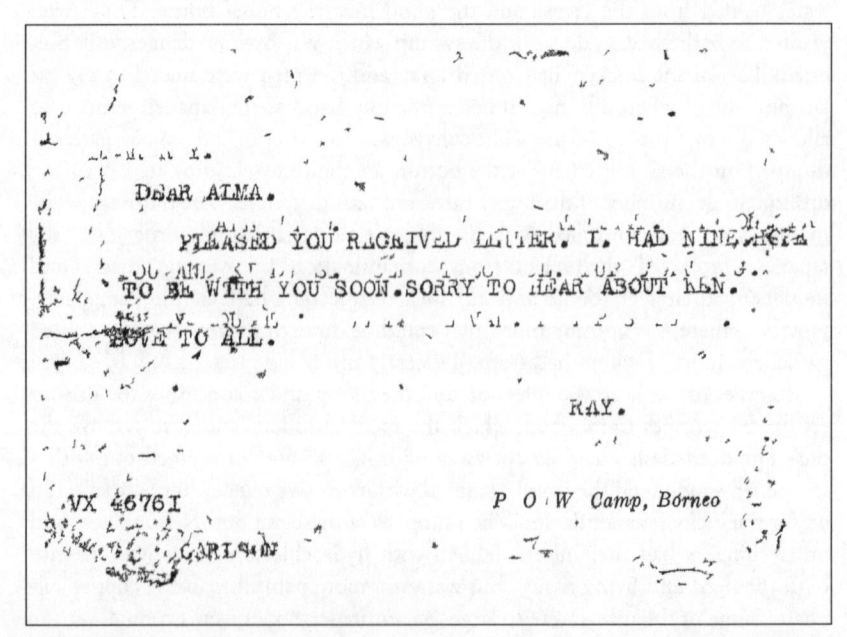

Ray Carlson's last postcard home, showing the 'secret' message typed above the legitimate one.

By the time the next card was sent, Ray Carlson had received mail from Australia — nine items in all. Sadly, one of the letters from his wife contained the news that his eldest son, Ken, had been killed in a motor-bike accident in August 1942. On this occasion the POWs were allowed to send four typed personal sentences rather than set statements, but there was little Ray could say, months after the tragedy, to comfort his wife Alma other than, 'Sorry to hear about Ken'. He did, however, hit upon a most ingenious way to get two messages home to his family. The legitimate one, to Alma, referred to their son's death, his nine letters and the hope that he would see them soon. The other message, to his son Ray, had been typed without a ribbon and was positioned slightly above the first. By holding the card under a strong light, the indentations of the secret message could be revealed. It was typical of Carlson that it ended with the exhortation — 'keep smiling'.

By the latter part of 1944 organised entertainment was non-existent. Prior to this, concerts had been held on a regular basis, despite the transfer of the officers' concert party to Kuching and the appropriation of the piano by Nagai and Moritake for their personal use. There was no shortage of first class talent among the rank and file. Eddie McAppion, the naval volunteer reservist turned army engineer from Western Australia, was never without his harmonica, on which he could play anything from Beethoven to bee-bop. Nelson Short, known throughout the camp for his melodious voice, had not taken any coaxing to put on an impromptu concert, which more often than not included recitations by one of the budding camp poets. Short was also a keen song writer, composing his own words and music, played on a small ukelele, which he had constructed from scrap three-ply timber and signal wire, using part of a comb for the frets and pegs from ground-down glass. Songs about home were his forte and there were more than a few moist eyes when Nelson, strumming away on his ukelele, launched into his favourite:

> *I'm dreaming of Australia,*
> *The land we left behind.*
> *Dreaming of the loved ones*
> *We could always bear in mind.*
> *Although its only fancy*
> *Our hearts within us yearn.*
> *But we'll make up for lost moments*
> *When to Aussie we return.*
>
> *There'd be sailing on the harbour,*
> *The Showboat our first choice.*
> *Or maybe we'd be dancing*
> *Listening to our sweetheart's voice.*
> *Although it's only fancy*
> *Our hearts within us yearn.*
> *Gee we'll make up for lost moments*
> *When to Aussie we return.*

Nelson continued to sing his songs to anyone who would listen until singing, whistling and even clapping were outlawed, but organised Amusing Hours were now a thing of the past. Hoshijima demanded a week's notice for any entertainment and, as the prisoners never knew whether there would even *be* a rest day, let alone when, they gave up trying to organise them. Wrestling and boxing matches which, following the amalgamation of B and E Forces had been conducted on the sports ground over at the Japanese barracks, had also ceased, along with the occasional sports days and cross country runs (around the camp perimeter with guards posted all the way), held to celebrate the Emperor's birthday or some other occasion.

There were no more games of pontoon under Gunboat Simpson's hut, nor two-up schools between the huts. The gambling ban was strictly enforced. Private Alan Taylor, caught playing 'housie-housie' by Kitamura, discovered that the punishment for disobeying this edict was severe. Captain Cook and Lieutenant Good protested but were forced to witness Taylor, aged 36, being subjected to a jujitsu punishment by Kitamura which sent him to hospital for a week. Another of Kitamura's victims was the unfortunate Gerald Fitzgerald, the ambulance man earlier accused of desecrating his shovel. This time he was caught smoking one of his precious Chesterfields on parade. Kitamura broke both his hands with a piece of wood. Even Padre Garland, while attempting to exchange a few words with an English prisoner, was viciously slapped across the face by one of the guards.

More and more men were on the sick list. As the workers had to tend the gardens and collect wood as well as labour on the 'drome, it was a daily struggle to fill the work quota, still 800 plus. Despite the pressing need to enlarge and improve the two runways and extend the road network, a task that required all the man-power available, the guards were as bad as ever. For some obscure reason, Gunners Robert Jillett, James Oliver and Charles Starkey, all of whom were older men, incurred the wrath of a guard while working in a party with Owen Campbell. The punishment — standing at attention in the sun for one and a half hours, without hats.

Aided by the evil Fukishima, who specialised in evicting the sick from the huts, Sergeant Watanabe had taken over the job of organising the working parties, making up the numbers, if necessary, with nursing and hospital staff. To ensure that the workers reported for duty with the minimum of fuss, the Japanese leaned heavily on the Australian senior NCOs who, in turn, leaned heavily on the men. The warrant officers and other senior NCOs, now elevated to the status of 'camp' or, in the case of Sticpewich, 'area' masters, formed the camp committee which controlled the day-to-day running of the camp and, with the exception of one or two, including the RAAF's Warrant Officer John Kinder, had succeeded in making themselves most unpopular. At the 'drome, the guards often took out their anger on those supervising the men, so this task had been delegated to junior NCOs, mostly unfortunate corporals, who lacked the authority to keep the men in line and stand up to the Japanese. Also, those who curried favour with the Japanese no longer bothered to conceal their actions. Lawrie Maddock, who kept the books in a private office and had his own room, generated ill-will by receiving extra rations, quinine and other preferential treatment from Hoshijima, who accompanied him daily to the 'drome, but it was Sergeant Hewitt who stirred up the most resentment. After one especially nasty confrontation, when he asked Moritake to punish POWs who refused to work, Richie Murray vowed to the others on parade that as soon as they boarded the ship back to Australia, Hewitt would get his just desserts.

Cook, the high-profile Sticpewich and the unfortunate Maskey, whose job as interpreter meant he had close contact with Japanese administration, all came in for criticism. Cook's popularity, now that he was in charge of the camp, had plummetted. However, while Cook and Maddock may have had valid reasons to dine and socialise with Hoshijima, Botterill and Short were two of those who failed to appreciate them. All they could see were senior administrative staff, to whom they derisively referred as 'white Japs', as well-fleshed in August of 1944 as they had been in February of 1942.

Sticpewich's elevation to area master had not improved his popularity. He had by now made himself indispensable to the Japanese and, as a consequence, enjoyed many privileges denied to the rest of the camp, including freedom to move around outside the wire, and extra rations, a benefit still extended to his 'technical staff'. While Bill Moxham, Botterill and Short were among those who regarded such a cosy relationship with the enemy as tantamount to collaboration, Sticpewich apparently saw it as a justifiable means to an end. He did appear to be concerned with the welfare of the camp as a whole, however, constantly adding to a growing list of grievances which he presented to Cook, who, because of apathy or outright antagonism from Hoshijima, did not bother to pursue.

When Cook decided to introduce a ruthless code of conduct, the situation really came to a head. Cook believed that the way to counter a lack of respect and ill-discipline was more rigid punishment. Prior to this, except on two occasions when, according to Hoshijima, Major Fraser had asked for one POW refusing to work to be punished, and another senior officer had requested Private Keith Rickerby be confined to Esau for misbehaviour, the men had dealt with misdemeanors themselves. Punishments were generally on a 'hut' basis, but, as a further public humiliation, the offender was forced to cross the muddy pond inside the camp — a signal to the other POWs that he had over-stepped the mark. Sometimes the initial punishment was far too effective. A young soldier who, despite his tearful protestations of innocence, was found guilty of stealing cash, was 'sent to Coventry' by Braithwaite and his mates. Then it was discovered that the real culprit was a rat, of the furry, four-legged variety, which had used the money to make a cosy nest for himself up in the hut rafters. Although the huts' occupants apologised to their unfortunate victim, the psychological damage had been too great. Retreating completely into his shell, he went into such a decline that he gave up the will to live.

In July 1944 Cook, finding himself unable to command the level of respect or obedience he required, embarked upon a new course of action. To Botterill's disgust, he began to report breaches of discipline to Hoshijima and also asked the commandant to build a new and larger punishment cage, capable of accommodating a number of offenders. Measuring a little under 3 metres by 6 metres it was positioned outside the wire near Esau, now reserved for short-term offences or as a 'softening-up' period for longer terms in the larger cage. As Hoshijima had ordered Moritake to crack-down on anyone trying to obtain extra food, neither cage was empty for long.

Sapper Hinchcliff, who was the first to be punished for infringing this rule while working out at the 'drome, was dragged back to camp. He was given the log treatment in the sun for 90 minutes, while the guards beat him. Before being caged, he was kept standing at attention for another two hours in front of the guardhouse, and whenever he relaxed his muscles he was kicked and beaten. He remained in the cage without food for the next seven days, sitting at attention except for a twice-daily visit to the latrines, and at each sentry change, when he was taken out and given a thorough beating by as many as four guards at a time. The only water he had was whatever he could manage to gulp down during the latrine breaks.

One of the next to experience Esau's cramped quarters was Botterill, sentenced to a week's detention by Cook for his alleged involvement in a duck theft. The ducks, which belonged to the officers, were being fattened in a pen near the cinnamon trees and it was only a matter of time before someone stole them. In a well-executed raid, Punchy Donohue and a couple of mates relieved the officers of their livestock while another accomplice, eighteen-year-old Keith Cox, kept watch. When the theft was discovered, an outraged Cook convened an inquiry in his office, assisted by Maddock and Hewitt. Botterill, who looked very much like Cox, was identified as a person lurking near the scene of the crime and was called in for questioning. When asked if he had stolen the ducks, he replied that he had not, but added, in his usual candid fashion, that he had definitely thought about doing so. It was enough for the 'magistrate'. Deeming that he had 'intent to steal', Cook sentenced Botterill to seven days in the cage. Meanwhile, since Botterill held strong views about dobbing, the real culprits went free.

Joining Botterill were Privates Len Annear and the incorrigible James Bowe, troublemakers of the first-order who had been sentenced to 20 days for their latest misdemeanor. It seemed that Annear and Bowe were destined to take up almost permanent residence in the cage. If it were not Hoshijima grabbing them for something, it was Cook. Their 20-day detention was followed by one of 44 and they had scarcely recovered from that when they were in again, this time for six weeks. There was no shortage of accommodation. By September there were three cages in operation — Esau, now on the hill behind the Japanese barracks; Captain Cook's cage opposite the Number 1 guardhouse, and another, of roughly the same size, next to the main guardhouse on the road leading into the Japanese barracks.

Botterill soon found himself in strife again. He agreed to act as 'cockatoo' while Gunners Les Grosvenor and John Holland and a dozen or so others pillaged a large amount of food from the camp's quartermaster's store, which was inside the wire. Although the hut was kept securely locked by the Japanese, the break-in was successful and the food distributed to the sick before all those involved, or thought to be involved, were arrested. Keith and his friend, 'Sticky' Allan Quailey, who was arrested simply because he was Keith's mate, were caged until Hoshijima decided upon a suitable punishment. By the time he had finished his investigation and sentenced Botterill to 40 days, 30 had gone past. They were possibly the hardest 40 days of Botterill's young life. Given neither food nor water for the first three, he was forced to keep on drinking on the fourth until he was ill. The small amount of rice issued on every second day after that was insufficient to sustain life, and Botterill and the others would have starved had it not been for the English cooks assigned to the Japanese guardhouse. Their final task every evening, before they returned to their camp, was to tip the kitchen left-overs and slops into the guard dogs' trough, which was near the cage. They endeavoured to empty the buckets during the cage residents' latrine break, allowing the prisoners, ravenous with hunger, to fight the dogs for the food. The contest was so fierce that on more than one occasion Botterill found himself wresting a bone from the mouth of an equally hungry canine.

The nights in the cage were as miserable as the days. No bedding or clothing other than a 'fondushi' loin cloth, was allowed, while overcrowding was so great that even when they all lay on their sides, four of the seventeen men still had to sit up. No one was permitted to wash or shave but there was compulsory exercise each day — physical jerks accompanied by a bashing so severe it reduced hardened men to tears. Kiyoshima (The Black Panther), Kawakami (The Gold-Toothed-Shin-Kicking-Bastard), Hayashi (Ming the Merciless) and Kunizowa, a bespectacled former schoolteacher known as Euclid, were the principal bashers, along with Kitamura, the jujitsu fiend, whose list of victims now included Captain Daniels, the English medical officer. The Black Panther, who loathed guard duty, was particularly vicious. Not content with sneaking up on prisoners at night and letting fly with the broom handle he always carried, Kioshima hit the caged victims with such gusto that he broke his stick in two. Kawakami, on the other hand, lived up to his alternate name by bringing his victim to his knees with the butt of a rifle and then kicking him in the shins. Ming the Merciless insisted that exercises be performed at top speed, bashing all those who could not keep up before forcing them to stand at attention for up to two hours. Euclid's speciality was to have POWs on the ground and then jump on their backs, giving those not nimble enough to get to their feet a hefty kick in the ribs.

When Botterill was released at the end of the 40 days, he was in an appalling condition — his body thin and wasted, his grimy skin bruised and battered, his hair and beard matted and his hands covered with scabies. The experience did nothing to break his indomitable spirit, nor that of Quailey, who was the product of a similarly tough, working class background. To Murray's dismay, both went under the wire the very next night to forage for sweet potato.

By this time, those stealing vegetable crops from the garden had developed a technique known as 'bandicooting', after the small Australian marsupial which rooted about for food, making it very unpopular with gardeners. Like the bandicoot, the POWs ventured out only at night. However, unlike the bandicoot, they left no trace of their visit. They pulled the entire plant from the soil, lopped off the leafy top and replanted it. A day or two later, when the foliage withered and died, the plant's demise was attributed to natural causes.

Murray, in an effort to curb Botterill's night-time excursions, had been busy cultivating a small patch of kang kong in the water-logged area beyond The Dead End Kids' hut. While kang kong could induce quite severe colic, it grew at a fantastic rate, but not fast enough for Botterill. Despite the extra greens, he was soon back in the cage for leaving the working party at the 'drome to forage for tapioca which, although watery, of poor nutritional value, difficult to digest, and toxic if not properly prepared, did provide temporary relief to a constantly empty stomach. Botterill was spotted by one of the Formosan guards while returning to the 'drome with his booty and given twelve days. On the way back to his hut after his release he was set upon by one of the guards, who gave him such a thrashing he was unable to move from his bed the next day.

Since the completion of the east-west runway in September, all efforts at the 'drome had been concentrated on finishing the north-south. However, with 400 Australians now in hospital, 200 classified as 'no duty' and another 150 employed in essential camp chores, it had become increasingly difficult to supply the 800 workers still needed each day. Despite the hardship, the men hung on, their morale having received an enormous boost shortly after completion of the first strip when, prior to the Allied push into the Philippines, reconnaissance planes were spotted high overhead. When strike aircraft began bombing Sandakan township and the airstrip a fortnight or so later, Hoshijima, fearing that the camp might also become a target, ordered a complete blackout at night. He also had Sticpewich organise a working-bee to make an enormous wooden sign, split into three sections for easy transporation, on which the letters P O W were picked out in white paint on a black background. The sign, measuring 50 by 15 metres was placed on the Japanese sports ground. A sunken area between the POW camp and the barracks, it was not as conspicuous from the air as Hoshijima had supposed. On 30 October when ten P-38 Lightning aircraft attacked the airfield, three planes peeled off from the main formation to straffe the camp. Unfortunately, while the third plane banked and aborted its attack, the two leading aircraft did not see the sign in time.

As the aircraft approached the camp, Braithwaite noticed one of the 'old blokes', fellow artilleryman Gunner Dan Mongan, another 39-liar, out in the open near one of the officers' old huts, which Braithwaite was occupying at the time. Dragging him under the hut, Braithwaite pushed him into a space hollowed out beneath a thick concrete slab which formed the floor of the ablution area. Protected by at least 10 centimetres of concrete and under one of the camp's most strongly built huts, it should have been the safest place in the compound. It wasn't. One of the heavy-calibre, armour piercing bullets, fired from an angle of 45 degrees, entered the sub-floor area. Passing through a solid timber support, a blanket hanging on a clothes line and two more pieces of timber, it hit the concrete floor and ricocheted away, but not before it had knocked out a sizable chunk of concrete, which took off the back of Dan's head. He died later that night, along with another mortally-wounded soldier, Private Clive Thorneycroft of Victoria. Another prisoner had been killed outright. In order to prevent a similar recurrence, Hoshijima ordered the POW sign to be moved immediately to higher, more open ground between the Number 1 and 2 Camps.

Suga, now promoted to the rank of Colonel, was lucky not to have been among the casualties. Visiting Sandakan on one of his six-monthly inspections he had flown back to Kuching at 9.30am, two hours before the Lightnings had made their strike. Bill Moxham observed that The Commandants of all the Borneos had looked decidedly out of sorts during his stay. For a start, there were none of his usual quips, the most memorable of which, delivered on previous occasions to both the Kuching and Sandakan camps, was destined to pass into POW folk lore. 'I am Major Suga', he had said. 'Some of you will probably remember me. I have been here before. I will give you three days' holiday — yesterday, tomorrow [which never came] and today' [for which there were about three hours of daylight left]. He had then added, quite seriously, the admonition that 'you must not try to escape otherwise you will be put in GAOL'.

When it had become apparent that Suga, looking extremely glum as he made his rounds with Hoshijima, was not going to address the camp as usual, Cook had prevailed upon him to say a few words. He invited them, for the first time ever, to sit down while he made an informal speech. Referring to air raids made on the township and airstrip earlier in the month, he assured them, 'What you see now, this bombing, is just the overflow from the Philippines. But you shortly will see our drive start and we will push back, back, back.' With that, he made his exit. The POWs never saw him again.

Some prisoners had taken great risks when the aircraft appeared, especially Padre Garland, who had run out to wave an Australian flag, hidden and kept especially for such an occasion. He was lucky. English prisoners who waved at the planes were killed as a consequence.

As far as the United States Air Force was concerned, the raid on the airfield had been most successful. Ever since the completion of the east-west strip there had been a stream of military aircraft landing and taking off and now 60 planes were destroyed on the ground. For the POWs there was a downside. The Japanese were in no mood to be magnanimous. Consequently the few official medical supplies that had been made available, the quinine and sulpha drugs to combat dysentery outbreaks, stopped. However as Dick Braithwaite, who swapped his watch for thirty quinine tablets, discovered, those with something to trade were still able to get supplies.

In November the ill men, and three of their huts, were moved from the Number 3 camp to the main compound. At first they were accommodated in the old hospital and the huts near the gate but, as time wore on and the numbers increased, accommodation huts were pressed into use. That month the death toll in the Australian camp, which had totalled only thirteen (including the air raid victims) since June, reached eighteen, while the British lost seven. According to the Japanese, numbers at this time stood at 2400 POWs and 3600 civilian labourers. The labourers received 680 grams of rice, 1.8 kilograms of sweet potatoes or 2.7 kilograms of tapioca, 225 grams of fish or meat and 500 grams of green vegetables a day, while the POWs' vegetable supplement had been cut completely in August, giving them little hope of combatting the combined effects of malaria, beriberi, dysentery and malnutrition. With so many on the sick list, the chapel which Botterill and Billy Young had so admired was a luxury that had to go, forcing the chaplains to call the faithful to services under The Big Tree.

In December deaths from malarial menengitis increased dramatically. When the Australian toll reached 35 and the British 21, Hoshijima called a halt to all coffin-making, citing a lack of timber as the reason — the same reason given for discontinuing with the cremations in January that year. Now all bodies were to be stripped and buried straight into the ground. Owen Campbell was one of those given the task of placing the dead, their nakedness covered by blankets or banana leaves, in a make-shift morgue in the elevated space under one end of the hospital/chapel hut until the burial party could deal with them.

In order to preserve some dignity for the naked corpses while transporting them to the cemetery, the burial parties devised a re-usable coffin. The body was laid on a narrow platform made from two 15-centimetre-wide planks, which was placed on a removable base, fastened to the side panels with four catches. Once the coffin was in position over the hole, the catches were released, allowing the body, still on its wooden platform, to be deposited neatly into the grave. Each grave was then identified with a tin marker onto which the relevant details had been etched by the camp's engraver, Dick Braithwaite.

One or two prisoners used these false-bottomed coffins to try and escape — a practice which came to an end when the Japanese discovered the ruse and began checking corpses by pricking the soles of the feet with a bayonet.

While the death toll at Sandakan was escalating it was far worse over on Labuan Island where, between September and December, more than one third of the 100 men who had left Sandakan with Captain Nagai died from malaria, exacerbated by a shortage of food. The compound at Victoria Golf Course had also been bombed, forcing a move away from the harbour to a new site at the 3 mile peg. It was here that Billy Young's mate, 23-year-old Henry Ford, who had volunteered to join the Labuan party in the belief that anywhere had to be better than Kuching, died from a combination of malaria and beriberi on 3 December.

Not all the deaths at Sandakan during this time were attributable to disease or malnutrition. In the case of Private Gordon Barber, the cage was responsible. One night about 20 November, Barber and Signalman Fred Weeks went under the wire, accompanied by Private Arthur Clement, a provost of strapping proportions and strength. Despite the cover provided by the blackout, all three were caught red-handed in the POW garden. Hoshijima called a parade. After giving Cook and all the camp masters, with the exception of Sticpewich and Kinder, a couple of sharp slaps across the face for not being able to control their men, he sentenced the culprits to a lengthy term in the cage. He also announced that in future anyone found outside the wire would be shot.

The three men spent the first five days in Esau, still up behind the barracks and out of sight of the rest of the prisoners. When they were released for transfer to the larger cage five days later, all three had been beaten. Barber, an 'old bloke' who had previously been looked after by Sticpewich with whom he was friendly, was in a bad way. When he went into Esau he weighed 76 kilograms and was in excellent health. When he came out he was considerably thinner and very weak. By this time the large cage near the Number 1 guardhouse had been moved. The new site, directly opposite the main guardhouse, was far worse than the old one, being close to a mosquito-infested swamp. On 8 December, within eleven days of being transferred to this cage, Barber was dead. According to Sticpewich, who saw the body, he weighed no more than 38 kilos. Although Cook was instructed by the camp committee to lodge a protest with Hoshijima over the treatment of the three prisoners, it seems he did not. While this may have been to avoid repercussions, it is more likely that, having just discovered a large-scale theft of food, Cook had not only asked Hoshijima to deal with the culprits but had requested the ringleaders be punished severely.

Although the theft was not detected until early December, it had taken place in November, when eight men — Sergeant Errol Bancroft (2/26th), Corporal Arthur Cross (2/30th), Gunner Norm Hewitt (4th Anti-tank), the 2/19th's Privates Ray Golding and Reg Temple (alias Moore) and that intractable threesome of Annear, Bowe and Donohue, mounted a successful raid on the main Japanese storehouse. It had been a daring undertaking. The White House, as the primary quartermaster's store was known, was outside the wire and only a few metres from the Number 1 guardhouse. After distributing dried fish to Private Noel Brett and other seriously-ill hospital patients, the raiding party had waited for the repercussions. Amazingly, nothing happened. The Japanese were unaware they had been robbed. About two weeks later, shortly after being roughed-up by Hoshijima for not controlling his men, Cook learned that rice and fish purloined from the Japanese store were being consumed in the camp. Cook informed Hoshijima. When a search of the huts revealed other food and stolen goods squirrelled away, Cook demanded that Annear, Bowe, Donohue and company be confined to the cage 'for the duration'.

Botterill was stunned. While Barber, who had died, and Clement and Weeks, both still in the cage, had been sentenced to a long period of detention, not even Hoshijima had handed down a sentence as severe as this. There was no way anyone could survive for an indeterminate period in the cage, especially Cross, aged 35, who was a good ten years older than any of the others. Evidently Hoshijima reached the same conclusion for, while the prisoners were still subjected to ritual beatings, as soon as any one of them became ill he was transferred to the hospital until he recovered. The other men, meantime, made sure that their caged comrades did not starve, bribing the guards to give them food.

At about this time, working parties of 20 men were dispatched to a nearby native garden in order to obtain vegetable supplies for both the garrison troops and the camp. There they were to dig sweet potato and pull tapioca. The locals had been refusing to supply crops in return for 'banana money', and the enforced appropriation of his produce certainly did not meet with the approval of the farmer, who argued violently with the guards. The POWs, however, had no qualms about receiving these stolen goods. After the Japanese had taken their disproportionally large share, there was still enough left for everyone in camp to receive 225 grams which, as the rice ration was down to 130 grams, was not insubstantial. But the extra tapioca ration and the caging of Annear and others did not stop hungry prisoners from seizing every opportunity to scrounge for food. Shortly before Christmas, while he was working down near the boiler house, Private Arthur Cull was caught. Although he tried to run away he was overtaken by Kitamura and Euclid, the current guard commander. Euclid beat Cull, aged 38, with a lawyer cane, before handing him over to Kitamura for jujitsu practice. Battered and bleeding, Cull was brought back to the camp and caged for fourteen days.

Christmas 1944 brought feelings of both elation and despair. The good news was that a heavy bombing raid by Liberator aircraft (B24s) at 11.00am put the airfield out of action. But Christmas dinner, described by Botterill as perhaps the 'best meal' of 1944, was hardly festive, consisting of pork soup and half a 440-gram-sized tin of rice and corn mixed with dried fish. The frugality of the meal was not, however, due to lack of cash on the part of the prisoners, most of whom had accumulated at least 10 dollars each. There was simply nowhere to spend it. The canteen had been defunct since September and trading was no longer permitted with the locals, who, after the Sandakan Incident, were prohibited from coming within 400 metres of any POW. In any case the farmers, as a form of passive resistance, had either retreated into the bush or cut back crop production. By this time the only person allowed to deal with the camp inmates was Goto, the Japanese merchant, and while he did his best, the supplies available for purchase were very limited.

Realising that the POWs, with roughly 20 000 dollars between them, had virtually no chance of spending their money in the foreseeable future, the Japanese 'banked' it for them in the Yokohama Specie Bank. Also, as there was nowhere to spend the money, Hoshijima returned to the Kuching Camp the 25 dollars which Ron Ollis had sent to his brother, John. The accompanying note, written on the inside of a recycled envelope containing the cash, made it clear that life at Kuching was a far cry from that at Sandakan. The officers, who sent their best wishes, were well. They had plenty of reading matter from the well-stocked camp library and Ron had received 20 letters from their mother and Leslye, the girl waiting for him back home. The Japanese administration at Kuching and Sandakan not only showed uncharacteristic compassion by allowing Ron's letters to be delivered, they had also dealt with previous gifts of cash most scrupulously, to the extent of insisting upon signed receipts, which were then returned to the donor.

Hoshijima also authorised an issue of clothing to about half the camp's inmates at the end of December. It was nothing much — either a cotton jacket or pair of trousers, but to those who were down to a ragged fondushi it was as good as Saville Row. Tailors such as Bill McDonald, who could whip up a pair of shorts from just about anything, ensured that most of the camp was by this stage wearing a fantastic array of clothing. Nelson Short, whose trousers had long since fallen apart, was one of those sporting a pair of non-regulation shorts, fashioned from an old kitbag by McDonald.

Although the airstrip was out of commission from the bombings, there was still work to be done. After the Christmas Day raid, 200 of the fitter prisoners were sent to clear up the debris and fill in the bomb craters so that the two undamaged planes, all that were left, could take off. As there were also quite a few partially-buried, unexploded bombs, a small demolition team was formed. Because of his slight build, Botterill was given the task of burrowing around the bomb's casing until he found and exposed the priming mechanism. It was a dangerous task and one in which Hoshijima, who enjoyed watching the explosions, took a great interest. With Murray and the others constantly urging Keith to take care, the commandant, who was standing at the edge of the excavation, inadvertently released the tension by leaning over the hole and shouting, 'Mind the bum, Keith'.

The repair work was a waste of time. Three days later there was another raid of such intensity that the working parties were out until 2.00am trying to fix the damage. The craters were no sooner filled than there was another strike, then another. And with each raid, the Japanese became more ill-tempered. No one was safe, not even Sticpewich. Very late one afternoon Euclid and Sergeant Watanabe arrived at his workshop demanding to know why he and his men were not back inside the compound. Unimpressed by the explanation that he was repairing a watch for Sergeant Itchikowa, Watanabe lunged at Sticpewich, who warded off the blow. The enraged guard then attacked the Australian with rifle butt and boots, knocking out his left incisor tooth. The scuffle ended when Sticpewich, who had grabbed the rifle, promptly handed the weapon back to his aggressor who, to save any further loss of face, immediately walked away. Sticpewich's victory, however, was short-lived. On their return Watanabe paraded the entire technical party outside the guard hut and ordered three of the guards to beat them up.

At 4.00pm on New Year's Day 1945, Noel Brett, one of those for whom the raid on the Japanese storeroom had been made, died. Officially, the cause of death was malaria. Although he was buried in the cemetery, there was no permanent grave marker. It appears that with scrap metal running out and Braithwaite unable to keep pace with the demand, the last Australian to have his grave properly identified was Private Thomas Watson, a 42-year-old ambulanceman from Parramatta, New South Wales, who died from beriberi and malaria on 15 December. Of the 34 Australian POWs who died that month, only three had identifiable graves. The rest, in a scheme devised by Cook, had their details recorded in a burial register and their gravesite marked only with a corresponding number.

Three other Australians who died in Borneo in December and lay in unmarked graves were the Python men, McKenzie, Rudwick and Brandis. Taken in June 1944 to Jesselton where the 37th Army had relocated its headquarters, they were held in Batu Tingi Gaol to await trial as spies. After a trial that was remarkably similar to that of Matthews, all three were found guilty and sentenced to death. On the afternoon of 30 December, blindfolded and bound, they were led up the fifteen wooden stairs to the gaol's gallows, a legacy of the previous British owners. Brandis, swollen up with beriberi, asked where they were being taken but his guide, a local man, replied that he did not know. Shortly after 3.30pm, with Chief Judge Colonel Maeda, Major Nishihara, Lieutenant Nagita, four other members of the judiciary and four Kempei-tai as witnesses, all three were hanged. While the Japanese had been keen to employ what was, to them, a novel method of execution, it would appear that in the case of McKenzie and one other, the cause of death may have been from a blow to the head with a heavy iron bar. Whatever the cause, they had faced their deaths bravely. According to Ahong, one of their escorts, each man had stood firm and erect upon the gallows.

Back at Sandakan, where the increased bombing attacks had forced the Japanese to abandon the airstrip, conditions at the camp had deteriorated dramatically. On 10 January, on Hoshijima's orders, the rice ration ceased. The

Australians were informed that from now on they must rely on the 105 bags which, fortunately, Lieutenant Good had put aside to cover such an emergency. Hoshijima, who had taken up residence at the Wongs' (Pop Wong being still in hiding) to take advantage of the protection offered by the POW sign, ordered that all rice, including the POWs' stockpile, be moved into his basement. According to the commandant's calculations the 105 bags, if consumed at the present rate of 130 grams a day, would last two months. On the assumption that, as they would no longer be expending energy on the 'drome it would be possible to subsist on less food, Good decided to eke out the supply longer, if possible. He set the daily quota at 70 grams — less than one tenth of the 1942 allowance.

Later that month, Dr Yamamoto arrived from Kuching, bringing with him five jars of atebrine, three jars of quinine (enough to give each prisoner one tablet each) and a small box of bandages. After observing the physical condition of the prisoners he informed Dr Picone that the best way to overcome beriberi was by more exercise and hard work. He was, apparently, unaware that the prisoners were receiving plenty of both. While work had now ceased on the 'drome, all those who could get to their feet were lined up by Fukishima each day and sent out to spread sullage, collect wood or forage for tapioca roots, sometimes from as far away as 16 kilometres. Only the truly bedridden were exempt.

On Australia Day 1945 Dick Braithwaite was one of those sent out on a tapioca party. After spending an exhausting morning pulling up roots by hand, the prisoners were ordered to bundle them into 40-kilo bags and carry them to the nearest road, about 3 kilometres away over quite rough terrain. Many of the men were ill. One, in particular, was so weak that once they were out of sight of the guards Braithwaite began a shuttle service to relieve him of his burden. As he moved back and forth along the track the Australian noticed a young Chinese farmer sawing wood near his house but, with Kiyoshima lurking nearby, studiously ignored him. As Braithwaite trudged past with his last load, his twelfth, the farmer handed him some native tobacco and indicated that he would like some tapioca roots in return. Unfortunately for both Braithwaite and the farmer, Kiyoshima was only a few metres away. Letting out a yell, he chased the Chinese down to the road, where he was caught and rifle-butted into submission. When Braithwaite turned up with his load he found Kiyoshima, Horijima and Tornika waiting for him. After belting him with rifle butts, kicking and threatening to shoot him, they were about to tie both men to the back of a truck and haul them the 8 kilometres back to camp when Warrant Officer Murozumi rode up on his bicycle.

Murozumi, who had been over-indulging in saki, was feeling in the mood for some fun. Forcing the farmer to his knees, Murozumi unsheathed his sword. After a few practice swipes, he placed the blade against the farmer 's neck, raised it high in the air and brought it down, cackling with laughter as he stopped just short of the vertebrae. He repeated the pantomime several times, spurred on by the sight of a tiny Chinese woman, apparently the victim's mother, tears streaming down her face, on her knees begging for mercy. Eventually tiring of the game, he turned to Braithwaite and asked if he had ever been in Esau, a question which filled the prisoner with dread, before ordering him to stand at attention until the last truck had been loaded — a process which was not completed until 10.00pm.

When they arrived back at camp, Braithwaite's companions ignored his advice that this would not be a good day to try and smuggle purloined tapioca past the guards. Believing that, as it was so late, the guards would not bother with a search, they decided to risk it. Unfortunately, when lanterns were produced by the sentries it became obvious that they were wrong. With Murozumi's attention focussed on the unfortunate tapioca smugglers, Braithwaite scuttled through the gate. His appearance back in camp created a minor sensation. According to those who had returned earlier, Dick Braithwaite had been beaten to death. Braithwaite, however, did not share in the general elation. Worried that once Murozumi had dealt with the tapioca smugglers he would refocus on him, Braithwaite visited Cook to seek his support and advice. Cook's response was brief and to the point. 'What do you expect me to do about it?' he asked. 'You got yourself into this and you'll get yourself out of it.'

Fortunately Murozumi's attention was diverted. Hoshijima had announced that 500 of the fittest prisoners, British and Australian, were to be moved to another destination. Tom Burns, confined to hospital, knew he would not be one of them. With so many sick, and so little food, he expected that for himself and many others, this Australia Day might well be their last. There were only two meals a day and the death toll in the Australian camp stood at 65 for the month and rising steadily each day. It was not to be wondered that Burns, sick in body and in spirit, had all but given up hope. It had been more than eighteen months now since the officers had escaped from Berhala. Apart from the air raids, there had been no indication that anyone on the outside was aware that the camp even existed, let alone that over 2000 Allied prisoners were dead or dying of starvation and disease. While there was not a prisoner in camp who did not fantasise of rescue and liberation, Tom and the other realists accepted that battalions of sun-bronzed Australian soldiers suddenly arriving on the scene was pretty much a pipe dream. With the airstrip obviously out of commission why would anyone think twice about Sandakan? Why would anyone give a damn about the POW camp?

For once, the rationalists were wrong. A number of people not only knew where the prisoners were, they were also very concerned. One, a young Australian army corporal, was very concerned indeed. He was in Nadzab, New Guinea, and his name was Paul Muir.

Chapter Ten
A PLAN EVOLVES

The AIF's Paul Muir was one of the few people outside the Allied Intelligence Bureau aware that small, specialised intelligence parties operated behind enemy lines. Since his secondment in 1943 to the RAAF's Number 4 Tactical Reconnaissance Squadron at Nadzab, one of Muir's tasks had been to plot information coming from agents under AIB's control — Coastwatchers, NEFIS (the Dutch undercover organisation) and SIA (Secret Intelligence Australia). He was not senior enough to know why this information was transmitted but he had observed that, generally, an Allied operation of some kind evolved at a later date.

In late December 1944 he had been called into the office of his commanding officer, Major Roderick O'Loan, for a 'Top Secret' briefing. Handing Muir a large scale map of the northern part of Borneo, O'Loan had instructed him to mark on it information which would soon be arriving from an AIB field agent there. Security, O'Loan stressed, was of paramount importance. The task was to be carried out in absolute secrecy at night and on no account was he to acknowledge the existence of the map or the contents of the signals to anyone, no matter how high in rank. Muir immediately set about finding a secure place to keep his map. He mounted it onto stiff cardboard and made a false compartment between two metal filing boxes in the orderly tent, enabling him to access it easily and, if necessary, hide it quickly.

It was not until the end of January that the first signals were passed to him from the cipher room. They were short and spasmodic, with a minimum of words — a sign that the agent was operating in the field and observing strict security.

The messages related to a POW camp at a place called Sandakan. He learned there was a large number of Allied soldiers imprisoned there, many from 8th Division units. Some had been moved and others were either dead or dying. As the days passed and more data came in about the movement of the POWs, some of whom were reported to have been murdered, Muir found it impossible to maintain his usual detachment. Was his good friend, Gunner Bill Thompson of the 2/15th Field Regiment among this group? However, although he became increasingly disturbed by the nature of the signals, Muir could do nothing more than record the progress of the POW column which appeared to be heading for Jesselton along a difficult and mountainous jungle track.

At the end of February, when the transmissions suddenly ceased, Muir assumed that the agent had met with foul play. Fretting about the fate of his countrymen he remarked to his commanding officer that surely a commando raid or some similar kind of operation could be mounted to assist the POWs. He was relieved when O'Loan intimated that such a plan was in train.

The forward Allied base was now operating from Morotai, an island in the

Halmahera group, captured by American troops the previous September. As it was within easy range of the Borneo coast, and the Americans were re-occupying the Philippines, Muir hoped that someone in AIB or General Headquarters had already done something positive about the situation. There was no doubt that the information was reliable. Some must even have come from a contact inside the camp itself, while details on the movement of the prisoners, collected by an unnamed Chinese, was so specific it must be originating from local field agents.

Muir had no idea of the identity of the signaller or his unit but there were only two groups operating in the Borneo area at that time — Saurez's men, who did not come under the control of, or report to, AIB, and a NEFIS party, code-named Apple, which did. Inserted onto the mainland by Catalina flying-boat from AIB's Morotai base on 13 January, Lieutenant O. Dijber and his Apple team had been instructed to collect intelligence prior to a planned Allied invasion of Tarakan, the oil-producing island to the south of Sandakan. Unfortunately, because of Japanese activity about ten days after their arrival, the party had been forced to move on. While they were unable to obtain much useful information about Tarakan, the mission was not a complete failure. Obeying an instruction issued on 29 December for AIB parties in Borneo to report all possible information, Dijber had continued to collect and transmit intelligence while awaiting his extraction at the end of February.

Whoever was sending the signals to Muir had tapped into the local intelligence network established by Python in 1943. Its principal agent was Mr B. S. Willie, Beluran's District officer, who was of Dusan and European parentage and an old friend of Gort Chester. He lived at Sapi on the Labuk River and was known to Gort as 'Sandshoe Willie', because of his habit of wearing on his feet only latex slip-on shoes. Sandshoe Willie, highly reliable and fiercely anti-Japanese, was one of only two agents in the area capable of collecting and delivering intelligence of the calibre being processed by Muir. The other one was Sin Yen, a Chinese from Sandakan, who had contacts with the local police, and through them, a link to the POWs.

At about this time Owen Campbell was out gathering wood near the Sibuga River, when he met a secret agent who had infiltrated the Sandakan area. Campbell, wishing to defecate, had been given permission to move away from the main party, provided he kept in sight of the guard. He had been scooping out a small hole about 100 metres away when a disembodied voice, speaking in English, told him to remain calm and to make no sudden move. Campbell was astonished to see a European soldier, dressed in jungle greens and beret and holding a type of sub-machine gun which he had never seen before, move into his line of sight from behind some bushes.

The mysterious figure, giving no clues to his identity, other than confirming he was not American, began to quiz Campbell about the number of able-bodied prisoners in camp. Campbell replied that several hundred had been moved and many were sick or dying, but he thought they could rake up about 400 fit men from the Australian compound. The soldier told him to obtain a firm figure from his commanding officer and he would return within a day or two, then melted back into the undergrowth. Campbell never saw him again. He obtained the necessary information from Dr Picone, but the soldier failed to keep the rendezvous. Who this visitor was, or where he came from, is still not known. What is known is that the only white Allied personnel operating in Borneo at that time were the Apple party, who wore jungle greens, berets and carried Sten guns, a new automatic weapon which had only been brought into use on secret operations the previous year.

On 5 March, shortly after the transmissions from the field agent ceased, Muir was admitted to hospital. When he was discharged ten days later he discovered his map and all the signals had been destroyed. As Major O'Loan, had been ordered to move his men out by the end of the month, he had burnt the lot. However, Muir's dismay was quickly dispelled. As the reason for the move was to support an Allied invasion of Borneo, the POWs would surely be rescued.

However, while the 9th and 7th Australian Divisions would, in due course, recapture Tarakan and Balikpapan in the east and Labuan in the west, the rescue of POWs was not, as Muir assumed, on their agenda. It was, nonetheless, high on General Blamey's list of priorities. At a special planning conference on 5 July 1944 Gort Chester, a mere fortnight after Python's evacuation to Australia, had submitted a draft plan which included the possible rescue of POWs in Borneo. While this proposal had been floated on 5 May, shortly after the return of Wallace, Steele and Kennedy, it was not until after Gort's arrival that it had evolved into a mission code-named Operation Agas, the Malay word for a gnat or sandfly. Far more ambitious than Python, Agas' objectives were to set up an intelligence network on the west coast, recruit and train a Chinese guerrilla army, carry out sabotage and establish contact with POW camps to organise escapes.

While Captain Ray Steele and Wallace, in particular, were eager to be involved in any proposal to rescue POWs, neither man was invited to have input into Agas. Steele, who had delivered a detailed and comprehensive report on the situation in Malaya and Singapore, was evidently excluded as his knowledge of the Sandakan area did not extend beyond Berhala Island. Wallace had given some very detailed information and possessed intimate knowledge of the camp and environs, but SRD had a poor opinion of him, declaring him to be 'very unreliable' and 'not the man to return' to Borneo. Furthermore, he was unable to keep his mouth shut.

Wallace, who had been seen in Sydney and Melbourne wearing his 8th Division colour patch, had attracted the attention of the public and press, as it was known that more than 18 000 men from that Division were in POW camps. By the strangest coincidence, Imelda Mosher, Ken Mosher's wife, a driver with 2 Australian Ambulance Unit which usually operated in country districts, had been detailed to transfer Wallace to a miltary hospital at suburban Concord after his arrival in Sydney. Noticing that he was 8th Division, but taking care not to betray her personal interest, she asked whether he knew of a Captain Mosher. As there was no love lost between him and Mosher, Wallace told Imelda that he was dead. Before she could discover anything further, Wallace was hustled away.

It was not until 1 August, almost a month after the meeting with Gort, that a further conference had been held to draw up details for the project. Three days later Lieutenant-Colonel John Chapman-Walker, SRD's Director, sent a letter, seeking official approval and allocation of submarine transport, to Colonel

Roberts at AIB who, if he concurred, would forward it to General MacArthur. In anticipation that approval would be granted, Major J. E. B. Finlay, Director of SRD's Planning Department, drew up final, more detailed plans. Meanwhile, Gort flew to Western Australia to recruit two Malay volunteers for the mission and discuss transportation requirements with Admiral Christie, Commander of Task Force 71, the United States submarine fleet based at Fremantle. Ten days later, on 18 August, he was back on the east coast, putting his hand-picked team through their paces at Queensland's Fraser Island Commando School.

On 22 August, almost three weeks after sending his request for approval to AIB, Chapman-Walker learned that Roberts had not yet forwarded the submission to MacArthur. This lack of co-operation between AIB, the pipeline to General Headquarters, and SRD was not new. The set-up at SRD had always been a sore point with AIB, while the Americans, apart from being highly suspicious of SRD's motives, were not keen to have maverick units operating in what they regarded as their patch. Furthermore Roberts had noted with some alarm that, under the directorship of Chapman-Walker, SRD had grown to be larger than all the other clandestine organisations combined, with the exception of the American-controlled Philippine guerrilla unit. Expansion, despite the misgivings of both Roberts and the Americans, was so great that by May 1944 it had been necessary to create a new post — The Directorate of General Staff, under the command of Lieutenant-Colonel H. A. Campbell, to co-ordinate all SRD plans, signals, intelligence and operations. Campbell, commonly known as Jock, was a former planter from Malaya who had started out life in Special Operations in 1942 as SOE's administrator for Operation Jaywick. Coming under his jurisdiction were Majors Finlay of Plans, M. Israel of Signals and Dick Noone, Director of Intelligence. The Operations Section had also been split in two — 'Nordops' under Trappes-Lomax and 'Westops', headed by Captain I. Wylie, which took in British North Borneo, Sarawak, Malaya and the South China Sea.

Despite this huge pool of personnel and resources, the Agas proposal was rejected by Colonel Roberts as the planning was very poor. The water at the planned insertion point was too shallow for the submarine to approach any nearer than 25 kilometres, and the proposal to form what amounted to a private army meant there was no possibility of the mission ever being sanctioned. As far as AIB was concerned, sabotage, armed resistance and other subversive activities must make way for intelligence gathering, coastwatching and the possible rescue of POWs.

Gort, who had made it quite clear it would be impossible to move about Borneo or set up his network once the monsoon season had begun, was annoyed by the delay. He had been aiming to leave in September, or mid-October at the latest. There was still time if SRD and AIB hurried. They didn't. It was not until 25 September that an amended plan was submitted to General Headquarters. Meanwhile, the training for the first phase of the plan (setting up an intelligence network and befriending the locals) continued and plans for the second phase, Agas II, which included the possible rescue of the prisoners, were developed further. On 10 October, as there was still no word from MacArthur, Gort went to Brisbane to hurry things along. He received the long-awaited permission from General Richard Sutherland, Chief of the General Staff, the following day but, on learning that no immediate submarine transportation was available, announced that approval had come too late. After consultation with his deputy, Major R. 'Nick' Coombe, a very peeved Chester signalled 'APPROVAL AGAS TOO LATE FOR IMMEDIATE ACTION OWING TO MONSOON. JANUARY NOW EARLIEST POSSIBLE.'

Although Gort's mission to the west coast was postponed until the New Year, plans for the proposed rescue operation developed rapidly. What had been a small sub-section of the Agas II project in August had evolved, by early November, into a highly complex operation. Code-named Kingfisher, the mission had only one aim — 'to evacuate and rescue all prisoners of war from the PW camps in the Sandakan area of British North Borneo'. Anxious to get Kingfisher underway, Chapman-Walker had dispatched a short appreciation to AIB in early November. By the 23rd he was seeking formal approval for the immediate insertion of an SRD party to gather vital up-to-date additional intelligence. In the meantime the planning for the rescue itself went ahead and by 3 December the final draft was ready.

It was to be a full-scale undertaking. As soon as an SRD party, headed by Captain Don Sutcliffe, British Army, had played its role by collecting last-minute intelligence, a paratroop battalion would be dropped in to secure the camp, the airfield and the town. The prisoners were to be evacuated by landing barges onto a hospital ship, which by this time would be waiting in the harbour. Sutcliffe's ground party throughout this rescue phase would be to direct and coordinate the operations. The planners had certainly been busy. Details had been provided by Wallace and pre-war civilians and added to excellent aerial photographic reconnaissance obtained on 24 October. Cartographers had then prepared large-scale maps showing land and sea approaches, drop-zones, beaches suitable for landing craft, Sandakan township, enemy installations and the airfield, along with plans of the camp itself, right down to the construction of the barbed wire fences, the positions of the sentry boxes and the hut layout.

These maps were accompanied by technical data dealing with the requirements of the paratroops, and pages of closely-typed intelligence information, covering every aspect of the mission from off-shore conditions, climate, topography, vegetation and anchorages to road networks, defences, known POW routines, names of Japanese officers and the Japanese order of battle. Information regarding the road network was so detailed it included not only a description of the surface, width and direction but the position of every path, bridge, village, hill and dale along each route. Based on this data, and the desire to drop the paratroops in one wave to maximise the element of surprise, it was calculated that a force of 612 men and 25 officers would be needed, possibly assisted by 40 airborne engineers. Three drop zones had been selected: the region north-west of the Sibuga river, the golf course and the area immediately west of the airfield. The paratroops would be transported by the military version of the Douglas DC-3 aircraft, known officially as a C-47 and unofficially as a 'biscuit bomber', a name coined in 1942 by Australian infantry fighting along the Kokoda Track, who depended upon supply drops from these highly reliable aerial workhorses. As each C-47 could easily accommodate 20 paratroopers and their gear, in this case special weapons containers, the maximum number required for the Kingfisher mission, including the engineers, was 34. However, by loading each aircraft to its capacity (23 paratroopers plus equipment), the number of C-47s required could be reduced to 30.

In mid-December, Kingfisher was approved. Perhaps it was the fear that the Japanese would massacre the prisoners when the Allies landed at Tarakan, or perhaps an improvement in relations between SRD and AIB following the appointment of a new Controller at the latter. Whatever the reason, on 15 December AIB's new boss, Brigadier Ken Wills, informed Chapman-Walker that Kingfisher had received MacArthur's complete approval. Ironically, although SRD had done all the preparatory work, Chapman-Walker was about the last to know the mission had been sanctioned. As early as 7 December General Sutherland, who forged strategic directions with MacArthur, had sent written instructions to the Commander, Allied Naval Forces, informing him of the operation and outlining the sea transportation requirements. A week later, Major Harry Beamer, by command of General George Kenney, chief of Allied Air Forces in the Far East, was writing with similar instructions regarding aircraft to Air Vice-Marshal William Bostock, the RAAF's Air Officer Commanding and also informing him that the United States 13th Air Force bases and facilities of the Commander, Aircraft Seventh Fleet, were at his disposal.

All that remained was for SRD to carry out the final, crucial intelligence mission. The party, which was to be inserted six weeks before the attack, had until ten days before D (attack) Day to relay the information. This meant that, if the ground party entered Borneo as soon as possible after 25 January, the prisoners could be liberated by the first week of March.

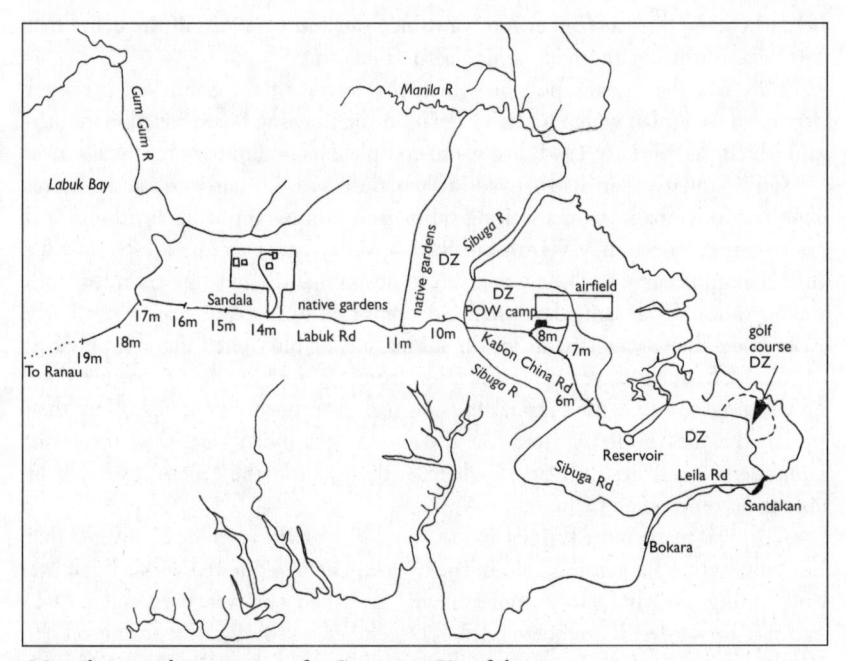

Map showing drop zones etc for Operation Kingfisher.

To date, SRD administration had done nothing to inspire confidence that it could meet the challenge. The delays in getting Agas approved and major problems experienced by Python, were only two in a succession of failures. Operation Falcon — thirteen planned sea-going raids on targets, stretching from Timor in the west to New Ireland in the east, was crippled because submarine transport had not been organised. All but two of the Falcon missions, hastily re-organised as air-sorties, were cancelled. Only one of these actually got off the ground, but it ended in disaster, resulting in heavy loss of life.

During 1944, things had gone steadily from bad to worse for SRD. While there were one or two successful intelligence gathering sorties into Dutch New Guinea, many proposed missions, having failed to gain approval or made redundant by the tide of battle, had been scrubbed. The outcome of others had been disastrous. The Python and Falcon project aside, the past 18 months had not been a good one for SRD. Blamey's decision to keep secret Operation Jaywick, intended as a propaganda exercise, had been disastrous. Intercepted signals had revealed that the Japanese believed the raid was the work of local people and prominent European internees. In the purge which followed, hundreds of innocent people had been murdered. Twelve months later, further signals had revealed that Operation Rimau, an ambitious plan to attack 60 ships in Singapore harbour (a mission described by its party leader, Jaywick's Ivan Lyon, as 'too big'), had ended in total disaster with all 23 men killed or captured. To date, another 19 agents had been inserted into supposedly neutral Portuguese Timor. Although most were presumed dead, there were growing suspicions that one, at least, had been compromised by the enemy — a major worry to SRD administration since tonnes of arms, equipment and stores, plus a small fortune in gold, had been dropped behind enemy lines at regular intervals since the end of 1943, in the belief that SRD was outfitting and maintaining a guerrilla army.

This was the organisation on which the rescue of the Sandakan prisoners depended — a plan which had now been on the drawing board for nine months and which, in February 1945, had yet to complete its preliminary reconnaissance.

On 7 January, Gort had arrived in Fremantle with his party and all his stores expecting to embark upon a waiting submarine. Almost immediately, things had gone wrong. Corporal Ma'erroff bin Said, a Malay agent recruited especially for the mission, became so ill he was taken to hospital and had to be excluded from the operation. That same day, when Gort reported to the Americans' Task Force 71 to make final arrangements for the submarine, he discovered that not only had Admiral Christie received no notification from SRD of the new departure date, he was unaware that the original mission had even been postponed. Gort then prevailed upon the RAAF to airlift the entire Agas party, with their tonnes of equipment and stores, to Darwin where, with any luck, the Americans might be able to accommodate them.

Gort was made more furious on his arrival in Darwin when he discovered that not only were aerial photographs of the insertion area, requested with a 'high priority' rating in early October, not available, they had not even been taken. SRD had not forwarded the request until 6 December and AIB, after sitting on the paperwork for almost a fortnight, did not realise until 6 January that it had been forwarded to the wrong agency. Almost beside himself with rage, Gort Chester pointed out to SRD and AIB administration that their hopelessly inadequate liaison had caused not only the current problems but also the postponement of the mission the previous October.

Unfortunately Gort's problems were not yet over. On 12 January, the day after they arrived in Darwin, Sergeant Graham Greenwood, a signaller recruited from the New Zealand army, was found to have jaundice, forcing Agas to urgently petition SRD for a replacement. While they were waiting, Agas moved into the old quarantine station, now AIB's 'Lugger Maintenance Section', the undercover name for a staging-post used by parties awaiting entry into the islands to the north of Australia. While the Lugger Maintenance Section was a very secure base, it was on an island in Darwin harbour and when the time came for Agas to leave, the stores had to be manhandled from the workshop, down a slipway and then across 200 metres of shoreline to a barge, which then had to be towed by launch to the submarine, moored some distance out to sea.

Fortunately the Americans had provided a submarine. On 15 January, much to Gort's relief, USS *Tuna* arrived in Darwin to take them to Borneo. The party now consisted of seven men. Apart from Chester, Nash and Coombe, a former District officer of Kudat, British North Borneo, there were two signallers, Lieutenant Fred Olsen, formerly of Python, and Sergeant Vic Sharpe. The remaining two were Corporal Kanun bin Abdul Gafu who, despite his non-European name and Malay heritage, had enlisted in the AIF and Corporal Jack Wong Sue, one of the few RAAF personnel recruited to SRD, whose mellifluous voice, with its rounded, cultured tones, belied his Chinese heritage.

The Agas party left Darwin on 16 January without the reconnaissance photographs. Reaching the entry point at Bisa Island, between Kudat and Kota Belud, on 28 January, Gort 's worst fears were realised. The enemy was in occupation. A periscope reconnaissance of the coastline between the island and Sikuti revealed what appeared to be buildings and radio masts as well as a considerable amount of smoke. Unable to find a secure entry point, there was no alternative but to return to Australia, a decision which was a problem in itself since *Tuna* was on a regular patrol and was not returning to base for some time. The ever-accommodating Americans agreed to divert USS *Bream*, about to return to Australia after a reconnaissance patrol in the South China Sea, to make a pick up. To their surprise, Agas found two of their SRD colleagues on board — Lieutenants John Sachs and Alex Hawkins who, as part of Operation Politician, had joined forces with the Americans in the hope of carrying out sabotage on enemy installations.

Other delays were occurring in Australia. Despite the stated urgency of the Kingfisher mission, its intelligence gathering party had not left. Amazingly, there had been no move to insert Sutcliffe's team by air, even though Apple had made a successful entry by Catalina on 13 January. Neither did SRD consider relaxing its timetable to allow the party to enter Borneo at the same time as, or even before, Agas I. There was no danger of being seen by patrolling enemy aircraft. Two days after Apple's insertion, SRD's Captain Tom Harrison, undertaking an aerial reconnaissance of the whole of British North Borneo, reported that, contrary to current intelligence, unescorted planes, including sole Catalinas, could now roam

British North Borneo's skies at will. He had also added that it was 'high time a full-time intelligence officer from SRD went forward of Brisbane'.

On 7 February, after receiving news that the Agas I mission had been aborted, three of SRD's senior administrators, including planning director Finlay, flew to Perth to meet Gort and Coombe who had transferred to an aircraft at Onslow, Western Australia and were now back at SRD's Western Base near Fremantle. Unaware that the 'radio masts' he had seen through the periscope were only two burnt, leafless trees, Gort informed his superiors that a west coast landing was out of the question. Python's old area in the south-east was also too risky, so he suggested that the new insertion point should be on the north-east coast, to the north of Sandakan. This was accepted. However, this time Gort was leaving nothing to chance. On 10 February he and Coombe departed for Morotai to arrange for a personal aerial reconnaissance of the insertion area, leaving SRD to organise another submarine. Once again the Americans came to the rescue. *Tuna* could be diverted to Darwin, provided Gort was ready to leave no later than 24 February. Otherwise, he would have to wait another month.

Although the aerial reconnaissance was a matter of extreme urgency, it was not until 18 February that Gort and Coombe were able to carry it out. From a Liberator at an altitude of 750 metres, they could see no sign of enemy activity anywhere near Sandakan Harbour or along the coastline to the north. The following day, when they arrived back in Australia to organise the men and stores, they were in for a shock. The original plan had been scrapped, along with some of the team. SRD had decreed that, as Agas I was switching to an east-coast entry point, Gort could also carry out Kingfisher's intelligence.

Apparently, the sudden decision to speed up Kingfisher's timetable was prompted by the realisation that, although some of the POWs had been moved, there was every chance the rest could be massacred when the Allies landed at Tarakan. MacArthur's headquarters had been aware of the possibility for some time, ever since intercepted Japanese signals had revealed details of orders issued in relation to the disposal of POWs. On 1 August 1944, in response to a question from Formosan POW headquarters to clarify instructions for 'extreme measures' to be taken against prisoners, Tokyo had replied:

1) The Time.
Although the basic aim is to act under superior orders, individual disposition may be made in the following circumstances:

a) When an uprising of large numbers cannot be suppressed without the use of firearms.
b) When escapes from the camp may turn into a hostile fighting force.

2) The Methods.
a) Whether they are destroyed individually or in groups, or however it is done, with mass bombing, poisonous smoke, poisons, drowning, decapitation, or what, dispose of them as the situation dictates.
b) In any case it is the aim not to allow the escape of a single one, to annihilate them all, and not to leave any traces.

It was only on reoccupying the Philippines that the Americans discovered these orders had become reality. On 14 December 1944, following the battle at Leyte Gulf, American forces had attacked Palawan, the most south-westerly island of the Philippine group and only 200 kilometres from the north-eastern tip of Borneo. At a camp on the cliffs above the bay of Puerto Princesa were about 150 American prisoners of war. Early that morning, the POWs had gone out to work but had been escorted back at noon and told to enter their air raid shelters as there were 'hundreds of American planes approaching'. Marine Sergeant Douglas Bogue described how they had only just taken cover when he heard a dull explosion, followed by screaming, laughing and the sound of machine gun and rifle fire. Looking out, he saw about 50 to 60 heavily-armed Japanese soldiers throwing buckets of petrol, which they ignited, into the neighbouring shelter. As the prisoners emerged, their hair and clothes burning fiercely, they were bayoneted, shot, clubbed or stabbed to death. Bogue's group made a run for it, only to be mown down by machine-gun fire. Forty ran the gauntlet and threw themselves over the cliff in an attempt to reach the beach, 15 metres below. Only four survived the fall. The following day they made their way through the jungle where they soon joined the guerrilla forces.

On 6 February the Philippine capital of Manila was retaken. MacArthur, fearing that 5000 prisoners, especially the 3700 civilian internees held at Santo Tomas University, might meet a fate similar to those at Palawan unless rescued prior to the main assault on the capital, ordered a heavily-armoured flying column to launch a lightning attack. The prisoners were liberated, but only just in time. The commandant, it was discovered, held orders from Tokyo to kill them all.

It was therefore clear that, in the event of an Allied invasion, the Sandakan POWs were in great danger. Yet Sutcliffe's Kingfisher team, which had been fully briefed and awaiting insertion for weeks, had not entered Borneo to collect the vitally-needed intelligence. And now, for some inexplicable reason, the carefully thought-out Kingfisher plan had been replaced by new orders which called for Agas I to take on Kingfisher's role as well as its own. Gort could not believe it. To set up a local intelligence network, organise a resistance movement, and collect Kingfisher's information, simultaneously, was impossible.

For a start, Kingfisher's planned Gum Gum River base, ideally sited for a close reconnaissance of the Sandakan camp and its immediate environs, had been scrapped in favour of a single base, well to the north, on the other side of Labuk Bay. Agas had also been instructed to collect information needed to facilitate the extraction of a Mr Chong, a prominent member of the chamber of commerce at Kudat, who was a 'high priority target' of considerable interest to General Headquarters. With hundreds of kilometres of mountainous jungle separating Mr Chong and Kudat on the far north-western tip of British North Borneo from the POWs and Sandakan in the east, Gort realised immediately that these tasks alone would require the full attention of two separate, on-the-spot, fully briefed teams.

Not surprisingly, Gort went into a towering rage. He ranted and raved about the idiocy of the new proposal, but it did him no good. SRD had the muscle, and used it. They delivered Gort an ultimatum. He was taken on the amalgamated missions or resign.

It was with very grave misgivings that Gort Chester left Darwin for Borneo on the afternoon of 24 February. Not only was he concerned about the work load, he was also worried about the composition of his party which, because of the amalgamation of the two missions, had been completely restructured. Of the original eight-man team, only Gort, Sue and Olsen remained and of this trio, only Jack Sue retained his real identity. Gort and Olsen might be known to the Japanese through the captured Python men, so they had adopted temporarily the names 'O'Keefe' and 'Maunder'. The new personnel included Scottish-born Sutcliffe, British army and an unknown quantity, replacing Coombe who had spent years of his life in Borneo. In Kanun's place was Lieutenant Don Harlem who, although a very able soldier, had never been in Borneo and had no chance of passing as a local. Graham Greenwood, fully recovered from his jaundice, had reclaimed his old position, making Vic Sharpe redundant. When the party reached Adelaide, Nash became ill. His last-minute replacement was Corporal Hywood, a very tall, strapping signaller whose given name of Amos had long ago been bastardised to 'A-mos-quito', which in turn had evolved into 'Skeet'.

The submarine was about half way to Borneo when Gort accepted he had two more problems. Sutcliffe lacked rapport with non-Europeans and he had a style of leadership more suited to the days of the Raj, which was causing a great deal of dissention among the men. Also *Tuna*'s commander, Captain Stefanides, was under orders to abort the mission if he considered his submarine to be at risk. It was fortunate, therefore, that the voyage was uneventful. Apart from a lone sampan, which had prompted a change in course as they neared their destination, they had seen nothing of interest. At 7.00pm on 3 March *Tuna* surfaced and closed on the insertion point, about 9 kilometres from Tagahan River, just south of Tanjung Tagahan. By 8.52pm the stores (including a huge amount of gold and currency to pay guerrillas, purchase boats and bribe locals) had been transferred from the submarine to a seven-man rubber boat and two folboats. Six minutes later, *Tuna* departed at high speed. As a precaution, allied aircraft had attacked all enemy patrol boats in the Sandakan area prior to the submarine's arrival, but Stefanides was taking no unnecessary chances at being caught on the surface in shallow water.

Paddling the large boat and towing the two folboats, the party reached the mouth of the river at about 2.00am. At dawn, aided by an incoming tide, they followed the river upstream for roughly 3.5 kilometres where Gort selected a site for the base camp — a patch of high ground on an island, completely surrounded by mangroves and nipah palms. As there were two villages close by, he cautioned the men not to betray their presence until the loyalties of the locals were ascertained. On 7 March, as soon as an emergency wireless link was established with the Dutch station at Darwin, the operational team — Gort, Jack, Sutcliffe and Harlem — left in two folboats to begin the first of a series of reconnaissance missions, paddling by night and resting by day. Signallers Olsen, Greenwood and Hywood remained behind to set up a permanent link with SRD's signal station at Leanyer, Northern Territory, on 10 March and maintain a listening watch. Not that they expected anything in the way of wireless traffic. Radio transmissions were restricted to emergency signals only, for the first three weeks.

The reconnaissance team members were lying in their hammocks in thick jungle near the Sugut River, about 16 kilometres from the base camp, when a Malay suddenly appeared out of nowhere. The startled Australians thought they had been ambushed by an enemy patrol, but their unexpected visitor was Samak, an ex-Custom's house boatman who came from Meninghatan, just to the north of the river. He was the answer to Gort's prayers. Once he had recovered from the shock of finding four men lying in hammocks in the jungle, he relaxed, reassured by the presence of Jack and the discovery that Gort spoke fluent Malay. He pledged his assistance, confirming that there had been a movement of POWs from Sandakan to Jesselton and also revealing that Sandshoe Willie was alive and well.

At this point Sutcliffe decided Samak was a security threat and wanted to shoot him. Fortunately Gort pulled rank, accepted Samak's offer of assistance and sent him on his way. Gort's faith in Samak was soon justified. Within days he had located Sandshoe Willie and let it be known that anyone who wished to join in the fight against the Japanese should report to Meninghatan. While Gort was certain Samak would continue to deliver, he no longer had confidence in Sutcliffe's ability to co-ordinate an intelligence network involving local people. When Mr Willie turned up a few days later, Gort accepted his offer to collect the intelligence they needed and bring it directly to the base for immediate transmission to Australia.

Leaving Willie and Samak to organise their contacts, the party returned to base for supplies. Gort was in camp when the signallers heard Agas' call-sign on the wireless. Although the party was under strict orders not to break radio silence for three weeks, SRD had added 'QSQ' to the call sign to indicate that the matter was 'very urgent, come on air'. Gort, against his better judgement, decided they had better respond. The message had originated from Agas' 'conducting officer', who wanted to know, 'Can you build an airstrip for dive-bombers?' Although Gort's reaction to this amazing communication was to ignore it completely, he couldn't resist replying, 'Cannot build airstrip. Do not have bulldozer.' The sarcasm was lost on SRD. The following day the wireless operator once more heard the Agas call sign, followed by QSQ. 'Can arrange bulldozer', signalled SRD. Finding it impossible to credit that anyone could possibly be serious about a handful of secret agents building an airstrip in some of the most difficult terrain on earth, Gort replied, 'Even with bulldozer do not have enough hands or tools. Only seven of us here.'

When SRD responded with, 'Captain Fisher on way to Palawan. Have organised barge, bulldozer, 20 men and tools', Jack Sue thought Gort would have an apoplectic fit. After letting forth a string of four letter expletives about the general level of intelligence at SRD, Gort had the wireless operator put an end to the nonsense with 'Don't send bulldozer. We're only having you on.' 'Restrict your amusement or be withdrawn,' replied SRD. 'Withdraw us then', challenged Gort, and with that, all transmissions about airfield construction ceased.

His supplies replenished, Gort continued with his reconnaissance, confident that Sandshoe Willie would collect the necessary information about the POWs. Willie had been told it was urgent. With thousands of Australian troops about to converge on Morotai prior to the invasion of Tarakan, there were less than eight weeks to gather the intelligence, send it to the base camp, transmit it to Australia and pull off the rescue.

As they knew that at least one massacre had taken place and another had only been narrowly avoided, it must have been a worrying time for those working at Allied Intelligence. Everything was in readiness. The elite Australian Paratroop Battalion, which had been training on the Atherton Tableland with its commanding officer, Lieutenant-Colonel John Overall, was on standby and there was a potential pool of 71 airworthy RAAF C-47s available, more than double the number required. However, no move could be made to mobilise the force, or even begin the last phase of training, until further intelligence was received from Borneo.

Three weeks passed. A short signal from Agas containing details of the Japanese garrison at Beluran was received on 28 March but SRD had to wait another week for the first information on the POWs to come through. As it was now only four weeks until the Tarakan landings the timetable was becoming increasingly tight. With the chances of obtaining all the information required to effect a rescue before the Tarakan invasion fading with each passing day, SRD's relief when they decoded Agas' signal on 3 April can only be imagined. The possibility of a wholesale massacre no longer existed. All the POWs had been moved! They were no longer in Sandakan! According to reliable information from a native chief in the Sugut area, north of Labuk Bay, the prisoners had been taken in groups overland to Jesselton via Lingkabau, Meridi and Ranau. Although the incidence of beriberi was reported as high and those unable to travel were shot, 'all signs indicate an enemy evacuation of Sandakan'.

On 10 April, Agas moved camp to Jembongan Island. Although the new site was about 6 kilometres off the coast and a good 60 kilometres north of the old base, Sandshoe Willie and his men continued to report regularly with whatever information they had collected. Six days later SRD's Captain Stringfellow, an intelligence officer now based at Morotai, removed any lingering doubt about the fate of the prisoners by reporting 'Transfer of Sandakan PW overland to Jesselton is confirmed. Some are being left at Ranau for the present. There is another group of about 500 at Meridi.'

With no one left at Sandakan, all rescue plans came to an abrupt and immediate end. While orders were set in train to stand down the paratroopers, who would be told only in mid-May that the mysterious mission for which they were training had been cancelled, SRD hurriedly took stock of the situation. By 19 April a new appraisal had been issued. In light of the Stringfellow announcement, SRD was to divert its energies elsewhere. 'Owing to information received about the POWs', Agas III, a reconnaissance mission planned for the west coast was now to have a higher priority — a decision which was vindicated on 30 April when 'latest news' revealed that 'troops in the area have been increased from the Philippines. Total strength is between 1500-2000. Some of them came overland from Lahad Datu using forced labour as porterage. Seen by agent. Shortage of arms and ammunition.' Reports had also been received that another 800-900 enemy troops en route to the west were now camped at Sandakan in the rubber estates along the road leading to the airfield, and another 200-300 near the old

Chinese school on the Sibuga Road. SRD agreed that the Kabon China Road, between the 2 and 9 mile pegs, an area which included The Eight Mile Camp, should be bombed as soon as possible.

On 1 May, the day after this signal was received, Australian troops invaded Tarakan. On 8 May Agas signalled that everything was pointing to Ranau as the final Japanese stronghold. Five days later the Sandakan area was bombed with such intensity that 600 Japanese troops stationed along the Kabon China Road were killed. Meanwhile, four British warships shelled Berhala Island.

Meanwhile, on 22 April, Rex Blow and Jock McLaren, who had spent the last 22 months fighting with the Filipino guerrillas, had reported to the Australian base at Morotai, where they met General Blamey. They had no inkling that a rescue had even been planned, much less cancelled, and Blamey was not about to tell them. Aware from locals who had arrived in Tawi Tawi to join the guerrillas that the situation in Sandakan was very bad, they urged Blamey to mount a rescue attempt and offered their services. The general promised that 'if it could be fitted in to other operations, we'll do it — and you two will be in it'. With that, he promoted McLaren to the rank of captain, Blow to major and sent them back to Australia on extended leave.

By the third week of May those at SRD advanced headquarters at Morotai were breathing a little easier. Although they had been too late to rescue the POWs, at least their fortuitous removal from Sandakan before the Tarakan landings had ensured that the bulk of them were alive. Chester, who had been extracted from Borneo by Catalina for a debriefing on 21 May, reported that, according to agents, a number of prisoners had died or been killed but the remainder, who had not been sent to Jesselton as previously reported, were now safely at Ranau. Japanese troops, described as 'first class, front line troops' were also pulling back in that direction but since the jungle routes, the same ones used by the POWs, had been identified, low level strafing of the track should take care of some of them at least.

On 22 May, when Captain Stringfellow issued his latest intelligence report stating, 'All PW have been moved from Sandakan to Ranau, where they now are', it was the signal for American PT boats and Allied aircraft to shell, strafe and bomb Sandakan and the surrounding areas. Five days later they did so, confident that the camp and its environs were now free of all Allied prisoners.

They were not. Although 455 POWs had been moved to Ranau in February and many had died since, more than 800 Australian and British prisoners were still alive. They were all there, in the compound at the Sandakan Eight Mile Camp.

Chapter Eleven
TO RANAU

The movement of the prisoners, begun on 28 January, was in response to an order issued by headquarters' General Yamawaki just over a fortnight before. On 13 January Captain Yamamoto Shoichi, commanding officer of the 25th Mixed Regiment currently based at Sandakan, had been instructed to move 360 infantry troops and a company of machine gunners to Tuaran, more than 400 kilometres to the west. He was to take with him 500 POWs from the Sandakan compounds to labour in the Tuaran-Jesselton area, where the garrison was being strengthened.

For the past three months the Yamamoto Butai, as the unit was also known, had been engaged in building fortifications in and around Sandakan, particularly near the airfield. However, since the airstrip was no longer viable except for small aircraft, and the Japanese High Command was concerned that, with the Philippines retaken, the military bases in Borneo's west would be targeted, the regiment received its marching orders. All shipping was at a standstill (apart from a decrepit steam-driven launch still operating between Sandakan and Kudat) and an airlift was out of the question. Both troops and POWs would have to make the journey on foot, overland.

Although various river systems linked by foot tracks formed a well-established route from Beluran to Tuaran, Yamamoto was ordered to take a more southerly route, developed less than six months previously. The new path, or rentis as it was also termed, had been cut or widened in three stages and linked the 42 mile peg on the existing Sandakan-Beluran track with Ranau, another 195 kilometres further west. The lower section, from the 42 mile to the head waters of the Sapi River, was surveyed and blazed by Sandshoe Willie (in his capacity as Beluran's Deputy District Officer) and his assistant Orang Tuan Kulang of Muanad, head of the local Dusan tribespeople. The middle section, from Sapi to Tampias, a distance of between 70 and 80 kilometres, had been the responsibility of Kanak, headman of Tendu Batu and chief of the Orang Sungei (River People), while the last part, following the line of an existing native foot pad, had been placed in the control of Ackoi, headman of Tampias. Once the lower sections had been defined, the entire track had been widened by Javanese and local coolies.

Believing it would be used solely by enemy troops, the fiercely anti-Japanese Willie and Kulang had devised the most tortuous and difficult route. Leaving the Beluran bridle path at the 42 mile peg, the track passed first through low-lying, swampy ground which soon gave way to rain forest, so thick and dense that no sunlight penetrated its lush canopy. Cutting the path at frequent intervals were a number of rivers, the largest of which were the Dusan at mile 33, Kolapis at the 44 mile, the Muanad (also known as the Munyed) at the 49½, the Pandan Pandan at about mile 58, the Mandorin at peg 60 and the Sapapiyau, a tributary of the

Sapi, at about mile 70. From Sapi the track roller-coastered due west to cross the Celo and Bonkud Rivers before climbing north-west towards Boto village on the upper reaches of the Labuk. From here the way turned south, along the Telupid River, before heading north west again. The tributaries feeding the Labuk, now known as the Kuanan, now came in quick succession — the Tapang (Papan), Baba, Tara Rangag, Tundom, Lolosing, Monkilau and finally, at Tampias, the Kegibangan. Near the Telupid, the real mountains began and the going became very difficult with the head waters of the Kuanan cutting through precipitous, jungle clad terrain of the Maitland Range. Once past Tampias, where the Kegibangan met the Kuanan, the old native track, less than a metre wide in parts, snaked on, to the 138 mile at Paginatan before beginning the final ascent across the Crocker Ranges to the Ranau plain at peg 164, another 42 kilometres to the west.

Hoshijima had been weighing the prisoners every week to make sure they were wasting at the required rate. He must have realised that there was not a single man in camp fit enough to undertake a forced march from one side of Borneo to the other, but it was not in his interests to question such an order. Official policy dictated that all POWs were to be disposed of and, with the Allies expected to attack the east coast before long, the fewer prisoners he had to deal with the better. However Yamamoto, whose concerns lay with his men rather than prisoners, sent his adjutant, Lieutenant Iino Shigeru, by small plane to Kuching. His instructions were to try and obtain a postponement until February to allow time to set up extra supply dumps along the route and, as it was the wet season, for the weather to improve. Major-General Manaki Takanobu, Chief of Staff of the 37th army,

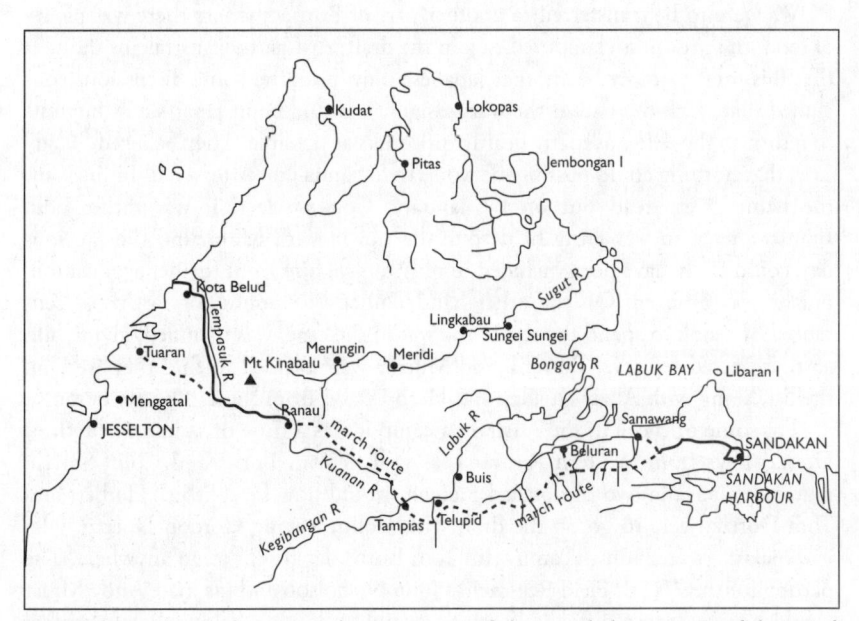

Map of British North Borneo showing route of the march between Sandakan and Ranau.

must have been well aware that, of 800 supposedly-fit Japanese troops who had set out to march north to Jesselton from Kawang that same month only 200 had arrived, yet he was unmoved. On 24 January Yamamoto received a telegram confirming that the order was to be carried out without delay. Furthermore, the journey was to be completed as quickly as possible.

The column was to be split into ten parties, each comprising about 50 POW and a similar number of soldiers, which would leave Sandakan at one day intervals. As the journey was expected to take three weeks, Japanese Headquarters had undertaken to set up food dumps and provide shelter at Muanad (49½ mile), Mandorin (60 mile), Boto (103 mile), Papan (120 mile) and Paginatan (138 mile). Once they reached Ranau, at the 164 mile, the POWs were to be handed over to Captain Nagai, who would march them to Tuaran. According to his junior officers, Yamamoto made it quite clear that any POW who became too ill to continue was to be left behind at one of the 'rest houses'. However, once these general instructions had been issued, Yamamoto sent for Lieutenant Abe Kazuo. A member of the 20th Independent Machine-Gun Battalion, Abe had been singled out to oversee the disposal of any POW who had been left behind and could not continue.

Killing those who became ill, or were wounded, far away from medical help, was nothing new. Indeed, Australian Intelligence was well aware of the hard line taken by the Japanese. Captured documents had revealed that, as early as January 1944, commanding officers had been instructed to take a similar acion with their own men if they caused 'too obvious an obstruction to the efficient execution of the withdrawal, unavoidable instances when sick and wounded must be disposed of are to be expected'.

On 26 January when Hoshijima announced that 500 of Sandakan's fittest POWs were to be transferred to another part of Borneo, where there was plenty of food, the prisoners clamoured to join the draft. At first the Australians thought that this might simply be another Japanese ploy, but after some discussions concluded that, with the end of the war in sight, it would be in Japan's best interests to return to the Allies as many healthy prisoners as possible. They believed, in any case, that nothing could possibly be worse than Sandakan. After a nail-biting wait, the names were read out on 27 January. Cook's selection was rather odd. Braithwaite, who was fairly fit despite the run-in with Murozumi the previous day, could easily have been included, if only to save him from further aggravation, but he was omitted. On the other hand, Punchy Donohue, one of those sentenced by Cook to spend the rest of the war in the cage, was included, giving him an unexpected reprieve. Botterill and Murray were pleased to find they were on the list, along with Allan Quailey and Herb Lytton from the 2/30th Battalion.

For some of those in the Australian camp it was a time of sadness. The three Dorizzi boys from Western Australia, as well as Tom Burns and Colin Smyth, reunited when the two camps had merged, would now be split up. Herbert and Tom Dorizzi were to go on the draft with Colin, leaving Gordon Dorizzi, who had malaria, to remain in camp with Tom Burns, far too ill to go anywhere. The parting for the 2/15th Field Regiment's John Nicholson and his mate Andy Miller would be even more difficult, for they would be leaving behind John's brother Gerard, who had died from malaria the day before.

Once the list had been read out, Hoshijima announced that all those being transferred would be issued with food, 30 grams of tobacco, a pair of second-hand shorts and shirt and, for those who did not have boots (about 90 per cent of the draft), a pair of latex-rubber slip-on shoes, which the Japanese called 'jikatabi'. He also gave permission for the POWs to slaughter several of their pigs and his horse, on which he had carried out inspections at the aerodrome. This gesture was not as magnanimous as it appeared. The novelty of riding the horse had long since worn off and the poor creature, as underfed as the prisoners, was nothing more than a bag of bones. Furthermore, the Japanese did not care for horse meat.

At 5.00 the following morning a good-sized crowd turned out to watch 55 Australians, under the control of Warrant Officer Charles Watson and Colin Smyth, and escorted by five Formosan guards, (including Kawakami, The-Gold-Toothed-Shin-Kicking-Bastard) march, out the gate and disappear down the track in the pre-dawn darkness. Also in this party were Dr Rod Jeffrey, the two Dorizzi brothers and a well-known identity from their machine-gun unit, Bob Chipperfield who, well over 2 metres in height, was believed to be the tallest man in the 8th Division, if not the entire AIF. Each prisoner had been issued with enough rations for four days — 1.35 kilograms of rice, just over 1100 grams of dried fish and 30 grams of salt.

Reaching the bitumen at the 8 mile peg, they did not turn left to Sandakan along the Kabon China Road as expected but right, towards Beluran. Waiting for them a mile up the road were Captain Yamamoto and 40 of his men, along with a mountain of hessian bags containing ammunition, rice and other supplies. As soon as the prisoners had been loaded up with various sacks which, in some cases amounted to a weight of 25 kilograms, Yamamoto set off with an advance party. After a delay of 24 hours due to heavy rain, the column followed with Captain Iino.

Botterill, Murray and Quailey, along with David Humphries, one of Botterill's 2/19th mates, left with the third party before dawn on 31 January. They were in high spirits, despite the miserable weather. No one in the 50-strong party had any idea where they were headed but, on reaching the Japanese camp at the 9 mile they found that, besides their own packs, rations and communal cooking gear, they were expected to carry mosquito nets and other baggage belonging to 47 members of the Yamamoto Butai. Ten sacks of rice, ten bags of ammunition and a dismantled mountain gun also had to be hauled. After breaking down the load for distribution among the prisoners, the Japanese officer in charge of the party, Lieutenant Toyohara Kihaku, ordered them to move off.

In spite of the rain and the weight of the rice sacks, which were passed from man to man at frequent intervals, they made it to the 18 mile peg, just beyond the Gum Gum River, on the end of the first day. By this time most of the party were marching in bare feet, having discovered that without socks and with the ground wet and sloppy underfoot, Hoshijima's rubber slip-ons were more often off than on. It was a toss up which was worse — lacerating feet on hidden roots, stumps and stones, or frequent falls. On the morning of day two they were well into the jungle. The muddy dirt-road which had begun at the 15 mile peg had degenerated at the 19 mile into a 1.5-metre wide, well-established but equally muddy path leading to Beluran. The initial section, skirting the large crocodile-infested, mangrove swamps of the Labuk River basin, was prone to flooding between the 22 and 42 mile and more especially between the 27 and 36 mile, where the track was cut by the Tindok, Dusun and Mandjang Rivers. As they neared the first of the swampy areas, Botterill was relieved to see that the track gave way to a narrow bamboo boardwalk, perched on poles about a metre above the slush. However, his relief was short-lived. The combination of split bamboo slats, mud and rain was far more deadly than any crocodile lurking in the swamps. Toyohara made it quite clear that as there were no medical facilities available, any prisoner or soldier who slipped from the boardwalk and broke a leg would be shot.

The next two days were horrendous and Botterill thought he must surely die. The heavy rain, coupled with the already swampy terrain, saw Japanese and prisoner alike struggling through knee-deep mud or trying to maintain a precarious footing on the short, sharp rises between. They were only half way through the swamps when darkness fell and, with nowhere else to sleep they had no choice but to collapse onto the boardwalk, eaten alive by swarms of voracious mosquitoes. Somehow, the next morning, all stood to tackle the mangroves once more. On the fourth day they were out of the worst of the muck and trudging along in the vicinity of the 46 mile,[1] a few hours into the march, when an Australian NCO, bloated with severe beriberi, fell behind. Unable to move his grossly distended legs and refusing offers by Botterill and others to help, he declared he could go no further. When Lieutenant Toyohara tried to jolly him along by saying there were only another 6 or 7 kilometres to go that day, the sergeant went berserk, shouting insults at the Japanese and pleading for someone to shoot him. When it became clear that it would be impossible to coax him to continue, Sergeant-Major Gotunda, with Toyahara's concurrence, agreed to put him out of his misery, as long as Warrant Officer Clive Warrington, of Divisional Headquarters Intelligence and the party's most senior Australian, gave permission. Warrington wrote out the necessary authority but Gotunda could not bring himself to do it. When one final attempt to help the prisoner, now raving and threshing about hysterically, failed, Warrington pulled the trigger himself.

That night they reached the 'rest house', a large open-sided hut built by Kulang on the eastern side of the Tankul Crossing on the Muanad River (also known as East Mandorin). Gotunda, who was travelling a few hours ahead of the main pack, discovered there was no food left there. As the prisoners had eaten almost all of their rice, this could have been critical. He, therefore, took a boat down the Muanad to Beluran, where he managed to obtain 30 kilograms of rice and a huge basket of vegetables.

That next night they camped out at the Mandorin River staging post near the 60 mile. Although they were out of the worst of the mud now, this section of the track, with its perilous river crossings, leeches as thick as pencils, mosquitoes and stinging March flies, was almost as bad. The POWs cooked their pooled rice in the 5-gallon billy can they carried, adding fern tops or any other edible bits and pieces they had found along the way to make it go just that little bit further. Their few blankets were threadbare but fortunately, as they were still fairly near the coast, it was not cold at night.

Toyahara's troops were well-disciplined, so much so that even in the depths of the jungle they stuck to their usual routine. After they had cooked their meal at night, reserving a portion for breakfast, the soldiers carried out their normal chores — washing and mending uniforms (now showing considerable signs of wear and tear), cleaning weapons and repairing boots on a small last. As soon as the morning inspection was over, carried out with the same precision and formality that one would expect on a regimental parade ground, the soldiers split themselves into three groups — one at either end of the straggling line of POWs and the other at about the middle. There was no fraternisation, although they offered the POWs a light for their tobacco and tried to keep their spirits up with an 'only one more mile' as energy levels dropped in the late afternoon. There was no ill-treatment either. The Japanese also religiously enforced a rest period of ten minutes every hour, to Botterill's relief.

The soldiers were intent on getting through the day's march and the POWs could have escaped at any time. Botterill considered this option but dismissed it. The jungle was a frightening place, and, in Botterill's opinion, you would probably die of fright out there on your own. With wild animals, including boars, elephants and orangutans and highly venomous snakes, he figured that the chances of survival were better on the track than off it.

Japanese army headquarters was supposed to have organised food dumps, with rice, tapioca or corn, at designated places along the route. However, the further they moved into the interior the more hit and miss the supplies became. The so-called rest houses, when they existed, were usually taken by the Japanese troops, forcing the prisoners to seek shelter in the roots of giant trees or, if fortunate, under ground-sheets and blankets. The soldiers took priority over the prisoners and there was often precious little to be shared among them. Most were suffering, to some degree, from beriberi, malaria and/or dysentery and, as the column began to string out, Lieutenant Toyohara sent the sick ahead of the main bunch each morning, hoping that an hour's start would compensate for their slower progress. It was not until about lunchtime that Botterill, among the fittest, caught up with them.

When they reached the 103 mile dump near Boto on about 11 February, they discovered only six cucumbers and a tiny amount of rice. The next guaranteed food stocks were almost 60 kilometres away at the village of Paginatan, on the far side of the Maitland Range. Things looked grim. Gotunda, realising that some of the POWs would never make it if they had to carry anything other than bare essentials, told them to dump the troops' mosquito nets. He then went on ahead to check on the situation at Paginatan. One of the Japanese corporals, ignoring Gotunda's instructions, ordered the prisoners to pick up the nets and get moving.

The Japanese did not offer to donate any of their emergency rations of dried fish, dehydrated buffalo meat or soya bean powder to the starving POWs. The Australians had to will themselves to keep going, one foot after another and then on hands and knees, sustained only by the cucumbers, fern fronds and an occasional frog or insect. Reduced by hunger and exhaustion to an almost trance-like state, Botterill moved like a zombie, not caring whether he lived or died. However, Murray, who had emerged as the group's unofficial leader, was still able

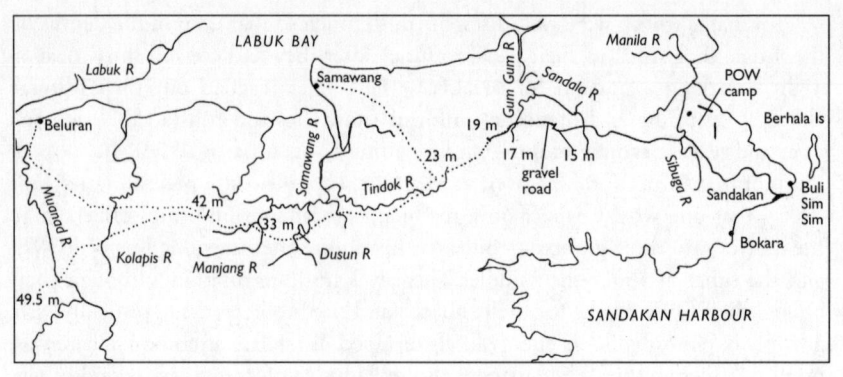

The track — Sandakan to Muanad River at the 49.5 mile.

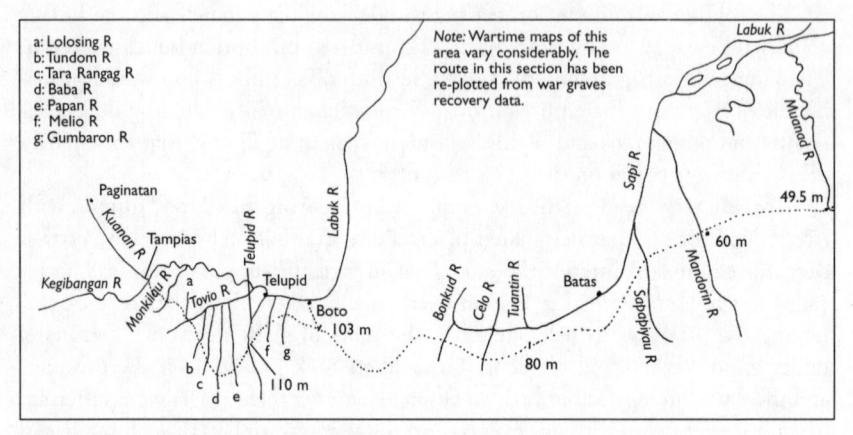

The track — Muanad River to Tampias at 133 mile.

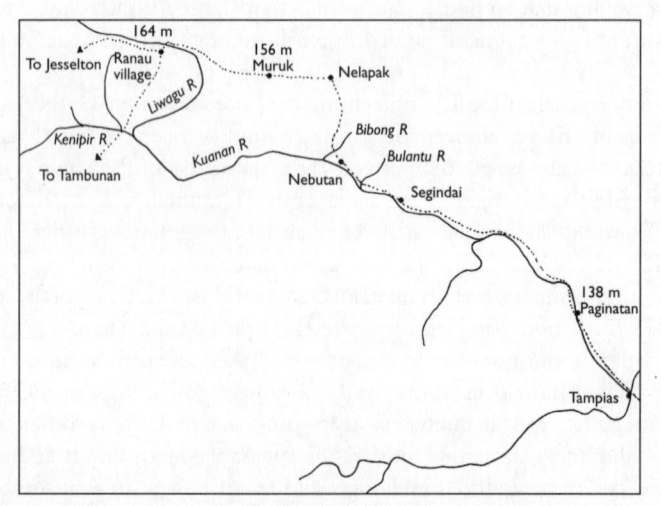

The track — Tampias to Ranau at the 164 mile.

to lend encouragement to those whose spirits were flagging. He stayed at the rear with the stragglers to give physical support to the weak and ill, but, despite his efforts, some did not make it over the mountain. David Humphries, ambulanceman Arthur Noakes, and Corporal Donald Palmer, an engineer, managed to struggle less than a kilometre beyond Milulu, west of the Tapang River, where the party had stopped on the night of 12 February. Noakes died at 8.00am and 50 minutes later Botterill stood by helplessly as Humphries and Palmer were shot dead by a Japanese sergeant and one of the privates. Anti-tank gunner Norman McLeod and Private Lawrence McLeenan, of the 2/18th Battalion, died just over 3 kilometres further on. Botterill knew his comrades were not the first to have died on the mountain, or along the track. His nose told him that others had met a similar fate.

The next day the 44 surviving prisoners staggered down the mountain and into Tampias, less than a day's march from Paginatan. They were more dead than alive. That they made it was due to the help of some natives, so small in stature they looked like pygmies, who had overcome their natural shyness to emerge from the jungle to offer the strangers tapioca in return for a couple of mess plates. It was not much, but, with no food at the Papan dump, it provided Botterill's group with the energy to reach Tampias, where some friendly Dusans gave them tapioca and sweet potato. Tampias was nothing more than a few small huts straggling along the river and a rest house at the foot of the hill. It boasted the only ferry along the entire track — a couple of canoes manned by two local oarsmen. The maximum number of passengers per canoe was two, so the POWs had an unexpected but very welcome rest while waiting their turn.

Paginatan may have been less than a day's march away, but it was all uphill. After the hold-up at the ferry, the column was now very spread out. Those at the front were hours ahead of the tail. Botterill and Murray had about 5 kilometres to go when they came across one of their party, crawling along on his hands and knees. As Murray volunteered to staybehind and help him, Botterill continued on his way. He had almost reached Paginatan when he met Sergeant-Major Gotunda. When Gotunda learned that the prisoners were still carrying the nets, and that one of the party was very ill, he hurried down the track to render assistance. He returned with only one prisoner, Murray. The other had been shot. At roll call at Paginatan they were one more short. Botterill had noticed a prisoner leaving the column not far from the village, and, as no one had seen any sign of him since, they assumed he had wandered into the jungle to die.

Paginatan village consisted of about 20 or so huts clustered along or near a wide, fast-flowing but shallow river. At the far end of the village was the rest house — large, roomy and by far the best accommodation to date. Their stay in the village, with its friendly family groups, chickens scratching about in vegetable gardens and a well-stocked food dump, was an almost unbelievable luxury. It was even better the following morning when they traded two blankets for a pig. It was not much bigger than an under-sized cat, and they were forced to donate half of it to the Japanese, but it was, nevertheless, a pig. Spurred on by the thought of pork stew that night, the prisoners headed towards Segindai, about 12 kilometres away at the 146 mile peg.

After Segindai the track, which had been rising and falling since leaving Paginatan, climbed very steeply for the next 7 kilometres, twisting through the Crocker Ranges, the beauty of which the prisoners could not appreciate. Botterill's group negotiated this section without loss of life, because, fortunately, three stricken with malaria had been allowed to remain behind at Paginatan until they were well enough to proceed. This was not the case with other groups and the climb from Paginatan, to date, had accounted for the lives of at least four POWs suffering from cardiac beriberi. Group 1's Bob Chipperfield had dropped dead on 11 February, 8 kilometres from Segindai, while the same fate had overtaken Herb Dorizzi 1.5 kilometres further on and electrical engineer Herb Ewing, one of the old blokes, a further 1.5 kilometres beyond that. Tom Dorizzi, unaware that his other brother, Gordon, left behind at Sandakan, would also die that same day, could do nothing more for Herb than remove his identity tags in the hope that he could take them home to Australia. When Group 2 passed through the same stretch two days later, the Japanese NCO recording the deaths reported that John Martin, one of John Barnier's AASC mates, had also succumbed to cardiac beriberi 5 kilometres from Segindai.

The recorder's job was merely to take down the names of all who died or dropped out, but he had no idea whether those unable to continue died as a result of illness or were given a *coup de gras*. Furthermore, some of the names appearing on his list suffered in the translation. Group 3's David Humphries became Hampaless, Albert Noakes turned into Knox and Lawrence Arthur McLeenan to Lawrence Assut Mcrenan. This particular record keeper was not the only one having problems. The name of Cyril Dempster, who had died of cardiac beriberi near the 80 mile on 6 February, had been corrupted to Cycle Lampster, while Group 4's Arthur Clement Ivan Ayton and John Nicholson, both of whom would die of heart failure near or at Tampias on 15 February, would enter the Japanese record as Alsaclement Tweeban Aiton and John Neulson. Thoroughgood was converted to Taragood and Coughlan to Cogran, Downey was Dawny while Flavelle became Flowell and Winning, Waning. George O'Malley's name date and cause of death (17 February, dysentery) and the place (near Manakdai) were not a problem, but his surname was transcribed as 'Olmeiley'.

Group 3 continued along the ridge towards Nelapak, 23 kilometres from Paginatan. They stopped for the night in a grove of kapok trees. The outspread branches, through which they could see the night sky, were a blessed relief after the perpetually dank, black foliage of the rain forest. It was bitterly cold, but with the pork stew simmering away, the discomfort was of no consequence. Everyone who had managed to find anything edible, such as wild tapioca, sweet potato or fern tops, had added them to the communal pot, including the find of the day, a huge melon. Salivating with anticipation, the men lifted the first spoonful to their lips, rolled it around their tongues and immediately began to retch. What the melon was they didn't know, but it had imparted a taste so vile and bitter that no one, not even the most ravenously hungry, could swallow as much as a mouthful. It was all too much for Allan Quailey, who wept with frustration and disappointment.

As they continued along the ridge the following morning it was obvious that something was the matter with Quailey. Murray stayed behind to help him, realising it was not just the beriberi and malaria, that was the problem. Quailey seemed to have lost the will to go on. They were a mile past Nelapak, on the ridge leading down to the Ranau plain, when he slumped against a large tree, refusing to go any further. Murray urged him to make one final effort but it made no difference. Murray caught up to Botterill to report that Quailey was dead. The Japanese had shot him.

Quailey had given up his fight for survival too soon. Because of increased Allied air activity over Jesselton, only Yamamoto's soldiers were to continue to Tuaran, as planned. The POWs were to remain at Ranau which was now only 18 kilometres away. Eight kilometres further along the ridge, where the Kananapan River cut the track at Muruk, was a large natural pool, abounding with fish and shaded by a huge tree. From here the track climbed again for 5 kilometres, passing through beautiful timbered country and giving a spectacular view of Kinabalu, the magnificent waterfalls which tumbled down its ancient lava peak clearly visible above a thick cloud band. At the end of the ridge the track descended rapidly for the next 5 kilometres, to a high-altitude, grassy plain. Three kilometres away, on the western side of the plain, was Ranau.

Nestled along the southern bank of the shallow, boulder-strewn Liwagu River, the two-street village created a hub from which tracks radiated to the north, south, east and west. Facing the river, in what was really a dead-end extension of the Tuaran-Ranau track, was a one-sided main street, boasting a district officer's residence, administrative offices, schoolhouse, police post, gaol, courthouse and two hospital buildings. A double row of Chinese shops (kedais), running at right angles to the main thoroughfare at the western end completed the village proper, while a native market occupied a grassy flat between the main street and the river bed. A footbridge spanned the stream, linking the village with a track leading north to Meridi and the Paginatan track from the east. Along the northern bank of the river, a little to the east of the bridge, were atap barracks belonging to a Japanese staging camp. About a kilometre further to the east, occupying a fair-sized chunk of the Ranau plain, and on the northern side of the Paginatan track, was a small airstrip. And between the strip and the Japanese barracks, on a slope where the Meridi and Paginatan tracks met, was a large atap hut in a rough bamboo enclosure — the POWs' new camp.

The hut, from which the previous occupants had recently been evicted, was separated from the staging camp by a small creek which flowed into the Liwagu River. Open-sided, it was constructed entirely of atap with the usual sleeping platforms, alive with blood-sucking vermin, each side of the main aisle. As there were no other facilities, the guards on duty occupied one end and the 'hospital' the other. 'Fit' POWs were in the middle.

Because of the lack of accommodation at Ranau, all POWs except groups 1 to 5 were ordered to remain at Paginatan. Major Watanabe Yoshio, who was in charge of the Ranau garrison and planned to use the POWs for coolie labour, was disappointed to find most of them in a poor state of health. Before he had left for Tuaran, Yamamoto had indicated that numbers were down but it was not until 19 February, when Group 5 arrived, that a roll call revealed the size of the death

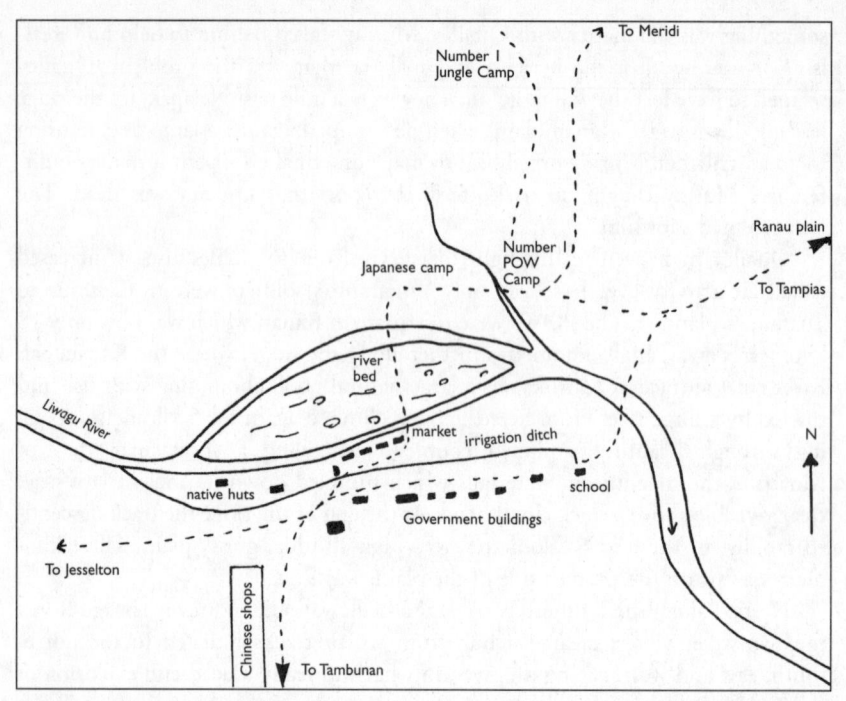

Map showing Ranau village, Ranau 1 Compound and Ranau Number 1 Jungle Compound.

toll. Of the 265 POWs who left Sandakan with these five groups, 70 (more than 26 per cent) had failed to complete the journey. Group 1, which had made the trip in a gruelling fifteen days, had lost twelve other prisoners apart from Chipperfield, Herb Dorizzi and Ewing. Group 2, which had started out with 50 POWs, had lost 20. The originally 50-strong Group 3 was down by ten, as was Group 4, which had left Sandakan with 55. Group 5, starting with 55 was now reduced to 40.

Eight more prisoners died shortly after arrival. Groups 1 and 4 seemed to have had the worst of it because of the additional baggage the POWs had been forced to carry and the speed with which they had been made to travel. However, not all the prisoners missing were known to be dead and not all the dead were prisoners. Thirty-five Japanese troops had died — some at the hands of the killing squad. And while Group 2's Lieutenant Hiraro had reported the non-arrival of 20 prisoners, he later revealed that five had escaped on 7 February, somewhere between the Mandorin and Sapi Rivers. No trace of them had been found.

One of the few locals who knew for sure that sick prisoners were being murdered was Kulang, Sandshoe Willie's friend and track co-surveyor, who was working on the staging camp at Muanad on 7 February when Group 5 arrived. Striking up a conversation with a tall, fair-haired prisoner who appeared to be in charge of the group, Kulang learned that one of the party, lying in the rest house on the eastern side of the crossing, was too ill to walk. Although the headman offered to care for him, Lieutenant Sato rejected the offer as he was worried a more senior officer might come by and report him. The next morning, when the group moved off, the incapacitated POW and a less ill companion were left behind. Not long afterwards, while the able-bodied man was boiling up some water over a small fire, two Japanese arrived on the scene and sent him on his way. As he left, he handed Kulang a photo of his family, on the back of which was an inscription, his name and the name of his sick mate. Two soldiers then placed the ill prisoner on a stretcher and carried him to a spot about 100 metres from the rest house. Soon afterwards, Kulang heard two pistol shots ring out. The victim was 39-year-old Sapper Len Haye of Western Australia and his companion Perc Carter, who had given Kulang the photo, a 26-year-old gunner from the 2/10th Field Regiment.[2] Four others from their party also perished that day. The 2/10th's Gunner Michael Rush, Bill Brady of the 2/19th, electrical engineer Harold Downey and Signaller Stan Reay, all died or were killed within the next 8 kilometres.

The remaining members of Group 5, and all others who survived the march, were to find no relief at Ranau. Dysentery broke out, claiming twelve lives in eight days. And as the regular soldiers had gone to Tuaran, they were once more at the mercy of the brutal Formosans who had made their lives such a misery at Sandakan. Hayashi (Ming the Merciless), Kawakami (The-Gold-Toothed-Shin-Kicking-Bastard), Kitamura Kotaro (the jujitsu exponent) and the equally evil Suzuki Saburo lost no time organising working parties, both inside and outside the camp area. When a small party was ordered into Ranau village to carry vegetables back to the camp, Botterill and Gunner Wally Crease of the 2/15th Field Regiment, whose real name was Gardner, volunteered. They took advantage of the excursion to engage in surreptitious conversation with a friendly Chinese cigar maker. He told them the way of escape lay across the mountains to the west — Jesselton, where the Chinese community would help them.

On 22 February, 20 POWs and some local people, accompanied by Suzuki Saburo and Hayashi, left for Paginatan with supplies for Japanese troops and the POWs still held there. Each man in the party carried a 20-kilogram bag of rice, brought up from Jesselton by coolie labour. Anyone who failed to keep up was a dead man. They were just past the 10 mile peg when two locals, Kangas and Batingi of Ganagana village, well ahead of the main pack, stopped to rest. As the others came into sight they were appalled to see that two guards were twisting a rope around the neck of one of the POWs, strangling him. The victim was stripped and dragged into the jungle, but not buried. Kangas and Batingi covered his remains with a ground sheet before rejoining the column. They had gone just over a kilometre when the guards shot the next prisoner, leaving the body beside a stream.

Three days after the rice party left, Captain Nagai, who had left Labuan on 9 February, turned up to take control of the camp and the rice carrying. When Botterill saw Nagai had brought with him several Formosans and a junior officer, Second-Lieutenant Suzuki, his hopes that the new commandant would curb the excesses of the guards, plummeted. Murray and Botterill, therefore, both volunteered to join the second rice-carrying party when it left on 28 February. They had made the right choice. The five-day journey — three up and two back — was exhausting and the guards killed anyone who could not keep up, but for those who kept their wits about them rice carrying could mean the difference between life and death.

Although the Japanese weighed the sacks at both the beginning and end of the journey, and watched the prisoners like hawks, the Australians devised a way of receiving a share of the rice. After hefting the rice sack onto their shoulders, they inserted the end of a hollow piece of bamboo between the stitches on the sack and siphoned rice from the bag into an empty water bottle, which was strategically placed beneath the sack. To cover the difference in weight of the sacks they dunked the sacks in the river as they neared Paginatan.

The unlimited rice, plus the snails, slugs, frogs and beetles they picked up along the way, were a godsend, but long term survival required a more reliable source of protein and vitamins. Botterill, using survival skills honed and refined as a child raised in Woolloomooloo, one of Sydney's most deprived areas, was the group's prime scrounger. Eyes which, at the age of eight or nine, had noted every fruit tree in the gardens of affluent Eastern Suburbs' residents, had no trouble spotting wild chillies, tapioca and ferns, while sharp ears easily detected the distant sound of a village dog barking, a well-trained memory marking the locations well.

He was accompanied on his nocturnal raids by Richie Murray and Ron Sullivan, a 30-year-old, auburn-haired AASC corporal who had also been attached to Brigadier Taylor's headquarters. Average in height but physically tough, Ron, second eldest in a family of nine, had been raised in the bush and was highly practical. A talented spin-bowler and batsman, he had played for the Country side in Country-City matches and was well known among the New South Wales' cricketing fraternity. Until the time of his enlistment he had worked on the family sheep and wheat farm, which lay in the shadow of the magnificent Warrumbungle Mountains near Purlewaugh, south-east of the New South Wales town of Coonabarabran.

The raiding party made its move after dinner when the guards, satisfied that the rice was stacked well out of the prisoners' reach, settled down for the night. They returned with goods ranging from a dog, bananas, green pawpaws and vegetables, all appropriated from the unsuspecting natives. Since the main stops were always at Muruk, Nelapak and Segindai, excess rice, and anything else which could not be eaten immediately, was wrapped in a leaf and buried for retrieval on the return trip, when the guards, more relaxed now that the rice was safely delivered, were far less vigilant.

Botterill returned from his first trip to Paginatan on 4 March to find that Perc Carter had died on 2 March and that Wally Crease and his mate Gunner Albert Cleary had escaped the day before. A search was mounted, but they were still at large when Rice Party 3 left three days later. Despite the prospect of an 80-kilometre trek to Paginatan and back, only five of the 20-strong party were not volunteers. The other fifteen, which included Botterill, Murray and Sullivan again, were only too keen to move away from a camp where the death toll for the month had already reached thirteen. The most recent death had been that of Group 1's Warrant Officer Charlie Watson, who had died from beriberi on 6 March.

The family photo which Perc Carter handed to Kulang at Muanad shortly before his mate, Len Haye, was murdered.

Kawakami, detailed to accompany the rice party, was probably as eager as the rice volunteers to quit Ranau, if only to avoid Lieutenant Suzuki. Infuriated that Crease and Cleary had escaped, he had punished the guards on duty at the time by sending them on a 4 or 5 kilometre run before lining them up for a bout of face slapping.

When the rice party returned to Ranau on 11 March, there were two more brand new graves in the cemetery. Tom, the last of the Dorizzi boys, and Jack Gaven, the talented wood sculptor, had died that day. Dr Jeffrey recorded details of all deaths, which he handed to the elderly Japanese interpreter, Sergeant-Major Fujita, for forwarding to POW Headquarters at Kuching. The funeral rites were basic. There were no coffins, nor anything to identify the graves. The naked body, placed inside a blanket slung from a pole, was carried to the cemetery and buried in a narrow, shallow ditch. Nagai took perverse pleasure in watching the burial party struggle along with their grisly burden, laughing aloud when they dropped it. Padre Garland was at Paginatan, so there were no religious services, but the burial party did spit on the bodies before covering them up, for that was the soldiers' way.

On 12 March, Botterill was coming back from burial detail when he saw that a prisoner, clad only in a fondushi and with his hands tied behind his back, was being given the log treatment at the guardhouse end of the hut. After more than a week on the run, Gunner Cleary had been recaptured. The guards, taking their revenge for their recent humiliation at the hands of Lieutenant Suzuki, were kicking and bashing him about the face and body with fists and rifle butts, charging at him with bayonets and jumping on the end of the 2-metre-long log at frequent intervals, causing him to shriek in agony. Every hour or so they forced the prisoner to his feet, causing further agonising pain as the blood flowed back to his lower limbs. At about 7.30pm, after five hours of non-stop torture, Cleary was removed from the log.

Kawakami and a fresh lot of guards started up again, early the following morning. They were still going strong when, shortly after midday, a member of the local Kempei-tai delivered Wally Crease to the guardhouse. Kawakami kicked

Cleary, still trussed to the log, under the sleeping platform, and now turned his attention to the recaptured escapee who, like Cleary, had been betrayed to the Japanese by locals keen to claim a reward. At about 6.00pm Cleary was dragged out from beneath the platform to join Crease on the log. For the next 90 minutes the guards indulged in the same hideous torture of the previous day, the victims' pleas for mercy only inciting their tormentors to further brutality. The ill-treatment continued on and off throughout the night, increasing in intensity at each change of the guard. Dawn brought no relief. By 7.00am Kawakami was at it again, desisting only when it was time to organise the day's working parties. Realising the guards were distracted, Crease, who had just been released from the log to get a drink of water, escaped. By the time they realised he had disappeared, he was well out of sight. Kawakami and Miajima, The English-Speaking-Bastard, were later sent to look for him, but returned empty-handed, provoking Suzuki to show his displeasure with another round of face-slapping.

Rice Party 4 left immediately after roll call that day, 14 March. It was a harrowing journey. They had only reached the 9 mile peg, early on the second day, when the killing began. One of the older men, Gunner Wright Albert Sheard, of the 2/10th Field Regiment, was too weak to go on. Refusing to let his companions help him, and taking no notice of his impassioned pleas for mercy, the guards hauled Sheard off the track and shot him. They split the rice he was carrying among the others and forced the party to move on.

They returned on 18 March to find that Crease had been shot in the jungle to the west of the camp shortly after his escape, and that Cleary, a rope around his neck and wearing only a fondushi, had been tied up ever since to a tree outside the hut. He was suffering from dysentery, lying in his own excreta and in a shocking state. Multiple bruises and blood blisters covered his blood-encrusted face and body, now a sickly shade of yellow. His tormentors no longer beat him with their fists, preferring instead to deliver kicks as they passed by, to hit him with rifle butts, to spit or urinate on him. Nagai, who had ordered Cleary's rations to be cut in half before leaving the camp on official business and Lieutenant Suzuki, who had assumed command in his absence, made no attempt to stop the brutality or provide the prisoner with shelter from the blistering sun during the day and the chill air of the evening. Cleary's condition deteriorated and his mates wept, unable to do anything other than beseech the Almighty to 'let the poor bastard die'. He lasted until 20 March when, as a further humiliation, the semi-conscious and dying man was removed from the compound and dumped, like garbage awaiting disposal, near a gutter at the side of the Meridi track. By the time his friends were allowed to attend to him, Albert Cleary was close to death. At the creek they tenderly washed away the accumulated grime and sludge from his wasted, battered body before carrying him back to the hut where he died, cradled in the arms of his mates.

Kawakami, who considered that 22-year-old Cleary had received his just desserts, warned the surviving POWs, 'if you escape the same thing will happen to you'. Rod Jeffrey, appalled at the barbarity of what he had witnessed, vowed, 'if any of us get out of here this atrocity must be reported'. But the chances of anyone staying alive long enough to do so were growing slimmer with each passing day. By 20 March, the day of Cleary's death, Botterill and the others had buried no fewer than 60 of their comrades. Forty-eight were in the original graveyard plot, about 100 metres to the east of the hut on the other side of a small gully. Cleary, classified as a 'criminal', was not allowed to be buried with his fellow soldiers, but the other dead were in a new cemetery 100 metres further up the hill. Most had died of dysentery, with beriberi claiming the next largest group, while about five or six carrying rice to Paginatan had met their end on the track. Among the last to be buried in the old cemetery were the incorrigible James Stuart Smith, who had forged the leave passes in Malaya, and Keith 'Shearer' Gillett, Billy Young's mentor who had organised the boxing matches at Sandakan. He had lost his fight for life on 14 March when, swollen with beriberi and racked with malaria, he had died shortly before dawn.

The day after Cleary's death, Botterill was once again on his way to Paginatan, with Rice Party 5. Although the 'fittest' were on these working parties, malnutrition and disease were taking effect. Every opportunity was taken to steal rice, but Botterill and his mates were no longer adding dog meat to the pot, after discovering that the village curs at Paginatan were feeding on the bodies of the dead buried there. They were however, able to trade some of their curry ration with the locals and with the guards. While the locals received 100 per cent curry powder in this exchange, the guards did not. The POWs had discovered that borer droppings, when mixed through the powder, not only bulked it out but were undetectable to the eye.

Murray and Botterill had only been back in camp two days when the guard commander announced that they must make yet another trip to Paginatan. The rice carriers dug in their heels. Their decision to go on strike did not meet with the approval of Captain Nagai, now back in camp. He stormed from his neat, white-washed, mud-rendered atap hut which his underlings had built him, and confronted Murray, the group's spokesman, with an angry, 'What's this I hear about refusing to carry the rice?' In response to Murray's laconic, 'That's right', Nagai barked, 'If you don't carry it, I'll march you all back to Sandakan'.

Coming from Nagai, this was no idle threat, and Botterill, Murray, Sullivan and seventeen others, most of whom were ill, left the camp on 28 March. Of the six trips to date, it was by far the worst. The prisoners were still in sight of the camp when the killing began. They had crossed the Ranau plain and stopped for the second 'smoko' part way up the first hill when it became obvious that one of the men, suffering from advanced beriberi, could go no further. The other prisoners begged for him to be allowed to return to the camp but the soldier accompanying them dragged the helpless man to the side of the track and dispatched him with a single shot to the head. The party was to lose four more of its 20 men. Two made it to Paginatan, only to die on the return journey. The party was 10 kilometres from Paginatan on 31 March, Easter Saturday, when, shortly after noon, Gunner Wallace Alberts, one of five Aboriginal soldiers to be sent to Borneo[3] and Botterill's bushie mate, Ron Sullivan, blacked out while tackling the hill near Segindai. Both men were unconscious, so the guard bayonetted them to death.

Back in Australia Mr and Mrs Sullivan and their youngest child, Helen, had just left the Coonabarabran's St Lawrence O'Toole Catholic Church after Easter

Saturday service. Instead of crossing the street to have a cup of tea and a bite to eat with Mrs Hennessy, whose son was also a POW, Mrs Sullivan got into the family car to leave. Puzzled by her mother's deviation from what had been a post-church ritual for as long as she could remember, Helen asked what was the matter. 'I can't face Mrs Hennessy just now', her mother replied. 'I know something terrible has just happened to Ron'.

Rice Party 6 had been somewhere between Muruk and Nelapak, on the way to Paginatan, when they had passed about 50 or so POWs, some of them in a very poor state indeed, coming from the opposite direction. As the rice party now retraced its steps back to Ranau, it was obvious to Botterill that not all had made it to their destination. Near Muruk, he noticed a body lying in a ditch to one side of the path. It was Private Noel Parker of the 2/20th Battalion and it looked as if he had been battered to death. When he arrived back in Ranau later that day, Botterill learned from Bill Moxham what had happened, not only to Parker, but to those who had left Sandakan with the later parties.

In the end, only nine groups had left on the march. Hoshijima had been ordered to send 500 POWs, but only 455 were anywhere fit enough to leave the camp.[4] Of these, 265 Australians had formed Groups 1-5, while the remainder, 90 Australians and 100 English, had made up groups 6-9. Group 6, the first mixed party, comprised 20 Australians and 20 Englishmen, under the control of 50 Japanese troops and three Formosans. Hoshijima was battling to make up the numbers and some of the 50 POWs in Group 7, the last of the purely Australian parties, were suffering with advanced ulcers, as well as malaria and beriberi. They were accompanied by 45 troops, while the 50-strong Group 8, which was entirely English, had 49 Japanese and three Formosans. The last party, under the command of Captain Abe, the officer also in charge of the 'disposal' squad, had 20 Australian and 30 British POWs. With this group were 50 troops and five compound guards.

These groups had not fared well. Their poor health, the greatly depleted food dumps and brutality of some of the Formosans, had accounted for the lives of at least 44 POWs between Sandakan and Paginatan, an overall death rate of just over 23 per cent. On 23 February, when Bill Moxham's party (Group 7) reached Paginatan after a nineteen-day trek, seven POWs and the same number of Japanese had dropped out. Although many in this group were quite ill, the death rate was by far the lowest at 14 per cent, or about half the average. As Moxham pointed out, the reason for this was simple. There were no Formosans and the troops accompanying them travelled light and carried all their own gear.

Holding torches to light the way, Watanabe and Moritake had escorted them from the Sandakan camp as far as the 9 mile, where Second-Lieutenant Sugimura Shunichi informed them he had been instructed to take them to Ranau 'to the best of his ability'. With the rain still coming down in torrents every afternoon, progress was slow, about 11 kilometres a day. Moxham's group had only reached the 21 mile post when one of the party had become ill with malaria. He struggled on to the 23 mile, but when it became obvious he could not continue, Sugimura sent him back to Sandakan with two Japanese soldiers and enough rations to sustain them on the journey. Shortly after their departure the prisoners were informed that the four days' ration — rice, dried fish and a small amount of salt and sugar issued at Sandakan — must now stretch to eight. On reaching Muanad, on about 10 February, they each received a handful of rice, supposedly enough to last two days, along with some potatoes and greens to be shared among 49 men. It was undoubtedly only because they were not carrying any baggage that they were able to go another 80 kilometres without losing any of the party.

The first to die was Gunner Albert Dale. Aged 38, he was about 3 kilometres from the night's stopping place west of the Celo River on 13 February when he collapsed from beriberi and dysentery. Moxham and three others were given permission to go back and bring him to the camp site but he died during the night. They buried him and marked the place, making him one of the few to have an identified grave along the track. Unfortunately, they were not allowed to do the same for Gunner Tom Coughlan who dropped out with severe malaria and beriberi several kilometres before. The Japanese allegedly went back for him, but Moxham never saw him again.

The next day, 12 kilometres west of the Celo River, another three dropped out — Private Ken Molde (who had changed his name to Dawson to enlist), Gunner Eric Fuller and another, too sick to go on. They were joined by two Englishmen, Gunner Bois Roberts and Leading Air-Craftsman Herbert Beardshaw from Group 6 which, as it was moving slowly, had been almost overtaken by the unencumbered Group 7. Moxham had no idea what had become of them, or the identity of a body from one of the earlier parties, lying in the middle of the track, shovel in hand. However, he did know that the next two who dropped out near Melio at the foot of the big mountain were shot by Japanese at a staging camp there. At Maringan he also noticed a body under a log beside the track. The dead man's colour patch was that of his sister unit, the 2/10th Field Regiment, so he stopped and examined the corpse. It was 35-year-old Gunner Gervin Williams, a member of Lieutenant Sato Tetsuo's Group 5, who had died on 15 February.

There had also been at least one escape. Four out of a group of five who had escaped early in the march had fallen foul of the Kempei-tai. After obtaining a boat from Sumin, who came from Sungei Batang, they had arrived at the village of Mumiang, to the south of Sandakan, where they were sheltered by the headman. When their presence was reported by a collaborator, they were taken back to Sandakan where all were tortured and four killed. The fifth, after allegedly disclosing who had given them the boat, was evidently spared. Sumin was not.

Group 6 had not lost the highest proportion of men (29 per cent), but it had suffered the most hardship. The Japanese officer in charge, Lieutenant Tanaka Shojiro, a 48-year-old veteran from the First World War, did not believe in travelling light. It had taken six POWs to carry his boxes and trunks, slung coolie-style on bamboo poles. Nor had he kept close enough control over the Formosan guards attached to his group. The prisoners, loaded down with baggage and trying to keep a footing in torrential rain as they staggered up the mountain between Milulu and Tampias, moved too slowly for the guards who started to beat them with rifle butts and sticks. When Private Roderick Richards, of the 2/10th Field Ambulance, took exception to being prodded in the back with a rifle, the guard's reaction was predictable. He tied Richards up and beat him to a pulp before shoving him over the side of the track. Moxham's party heard moans coming from the undergrowth as they passed the spot the following morning. The POWs and guards who scrambled down the slope to investigate found Richards, in great agony and partially paralysed, lying at the bottom of a gully. He was helped along by his rescuers but the severity of his injuries forced him to fall out before they reached Tampias.

There were twelve other POWs missing from Tanaka's Group 6 when it reached Paginatan. The first to fall by the wayside was Englishman Joseph Sarginson, a 26-year-old air-craftsman from Durham. Stricken with beriberi, he was struggling through the mud and slush 5 kilometres east of the Mandorin River on 9 February when he could go no further. He was not missed for some hours. Two POWs with medical training, and a Japanese soldier, were sent back to look for him, but could find no trace. The next morning an advance party from Group 7 reported that they had seen his body lying beside the track. The next two died before reaching Boto, while the high country beyond had claimed another six, including the 2/10th Field Regiment's Gunner Basil Smeeton, who had enlisted in New Guinea.

Despite this party's high death toll, not all had died en route. Unable to go beyond the 27 mile peg, the AASC's Driver George Carter, aged 23, who had sprained his ankle, and an Englishman suffering from malaria, had been sent back to Sandakan by the lieutenant, along with two Japanese soldiers, also too ill to continue. The decision to allow him to return to camp must have come as a surprise to Carter. Only two or three weeks before, he had been so badly beaten by guards for saluting an Australian officer that he was black and blue from the hips down. Both Carter and his companion arrived back at Sandakan safely. Two others, left behind at Boto with beriberi, also recovered sufficiently to come on with Moxham's group.

The last two parties, Groups 8 and 9, had found the march very hard going. Their generally poorer health was exacerbated by the depleted food stocks at each dump and a track which had been churned to mud by the previous groups. Lieutenant Horikawa Koichi, who was in charge of Group 8, was at a loss to know why they had been ordered to undertake such a journey in such appalling conditions. He lost seven of his 46 soldiers and thirteen POWs, the latter representing 26 per cent of the group. Four POWs, stricken with malaria, were left behind at Boto, along with Japanese Privates Chojin Toshio and Araki Gensuki. None, including the soldiers, were ever seen again.

Group 9, composed of the highest number of sick and to which Lieutenant Abe Kazuo's killing squad had been attached, had the highest mortality rate — 36 per cent. It was not until Muanad that Abe first detailed two of his men, Privates Endo Hiraki and Sato, to attend to the stragglers. The first victim was shot by Sato somewhere between Muanad and Boto, a stretch that claimed the lives of seven others, all said to have died from natural causes. Sato disposed of the next straggler shortly after reaching Boto, while another five, left behind by previous parties, were also dispatched by him, the fatal bullets evidently fired without any qualms. If Endo can be believed, he had no stomach for killing. Unable to put five desperately ill men out of their misery he took the soft option, leaving them to die beside the track without food or water, a decision he later regretted. By the time the party arrived at Paginatan, only 32 out of the original 50 were left alive.

Paginatan was not destined to be a refuge for those who had survived the rigours of the march. Of the 182 prisoners in groups 6-9 who had not been recaptured or returned to Sandakan, 138 had reached the village, only to discover that with the departure of the soldiers they were now at the mercy of the guards. Most of these men had been brought in from one of the western garrisons but also there were Sandakan's brutal Suzuki Saburo and Hayashi (Ming the Merciless), who had been sent from Ranau with the first rice party. The beatings began again. No one was spared, especially the sick, whose debility the guards seemed to find annoying. Warrant Officer Kinder tried to protect the men but he generally ended up receiving a bashing. The poor food, lack of medical attention and harsh treatment took a dreadful toll on those whose energy had been sapped by the march. Despite the tireless efforts of ambulanceman/chaplain Alan Garland, they died like flies. After only a month, of the 138 who had arrived at Paginatan, only about 60 were still alive. Padre Garland was not among them, having died on 18 March. He and the others now lay in shallow, unmarked graves along the banks of the river, along with a prisoner named Smith, who had come from Ranau with one of the rice parties and, unable to bear the thought of the return journey, had cut his own wrists.

On 26 March, between 50 and 60 Paginatan survivors were ordered to move to Ranau. With fiends such as Hayashi and Suzuki Saburo in control, it was to be a five-day, nightmare journey. Setting off at 7.00 each morning, the POWs were given a set distance to cover each day and the guards beat anyone who lagged behind. Sometimes it was 10.00pm before they completed the day's trek, only to be then sent off to scrounge for food. Although the guards traded the POWs' blankets, boots and clothing with the natives for pigs and sweet potatoes, the prisoners saw very little of it — a few sweet potatoes and, on one occasion, the skin of a pig. About 46 reached Ranau alive.[5] The rest had either died from their illnesses or been dispatched by guards in circumstances described by Kinder as 'wicked'. Noel Parker, whose body Botterill had seen beside the track, was one such victim. Bloated with beriberi, he had been getting along all right, although not fast enough for Hayashi. The Formosan refused to leave Parker alone, forcing him along at such a rate that even with Moxham's and Kinder's help, he could not keep up. When Hayashi, who had gone ahead, looked back and saw that Parker could go no further, he stomped back along the track. He beat Parker about the head and shoulders with the butt of his rifle until he fell to the ground, then ordered Kinder and Moxham to move on. However, on hearing Parker's screams, Kinder returned. He pleaded for Hayashi to stop but the Formosan had not been dubbed Ming the Merciless for nothing. Swinging his rifle at Kinder, he turned again to the task at hand, beating Parker without let-up for another ten minutes, by which time he was no longer alive.

When Botterill had returned to Ranau on 1 April with Rice Party 6, it was to discover that the Paginatan survivors who had arrived the day before had swelled the total number in camp to about 150. Of the 452 POWs who had finally embarked upon the march itself, at least 302 were now dead. The main march had accounted for 123, the Paginatan camp for 69, Ranau for 89, the just completed Paginatan-Ranau march and the six rice journeys for about 21. Rice Party 6 was the last. As five had died on the most recent trip, and the rest were barely able to move about the camp, let alone march any distance, Nagai called an end to it. In future the rice, which was still needed to supply troops passing through on their way to Jesselton, would be taken to Paginatan by local coolies.

It was just as well that, by this time, the Japanese had moved out of the end of the POW hut and into a new guardhouse, erected some metres away. Three-quarters of the space was now devoted entirely to the sick and dying, most of whom were dysentery patients. Those unable to control their bowels moved under the huts and tried valiantly to scratch a hole in the earth with their dixies, or, in some cases, to use them as emergency chamber pots, but the stench was appalling. Slick with bloody mucous and excreta, the bamboo slats, as well as the patients themselves, attracted myriads of flies which, in turn, contaminated everything on which they settled. The others could do nothing to relieve the suffering. After scraping away the encrusted filth from the sleeping platform, men went to sleep at night not knowing whether the person either side of them would be alive or dead when the new day dawned. Each morning on waking, Botterill checked the man lying alongside him. If, as was often the case, he had died during the night, the body would be stripped and the clothing distributed to the living, before he was taken on his last journey up the hill to the ever-expanding cemetery. Those who knew their end was near could only wait. The eyes of the dysentery patients, enormous above gaunt, sunken cheekbones were a stark contrast to the almost indistinguishable slits in the suety, moon-like faces of the beriberi sufferers. The dying watched those still on their feet, silently pleading for help; help which, to Botterill's great distress, he was unable to provide.

It was at this time that Botterill, his head and legs swollen with beriberi, gave up the will to live. Ranau had become a place so dreadful it defied the scope of normal human experience; a place at which the barest necessities of life no longer existed; a place which Botterill, surrounded by muck and death and slime, now reduced to the simplest of terms: 'no toilet paper, no comb, no soap, no toothbrush, no clothes, no food, no medicine. But plenty of lice, plenty of bugs, plenty of crabs, plenty of mites, plenty of flies, but above all, no hope.'

Richie Murray, outside chopping wood, learned that Botterill had taken himself to the end of the hut to die. He reacted instinctively. There was no way he was going to allow his best mate to give up now. He hauled Botterill from what would have been his death bed, helped him outside, bullying him to keep going and forcing him to stay on his feet and help gather wood. Murray's dogged refusal to allow his friend to die, or perhaps the enforced physical activity which helped purge the toxic fluid build-up from his body, worked. Instead of dying, Keith Botterill turned the corner.

By the last week of April, there were less than 60 left alive. Morale had also deteriorated rapidly during the past month, the need for survival peeling away the last vestiges of civilised behaviour. It was now a case of every man for himself. Not even Dr Jeffrey had risen above it. Forsaking the sacred Hippocratic oath which had hitherto sustained him, he refused to administer to the men. He was, however, treating the Japanese and trading his medical equipment in return for extra food for himself, telling the sick and dying he was 'doing it for their own good'. His record keeping was now a low priority and the date of death and the name of the deceased were the only details passed to the Japanese. Those who had mates still stuck together, but even they watched each other at meal times, in case one received a teaspoon more of the watery slurry. As the rice carrying expeditions had been discontinued, the opportunity to obtain extra food had ceased. Food was so scarce that Botterill and Murray were supplementing their meagre ration with tiny, immature pawpaws, which they had found on a tree growing near the hut. They knew that the rock-hard, unripened fruit would make them ill if eaten in its natural state, so they had grated it on a piece of tin, through which nail holes had been punched, before adding it to the pot. When the pawpaws had all been eaten they moved onto the leaves, and finally the trunk.

Meanwhile, the steady stream of information on the POW situation was continuing to flow to SRD from Gort Chester's Agas headquarters on Jembongan Island, north of Sandakan. With the recent news that the POWs in Sandakan had all been moved to Jesselton, interest had turned to Ranau which, judging from the reports of huge enemy troop movements, was being turned into a stronghold. Consequently, on ANZAC Day, 25 April, American Air Force planes were ordered to make a concentrated attack on both the airstrip and the nearby Japanese barracks. As Lightnings tore overhead, unaware that the lone atap hut between the airstrip and barracks was filled with ill and dying POWs, the Japanese and prisoners ducked for cover. When the dust settled, two prisoners and a number of Japanese troops were found dead. The camp was no longer tenable. Two days later, the 56 surviving prisoners and their guards abandoned the Ranau Number 1 Camp and headed north-west, into the jungle.

Chapter Twelve
'ANNIHILATE THEM ALL'

They didn't go far. Skirting the cemetery they continued around the side of the hill for about a kilometre or so to a small jungle clearing, where there were three or four abandoned native huts. Originally designated as Sinarut Camp, the name of a nearby village, the guards also called this place Ranau Number 1 Jungle Camp, a label which would later cause it to be confused with the old Ranau Number 1 Compound.

The Japanese grabbed the first hut, the one closest to Ranau. The Formosan guards were in another about 40 metres away while the POWs were 50 metres beyond that, in sight of their guards but far enough removed to ensure that the sight and smell of their emaciated, filthy bodies offended neither Formosan nor Japanese sensibilities. This hut, measuring roughly 8 metres square and elevated only 30 centimetres above the ground, had a small lean-to cookhouse, with an open fireplace, erected on one side. A detached kitchen for the Formosans and the Japanese, was a short distance from the guards' hut. There was no perimeter fencing but the POW hut had been encircled with a double-strand barbed-wire fence, erected about a metre from the walls.

There were six fewer Japanese at the new camp. Major Watanabe, who gave the order for the move, remained in Ranau with the occupation garrison. Captain Nagai, with subordinates Beppu, Okada, Takahara and Ishii had gone off along the Tambunan track south of Ranau, to investigate the establishment of another compound. Lieutenant Suzuki was left to oversee the POWs and the remaining guards — a group of about eight or so including Suzuki Saburo and Kawakami. Rod Jeffrey was the most senior POW officer, but the camp leader was now Warrant Officer Kinder who, although an airman, had earned the respect of the troops by his willingness to stand up to the Japanese at Paginatan. It was Kinder, with the help of men such as Moxham, who held this small tribe together.

The POWs at the new camp were detailed to various tasks. Botterill, Murray and Moxham, among the fittest, were sent with a working party to remove atap from the old camp and carry it to the site Nagai had inspected, about 8 kilometres south of Ranau village. They were hard at work when the Lightnings came on what had become a regular strafing run. Botterill dived into a slit trench ditch while his two mates scuttled into one of the Japanese bunkers. They were unaware that the object of the pilot's attention was not the airstrip, which would be put out of commission once and for all on 30 May when eleven 1000 pound (450 kilogram) bombs were dropped on it, or the village kedai, which had been burnt to the ground by a previous raid, but the very bunker in which they were sheltering. Fortunately the gunner's aim was off.

As soon as it was safe to venture out, the prisoners gathered up the atap and proceeded to a small, partially-cleared valley, surrounded by lush jungle and through which flowed a pleasant stream. Since Captain Nagai, the only person in authority who spoke English, was nowhere to be seen, they were unable to determine the reason for the lean-to shelters being erected by local coolie labour. They then returned to Sinarut and more menial chores, keeping one ear cocked for the sound of Allied aircraft which had, during previous raids, dropped several bombs uncomfortably close to the camp. Lieutenant Suzuki had insisted initially that all POWs remain in their hut during air raids, but had agreed to allow them to take cover in the jungle, on condition that no one took advantage of this concession by attempting to escape.

It was not much of a risk. They were too weak to go far and there was little chance of obtaining food outside the camp. Botterill, however, had located a secret Japanese rice cache while out on a working party. He had been collecting wood down near the old camp when he was ordered to stow a sack of rice in a small, cellar-like food store. Cut into the slope near the main cemetery and just off the foot-pad that linked the old camp site with the new, the store-house was so inconspicuous that, up until that time, not even the sharp-eyed Botterill had been aware of its existence.

On 6 May Rod Jeffrey, who had been ill for weeks with beriberi, died. Ransacking what was left of his medical kit, the prisoners found several scalpels with which they were now able to lance their boils. The next day they buried ambulanceman Colin Smyth, Tom Burns' mate. There was no proper cemetery here. The new camp was surrounded by jungle and burial places were scattered about the few areas cleared of foliage. Individual graves were also a thing of the past. By this time the fit were scarcely able to raise enough energy to scrape out even a shallow hole with a chonkol, so the burial party, whenever possible, opted for mass graves. However, during the first week of May Botterill, Murray and three or four others were ordered to transport five bodies, slung in a ground sheet, to a small plot in a clearing. They had buried only the first three when Murray saw a baby goat, about 10 metres away. He dived on the creature while Botterill dispatched it with the chonkol. While the rest of the party diverted the guards' attention by industriously digging a new grave for the two remaining bodies, Murray wrapped the tiny carcass inside the ground sheet.

Another mass burial took place a week or so later when, following the death of ten POWs, including Warrant Officer Warrington and Herb Lytton, the only POW in camp who still owned a decent shirt. The burial detail selected a spot, about 35 metres further down the track towards Ranau. As Herb Lytton also had a leather wallet, stuffed full of papers, Botterill left the shirt on the body and placed the wallet in the breast pocket, in the hope that at some later date his remains might be recovered and identified.

A rumour circulated at this time that the fit were to be marched to another camp in a fortnight or so, possibly as far away as Jesselton. Knowing they could not survive another forced march, Botterill and Murray agreed to escape as soon as the move was announced. On the basis that, if they ran into trouble, eight fists would be better than four, they invited two more to join them — Corporal Norm Allie from their own battalion and Norm Grist, a steady, reliable private from the 2/30th. Aware that the local population could not always be trusted, they agreed that a successful escape depended on two things. First, they must build up their strength in order to get as far away from the camp as possible. Second, it was vital they take reserve food stocks with them to avoid reliance on outside help. However, if contact with the local people were unavoidable, Norm Allie would be their spokesman. He was Asian — the son of Charles Mohamet Allie, who had emigrated to Australia and lived at Battery Point, Tasmania.

That night, Botterill led the others under the wire and down the track to the food store, which was not locked. They removed a 20-kilogram sack of rice, and a small wooden box, rearranging the rice bags carefully to leave no sign of the theft. In the cemetery, they stopped and examined the spoils. The box contained a dozen or so draw-string, calico bags containing about twelve small, all-day suckers and the same number of biscuits, of a type generally known to sailors as 'hard tack'. After burying the box among the graves, the men returned to the camp, where they gave a bag of biscuits to four of their mates, who had agreed to act as cockatoos and keep an eye on the two Formosan guards. Some of the food was distributed to the others, particularly the sick, and the remainder split into four equal parts. Allie, Botterill and Grist secreted three of them in the jungle while Murray hid the other, in the low sub-floor space under the hut, for current use.

Five days passed. On the afternoon of 20 May, while the prisoners were going about their usual chores, one of the guards, for reasons that have never been ascertained, squatted down and looked under the POW hut. Spotting an empty calico bag, he called to a colleague and the pair uncovered the theft. Lieutenant Suzuki immediately called a muster, ordering the camp's 30 surviving prisoners to line up in two ranks. Botterill whispered to Murray, who was standing in the front row, 'Don't panic. Don't say anything. They can't shoot us all.'

Stealing rice was a capital offence and Suzuki had worked himself into a frenzy. Ranting and raving, he stormed up and down, waving the biscuit bag about and demanding that the culprit confess. Botterill was poised for flight, but no one moved. Then, to Botterill's horror, Richie Murray stepped forward. In a clear, firm voice, he told Suzuki that he had stolen the food and that he, and he alone, was responsible.

He was taken at bayonet point to a tree outside the Japanese hut and tied up while the rest of the prisoners were told to get on with their work which, for Botterill, was cutting wood down at the Formosan quarters. He couldn't see what was going on but he figured that Suzuki would keep Murray tied to the tree overnight. After dark he would cut Murray loose and escape, possibly with Allie and Grist as previously planned. They would have to flee immediately, of course, but, with the rest of the stolen food still safely hidden in the jungle, at least they would have a fair chance of making a good break before the alarm was raised.

About an hour later Botterill looked up to see Murray disappearing down the track under escort. He couldn't identify the guards but some English prisoners, working in the main kitchen on the other side of the Formosan hut, had a clear view. They watched, horrified, as Suzuki, accompanied by a guard escort which included Kawakami (The Gold-Toothed-Shin-Kicking-Bastard), Mori Shoichi and Yoshiya Kinjo, took Murray, who had been savagely beaten, down the track at bayonet point. Twenty minutes later the guards returned without him.

Botterill's worst fears became a hideous reality when Kawakami swaggered down to the Formosan hut and made a great show of wiping his bayonet on the grass, boasting to his fellow guards that he had 'blooded his blade' on the prisoner.

Botterill was shattered by the realisation that his friend, the only true friend he had ever had, the man he had loved like an elder brother, was dead. But the nightmare was just beginning. Kawakami, convinced that Botterill was also implicated in the theft, pushed the ashen-faced prisoner up the steps of the hut and forced him inside and to his knees. Picking up Suzuki's sword, which the guards had been ordered to polish, Kawakami drew the cold steel blade across the back of Botterill's neck. Botterill appealed to Memora, who was watching, begging in a mixture of Malay and Japanese, 'Please tell Kawakami I didn't steal his rice'. Memora, one of the few Formosans who had ever exhibited any common decency or kindness towards the prisoners, turned to Kawakami and said, 'You've already killed his friend. Leave him alone. They're dying like flies and will all be dead soon.' Kawakami removed the blade from the neck of his terrified captive, placed a boot against the small of his back and sent him sprawling down the steps.

After Richie Murray's death Botterill retreated into himself, functioning like an automaton, numbed by grief but unable to weep. He believed that Murray had been murdered near the main cemetery at the old camp and tried to look for the body while out on a working party but, to his great and everlasting sorrow, he failed to find it. Keith Botterill had buried every prisoner in the camp. To be unable to perform this final act for a man who had so passionately wanted to live but had, in the end, deliberately and selflessly sacrificed his life for his friends, was almost too much to bear. And yet, in spite of the misery that threatened to overwhelm him, Botterill did not cave in. Indeed, Murray's death had the reverse effect, strengthening Botterill's resolve to live at a time when many others had simply given up. He had to accept the fact that his mate had died, and in a hideous manner. However, what he did not have to accept was that those responsible would get away with it. Botterill had not only to go on living, he also had to survive, for Murray's sake.

It was going to take a great deal of luck and a great deal of willpower. The intractable Punchy Donohue, one of the few to survive the rigours of the cage, died on 30 May and by 9 June only 21 of the 56 who had arrived at the jungle camp were left alive. Ten were still on their feet, but the remainder were ill or close to death. Warrant Officer Kinder had pulled through the dysentery epidemic, only to come down with malaria and another bout of dysentery. Moxham, who was nursing him, knew only too well that a man might shake off a severe case of dysentery, or malaria, or beriberi, but not two of them together, especially with malnutrition, tropical ulcers and parasitic worms added to the mix. In the early hours of 10 June, Kinder died. Moxham, who buried him, marked the spot with a wooden cross on which he carved the airman's name, making him the only prisoner buried at Ranau to have a properly identified grave.

Later that morning the prisoners were told that all those who could walk were to go to a new camp. Botterill, unable to face yet another move, stayed in the hut with the sick instead of lining up with the others. The absence of the prisoner known to the guards as the 'wood soldier' was immediately noticed. Botterill was ordered to pick up his pathetically small bundle of possessions and move off with the others. They left behind 36 dead, another nine so close to dying it no longer mattered and Norm Allie who, although not well himself, had remained to look after them. He told Moxham that if things looked bad he would try to bury some records or notes under the hut.

Of the 452 sent to Ranau just over five months before, these ten emaciated creatures, Allie and the nine who were sick, were all that remained.

At Ranau village they did not turn to the west in the direction of Jesselton, as they had expected, but south. Their destination was the Ranau Number 2 Jungle Camp, to which Moxham and Botterill had carried the atap. They were not told the reason for the change in destination — Allied warships were approaching the west coast. Escorting them to the new camp were two guards, Haneda Miyoshi and Toyoda Takashi. Botterill and Moxham had been given the task of transporting a huge, cabinet-model gramophone belonging to one of the Japanese but, fortunately, the guards were in no hurry and the entire party reached its destination without mishap. A couple of days later Suzuki and the rest of the guards from the Sinarut camp arrived. They were alone. Allie and the others had been murdered some hours after the others had left.

It had not been until quite late in the afternoon that Suzuki had announced to Sergeant Iwabe Shigaru that the sick POWs were to be killed. Two had died during the day, so the group numbered eight: six stretcher cases, Allie, and one other who was still able to walk. Kawakami, Suzuki Saburo, Hayashida Mitsujiro (who had accompanied Group 1 from Sandakan), Ishii Fujio (who had come up from the new camp site), Yanai Kenji and Suzuki Taiichi were ordered to carry the six stretcher cases to a clearing where Kinder and 21 others had been buried. Meanwhile, Takata Kunio took up a position another 50 metres down the track in case any locals unexpectedly appeared. The first two prisoners were shot where they lay by Lieutenant Suzuki with his pistol. While Suzuki Taiichi looked on, he also shot one of the next two, leaving the other for Iwabe to dispatch with his rifle. The next pair was killed by Kawakami and Ishii, the latter taking two shots to do it. The last pair, evidently the two still on their feet, were taken aside by Takata, Yanai and Suzuki Saburo, who had not as yet participated in the killing. They were lousy shots. Their unfortunate victims urged them to hurry up and finish them off, but they each had to fire another round before life was pronounced extinct.

The guards at the new camp now outnumbered the prisoners. The site had been well chosen and there was little chance of anyone seeing it from the air. Although the track to Tambunan ran through fairly flat forested country initially, 8 kilometres to the south of Ranau (near the 110 mile) it cut through a small, steeply-sided valley, before crossing the Kehunut River, just east of its junction with the Kenipir. It was here, on the southern side of the river valley just below the junction, hidden by thick, overhanging rainforest, that the new camp had been erected. It wasn't much — four atap huts for the guards and another for the quartermaster's store, with a small lean-to for the POWs further up the hill.

The smaller of the four huts, set apart from the other three, was designated for the exclusive use of officers. There was only one occupant, Lieutenant Suzuki.

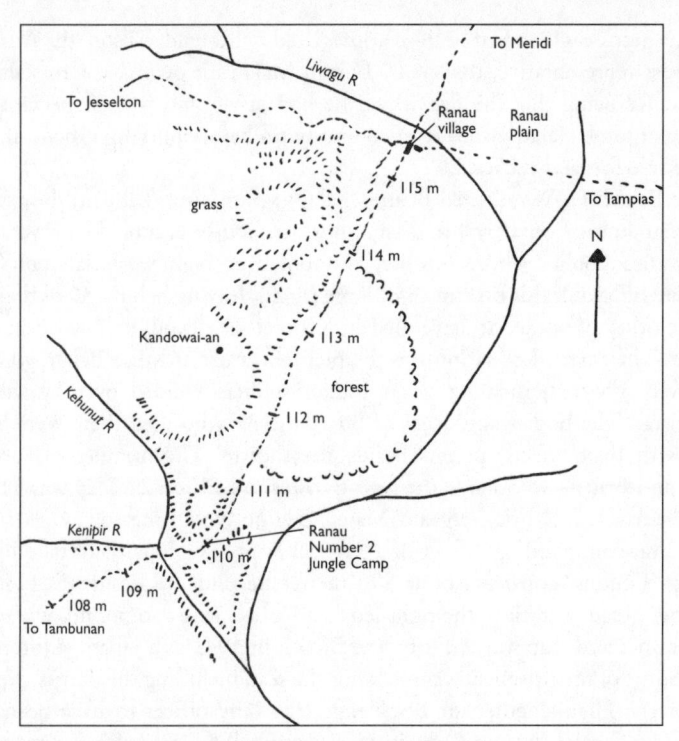

Map showing position of Ranau Number 2 Jungle Camp

Captain Nagai had left Ranau for good, transferred in late April to Tenou, his well-timed departure demonstrating yet again a remarkable talent to be far away from the scene of any 'unpleasantness'. He left Sandakan and Ranau before the deaths began to escalate and had been absent from camp when Cleary was murdered. His transfer from Labuan Island had been most opportune, as well. The first few months for the 300 POWs sent to Labuan had not been too bad. Although they were poorly-clad and very thin, they had managed to remain cheerful, singing rousing renditions of 'Tipperary' as they toiled in the swamps. However, the poor rations, overwork and malaria were too much. Almost half died during Nagai's six month administration and, by the time Colonel Suga ordered his successor, Sergeant-Major Sugino, to move the prisoners to Kuching six weeks later, the death toll, which now included Dead Ender Joey Crome, had risen to 188.[1] All had been buried with due solemnity, each corpse draped with a Union Jack flag, used specifically for that purpose. On 7 March, shortly after the 112 remaining POWs and their fifteen Formosan guards had departed for Kuching, Corporal L. Malau, one of the many thousands of Dutch-Indonesians brought to Borneo to provide a labour force, entered the abandoned compound in search of food. Under the administrative building he found the flag, on which were inscribed between 30 and 40 names which, he assumed, were those of the deceased.[2] Although Malau owed no allegiance to the British, he was a man of great humanity. At Kuching he had supplied eggs and other delicacies to sick

POWs, a gesture which had been so appreciated by Ronald Wilson, the Australian Red Cross representative, that he had given Malau his own Red Cross shoulder insignia. Knowing that the flag which he had just found was of special significance, Corporal Malau placed it in an empty tin before burying it beneath a distinctive tree for later retrieval.

The British POWs reached Brunei, a day's sailing from Labuan, the next day. They were housed on arrival in a large hut, previously occupied by several hundred Javanese coolies, whose jobs they also took over. Eight weeks later, on 8 May, they were off again, this time in three large trucks, leaving behind 30 of their dead and one other presumed to have died in Kempei-tai custody following an escape attempt. Their next destination was the picture theatre at Kuala Belait, where the 81 survivors were joined by seven Indian soldiers handed over by the local Kempei-tai. The bodies and ashes of 30 of the 37 who died there were buried, along with their effects, in pits beside the theatre. The number of survivors, Indian and British, who made the next transfer to Miri on 27 May was 51.

On arrival at Miri, Sergeant-Major Sugino was ordered by Lieutenant Nishimura, commanding officer of 20 Aerial Supply Company, to take his prisoners to Tanjung Lobang. About 500 metres beyond the Resident's House, in Residency Road, a track to the right led to a barbed-wire compound, where there was a timber and atap hut, built by the British in 1941 as a Japanese internment camp. Some of the prisoners were sick but the rest, including the party's two medical officers, Flight-Lieutenant Blackledge (the only officer to have been transferred from Sandakan) and Captain C.F. Campbell from Kuching, were reasonably fit and well. Twelve days later, on the afternoon of 8 June, news was received that Allied warships were approaching the west coast. At 8.00pm Sugino ordered the POWs, now numbering 46, to move down a jungle track, taking a small bundle of personal belongings with them. At midnight, having reached the Riam Road, they stopped and rested near the old police station at the 3 mile until 4.00am when Campbell, along with fourteen of the 20 fittest prisoners, returned with five guards to the Residency Road compound to pick up rice, salt, office stores and medicine. They returned six hours later, only to depart at 1.00am for a second load. While they were away, two of the sick prisoners died.

Meanwhile Sugino had sent a message to Nishimura informing him that, as warships were approaching, he had moved the remaining 44 POWs out of the compound. According to the commandant, he was now ordered to take his prisoners into the mountains, where it would be 'safer'. They set out at about 8.00pm. Two hours later they reached the 6 mile peg and a small deserted house, set on a rise in a large clearing to the left of the road, where they stayed for the night. At around noon the following day Sugino went to a spot about 100 metres from the house, where he burnt all documents and letters belonging to deceased prisoners. Three hours later the same fifteen carriers, with Naga and three other Formosan guards, set off once more for the old compound, leaving 28 POWs, in the care of Blackledge, in the camp. It was now 10 June, the date on which the Australian 9th Division landed at Brunei Bay, less than 200 kilometres away. What occurred next appears to be perfectly in keeping with Japanese policy — a policy which Sugino's Ranau colleague, Lieutenant Suzuki, had implemented a couple of hours previously at the Sinarut camp. When invasion, and therefore liberation, appeared to be imminent, Tokyo had instructed there was only one way to deal with prisoners — 'annihilate them all and not leave any traces'.

According to Sugino, at 7.00pm five or six POWs, led by 32-year-old Sergeant C. Ackland, jumped up from where they were sitting outside the house and tried to escape. He ordered the guards to open fire on those fleeing but, in the confusion, some of the bullets were 'inadvertently' directed at the house, causing other prisoners to come out. As they did so they were shot or bayonetted by the guards. The sick, trying to crawl out of the way, were also killed. Sugino said he did not give an order to cease firing as he was 'so excited' he 'didn't know what was happening'. He did not take long to recover his composure or to decide what to do next. Leaving some of the guards to begin burying the massacre victims in a nearby swamp, Sugino and six or seven others set off down the road where they intercepted the stores-carrying party, resting near some huts at the 5 mile peg. Shortly afterwards Lance-Corporal Kaneko and eight members of Nishimura's unit unexpectedly appeared on the scene, which was most providential since, by this time, Sugino was ready to dispose of the remaining prisoners. According to Sugino, one of the white POWs suddenly tried to make a run for it, despite the fact that there were at least 21 armed guards and soldiers standing only metres away. Once again, evidently overtaken by uncontrollable feelings of excitement, Sugino gave the order to open fire. All those not killed outright were finished off. Leaving his men to bury the dead, he departed to the 6 mile to check on the progress of the other burial party and fire the house to destroy all further evidence. His task complete, he repaired to lodgings at the 7 mile, where he apparently had no trouble falling asleep. He had certainly served his Emperor well.

Of the 300 POWs who had arrived at Labuan the previous year, not one was left alive.

Lieutenant Suzuki, meanwhile, was doing almost as well with the ten at Ranau. Nine days after arriving at the Number 2 Jungle Camp, only six who had walked in from the Sinarut compound were still in residence — five Australians (Botterill, Moxham, Grist, Sergeant Stacy and 28-year-old Sapper Arthur Bird,) and one sole Englishman (Gunner Norm Frost, aged 30). The other four, Evan Davies (died 16 June), Rolf Newling (13 June), Stan Roberts (13 June) and Colin Wright who, with no doctor available, had died from appendicitis on 19 June, were buried in a swampy area not far from the quartermaster's store.

On 26 June the six survivors looked up from their chores to see a ragged, bedraggled column enter the camp area. Botterill and Moxham, with their washboard ribs, filthy tangled hair and matted beards did not look too good, but they were a good deal better looking than most of this lot. It was not until they recognised Sticpewich and Captain Cook who, along with most of the technical party and the officers were in surprisingly fit condition, that the penny dropped.[3] The new arrivals had come from Sandakan.

Lieutenant Suzuki had no intention of allowing the six to have any contact with the newcomers. They were ordered to camp out in the open on the other side of the valley, using whatever cover they could find under bushes, pieces of blanket and ground sheets. When working parties were organised to collect atap for a hut as well as fetch firewood, water and vegetables, the two groups saw more of each other but, even then, it was not for several days that Botterill and Moxham were able to exchange any news. The Sinarut guards, wanting to catch up with their former Sandakan colleagues, stopped for a chat while escorting Botterill's group on a working party. Taking advantage of the unexpected break, Moxham and Botterill gathered what details they could before the guards noticed the exchange and put a stop to it. During the reprimand which followed, Saburo Suzuki demanded Moxham hand over the English lumber jacket he was wearing. Unfortunately Moxham lost far more than his jacket. Concealed inside the lining was a map of British North Borneo.

Dr Picone, with whom the pair had made contact, was left in a state of disbelief. He and Cook had assumed that the others from the first march were elsewhere — out on some working party, perhaps. His group had suffered great losses on their march, but he was appalled to discover that this was it — six alive out of 452. For their part, the six were just as appalled to learn that the 142 Australians and 41 British who had just arrived were probably all that were left out of the 1900-odd prisoners they had left at Sandakan five months before.

With the food ration at Sandakan set at 70 grams of rice a day, the prisoners' condition had deteriorated alarmingly in February, making it impossible for Colonel Suga to carry out an order to put 50 men to work repairing the airfield. Rather surprisingly, Hoshijima allowed the prisoners to go fishing in the freshwater drains near the camp twice a week, but the catch was hardly worth bothering about — generally no more than 40 tiddlers, averaging about 2 centimetres each, just enough to give half-a-dozen hospital patients a taste. Men became so hungry that they ate anything that moved — grasshoppers, snails, beetles and, if they were lucky enough to find them, rats. Nelson Short had discovered that slugs, lured from their hiding places with damp leaves placed on the ground, were quite palatable when threaded onto a piece of wire and roasted over coals.

The death toll in the Australian camp had escalated from 57 in January to 119 in February and then up to 204 in March. One of those who had died in March was Bill Thompson, friend of Paul Muir who had been monitoring Apple's transmissions in New Guinea. April saw the deaths of another 164, including George Carter, one of those sent back to Sandakan from the march, with roughly the same number in May. Billy Young, still languishing in Outram Road Gaol, lost two of his special mates during this time. John 'Snowy' Bryant, Shearer Gillett's fancied boxer who had lost 'The Big Fight' to Punchy Donohue, died on 29 March and the fatherly, protective Bob Shipsides, five days later. On 29 April the camp lost its finest intellectual mind with the death of Bill Bundey, the South Australian barrister. There was no hope that Bill Ney, the bushie from Gollan, would ever see his brother Ivan. Stricken with malaria in mid-April, he died on 2 May. During the same four-month period, the British lost 234 — 60 in February, 70 in both March and April and 34 in May — bringing the death toll in both camps during this time to more than 1000. By the end of May, the number of British and Australian prisoners still alive would be just over 800.

Although rice was cut out completely in April and replaced by tapioca and sweet potato, not all deaths had been attributable to illness or malnutrition. Eight, including almost all of those confined 'for the duration' by Cook, had died as a result of being caged — Ron Tyrrell, one of Christie's ordnance store mates, on 7 February, Len Annear on 20 February, Norm Hewitt, Ray Golding and Arthur Cross on 5, 10 and 23 March, Reg Temple and John McCarthy on 3 and 9 April and Jim Bowe on 5 May. Fred Weeks and Arthur Clement, sent to the cage with Barber by Hoshijima, were also dead — Clement on 9 March and Weeks on 4 February. Exactly one month after Weeks' death, Private Jack Orr had been shot dead.

Hoshijima had stated that anyone going outside the wire would be severely punished. Yet prisoners driven by hunger had continued to run the gauntlet. Some, caught going out through a drainpipe down near the swamp, were put in the cage where at least one of them died. When even that failed as a deterrent, Hoshijima put the camp on notice that prisoners found outside the wire would be shot. Orr had been in the habit of sneaking out at night to scrounge tapioca and sweet potatoes. On the night of 4 March the POWs in the Australian compound had been woken by the sound of a rifle shot, very close at hand. Sticpewich, who understood a fair amount of Japanese, heard Troita, one of the guards, say, 'He is dead'. Above the babble of a dozen or more Japanese voices, Hoshijima was then heard to say, 'Remove the body', before ordering Moritake to take a tally of the prisoners. On the second count it was revealed that Jack Orr, of the 2/10th Field Ambulance, was missing.

Cook was called to formally identify the body at 6.00am the following day. It was obvious to even a layman that Orr, now lying on the POW sign, had been shot in the back. The wound in the chest, where the bullet had exited, was much larger than that at the point of entry. The burial party, sent to retrieve the corpse with Doctors Picone and Oakeshott an hour later, was even more observant. The powder marks on the body and the enormous amount of blood found beside the fence showed that Orr had been shot at very close range and the body then removed, to make it appear that he had been shot on the run, well outside the wire. Orr had been killed by Hinata 'Sourpuss' Genzo whose admiring colleagues declared him a 'bagous [good] shot'.

Hoshijima decreed that, as Orr had been outside the wire in direct contravention of camp regulations, a group punishment was in order. He cut rations to the entire camp for 24 hours.

About six weeks later Hoshijima decided to move the British into a wired-off area of the Australian compound. Numbers were well below 1000, including 400 in hospital, so everyone could fit. They were separated by the wire, but the seven Australian officers could at least see their nine British counterparts. Of this group, Lieutenant Geoffrey Chopping, aged 26, was possibly the only one to have been a guest of the Kempei-tai. In January Air-Craftsman M. Soorier had escaped from the Number 2 Compound. If anyone had a chance of remaining at large it should have been Soorier. Born in Ceylon, he lived in Serembang, Malaya and, consequently, not only looked like a local but also spoke their language. His luck ran out and it appears that under torture Soorier implicated Chopping, who was taken to Kempei-tai headquarters and placed under arrest. Interrogated for two days, he was eventually returned to the compound. Soorier was not. He died in custody on 3 April. The Japanese said the cause of death was malaria.

In mid-April Hoshijima's superiors also confirmed that the remaining Australian and British POWs were to be removed to Ranau. The notification of the impending move followed an announcement on 17 March by Japanese war minister Shibayama Keneshiro, as a result of the liberation of the American prisoners. Hoshijima had been instructed that,

PRISONERS OF WAR MUST BE PREVENTED BY ALL MEANS AVAILABLE FROM FALLING INTO ENEMY HANDS. THEY SHOULD EITHER BE RELOCATED AWAY FROM THE FRONT OR COLLECTED AT SUITABLE POINTS AND TIMES WITH AN EYE TO ENEMY AIR RAIDS, SHORE BOMBARDMENTS ETC. THEY SHOULD BE KEPT ALIVE TO THE LAST WHEREVER THEIR LABOUR IS NEEDED. IN DESPERATE CIRCUMSTANCES, WHERE THERE IS NO TIME TO MOVE THEM, THEY MAY, AS A LAST RESORT, BE SET FREE. THEN EMERGENCY MEASURES SHOULD BE CARRIED OUT AGAINST THOSE WITH AN ANTAGONISTIC ATTITUDE AND UTMOST PRECAUTIONS SHOULD BE TAKEN TO ENSURE NO HARM IS DONE TO THE PUBLIC. IN EXECUTING EMERGENCY MEASURES, CARE SHOULD BE HAD NOT TO PROVOKE ENEMY PROPAGANDA OR RETALIATION. PRISONERS SHOULD BE FED AT THE END.

Immediately after the order to move, Colonel Takayama Nikoichi, a senior staff officer from 37th Army Headquarters, arrived. The purpose of his visit was to inspect the local defences, as, since 11 April, Australian and American aircraft had been pounding not only Tarakan but also Kuching, Surabaya (Java), Bali and shipping in the Celebes Sea and Macassar Straits. Takayama noticed the large POW sign, still prominently displayed just outside the wire. He also observed the poor condition of most of the prisoners. Consequently, before he returned to Jesselton, he agreed with Hoshijima's proposal that they should be shifted, not to Ranau, but to Kemansi, a large Japanese-owned estate on the lower reaches of the Labuk River, easily accessible by boat.

On 26 April, the day before the Australian invasion force left Morotai to retake Tarakan, Hoshijima received two sets of marching orders — the POWs' and his own. The first confirmed the POWs were to move to Kemansi as he had suggested and he sent Moritake and two guards to organise atap to build the necessary accommodation. The second order relieved Hoshijima of his command, replacing him with the evil, lecherous Captain Takakuwa Takuo. According to Hoshijima, the reason for his sudden removal was his decision to display the POW sign. While his transfer was probably because, with the airstrip out of use, his engineering expertise was no longer required, there is no doubt that Hoshijima had over-stepped the mark. He was ordered to remove the sign at once.

On 29 April, three days after his new orders, Hoshijima organised a fishing competition for the camp and hosted a farewell dinner to which all Allied officers were invited. First prize in the fishing competition went to the Japanese quartermaster Sergeant-Major Ichikawa Takehora, with second prize going to Lieutenant

Good and third to an English officer. According to Hoshijima, the dinner party held that night was a most memorable occasion, with the chief guests-of-honour, Captains Cook and Mills, delivering most moving speeches in which they expressed their profound and lasting gratitude for Hoshijima's many kind acts during his administration — statements which were backed by signed testimonials. Hoshijima recalled that, during the course of the dinner, he and Cook agreed to maintain their friendship. Cook had apparently confided to Hoshijima that, because 'he was good and a man of righteousness', the Australians had honoured him with a special nickname — 'trump'.

Nineteen days later this 'good and righteous man' had chalked up another murder. Officially, the victim, Signaller William Constable, one of Matthews' men, had died from malaria. While Constable, like most of the prisoners, had suffered from chronic malaria, it was not illness that had caused his death on 18 May. It was a sixteen-hour beating, delivered with great severity four days before. Although Hoshijima had left on 17 May, the responsibility for this death, and the deaths of all those who had been beaten, over-worked or maltreated during his three-year administration, lay squarely on his shoulders. Lieutenant-General Yamawaki and Major-General Manaki deliberately withheld food, drugs and medical supplies from the POWs, but it was Hoshijima who had stopped supplying rice to the prisoners three months before being officially ordered to do so.

It was later claimed that the shortage of food was a result of Sandakan being cut off from the rest of the South-East Asian Co-Prosperity Sphere, and that medical supplies were unprocurable. Yet the Japanese had no trouble amassing huge stockpiles of commodities. Under Hoshijima's house were no less than 90 tonnes of rice and 160 000 quinine tablets, while at the Japanese barracks, stacked in the barber shop and a bomb-proof store, were at least another 54 tonnes of rice. Also on hand were 786 000 quinine tablets, 19 600 vitamin A and D tablets, large numbers of vitamin B and C tablets, hundreds of Red Cross parcels and an enormous amount of medical supplies and surgical equipment. Despite this abundance of food and drugs, not a single tablet or bandage or grain of rice was given to the prisoners.

Their captors did not even allow the prisoners the unauthorised use of a light bulb. Dr Picone, faced with a patient in need of dire surgery for a ruptured duodenal ulcer had borrowed a globe from the guardhouse. Discovering that not only was an 'unauthorised' operation taking place but the light being shed on the patient was coming from an 'unauthorised' globe, Moritake had Picone hauled outside, where he was beaten soundly before being made to stand to attention for two hours, leaving the patient lying on the operating table.

On 20 May, three days after Hoshijima left the camp, Takakuwa received new orders from General Manaki's 37th Army Headquarters, which were confirmed by Colonel Suga. All POWs, regardless of their condition, must move to Ranau as previously ordered. The reason given was insufficient food stocks at Kemansi but Army headquarters were well aware that the Sandakan-Ranau track was extracting a frightful toll. Of the eight Japanese battalions ordered to make the journey from Sandakan to Jesselton, 8500 died. Earlier that month Major-General Akashi had marched from Sandakan to Ranau with 150 cavalrymen, only to have 90 perish on the way. The Okumura Battalion, which was forced, because of a mix-up in operational plans, to march from Jesselton to Sandakan and then back again, lost 889 of its 1025 men, while the 2150-strong Iemura Battalion, travelling from east to west only, lost 1226. It was patently obvious that, while the first Ranau march had been a march *to* death, for the remaining Sandakan prisoners this would be a march *of* death.

Captain Takakuwa was not at all keen to march more than 800 ill and dying men across 260 kilometres of such difficult terrain. He sent a telegram to Jesselton, advising that, as almost half the POWs were stretcher cases, and another 200 could not walk, he estimated that only about one-fifth would reach their destination. While he was awaiting a reply the air raids, which had resumed on 13 May at Gort Chester's urging, continued. Although Sandakan had been bombed and strafed on a number of occasions, this was the first time since October that the camp had been a deliberate target — a target which the pilots concluded was now quite safe to attack. Intelligence reported that all POWs had departed, and this was obviously correct as the large and prominent POW sign, which had been in place for more than six months, had now been removed.

An air raid on 23 May took the lives of a number of prisoners, including Ray Tinning, Richard Toombs and George Weissel. Others, caught in the open while out gathering wood, were also killed, along with a guard named Horijima. Almost all of those known to have died on this day were older men, the oldest being Toombs, aged 51.[4] The next day Dick Braithwaite was visiting Gunner Cec Glover, who was ill with diphtheria, when he heard the sound of falling bombs. Braithwaite instinctively threw himself to the ground. When the air cleared, he discovered that Cec was dead — his leg had been blown off by the blast. Electrical engineer Fred Launder was just as unlucky. A bullet took the top off his skull, killing him instantly. The next day Charles Speake, of the AASC, was killed in a similar raid.

Braithwaite had another near miss 24 hours later. He was lying on his bunk trying to fend off an attack of malaria when the first bombs exploded. As the timber wall opened up and a jagged piece of shrapnel spun towards him, he swung himself into a sitting position. As he did so the red-hot metal went between his legs and out through the wall behind him. Staggering out of the hut, he headed for the slit trenches which he and his hut-mates had dug underneath. As he and fellow artilleryman Allan Shaw, who was very weak with dysentery, flattened themselves against the hut wall, holes appeared in the wooden boards beside them, spurring them to further effort. They were too slow. The next burst shattered Allan's elbow. Fortunately Braithwaite was able to get him into a trench where one of the others quickly applied a tourniquet. Gunner Shaw must have been made of iron. The next morning, when Braithwaite went to see how he was getting on, he was sitting up, giving cheek. Although he survived the raid, Vic Brabham, Jim Drinkwater, Sam Platt and 41-year-old Percy Humphries, who belonged to the same AASC company as Barnier, did not. Neither did John Munro, also of the AASC, who died on 28 May as a result of his injuries.

On 27 May the Australians and Americans, acting upon information supplied by Gort Chester that all POWs were now in Ranau and the Japanese garrison at

Sandakan was on the move, launched a massive combined aerial-naval attack on Sandakan. Shortly after dawn while aircraft screamed overhead, bombing and strafing everything in sight, PT boats shot up the harbour and foreshores, drawing enemy fire as they launched torpedoes which exploded under the docks, rendering the harbour facilities useless. Naval personnel from another group of PT boats not only entered the Sibuga River unmolested, they came ashore. When the raid, which lasted just on three and a half hours, was over, almost every building in Sandakan, including the Roman Catholic Convent, was severely damaged. So too was Japanese pride.

Such a loss of face could not be ignored. As soon as the raiders had departed a party of Japanese marines from Captain Aida Hideo's Special Attack Unit stormed into town. On the assumption that the Chinese community was assisting the Allies, they entered a number of houses, bayonetting men, women and children. Meanwhile, Colonel Otsuka, Military Commander of the Sandakan area, gave orders to round up all citizens who spoke English. The most prominent among them were then beheaded, including a young Chinese woman from Shanghai.

The following morning the local Japanese garrison, the Otsuka Unit, received a message from army intelligence to expect one Allied division to land at Sandakan and another at Kudat, on Borneo's north-western tip. The garrison therefore withdrew to the 11 mile, which meant that the POW camp was now in front of the defending soldiers. Colonel Otsuka, convinced that landing barges and enemy paratroops would soon appear, ordered Takakuwa to move the prisoners out of the camp, evacuate Japanese patients from the local hospital and destroy everything.

Munition dumps were still exploding at 9.00am the next day (29 May) when Takakuwa, accompanied by his adjutant, Lieutenant Watanabe Genzo and Ichikawa, the quartermaster, arrived at the camp for an inspection. Fifteen minutes after their departure the huts in the Number 3 compound were set on fire. At about 10.30am all prisoners were given ten minutes — a deadline which was extended to half an hour — to clear the camp and reassemble in the garden area of the Number 2 compound, opposite the main guardhouse at the entrance to the Japanese barracks. Three of the seriously-ill stretcher cases died before they reached the gate. One was HMAS *Perth*'s Able Seaman G. Morriss whose shipmate, bandsman Henry Kelly, had died the previous January. As there was no time for a proper burial, they were hastily interred in a slit trench between the huts.[5]

The last stretcher case had just been carried out the gate when Number 1 camp was enveloped in fire. Most of the prisoners were now convinced that the Allies must be about to land, especially when Catalinas flying overhead passed so low they could see the faces of the American crews standing at the open doorway. The fact that the sick had been included in the move added even more weight — a sure sign that arrangements were in train to hand them over to medical teams for immediate evacuation.

At about 3.30pm, following the instruction that 'prisoners should be fed at the end', the camp staff butchered and cooked five pigs — which further fuelled speculation that liberation was only a matter of hours away. About half the camp had been served when Cook received another order. All those fit enough to walk must assemble beneath The Big Tree, ready to move within the hour. At 7.00pm this was amended to 500 Australian and 100 British prisoners who were to form themselves in batches of 50 and line up along the road as they were going on 'a short journey'. The sick, Takakuwa assured them, would be transported to their destination in trucks. Almost everyone capable of standing reported for the muster. Nelson Short lined up, ignoring the advice of one of the older men who, noticing Nelson's beriberi legs and ulcerated toes, urged, 'Don't go. The war's over. They'll send a truck to pick us up.' Nelson was not the only 'walking wounded' eager to make the march to freedom under his own steam. The ulcer cases were there, hobbling on sticks and crude crutches, their shin-bones exposed from ankle to knee, as were the men with advanced beriberi, lumbering along on inflated, tree-stump legs. So too were those with dysentery, and the severely malnourished, their abdomens so sunken and shrunken it looked as if they were fused to their backbones.

Even with these ill men included, only 536 could be rounded up. An officer or senior NCO was appointed to lead each group. Heaslop had 50 hospital patients (Group 1), Sticpewich (Group 2), Padre Wardale-Greenwood (Group 3), Oakeshott (Group 4), Picone (Group 5), Warrant Officer Jonathan Dixon of the 2/18th Battalion (Group 6), Cook (Group 7) Good (Group 8), Flying-Officer Burgess (Group 9), Dr Daniels (Group10), and Lieutenant Chopping (Group 11). The first ten parties had 50 men in each while the last had 36. Groups 1-8 were purely Australian, Group 9 was mixed and the last two were entirely English.

Only about 100 of the 536 could be classified as fit. Cook was one of these, as was Sticpewich and his technical party. They had received extra rations from Ichikawa but were also the camp butchers, as Sticpewich had, at one time, worked in an abattoir. Maddock who had enjoyed the patronage of Hoshijima and had received extra rations and quinine to counteract malaria, was in noticeably better condition. The cooks, and other camp staff, were reasonably fit, too. The rest, in Takakuwa's words, were 'very weak and thin'. Fat or thin, all would have to go for Takakuwa had received no clarification of his orders. Although Lieutenant-Colonel Iwahashi Manabu would later claim he had agreed to evacuate only fit prisoners and that a message to this effect had been sent on 26 May, with a request for 'high priority' wireless transmission, it is doubtful this story is true as Takakuwa was later reprimanded by his superiors for taking it upon himself to leave 288 sick POWs behind.

John Skinner, aged 31, elder brother of Ted, was one of the 288. The Skinner boys, both members of the Medical Corps, came from Tenterfield, on the New England Tablelands of New South Wales. They had consecutive army numbers and had been together since enlistment, so it must have been extremely difficult for Ted, a quiet and gentle man, to be separated at this late stage from his sick brother. As George Plunkett was remaining in camp, he and fellow survivor from the X Battalion massacre, Jacky Ings, were also parting company, as were John Barnier and Johnny O'Donohue who had lost their other great mate, Jacky Jackson, on 29 April to malaria — which left Albert Anderson's six children fatherless twelve days later. Braithwaite's mate, Freddie Thompson, had been hit in the ankle by flying shrapnel during an air raid and as the doctors had not had time to remove the metal, he too was remaining behind. Others included Tom Burns, Eric Tomkyns, Ray Carlson, Ron Moran and five of the eight British officers — Captain Mills, Lieutenants Rolfe and Young and Flying Officers Cressey and Linge.

It is not known how many of the officers were ill, nor is it possible to establish whether some of the 288, particularly those with medical training, were carers, rather than patients. What is known is that, as the Japanese expected an Allied landing to take place the following morning, the camp was abandoned at 8.00pm on 29 May. As the eleven groups moved off, each group escorted by a contingent of 'old soldiers' to make sure no one escaped or lagged behind, the kitchi guards moved among the stretcher cases, trying to force a few more to their feet before setting fire to most of the administration buildings.

Expectations among the prisoners on the march were high. However, when the leading group turned right at the 8 mile peg instead of left to Sandakan, morale sunk to its lowest. They all knew where they were headed — into the interior. They also knew that most would not be able to go far. George Carter and the others who had set out on the march in February, only to return a week or so later, had told them what lay at the end of the bitumen. Sticpewich's party, which was composed of eight fit men from his technical staff and 42 hospital patients, had trouble almost immediately. Charles Forrester of the 2/19th had struggled as far as the 9 mile when he decided he had had enough. He made his way back to the camp, evidently without any trouble. By the time they reached the 12 mile where Watanabe issued each group with two 40-kilogram sacks of rice (about 200 grams per person, per day, for ten days) and a pencil and paper to compile a nominal roll, six more men had been lost. Four were so ill Takakuwa had sent them back to camp in a truck at the 11 mile, while the other two had simply disappeared.

They stopped for a two-hour rest in the early hours of the morning but were then moved on, the Japanese intent on getting as far away as possible from Sandakan before dawn. It did them no good. Shortly before noon they were spotted by Allied planes as they rested in a clearing, and were forced to remain hidden for the remainder of the day. During this time Jacky Ings died. The next day they only covered about 6 kilometres. Although there was a rest period of twenty minutes or so every hour and a half, the men were exhausted by the time Takakuwa called a halt, sometime after 3.00pm. At 5.00pm a Japanese soldier visited each of the groups, relieving them of about 13 kilograms of their rice ration and issuing instructions for the order of march. From now on the groups were to consolidate into three large parties. Groups 1, 2, 3 and 4 were to be in the first; 5, 6, 7 and 8 in the second and the remaining three in the third. These parties were to move off at half-hour intervals, starting at 6.30am (Tokyo time) and rotating the sequence so that a different party was leading each day.

The next morning, when Sticpewich called the roll, he discovered his group of 50 was down to 38, five more having dropped out. He was unaware, at this stage, that those who lagged behind were being dispatched by a two-man Formosan murder squad, under the command of Lieutenant Watanabe. The murders, usually by a bullet but quite often a savage blow to the head with a rifle butt or one of the victim's own crutches, were carried out, officially, by Fukishima

Maseo (The Black Bastard) and Sergeant-Major Tsuji, and unofficially by anyone else who cared to participate. Each morning those unable to travel were placed in groups and left for Fukishima and Tsuji, who brought up the rear.

Progress was slow, especially for those carrying Japanese equipment as well as their own gear and rice ration. On day five the Japanese stepped up the pace, prodding, bashing and bullying anyone who could not keep up. As a result, from 2 June onwards the number of prisoners unable to join the column each morning increased dramatically. The Australians lost 26 that day, six more than the first four days combined. Some were seized with rheumatism so severe they could not move their limbs. Others who had been shuffling along with ulcers and beriberi or doubled up with dysentery, simply found it impossible to get up and get going, not even when bashed or belted by the guards. Two who dropped out were the 2/29th's Alec (Tony) Webster, who collapsed at the side of the track with beriberi and malaria, and Gerald Fitzgerald, the ambulanceman who had been singled out for severe punishment earlier in the year. Gunboat Simpson also died that day but not at the hands of the executioners. He walked away from the column and into the jungle near the 20 mile.

At the 10.00am break, when they stopped for the first of two meals of the day, Lieutenant Good, the quartermaster, issued 450 grams of salt and about a kilogram of sugar to each group. To prevent the Japanese 'requisitioning' this precious ration, Sticpewich and Padre Wardale-Greenwood distributed it evenly among their men. When the marauding guards, as expected, came to confiscate it later, Sticpewich and the Padre told them it had all been eaten.

The muddy areas along the Labuk tributaries took a heavy toll, so that strong-willed men who might otherwise have been able to go on simply dropped with exhaustion and weariness. Eddie McAppion, the harmonica player who loved the sea, died at the 26 mile, within smell, if not sight of it, on 4 June — the same day as Vic Johnston and Harry Hewitt, the camp master who had so enraged Murray, both of whom died near the 37 mile. Neil Christie, who wanted nothing more than to return home to his family and raise chooks, lasted another day before dying from malaria and beriberi at the 43½ mile.

Sticpewich and the others were now well aware of the fate of those who fell behind. One of the guards warned that all who stopped would be dead, while the sound of gunfire at regular intervals throughout the day made it only too clear what was happening at the rear of the column. Those who dropped out faced their death with dignity, giving their mates messages for their loved ones, and any valuable keepsakes and food they still had, then shaking hands with them for the last time. When the moment of death came they did not, however, submit meekly, shouting curses and insults at their executioners and demanding that they hurry up and get it over.

The names of those who could not continue or who had died during the night were recorded. The date and cause of death (always cited as malaria, beriberi, dysentery or, occasionally, 'extreme exhaustion of the whole body') were fairly diligently noted, but Takakuwa's men were not nearly as particular as their counterparts on the first march when it came to recording the place of death. The notation beside the names of many of those who died on this second march was an all encompassing 'East Coast Residency, Sandakan'.

While at least 113 Australians had died in the first eight days, the blackest day was 7 June when about 35 prisoners, first tied together by their genitals, were massacred at the 55 mile peg, about 8 kilometres from the Tangkul Crossing. One, at least, who pretended to be dead, managed to escape. The lone Australian, aged about 30 and wearing nothing but his slouch hat, boots and a singlet, arrived a few days later at a house at the 15 mile occupied by Hee Choi, his brother and sister-in-law, and their three children. He asked Choi for help. Although terrified of reprisals, the family gave him some Chinese clothing and found him a safe place to hide in the jungle. The two brothers took him food at regular intervals and at night, when there was less danger, brought him into the house to sleep.

The Hee brothers were taking the most terrible risk. The Kempei-tai, before decapitating anyone suspected of harbouring escapees, had introduced a new and diabolical torture. After the usual water and log treatments, beatings and the like, the Kempei bound the accused with wire to the trunk of a rubber tree, so that his feet could not touch the ground. One end of a length of wire was then looped around the testicles. The other was wrapped around a house brick, which was then balanced on the victim's head. The Kempei-tai then slashed the tree trunk so that the latex dripped down onto the brick. As soon as the brick was coated sufficiently with highly flammable liquid rubber, they ignited it, causing red-hot gobs to drop onto the naked flesh of the victim, who would flinch. As the brick toppled to the ground the wire cut through the scrotal sac, castrating him.

The remainder of the column, meanwhile, moved further and further into the interior. That morning they had been issued with another ten days' rations, which were to last them to Boto, more than 80 kilometres away. Owen Campbell, in Group 5, very much doubted he could make it that far, while Braithwaite, in Group 4, among the fittest of the non-camp staff, weighed about 41 kilograms and was suffering from recurring attacks of malaria as well as blackouts. The 30 quinine tablets he had traded for his watch earlier in the year had long since run out and there was no chance of getting any more. Perhaps the only prisoners not suffering from malaria were Nelson Short, who seemed to have a natural immunity, and Maddock who, through Hoshijima's influence, was still getting his regular dose of life-saving quinine. The sight of human remains and personal effects belonging to the first march victims, which were scattered along the track, was also hardly reassuring. Although they had seen one skeleton, his mouldy slouch hat lying nearby, propped up against a tree near the 42 mile, it had not been until after the Tangkul Crossing that the gruesome evidence had become more apparent — rotting webbing, bits of discarded footwear, corroding utensils, faded photographs, tattered papers and pay books, and, far more chilling, bleached bones picked clean by ants and scattered by wild animals.

Braithwaite first ran into trouble just past the 55 mile peg. He was trying to struggle up a sharp, greasy incline when one of the guards, holding the barrel of his gun like a baseball bat, flattened him with a vicious blow to the kidneys. Braithwaite turned his head in the nick of time and the second blow glanced off his mouth. The next, however, slammed into the side of his head, rupturing his ear drum, while the kicks and blows which followed rendered him semi-conscious. The guard ratted Braithwaite's clothes and kit for food and valuables, then left him for dead. The prisoner was still fighting for breath when the tail-end of his party reached him. 'Come on son, you can make it', urged Bob Sykes, a warrant officer from Braithwaite's unit, giving him the encouragement he needed to struggle to his feet. As he staggered on, he heard the sound of distant, concentrated firing. Unaware that the automatic fire was the sound of the massacre, he assumed the Allies were landing, somewhere to the north.

Shortly after, the column was attacked by three Allied aircraft whose pilots, acting on information transmitted by the Agas party, concluded the marchers were all Japanese evacuating to the west coast. The planes came in for a low-level strafing run, sending Japanese and prisoners in all directions. Owen Campbell and four companions realised they might never have a better opportunity to escape. In the confusion, Campbell, Ted Skinner, Sid Webber, Ted Emmett and one other, who Campbell thought was named Jack Austen, but was almost certainly Private Costin of the AAMC,[6] stopped long enough to ransack the kits of the Japanese soldiers. Loaded up with 5 or 6 kilograms of rice, half-a-dozen tins of salmon and protein-rich, dried soya bean powder, they plunged into the jungle on the northern side of the track. Terrified of bumping into Japanese stationed along the Labuk, they headed inland, away from the river.

Meanwhile, Braithwaite and the rest plodded on. The following afternoon, 8 June, they arrived at the Mandorin River staging camp. A log, slick with mud and with nothing to prevent them from slipping into the fast-flowing waters but a wire hand rail, spanned the river. One prisoner, overcome by vertigo, froze midway, blocking any further progress. He would have been shot by a pistol-toting Japanese civilian standing on the other side had Sticpewich not intervened. He went back across the log, rescuing both the soldier and his gear, which was immediately appropriated by the civilian. At least three Australians, including the 2/30th's Jack West, lost their footing on this 'bridge' and were swept to their deaths.

That night Braithwaite discussed the possibility of escape with his good mate, Wally Blatch. Although Blatch offered to join him if he really wanted to give it a try, Braithwaite decided that when and if the chance arose he would go it alone as he would only slow down his much stronger friend. The next morning he felt so weak he contemplated suicide but changed his mind when his friends held him up during roll call so that he would not be left behind to be killed. The men tried to get six others to their feet, but their legs simply refused to support them. Two were friends of Braithwaite — 36-year-old Jake Mildenhall and Rex Hodges, 26, of the AASC. Also left behind was Ozawa, the interpreter, who had been wandering around in a most disoriented state. No one left behind was safe. Shortly Ozawa too would be dispatched with the same indifference shown to the prisoners.

Not long after moving off, Braithwaite heard shots ring out. He was sure that unless he could escape he would be next. Carrying on for about a kilometre and a half in a state of near collapse, he reached a gully where large trees blocked the way, necessitating a difficult detour which unexpectedly created a gap in the column. Finding himself alone, Braithwaite ducked off the makeshift path to the left and into the jungle. He had gone no more than 15 metres when he heard the guards coming along the track. With his progress blocked by a fallen tree, he dropped to the ground and froze. It was not a good place to lie 'doggo'. There was hardly any cover and the leaf litter was swarming with huge ants which, although they crawled all over Braithwaite's body, fortunately did not bite. His throat began to tickle, the irritation becoming so bad he could no longer ignore it. Lifting his head to cough, he found himself staring at a guard who unslung his rifle and gave the impression he had seen the fugitive, yet moved on. After the last of the Japanese had passed by, at about 3.00pm, Braithwaite left his hiding place and started back down the track. Rounding a sharp bend he almost ran headlong into a lone Japanese. Luckily, Braithwaite saw him first. He hit the guard with a heavy branch, smashing his head again and again as he unleashed three years of pent-up hatred and anger. When it was over, he dragged the body from the track and concealed it as best he could. He returned to the river and scanned the area carefully for any signs of life. A couple of Japanese were resting in their overnight shelter on the opposite bank, but that was all. Mildenhall, Hodges and the others were nowhere to be seen.

Campbell's group, and Braithwaite, were not the only ones to have left the column undetected. Defections had been taking place ever since the parties left Sandakan. Warrant Officer John Frazier, an electrical engineer, and Sergeant William Coulter, of the AASC. who were both in good health, had slipped away on 3 June. John Fletcher, one of Barnier's AASC pals, also managed to escape the day after Braithwaite, somewhere in the vicinity of the Sapi River. When Alexander Willmott, of the 2/20th, escaped is not known. In the absence of any firm information his 'date of death' remained a blank, forcing Japanese POW headquarters in Kuching to invent the necessary details in order to keep the record straight. According to Headquarters, Willmott died in Sandakan of malaria on 10 January. Coulter was also accorded a false date of death, 3 March at Sandakan, but for Warrant Officer Frazier there was no record at all.

Malaria was also the reason given also for the sudden death of the Group 6 leader, Warrant Officer Jonathan Dixon, who was murdered somewhere between the Mandorin and Sapi Rivers on 9 June. A day or two before, Matsuda Kenji known to the POWs as 'Top Hat' or 'Gentleman Jim', had tried to persuade Dixon to trade a gold ring he was wearing for a few pieces of tapioca and some salt. Unable to coax the prisoner to part with it, Matsuda bided his time. His chance came on 9 June when Dixon, aged 44, decided to leave early with the leading party so that, when he exhausted his energy later in the day, he would not fall behind. Matsuda realised that Dixon was not in his correct group and challenged him. Explanations were useless. The guard hit Dixon over the head with a stout branch, knocking him off his feet. The next swipe caught him above the eye, felling him instantly. He later regained consciousness beside Gunner William (Jimmy) Barlow. Top Hat, armed with a light machine gun, stood over them and, despite their pleas, refused to allow them to move on. Whether he or the execution squad finished the pair off was never established. The acquisitive Matsuda now had what he wanted — Dixon's gold ring.

In the week following Braithwaite's escape, the death toll hovered around two or three a day. One of those who died during this period was Wally Blatch who, fitter than most, may have been one of those siphoned off to join a group of POWs carrying rice between the the 18 mile peg and Boto. He died of acute enteritis at the Tuanintin River, near the 80 mile peg on 16 June.[7] To supplement their 70-grams rice ration, the POWs were now adding anything edible to the pot — fresh-water shrimps, frogs, snails, lizards, grasshoppers, wood grubs, a monkey and, on one occasion, the forequarter, head and intestines of a tubercular, parasite-ridden pig — the Japanese having claimed the rest.

As the main column entered the area to the west of Boto, the death toll began to climb rapidly. The poor rations and the gruelling terrain did not help, but the Japanese were now nominating those who were to remain behind each day. Each morning, anyone in poor shape was culled from the pack. Fred Glover, whose twin brother Cec had been killed in the bombing raid on 24 May, died near Milulu on 18 June. The next day, negotiating the energy-sapping climb between Milulu and Tampias, Sticpewich witnessed the murder of Arthur Albress, aged 41, who had dropped out. Another 200 metres further on, Sapper Bertram Evans, who had worked for the Perth Tramways as a conductor, met the same fate. At about 1.30pm the column was a about 2 kilometres east of Tampias, having just struggled to the top of the range, when Padre Thompson, marching under difficulties with a large superating ulcer on his foot, was removed from the line by Watanabe and Tsuji and ordered to go no further. Between 16 and 20 June, when the column arrived at Paginatan, Thompson and at least 35 other Australians perished.

The surviving Australian padre struggled on. Harold Wardale-Greenwood had comforted the dead, the dying and the disconsolate for so long that he was now broken physically and spiritually. He had lost his faith in a God who, he believed, had forsaken them. Indeed it would have taken a man of superhuman faith to have believed that such death and suffering was God's will.

On 24 June they were at Muruk, only two day's march from their destination, when the track claimed 29-year-old signaller Norman Cummings and the AASC's Douglas McKenzie, aged 44, who were last seen sitting on a log at the 8 mile peg. The 2/18th's Corporal Bob Greenwood, of Quirindi, staggered to the next peg before collapsing with acute enteritis. The Australians lost eleven more men between Paginatan and the camp, with the 2/20th's Joe Steel almost making it and Owen Smith, of the 2/18th, dying shortly after arrival. When they lined up on the night of 26 June for tenko, only 183 of the 529 who had been present at the 12 mile answered their names. However, not all the missing were necessarily dead. There was an unknown number of POWs who, according to the locals, were carrying rice between various places along the track, while others were reportedly being used as coolie labour on the northern Beluran-Meridi route.

Some of the escapees also were still alive. One of them, Dick Braithwaite, was not only alive. He was at Tawi Tawi, safe and sound and in Allied hands.

Chapter Thirteen
'AS THE SITUATION DICTATES'

As the small native craft, skippered by Sapi villager Sapan, had drawn alongside PT boat 112 off Libaran Island, Dick Braithwaite heard the incredulous voice of Lieutenant James, USS *Oyster Bay*, exclaim in accents undeniably American, 'Whadda ya know? It's an Aussie.' After six days on the run, he was safe. The next day, 15 June, the Australian's 28th birthday, he was at Tawi Tawi, pouring out details of his amazing escape.

When he arrived back at the river Braithwaite had been unable to see any sign of Mildenhall and Hodges, whose bodies had been concealed beneath a pile of leaves. Suppressing an urge to cross the log and raid the kits of the two sleeping Japanese he had followed the river downstream, towards the Labuk estuary, confident that the firing he had heard after leaving the Tangkul Crossing had come from American PT boats. That he was was alone did not worry him as he had seen bare footprints in the mud along the river bank and thought he might soon come across other escaped prisoners. However, when night fell and he was still alone, he propped himself up against a tree and fell into a fitful sleep.

The next day was very hard going. The way was often blocked, forcing him to cross and recross the river until he gave up following it. But being away from the stream was far worse. Paths that appeared to be man-made tracks were more often than not animal pads leading to dead ends. Then, when he did find a proper track, he almost ran into a Japanese patrol. He had plodded on for the next three days, often losing his sense of direction and ending up in snake-infested swamps or impenetrable thickets. Once, in the dark, he had stumbled into a huge swarm of army ants which, even after he climbed a tree to get away from them, attacked his bare feet until they were raw and bleeding. Exhausted, and weak with hunger, he eventually relocated the river. The thick jungle made it impossible for him to proceed further, and he was considering making a raft when he spotted an elderly fisherman in a small boat. The Australian called softly in Malay. After a few anxious minutes, the old man paddled over, motioned him to hop in and they headed swiftly downstream.

They soon came to a village, built on stilts over the water and on a wide bend, not far from where the Mandorin River joined the Sapi before emptying into the Labuk. Braithwaite could not have come to a better place. The village was Kampong Sapi, home to Sandshoe Willie, and his rescuer was none other than the headman, Abing bin Luma, who had been on his way upstream to inspect his fish traps when Braithwaite hailed him. As he attempted to climb the ladder to Abing's house, Braithwaite, unable to summon any more energy, collapsed. A large Japanese camp was sited at the mouth of the river, less than 5 kilometres away, so Abing's son-in-law, Amit, who had been bathing one of his children in the river when he saw the boat approaching, wasted no time getting the visitor indoors and out of sight. Amit gave Braithwaite food, then hid him behind a false wall where the family kept the rice supply. The village elders arrived shortly afterwards, bearing gifts, sweets and other delicacies and bringing with them a Filipino, Abdul Raschid, who spoke excellent English. Raschid, whose real name was Loreto Padua, was a former employee of one of the large timber companies. His wife and child had been murdered by the Japanese and he was now wanted by the Kempai-tai for his high-profile, pro-guerrilla activities.

Braithwaite learned from Raschid that the villagers, too, wanted to contact the Allies. While Braithwaite wanted to get away from the Japanese, the elders wanted him to act as their emissary, to ask the Americans to stop strafing their village from the air. Abing and Amit supplied him with a boat, and an escort — Abing, Raschid, Sapan, and a crew of five — Omar, Sagan, Buang, Salim and Mangalong. Braithwaite had no money with which to repay Amit, who was unable to go with them, so he gave him two fountain pens as a token of his appreciation. At about 10.00pm they set off. A decoy boat, with a crew of two, went ahead in case of trouble. From time to time, in order to avoid other craft, they were compelled to pull into the shadows and drift along the shoreline, but neither vessel encountered any problems. It was so peaceful that Braithwaite, hidden under a blanket of banana leaves, fell asleep. The following morning he awoke to discover they were on the open sea and on their way to Libaran Island where, two days later, they hailed the passing PT boat.

The Americans transported Braithwaite safely to Tawi Tawi and sent news of his rescue, along with a rundown on the true situation at Sandakan, to their Australian allies. Towards the end of June, Australian Military Intelligence advised Allied Land Headquarters that:

AT SANDAKAN JUNE 1 500 AUSTRALIAN AND BRITISH PWS MOVED WESTWARD FROM PW CAMP WHICH WAS DESTROYED BY JAPS. 150 PWS TOO SICK TO WALK REMAINED. FATE NOT KNOWN. PRISONERS DROPPING OUT OF MARCH BELIEVED SHOT. THESE PRISONERS NOW BELIEVED TO BE IN VICINITY BELURAN OR LABUK BAY. EFFORT BEING MADE TO CONTACT.

'Effort being made to contact' was an understatement. SRD had gone into immediate damage control mode on receipt of Braithwaite's information. Things could not have been worse. The entire rescue mission had been, to use the parlance of the rank and file, 'a right cock up' from beginning to end.

First, there was the interminable delay in getting Gort into Borneo, only to learn that the POWs had been moved to Jesselton. On the strength of this incorrect intelligence, Kingfisher had been cancelled and Ranau, reported to be a Japanese stronghold, bombed. Then, when further information revealed that a large number of POWs, who had been in Sandakan all the time, had recently been removed to Ranau, SRD had urged full-scale attacks on Sandakan and the 'empty' Eight Mile Camp. A fortnight later Gort Chester, in Morotai for a debriefing following his mission to the west coast, had revealed the chances of rescuing the POWs from Ranau looked hopeless. The area where the prisoners were believed to be was too heavily defended to attempt a commando-style operation and the prisoners would be in no fit state to be moved. And now, ten days later, this bombshell from Braithwaite revealed that Sandakan had not been abandoned, that hundreds of prisoners had still been in the camp when it was bombed and strafed, that planes had attacked the retreating column and that a large number of sick had been left behind. The situation demanded drastic and immediate action.

Not so immediate, however, that anyone in the regular services should know about it. Air force planes were constantly attacking Sandakan and the Ranau track, yet it was not until 26 July that RAAF command learned, by sheer chance, that POWs were still at The Eight Mile. This resulted in an immediate and self-imposed ban on any further strikes. General Blamey did not alert the RAAF to the real situation. He did, however, order SRD to insert another party, Agas III, into North Borneo immediately. Unlike other Agas teams, which were now concentrating on guerrilla warfare, the aim of Agas III was to conduct a general reconnaissance of the Ranau area for 1 Australia Corps, now in Brunei. Although discussions had been going on between SRD and the regular army since 4 June, the receipt of Braithwaite's intelligence had suddenly increased the pressure. When Gort Chester returned to Jembongan on 21 June from his latest debriefing he had company — Flight Lieutenant Ripley, a former member of the British North Borneo Police Service. Ripley, who was to collect a signaller from Agas Control at Lokopas, was to proceed immediately, with a small party, to Ranau via the Sugut River route to gather intelligence, assess the POW situation, investigate the food position and report on the state of the airstrip. As the route they were taking — canoe up-river to Meridi and then on foot to Ranau via a recognised track — was well-established, it should not be too long before Ripley had a true picture of the situation.

A day or two after Ripley's departure from Morotai, Jock Campbell, recently appointed to SRD's top post and a man who, to date, had never ventured anywhere near the front line, moved out of his office and into the field. His destination — Libaran Island, Borneo.

Gort Chester, back on Jembongan Island, was an extremely worried man. In May, following the cancellation of the rescue plan, SRD had reorganised Agas I, freeing its members to concentrate on their other objectives — recruiting and training a guerrilla army, organising strikes against the Japanese and collecting general intelligence for the Allied invasion of Labuan and Brunei. Agas therefore had been reinforced and split into sub-parties. While the recently arrived Lieutenant H. 'Jock' Hollingworth remained at Jembongan to continue training guerrillas, Sutcliffe and Harlem had gone off to establish a new base on the Sugut River. From here they were to proceed to Telupid and Meridi to harass the enemy, disrupt their lines of communication, and obtain more information on the POWs, reportedly moving along both the southern and northern routes. This had left Chester, Jack Sue, Skeet Hywood and local agent Mandor Ali free to undertake a reconnaissance of the west coast.

Gort's party, due almost entirely to Jack Sue's and Mandor Ali's ability to pass themselves off as locals, had achieved their set objectives. Unfortunately, Sutcliffe and Harlem had not. They were side-tracked from their plan when they decided to attack the village of Aling, near Lingkabau, where 30 Japanese were reported to be garrisoned. The enemy, who were expecting them, had put up a fierce and prolonged resistance. The attacking force finally emerged victorious, but the local guerrillas had lost their taste for battle. They deserted in droves, forcing Sutcliffe and Harlem to return to base and regroup without ever reaching their destinations, much less obtaining information on the whereabouts of the POWs.

Since Agas had been confident that they were passing on 'reliable information' on the movement of Japanese troops and the evacuation of the camp, Braithwaite's revelations had been devastating. Until now Gort had no inkling that the intelligence network which had served Python so well had fallen apart, no idea that Willie's agents, terrified of reprisals, had relied on gossip and hearsay for their information rather than first hand observation, and no idea that, because of the hideous purges following the ill-fated Double Tenth uprising, enemy collaborators had made the gathering of information a very 'hit-and-miss affair' indeed. Unable to believe that Sandshoe Willie's men, previously so steadfast and reliable, could possibly have got it so wrong, Gort and Jack Sue paddled south to check on the situation for themselves.

They hid themselves in dense undergrowth along the track to the east of the Beluran turn-off. Although Gort and Jack were used to the harsh realities of war, nothing could have prepared them for what they now saw. Into their line of vision came a contingent of Japanese guards, followed by four skeletal creatures, so starved and emaciated they looked more like mummified corpses than human beings. The instinctive reaction of both men was to rush out, kill the guards and liberate the prisoners, but their training and experience told them to remain hidden. Nothing could be gained by breaking cover. Indeed, to show themselves could jeopardise any remaining chance of rescuing the others. And even if they released the prisoners, what next? They were miles from base, had no medical back-up and no way of transporting men as sick and weak as this back to the folboats, much less back to Jembongan. And so Gort Chester and Jack Sue lay still, watching their countrymen shuffle down the track and out of sight. It was the hardest thing either of them had ever done.

The men Gort and Jack had seen were from Sandakan, the remnants of a third group which had left The Eight Mile in two trucks some days before on the orders of Moritake. He and Hinata Genzo had returned from Kemansi on 1 June, bringing with them written instructions from Takakuwa that all POWs still alive must either be sent to Ranau or disposed of by some other means. In mid-June, in accordance with these orders, and by which time communications disrupted by the attack on Sandakan had been restored, Moritake had selected 75 POWs still on their feet to walk to Ranau, accompanied by Formosan guards Nishimura Mizuo and Ichikawa Takegoro and 55 soldiers, most of whom were not in good condition themselves.[1] Thirty-seven of these troops were from the Okuyama Battalion, under the command of Lieutenant Iwashita. The rest were evidently from the Okumura Unit.[2]

By the time the prisoners had reached Gort and Jack Sue, somewhere in the vicinity of the 40 mile peg, only four were left alive. Some, too ill to proceed, had been shot dead as they disembarked from the vehicles at the 15 mile. At least seven more had been shot less than a kilometre further on, on the orders of the Okumura Unit's Corporal Katayama, who was bringing up the rear. Two more were also slain here, not by the escorting guards but by Sergeant Hosotani Naoji, a member of the Sandakan Kempei-tai. Hosotani had already killed five Chinese, suspected of collaborating with a guerrilla group operating among the islands near Sandakan Harbour. He had shot the first two, Sui Chong and Ten Pek, in a rubber plantation near the 1½ mile post on 27 May, the day of the Allied attack on Sandakan. The next victim had been dispatched a week or so later at the 1 mile, while the last two had been shot in a rubber plantation near the 9 mile.

And so, having made his way progressively along the track, disposing of his victims as he went, Hosotani had reached his billet at the 15½ mile, where he became ill with malaria. He was still recuperating when the third march passed by. He had learned from a local named Chen Ten Choi that six Allied soldiers had been shot, and was not surprised when Katayama, who had to move on, approached him the next morning requesting that he shoot any stragglers. Shortly afterwards Hosotani saw two POWs, who had survived the shooting, resting behind the house of Chim Kin. They were dressed in rags and he did not know their nationality but assumed they were Australian, as both were wearing slouch hats. He borrowed a gun from Yaten, a Malay police boy who was billeted with him, and returned to shoot both prisoners in the head. Later, he shot dead another, who had escaped.

Details on the fate of the rest of the party would never be known. The sole survivor, Formosan guard Private Ichikawa, died at Jesselton before he could make a statement. However, Aman bin Aras, a Javanese superintending coolie labourers between the 17 and 42 mile watched the column pass by and later reported that by the time the marchers reached the Beluran turn-off only four POWs, the four seen by Gort and Sue, were left alive. The rest had been murdered before they reached the 30 mile peg.

A reconnaissance carried out by Rex Blow a few days later at the end of June would not shed any further light either. His recuperative leave now over, he had been sent to Libaran Island with orders to infiltrate the area near Sandakan and find out just what was going on. Recruiting a local who owned a canoe, he paddled up the Labuk estuary and into the Samawang River whose upper reaches, as the Dusan, cut the Sandakan-Beluran track near the 33 mile peg. Following the track a short distance to the west, Blow felt sure it had been subjected to some fairly heavy foot traffic recently. This was confirmed by several locals who assured him that the camp had been vacated and that all the POWs had been marched off in the direction of Ranau. Blow returned to Libaran Island without checking any further.

In fact, although 75 had left the camp on a third march, and over 130 had died, there were still between 80 and 90 POWs still alive at The 8 Mile at the end of June. After the departure of the second march they had been corralled behind a double run of barbed-wire in the Number 2 Compound, directly opposite the Japanese barracks. Although they had access to the small dam and the stream which fed it, food was limited. Moritake had traded most of the 23 bags of rice, which Takakuwa had left behind for the sick, for vegetables for himself and his men. Rations, which the POWs had to cook for themselves, now consisted of a small amount of rice, tapioca, a little coconut oil, wild kang kong and whatever bits and pieces the faithful Chinese were able to slip beneath the wire. They had established a makeshift camp in a small grove of rubber trees. Their humpies, constructed from sticks, blankets, ground sheets and whatever else they could find, were very primitive but they did afford some protection from the worst of the elements. Furthermore, despite their desperate circumstances, they were still a close-knit group. Mateship had bound the Australians, in particular, during the past three years and it did not break down now. The stronger still helped and protected the weak, the more able-bodied tended the sick, now too ill to move from their shelters. The fitter, or those with some kind of medical training, had established a rudimentary aid post in an old guard box near a clump of bananas. They stocked it with a few basic supplies from stalwart Chinese and from Red Cross parcels which the Japanese had finally decided to release.

For so many the struggle to stay alive was too great. Trevor Dobson, whose song about the Ringle Rangle Ram had kept the Dead End Kids entertained, died on 10 June and gentle John Barnier, the idealistic and patriotic young schoolteacher from Grafton, on 12 June. Two days later George Plunkett, who had survived against the odds for so long, also lost his fight for life while Ray Carlson, devoted father of eleven, died on the 22nd. His death was followed the next day by that of the gravelly-voiced Nutsy Roberts, Mo Davis' mate, and, 48 hours later, by that of Gunner Eric Tomkyns, the Indian-born schoolmaster from Warialda who had so loved the Australian bush. Youthful Ron Moran, the machine gunner from Western Australia, whose failing eyesight had sent him to Sandakan, lost his tenuous hold on life on 28 June.

They, and all the others who died in this compound, were buried, closely packed and head to tail, in slit trenches just outside the wire. Before carrying out the burials the four Javanese coolies, who had been assigned to this task by Moritake, stripped the bodies of any identification.

Moritake, Sergeant-Major Murozumi and the other fifteen Formosans guarding the camp did nothing to alleviate the suffering or the misery. The guards still displayed no compassion to the prisoners in their care. Nor did they conceal their attitude from a young man in their employ, Wong Hiong who, with fellow Chinese Wong Bow Sang, Tshu Khi and Wong Yin and the pro-Japanese Ali Asar, worked at the Japanese barracks. Hiong, small of stature and looking much younger than his fifteen years, worked as a kitchen-hand and was regarded as something of a pet by the Japanese, who called him 'Kodomo', the Japanese word for 'child'. Unlike his co-workers, he had the run of the camp, enabling him to see what others did not. The callous disregard of the guards distressed him and he did not understand how his employers could sanction the beating of such ill and weak men, or force them to stand for protracted periods while holding water barrels above their heads.

One evening, after the third march had left, Hiong saw that one of the POWs had been placed in the punishment cage, which was similar in construction to Esau but with barbed-wire sides. Although the prisoner was very thin, and his hair and beard long, Hiong recognised him as the chief administrative officer from the old Number 2 Camp. The man's name was too difficult to pronounce so everyone, from Moritake down, simply called this prisoner 'Honcho'. He was quite tall (but not nearly as tall as Chipperfield, the giant, red-headed Australian called 'tinggi', the Malay word for 'high') and had a distinctively hooked nose, ginger moustache and receding reddish hair. He wore a peaked cap, long khaki trousers, black boots and a khaki shirt which bore a senior officer's insignia. Hiong liked this man, believed to be Captain Mills, very much.[3] Honcho often winked at him as he went by and made a sign with his fingers, evidently a V for Victory, when the bombers came over.

Honcho had been placed in the cage after Nishikawa, a Formosan civilian investigating the disappearance of a pig from the sty, had discovered pieces of pork in the prisoner's cup and plate — evidence which had given Honcho no option but to admit he had killed the pig and distributed it among his fellow prisoners. When Hiong went to the latrines at about 6.30am on the day after Honcho's arrest he saw the prisoner, smoking a cigarette, sitting on a chair outside the Japanese office, flanked by guards Hinata Genzo and Fukuda Nobuo. About 20 minutes later, as Hiong returned, he saw that Honcho, dressed only in a loin-cloth and very weak, was being helped along by the same two guards. Moritake, carrying a hammer, brought up the rear. Hiong watched as the small procession stopped at a large wooden cross, erected about 75 metres from the cookhouse and 30 metres from the office.

Hinata supported the prisoner firmly against the upright while Moritake mounted a small stool which Nishikawa had brought from the office. Then, while Hinata pressed his body against the victim to hold him still, Mortitake drove a long nail into the palm of the prisoner's outstretched right hand. He ordered Hinata to stuff a piece of rag into Honcho's mouth to stifle his screams. Moritake repeated the process with the left hand, then nailed both the prisoner's feet to a horizontal board on which he was standing. Finally Moritake drove a 20-centimetre-long nail through the centre of Honcho's forehead. He then took a butcher's knife and cut two pieces of flesh from the prisoner's abdomen, which he set aside on a wooden board brought especially for the purpose. Donning a rubber glove, he slit the torso from neck to navel, removing the liver and the heart, which he cut in two. He had just finished slicing away more flesh from the thighs, arms and abdomen when, Hiong, hiding under the barracks, heard the Japanese cook calling him from the kitchen.

When Hiong emerged ten minutes later, on the pretext of wanting to urinate, he heard Moritake, still at the cross, shout for Nishikawa who then hurried off in the direction of the Number 2 Compound. He returned about 30 minutes later with two POWs who were ordered to pick up the board and its grisly exhibits. The prisoners, escorted by Moritake and his three henchmen, were marched back across the road to the camp where the other prisoners had been lined up. The remains of the corpse were left hanging on the cross to decompose.

In the middle of July, Moritake piled wood faggots around the remains, saturated everything with kerosene and set it all alight, destroying all physical evidence of his appalling crime. The prisoners, of course, were of no consequence as Moritake had no intention of leaving any witnesses. By the end of June there were only 65 Australians and 22 British left alive. By the second week in July, when Moritake received orders from Takakuwa to leave for Ranau as soon as possible and dispose of the POWs along the way, there were still 48 left. Twenty-five of these looked as if they were close to death, so Moritake decided to dispose of the rest immediately. Late in the afternoon of 13 July, 23 Australian prisoners, including Tom Burns and William Steen, a 35-year-old driver from the AASC, were marched out of the camp and down the road towards the airfield. Accompanying them were Murozumi and twelve other guards. Moritake, who was ill with malaria, Kanazawa, Nishimura and the Japanese cook remained behind to guard the others.

Tom Burns had taken with him his pack containing his diary, Christmas menu of 1943 and sundry other precious bits and pieces. He, for one, seemed to have no idea this walk would be his last. As they approached the bombed-out barrack buildings and an abandoned Chinese house near the air strip, the column turned off the road and entered a rubber plantation on the left. About 30 metres in from the road was a trench, 10 metres long, 1 metre wide and about 1.5 metres deep, which had been dug as part of the airstrip defence works. A crescent-shaped dirt revetment, built to provide cover for the defenders, was on the side of the trench closest to the strip. The prisoners were split into two groups and lined up at each end of the trench, while the guards formed two squads a few metres away. Some of the guards were uneasy about participating in a massacre, so Murozumi stood about three paces behind, ready to enforce the order with his pistol, if necessary. A volley of shots, clearly audible to Hiong back at the camp, rang out.

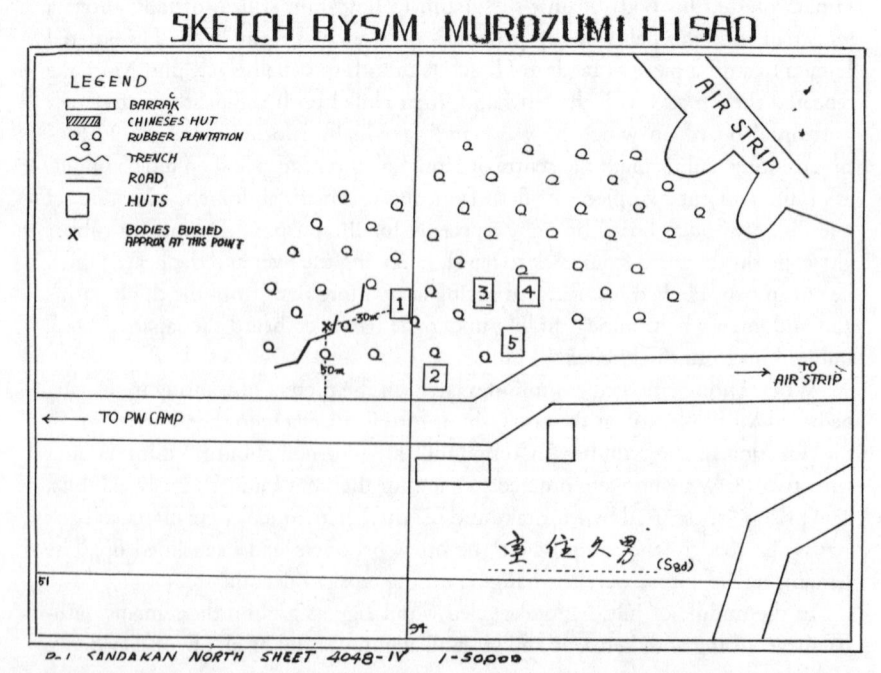

Sketch map by Murozumi, showing the place where Tom Burns and his 22 companions were murdered.

The bodies of the men were rolled into the trench and covered with soil pushed down from the revetment. Murozumi then ensured that the paperwork recorded that each of the 23 had died of natural causes. He entered the dates of death over a period of a few days, from 13 to 15 July to make the sudden rise in the death toll less obvious. It was an unnecessary ploy. Hiong, who had asked what the shooting was about, was satisfied with the explanation that the guards had been out hunting and had bagged 23 ducks.

Moritake died four days later. He was buried, dressed in full ceremonial uniform, in the Japanese compound, not far from the administrative office. Moritake's demise made conditions even worse for the three English and fifteen Australians who had outlived him, as he had given away the rest of their rice to his favourite prostitutes, as a parting gift. Subsisting on a diet of kang kong and tapioca, the prisoners were now so weak they were compelled to eat their meagre ration uncooked. Yet, despite this, a handful still hung on. The last English officer, Lieutenant Young, died on 26 July. The following day The Turk also died, his stash of diamonds and gold, hidden in the hollow of The Big Tree back at the Number 1 Compound, apparently untouched.

On 1 August there were nine Australians and one British soldier alive. Four days later, when Ali Asar was sent to deliver an armful of kang kong, four Australians had died, as no other food had been sent in for the past week. Hiong had been sneaking some food to them, but his activities had come to an abrupt end when he was seen exchanging salt for a pair of shorts with Ted Skinner's brother, John, and punished with a beating and a warning that, if he did it again, Murozumi would cut off his head. The five survivors — Skinner, 31, Ernest Woodley, 26, Ivan Sinclair, 36, John Davis, 34, Walter Hancock, 42 and the lone Englishman, Harold Rooker, 31 — asked Asar to bring more food but he was unable to do so, as Murozumi had recently ordered that any Malay or Chinese worker who went near the compound would be shot. That day, Woodley and Sinclair died. Davis and Rooker died four days later.

When dawn broke on the morning of Wednesday 15 August, John Skinner was alone.[4] His mate, Walter Hancock, had died during the night. Skinner was still lying beneath his shelter of blankets and ground sheets when, shortly before 7.00am, Murozumi led a contingent of guards into the compound. Hiong, who had secretly followed them, despite explicit instructions from Murozumi to remain in the barracks, climbed a nearby rubber tree and watched as Nishikawa Yoshinori, Fukuda Nobuo, Nagata Shinichi and Goto Yoshitaro strode over to one of the shelters and dragged Skinner to his feet. They drove Skinner outside the wire, lashing out with fists and boots, and up the slope to where Murozumi, sword in hand, was waiting beside an open slit-trench. Murozumi positioned himself to the left, legs astride. Hinata Genzo forced the captive to his knees and Nagata tied a piece of black cloth around his eyes. Gripping it with both hands, Murozumi raised his sword high above his head, pausing only momentarily before bringing it down, in one tremendous swipe, to decapitate Sandakan's last prisoner of war.

Five hours later the high-pitched voice of Emperor Hirohito announced, on national domestic radio, that Japan had surrendered to the Allies.

While the rest of the western world rejoiced at this long-awaited announcement, Colonel J. Wilton, an Australian Army officer at General Staff Headquarters had other matters on his mind. On 15 August, unaware that Murozumi had, that very day, disposed of Sandakan's last prisoner of war, he submitted a proposal to rescue a possible 200 POWs thought to be alive — 120 at The Eight Mile Camp and the rest in small groups along the Sandakan-Ranau track. Within 24 hours, 1 Australia Corps had not only approved his proposal, it had come up with a plan and ordered the Commander of the 26th Australian Infantry Brigade, at Tarakan, to carry it out. A composite force, made up of members of the 2/4 Commando Squadron, 2 Australian Field company, 2/11 Field Ambulance, 2/43 Australian Cipher Section, ATIS (Allied Translation and Interpreter Service) and FELO (AIB's propaganda section), all under the command of the Squadron's Major Irving, was put on two-hours' standby. The RAAF, whose C-47s had been integral to the aborted Kingfisher plan, continued to put its wholehearted support behind a possible rescue and pledged its maximum co-operation in any attempt to recover the prisoners. At the same time SRD's Flight Lieutenant North, Captain O'Keefe and two signallers, along with Royal Australian Naval frigate *Gascoyne* and corvette *Kapunda*, were ordered to proceed to Tarakan immediately.

As soon as the ships arrived on the morning of 18 August they were loaded with 250 tonnes of stores, including tents, folding beds, blankets, mosquito nets and pyjamas as well as sufficient food and medical stores to sustain 250 troops and up to 200 POWs for 25 days. Included in the canteen stores were 24 dozen bottles of beer, 240 packets of Minties, 288 packets of chocolate, 144 tubes of toothpaste, 26 cartons of chewing gum, and a huge supply of custom-made cigarettes, tobacco and cigarette papers. Meanwhile, O'Keefe and the signallers went by PT boat to Libaran Island via Tawi Tawi, where a flotilla of PT boats and shallow-draught river gun boats, to be used for the rescue, were stationed. On arrival at Libaran, the signallers established wireless links with *Gascoyne*, Tarakan and Tawi Tawi, and O'Keefe organised native guides and carriers and collected information on the condition and health of the POWs, as well as details regarding waterways which might be suitable for the evacuation.

On 17 August, the RAAF dropped 1000 leaflets in Sandakan and along the track. They were designed to ensure both the Japanese and POWs knew the war was over and carried an instruction written in Malay and Japanese, for anyone finding a leaflet to deliver it to the nearest POW camp.

> *On August 14 1945, the Japanese Government informed the Allied government that they would accept the terms of the Potsdam Declaration, and the Emperor of Japan issued instructions that all Japanese forces lay down their arms.*

> *One of the clauses of surrender terms was that all Allied Prisoners of War should be looked after by the Japanese forces and concentrated in those areas where they would be readily accessible to Allied transport.*

> *We have addressed messages to the Japanese forces in this area asking them to carry out the terms of the Emperor's instructions. In the meantime until we arrive you should act with restraint.*

We know what this news must mean to you, and we who have been separated from you for so long are concentrating everything possible on your immediate release. Because of the distances which separate the Allied forces in the area there may be a lapse of some time before this can be arranged.

In the meantime keep your spirits up because we will be with you shortly.

At 9.00pm on 19 August, 26th Infantry Brigade signalled Corps Headquarters that the force would be ready to leave the following day at noon. It was all too late.

On 20 August, General Headquarters stood the troops down and cancelled the entire rescue mission. They had learned that there was definitely no one left alive at Sandakan. That same day, Murozumi ordered the destruction of the prisoners' personal effects, set fire to the barracks buildings and abandoned The Eight Mile Camp. But, if Murozumi thought that he had eliminated all the evidence and all the witnesses, he was very much mistaken.

On 28 July, thirteen days after Braithwaite had been rescued from Libaran Island, Owen Campbell was on United States aircraft carrier *Pokomoke*, giving details of his amazing escape to an incredulous Major Dick Noone (British Army) — SRD's Director of Intelligence. After leaving the column on 7 June, Campbell and his companions had continued to head away from the coast, aided by a compass which Emmett had somehow managed to keep hidden. They covered only about 1.5 kilometres the first day, stopping now and again to fish the creeks, using lines also belonging to the resourceful Emmett. The next day, by which time they had travelled 10 kilmoetres, they turned towards the coast, only to be held up on 9 June when Campbell came down with malaria. Fortunately, one of the party had quinine and they were on their way again within 24 hours, but were halted once more when Skinner was stricken with dysentery. When it became obvious after two days that he was too ill to go any further, Campbell, who had quite severe beriberi, elected to remain with him while the other three kept going in a north-easterly direction towards the coast, marking their trail as they went. Campbell stayed by Skinner's side for three days, ignoring his pleas to leave him and go after the others, . On 16 June, as their food ration had run out, Campbell left Skinner alone while he went to a nearby creek to fetch water and scrounge for something to eat. When he returned, his mate was dead. He had cut his throat with a lid from one of the empty salmon tins. The next morning, Campbell buried Skinner in a shallow grave onto which he rolled small logs and stones, then he too set off for the coast.

Campbell, sustained only by freshwater crabs and an unidentified animal which he caught and ate raw, tracked the others to the Mandorin River, where he came upon Costin, ill with dysentery and malaria, sheltering under a blanket about 60 metres from the river bank. Emmett and Webber were away fishing, but on their return the four men agreed that their only hope was to appeal to the locals. Late that afternoon they heard the sounds of a boat. Emmett and Webber ran to the bank, where they called to the two occupants, Malay fishermen. As they paddled towards the Australians a Japanese soldier, previously hidden from view at the bottom of the boat, opened fire. Emmett and Webber, shot through the head and chest, fell into the river and disappeared. Campbell, who had been some distance behind them, was not spotted.

The Japanese soldier made no attempt to come ashore and Campbell was able to make his way back to the blanket shelter. Living on soya bean powder, he remained with the rapidly weakening Costin, who died in his sleep three days later, on the night of 21 June. Campbell pushed on the next morning, covering not much more than 3 kilometres before night, and rain, started to fall. The following day, while attempting to cross the 270-metre-wide Mandorin River on a log, a Japanese soldier standing on the bank saw him and opened fire. Campbell sustained a bullet wound to the left wrist, but was able to swim underwater the rest of the way and hide among the mangroves. The soldier fired three or four more shots into the undergrowth, but made no attempt to cross the river and look for him.

For the next nine days the Australian pushed on, eating whatever he could find — fungus, raw fish and crabs. Delirious for much of the time, he conversed with his dead mates, convinced they were still beside him. On 2 July, ten days after leaving Costin, he was asleep under a tree when a wild pig tried to take a bite out of his knee. Campbell awoke just in time and poked a stick in the pig's eye, driving it off. The next morning he followed the animal's trail and reached the Muanad River. He was hiding among the mangroves, trying to raid a fish trap, when he spotted a small canoe which seemed to be avoiding other river traffic. In response to his call ('Abang', the Malay word for elder brother) the canoeist paddled over and told him to stay where he was. About 45 minutes later the man returned, with a friend. They instructed Campbell to douse himself with water before climbing into the canoe so that they could claim they had fished him out of the river if stopped by a Japanese patrol boat from a large camp, only 300 metres downstream.

Campbell's rescuers, Galuting and Lap, were from Kampong Muanad, home of Orang Tuan Kulang, chief of the Dusans, friend of Sandshoe Willie, surveyor of the Sandakan-Ranau track, secret SRD agent and one of the fiercest enemies of the Japanese. His loyal followers soon had Campbell across the river and safely hidden in a house. After dark Galuting and Lap transferred him to a new kampong, deeper in the jungle, which the villagers had built to avoid harassment by the Japanese. Here, at the house of the acting headman, Salium, Campbell was given a bath, clean clothes and a bowl of soup. Kulang himself arrived later to find that Campbell had graduated to eating rice and prawns and was regaining his strength. He had just finished cutting a rentis for SRD in the Bongaya River area, about 40 kilometres to the north of the Labuk, and had taken a few days off to see what was happening back at the village.

Campbell was still emaciated and suffering from beriberi and recurring malaria, but regular meals had put a bit of flesh on his bones, while a haircut and shave, administered by Kulang with the aid of an ancient cut-throat razor, had greatly improved his looks. Kulang decided he could be moved. Campbell, accompanied by Kulang and a number of villagers, made his way through the jungle to the Kolapis River, roughly 5 kilometres away, where they boarded two prahaus. Three days' paddling brought them to the entrance to the Labuk, and another three to the mouth of the Bongaya. Seven hours later Campbell was delivered into the capable hands of Kulang's 'boss' — Agas party's Lieutenant Jock Hollingworth.

Hollingworth was expecting them. Earlier that day he had been manning an outpost on the river with a small force of guerrillas when a runner arrived with news that Kulang was on his way upstream with an escaped POW. It was obvious that Campbell required immediate medical attention, so Hollingworth, who had been left without a wireless transmitter following the recent departure of Harlem to a base further up the river, sent a runner after him. In the early hours of the following morning, 21 July, the runner returned, bringing with him Signaller Kelm and a transmitter. Five hours later, Hollingsworth was receiving instructions from Sutcliffe. He was to contact Morotai and arrange for Campbell's evacuation by flying boat.

Mid-afternoon on 23 July, Hollingworth and Campbell, accompanied by Kelm, Kulang and a small party of guerrillas, paddled downstream in a large prahau to the rendezvous, set down for 8.30am the following day at Kandawan Island, off Kuala Bongaya. They reached the river mouth with an hour to spare but, although they waited an hour past the appointed time, saw no sign of any aircraft. There was no possibility of returning to the camp. The river was in full flood and Campbell, who had lost consciousness during the journey, was lying in a state of delirium in the bottom of the boat. At. 9.30am Hollingworth ordered the prahau to put to sea. About 11 kilometres off-shore they sighted a Mariner aircraft, circling in the distance. Shortly afterwards Campbell was tucked up in a hospital bed on board *Pokomoke*, anchored off the coast.

Four days later the escapee was debriefed by SRD's Dick Noone. Despite intensive medical treatment, he was still physically debilitated by malaria and his skin was a mass of dry scales as a result of a severe vitamin deficiency. His weight, a hefty 76 kilograms before captivity was now down to 44, and four of those were fluid, trapped in his tissues, the effects of beriberi. Some of the details he recounted to Noone were a little confused, but the intelligence officer heard nothing which gave him reason to hold out hope for the rest of the prisoners Campbell had left on the march. In the absence of any other information, they would have to wait until Ripley and his men arrived to check on those at Ranau.

Ripley had left Morotai expecting to pick up a signaller from Lokopas, only to find that the three wireless experts — Nash, Greenwood and Olsen — had moved. They were now with Agas II's Nick Coombe, British Army, on the Bengkoka River at a place called Pitas, kilometres away on the other side of the Paitan-Maradu peninsula. A signaller was integral to the mission, so Ripley had no alternative but to chase after them. The journey was not easy. A native boat could take him only as far as Melobong and he had to travel the rest of the way on foot. When he eventually arrived at Pitas, it was to discover that not one of Agas's four signallers was available. By the time Signaller Skeet Hywood flew in by Catalina from Morotai it was 8 July and time was running out. With Pitas so far away from the Sugut River mouth, Ripley scrapped the original plan. Instead of approaching Ranau from the east, he would travel south, down the Bengkoka River and then strike out across the Crocker Range for Meridi.

Why Major Coombe, or one of Agas' other field officers, who knew that the vast region beyond Bombong Bombong was uncharted territory, did not arrange air insertion for Ripley and Hywood is a mystery. If Ripley had been ordered to return to Morotai, he would have had at his disposal SRD's exclusive air wing, Flight 200, which was experienced in dropping SRD teams into Borneo from specially converted B-24s. Indeed, Major Coombe himself, along with his four-man party, had been parachuted into Lokopas from a B–24 on 5 May. Within hours of arriving back at Morotai, Agas III could have been on its way, if not to Ranau itself, then to a drop zone infinitely closer than where they were now. But it was not to be.

On 8 July, Ripley and Hywood, accompanied by police constables Sampura, Ampun and Jalil, left Pitas for the south. Little did they realise that between them and the POWs at Ranau lay some of the most difficult terrain on earth.

Chapter Fourteen
AND THEN THERE WERE SIX

The prisoners at the Number 2 Jungle Camp had no idea that Ripley was on his way, or, indeed that anyone on the outside world was aware of their situation. For those who had arrived on the second march, Ranau had become hell on earth. They barely had time to draw breath before they were split into working parties — cutting bamboo, collecting wood, carrying out general fatigue duties for the guards, marching back and forth along the track to the old airstrip camp to collect atap for the hut, and transporting 20-kilogram bags of rice and vegetables (the lion's share of which went to the guards) from a dump about 3 kilometres south of the village. This labour was gruelling, but it was nothing compared to the workload of the half-dozen unfortunate men assigned to the officers' quarters — nine of whom died from exhaustion hauling water, 130 buckets a day, up the steep slope from the creek to the Japanese huts.

The POWs were forced to draw their own water downstream from the place where the guards bathed, washed their clothes and urinated. The incidence of gastro-enteritis therefore rose sharply. Doctors Picone and Oakeshott worked around the clock to provide what comfort they could for the ill, and, although Takakuwa refused to relinquish any medical supplies, Sticpewich's friendship with Takahara, one of the guards, ensured that he received not only a steady supply of extra food, but also atebrin and quinine, which he passed to the doctors. Takahara knew Sticpewich and most of his technical party well. He had been transferred from The Eight Mile Camp in June 1944 because of fraternisation with the prisoners, but until then had kept them supplied with food and drugs and carried messages to native contacts outside the wire. When Takahara had realised that his old friend Sticpewich was among the new arrivals in Ranau, he sent a message to him through a member of the technical party.[1] Later, when Sticpewich made his way to the cookhouse, Takahara was able to slip him a bottle of anti-malarial drugs and signal that he had also left a bunch of bananas — an arrangement that worked so smoothly it was repeated on numerous occasions.

The two medical officers not only ministered to the sick but also had to contend with others who lay down in the mud of the compound and refused to move. Such behaviour was understandable from men who were by no means fit, but their malingering made life even more difficult for their comrades who, with the meagre work force diminished, had to work even harder. The lack of sanitation, the starvation rations, the overwork, the generally poor health and the beatings, accounted for the lives of at least 25 Australians between 26 June and 7 July. The burial detail found it more and more difficult to drag the dead to the cemetery, let alone scrape out a grave. And, as Japanese tempers, frayed by depressing news from the front, snapped, the officers were far more inclined to beat their Formosan underlings who, in turn, stepped up their physical attacks on the

POWs. Almost anything could lead to a severe bashing — leaving the restricted area to defecate, not moving the dead to the cemetery quickly enough, being too slow in carrying out orders, or, simply, being a prisoner of war.

The only people immune from this barbarism were members of a small, select band of POWs who, by being 'held in reserve', were able to avoid contact with Japanese officers and guards. One of those keeping a low profile was Cook, who had handed over his command to the dominant Sticpewich, now in a position of great influence and power. In addition to carrying out Cook's duties, organising working parties, and keeping camp records, Sticpewich also oversaw the cookhouse, the distribution of rations and hut construction. On the three occasions when meat was provided, he organised the slaughtering of cattle, appropriated from the Ranau villagers and kept in a compound about 500 metres south of the river, on the eastern side of the Tambunan track. A guard shot the beast (or beasts, depending on the size) and it was the task of the POWs to dress the carcass before lugging it back down the track, along with the head, hide and entrails. Between 310-350 kilograms of beef were distributed to various Japanese units along the way. The POWs were given the leftovers — the stomach and intestines.

On 1 July, while accompanying the eight-man slaughter party to the cattle pen, Sticpewich fell into conversation with one of the two Formosan guards. Nakamura Koji, who had been beaten up by Takakuwa and Suzuki for carrying a dirty rifle, was feeling aggrieved. He told Sticpewich that he believed that Sandakan had been occupied, a rumour the Australians had already heard, and spoke about the great differences in the way Australians and Japanese treated their prisoners of war. Nakamura, who was aware of the situation in Australia from letters written by his POW father, apologised for what he had done in the past and offered his friendship. After declaring that the Japanese were no good and would kill all their prisoners, he confided that he would commit suicide rather than surrender to the Allies. Sticpewich remarked that if any Australian were in a similar position, he would shoot the officers he disliked and then, as he was going to die anyway, kill himself. Nakamura listened carefully to Sticpewich's words. By the time they had reached the cattle compound he had made up his mind. 'Beso sia mati — tomorrow I die', he vowed, and so, too, he said, would Takakuwa and all officers who had treated him badly and killed Australians.

The Australians readied themselves to seize control of the camp. The next afternoon at about 5.15, in the expectation that he would soon be replacing Takakuwa as camp commandant, Captain Cook left wherever he was being kept 'in reserve' and made his way towards the Japanese officers' quarters. Without warning Nakamura burst into the officers' hut. Before they realised what was happening he had shot dead the hated Lieutenant Suzuki. Unfortunately, he only managed to wound Takakuwa in the thigh and slightly injure two others — the callous medical orderly Sergeant Fugita and Takakuwa's batman. Cook, standing nearby, was grazed slightly by a stray bullet. Although Nakamura tossed a hand grenade into the room, everyone else escaped without a scratch as the would-be assassin, in his panic, had not removed the priming pin. Nakamura then placed his rifle to his own head and pulled the trigger.

The only Japanese with any medical training, Fugita, had been injured in the fracas, so Doctors Oakeshott and Picone were ordered to attend the wounded. Suzuki's body lay in the hut until the next evening, by which time POW working parties had gathered sufficient wood for a funeral pyre. The disgraced Nakamura was buried in an unmarked grave. The day after the shooting Lieutenant Watanabe, acting commandant, lined up the Formosan guards and berated them for 40 minutes. As a result, their brutality towards the POWs increased dramatically.

On 6 July, four days after Suzuki's murder, Botterill and Moxham were ordered to join a cane-cutting detail. When the men lined up about 50 metres from the compound area and realised they were a few short, Maskey, in his role as interpreter, was ordered to report the deficiency to Fukishima Maseo, now overseeing working parties. Fukishima stormed down to the POW area and dragged Sapper Arthur 'Dickie' Bird and another POW to their feet. Refusing to listen to Bird's pleas to be excused from work as he was suffering from malaria and beriberi, as well as a large leg ulcer, Fukishima ordered the party to move off. They had only gone about 10 metres when Bird collapsed, saying, 'I am too crook. I cannot come.' Botterill and Moxham tried to help him to his feet, but Fukishima appeared on the scene, cursing and swearing. Bird tried to explain that he was ill, but the enraged guard knocked him to the ground. Maskey attempted to intervene but was pushed out of the way. Fukishima then went berserk, kicking Bird about the face and body. He had not stopped when the working party was ordered to move off, a good ten minutes later.

When the men returned shortly before 5.00pm, Botterill saw that Bird was lying on the ground, about 3 metres from where they had left him. They tried to carry him back to the hut but after 30 metres or so the agony was so great Bird asked to be put down. Botterill realised that it was no use sending for the medical officers. Without drugs and surgical instruments there was nothing either Picone or Oakeshott could do. Bird, who had lapsed into a coma, died two days later.[2] According to the official Japanese record, the cause of death was malaria. An appalled Oakeshott, who was responsible for filling in the paperwork, exhorted anyone who survived, or managed to escape, to ensure that those responsible for Bird's murder be brought to justice.

Botterill and Moxham were not there to witness the burial. On 7 July, Watanabe ordered the five surviving members of the first march (Botterill, Moxham, Stacy, Grist and Frost) to join the rest of the prisoners. There were now about 100 left at the Ranau camp — a camp which Botterill was certain would be inhabited only by the dead before very long. It was an opinion shared by Moxham who had learned from the guard, Memora, that orders to this effect had been issued. The Black Bastard's attack on Bird had helped them to make up their minds. They would escape that very night.

Still believing that, if they ran into trouble, four men were better than two, the pair quietly canvassed those nearby to see if they would join them. Some, including Norm Grist, were too ill; others, who had heard what happened to Crease and Cleary, were too scared. Nelson Short was not. Neither was the 2/10th Field Regiment's Frank 'Andy' Anderson, a 25-year-old gunner who, in civilian life, had been a window dresser for Allan & Starks, a large Brisbane department store. When their mate Les Fitzgerald, who was too ill with malaria to make the attempt, told them that Botterill and Moxham were looking for volunteers, both asked if they could come. As Nelson looked as if he had a bit of go in him and Andy, although he had an ulcer on his foot, was obviously a game enough bloke, Botterill and Moxham agreed to take them.

While Nelson had nothing but the clothes he stood up in — the kit-bag shorts made by Bill McDonald — Botterill and Moxham were reasonably well-equipped. They no longer had Moxham's lumber jacket or map, but they did have a spectacle lens which they could use as a magnifying glass, a jack-knife and a battered kerosene-tin billy, as well as extra clothing donated by those who would have liked to come but, because they were too weak or ill, could not. After saying goodbye to Fitzgerald, and promising to visit his family if he made it home, Nelson ate his cup of watery rice and settled down to wait. There was no proper shelter for any of the prisoners, not even for the sick, and the rain, which had begun earlier in the day, was now falling steadily. It was during this period that two men near Short, ambulanceman Corporal Bob McEwen, and another young soldier, died. The soldier's final act was to call for his mate, Bluey, to whom he handed his last, and most treasured possession — his mother's wedding ring.

At last it was 9.00pm and time to go. They had agreed to give Cook, and all senior officers, except two, a wide berth. Crawling over to where the two doctors, Picone and Oakeshott, were huddled under a pile of branches, the men shook hands and said they were leaving. Wishing them the best of luck, the medical officers handed over a wad of Japanese money saying, 'It might help you. You might be able to bribe the natives.' When the men took their leave, they had more than just the doctors' cash. Figuring that his need was the greater, Moxham had appropriated Oakeshott's boots.

They made their way, hanging onto the man in front, Indian-file, towards the camp perimeter. They had gone only a few metres when Moxham blundered into something. It was a small, one-man humpy, constructed from a ground sheet and a few branches, supported by four bamboo sticks. Trying to regain his balance, Moxham trod on the unfortunate occupant, Englishman Norm Frost, who immediately jumped up and grabbed the intruder. Realising it was Moxham and that he was wearing a pack, Frost asked, 'What's up?' To his everlasting regret, Botterill did not tell him, but whispered instead, 'Shut up. We'll be back soon and we'll fix up your tent.'

The rain, coming down in torrents, was a mixed blessing. It hindered their progress, but it had driven all but one of the guards into a lean-to shelter. The other, on picket duty, was sitting on a nearby log. As the four men neared the shelter, they drew straws to decide who should take the lead. Botterill 'lost', but luck was with him. The guards were all standing around a fire, while the lookout was smoking, each draw of his cigarette betraying the movement of his head. Safely past, the Australians headed towards a rice store, which Botterill and Moxham had previously located about 5 kilometres down the track. Again they were in luck. The store was unguarded and, although there was a lock on the door, it was secured only with a twist of wire. Filling their haversacks and billy with enough rice to last a week or so, the men continued on to Ranau.

They sneaked through the sleeping village and turned west, down the Tuaran track in the direction of Jesselton, well over 100 kilometres to the south-west. Realising that it was essential to put as much distance as possible between themselves and the camp, they kept going all night. By the time dawn broke the rain had stopped, enabling them to leave the track and make their way down the mountainside, where they sought refuge in a small cave beside a stream. With the aid of the spectacle lens and kindling scraped from a bamboo cane, they soon had a billy of rice boiling merrily over a small fire.

They stayed in the cave, which they camouflaged with foliage, for the next six days. There were no shrimps or fish in the creek but growing nearby were plenty of green bananas, which they cut up and cooked with the rice. However, on the night of 14 July, realising they were becoming progressively weaker, the four men climbed back up the hill and once more set off for Jesselton. They had not gone far when they came to a Japanese police hut. Outside the hut was a post, and tied to the post was a horse — a horse which could provide transportation and, ultimately, food. Unfortunately the animal was not at all co-operative. They were forced to abandon the plan when a policeman, hearing the racket, stomped out onto the hut's verandah and yelled for the horse to be quiet.

The next day, after a cold and miserable night in the open, they found an abandoned hut. Short's dark, wavy hair and deeply-tanned skin, acquired from the march, made him less conspicuous than his companions, so he was elected to keep guard while the others took a nap. He evidently made a convincing Malay. A lone Japanese soldier, who came upon him unexpectedly, thought he was a local and asked for a match. Short, panicking, shouted a warning and took off along the slope, just as Botterill emerged from the hut. Perhaps it was Botterill's wild appearance, or the possibility he was suffering from a highly contagious disease. Whatever the reason, the soldier took one look at him and fled.

Realising that the incident would be reported, Botterill, Moxham and Anderson rustled up Short, hiding in the long grass, and headed down the mountainside. Anderson had become ill with dysentery by this time, so, when they came upon another hut, they called a halt. From inside they heard the sound of footsteps approaching. It was Baragah (pronounced 'Bariga') Katus, a middle-aged Dusan farmer, headman of Batu Lima village and owner of the hut. Baragah, who was on his way to deliver a huge bunch of bananas to the local garrison, had been forced to give up his large farm to work as a tailor for the occupying forces and was very anti-Japanese. Assuring his unexpected tenants that he was 'kowan' — friend — he gave them 40 huge bananas, ten each, and promised to return with some more food.

Baragah had been gone for only a short time, when Short looked up to see an unarmed Japanese soldier heading their way. They barely had time to agree on a plan of action — Botterill and Short would keep him talking while Moxham dispatched him with the jack knife — when he stuck his head inside the hut and asked if they had a watch. Finding they did not, he then asked about food before mentioning that four prisoners had escaped. Feigning surprise, the men explained they were out on a working party but were waiting for their guard to return with some medicine as they had become ill. Anderson certainly looked ill, but whether they were believed or not they never had a chance to find out. The soldier took off to seek cover on hearing the sound of approaching aircraft. As soon as he had gone, the others picked up Anderson and headed into the jungle.

Baragah found the fugitives at noon the next day, He had smelt the smoke from their fire on which they were cooking what was left of their rice. He quickly doused the flames and told them that the alarm had been raised. The Kempei-tai, who were offering bags of rice and salt for every escaped prisoner turned over to them, were not far away. He handed over a parcel of food containing his own mid-day meal with the assurance he would return, and ordered them to stay out of sight. When he came back a few hours later he took them further into the jungle, where he built a small lean-to shelter beside a creek. However a week later, worried that a constant stream of visitors from the village would alert the Japanese, Baragah moved them to a new site, 200 metres west of the 5 mile peg on the Ranau-Tuaran track. Here, on a steep mountainside about 200 metres below the track, he built another, more substantial hut in a small clearing near the Kehunot River.

Their faithful friend kept them supplied with food, but Andy Anderson continued to deteriorate. He died on 29 July, a few days after moving to the new hiding place. His mates, lacking the energy to dig a grave, took him to a spot on the far side of the river, where they covered his body with dirt and small stones. The next day they buried him properly as a marauding animal had discovered the site.

A couple of weeks later, Baragah reported that only about 20 of the 70 Australians and 30 English they had left at Ranau were still alive. However, the news had little impact on the three men. The close confines of the hut, coupled with the uncertainty of their continued existence, had taken its toll. The mateship which had sustained them when facing the common enemy had evaporated, replaced by wariness and distrust. It was a case of every man for himself, especially at meal times. Each watched every move the others made, lest someone take more than his fair share of the food. They were beginning to hate the sight of one another, when a village youth named Kaingal rushed into the hut about 15 August with the news that his friend's cousin had seen white soldiers at a camp in the jungle, north-east of Ranau. After six long and gruelling weeks, Flight-Lieutenant Ripley and the Agas III team had made it!

Leaving Pitas on 8 July, they had travelled down the Bengkoka River before striking south-east to Melinsau, which they reached on 16 July after a most arduous overland journey. En route they had been joined by headman Andong Ajak, a wiry old fellow of indeterminate age, who had run for two days from Pitas to catch up to them. The party by now was in urgent need of food, but as no suitable drop zone could be found they moved on to Kiayap, arriving on 22 July. Three days later ten storpedoes (stores containers) were parachuted from one of SRD's B-24 aircraft. As all missed the target, the team wasted the next three days scouring thick jungle in order to find them. Even worse, instead of sending the six tins of 'compo rations' which Ripley had requested, for reasons known only to itself, SRD had dropped almost 1.5 tonnes of stores. In a master piece of understatement Ripley reported that this enormous over-catering 'was a source of trouble almost to the end of the trip'.

Learning that the Japanese based at Meridi and Merungin were raiding nearby communities for food and could create problems for the party, Ripley made repeated requests while at Kiayap for both sites to be bombed. Meridi was never attacked but, on 2 August, United States Kittyhawks made a strike in the vicinity of Merungin. Neither the village nor its Japanese occupants were hit. The sole casualties were a cow and pig belonging to the pro-British headman, Dampulok. Slowed by the need to by-pass Merungin (still full of Japanese), the difficult mountain terrain and the problem of finding anyone to help carry the over-abundance of supplies, it was not for another five days that the party reached Lansat. The next day they had a visitor. It was Zimban bin Dittuan, a member of the British North Borneo constabulary. He had come from the village of Sumaang, a few kilometres to the south-west of Ranau, with news that two escaped POWs were living in the jungle, not far from his village. He had brought with him a note, dated 5 August, addressed to the Commander in Chief, Allied Forces, Jesselton. The message, written in firm, well-formed handwriting on a piece of scrap notepaper, was unexpectedly formal. The sender, forwarding this 'dispatch' in 'accordance with Article XXIX, Articles, Laws and Customs of War', was QX 9538, Warrant Officer Class 1, William Hector Sticpewich, 8th Division, AASC.

Sticpewich had waited for more than three weeks after Botterill and the others had escaped, before making his own break. As was to be expected, the disappearance of the four prisoners had resulted in serious repercussions. After calling a general parade, Watanabe had confiscated that day's vegetable ration and cancelled all future supplies. From now on the camp inmates were totally dependent on 70 grams of rice a day. However, despite the reduced food intake, work parties were sent out as usual. On 8 July, a road mending gang, made up of coolies and Australian POWs, was working near the 111 mile when an air raid started. The Japanese guards scuttled into a nearby hole, while five Australians and Janan, a worker from Kampong Matang, dived for cover in some long grass. Now out of sight of the guards, Janan gave the prisoners some cooked rice, while ambulance-man Private Wally Read, aged 25, asked him to look after his leather wallet, containing a photo of five children, on the back of which was also written the name of Driver Les Hardy, a 41-year-old ambulance driver who had died in Sandakan on 19 May. Handing over the wallet, Read, who spoke a little Malay, said, 'Hold these things for me until I collect them. If I don't collect them you will know that the Japanese have killed me.' As soon as the raid was over the Australians and the coolies went their separate ways. They did not meet again for, by 15 July, when the rice ration was further reduced, most of the survivors were so weak that rice-carrying and road work ceased. However, they were still required to continue with the hut construction under Sticpewich's supervision, and service the Japanese officer's quarters, where water-carrying was extracting a huge toll. All but two of the eighteen or so assigned to this chore between 2 July and 20 July died, the exceptions being Nelson Short, who had escaped, and Driver Owen Evans, of the AASC.

Sticpewich's construction workers completed the hut on 18 July. The following day a total of 72 POWs moved into the bamboo and atap building, which measured roughly 9 metres long and a little under 6 metres wide. It had no sides and no sleeping platform, but for men who had been lying in ankle-deep mud in their own filth for the past three weeks, it was the POW equivalent of 'The Ritz'. Forty occupied the hut proper while the rest, all dysentery patients, were relegated to the sub-floor area in an attempt to prevent further contamination. As the number of deaths had begun to escalate in the first week of July, another cemetery had been established on or about the 10th, about 25 metres up the slope from the new hut. The burial parties were now so debilitated that it took two and a half hours to scrape out a shallow grave large enough to take up to eight skeletal corpses, and another hour and a half to bury them. Sticpewich, who candidly admitted he 'was never really starving', was still by far the fittest. He continued to run the camp, control the rations and keep death records up to date, watched closely by a Japanese officer to make sure the cause of death was noted as malaria, dysentery or some other 'natural' cause.

By 28 July Sticpewich would record that no less than 119 Australians and fourteen Englishmen were dead. Harry Longley, Billy Young's larrikin mate, died on 5 July, Norm Grist, who had been too sick to join Botterill in his escape, on 10 July and Les Fitzgerald, who had tipped off Nelson Short, five days later. Three of the officers died within a week of each other — quartermaster Gordon Good on 13 July, Padre Wardale-Greenwood on the 18th and Jim Heaslop, the canteen officer, the next day. The English chaplain, Padre Wanless, had died on 30 June. Without his patron, Hoshijima, on hand to enforce his order that 'this man must not die', Laurie Maddock was vulnerable. His supplies of quinine could not protect him from dysentery which killed him on 24 July along with Botterill's English pal, Norm Frost. Twenty-four hours later Sergeant Richard Stacy, sole survivor of the first march, was dead.

Ambulanceman Sergeant Robert Horder, aged 48, had been in fair condition up until 8 July and may have survived longer had he not caught Suzuki Saburo and another guard rifling his gear. They had helped themselves to his watch and ring and Horder loudly called them thieves and mongrels. In return they kicked him into insensibility. He died during the night, never regaining consciousness. In accordance with Japanese instructions, Sticpewich recorded the cause of death as malaria.

On about 22 July, Owen Evans, who had survived the water-carrying but was still working at the officers' quarters, was held responsible for failing to stop one of the other Australians stealing vegetables. He was given such a beating that he lost the use of both his arms and the partial use of one leg. He attempted to carry out his duties still, but two days later he was brought to the hut where Dr Picone diagnosed severe internal injuries.

On 26 July a guard named Yoshikoa, supervising the burial of the dead, bragged to Sticpewich he had seen an order, from the Japanese High Command, that all POWs were to be eliminated. As Sticpewich knew he had tried, a few days earlier, to obtain a hypodermic syringe in order to inject ill prisoners with petrol, the Australian had no reason to disbelieve him. That night the guard, strengthened after the previous escapes, was doubled. At 9.00 the next evening Sticpewich extinguished the fire at the cook house and was walking towards the creek when he was grabbed by Takahara who whispered, 'You go now. Go jungle. You stay you will be mati [dead]. I see Captain Takakuwa's papers. Papers say all men be mati here.'

This warning, on top of the other incidents, could not be ignored. There were now 42 prisoners left alive — 32 Australian ORs, three Australian officers, four British ORs and three British officers. Amazingly, the old blokes had lasted the longest. Of the 32 Australian ORs, thirteen were aged in their 30s, six were in their late 20s while Bill McDonald, the tailor, and Frank Fitzpatrick, were aged 44 and 45 respectively. Those raised in the country were also over-represented.[3] However Sticpewich, who had decided to escape, approached only four. In his opinion, the other 37 were either 'too incompetent' or too sick to make the attempt. Eight, who were comatose, were unlikely to survive the night. Sticpewich asked Dr Picone, who was fit enough, to join him but he elected to stay with the men. Dr Oakeshott also refused, pointing out that even if he went he would only be an encumbrance as he had a large ulcer on his foot and no boots. He suggested, however, that Sticpewich take Herman 'Algie' Reither, of the technical staff, who had spent time in the cage during the Sandakan Incident. Although ill, the 38-year-old Reither was willing to give it a try. Cook, who had fully recovered from the bullet graze received at the time of Suzuki's murder, was also asked to join them, but declined on the grounds of ill-health. Nevertheless, he evidently considered that he had a good chance of surviving, for, despite Sticpewich's pleas to hand over the camp records, including the key to the numbering system which identified the hundreds of unmarked burial plots at Sandakan, he refused to give them up. However, he did agree to place them in a tin and bury them beneath a large tree in the compound, should his survival be in doubt.

At about 9.30pm, 28 July, after Sticpewich had cooked and served the evening meal as usual, he and Reither slipped out of the camp. They didn't move far — just up the track a short way, where they hid in the jungle for the next 24 hours, observing the camp and the movement of the search parties which had been sent out to look for them. At dusk, after watching the returning search parties line up for a brisk round of face slapping, the fugitives made their way towards Ranau. They sought shelter that night in the hut of Ginssas bin Gunggas, who hid them under a grass mat when a lone Japanese dropped by. What happened next is not at all clear, but by the time they stumbled into the hut of peasant farmer Dihil bin Ambilid, near the village of Sumaang, south-west of Ranau, Reither had sustained injuries to his stomach, arms and legs. Dihil had heard shots on the night of 29 July and thought the wounds had been caused either by a bayonet or bullet. Neither Sticpewich nor Reither enlightened him, so he never knew what had happened or who was responsible.

Dihil, also known as Godohil, was a Kadazan Christian. He refused to betray the fugitives despite the posted reward of 2000 Borneo dollars, the equivalent of two years' pay for a high ranking civil servant. For over a week he harboured them, hiding them beneath grass matting or in the jungle if the Japanese were in the vicinity. His brother-in-law, Zimban, agreed to walk to Jesselton with Sticpewich's note, in the hope of contacting the Allied forces he knew had landed on the west coast. However, when Zimban learned that white soldiers had arrived at Lansat, he went immediately to Ripley. When Ripley received Sticpewich's message on 8 August, he sent the Lansat village headman, Orang Tuan Gilenki, back with Zimban with medicines and food.[4] Unfortunately they arrived too late to save Reither. Weakened by dysentery and his injuries, he had died that day.

Meanwhile, Ripley's team moved closer to Ranau, setting up a new base on 9 August at Narawang, south of Lansat. The next day Gilenki and Zimban arrived at the camp with Sticpewich, who had made the journey on horseback. He told Ripley that Moxham and three others had escaped on 7 July and that on 28 July, when he and Reither had left the camp, there were 40 left. As local people had reported that up to 20 of these POWs were still alive, Zimban agreed to try and smuggle food and medicines to them, while other agents undertook the task of trying to locate Moxham's group. Ripley, charged with the responsibility of rescuing and evacuating the Ranau POWs, was therefore unprepared for a signal which he received on 12 August. It was from Gort Chester, who instructed him to 'STOP ALL FURTHER ACTIVITIES. DO NOT WANT TO AGGRAVATE DANGER OF POWS BEING KILLED.'

However, news of Agas III's arrival had already reached Baragah's village via Kaingal's friend's cousin, but when Kaingal rushed into the hut with his third-hand news, the three Australians did not believe him. It was not until Baragah arrived with his brother Gunting, confirming the information and asking Moxham to write a note for them to deliver to the white men, that hopes, and morale, rocketed. Addressing his message to 'OC in charge of English or American Forces', Moxham wrote in a clear, neat hand.

> *We are three Australian prisoners of war. We escaped from camp early in July as Nippon was starving all men. They were dying six and seven a day. After a few days out this dusan O.T. [Orang Tuan — headman] found us and has looked after us ever since, building a little hut in the jungle. We are still in very weak condition but quite OK. O.T. Baragah is a Tuan Besar [big chief] around here and you will find all the Dusans very friendly and sincere.*
>
> *Today they called in and wanted me to write this note and one O.T. Baragah and O.T. Gunting are going to contact you. Hope it will not be long before I see you as to my knowledge about ten or twenty men (prisoners) left out of 3000 or more. Do all you can for Baragh [sic] (pronounced) Bariga.*
>
> *[Signed] Bdr Moxham.*
>
> *NX 58617 Pte Short, NX 42191 Pte Botterill, NX 19750, Bdr Moxham anxiously waiting to hear from you. We are 5 miles from Ranau.*

Twenty-four hours later Baragah was back, asking Moxham to write another note as heavy rain had prevented him from delivering the first. Using a page torn from an exercise book, Moxham repeated his message, signed personally this time by his two companions as well as himself. On 17 August, Baragah, who had been met en route by Agas agents, delivered his note to Ripley. The next day he was back at Sumaang, accompanied by Andong Ajak and with medicines, vitamin pills, a box of Bell's Wax Matches, powdered milk, a packet of Lifesavers, and a note. The joy

> Baragah
> O.C. in charge of English or American forces
> This is my second note to you.
> We are led to believe that there are
> English armed forces 15 miles from here
> Baragah the man taking this note
> is a Juan Besar Dusun.
> He owns quite a big farm here
> & I knowing him as I do can fully
> vouch to say he is trustworthy
> & sincere & anything he can do
> for you I know he will do
> All the dusuns are the same &
> they hate nippon. Nippon is taking
> all they have left now, the pigs &
> fowls. I wrote a note to you
> yesterday but Baragah informed me
> today that on account of the rain
> they did not go. Tonight they are
> going & I hope they contact you O.K.
> Three of us are camped here in
> the jungle, we escaped from camp
> as would only have died there on one
> meal a day. Baragah picked us up
> a few days out & has looked after
> us ever since. Could give you a lot of
> information but will wait until I hear
> from you.

The second note which Moxham sent to the Agas III party with Baragah.

evoked by the first part, 'The war is finished', was dampened by the rider which instructed them to, 'stop where you are because the Japanese are hostile'. However, a day or two later, Baragah, who had taken some sweet potatoes to the rescue team, returned from Narawang, with another note telling them to 'come to us'.

By this time, following information from Ripley that some POWs had escaped, Agas had been reinforced. On the morning of 18 July, Major J. Forster, of the Indian Medical Service, Captain Henry 'Wings' Nicholls, Sergeant Jack McNeale, Corporals Eric 'Baldy' Gore (signaller) and Les 'Blue' Grinham (medic), along with Privates John 'Lofty' Hodges and Norm 'Sally' Wallace, had parachuted onto a specially-prepared drop zone at Lansat. On the 20th the entire party, except for Blue Grinham who remained behind at Narawang to look after Sticpewich, moved to Silad, about 15 kilometres from Ranau, where Forster and

Wallace had set up a base the day before. While the new arrivals were settling in, the other two made a close reconnaissance of Ranau.

It was not until 24 August that a runner arrived at Silad with news that the escapees were on their way. The journey had taken three days and one night and had been a slow and painful process. Baragah and Adong Ajak had mobilised about 30 locals to act as bearers, but the makeshift bamboo and rattan stretchers had proved to be too hard for the Australians' bodies to bear. They were reduced to shuffling along, leaning heavily on sticks, traversing remote, barely discernible jungle trails that were a challenge for even the sure-footed, let alone men who could not lift their feet any more than a centimetre or so above the ground. On day two they heard the sound of rifle fire. Worried that the Japanese were nearby and they might not yet make it, they marched through the night, their way lit by the light of flaming bamboo torches.[5] Botterill and Short, at the head of the line, were slumped over beside the track on the third day, sure they could not go any further, when they heard the tramp of heavy footsteps. They were expecting the worst, when an undeniably Australian voice boomed, 'How ya going, boys?'

The two men looked up to see a sight they would never forget. Lofty Hodges, tall and strapping, clad in jungle greens and cradling his pistol like a toy, was the embodiment of everything they had fantasised and dreamed about during their three and a half years of captivity. Hodges, in turn, could scarcely credit that the bearded, ravaged, pathetic creatures staring at him with a look of profound wonder had once been Australian soldiers. Short was so swollen with beriberi his limbs and torso resembled grotesquely stuffed sausages, while Botterill was not much more than a skin-covered collection of bones, apart from a scrotal sac so distended with fluid it had to be supported in a knapsack to allow him to walk.

Would they like a cup of tea? Milk? Sugar? Biscuits? A piece of chocolate? A cigarette? The kindness and compassion of Hodges and his companions, after years of brutality and deprivation, was overwhelming. Botterill sat down and wept. The rest of the day passed by in something of a blur. Major Forster, summoned by a runner, arrived on the scene, ticked off Hodges for giving them chocolate and then set about supervising their evacuation to the Silad base. Botterill and Moxham, the weakest, were carried on army stretchers. The extroverted Short made his triumphal entry into the camp under his own steam.

Botterill was the most ill — so sick that Forster told Hodges he would not last the night. However, having been to hell and back, Botterill was not going to give up the fight now. When dawn broke he was still alive. For the next three weeks Hodges, Botterill's self-appointed guardian angel, looked after him like a baby, carrying him to the latrine, bathing him in the creek, making sure he followed Forster's instructions — to eat plenty of Marmite — and generally attending to his every need. The condition of the three men had a profound effect on Hodges, a man often described as a 'gentle giant'. At first he had been shocked and immensely sad to think that his countrymen could have been reduced to this state by other human beings. However, this sadness had soon given way to anger, an anger which later stirred him to uncharacteristic physical violence when two captured Japanese soldiers, brought into the camp, tried to make a break. The first he simply threw to the ground. The other he knocked unconscious.

Botterill was so ill that it was some time before he realised there was another escaped Australian in camp — Sticpewich. He did not like Sticpewich, but neither his presence, nor the revelation that he was possibly the only other survivor, bothered him much. Not so Moxham. Moxham's enmity for a man many had considered, at best, to be opportunistic, his loathing, which he had kept under control for so long, erupted. He swore that as soon as he regained his strength he would tear Sticpewich apart, a vow taken so seriously by the Agas team they felt compelled to accommodate them in separate tents. None of those outside the POW circle could ever hope to understand the depth of resentment Sticpewich had engendered among many of his fellow prisoners, but they noticed that the warrant officer was in amazingly good condition. He had been thin, weak and slightly incoherent when he arrived at Narawang, but he was nowhere near as emaciated as the other three, nor suffering anything like the same degree of ill-health. Whereas they were still shuffling, shambling shadows of their former selves, Sticpewich had regained his vigour within a matter of days. His fellow Australians could not condone Moxham's threat of violence, but they could definitely understand it.

Meanwhile, the locals continued to visit the escapees, bringing parcels of food and other small gifts to help raise their spirits. The gift which brought the most joy was a small, partly-domesticated monkey, which had been captured by villagers and kept tethered to a length of chain. The escapees soon realised that the poor thing, like them, craved affection. The men enjoyed the company of their furry friend, who groomed them constantly and delighted in running his tiny, delicate fingers through their hair looking for salt. Australia had strict quarantine laws, but Nelson, who was very taken with the monkey's antics, wanted to take it home. However, the monkey had a mind of its own. One night, finding its chain had not been properly secured, it escaped into the jungle. Although Botterill missed the company, he understood exactly how it felt.

Ripley had been trying to arrange for their evacuation by air. It was harder than he expected. An airstrip, started on 24 August, had been made in a clearing about 2 kilometres away, and a supply of petrol dropped by parachute, but the two-seater Austers summoned for the intended evacuation were unable to land because of the surrounding jungle. On 14 September the entire party, with the exception of Grinham, who remained behind to look after the escapees, moved to Todagan village with the aim of repairing enough of the Ranau airstrip to allow the Austers to land. There were still a large number of hostile Japanese, either in the area, or passing through it on their way to the west, who might feel inclined to shoot at them, so the appraisal of the strip was carried out at night. Forming a line abreast, the men moved slowly down the runway, counting the paces and using their feet to feel for any irregularities in the surface. These were then measured, noted and plotted on a grid. Once the whole surface had been covered, the plot was examined to decide which part of the strip would be easiest to repair. The craters were filled in by a local labour force at night, using soil delivered to the side of the strip. By day, the Australians filled in any spare time by disarming enemy troops caught retreating along the Sandakan-Tuaran track, which cut across the strip at the southern end.

On 18 September, Grinham, with his charges mounted on horseback, made the 10-kilometre journey from Silad to Tudangan, a small village north of the airstrip on the Ranau plain. That day members of the Agas team, ousting sixteen Japanese living in two houses near the village, came across the scattered wreckage of a Kittyhawk in the jungle, just off the Poring track, about 5 kilometres northwest of Ranau. Still strapped in his seat were the skeletal remains of the pilot. He was twenty-five-year-old Flight Lieutenant Harold Cooper, of the RAAF.[6]

Not all the Japanese in the area had been rounded up. Leaflets had been dropped when it was discovered that the Ranau garrison's radio had been destroyed by Allied bombing, but many Japanese had simply refused to accept that the war had ended. The Kempei-tai in Ranau, in an effort to suppress the news, offered the locals one dollar for every leaflet handed in, or a dollar and a bag of salt, for every ten. Thirty troops at Napong, west of Lansat on the Langonan River, also had no intention of surrendering. Arming themselves with machine guns and rifles, they announced they were staying. Closer to Ranau, another Japanese soldier tried to shoot Botterill.

Botterill's health, after almost a month's tender loving care, was now much improved. He was still very much underweight and suffering from a variety of tropical complaints from hookworm to recurrent malaria, yet he felt well enough to take a walk down to the airstrip, a walk he had made several times before, to look at an Auster plane which had just landed. As he ambled along something whizzed past his head. When it was followed almost immediately by a loud crack he realised someone was firing from long grass, 300 or 400 metres away, and that the target, without a doubt, was him. He crouched over and moved as fast as he could to the plane, where the laconic Australian pilot told him not to worry, he would soon be on his way home.

The pilot was right. On 20 September five Austers, carrying the four evacuees and Major Forster, lined up on the Ranau strip to evacuate them to the 2/4th AGH at Labuan. As Botterill moved towards the plane a Japanese prisoner tried to attack him but was thwarted by the ever-vigilant and ever-protective Hodges. Moxham, too, ran into trouble. His plane, piloted by Flight Lieutenant Cocks, crashed on take-off. Cocks was unhurt but Moxham gashed his forehead. The Auster was a write-off. Fortunately, the plane carrying Forster turned back, and Moxham, after receiving attention for his injury, was evacuated in his place.

Meanwhile, prisoners who had been transferred from Sandakan at one time or another had also been liberated. The first group to be set free was from Outram Road Gaol, where conditions had, as expected, been appalling and the rice ration barely at subsistence level. Yet the death toll there had been surprisingly low, for, unlike those at Sandakan and Ranau, these inmates had been fed three times a day. Six — Privates Allen and Shelley, Sappers Davis and Marshall and Corporals Small and Fairey — had died of illness. The other 24, kept alive by sheer willpower and determination, included the irrepressible Billy Young, his mate M.P. Brown, and Rod Wells, who had retained his sanity while in solitary confinement by performing complicated mental tasks. At one stage Rod and Billy had shared a cell where, to help pass the time, the brilliant young lieutenant had introduced Billy to the world of atoms, valency and other scientific wonders.

The first real indication, other than constant air raids, that the war might be nearing its end was on 15 August, when, in place of their usual bowl of water, some of the prisoners were given milk. Four days later, they were summoned from their cells. Unable to bring himself to admit that Japan had surrendered, the interpreter side-stepped the issue by announcing, 'Today we are sending you back to Changi Prisoner of War Camp ... But you must come back later, to complete your sentence.' For Billy, who had been expecting more than a few bland words, the proclamation was something of an anti-climax. The realisation that he was free did not hit him until he arrived in Changi, where he was lifted gently from the back of the truck by a beaming Paddy O'Toole and welcomed back to what was left of the battalion.

Four days later the Kuching prisoners were ordered to assemble. Although most of them had already heard, via a clandestine radio, that the war was over, it had taken Colonel Suga over a week to make the official announcement. Because of the large number of POWs and internees in the camp, it was not until 15 September, the day on which they were all to have been massacred, that the bulk of the prisoners were finally moved out. The 1500 survivors had had a narrow escape. On Suga's desk were orders to march the men to Dahan for extermination and to poison all the women and children.

Although 600 British ORs required to work on airfield construction and 300 civilians had died, Mo Davis and the 33 other Australian ORs, the two 'contaminated' British ORs, 144 Australian officers and 30 British officers had survived. The British had lost only one officer, Flying Officer Richard Caruth, who had died on 22 June 1945, but there had been five deaths among the Australian officers — all of them in 1945. Lieutenant Peter Stewart and Captain Cyril Young had died in July, Lieutenant Bradford Pascoe-Pierce the day the war ended, while three days later Lieutenant Frederick Flett had succumbed to tuberculosis. Major George Campbell, who had been arrested following the escape of the AASC men in 1942, died of a heart attack and malaria on 2 September.

Although Dr Jim Taylor had survived Outram Road, the Sandakan civilians serving their sentences in Borneo had not fared as well. Dr Stookes was executed at Jesselton airport, along with four other prominent Europeans, on 7 July 1945. The indefatigable Mrs Cohen was also dead. According to one report, she was placed inside a barrel which was then rolled around until she died. The Japanese claimed that she drowned at sea while being transferred to Sandakan. Of the local people imprisoned, Amigaw, Mandor Kassim, Sidek and Soh King Seng all died.

Back at Ranau, Ripley's men were still endeavouring to come to terms with what had happened. The entire team, apart from Dr Forster, who had been evacuated by air four days after the four survivors, stayed in the area for some weeks, chasing up recalcitrant Japanese, keeping the peace and trying to make some kind of sense of the mass of information, passed by word of mouth, about the fate of the Ranau prisoners. By the time they were evacuated, their worst fears were confirmed. Not one of the 34 men and six officers alive when Sticpewich left the camp on 28 July had survived.

Of the 2434 POWs incarcerated in The Eight Mile Camp, there were only six left.[7]

Chapter Fifteen
'AND NOT LEAVE ANY TRACES'?

Takahara's warnings had proved correct. At 8.00am on 1 August, four days after Sticpewich's escape, Captain Takakuwa called a conference of his officers and NCOs, attended by Lieutenant Watanabe, Sergeant-Majors Tsuji and Itchikawa, Interpreter Fujita and Sergeants Beppu and Okada. Sergeant Iwabe, who was out looking for Sticpewich, and Sergeant-Major Fujita, the medical orderly who had been wounded during the Suzuki shooting, were absent. Takakuwa informed his men that the recent 'regrettable' escapes and the fact that many POWs were too weak to be used as a labour force, had prompted his decision to implement the orders lying on his desk. He then read out the names of the 32 surviving prisoners, who had been divided into three categories. Takakuwa announced that Okada was to organise the 'disposal' of all those too ill to walk, Beppu the five officers, and Tsuji the rest. The sick, who were of no practical use and only an encumbrance, were to be killed immediately. At about 11.00am, while four guards kept watch over the rest of the camp, Okada and nine Formosans descended on the POW hut.[1] Maskey, Owen Evans (still alive despite his internal injuries), and fifteen other dying prisoners were removed from the hut and taken up the hill to the cemetery, where two holes had been dug. With the exception of two men, who crawled all the way on their hands and knees, the rest were so incapacitated they had to be carried on stretchers.

The prisoners either sat or lay on the ground, while Okada issued his instructions. He then gave a practical demonstration of what he required by shooting the first prisoner through the head himself. Morioka Teichichi and the other eight guards killed the rest.[2] While most were shot through the head, one, at least, was finished with a crushing blow to the skull. Watanabe, who had watched the executions from a distance, arrived in time to supervise the burial. Those murdered were placed in one grave, while the bodies of twelve who had died since 27 July were interred in another.

The remaining fifteen prisoners were not eliminated immediately. They were still alive on 25 August when a local confirmed a previous report that approximately 20 were being held under close guard. One of Ripley's agents, a man named Salunti who came from Sinarut, had also visited the camp twice — once on 11 August and again two days later. He had gained entrance to the camp in the guise of a vegetable vendor, and there he saw several prisoners moving about and another tied to a tree. During the next week Kambating of Kandowai-an, a village to the north-west of the camp, also brought vegetables. As he passed the 113 mile peg, 4.5 kilometres from the main compound, he saw about ten prisoners, dressed in ragged shorts and wearing slouch hats, building a hut. These were all who remained of more than 980 NCOs and privates who had set out from Sandakan.

On 27 August, five days after surrender leaflets had been dropped in the area,

Takakuwa, knowing the war was over, ordered Sergeant-Major Tsuji to take the ten POWs working at the 113 mile down the Tambunan track and dispose of them at a previously determined location. The prisoners had been handed sacks and told they were going to collect provisions, so probably suspected nothing. Near the 112 mile peg they were seen by Jaimi bin Gunsand (also known as Edmuno) of Ranau, who noticed all were thin and dressed in rags. When they were about 500 metres south of the main camp, Tsuji called a halt near a large tree. The eleven guards in the escort surrounded the prisoners, who were told they were to be killed and asked if they had anything to say.[3] According to the guards, the POWs were given food, water and cigarettes, which they smoked while Tsuji issued the guards their instructions. The ten prisoners were then taken, one by one, about 200 metres down a path on the eastern side of the main track, shielded from passers-by by a small hill. The killing field had been well-chosen. Fukishima, 'The Black Bastard', was instructed to kill the first prisoner. Amazingly, although he had beaten various prisoners, killed dozens on the march and kicked Arthur Bird to death, he now claimed he could not bring himself to do it. Tsuji, in a fit of temper, grabbed the rifle, barked, 'Do it this way', and shot the prisoner dead from a distance of 3 metres. Nishikawa killed the next while Toyoka shot the third. The remainder were killed in quick succession, one of them by Moritake Maseo, a Kempei-tai corporal who had beaten natives to death at Jesselton and had no qualms about carrying out his task. The eighth prisoner, when asked if he had anything to say, said, 'shoot me in the forehead', which Takeuchi did. When Kaneshige, who was to kill the last prisoner, hesitated, the ever accommodating Suzuki Saburo did it for him. No one attempted to escape.

When it was over, the bodies were buried in a mass grave beneath a large tree. All 30 Australian and four British ORs still alive when Sticpewich left the camp on 28 July were now dead, among them Bill McDonald, paymaster John Codlin, Billy Young's mate Jimmy Finn and the last of the Alumny Creek boys, Johnny O'Donohue.[4] When Tsuji returned to camp and reported that some of the guards had developed cold feet, Takakuwa lined them up and gave them all a tongue-lashing.

At about 12.30pm that same day the five surviving officers — Cook, Oakeshott, Picone, Daniels (the British medical officer) and Burgess, the RAF liaison officer — were informed they were to go to Kempei-tai headquarters at Ranau for interrogation. Accompanying them were Kawakami, The-Gold-Toothed-Shin-Kicking-Bastard, who was by this time a seasoned killer, his only slightly less bloodthirsty mate, Yoshio Kinjo, who had been involved in Murray's murder, Hashimoto 'Smiler' Miseo, who had come from Sandakan with the second march and had killed at least one POW, and three others — Nagahiro Maseo, Yamomoto Jiro and Oyama Tatsuo, also known as 'Potato Jones'. Suzuki Saburo and Nakayama Tameo were to follow, after an interval, with shovels. Sergeant Beppu, although feeling unwell, had been instructed to oversee the disposal and went on ahead. After about 500 metres he stopped. Leaving a prearranged marker on the western side of the track near a short-cut leading to the 111 mile peg, he crossed over to a rice store on the other side and sat down to wait. When the guards, who had been told to watch out for the marker, reached the assigned spot, they halted. The five officers suspected nothing. After he had given permission for everyone to smoke, Beppu told the prisoners to move into some shade about 50 metres away and have a rest as it was such a hot day. They must have felt relaxed, for Doctor Daniels removed his shirt and some of the others their belts. While Yoshiya and Oyama positioned themselves in case anyone tried to escape, Beppu issued his instructions.

Beppu ordered 'shoot'. Hashimoto Maseo, who had Daniels in his sights, and the three other guards, opened fire on the prisoners. One officer, evidently not killed instantly, was finished off with a blow to the head which cleft his skull almost in two. Yoshiya and Oyama then moved to the side of the track to deter any inquisitive locals who might happen along. As soon as bodies had been buried in two graves, dug by Suzuki and Nakayama, the party returned to the camp. The killing squad made no attempt to camouflage the graves, obliterate the huge pools of blood or dispose of the belts, Burgess's distinctive RAF cap or Daniels' shirt, which still had his thermometer in the pocket. Watanabe let it be known that all POWs had been moved to Tambunan, and then burned all incriminating material, including the POW records which Cook had handed him for safekeeping instead of burying them beneath the tree, as promised to Sticpewich. Two elderly guards were left behind, evidently to finish the tidying up, then Watanabe evacuated himself and all his staff to Tambunan. When Kabiaru of Mangawo village came to deliver some vegetables a few days later he found the camp empty, except for the two disgruntled guards, who were annoyed that he was a day late as they were packed up and ready to leave.

Despite Watanabe and Takakuwu's best efforts to conceal their crimes, they did leave evidence behind. Ripley had been receiving information from several agents as well as locals, including Jaimi bin Ginsund, who was chief clerk to the garrison commander at Ranau, and had also seen the prisoners on the track. And, unbeknown to Ripley, at least one other SRD agent was also operating in the area. Chester, learning that the POWs were to be moved to Tambunan on 27 August, had ordered one of Agas I's agents, under the control of Stan Neil, to make a reconnaissance, with a view to rescuing them en route. That day the agent had hidden himself beside the track and waited for the POWs to come along. When no one appeared, he retraced his steps towards Ranau, finding on the way evidence of the officers' murder. Another of Ripley's contacts, who was searching for clues as to the POWs sudden disappearance, found a pile of hats and caps beside the track near the 110 mile and what appeared to be a large grave. Shortly after, Kabiaru, on his way home after delivering vegetables, came across the same pile of hats and caps, a length of rope and a vast amount of congealed blood. A few days later, while taking the short cut near the 111 mile peg, he too stumbled across the officers' graves, which he reported were less than ten days old. Meanwhile, villagers who had entered the now dismantled and empty compound reported the discovery of five wooden POW number tags. Only one, number 708 belonging to Ron French, had a name on it, so they had no way of establishing that the others belonged to Lieutenants Good and Heaslop, Sergeant Stacy and Warrant Officer Ken Allsop, of the RAF.

On 21 September, with the four escapees safely on their way to Labuan,

Ripley, accompanied by four Agas III team members and five guerrillas, marched into Ranau. It was pouring with rain and Ripley was in no mood for niceties. Before the 200 enemy soldiers and guards stationed at the ten barracks in and around Ranau knew what was happening, they had been relieved not only of their weapons, which the Australians burned, but also of all fountain pens, watches and other goods which Ripley deemed to have been obtained from POWs. Lieutenant Ohkanda, the Japanese commander, was outraged, so outraged he later lodged an official complaint with 9th Division Headquarters. It did him no good. And in any case, Ripley's haul of thirteen wrist watches, 28 fountain pens, six propelling pencils, four pocket watches, eight wallets, one pair of opera glasses and one pair of field glasses, was only a fraction of what had been looted, and then incinerated in an attempt to destroy the evidence. Furthermore, three of the wristwatches were inscribed. They belonged to Private Norman Jenyns and Sergeant Michael Baxter who had died at Sandakan in June, and Sapper Bernard Rowley, who had perished at Paginatan in March.

Ripley released about a dozen Javanese slaves, then gave Ohkanda 24 hours to concentrate the sick at a nearby Japanese hospital and 48 to parade all other Japanese soldiers, guards and civilians at SRD's Ranau headquarters. When 170 presented themselves, as ordered, at 11.00am on 23 September, Ripley lined them all up and made them salute the Union Jack, before sending them, on foot, across the mountains to Jesselton.

Ripley, who had been forbidden to attempt a rescue of the Ranau POWs, realised that the entire mission, apart from the recovery of the four escapees, had been a disaster. He now focussed on collecting as much intelligence as possible in the short time that remained before he and his team were extracted to Agas headquarters at Kaniogan Island, north of the Bongaya River. On 3 October, the day before they left, police constables Sampur and Solum, who had been sent to Boto to verify whether the POWs acting as coolie labourers were still alive, returned. As had been suspected, they had found no trace of any living prisoners, but they had learned that two white men, who had come from Kaniogan Island, had taken away one of the locals who had information on four POWs who had escaped near Telupid.

The unidentified white soldiers, about whom Ripley knew nothing, were members of a patrol dispatched from Kaniogan by Gort Chester on 20 September. Japanese were still active in the area, so the three Agas I men, Harlem, Roberts and Russell, were accompanied by four guerrillas, four police boys, one guide and five coolies. Their mission was to travel by boat between Beluran and Boto and carry out a reconnaissance of all villages. As they were the first investigating team to arrive on the scene, they soon amassed intelligence. At Telupid they met village headman Orang Tuan Gundi and also Panglima Hussen, who handed them a *Radio Rubbish* concert programme, on the back of which were the names of Sergeant Les Hales and Privates Bill Marsh, Tom Patterson, Keith Rickerby, Jack Kearney, Darcy Pryor, Gene Parham and Frank Reardon. He also produced a sworn statement, signed by four escaped POWs, stating they would each pay him 400 dollars if they reached Allied lines. The signatures were those of Fuller, Dawson (Molde), Roberts and Beardshaw.

The four had left the march on 14 February, having no desire to meet the same fate as ten of their companions, who had dropped out with exhaustion and been murdered. The Australian pair fled to the east and the two Englishmen, Roberts and Beardshaw, towards the Labuk River, where they intended to hide for a day or two. As the Australians made their break they were seen by the guards, who opened fire, hitting Molde in the elbow. Three days later, Hussen, a tall, grey-haired, moustached Dyak, made contact with the Englishmen, who were hiding near the Labuk River at Telupid. After taking them to his house, he scouted the surrounding jungle, returning a short time later with the Australians who had also decided to move west, towards the river. Hussen explained to Molde, who understood some Malay, it was too dangerous to keep them at Telupid and took them instead to Kemansi, a small village a kilometre or two away, where he handed them over to the care of the headman, Orang Tuan Onsi. As Kemansi, too, was prone to visits by the Japanese, the 20 families who lived in the village built them a small hut in the jungle. Their physical condition was so poor they were unable to move on, and, as the only available food was tapioca and a small amount of rice, they gradually became weaker. The villagers did all they could with their limited resources, but Roberts died in early March, Molde at the end of the month, Fuller five days later and Beardshaw in May. Apart from their names and their marked graves in the jungle, there was no further information available as the prisoners used their diaries for latrine paper.

Gundi also had other, very disturbing information. Some of his men, in Paginatan in June, reported that ill prisoners had been shot in cold blood there and that one, at least, had been dismembered and eaten.

On his return to Kaniogan, Russell was ordered to Sandakan, where he was to join Number 3 Australian Prisoner of War Contact and Inquiry team, more commonly known as 3 PWC&I, whose Captain Mort had already submitted a preliminary report, based on information obtained from the four rescued Ranau escapees. He was only one of a number of officers heading various teams sent to Borneo to conduct a series of tasks, ranging from war crimes investigations to preliminary war graves recovery. His unit was split into sub groups — at Sandakan, Ranau, Labuan, Jesselton, and the track from Sandakan to Tampias, the group to which Russell had been seconded. In addition, Lieutenant Campbell was to make separate inquiries at Kaniogan, where Agas had its main base.

Campbell, who flew immediately to Kaniogan, had finished his report by the time the main Sandakan team, under the command of Captain G. Cocks, arrived at its destination on 17 October. They were by no means the first on the scene. An occupying force of soldiers from the 9th Division, who had sailed from Labuan on HMAS *Deloraine*, had disembarked some weeks before to disarm the garrison and restore some order to the town. They too had found the Japanese in possession of a large number of items, either traded or stolen from POWs. Unfortunately, instead of collecting them and sending them back to Australia for identification and possible return to the next-of-kin, as Ripley had done, the occupying soldiers had kept them as spoils of war. Some individuals had one or two items, but two brothers from Western Australia had quite a haul, including Governor Tanuke Kumabe's medals, which they were forced to return when the owner complained. Although many of the items were inscribed with names and initials, it appears little, or no, attempt was made to find out to whom they belonged. It was not as if identification were difficult. Fifty-two years later it would take only a matter of minutes to establish that the owner of a watch, on which the initials J.H.K. had been scratched, was Corporal John Henry Knowles of Lancashire, England, who had died at Sandakan.

The Sandakan Contact and Inquiry team, on arriving at The Eight Mile Camp, was confronted with a dismal scene. The POW huts were either burnt or derelict and the compounds completely overgrown. The growth was so rampant that the barbed-wire fences had all but disappeared beneath the vines and grass. However, as the 23 Australian War Graves Unit (23 AWGU), which had arrived from Labuan on HMAS *Latrobe* the previous month, had rounded up a Japanese labour force, removing the vegetation was not a problem. In the ten days that he was at Sandakan, the team's commanding officer, Captain R. A. Houghton, had established that 26 POWs had been buried in the civil cemetery and located the Number 1 and 2 POW Cemeteries at The Eight Mile Camp, as well as several bodies between the camp and the 20 mile peg. Although Houghton had taken a Japanese officer with him, a third cemetery, thought to be out near the airfield, had not been located. As only 145 graves had been marked in the first POW cemetery and 80 in the second, Cocks was hopeful of finding, among a pile of confiscated Japanese records which the ATIS people were translating, a burial plan which would identify the rest.

Almost immediately his team began a systematic search of the two compounds, which the war graves unit had begun. Very little, other than buttons, badges and shoulder titles had been found in the burnt out Number 1 camp, but a search of Number 2 revealed a large number of identifiable items, ranging from paybooks to mess gear, oddments of clothing (including Dick Braithwaite's heavyweight wool jacket), webbing and other equipment, identity disks, Japanese number tags, cigarette cases, wallets, watches, badges, buttons, insignia and numerous other bits and pieces. There was even a metal identification plate from one of *Yubi Maru*'s life rafts, souvenired by Private Tom Robbins, of South Australia. As most of the personal papers and effects had been concentrated in small bundles and protected from the elements with a blanket or piece of sacking, they were in very good condition. Three items known to belong to Australians were Albert Anderson's non-issue metal identity tag (a map of Australia resting on a boomerang), Ron Moran's paybook and one of the signed, hand-coloured, 1943 Christmas menus which Tom Burns and his mates had made. Also found were items belonging to the British, including Lieutenants Young's and Rolfe's haversacks. However, perhaps the most poignant relic ever found was a baby's silver Christening mug, rather battered and minus its handle, but nevertheless with its inscription 'Bridget Catherine from her Godmother, September 1940' still intact. By 21 October a preliminary report, with a map of the cemeteries and full details of the 154 items recovered, was on its way to 9th Division headquarters.

The next day Lieutenant Robertson discovered the stretchers near the banana palms and the remains of the guardbox-cum-aid post. Rummaging through the wreckage of the small hut his searchers found a set of surgeon's instruments, only

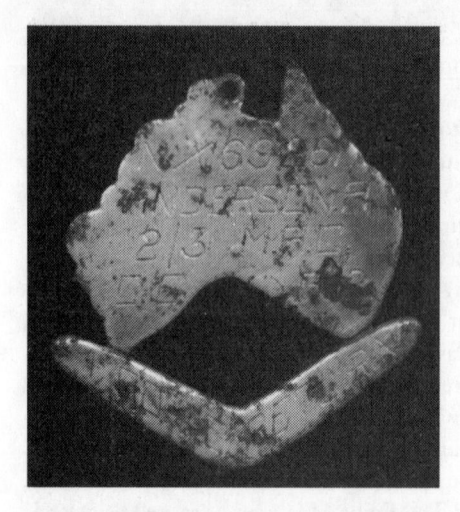

Albert Anderson's (non issue) identity tag, recovered from the slit trenches in the Number 2 Compound, where the sick were confined after the second march left.

slightly rusted by the rain, vials of anti-dysentery vaccine and piles of filthy dressings and bandages. Also scattered over a wide area were four small cartons of paybooks, too badly affected by the weather to decipher, and Red Cross boxes. The discovery of a bucket of prepared rice, blankets and personal items near another group of stretchers suggested that the owner, or owners, had been removed from the area without warning. On 20 October the Japanese labourers were ordered to open the filled-in slit-trenches. The bodies, stacked one on top of the other, were not exhumed, but Cocks calculated that more than 250 were buried there. The only identity tag discovered was that belonging to Ray Irving of Victoria, but as it had become detached it was impossible to say which body was his. That 'dog tags' were missing was not surprising. They were made from a type of compressed, cardboard-like material strung on a leather thong. Although the disks were fine for desert warfare, few had withstood the ravages of a tropical rain forest climate. Continuously bathed in sweat, and saturated by monsoonal downpours, most had long since rotted away. Those that had remained intact had been removed by the Japanese.

While Cocks' team was occupying itself at the compound, Squadron Leader F. Birchall, RAAF, was busily collecting evidence for war crimes trials. On 24 October he interviewed several deponents, including Hee Choi, one of the two brothers who had hidden the young Australian soldier seeking refuge after the massacre at the 55 mile peg. Throughout June, at great personal risk, they had continued to care for the prisoner, who had been beaten so badly he was lame in one leg, carrying him into the jungle at 6.00am each day and fetching him again each evening. Unfortunately, they could do nothing to combat the effects of tetanus baccilus. In about mid-July, the soldier, who spoke Malay, said 'Don't worry about me. I am going to die. When the Australians land here, tell them all about me and show them where you have buried me.' Before he became completely incapacitated, he wrote a testimonial, so that his hosts would be rewarded. Shortly afterwards, the soldier's condition deteriorated rapidly and he died. Choi, terrified that the Japanese might search the house and find the incriminating paperwork, burnt it, thereby consigning the soldier to eternal anonymity.

Two days later, on 26 October, acting on information from Chen Kay, Chin Kin and Lo Tong, who had witnessed the murders of the prisoners at the 15½ mile peg, Birchall interviewed and obtained a full confession from Hosotani, the Kempei-tai sergeant who had killed them.

Although the reason for Russell's secondment to 3 PWC&I was to carry out a thorough search of the track as far as Tampias, on 2 November 9th Division Headquarters unaccountably revoked its own plan. Instead of proceeding to Tampias on foot, Cocks and Russell now had to travel up the Labuk and its tributaries by boat and confine themselves to an information gathering exercise. At no time were they permitted to move any further than one mile from the river. Between 13 and 15 November, with headman Kulang as guide, they conducted a superficial reconnaissance of the track between the Gum Gum River at the 17 mile and the Tindok River at the 28. Although Russell described the search as 'rather useless', he nevertheless reported that within half a mile of the 17 mile peg they had begun to find clothing, belongings and skeletal remains of POWs who had passed that way. By the time they reached Tindok, they had recorded the locations of 20 bodies, only three of which had been buried. At the 23 mile they had also found a drinking cup belonging to Wilfred Bennett, of the 2/19th Battalion, who had died in Ranau in July. As Kulang and Police Constable Kamon, who was also accompanying them, had seen large numbers of bodies further up the track, Russell was anxious to make further inquiries as soon as possible, before the monsoon really set in. It was not just the number of corpses which bothered him. Kulang had also cited another case of cannibalism, which had occurred on 4 August.

This allegation, along with the claims made by Hussen, Gundi and others that prisoners had been shot, butchered and eaten by Japanese soldiers at Paginatan, was taken seriously. According to Kulang's brother, Liap, two members of the Kempei-tai had shot dead two prisoners near the village of Muanad. After the scabies-infected arms and legs had been cut off and thrown into the river, the torsos were loaded into a boat and taken down-stream towards the large Japanese camp. News of this atrocity had travelled far and wide — Campbell had recorded the same story from informants at Kaniogan. The local people explained that, as enemy troops were very short of food, the POWs had been 'culled' from the pack.

While cannibalism is abhorrent to the western mind, it was not uncommon for Japanese soldiers to eat the flesh of the enemy. In fact, it was encouraged. On 1 November 1944 Major-General Aotu, 41 Division Infantry Group Commander, in a speech to his troops had stated 'Troops must fight the Allies, even to the extent of eating them'. Seventeen days later, in case there was any doubt about who could or couldn't be eaten, an official memorandum was issued to inform all troops that, 'Although it is not prescribed in the criminal code, those who eat human flesh (except that of the enemy) knowing it to be so, shall be sentenced to death as the worst kind of criminal against mankind'. Evidently, this was not clear enough. A fortnight later, when rumours became prevalent that Japanese soldiers were eating their own dead, an order was issued from 18th Army Headquarters reminding troops they were permitted to eat the flesh of Allied dead but must not eat their own.

On 15 November the Inquiry team returned to Sandakan to begin its journey up the Labuk in two prahaus. Cocks, Russell, Corporal G. Lee (also of 3 PWC&I) and Private K. Cowell (representing 23 AWGU) were in one, and Kulang, Kumon and five Dusan carriers in the other. Russell found the trip extremely frustrating. They were forced to row much of the way, as the tide and wind were against them. It took three days for his boat to reach Muanad, while Kulang's, which broke its mast and had to return to Sandakan, took even longer. At 8.00am on 20 November the entire party set off by canoe to Ulu Muanad, where the track met the river at the Tangkul Crossing. There was no way they could miss it. The large Japanese staging camp, sprawling across both river banks, was still standing. Although the area was partially flooded they discovered the remains of seven POWs, 100 metres south of a rest house on the western bank. They then returned to Muanad for the night. The following morning they woke to find that, owing to heavy rain, the river had risen 60 centimetres overnight. It was also flowing so swiftly that even with six men paddling it took six hours to reach the crossing. It was after 2.30pm when they disembarked to begin a search to the east. At this point, as the track ran parallel to the river for about 3 kilometres, they were able to go as far as the 47½ mile peg. All they found were a skull and Australian hat, two blankets, another hat, a pair of shorts and a towel. Russell tried to examine the clothing for identifying marks but the fabric was so rotted it fell apart. As flooding made further searches difficult, they returned to the crossing where they spent the night in the POW rest house. Early the next morning the party split in two, extending the search to both sides of the river. However, as there had been further rain overnight, those on the western side were forced back after the water rose from thigh-high to 2 metres. The eastern group met with a similar experience. The area covered the previous day was under deep water and one of the footbridges had washed away. Returning to the crossing they found one complete skeleton, dressed in Australian clothing, in thick undergrowth about 100 metres from the river. Unfortunately, although the body was found close to the place where Len Haye was murdered, there was no attempt to verify its identity. Unable to search the track further, they combed the area around the rest house, where they found Haye's mess tin and several black and tan army boots.

Russell was very disappointed with the results of the search. The remains, all completely decomposed and with no form of identification, were lying in deep mud. While some skeletons were intact, many had been scattered, either by foraging pigs or floodwaters. Although it was impossible to determine cause of death, none of the skeletons he had seen showed any signs of violence. However, according to Kamon and his friend Segulu, also a policeman, there were at least 53 bodies between the 28 and 50 mile pegs. The previous October both policemen had been sentenced to gaol after being found guilty of dumping a large amount of rice, raided from the main Japanese store during an air-raid, into Sandakan harbour. In April, when the gaol had been bombed, they had been sent to the track to work as coolies and, in June, Kamon had walked along the Tindok-Muanad section of the track. Between the 28 and 35 mile pegs he had seen eight bodies, and between the 35 and 50 miles, another 30. Segulu reported he had been working at the 27 mile when a party of 100 POWs had arrived. Many had looked quite fit but the rest were suffering from beriberi and malnutrition. The following morning he had seen the bodies of two men who had died during the night from natural causes. Later, while walking to the 36 mile, he saw the body of a prisoner, who he thought had been shot, lying in the middle of the track, and two more, covered with leaves. His next move was to the 45 mile, near Kolapis, where he saw one body covered with a blanket. He returned to the 28½ mile a few days later. The night he arrived he saw two Japanese and two prisoners, wearing Australian hats and looking quite fit. The following morning one of the guards, Kabatu San, took the prisoners into the jungle. He was wearing his sword. When he emerged 30 minutes later, he was alone.

Kamon had escaped from his hard labour while carrying rice back to Sandakan from the Tangkul Crossing. He arrived at the 17 mile and was harboured by a friendly Chinese, Chong Kwey. Chong showed him the remains of an escaped prisoner, who had been hiding in the undergrowth, about 200 metres from his house, when a Japanese had seen the smoke from his fire and shot him dead. Villagers from Gumbaron also had information about a POW who had been left at the side of the track by the Japanese (possibly one of those left behind by Endo Hiraka, who said he had no stomach for killing) as it was believed he would die within a few hours. However, he was found by the villagers, who hid him in the jungle about 90 metres away from the track and fed him. He may have survived, had the Japanese not ordered all able-bodied men in the village to paddle to Tampias, thereby cutting off his food supply. When they returned ten days later, they went immediately to the prisoner, but he had died in the meantime from dysentery and starvation. Kulang, who had already reported the murder of Les Haye and handed over the photograph given to him by Perc Carter, also disclosed that on 24 October, after a brief search, he had found the remains of ten POWs near Tindok. As the bones were very weathered, he believed they were from the first march. He also had other information to impart, not about victims of the marches but the fate of some of those who had been diverted from the second march to carry stores between the Tangkul Crossing and Boto. Six had been shot at Muanad on 27 August, the date of the Ranau massacres, while a Chinese named Ah Chang reported that another 54 had been shot to the west of Muanad the same day. Kulang was emphatic that these men were definitely rice-carriers and had not, at any stage, ever proceeded past Boto.

Not all those who came forward had information relating to POWs. The locals and thousands of imported labourers had suffered as hideously as the prisoners. Of the 4,000 Javanese working on the Sandakan airstrip, only two or three had survived. Now that the war was over, victims, or the families of victims, were anxious to impart whatever information they had — from the names of 25 known war criminals and a similar number of collaborators and black-marketeers, to war crimes which encompassed massacres of entire villages and the bayonetting of babies tossed into the air. Constrained by their orders and prevented by floodwaters from further investigations, the best the inquiry team could do was to forward the informants' statements, along with various relics which had been handed in, to 9th Division Headquarters. Those who held POWs' possessions were worried they might be branded as collaborators, against whom The Mumiang Volunteers, a local underground organisation committed to the apprehension and punishment of such individuals, were extracting swift summary justice. Russell, therefore, urged that they be interrogated before they disposed of the goods. He also exhorted his superiors to send recovery teams in as soon as practicable, to locate and remove to a cemetery the large number of bodies believed to be lying along the 260 kilometres of track. However, he and Cocks concluded that, even when the monsoon was over, the recovery of these remains would be 'a colossal undertaking'.

Meanwhile, other teams had been conducting similar enquiries in the west. The two groups covering Labuan, Brunei and Miri, where inquiries had begun as soon as the 9th Division had secured the area, had a substantial head-start. The Tanjung Lobang compound at Miri, first entered on 17 June, had been combed for evidence on several occasions while a POW Liaison team had conducted a thorough search of the Brunei-Miri sites between 26 July and 1 August. Corporal Malau, who had buried the Union Jack with the inscribed names on it (which the POWs had used to cover their dead at the Labuan compound), came forward but unfortunately, when the flag was retrieved it was in poor condition as the tin in which he had placed it had no lid. In any case, it was useless as a means of identification. None of the names on it belonged to any of the POW who had been imprisoned there. However, as Captain Nagai and Sergeant-Major Sugino had also been rounded up and interrogated, along with any locals with information to impart, by the time the two two-man inquiry teams — Captain D. Worrell and Corporal J. Nagel in one, and Captain A. Boyland and Sergeant D. Whitelaw in the other — arrived at Labuan on 20 October, virtually all their work had been done for them. Sugino, the officer in charge when the majority of the POWs had died, had been most forthcoming, and there was very little that was unknown about the fate of his victims. Although no nominal rolls appeared to have survived, they were able to compile death dates from Japanese records and trace the movement of prisoners from personal belongings found at the various sites, as well as names scratched on hut walls.

Investigations at Labuan were all but complete, so the two teams detoured to Jesselton on 31 October. Although it was now three-and-a-half years since the POWs had left, the teams were nevertheless able to locate all remains and obtain extra information which, when added to that gleaned from Nagai's previous interrogation, gave a fairly clear picture. What they could not establish, at this stage, was whether or not the Jesselton prisoners had been badly treated.

The remoteness of the region hampered the investigations of the Ranau group. They did not begin until 12 November. On 3 November the team had flown as far as Keningau, about 160 kilometres to the south of Tambunan, but it had taken another nine days to walk to Ranau. The ten-man party, headed by Captain Mort, included a civilian interpreter, Mr G. S. Sundang and eight members of the AIF. Seven were from various recovery units. The eighth was Warrant Officer Bill Sticpewich who, unlike his still-hospitalised fellow escapees, had not only recovered fully but was pronounced fit enough to walk the 320-odd kilometres from Keningau to Ranau and then back again. Mort divided his investigations into four key areas — the original Ranau compound, the Sinarut camp, the final compound on the Tambunan track, and local villages. Unaware that the Japanese had labelled the various compounds Number 1 Ranau Camp, Number 1 Jungle Camp and Number 2 Jungle Camp, he dubbed them PW Compounds 1, 2 and 3 — which would later cause one camp to be muddled with another. Although they had been given only seven days to carry out their enquiries, the team was not starting with nothing. Botterill and Moxham had given a good idea of where to find the burial sites at all three camps, while Sticpewich was at hand to assist with the third. By the end of a week, the time span allotted by 9th Division Headquarters, they had collected a pile of relics from the various sites and located, for the war graves teams, the graves of Anderson, Reither and Flight Lieutenant Cooper, the Kittyhawk pilot, as well as most of the mass burial sites. Locals had pointed out various other burial plots, including two bomb craters, thought to hold as many as ten bodies. Some of these were now enclosed with bamboo fences. Kabirau had also taken Lieutenant S. Sergeant, a war graves registration officer, to the place where the five officers had been buried. The lieutenant recovered the clothing and, as the graves had been disturbed by pigs, was able to establish that the bodies were those of five Europeans. He also picked up two spent .25 cartridges, evidently ejected from Beppu's pistol, lying on the ground about 1.5 metres away. At the 110 mile, Sergeant examined the area where the ORs had been massacred, finding an amount of clothing as well as a set of dentures. The second cemetery at the Number 2 Jungle Camp also yielded up evidence, including blood-soaked stretchers and a badly-fractured skull, thought to be that of the last man murdered.

A search of the three compounds had also turned up a variety of objects, ranging from identity tags to personal papers and clothing oddments. Apart from two metal plates belonging to Private Percy Addison and Sapper Vic Jones, the bulk of the items recovered from the airstrip camp were either army issue identity disks or Japanese POW tags. The team had no way of identifying the owners of the Japanese tags but the names on the six regular tags were clearly decipherable — Herb Dorizzi, Bill Leadbeatter, Bill McGee, Tom Skinner and Charles Watson, all of the AIF, and John Madeley, Royal Army.[5] All, apart from Herb Dorizzi who perished on the track, had died at the camp. It appears that Herb's tag was taken to Ranau by his brother, Gordon, who had died there.

Apart from a few odd badges, eleven items only were recovered from the Number 1 Jungle Camp, which was not surprising, as only 56 POWs had made the move there. The items that were marked were not of much use. The only identity tag found was that of Basil Lock, who had died at the airstrip camp shortly after arrival, while other bits and pieces belonged to men who had died a long time before or, in the case of garments from the Selarang clothing pool, had never set foot in Borneo. The searchers had more luck at the Number 2 Jungle Camp. Items here ranged from a housewife (army terminology for a mending kit) marked with the name of ambulanceman John Parsons, who died at the camp on 12 July, to a greatcoat belonging to Joe Platford, who had died in Sandakan on 23 May. Various identity disks and Japanese tags were also found, among them those belonging to infantryman John Burke, baker Henry Frost, Sergeants Len Doyle and Wes Mann, and ambulanceman Edmund Noonan, a bushie from Kyogle,

New South Wales, whose brother Bill had died in the same camp on 23 July, exactly a week before him. As was the case in the other Ranau and Sandakan camps, marked haversacks, towels and clothing, passed from one person to another or taken from the clothing pool, would prove to be virtually useless as a means of identification.

This was true, too, for the dozens of articles of clothing handed in by villagers, who had often exchanged food in return for clothing. Out of almost 60 objects surrendered to the inquiry team, only four were traceable to Ranau prisoners — an officer's hat and haversack belonging to Gordon Good, Tony Fahey's pack, and a dixie belonging to Richard Gellatly. Several of the surrendered items, such as a haversack and jacket belonging to Leo McCarthy and Vic Leinster, both of whom had died at Paginatan, and a jacket, marked with the name of Arthur Ellis (who had made it as far as Maringan), had evidently been traded en route to Ranau. If the investigators were surprised to find that anyone had taken a greatcoat to Borneo, they must have been astounded to discover that Platford had taken two — the one found at the Number 2 Jungle Camp and the other handed in by a villager. While all these items were of interest, the one thing they wanted to find above all else was the tin containing the camp records. Although they dug all around the tree where Cook had promised to bury them, they found nothing. The loss of this paperwork was devastating for, without it, identification of hundreds of unmarked graves was impossible. Unable to locate the tin, but with the main burial places noted, and the relics collected for possible identification, the Ranau team departed, not for Keningau as originally planned, but for Jesselton, which was about only half the distance. Although it had been envisaged that there might be some investigation of the track, the team had limited its search to the three Ranau sites. Any further search would have to wait until the arrival of the war graves recovery teams the following year.

Although the various searches were superficial in terms of a body count, they were more that sufficient for the needs of war crimes investigators. As soon as hostilities had ceased they had begun to collect their evidence — interviewing survivors (including civilians and the POWs moved to Kuching), interrogating Japanese personnel, confiscating records and hunting down known or suspected war criminals. Topping the list were General Baba, Borneo's most senior officer (who had managed to avoid being assassinated by Roland Griffiths-Marsh, an SRD field agent sent from Australia for that specific purpose), Major Suga, Hoshijima, Yamamoto, Abe, Takakuwa, Watanabe, Nagai and Sugino. Not too far behind were guards such as Kada, Suzuki Saburo, Kitamura, Fukishima, Kawakami, Beppu, Kiyoshima and Hayashi, as well as Ehara and Hosotani of the Kempei-tai. And there were many others. By the time the investigators had collated the Sandakan-Ranau list, there were between 150 and 200 names on it.

Some, such as Mad Mick Kada, who had attacked Darlington, and Bulldog Ehara, responsible for the tortures during interrogations over the Sandakan Incident, fled, never to be seen again. Others, such as Ishikawa Takeo, the Sandakan quartermaster, managed to die of disease before the prosecutors had time to swoop. Colonel Suga, who had little hope of avoiding the gallows, cheated the hangman by cutting his throat with a table knife. His last request, for his batman to burn incense beside his body, was only partially realised. With no incense available, he had to make do with a mosquito bomb. At least Suga had the courage of his convictions. Despite repeated assertions by the Japanese that they would commit hari kari rather than surrender or be taken prisoner, no one at Sandakan or Ranau followed Suga's lead — not even the haughty Hoshijima. The rest were rounded up and placed in compounds, until such time as they were either charged, or repatriated to Japan. Those in command assumed that, as they had systematically disposed of the entire Sandakan-Ranau POW population, they were immune from prosecution, while their underlings were confident they would soon be on their way home, not least because of British policy.

Lord Louis Mountbatten had announced, as soon as hostilities ceased, Allied policy in regard to war criminals. Anyone who had committed war crimes should be tried, but 'no one should be charged unless there was very strong *prima facie* evidence that he would be convicted on evidence which could be clearly seen to be irrefutable'. The reason for this was not to prevent vexatious allegations clogging up the system, but to protect the image of the British Empire. According to Mountbatten, 'nothing would diminish our prestige more if we appeared to be instigating vindictive trials against individuals or a beaten enemy nation'. He seems to have been worried that the Japanese public might view the aggressive pursual of war criminals as something which was not altogether 'cricket'.

Identification was always going to be a problem. For a start, to Western eyes all Asians look similar, as Westerners do to them. Second, many had identical or similar names and, third, quite a number were known only by their nicknames. Finding someone identified only as Masturbation, Ramona (his favourite song) or Coffee King was going to take some doing. Consequently, apart from the key players, most of the Japanese and Formosans in the surrender compounds at Labuan, Beaufort and Papar felt sure that they would be on their way home before long. What a shock it must have been for the Sandakan and Ranau personnel, lined up for an identity parade, to come face to face with none other than Warrant Officer Bill Sticpewich.

The high profile criminals were to be tried first, with the trials set down for early January. Short, Botterill and Moxham, now in Australia, were still far too ill to be flown to Labuan to testify, so sworn statements had been taken down by Mr Justice Mansfield in Sydney on 16 and 19 November. Exactly a month before, Sticpewich too had made statements, one to Mansfield and the other to investigator Captain G. S. Ruse, who he had met when the four survivors were evacuated to Morotai. On 3 November, after the other three had been flown home for further medical treatment, he and war crimes investigator Captain Brereton had visited the Labuan compound where Sticpewich formally identified Japanese prisoners 6, 7, 9 and 235 as Hoshijima, Nagai, Watanabe Genzo and Sergeant Watanabe. This was not Brereton's first encounter with the accused. He had interrogated them all about six weeks before.

On 29 December, Captain Athol Moffitt, a young Sydney barrister from the 9th Australian Division, who had been sent to Brunei in October to assist in civilian trials, received orders to report to Labuan. He was to act as prosecutor in the trials of several Japanese war criminals, which were to be held as soon as possible as the 9th Division was ready to pull out of Borneo. The first, that of Hoshijima Susumi, was scheduled to begin on 8 January. On New Year's Eve, Moffitt swapped his palatial digs in Brunei (a pre-war government residence) for an army tent in Labuan. Almost immediately he set about reading and evaluating the evidence, which included 50 sworn statements, collected by the investigating teams. Although under the rules laid down for war crimes trials it was not imperative for deponents to appear in person at a hearing, Moffitt discovered he would not be forced to rely purely on the sworn statements of the survivors to prove his case. He had a witness. William Hector Sticpewich was not only fit, he was being flown from Australia to testify.

The witness arrived on Sunday 6 January, two days before the trial. He struck Moffitt as 'fairly rough' but, as events would prove, his strong personality and ability to present his evidence in a convincing manner would make him a force with which to be reckoned. The trial lasted twelve days. Its main thrust was that Hoshijima was responsible, at the very least, for the deaths of all prisoners at Sandakan from January 1945 until May, when he was relieved by Takakuwa. Although his primary defence, that he was acting on superior orders in regard to the rice cut, was vigorous, it was doomed from the start. His own Quartermaster Arai, supported by other Japanese staff, made it quite clear that it was Hoshijima himself who had cut the rice ration, three months before officially ordered to do so. An attempt to blame the deaths on a shortage of medicines also failed. There were dozens of Red Cross boxes in storage, and the court learned that not only had Dr Taylor enough quinine on hand to supply the whole of North Borneo for two years, but Hoshijima had refused to accept any of it. He then claimed that all food and medicines which he had received were equally divided among the Japanese and their prisoners — an argument which fell apart when he was asked, if his claims were true, why 1000 prisoners but only one Japanese died. His credibility, already in shreds, reached zero when he answered that such a disparity could be explained by three things — the prisoners' inability to withstand the tropical climate, the stress of being incarcerated and then, in 1945, their anxiety at the prospect of being released. His claims that he had been kind to prisoners, so kind that he had sacrificed his beloved horse for food, were also unconvincing as was his assertion that he had instructed his guards also to be kind. By the time the sworn statements were presented and Sticpewich took the stand, Hoshijima was finished. Sticpewich left nothing out — the cages, the beatings, flying practice, the starvation rations, the ill-treatment of the sick, the shooting of Orr, the tortures and the truth about the horse. He even included the stories, believing them to be true, that Billy Young had died as a result of his eyes being gouged out and that Darlington's arm had been broken. Hoshijima could only deny or try to side-step the allegations, including the fantastic assertion that the one and only POW who had died in the cage had died of malaria. However, although he had spent much of his time chatting and laughing with his defence team, eventually the strain began to tell. On 16 January, eight days into the trial, he claimed he was unwell with malaria and asked for an adjournment. The two-day break only delayed the inevitable. On 20 January the court brought down its findings. Verdict: guilty of all charges. Sentence: death by hanging. Hoshijima, who showed no sign of emotion, merely clicked the heels of his highly polished boots, made a precise 180-degree turn and marched from the room.

A fortnight later he lodged an appeal, against both the finding and the sentence. 'I was found guilty and sentenced to suffer death by hanging by the general Court Martial of 9 Aust. Division at Labuan on 20 January 1946', he wrote. 'This was quite beyond my expectation and I still cannot understand at all why I was found to be so ... I am afraid that the court did not care to take all my efforts and endeavours made for the benefit of the PWs during the hardest times since October 1944 into consideration ... You can see how I had been worried about everything, especially in procuring food and medicine for them and how I had done my best... It is not an exaggeration to say that everything that had been given to PWs was the result of my efforts during day and night. To my great regret all persons in the camp had not been aware of my efforts which I had made outside the camp ... Now confined in jail my only wish is that either Captain Cook or Captain Mills who had known me well could still be alive.' He also wished that he had been provided with a better interpreter, a comment which did nothing to further his cause since he spoke English quite well and had spent a great deal of time during his trial arguing points of grammar and improving the interpreter's translation. He finished his appeal on an emotional note, citing homesickness and concern for the fate of his family as further reasons for leniency, an amazing plea given his lack of compassion towards the prisoners in his care.

The trial proceedings and the appeal were sent to an independent legal review board. As it could find no cause to overturn the findings of the court, or any grounds for mitigation, the sentence was confirmed and a death warrant issued by General Sturdee. At 9.30am on 6 April 1946, Captain Hoshijima Suzumi, a man who described himself as 'cultured', was hanged at Rabaul. He was allowed to write ten farewell letters, which he handed to a Buddhist priest, but the Australians had acceded to no other requests — neither scissors to enable him to send a lock of hair and toenail parings to his relatives, nor morphia to dull his senses. He was defiant to the end. As he mounted the thirteen steps to the gallows he shouted, 'Tenno kaika Banzai' — 'Long live the Emperor'. When a provost tried to silence his bellows with a series of rapid slaps across the face, Hoshijima retaliated by sinking his teeth into the officer's hand, drawing blood. The executioner, however, held the trump card. The last thing Hoshijima heard, as the trap door fell from beneath his feet, were the words 'This is for the Aussies you killed at Sandakan'.

He was not the only one to die that day. By the time his execution took place, the Australians had already hanged Takakuwa, who had been found guilty, along with Watanabe, on 5 January after a trial lasting only three days. In proving they had ordered the murder of POWs on the march and at the Number 2 Jungle Camp, the prosecution had considerable help from the guards, who incriminated both officers. By the time the evidence had been presented there was no doubt about their guilt, especially when Takakuwa admitted to it. Watanabe, who was deemed to be slightly less guilty than his co-defendant, was taken to Morotai, where he was shot at 7.00am on 16 March. As there were no gallows at Morotai, Takakuwa was transferred to Rabaul, where his execution was set down at

8.00am, on the same day as that of Hoshijima. Unlike Hoshijima, he did not ask for drugs, but he had requested beer and cigarettes with his last meal, a request which was denied. He also asked for fresh clothing, which was delivered, only to be snatched away by an AIF officer who, on seeing it was Australian army issue, shouted 'You won't swing in that uniform'. As he was led to the gallows, Takakuwa was heard to mutter in Japanese 'I will pray for the Emperor'. A green handkerchief was placed around his eyes and a second later the trap was sprung.

Those involved in the Ranau massacres had no hope of avoiding retribution either. As the investigating officers applied pressure most admitted their guilt, hoping to gain favourable treatment by implicating their colleagues at the same time. However, while the confessions had the normal inconsistencies, there was one fact on which just about everyone agreed. They were adamant that the killings had all occurred on the same day — 1 August, a good fortnight before the war ended. Although, during interrogation, one or two admitted that the 'fit' had been killed at a much later date, the rest of the accused refused to budge, declaring that the Agas agents and other eyewitnesses could not possibly have seen POWs after 1 August, as all were dead. In the end, the date was not an issue, which was fortunate for the accused, none of whom was executed, as POW Headquarters in Kuching had invented dates of death for the victims, only one of which was 1 August.

Yamamoto, Abe and the officers in charge of the nine groups on the first march were also tried, not once, but twice. Moffitt, prosecutor at the first trial held at Labuan between 23 and 28 January, managed to obtain his convictions, based largely on the sworn statements of Moxham and Botterill. Ten were sentenced to death, found guilty of either murder or of forcing prisoners on a march which resulted in death. Yamamoto and Abe were to hang, while the rest, including Sergeant-Major Gotunda, were to be shot. Captain Tanaka received life imprisonment. Fortunately for Gotunda who, because of ambiguities in Botterill's statement, had been identified as one of the killers, the reviewing body ordered a re-trial. Its members agreed that while the charges of murder were supported by the evidence, legal advice as to whether the evidence supported the forced march charges was conflicting. Consequently, none of the convictions or sentences could be confirmed. As soon as the two witnesses were well enough to travel, a new trial must be held at Rabaul.

In May, Botterill, Moxham and Sticpewich, who were all required to give evidence at other hearings, arrived in Rabaul. The Japanese lawyers representing the eleven accused had plenty of time in the intervening months to prepare a new defence. During the proceedings, which took place between 20 and 27 May, the defendants constantly changed their original statements and asserted that the punishing timetable for the march had been laid down by Japanese Headquarters. However, despite their best efforts, the new defence failed. Apart from Gotunda, who was acquitted on Botterill's testimony, and Sergeant Sato, who had died, the rest were found guilty as charged. This time, however, only two were to forfeit their lives — Yamamoto and Abe. Both were to hang. The rest were sentenced to ten years' imprisonment. Yamamoto and Abe were executed at Rabaul on 19 October.

The three witnesses were to have a busy time at Rabaul. Between 25 and 30 May they appeared for the prosecution at no less than three separate trials. One involved Fukishima The Black Bastard who, in January, had been sentenced to fifteen years gaol, along with the rest of his killing squad, for the murders of the ten ORs at Ranau. He was now being tried, for the second time, for the murder of Arthur Bird. And this time, Botterill and Moxham were determined to get him. Although they had perjured themselves at the first trial by declaring that Bird had died on the night he was beaten when, in fact, he had lasted until 8 July, and that he had been examined by Dr Picone, the reviewing panel deemed there was insufficient evidence to prove he had caused Bird's death. At the retrial the pair decided to enlist the aid of Sticpewich. They did not like Sticpewich, but they realised he was a consummate performer in the witness box. As Botterill pointed out, Sticpewich could argue black was white and he would be believed. Furthermore, because he had an excellent memory, he was the best liar Botterill had ever met.

Sticpewich, in fact, had been out of the camp on a work detail when Bird was attacked. However, by the time the other two had filled him in on the fine details, to which Sticpewich had added his own little touches, he was able to recount a blow-by-blow account of the incident. The court believed the story, and sentenced Fukishima to death. However, in the end, Sticpewich's perjury, along with that of Botterill and Moxham, was for nought. The reviewing body failed to confirm the sentence.

Moxham and Botterill had more success with another case — the murder of Albert Cleary. Suzuki Saburo and others had sidestepped the death sentence for the massacre of the sick at the Number 1 Jungle Camp, so they decided to 'stitch him up'. They accused him of Cleary's murder, along with the two actually responsible — Kitamura Kotaro and Kawakami Koyoshi. Kitamura, the jujitsu exponent, had already received a fifteen-year gaol term for maltreatment of prisoners on the march, and was about to be tried for the murder of Noel Parker. Kawakami, The-Gold-Toothed-Shin-Kicking-Bastard, tried in January at Labuan, was also serving a fifteen-year sentence — for the massacres of the sick at the Number 1 Jungle Camp, and the officers at the Number 2. Lieutenant Suzuki, who had ordered Murray's murder, was dead, so Botterill was particularly keen for the court to convict Kawakami who, although he had come back and boasted of his part in the killing, was not being tried for this particular crime. The investigators had enough evidence, but as it had been obtained from a Formosan 'stoolpigeon' placed in Kawakami's cell and masquerading as a war criminal, they did not want to blow his cover. They did, however, tell Botterill that Kawakami had confirmed Murray had been bayonetted to death on the track leading to the hillside cemetery and that his body had been tossed into a bomb crater. Botterill, therefore, followed the Cleary murder trial, at which he was giving evidence against Kawakami, with more than usual interest.

The trial for the murder of Albert Cleary began on Saturday 25 May. It lasted three days but as Sunday was a lay-day, it did not conclude until 28 May. Botterill, who had witnessed Cleary's torture and death, was a powerful tool for the prosecution, his still-frail figure a tangible reminder of what had occurred in North Borneo. Kawakami, who admitted slapping Cleary three times and being 'filled with hate', nevertheless claimed that the prisoner, who showed no signs of bruising, was ill and had been taken to 'the patients' room' where, unfortunately, he had died. Medical Officer Okada Toshiharu swore that the cause of death, as reported by Dr Jeffrey, was 'acute inflammation of the intestines'. However, this evidence was effectively countered when, under cross-examination, Okada admitted that he had not seen the body, only the paperwork. Co-defendent Kitamura took a different tack. By putting the dates of his escort duty with the rice-party back a week, he claimed he was out of the camp at the time of Cleary's torture, and, in any case, he had never struck anyone at Ranau although he had smacked five or six POWs across the face at Sandakan. Suzuki's defence was that he was not in Ranau at all during this time but had gone to Paginatan on guard duties — a claim supported most strongly by both Kitamura and Kawakami. Suzuki also produced Hayashi Yoshinori, who testified that he and Suzuki had gone to Paginatan with the first rice-party at the end of February and had not returned until the end of March, when Moxham's group had been transferred to Ranau. Hayashi told the court that, 'I think Moxham would know that Suzuki returned to Ranau at the end of March'.

Botterill had spoken up in the defence of Gotunda and would later speak up for Toyoda, the wood party guard, but there was no way he, or Moxham, was going to testify on Suzuki's behalf. Quite the opposite. Moxham was prepared to lie under oath. He stated categorically that Suzuki had arrived at Paginatan with the first rice-carrying party in February and had returned to Ranau six days later. Suzuki's defence was blown apart. The court believed Moxham and Botterill. So did the review board. Despite a lengthy appeal, which attacked various discrepancies in the prosecution's case, the sentence of death was confirmed. On 18 October all three were hanged at Rabaul.

The third case in which Botterill and Moxham were involved was the murder of Noel Parker, for which Hayashi was on trial. He had already told the court during Suzuki's trial that he had been stationed at Paginatan and had escorted the last of the prisoners to Ranau, so he had no hope of 'absenting' himself from the scene. Moxham testified to every sickening detail of Parker's murder, taken down by investigators months before, and Botterill verified that he had seen the battered body lying beside the track. The verdict of the court was inevitable — death by hanging. Hayashi appealed but there was no mercy from the review board. On 2 August General Surdee signed the warrant of execution. Ming the Merciless had 29 days to reflect on his fate. He was hanged at Rabaul at 10.00am on the last day of August 1946.

Noel Parker's next-of-kin knew nothing of this. Very little of what had taken place at either the Labuan or Rabaul trials was reported in the press. Indeed, very little information about the fate of Australians who had fallen into Japanese hands had ever been reported. The suppression had initially been enforced by the Army Department when it reviewed a dispatch, written by a war correspondent by the name of Eager, twelve days after the Australian landings at Labuan in June 1945. Eager had compiled a report destined for *The Sydney Morning Herald* and Melbourne's *Age* newspapers, revealing atrocities which had taken place in the area. Publication was bound to create anxiety among the relatives of the 2000

Australians known to have been sent to Borneo, and official reaction was immediate. In a signal to 1 Australia Corps, the Brigadier, Director General of Public Relations, decreed 'Eager's story is such that its publication cannot be permitted'. However on 7 July the censor did allow transmission of a cable from another correspondent, Allan Dawes, who had written a grim, but generalised report on POW conditions in Labuan. By 25 July more-detailed material, gleaned from local eyewitnesses, Australian soldiers and liberated European civilians, was awaiting clearance. One of the dispatches was from Eager, who included information on atrocities against local people about which the Australian senior investigating officer in Borneo knew nothing. The newspaperman had the censor over a barrel. Realising that the story would break sooner rather than later through Dutch and American channels, the Brigadier decided the time had come to allow the publication of the less offensive dispatches and issue, simultaneously, a Ministerial statement. Unaware that only a handful of Australian prisoners had been sent to Labuan, Army Minister Forde released his statement, headed 'Australian Prisoners of War in Borneo'.

Shortly after the AIF landed on Labuan Island in North Borneo, evidence was obtained that Allied prisoners of war had previously been held there by the Japanese.

As the result of considerable enquiries and interrogation of natives, it is believed that early in 1944 some 200 to 300 Allied prisoners of war, including Australians, were brought to the island, probably from other parts of Borneo. During 1944 and up to March 1945 it seems that about 200 of the men died and were buried on the island in circumstances that render identification extremely difficult.

In March last those still living were moved across to the Borneo mainland where further deaths occurred. The survivors numbering about 30 were then moved southwards; but after travelling a short distance are reported by many natives and others to have been shot by their Japanese guards.

Whilst every endeavour will be made to identify as many as possible of the Australians involved in these tragic happenings, it is feared that identification will be inconclusive and incomplete and that some time will elapse before the identities of all the men can be established. Any information which the Army can assess as authentic will be passed to the next-of-kin with the least possible delay.

It is impossible to find words adequate to describe my feelings about this latest evidence of the inhuman barbarities of the Japanese. To starve and kill defenceless captives is surely the very depth of infamy.

I make this announcement with the greatest regret and appreciate how distressing it will be to next-of-kin of men still held by the Japanese. But as the story will inevitably be published I feel that it is best to inform the Australian public in this way, rather than have them obtain their information solely through other channels.

While the issue of such a statement was unavoidable, it only added to the anxiety. Who were these POWs? What were the circumstances which rendered identification 'extremely difficult'? Had they been tortured? Mutilated? Beheaded even? Rumours abounded, with the *Canberra Times* reporting that 100 prisoners from the 8th Division had been recovered alive. Desperate for more information, the relatives in Sydney formed an association headed by a Mr Sydney Smith who called a mass meeting at the Sydney Town Hall on 7 August in the hope that a representative from the government would accept an invitation to speak. The relatives turned up. The spokesman did not.

Eight days later, on 15 August, the war ended, putting an end to the censorship which had been in force since September 1939. About six weeks later, Eager compiled a lengthy and graphic report on the fate of the Borneo POWs. His sources must have been excellent, for, although the investigations had only just begun, his report was fairly accurate. Evidently wishing to avoid interference from the Australian military, he submitted his report to MacArthur's headquarters, who, in turn, passed it for publication. When Eager's actual copy arrived at army signals for transmission to Australia, Major Huon, believing that the story would only cause distress to the relatives of the men listed as 'missing', decided to put a stop to it. Wartime censorship no longer applied and, as restrictive 'D' Notices issued to the press, which were in force in Britain, had yet to be introduced in Australia, Army Headquarters promptly invoked a regulation which prohibited 'any mention of [personnel] missing or believed killed except through official army channels. Correspondents all theatres should be advised of this policy.' In addition, all reports leaving areas previously under Japanese control must be couched in general terms and on no account were they to include specific details which might identify individual POWs, camps or units of troops.

While army authorities could control overseas correspondents, they had no control over reports released by the government. On 22 August the Melbourne *Herald* had revealed that 'the most ghastly story yet told of Japanese barbarity and brutality is expected to be released soon by the Minister for External Affairs' . The newspaper was referring to a report, compiled by Sir William Webb, Australia's leading jurist, for the International War Crimes Commission. Most of the atrocities had taken place in New Guinea and although the report had yet to be released, the *Herald*'s account left nothing to the imagination. On September 11, Webb's report became public and the newspaper accounts of murder, rape, cannibalism, bestiality and brutality even more graphic. Six days later, on 17 September, under the headline 'Heavy Toll of POWs in Borneo', the *Argus* broke the story of the death marches. The difference between the two news items could not have been more marked. The stories on the Webb Report had covered almost an entire page. The Borneo report, consisting of death toll statistics and flat, generalised statements about the marches, had been reduced to one thin column, 16 centimetres in length. As this was the first anyone had heard about a death march, the item, brief as it was, opened a floodgate of enquiries and started up yet another round of rumours. On 27 September, in response to a request from Mr C. F. Aldermann, Member for the ACT, Forde issued a further press statement. Again under the heading 'Australian Prisoners of War in Borneo', the Minister announced that,

> *Specially trained Army officers are making every effort to locate AMF prisoners of war in Borneo and trace those still reported as missing in that area.*
>
> *The task is proving very difficult as, from information so far received, it is known that prior to the Japanese surrender prisoners of war were moved by the Japanese from their known locations to other parts of Borneo.*
>
> *Every endeavour is being made by the interrogation of recovered prisoners of war in Borneo and Japanese personnel to obtain information relative to the movements of prisoners of war in that area, and the fate of those still posted as missing. All such information is being actively pursued.*
>
> *The task is proving more difficult owing to the Japanese having burned down the Sandakan prisoner of war compound in which Australian prisoners of war had been confined after the prisoners of war had departed, thus preventing the obtaining of any evidence which might otherwise have been available.*
>
> *While it is sincerely hoped that the efforts to locate further prisoners of war will be successful, from advice already received it is feared that the death rate amongst prisoners of war will be high, due mainly to the meagre food rations issued by the Japanese and the apparent lack of medical facilities for the sick. Information received indicates that whilst some graves of prisoners of war at Sandakan bear the name of the deceased member and in some cases his regimental details, many are without any means of identification. The Japanese have been ordered to prepare a nominal roll of all deceased prisoners of war in this area.*
>
> *Food, medical supplies (including blood, penicillin and sulphur drugs) and medical personnel have been flown in to meet all emergencies, and the evacuation of those so far recovered is proceeding with all haste, subject only to fitness to travel.*
>
> *The Commonwealth Government fully sympathises with the next-of-kin and relatives of these men, and they may rest assured that no expense or effort will be spared to trace their ultimate fate. As definite information comes to hand, the next-of-kin will be immediately advised.*

Platitudes from the Minister for the Army were not what the public wanted to hear. The war had been over now for eight weeks and still the families of the Borneo men had heard nothing, apart from a small item on 11 October to the effect that investigators were currently collecting evidence against 66 suspected Japanese war criminals. A letter published in Melbourne's *Herald* on 13 October was indicative of the anguish being felt by the next-of-kin, desperate for news, any news. 'Waiting' of Thornbury wrote:

> *When are we to be given news of our men who were captured by the Japanese in Borneo? The suspense is terrible. It is months since the first Allied landing in Borneo and weeks since the official surrender, yet, apart from one horrible report (the death marches from Sandakan), there has been no official statement about these men. Surely something is known. I think it's time the facts were published.*

The Army was just as frustrated as the public. But the reality was that very little information at all was held about individuals and what there was, was scant and often conflicting. The Japanese had produced a roll with the name of every prisoner, date, place and cause of death but many of the entries were quite at odds with records recovered from the various camps and the main Kuching office. There was nothing sinister about the discrepancies, which were the result of the Japanese central office not receiving information on POWs who had died at Sandakan after 29 May, at Ranau in August, or those who had escaped from the march. Consequently, when 9th Division ordered POW Headquarters to provide a nominal roll, any POW for whom no details had been received, was given a fictitious date, place and cause of death.

Unfortunately, the survivors had not been much help either. While at Morotai, Botterill and Sticpewich had been shown photographs and a list of E and B Force names provided by Ray Steele and Colonel Walsh (who had just been liberated from Kuching), but the results had been disappointing. Botterill, still in a state of trauma and due to be evacuated to Australia for intensive medical treatment that afternoon, had 'showed a disinclination to give information' — an attitude which did not go down well with Lieutenant L. McGinley, the officer conducting the interrogations, who denounced him as being 'uncooperative and devoid of a sense of responsibility'. Sticpewich, on the other hand, had been eager to impart information — far too eager. As a result, information he had given at Labuan now conflicted with information provided at Morotai, though how either he or Botterill could possibly be expected to relate photographs of healthy, well-fed soldiers taken in 1940-41 with the bearded, skeletal creatures of the POW camp is beyond comprehension.

On 24 October, Army Headquarters discussed the problem. As a senior officer at 2nd Echelon (in charge of records) pointed out, 'The information is very vague. Sticpewich frequently shows men having died on one of the marches from Sandakan and both Braithwaite (whose reports are all based on hearsay) and Campbell (own knowledge) state that death occurred at Sandakan some months earlier. No definite dates of death are given at all [by the three survivors] beyond those who were killed in air raids.' Although pressure was mounting to release whatever information was held, the problem of what, or what not, to tell relatives continued. On 2 November a memo was sent to the commanding officer of 2nd Echelon, requesting he consider sending out a general statement to next-of-kin as 'there has been pressure by people from Headquarters 8th Australian Division staff that they should be permitted to send out some such circular, which I think would be unwise, but as many unwise things are being done today they might either do it or be given permission to do it unless we forestall them. It would require to be a most carefully worded letter but I suggest it is one which we require to consider immediately.'

The prospect of staff at 8th Division taking matters into their own hands evidently propelled the Army into action. On about 19 November, Richie Murray's widow received, by registered mail, her version of the 'carefully worded' letter, dated 17 November. A Lieutenant J. Findley, signing on behalf of an (unnamed) Lieutenant-Colonel, Officer in Charge of New South Wales Echelon and

Records, informed Margaret Murray that:

> *It is with much regret I have to advise you that although every effort has been made to ascertain the whereabouts of your Husband, NX 33361 Pte Richard Murray, who is recorded as a Prisoner of War in Japanese hands Borneo, no information has as yet been received concerning him.*
>
> *An examination of documents so far supplied by the Japanese authorities has failed to reveal any record of him, but it is thought that in all probability he was one of a number of Australian prisoners of war who were located in North Borneo and would be one of those who, although weakened by the conditions prevailing in the prisoner of war camps, were sent out by the Japanese on forced marches to a place some miles distant from their original location.*
>
> *Now that an examination of the Japanese records has been completed it is considered you should be informed that the Military Investigators have come to the conclusion that he probability of your Son [sic] being recovered alive is very remote.*
>
> *In the light of what has happened in Borneo and the added knowledge that the Japanese destroyed evidence of value to the Allied Forces, it will be most difficult in many cases to supply any definite information for a lengthy period as to the fate of members unaccounted for in Japanese records. Inquiries are, however, being continued and at the present time a party of Australians is investigating the routes taken by prisoners of war during their enforced marches. Pending the finalisation of such investigations the records of Pte Murray will be endorsed as follows:-*
>
> *'Previously reported "Prisoner of War" now posted as "Missing believed deceased, cause and date unknown".'*
>
> *It is known that typewritten postcards have recently been received in Australia bearing a Borneo address and it is desired to state that if one of them has been received by you it should not be accepted as evidence that your Husband was alive and well at a recent date, as an examination of such mail discloses that where it was dated, it was written between March and August 1944.*
>
> *Your prolonged anxiety and distress occasioned by the absence of news is fully appreciated and you are assured that immediately anything is known concerning Pte Murray you will be informed by NSW Echelon and Records, Broadway Sydney.*

The families of other POWs, whose deaths had definitely been established from Japanese records, were notified only by telegram. On 2 October the parish priest arrived at the Sullivan farm at Coonabarrabran bearing an envelope. Its contents confirmed what Mrs Sullivan had known all along — that Ron had died on Easter Saturday, 1945. Four weeks later the dreaded telegrams were delivered to Doris Anderson at Glebe and the Barnier family at Grafton, who learned that Albert and John had died at Sandakan. It was a scene which was to be repeated time and again the length and breadth of Australia. By 3 November *The Sydney Morning*

Herald was setting aside an entire page of paid death announcements in a Roll of Honour, containing the names of many of the Borneo victims. Just over three weeks later Mrs Murray also received a telegram, updating the information sent by letter. Private Richard Murray was now posted as 'deceased, cause not stated, on 20 May 1945'.

Although Botterill, Moxham, SRD, 3 PWC&I, and war crimes investigating officers had known for months what had happened to Richie Murray, neither 2nd Echelon nor his wife and family were ever informed of his fate. Like all other next-of-kin, they remained in the dark, unaware that vast amounts of information had been compiled by various units, all of whom had carried out their tasks most diligently. One reason was, that while all of this information eventually reached Army headquarters, none of it was ever collated or coordinated. The other was far more sinister. The Australian Government, SRD administration and General Sir Thomas Blamey had all, for various reasons, embarked upon a policy of deliberate and wilful suppression.

Chapter Sixteen
'A MOST REGRETTABLE BUSINESS'

The war crimes trials began in January 1946. Army Headquarters had no jurisdiction here, for all war crimes trials were held in open court and anyone who attended heard every scrap of evidence. Yet the press, not usually noted for its reticence, entered into a gentlemen's agreement with the Australian Government to reveal nothing but the most scant details. The rationale behind this decision, which was to cause immense grief and torment to the relatives of dead POWs in the years ahead, was that the story of Australians held by the Japanese was too appalling to be disclosed. Consequently, while the entire world knew everything there was to know about atrocities perpetrated by Nazi Germany in Europe, the families of POWs held in Japanese-occupied territory were given no information.

The generalised statements appearing in the press about Borneo did more harm than good. While the public knew prisoners had been marched to their deaths from a place called Sandakan, they had no idea of the identity of the participants, or that the majority of prisoners had never left the main POW compound. With no specific details available, every mother, every wife, every child of the 2800 Australian and British POWs originally sent from Singapore to Sandakan imagined the worst. This was fuelled in later years by articles and books which concentrated on the Sandakan-Ranau marches.

The press could have printed the facts at any time after the war. However, apart from the *Age* in Melbourne, all followed the government line, oblivious to the fact that, by supressing the details, the only people they were protecting were the perpetrators of the crimes. Readers of the *Age*, however, were quite well informed on both the Ambon (where almost an entire battalion of the 8th Division had been wiped out) and Borneo trials. On 2 January the paper published a detailed account of the trial of Hosotani, who had been sentenced to death by shooting for the murder of the two Australians at the 15½ mile. This was followed on 5 January with a report on the Ranau massacres, including a run-down on the charges and the names of the accused. Six days later readers were given the grim details of the charges levelled against Hoshijima, who was quoted as having said, 'The sick are useless. They should not be tended or fed'. There was also a commentary on his light-hearted behaviour in court. Meanwhile, in direct contrast to the *Age*, leading papers such as *The Sydney Morning Herald* had studiously avoided all reference to any of these trials, as had the scandal sheets. However, not all news stories coming out of Borneo, nor all war crimes trials, were being spiked. On 3 January *The Sydney Morning Herald* reported that Australian occupation troops in Labuan were to be replaced by Indian Army personnel. The next day, while still ignoring the Labuan trials, the same paper gave details of the Bataan death march in the Philippines, which had claimed the lives of thousands of American and Filipino soldiers.

The dearth of information about atrocities against Australian POWs did not go unnoticed. Under the heading 'The Sandakan Diggers', an unidentified correspondent to a periodical magazine, to which the Barnier family subscribed, asked, 'Why has the press given so little publicity to the ill-treatment of Australian Prisoners-of-War? Is it sheer indifference, or does it spring from a desire not to harrow the feelings of bereaved relatives? Nobody seems to know who is responsible for the secrecy. Some blame the military, others the department of Information. That a hush-hush policy exists is all too evident.' The letter struck a chord with John's mother, Marie. She clipped the letter from the page and placed it among her mementos where, with the questions never answered, it would turn brown with age.

On 16 January the same questions were posed to a far wider audience when the columnist of 'The Serviceman', a regular feature which appeared in the *Bulletin*, a respected, Sydney-based news periodical, drew his readers' attention to a 'remarkable feature of current press reporting' — the avoidance of any reference to the Ambon and Labuan war crimes trials. Writing under the pseudonym of Ek Dum, columnist Malcolm Ellis was a forthright and fearless senior staff writer who described himself as 'next but one to the editor'. After observing that, 'the greatness of a nation can always be measured by the price it puts upon the citizens', he launched into a tirade about the way in which the trials were being held and the failure of the press (with the exception of the *Age*) to report them. 'One would have imagined', he thundered, 'that the trials would have been staged in a manner which would have done justice to the solemnity, and magnitude, of the occasion, before a tribunal whose eminence could have left no doubt in the eyes of the world that justice had been done majestically — in such a manner as to warn potential future offenders and exhibit the dignity of the Commonwealth. However, the trials are being carried out by minor military courts, the prosecutions in the hands of captains and lieutenants whose names are unknown even to those most familiar with the law in the Commonwealth. And the press has little interest in what is going on ... they are more concerned with the affair of a party of office girls, alleged to have been "smuggled" by the US Army to Manila, and the proceedings against a Sydney evening paper reporter, with the killing of a lady bookie in her tobacco kiosk, than with the trials of the murderers or torturers of 3000 Australian soldiers.'

Ellis devoted the remainder of his column to giving a lucid and accurate account of the evidence presented to the courts to date, including details of the march, which Takagama Hikoichi of Japanese headquarters described from the witness box as 'a most regrettable business'. On 6 February, possibly in response to the *Bulletin*'s stinging attack, *The Sydney Morning Herald* finally carried an item about the Labuan trials, based upon a letter written by Athol Moffitt, who revealed that Yamamoto and others had been sentenced to death and that he, Moffitt, had prosecuted the case. Apart from that, there was nothing which had not already been reported by the *Argus* months before. However on 12 March the paper managed to raise false hopes by reporting that RAAF Catalinas and Thunderbolts were sweeping the sea near Great Masalambo Island, between Java and the Celebes, looking for two AIF officers. According to the report the pair, last seen twelve months previously near the island in a small boat, were 'members of a special unit escaped from Borneo'.

The report was a beat-up. The place, date and nationality were right, but that was about it. The two soldiers, Lieutenants Clifford Perske and John Sachs (the same John Sachs whom Gort had met on USS *Bream*) were SRD operatives who had been captured in March 1945 after trying to blow up shipping near Great Masalambo Island. By the time the search was mounted both had been dead for almost eleven months, beheaded at Surabaya on Good Friday 1945, along with two American airmen, sole survivors of a plane which had crash-landed into the sea after dropping bombs on Sandakan in October 1944.

Finally, on 7 April, *The Sydney Morning Herald* made what appears to be its only other report on the Borneo story — the executions of Takakuwa and Hoshijima. This was followed up with a similar, but longer story the following day when Max Coleman, who had attended the executions, filed his eyewitness report in Sydney's *Sunday Sun*. Even then, those who had been scanning the papers each morning in the hope that new facts might emerge were to be disappointed. Apart from a brief paragraph stating that the two accused had been found guilty of murder and torture, the rest of the item was devoted to a description of the demeanour of the condemned as they were led to the gallows. Perhaps watered-down accounts of the trials were not worth bothering about, perhaps there was a feeling that the horrors of the war were best forgotten. Whatever the reason, by the time General Baba, found guilty of ordering the second march and failing to prevent the first (ordered by his now-deceased predecessor), was hanged at Rabaul in August 1947, the papers were no longer interested.

The relatives, however, still yearned for information. So did the army record-keepers at 2nd Echelon, who had been trying for months to obtain access to Japanese interrogations, and personal papers recovered from POW camps, which might throw light on the fate of some of the prisoners. It was all to no avail. As the trial paperwork was unavailable from the legal department until after the hearings and any subsequent appeal, the only way for 2nd Echelon personnel to obtain any casualty information on personnel was to hope that the newspapers would report it (which, with one notable exception, they did not), or to go to the courtroom and take notes themselves.

Unaware that Army Records was denied access to war crimes investigations, the Melbourne *Sun* published a graphic account of the deaths of a Tasmanian soldier, Corporal J. Armstrong, and a British Army gunner by the name of Martin, who had been murdered near Kopang, Timor, on about 12 June 1943. At the trial, held in Darwin and therefore far more accessible to the press than any of the other venues, it was revealed that the unfortunate Armstrong, helpless and blindfolded, had tried to elude his executioners by running round a village before he was cornered and shot. As neither the records' department, nor Armstrong's relations, had any idea that he was anything other than 'missing' until they read the paper, the publication created much distress and embarrassment for everyone concerned. The incident did not, however alter the status quo — if the records' department wanted casualty information it would have to wait until after confirmation of the sentence. Even then, a tight rein was kept on the paperwork. Before allowing it out of their sight, legal personnel attached a covering letter to the file to remind those perusing the evidence that 'the information contained in these proceedings will not be disclosed to the press'. This instruction was not an attempt to cover up irregularities in trial proceedings, as was claimed by some writers decades later, but to ensure that the names of victims remained confidential.

When May 1946 rolled into June and there was still no further information forthcoming, the Victorian Branch of the Returned Servicemen's League (RSL) put pressure on the government to release the contents of The Webb Report, tabled in Federal Parliament months before. Although Mr Sinclair, Secretary for the Department of the Army, wrote a sympathetic reply, giving a broad outline of what was known to date and expressing the hope that war graves recovery units might shed further light on the matter, he advised that

> With regard to the request that Sir William Webb's report… be made available, it is desired to advise that it is considered both inadvisable and undesirable that any information contained in the report, other than that which has already appeared in the Press, should be released to the general public. This decision is prompted by a sympathetic consideration for the personal feelings of the next of kin of those unfortunate members of the Australian Military Forces who were subjects of such brutal and inhumane treatment at the hands of their captors.

By way of consolation he added that,

> On cessation of hostilities immediate action was taken to arrest all Japanese in the area connected with prisoners of war, and in addition, every endeavour is being continued to bring to trial all those Japanese responsible for this outrage. Those already apprehended and found guilty have been dealt with.

Sinclair's assertion that 'every endeavour' was being made to bring to trial those responsible for the outrage was not quite true. One particularly high profile war criminal was to go free. It was Captain Nagai, Hoshijima's number one accomplice, and he was not merely being set free, he was to be repatriated to Japan.

When Botterill had learned, early in the piece, that Nagai had been caught, he had returned to Australia to recover from his ordeal confident that Sticpewich would provide more than enough evidence to bring him to court. His confidence was misplaced. Sticpewich, who had once described Nagai as 'one of the worst criminals', formally identified him for Captain Brereton at the Labuan compound, but that was as far as it went. When Botterill arrived in Rabaul he was unaware that Sticpewich had undergone a complete about-face. Having previously shot Nagai's sworn statement full of holes, he had failed to denounce him to the war crimes investigators, who had let the suspect go. Botterill, in his naivety, gave Sticpewich a lengthy statement listing Nagai's many crimes, which he asked him to hand to senior investigating officers, and urged him also to raise the matter at the International War Crimes Tribunal in Tokyo, where Sticpewich was to give evidence later in the year. It was the last Botterill, or anyone else, ever saw or heard of the list. Although he had thought Sticpewich's sarcastic comment, 'What do you want to do? Hang every Jap in Japan?' rather odd at the time, he had no idea the pair had formed some kind of alliance — an alliance that became so close a few months later, when Sticpewich was in Tokyo, that he and his 'always best friend', 'Peter' Hirowa Nagai, seriously contemplated writing a book together.

Although Australia actively pursued war criminals until 1950, the execution of General Baba at Rabaul in 1947 wound up the last of the Borneo trials. Of the 898 names on the Borneo 'wanted' list, investigators had arrested at least 444. Of the remaining 454, 36 had died, sixteen had left Borneo, 33 could not be traced and 131 had not been located as they had given false names or there was not enough evidence to bother. Another 238, including Nagai, had been released after simple interrogation. These figures reflected the general clear-up rate by Allied investigators throughout the Far East. Of the 25 A Class criminals convicted, seven, including Tojo, the Minister for War, were hanged and sixteen sentenced to life imprisonment for 'Crimes against Peace'. Another 5700 B and C Class criminals were brought to trial for murder and crimes against humanity. Of these, 3000 were convicted and 920 executed. These statistics, which appeared impressive, were not equal to the carnage they had wreaked. One Japanese was sentenced for every 50 Allied prisoners held in POW camps, while one was executed for every 250 prisoners who died.

Of those who had been tried for crimes committed against Sandakan prisoners, eight had been hanged and at least 55 sentenced to prison terms ranging from two years (for general maltreatment) to life (for murder). While many of the sentences were quite hefty, they were not worth the paper on which they were written. In April 1952, when a peace treaty between the Allied powers and Japan, to which Australia was a signatory, preventing the further prosecution of any wanted criminals came into effect, all prisoners still in Allied hands were transferred to Sugamo Prison, Tokyo. As a result of pleas for mitigation all were free by December 1958. The longest sentence ever served by any Japanese war criminal convicted at any Allied trial was less than thirteen years.

Meanwhile 31 Australian War Graves Unit, under the command of Captain Johnstone, had arrived at Sandakan from Labuan in March. As the work of recovering the remains and reburying them in a proper cemetery was expected to take some time, especially since the area was extensively overgrown, the unit built a substantial camp near the site of the Eight Mile POW Compound. Included in the party was Corporal Graham Robinson, a photographer. There was also a sign writer, Corporal Peter Beaumont, on call, but, as his services were not required until the crosses were ready, he remained at 8 Unit's headquarters camp at a rubber estate near Menggatal, about 20 kilometres from Jesselton.

On 27 March a labour force of about 100 Javanese coolies and Japanese soldiers held in the Sandakan compound began the mammoth task of clearing the rampant undergrowth from the main cemetery sites. The going rate of pay for the coolies was 60 cents (Malay) a day, which was about 2 shillings in Australian currency. Meanwhile, the officers began a survey of the area to select a site for a cemetery large enough to hold all the bodies recovered from Sandakan, the track and Ranau, as well as all those killed in action during the fighting at Tarakan and Balikpapan. As no other suitable site could be found, they decided to use part of the defunct airstrip. On 6 June, as soon as a road had been constructed to the new cemetery and 2000 wooden crosses, costing 4 shillings, 11½ pence each, had been ordered from a local supplier, the exhumations commenced. By 21 June, Johnstone reported that all bodies had been recovered from both the civil and the Number 1 POW cemetery. Although only 52 Australian and 108 British graves were identifiable, it was possible to categorise many of the others as 'unknown Australian' and 'unknown British' when the locals assured the recovery teams that the two nationalities had been very careful in the early stages to bury their dead in separate parts of the cemetery.

Ray Battram, one of the Australians involved in the Number 1 Cemetery exhumations, was rather taken aback on opening the rough wooden coffins to discover that the remains, some of which had been buried for up to two years, were far from skeletal. The torsos were no longer intact, but the flesh on the limbs and head was pretty much preserved, as were the hair and whiskers. Some even had a touch of colour in their cheeks. Although the eyelids had gone, exposing marble-like eyes, the facial features were not sufficient to allow positive identification. In any case, as soon as the remains were exposed to the air, rapid putrefaction set in. That many of the corpses were fairly well preserved was most likely due to the exclusion of air in the wet, clayey soil and/or a phenomenon known as adipocere, which occurs when a corpse is immersed in water or buried in heavy, damp earth. Not all bodies were well preserved, especially those wrapped in blankets or wrapped in banana leaves, and three or four, buried alongside the marked graves, showed evidence of deep cuts to the back of the skull, consistent with having been inflicted by a sharp blade, possibly a sword or chonkol. It was not possible to determine whether the injuries had been inflicted before or after death, or if they were even the result of careless work by gravediggers. However, had there been any evidence at all (for example the skulls being severed from the spine) to indicate that death was due to beheading, the paperwork would have been clearly marked as such and the war crimes investigators called in. Notes were taken of all the bodies recovered, for a possible match against existing dental records, and anything else which might be able to assist with later identification was recorded.

Kulang had volunteered his services to assist in recruiting labour, locating burial sites and collecting information, and work continued steadily through July. On the 22nd of that month word was passed around that a bonus of 10 cents local currency (3½ pence) would be paid for each new set of remains located. Two days later six bodies, which had been buried by locals, were disinterred at the Sandala Estate, in the vicinity of the 15 mile. Three were identifiable — Fred Jordan of the RAF and two Australians, Bombardier Harry Treseder and machine gunner Standish Haly. All had escaped, Treseder on 15 May, Haly and Jordan in mid-June.

Meanwhile a three-man detachment, under the command of Lieutenant L. Brazier, had gone up-river to begin a search of the track between Boto and Paginatan, where they were to meet up with a detachment from 8 War Graves Unit, currently covering the Ranau area.[1] Accompanying Brazier's team were Kulang and his friend Kanak, who they picked up at Tandu-Batu, and a large number of locals, who were hired to hack away the jungle and transport the remains to various points along the river for transportation back to Sandakan. As Captain Cocks, who had carried out the initial survey the previous year, had pointed out, it was a colossal undertaking.

The cutters moved off first, followed by sixteen searchers who were spread out 20 metres either side of the track, with the carriers bringing up the rear. When evidence of remains or relics was discovered, the carriers were dispatched into the immediate area to look for scattered bones, articles belonging to the prisoners or any further evidence. These were all logged with the date and place of recovery and, in the case of actual remains, with a multi-digit, coded reference number. While the cutters and searchers moved ahead, the carriers, after wrapping and tying the upper bones in one strip of canvas and the lower in another, tagged the bundle with its reference number before packing it into a large woven basket, shaped like an ice-cream cone and known as a boongan, which they carried on their backs. Between Celo and Tampias they recovered the remains of 36 men, but only six were identifiable — Private Reuben O'Connor of the AAMC and Gunner Albert Dale who died near Boto, and escapees Roberts, Molde, Beardshaw and Fuller at Telupid. Another body (Gunner John Nicholson) found at Tampias itself, was later (erroneously) identified as that of Padre Thompson, who had died about 3 kilometres further east.[2] No bodies were recovered between Tampias and Paginatan. However, on discovering that the number buried at Paginatan was substantial, the carriers were put to work constructing rafts to float the bundles down the river to Tampias.

When they arrived at Paginatan on 31 July, Sergeant Roberts of 8 AWGU was waiting for them. He had completed his search of the track and was on his way back to his base at Ranau when he was ordered to return to the village to make contact with the other team. Having previously come off worst in a demarcation dispute with 31 Unit as to who should search where, he was probably not too pleased to be recalled, especially since he had left full details of his search with the Paginatan village headman. At least he was not on foot. As the track from Paginatan to Ranau was well defined, Roberts, his assistant and the interpreter had all been provided with horses. A kilometre to the west of the village his team had located a cemetery containing the remains of 46 POWs, bringing the total found in the area to 64. Although these remains were officially assigned to 31 Unit's tally, for some reason it was decided not to float them downstream to Tampias as planned, but send them to Ranau by coolie train, along with any bodies located along the Paginatan-Ranau track. Although at least twenty POWs had died along this stretch, Roberts found only four — one body each at the 11, 9, and 7½ mile pegs and another 1¼ miles further on.

Evidently the war graves units were not given access to statements made by survivors for war crimes trials, or to information collected by other investigating teams, or to any of the death records. Had they done so they would have realised that the body at the 11 mile, which Roberts had found lying near a big tree, was that of Quailey, and the one at the 9 mile was Sheard's. The other two, owing to problems with translation, were not as straightforward, but a short list of two could be deduced for the 6¼ mile body — Private Henry Morris (who had become 'lost' in the records when his name was transcribed as 'Maurice') and Gunner Ken Perry, both of whom had died on 18 February near the 6 mile peg. Further research would have revealed that the fourth body was almost certainly that of Gunner Roy Walter, who had died near the 7½ mile peg on 24 June, while on the second march.

As soon as 31 Unit had cleared the Paginatan area, the team returned to Boto. Once they left Boto and began to cover new ground, problems arose with the labourers, who proved to be such poor workers that they were paid off at Sapi at half-rates and sent back to their villages in disgrace. In the 64-kilometre stretch between Boto and Mandorin, four bodies only were recovered. At Muanad, it was a different story. Sixty-one bodies were recovered in a 5-kilometre stretch, 48 near the site of the Tangkul massacre.

At Muanad, Brazier encountered another problem — Sticpewich, who had arrived from War Graves Headquarters at Macassar to assist with the track search, only to find it was almost over. The two did not get on well as Sticpewich was senior in years, but not in rank to Brazier and was highly critical of the way in which the search was being conducted. As they moved along the track, he observed the lieutenant's methods closely. He also quizzed one of Brazier's men, Private Outram, who had joined the team. By the time they reached the 17 mile, five bodies only had been recovered. Arriving back at Sandakan, Sticpewich went immediately to Captain Johnstone to complain about the inadequacy of the search. His main criticism was Brazier's lack of personal supervision over the labour force who, in his opinion, needed careful watching to prevent them taking shortcuts in the search pattern. Johnstone did not take kindly to this attack. After making it quite plain that he regarded Sticpewich as an interloper, he reminded him that he was a mere warrant officer who was simply attached to the unit and was therefore of no consequence. He did, however, eventually agree to his re-searching the track between Paginatan and Sapi. Taking Private Curry with him, Sticpewich returned up-river to Beluran where he hired 22 locals to act as searchers and another 28 as carriers. While Curry waited for him at strategic points along the river, Sticpewich moved along the track from west to east.

Between Paginatan and Tampias, an area which had yet to yield a single body, he located six sets of remains. Between Tampias and Sapi he found another fourteen, including that of Rod Richards, who had been rescued from the gully on the Milulu mountain by Moxham, only to die a few kilometres further on. He was most put out, on returning to Beluran expecting to receive instructions to search the section from Sapi to Kolapis, to be ordered to return to Sandakan. In the meantime, Brazier had begun another re-search, from Kolapis to the 17 mile, which would result in the recovery of another 44 bodies. After twiddling his thumbs for the best part of a week, Sticpewich was shunted off to Ranau, where 8 AWGU was having trouble finding one or two of Lieutenant Sergeant's previously marked locations.

He learned that the Ranau recovery team, under the overall command of Captain T. J. Collins, had arrived on foot from Tamparuli on 9 July with Sergeant's list of locations, expecting to be gone within six weeks. However, while the number of prisoners who had died at Ranau was far less than that at Sandakan, the job of recovering them was far more difficult. All the burial sites, along with tracks leading to them, had been completely obliterated by vines and jungle growth and none identified, with the exception of the first camp, which had a sign written in Japanese proclaiming it to be 'British and Australian Soldiers' Cemetery — Borneo Prison Compound Section 2 — Identities Unknown'.

Furthermore, when the bodies were located, the logistics involved in transporting them to Jesselton, for trans-shipment by sea to Sandakan, were very difficult. Unlike 31 Unit, which was able to transport its recoveries back to Sandakan by river, the Ranau remains had first to be packed up and carried across the mountain range to Tamparuli, where headquarters' staff at the Menggatal Estate had arranged for their transfer to Jesselton by motor vehicle. At Jesselton the bundles were removed from the boongans and repacked into custom-made wooden crates, large enough to hold about 40 bundles each, before being dispatched to Sandakan by coastal steamer.

The exhumations had begun on 11 July. Corporal Clerk and a labour squad, guided by Baragah who had helped bury Andy Anderson, headed west to recover the body, while the remainder of the unit, along with a mandor and 35 labourers, began work at the locations indicated by Sergeant. The first two, enclosed within a bamboo fence, were to the north of the hut area and contained the remains of two prisoners. The first, marked with a cross, was that of Herman Reither. It appears that his body had been removed by locals from the jungle near Dihil's house, where it had evidently attracted the attention of pigs, for burial near the first compound. There was not much to find — the top portion of the skull was missing, but the jawbone, thigh and knuckle bones were present, along with a rough wooden cross on which Sticpewich had scratched his details when he was first buried. Although the searchers dug to a depth of 2.4 metres inside the enclosure, which Sergeant had estimated might contain up to twelve bodies, they found only one other. The skeleton was intact but there was nothing to give a clue to his identity, except perhaps the right-half of a pair of glasses, found about a metre away.[3] Skipping Location 3, the bamboo-fenced main cemetery, the team moved further north, towards the 2nd Jungle Camp. About 180 metres past the cemetery, and about 20 metres to the right, they found a bomb crater, also surrounded with bamboo, which Sergeant had estimated contained up to twelve bodies. They found one skeleton only, completely intact but unidentifiable. Before moving on, they continued with their policy of making careful notes and a small sketch map of the grave which, along with a broken pipe found beside the remains, would be forwarded to headquarters.

The next day, while Roberts and Clerk set off for the 110 mile on horseback to try and locate the two known cemeteries and the mass graves of the officers and ORs, the remainder of the team began work at the Number 1 Jungle Camp. The first plot opened revealed the bodies of ten men. It too contained personal bits and pieces — buttons, a magnifying glass, a tobacco pouch, a pipe, a wide brass ring, a small jar of 'Earth Balm' ointment, a piece of broken comb, a water-bottle, an enamel mug and the remains of a peaked cap. But it was the wallet found on the second body exhumed which was the most important find. It was full of currency of various types and denominations and wads of paperwork, including a Will, witnessed by Padre Garland and Air-Craftsman Fred Campling, of South Africa, and signed by Robert John Roberts, an Englishman, all of whom had died at Paginatan. Also in the wallet was a faded French postcard, part of a letter and a notebook, previously the property of Air-Craftsman Donald Elliott who had died at Paginatan on 17 March. It was hoped that this fantastic assortment might be able, on future examination, to assist in the identification of the corpse. In the end, none of it was of any use. The only person alive who knew the identity of the soldier buried with a wallet stuffed full of paperwork was Botterill, who had buried the man, and no one thought to ask him. Indeed, possibly because of Lieutenant McGinley's earlier, cutting remarks, no one thought to ask Botterill anything. Had they done so, they would have discovered that the custodian of the random paperwork belonging to those who had died at Paginatan, was Herb Lytton. They would also have learned the identities of many more, including Cleary, Crease, Murray and five who, inexplicably, had been buried in a small clearing in two separate graves, only a few metres apart.

By 17 July, six days after beginning the search, the unit had exhumed 141 bodies, including 124 from the large Ranau 1 Cemetery. Seventy-seven of them, packed into 33 boonguns, were taken to Tamparuli by native carriers, along with another eight containing records and the three packets of personal effects to be forwarded by registered mail to Macassar headquarters. It would be some time before the accompanying unit personnel returned with a fresh group of carriers, as the round trip took a minimum of nine days.

With work progressing satisfactorily at the northern compound sites, attention swung to the 110 mile area. As there was no accommodation, the workers had to walk the 8 kilometres there and back, a trek which ate considerably into their day. The massacre sites and the second cemetery were found without too much bother but it took some time before they found the first cemetery, containing 41 graves with another four in swampy ground a few metres away. Determined to find the camp records, a detachment camped at the site, but on 5 September, after four days of fruitless digging, the search was abandoned.[4] Meanwhile, the searchers at the Number 2 Jungle Camp located the two small plots where Murray had killed the goat, and a few days later the main cemetery site holding the remains of 30 men, including those of Warrant Officer Kinder, the only person in the whole of Ranau to have a marked grave. The discovery of these two sites brought the total number of bodies recovered from this compound to 46, which was a 100 per cent success rate. Results had not been as good at the Number 2 Jungle Camp where only 166 of the 187 believed to have died there had been accounted for, a deficit of 21.[5] Another body, probably that of an escapee from this camp, was found about 7 kilometres west of Ranau, to the south of the Jesselton track. Numbers were also down at the first compound but a concentrated search eventually revealed the site of the original cemetery on the other side of a gully, 20 metres to the south-east of Reither's grave. It contained 48 bodies, bringing the total for this camp to 169 out of a probable 170. Of the 403 prisoners believed to have died at the three Ranau camps, 382 had been recovered.[6]

The efforts of the war graves units in general did not, however, meet with approval of Sticpewich who, after his brief secondment to 8 Unit, had left for Tokyo, via Singapore, to give evidence to the International Tribunal. In early 1947 he returned to Borneo, expecting to resume his work with 31 Unit, which was still making recoveries in the Sandakan area. Their most recent success had been the discovery of the mass grave out near the airstrip, from which they had recovered the bodies of Tom Burns, Bill Steen and the 21 other Australians, along with the haversack containing Burns' diary and other personal papers.[7] To Sticpewich's chagrin, he was informed quite bluntly that he was not wanted and told to return to general headquarters at Macassar, which he did. After airing his grievances to Major Reavell, he discovered that general headquarters was under the impression he had re-searched the entire North Borneo area. When told this was not the case, the major undertook to allow him to return, provided he put his case in writing. However, by this stage Sticpewich had had enough. Having been 'messed about so much in the past' he announced that he would return home as arranged. Furthermore, he told the major he 'would not tolerate any of the past treatment, as he had no authority for rank' and intended to make a statement, a copy of which would be forwarded.

It was no empty threat. By early March, Sticpewich had laid it on the line, and in writing. While the War Graves Director agreed that, as it was their 'bounden duty to make all possible recoveries', a second search should be undertaken, he noted that Lieutenant Brazier had also recommended a second search. As Brazier had now been demobbed, on 17 March Sticpewich got what he wanted. He would leave for Borneo as soon as practicable and, to make his job when dealing with locals easier, he would be elevated to the rank of lieutenant. He was still in high spirits over his promotion when he ran into Mo Davis in a Sydney pub.[8] On learning that Sticpewich was returning to Sandakan, Mo mentioned that a search of the hollow trunk of The Big Tree, where POWs, including The Turk, had cached their valuables, might be in order. Whether he carried out a search, or whether others had beaten him to it is not known. However, he did, shortly after arrival at the compound, burn The Big Tree to the ground.

Those who regarded Sticpewich as something of an upstart were in for a surprise. He may have been abrasive, self-opinionated and egotistical, and his motives, possibly driven by feelings of real or imagined guilt, may have been open to question, but he was determined to get a result. On 17 June, six weeks after beginning his search, he would recover another 109 bodies. The groundwork was laid by 31 Unit, whose members re-searched the Sandakan cemeteries and also supplied on-going support. Captain J. Burnett had started in April by making a quick reconnaissance of the lower Labuk River to spread the news that the search would take place, check the condition of the track and ascertain what labour and rations were available. By the time Sticpewich, Sergeant E. Bunter, Kanak and three native assistants arrived at Ranau to begin their search on May 4, 31 Unit personnel had established strategic food dumps along the river with enough rice to feed an anticipated labour force of 180.

The searchers found no more remains at the Ranau Number 1 Jungle Camp, which was not surprising as there had been a 100 per cent recovery rate. However, when word circulated that 5 dollars (Malay) would be paid for the recovery of remains, a local policeman came forward with information (obtained the previous day from a villager too timid to be identified) which led them to four bodies, about 7 kilometres to the north-west of the camp near the head waters of the Liwagu River. As no one (apart from Crease, who had been shot at the edge of the jungle on the far side of the Ranau camp) had escaped from the northern compounds, the remains were probably those of prisoners who had tried to escape after Sticpewich had left. Whoever they were, it was clear that all had not died of natural causes. The front section of one skull was smashed in and the jaw and lower facial bones shattered on the other. The cause of death of the other two was not able to be determined.

No bodies were found in the Ranau 1 Camp cemeteries, but Sticpewich did locate one set of remains, along with a dixie and shirt, buried in a shallow grave 200 metres west of the compound, near the place where the Japanese had told Botterill that Crease had been shot. However, as both he and Moxham were in Australia, and as no one ever consulted them about possible identifications, the bones were recorded, and for the next five decades remained, as an 'unknown Empire soldier'. Before quitting the site, the party excavated a slit trench which had been used as a latrine. They found no bodies, but they did recover two mugs, two dixies, two water bottles, one ground sheet and one gas cape.

It was a different story at the Number 2 Jungle Camp where the searchers discovered a large number of bones, evidently brought to the surface by heavy rain and foraging animals. A complete skeleton was found lying on the ground at the extreme edge of the large cemetery and, as there was a bullet hole through the skull, it was deduced that it was one of the seventeen massacre victims. A thorough excavation of the smaller cemetery also turned up numerous relics, sets of false teeth and one set of remains, while another skull (the eighth) was found lying on the ground at the 110 mile, where the ten ORs had been killed. When the entire area was dug up a large number of bones were discovered, but there was still no sign of the ninth and tenth skulls. For some reason, none of the scattered bones collected from the Number 2 Jungle Camp was returned to Sandakan for interment. Instead, they were placed in bags and reburied at the various sites.

On 16 May, when it was obvious nothing further could be found at Ranau, the team began to search the track. Instead of covering 20 metres either side, as Roberts had done, Sticpewich was instructed to extend the distance to 270 metres. Although the search netted twelve bodies not previously located, the four found near Muruk were no more than 13 metres from the path while the headman at Nebutan led them to another five. Acting on information provided by eyewitness Kangas they also found a cranium, all that was left of the POW strangled while on the first rice-carrying party. A kilometre or so further on was the body of another rice-carrier, the one who had been shot on the flat beside the creek. Near the place where Sullivan and Roberts had died they spotted another skull and, after further digging, recovered the rest of the bones and mess gear, lying under a layer of silt. These remains, along with the other eight so far recovered, were each wrapped in a two-metre length of hessian and sent down-river by raft to Paginatan, where they were transferred to prahau by Captain Burnett, who had come up from Sandakan.

If Sticpewich's opinion of the quality of the previous search was low, by the time he left Paginatan it was a great deal lower. While Roberts and Brazier could have been forgiven for missing six skeletons lying in the jungle (whose locations were now disclosed by villagers), Sticpewich could find no excuse for missing 38 complete skeletons buried in the cemetery. On the other hand, Sticpewich was not infallible. Between Paginatan and Sapi, the area which he had insisted on searching in 1946, the team found a number of relics, including a mess tin belonging to the 2/18th Battalion's Alf Lever, and another ten bodies — three near a small shelter and four, one of whom was dressed in a British army uniform, beneath a dead tree. Further down the track, in the area in which Sticpewich had accompanied Brazier, they found 34 more. A final body, recovered at the 16½ mile on the way back to Sandakan, brought Sticpewich's tally to 109 which, when added to another five recovered by 31 Unit personnel between Paginatan and Sandala, made a grand total of 114.

But it was in the Sandakan area that they found the most. The work carried out during the first search was not nearly as exacting as it might have been. By the time 31 Unit re-excavated the two cemeteries and two compounds, another 228 bodies were located, along with a vast number of bones. On reopening the two cemeteries it was discovered that previous workers had often removed only the skulls, arms and leg bones. The remainder of the skeleton, still lying in coffins or on the false-bottom wooden slabs, had simply been left in the ground. Thirty-one additional bodies were recovered from the Number 1 Cemetery, 118 from the Number 2 and a further 76 from the slit trenches in the Number 2 Compound. Three more were found in the Number 1 Compound. Because of the ambiguities in Wong's poorly translated evidence, the recovery teams were still looking for the remains of the prisoner believed to have been crucified, and the discovery of nails alongside one of these last three bodies was noted. When a fantastic story surfaced in a newspaper article some years later alleging that a British POW had been crucified on a tree as punishment for having a bible, there was some speculation that this was the victim, despite the fact that Botterill, to whom the story had been attributed, denounced it as rubbish. Why the nails were beside the body was never established. Perhaps, like so many other POW bower-birds, this man had collected anything which might come in useful some day. Perhaps, like Botterill, who had at one stage swapped his cigarette ration for nails, he saw them as a tradable commodity. Who he was also remains a mystery. But it is likely, since his lower leg had been amputated, that he was one of the hospital patients who died while being moved on 29 May.

Of the 228 remains recovered, only three were identified at the time. Two were found in the Number 2 Cemetery — 27-year-old Neville Porritt, of Victoria, who had died on 20 May and South Australian Edward Robertson, aged 44, who had died five days later. The other was that of Sydney Osborne, a machine gunner from Western Australia, who had died at the Number 2 Compound on 21 June. That he had been found at all was due to a concentrated effort to locate the remains of the unnamed Australian prisoner known to have been beheaded by Murozumi. Although, when the body was finally exhumed, located and the cause of death was obviously by beheading, the fragmented nature of the existing records, along with some very poor translations of Wong's eye-witness accounts, would ensure that his identity (John Skinner) would remain a secret for another 50 years. Three other bodies were also recovered at this time from the slit trenches. A wallet, containing corroded medals and a waterproof watch was found on one of them but unfortunately the inscription 'Concord Good Wishes', engraved on a gold plate on the back of the watch, was too vague at the time to assist with further identification.[9]

So was information which had been received at Paginatan regarding the fate of two escaped POWs, apprehended by pro-Japanese Angkop Gampilo Dulagag Endong, who lived near the 8 mile. Although one, who had not been tied up, had regained his freedom for a short period, he was soon recaptured in a small hut in the jungle and taken with his companion to Nelapak, where he was handed over to the Japanese. What became of him was not known, but according to villagers the other had been murdered at Muruk. As information such as this was not deemed to be of any real significance, it was not included in Sticpewich's report to Lieutenant-Colonel Chapman, Director of War Graves Services, entitled 'Research of Sandakan-Ranau Rentis, Ranau Area and Paginatan'. Under normal circumstances, the news that 109 additional bodies had been recovered should have been grounds for hearty congratulations. Unfortunately Sticpewich's report, while giving details of the recoveries, also commented on a number of other matters, including a scathing assessment of the way in which 8 and 31 Units had carried out their searches. Such carping observations did not go down well with Chapman who noted 'that Lt. Sticpewich is critical of all personnel, except himself, who took part in the previous searches'.

Chapman had good reason to be pleased with the work of all those concerned in the search. When the recovery unit finally wound up its search at Sandakan it had located 1358 bodies, which accounted for all but 23 prisoners known to have died from that camp. However, as some were cremated and another five had died in Kempei-tai custody, the only body they hoped to find but did not, despite a lengthy search, was that of the crucifixion victim (who had been cremated). The final recoveries did not wrap up the work of the War Graves Services. Although a beautifully laid out cemetery, with rows of pristine white crosses inscribed by Corporal Beaumont, had been officially dedicated on ANZAC Day 1947, drainage was found to be a problem, something which came as no surprise to Botterill. In 1949, all the remains were exhumed and transferred to another cemetery at Labuan Island where, in due course, proper headstones, too many of which were marked as simply 'unknown', were erected, along with walls on which were inscribed the names of the missing. Not all the victims were laid to rest. Of the 1787 Australians and 641 British (a total of 2428) known to have perished at Sandakan, Ranau or along the track, 2163 remains were recovered. Of the 300 European and seven Indian soldiers known to have been at Labuan, Brunei and Miri (some of whom were cremated) at least 236 were recovered. While the recovery rate at Ranau 1 and the Number 1 Jungle Camps was 100 per cent, six were still missing from Jungle Camp Number 2. No traces were found of Soorier, the four escapees said to have been tortured to death or another 236 who had died at Paginatan, on the three marches, rice-carrying, or while attempting to escape. While some, especially at Paginatan and the lower section of the track, were washed away by floods and others were scattered by wild animals or died somewhere in the jungle, a good proportion of the missing were undoubtedly those siphoned from the second march to act as coolie labourers and who, consequently, died far away from the track. Unfortunately, information from local people that POWs were being moved along the northern route was never followed up. Neither was a report from an RAAF pilot who had spotted a number of crude graves marked with crosses in a clearing when sweeping low over the Beluran area.

The pledges made by prisoners to the local people who had assisted them were followed up and honoured if possible. That many had placed their lives at risk to succour and assist POWs first came to light in early 1946, when 31 AWGU was approached by villagers bearing chits and testimonials signed by members of the AIF. When the information reached the ears of Colonel Griffin, at the Directorate of Prisoners of War and Internees in Melbourne, he made representations to Frank Forde for an experienced army officer to be sent to Borneo to investigate the claims. On 25 November 1946 Colonel Harry Jackson arrived at 8 AWGU's bungalow on the Menggatal Estate. While he was awaiting the arrival of three other Australians — Colin Simpson (a writer) and Bill MacFarlane (a radio technician) from the Australian Broadcasting Commission, and Major Dyce, currently serving with the British Army — he interviewed his first claimant. Andu bin Patrick, previously a forest scaler from the Experimental Farm, produced a note signed by Rus Ewin attesting that he had provided the Australians at Sandakan, particularly during Christmas 1942, with eggs, pork and other delicacies. The note also said that Andu had given Ewin 100 dollars — a claim that was dismissed when Jackson discovered that this addendum had been written by the claimant himself.

On 4 December the four Australians, accompanied by a baggage train of mostly Dusan coolies to carry provisions and gear in boonguns, set off by jeep for the foot track linking Tamparuli with Ranau. Four days later Jackson made his acquaintance with Baragah, Gunting and Sumping, three of those who had been involved in the rescue of Sticpewich, Botterill, Moxham and Short. The next visitor was Ginssas bin Gungass, who had first harboured Sticpewich. He was so badly affected by beriberi that he could hardly walk, and arrived astride a water buffalo, led by his small son who was almost crippled by the large tropical ulcers on his feet. After they were given medical attention and drugs for on-going treatment, they made they way painfully home, proudly clutching the bundle of money and clothing the Australians had given them. Others then came forward, scarcely able to comprehend that Jackson and his team had come so far to honour the promises of dead men. Two of the most notable informants were Jahan, who brought in the wallet belonging to Wally Read, (whose photograph he identified in Jackson's collection) and Pelula, of Kampong Paka, who handed over a gold locket with a photograph of a woman inside, which a tall, grey-eyed prisoner, aged about 30, had thrown to him in return for five cakes. Pelula did not know the soldier's name but recalled he had very few upper teeth and dark brown hair which was inclined to curl. After MacFarlane had recorded the stories, the colonel gave them clothing, medicines and money, with the assurance they would receive further cash through the British District Officer when the information had been relayed to authorities in Australia and England. While the villagers were grateful for the gifts and pledge of further compensation, the thing which thrilled them most was the promise that all would receive a Certificate of Appreciation, which they called 'Letters of Good Name'.

Women too came forward. Tima's story was typical of many. Sucking her teeth and shaking her head at the memory, she described the prisoners she had seen as

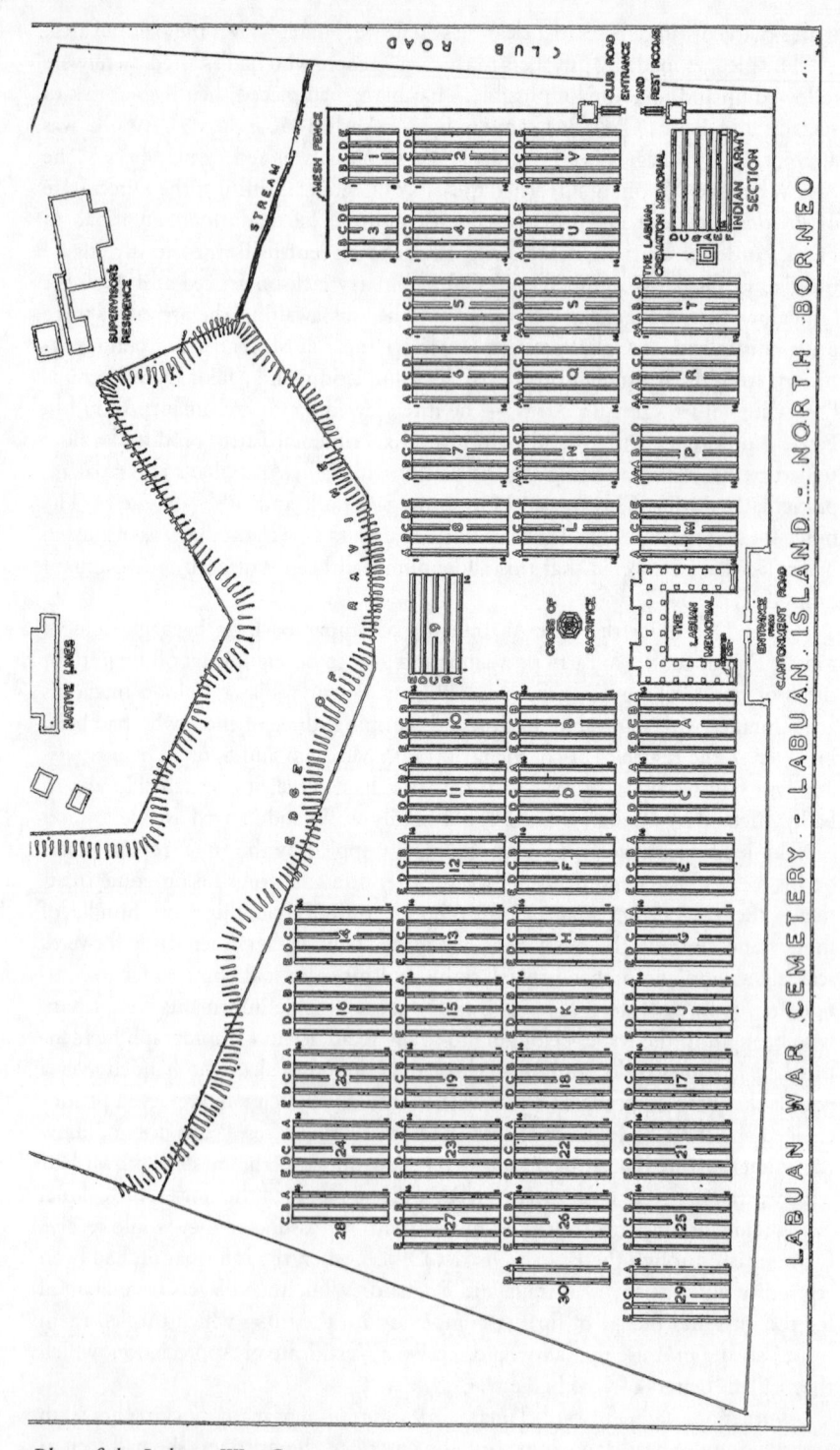

Plan of the Labuan War Cemetery.

'very thin, weak and sick looking...without boots, some without shirts, all had long beards, long hair and walked with bowed heads that swayed from side to side. Whenever they passed they made signs with the fingers and mouths that they were hungry and wanted food'. At Paginatan, which the team reached on 12 December, another woman named Burih told how she had given food to the prisoners as they had passed her house. Her husband had died of malnutrition shortly after the marchers had moved on, leaving her and their small daughter to fend for themselves, so she was undoubtedly grateful for the gifts she received in return for her charity. Leaving Dyce and MacFarlane to continue to Tampias, Jackson and Simpson retraced their steps to Ranau, where Jackson spent two days interviewing another 48 claimants before returning to Tamparuli on 18 December.

The following morning, after making arrangements for payments to the petitioners, he interviewed Halima binte Binting and Halima binte Amat, the widows of Matusup and Wong Mu Sing, who had been executed with Lionel Matthews. Aged only 20 and eighteen years at the time of their husbands' arrests, they now lived near Jesselton — Matusup's widow and their baby with her brother and Mu Sing's widow with a Chinese family for whom she worked in return for her keep. That night another survivor from the Sandakan Incident, sporting highly polished boots, a dashing scarlet sash and a grey serge forage-cap, all of which proclaimed him to be a member of the North Borneo Armed Constabulary, turned up on Jackson's doorstep. It was Sergeant Koram — ex-corporal, conspirator, escapee, saboteur, Japanese census-taker, guerrilla fighter and Allied secret agent, who had more lives than a cat.

Just before the purge in October 1943 which had wiped out the Kinabalu guerrillas, Koram had become ill and returned to his father's house at Pensiangan. As soon as he had recovered he marched off boldly to the nearest Japanese post to 'confess' he had helped eight POWs escape from Berhala Island and offered himself as a spy by way of atonement. Within days he was on a plane to Sandakan. After fifteen days' leave, generously granted by his new employers, he had set about the task of tracking the fugitives who, he had assured the Kempei-tai, were still in Borneo. Six months later he was back at Sandakan, having completed a round trip from one side of Borneo to the other, taking in the major Japanese troop centres of Ranau, Keningau, Beaufort and Jesselton on the way. Reporting that he had seen no sign of the fugitives, he had offered to continue the search, this time to the south. The Kempei-tai agreed, completely unaware that their number one spy was busily sketching Japanese installations and collating information on military movements for the Allies. However, Koram had no hope of getting away with this subterfuge indefinitely. On 1 May 1945 he was betrayed to the Kempei-tai at Segama, near Lahad Datu, on the south-east coast, and arrested. Five days later he escaped, fleeing across the Sibutu Channel to Tawi Tawi, taking his dossiers, reports and sketches with him. Interrogated by Colonel Saurez, he was evacuated to Morotai where he had been recruited by SRD. From mid-July until 13 October 1945, by which time all hostilities had ceased, he was assigned to Agas IV — an information gathering team headed by Rex Blow, which had been inserted into Semporna, on the south-eastern tip of British North Borneo. And now here he was again, proudly bearing Sergeant's stripes to which would be added, in due course, an MBE, in recognition of his outstanding loyalty and service to the Empire.

On the night of 25 December, Christmas Day, Jackson's team sailed on SS *Darval* for Sandakan, stopping off at Kudat to interview Johnny Funk, now working for the public works' department there. Although he was still far from well following his ordeal, he had prepared a lengthy statement with details of the various roles played by those involved with the Sandakan underground. Arriving at Sandakan three days later, the Australians went immediately to the 31 Unit camp, where they found Captain Johnstone had created excellent publicity about their visit by posting notices in English, Chinese and Malay all around the district. Early the next morning Jackson was visited by Magdalene Funk and Mrs Lagan, widows of Alex and Ernesto, and not long after by Sini and his wife Siti. With each interview more and more details began to unfold, enabling Jackson, who worked far into the night, to piece together the vital role played by the local civilians.

From Sandakan the Australians moved by launch to Muanad on 11 January, where Jackson located those who had helped Braithwaite and Campbell after their escape. After a short walk along the track from the 11 mile and an inspection of the overgrown Eight Mile Camp, the team left for Jesselton and home — Simpson and MacFarlane with enough material to make a documentary, which would be broadcast on ABC radio on 31 May, and Jackson with a swag of recommendations. The Australian Government honoured its promises: twenty-two Certificates of Appreciation, 58 demands for cash, including £24.10.0 from Baragah and £39.0.0 from Gunting; rewards totalling £5377.1.2 to people such as Salleh, Surat Min and Apostol, each of whom received £92.18.2; pensions to the widows of all those executed, which ranged from £823. 19.2 for Mrs Lagan, who had been left with four children to support, to £313.10.10 for Mrs Wong Mu Sing and Mrs Matusup who had no dependents. A similar amount was paid to Daiman bin Barano, an SRD runner who had been wounded in 1943 and was still on crutches. Paddy Funk, who had been beaten up and sentenced to six years' imprisonment, wanted no reward or compensation. All he asked for, and received, was £73.0.0, to help with medicine and medical treatment.

Jackson's report was ready by August 1947. Devotees of 'The Serviceman' column in the *Bulletin* were rewarded on the 8th of that month when Ellis printed a precis of the sections which had been made public. However, while Jackson's account was couched in far more emotive and evocative language than anything previously released, there was nothing in the *Bulletin* that had not been said before. A few months later, at the end of 1947, the work of the recovery, inquiry and war crimes teams was over and the mountain of paperwork filed away with the relevant government departments, awaiting removal to archives, where it would be locked up, away from the public gaze, for a minimum of 30 years.

With no way of gaining access to any of the details contained in the voluminous government files, the relatives of the Borneo POWs had to make do with small, pathetic piles of mementos — faded photographs; letters sent home before Singapore's fall; the POW postcards; a few yellowing news reports, the Minister for the Army's 'it is with deep regret' telegram and, for the lucky few, relics recovered from the camps which had been returned to their rightful owners. But what they wanted, above all else, was hard, factual information. Yet it was the one thing they were not going to get, either from the army or any other agency or organisation. However, while the army was motivated by a genuine, if misguided, concern to withhold information from grieving next-of-kin, the motives of SRD's senior officers and General Blamey, to whom they were answerable, were far less honourable. A total of 2428 Allied prisoners, many of whom could have, and should have been rescued from the Sandakan POW camp, had perished. Six only had come out alive — a survival rate of just 0.25 per cent — making it the nation's greatest single catastrophe of the war. If the government, or the public, ever learned the reasons why a full-scale rescue mission, after months of planning, had not taken place, the consequences would be horrendous. The disastrous Kingfisher project must be kept secret at all costs.

As SRD was itself a highly secret outfit, this did not present a problem. Very few inside the organisation knew Operation Kingfisher had ever existed and even fewer knew the details. The only other person besides Blamey and the senior administration who knew precisely what had happened was Gort Chester, and as he had died of blackwater fever at Jesselton shortly after the war, the chances of anything leaking out to the public, or worse, the press, was extremely remote. The paperwork was even less of a problem. Decades later, when the Kingfisher working files were released for public access, they were a model of neatness and organisation. There was no mass of memos, signals, assessments, comments and other potentially-explosive information as found in other SRD files. An account of Special Operations Australia, being compiled by SRD staff as an Official History, was no problem either. A bit of judicious filleting of the Agas 1 documents was all that was needed to wipe months of bungling, ineptitude and poor decision-making from the official record. Anything of a potentially embarrassing nature, such as Gort's comments about the shortcomings of SRD's senior administration or the string of bungles which had affected the Python mission, were also easily fixed. A few deft marks with the editor's blue pencil, along with the instruction 'not to be included in the Official History' and they too no longer existed. By the time SRD administration had finished, Kingfisher existed only on paper, as a rescue plan which had never come to fruition. In the end, the sanitisation of the multi-volumned Official History was an over-kill. Although a brief account of SOA was later published in a volume of *Australia in the War of 1939-1945*, the Australian War Memorial's Official History, the full-length version never made it onto the shelves. Indeed, the public would have remained ignorant for decades, possibly forever, that a rescue mission had ever been contemplated, had it not been for the furore which erupted following a speech delivered at a conference in Melbourne on 19 November 1947.

The occasion was the opening of the 2nd Annual Conference of the Australian Armoured Corps Association and the speaker was former wartime general and ex-SRD chief, Sir Thomas Blamey. Sitting in the audience were members of the paratroop battalion which had been training on the Atherton Tableland for a 'secret mission' when they had been inexplicably stood down before they reached the final briefing. As they had no idea where this mission was to have been or what was involved, they were quite unprepared when, after raising the subject of the Borneo POWs, Blamey dropped a bombshell.

> *We had high hopes of being able to use Australian parachute troops. We had complete plans for them. Our spies were in Japanese-held territory. We had established the necessary contacts with prisoners at Sandakan, and our parachute troops were going to relieve them.*
>
> *The parachute regiment didn't know what was planned, of course. But at the moment we wanted to act, we couldn't get the necessary aircraft to take them in.*
>
> *The operation would certainly have saved that death march of Sandakan. Destiny didn't permit us to carry it out.*

Why Blamey recounted this is unfathomable. Perhaps he was trying to relate to his audience, perhaps he wanted to add a bit of colour to what was an otherwise pretty straightforward speech. However, it is far more likely, in an attempt to deflect questions which might be raised at the conference by the paratroops, that he wanted to ensure once and for all that any blame for failing to rescue the prisoners was directed not at him but at someone else — a scapegoat he had selected more than two years before — America's General Douglas MacArthur.

Of all those involved in the Kingfisher debacle, the person who had most to lose if the facts ever became known was Blamey. A highly-revered, but at the same time often-reviled public figure, Blamey had already been involved in two high-level scandals during the 1930s while serving as Victoria's Chief of Police. The first involved the use of his police badge during a raid on a house of ill-repute — an episode which led to his non-admirers, including an alienated press and, later, his own troops, dubbing him 'Brothel Tom'. The second was far more serious and ended in a Royal Commission. In 1936, having served for eleven controversial years as Victoria's top policeman, Blamey had attempted, for reasons which he never disclosed, to cover up what appears to be a most irregular shooting incident involving the Superintendent of the Criminal Investigation Bureau (CIB). When whispers circulated that the shooting had not been self-inflicted, nor accidental, as had been claimed, an official, top level inquiry was instituted at which Blamey was forced to testify. His performance was less than convincing. In summing up, presiding judge Mr Justice Macindoe had declared 'I tried my best to steer him to the true story, but he was immoveable'. The reason for his perjury was that the reputation of the force which he commanded 'might be endangered if the whole truth was disclosed'. Lying to a Royal Commission did nothing to enhance Blamey's standing with either the Victorian Premier, or a disenchanted public. He was forced to resign.

However, in the twelve years since his demise as Police Chief, he had carved for himself a position of power and influence, as Commander-in-Chief of the AIF. Although he had left the army in 1945, he was well-connected politically and socially, with many friends on the conservative side of politics and just as many enemies on the left. His Achilles heel was SRD, an organisation he had headed and whose reputation, therefore, had to be defended at all costs. Indeed, he had already demonstrated an amazing talent to do so. Immediately after the war he had successfully covered up the series of blunders and security breaches by SRD which had resulted in the enemy receiving regular supplies of stores, ammunition, weapons, gold and money, dropped into Portuguese Timor over a two year period. Eventually, as a result of this negligence, 32 men sent to Timor on various missions had lost their lives. Determined to keep the entire affair under wraps, Blamey had forbidden all SRD personnel to testify at war crimes trials involving Japanese based in Timor, in case word of what had happened leak out. With the prosecution forced to go to trial without a single witness, the defendants, who were facing capital charges, were given gaol terms of three months.

Mid-1945 had been a nightmare period for those controlling SRD. At about the same time they had learned there was a problem in Timor, the Borneo mission had been in ruins. Faced with a calamity of huge proportions, the repercussions for which would be immense, they had begun to lay the groundwork for a massive cover-up. Shortly after SRD realised the extent of the disaster key men outside the organisation, such as the paratroop regiment's commanding officer, John Overall, were led to believe that the rescue plan had been aborted as MacArthur had refused to supply the necessary transportation. There was no reason to disbelieve it. By February 1945, the relationship between the two generals had deteriorated to such an extent that Blamey had written a long letter to Prime Minister Curtin about MacArthur's attempts to undermine his authority. Of course the story told to Overall was arrant nonsense. But those who knew the truth, apart from Gort Chester, were confined to Blamey and a small handful of very senior administrative officers, all of whom had vested interests. Gort Chester, however, had not kept quiet. Infuriated, first by SRD's long-term incompetence and, second, by the steps being taken to cover it up, he had returned to Borneo in May from his Morotai debriefing in such a rage that he had told his trusted companion Jack Sue 'You know what they're going to do? Blamey's going to shift the blame for all their bungling onto MacArthur'. And now, two years later, that is exactly what had happened. It was not much of a gamble. The egotistical MacArthur was not a popular figure in Australia and, in any case, he was now out of the picture, busily restructuring post-war Japan. All incriminating SRD paperwork was locked away, cleverly filed or sanitised, and its personnel dispersed far and wide. Besides, all were bound by an oath of secrecy, an oath so stringent it even prohibited them from disclosing they had been paid 'danger money'. Best of all, the wild card, the outspoken, no-holds-barred Gort Chester, the only person game enough, or senior enough, to have blown the whistle, was dead.

Blamey's announcement at the conference created a sensation. Within hours of its delivery the Melbourne *Herald* had printed a transcript of the relevant part of the speech under the headline 'DESTINY STOPPED P.O.W. RESCUE — NO PLANES SAYS BLAMEY'. The response from an outraged public was predictable and immediate. If what Blamey said was true, and there was no reason to doubt it, who was responsible for denying the planes? An answer was not long in coming. In response to a barrage of questions put to him shortly after his announcement, Blamey expanded on his previous story by declaring that the planes and ships were required by the 'Higher Command' for 'another purpose'. What this purpose was he could not say as it was all very 'hush-hush'. As the 'Higher Command' could only be General MacArthur, and the 'other purpose' could only be attacking targets, which at that stage of the war was not top priority, the hounds were immediately baying for blood. 'If', stormed the RSL's vocal Victorian Branch, 'aircraft were not available when they were wanted by the General Officer Commanding [Blamey], for what must surely have been a more worthy purpose than the speculative bombing of Japanese bases, then the public should be told why.' The demands made by the RSL were soon echoing through the hallowed halls of Parliament House, Canberra. During 'Questions Without Notice' Mr Falkinder, Liberal Member from Tasmania, asked Ben Chifley, now Prime Minister following Curtin's death on 5 July:

> *Has the Prime Minister seen press reports of a statement made by Sir Thomas Blamey to the effect that in 1945 the Australian Command prepared a plan which would have obviated the subsequent tragedy of the 'death march' from Sandakan? That plan involved the employment of Australian paratroops but, according to Sir Thomas Blamey, it had to be abandoned because aircraft were not available. Will the Prime Minister state the reason why aircraft could not be provided at that time and obtain a full report for the information of honourable members?*

Not having the slightest idea that a rescue plan had ever been contemplated, Chifley could not do much, other than state what he knew and stall for time by replying:

> *I have not read any report of such a statement by Sir Thomas Blamey, and I have no recollection of any other report which appeared in connection with the matter.*

He then inadvertently consolidated Blamey's claims by continuing

> *Operations in the Pacific Campaign were carried out under the direction of General MacArthur. I imagine there were many instances in which sufficient planes were not available for the conduct of the war in the Pacific ... at times the number of planes available was extremely small ... Whatever action was taken in the matter ... would, I presume, be taken only after consultation with General MacArthur or the Air Officer Commanding in the South West Pacific. However, I shall make inquiries to ascertain whether there is some information which I can give ...*

The next day, Mr Quealy, from the Defence Secretariat in Canberra, was dispatching copies of Falkinder's question and Chifley's reply (taken verbatim from the unrevised and confidential *Hansard Report*) to heads of various departments. Quealy was then able to receive advice on which to brief the Prime Minister. By 25 November he had learned that 'during the War the Prime Minister, as Minister for Defence, carried Ministerial responsibility for policy for operations which were under the control of General MacArthur'. Furthermore, there was 'no record of the receipt of any report on the matter' to Chifley from Blamey, nor was there any reference to it in operational reports made by the Chiefs of Staff to the Advisory War Council.

Quealy then requested further comments from the Chiefs of Staff. Within 24 hours he had them. They advised that, first, there was no record at Army Headquarters of any personal action being taken by Blamey in the matter.

Secondly, they could find no record of any official request being made to General MacArthur or to Air Marshal Jones at RAAF headquarters for the provision of aircraft for an airborne invasion for the rescue of prisoners of war from Sandakan prior to the death march. Furthermore, although the possibility of carrying out an operation to rescue prisoners prior to the death march was evidently examined at Advanced Headquarters, as the plan did not proceed beyond the planning stage there was no written record of it. The Chiefs, evidently to deflect any criticism which may be directed towards them, then went on to point out that any rescue would have required a far larger force than a paratroop battalion — amphibious landing craft and naval support — and, in February 1945, the date of the first march, there were 1200 enemy troops in the area.

That no paperwork could be found, was true. Blamey, in his role as the Army's operational commander, had a habit of keeping his plans to himself, one of the reasons being so that the Chief of the General Staff, Major-General John Northcott, and the Adjutant-General, Major-General C.E.M. Lloyd, would not inadvertently reveal them to the Minister for the Army, Frank Forde. Furthermore, the Chiefs did not know that it was no use looking in regular departmental files for information about any firm rescue plan, or indeed, for information regarding any undercover activities in which SRD had been involved. For an organisation which indulged in activities about which no outsider, especially a government which might one day be called on to deny all knowledge, must ever know, total secrecy was central to its very existence. The advice received from Air Marshal Jones in Melbourne, who had not been told of the Kingfisher project, was also true. While Air Vice-Marshal Bostock had received his instructions from General Kenny to supply 30 C-47 aircraft when needed, the matter had gone no further as the Kingfisher mission had collapsed long before that stage of the project was ever reached. Furthermore, there was no chance of Bostock enlightening Jones as to what was going on. The relationship between the pair, who had a long-running and bitter feud, was so acrimonious that, if forced to communicate with one another, they did it through an intermediary.

Meanwhile, Malcolm Ellis at the *Bulletin* had taken up the cause with a vengeance. On 26 November, after declaring 'the whole position is a scandal and has always been a scandal', he told his readers that the government had known since 1944 of the situation and had even sent arms and ammunition to assist the POWs in their planned uprising — information leaked to him by Macalister Blain, now back in parliament and sitting on the opposition benches. However, while Ellis' sentiments reflected the public mood, his analysis of the facts was wrong. Unaware that SRD existed, he had made the mistake of thinking its activities were those of the government. Therefore, he accused Chifley of falling back on 'the government's old whine that the conduct of the Pacific campaign was under the command of General MacArthur' and declared that if Chifley could not remember any discussion of plans to rescue the 'unfortunates' of Borneo, he was not fit to be Prime Minister. Warming to his theme, he informed his readers that the plight of the prisoners had been raised at the War Advisory Council by Sir Earle Page, but that the matter had been treated with contempt — an allegation found to be without foundation when the Council's minutes were checked.

The columnist, who made no secret of his conservative political alliances, declared the reason for this lack of interest was because 'Federal Labor' was too busy trying to ensure that it would have 'totalitarian powers after the war to worry about a few POW'.

A week after this outburst Chifley delivered to the parliament the statement Quealy had prepared in response to Falkinder's 'Question Without Notice'.

I am informed by the Army authorities that there is no record at Army Headquarters of the personal action taken by General Sir Thomas Blamey in this matter. The Army authorities state that the records held by them do not disclose any operational plan for the rescue of prisoners of war from Sandakan in 1945.

Also, there is no report or representations by General Blamey to the Prime Minister ... to whom he had the right of direct access and communication on operational matters affecting the Australian Army. Similarly, no report or submission was made to the Advisory War Council by himself or his Deputy. I mention this only to show that the matter did not receive consideration on a governmental level, nor was there any request for representations by the government to the Commander-in-Chief, SWPA [MacArthur] in support of any plan.

What Chifley said was true. No one in government, or wider military circles, had the faintest idea what Blamey was talking about. Blamey agreed. The following day he told reporters in Melbourne that, 'It had nothing whatsoever to do with the Government as it was a matter for the High Command. It was out of the Government's hands.' However, having been made to look a fool by the Prime Minister, he added that 'most people know that Allied High Command operational plans were not submitted to the Australian Government. Apparently Mr Chifley doesn't — so what he has to say doesn't concern me'. Then, to make it quite clear he would enter into no further discussion, he told reporters he had said all there was to say.

On 17 December under the headline 'The Government and Sandakan', Malcolm Ellis examined the question of whether a rescue could have been carried out. His main thrust was that no move had been made to rescue the prisoners, even though, as the maps accompanying his article showed, on 15 January 1945 Allied troops were no further than 400 kilometres away, and in May were within sight of the coast. Furthermore, Macalister Blain, who had been accused by his parliamentary opponents of using his gold pass in an attempt to gain favours from the Japanese, now supplied Ellis with details of the underground which had not hitherto been made public. The Government, Ellis declared, had a lot of explaining to do. In a follow-up article he called for the tabling of Blain's letter to Forde, Steele's report, the reports of all intelligence agents who had been in Borneo from 1943 onwards, and details of the rescue plan mentioned by Blamey.

His demands for an inquiry would never be met. Even had Chifley wanted to embark upon such a course of action, he would have failed. While the government had access to Blain's note and Steele's report, neither of which would have shed any light on the matter, the contents of secret SRD files would never be released to it, let alone tabled in parliament. Consequently, Blamey could say what he liked. He could even lie. In a further attempt to blacken MacArthur's name he told Air Marshal Jones that, while he had not submitted his rescue plan to the Australian government or other authorities, he had raised it with MacArthur, 'who did not favour it'. If Jones wondered what the publicity-seeking American general, who had covered himself in glory following the rescue of the Manila POWs, could possibly hope to gain by taking such a stance, he kept it to himself. Ellis too failed to raise the same question, his right-wing political leanings evidently blinding him to the possibility that Blamey could once more be lying. And so, apart from the Prime Minister, who had received nothing but ridicule for his trouble, no one publicly questioned the veracity of Blamey's claims. With his statements allowed to go unchallenged, General Douglas MacArthur, the commander who had given Operation Kingfisher his unqualified support, the man who had provided the submarines for SRD to carry out its secret operations, who had pledged logistical support for the RAAF's C-47s when the time came and who knew, beyond all doubt, that such a rescue could be pulled off, became the scapegoat for Kingfisher's failure.

The evidence which would have proved otherwise was either in the United States or filed carefully away. While the correspondence confirming MacArthur's support for Kingfisher was in planning files, the copies of the letters from Kenny and Sutherland to Bostock and the RAN, concerning the supply of aircraft and ships for Kingfisher, were in a mountain of general correspondence dealing with mundane matters (such as new tyres for a jeep), where they were destined to become simply two more bits of paper. And while there was other, more accessible paperwork to show that the entire Kingfisher plan had been based on the use of C-47s, 'the one type only available in Australia', it would take days of trawling through maintenance records to prove that when MacArthur was supposedly denying aircraft to Blamey, the RAAF had a pool of no less than 71 C-47s from which to draw the 30 needed for the paratroop assault.[10]

The one person on the outside who knew the truth about Blamey and MacArthur could do nothing. With Gort dead and the evidence he needed quite out of reach, Sergeant Jack Sue was no match for the General. Who, in a country obsessed by the 'yellow peril' to the north, would possibly believe the uncorroborated testimony of the Chinese Jack Wong Sue against the word of an immensely powerful, Anglo-Saxon, highly-decorated general — a general who, on 16 September 1950, despite fierce resistance from the opposition ranks, would be elevated, virtually on his death bed, by a conservative government to the exalted rank of field-marshal?

SRD and Blamey had done their work well. With no evidence, no witnesses and no one to ask any awkward questions, the story of what had really happened was safe.

Sandakan had become World War 2's most deadly secret.

EPILOGUE
Epping NSW

It is just on lunch time, 1 March 1996, as I thread my way past diners in a small, up-market bistro to a corner table where a frail, thin, elderly man is seated in a wheelchair, waiting for me. A pair of very blue eyes, partially shadowed by bushy eye-brows, look up at my approach. They belong to Keith Botterill, Sandakan survivor, who is now terminally ill with emphysema. Seated alongside him is a younger, far more robust man. He is Frank Murray, Richie Murray's son. On the other side of Botterill is Maureen Devereaux, a gentle, compassionate woman whose warm, welcoming smile gives no hint that 55 years before she had stood against the picket fence on Grafton Railway Station, sobbing uncontrollably as her much-loved older brother, John Barnier, went off to war.

It is my close relationship with all three which has brought me here for lunch. It was in 1992, while I was addressing an audience, that Maureen Devereaux had made herself known to me, as the cousin of one of the soldiers who had died on SRD's Operation Rimau, the subject of my then, recently-published, book. While chatting afterwards she had suggested I tackle the Sandakan story as my next project. However, as I was aware several writers had already made an attempt, I told her that unless I discovered something new which would warrant an in-depth investigation, it would have to wait. We nevertheless kept in touch and the following year, as a result of her friendship, I met Keith Botterill, and through him, Murray's son, Frank. At the time of my meeting the two men, our mutual interest lay in the Malayan Campaign, a subject I was currently investigating following allegations earlier that year that Australian cowardice had been responsible for Singapore's fall.

However in 1995, while sitting in on a recorded interview with Keith for the 50th anniversary of the end of World War 2, my interest in Sandakan sharpened dramatically. The young television interviewer, who had obviously not been properly briefed for her assignment, was making heavy weather of it. Keith was quite ill, and his patience was running out, as he tried to get across to her the fact that Sandakan was Australia's greatest tragedy of World War 2. Sitting in an oversized chair, dressed in a natty blue-striped shirt with a white collar, red bow-tie and matching braces, he was finding it difficult to breathe and looked even more frail than usual. As I listened to his attempts to explain the story in the three-minute allocated time-slot, I realised what a terrible burden he had to bear for, although six had survived, only three were left alive.

Bill Moxham who, before the war, had thrived on living dangerously, had been so profoundly affected by the horror he had experienced that he had taken his own life in 1961. Sticpewich had been killed in 1977 in Melbourne while crossing the road. Dick Braithwaite, who had managed to live a more-or-less normal existence with the help and support of his wife, Joyce, the widow of his best friend Wal Blatch, had died from cancer in December 1986. Of the three who were left, Owen Campbell rarely gave interviews and while the extroverted Nelson Short, who would die in October from a heart-attack, was available, his recollections were not as sharp as Botterill's. Ultimately, if the media requested an interview, it was Botterill who shouldered the responsibility for speaking up for his dead mates.

The advice, given to him and all POWs by well-meaning officers post-war, had been to go home and forget all about it. Yet how could he? With a constant stream of Sandakan relatives knocking at his door by day in search of news, and tormented at night by nightmares in which he relived again and again the horrors he had experienced, he could never forget. Although he had tried to live a 'normal' life with marriage and children, the strain had ultimately taken its toll so that for some years he lived by himself. However as time passed he had come to terms with the fact that he was never going to forget, that not a day would go past when he did not think of his mates, especially his best mate, Richie Murray. Consequently, when Frank Murray had tracked him down in 1994 it had been an indescribable moment for both men. For Frank it was being able to put real flesh and blood on the distant, shadowy figure who had been his father, for Keith it had been the joy of discovering that Richie not only had a grown-up son but that he looked very much like him. The memory of Richie Murray, one from the viewpoint of a seven-year old boy, the other from his soldier mate, forged a bond between the two men which ran far deeper than normal ties of blood or friendship.

While I sat on the sofa, out of camera range and waiting for the interview to end, I had reflected how different Keith's life might have been if more of his fellow prisoners had survived; if he had been able to get the support available to say, survivors of the Burma-Thai railway; if he had others to help him tell it how it was to a generation to whom the war of 1939-45 was a very long time ago. Letting my mind drift on what might have been I thought of General Douglas MacArthur, the man history held responsible for the failure to rescue the prisoners. To deny Australia the use of planes to save hundreds of POW lives at a time when the war was winding to its inevitable conclusion, seemed an incredibly callous act — too incredible to be true. It was as if a flashbulb had exploded in my head. Was the story true and if so, what was the proof, and where was it?

And so began an investigation which would take almost two years, an investigation which, once begun, would keep on growing as one piece of evidence led to the next, until the whole sorry picture had unfolded. Some of the information found was already known. Most of it was not. And that which was known was sometimes unreliable. While the survivors' statements were invaluable, Sticpewich's tendency to present hearsay as first-hand experience was a problem. So too were ambiguities and poor chronological arrangement of events in his and many of the other survivors' statements — a difficulty which could only be resolved by comparing one statement with another and with other Allied and Japanese records.

I also found that some long-accepted 'facts' were not facts at all, the most notable being the allegation that a diary kept by 'a foolish officer' (Rod Wells) was responsible for Matthews' death. This allegation, a result of camp gossip and rumour by those who had seen Wells compiling his various reports, had gained great credibility when Sticpewich presented it as fact during a war crimes trial, the transcripts of which then entered the public record. Interestingly, while some thought it incredible that Wells, a highly intelligent man who had taken great pains with security, could be stupid enough to keep a record, written in plain English, in the camp, no one ever asked him about it.

Jack Sue, who had been awarded a Distinguished Conduct Medal in recognition of the great risks he had taken while gathering intelligence on the west coast, was another who had fallen victim to vicious rumour-mongers. Without bothering to check their facts, they declared that he had been on the other side of Borneo when the second death march left and that if he had witnessed it, as he claimed, why did he not do something? Had they had enough decency to confront him, they would have discovered it was the third march he and Gort had seen and that having to stay hidden and do nothing at all had been the hardest thing they had ever done. One other widely believed 'fact', that went by the board early in the piece was the oft-quoted statistic that 2500 POWs had been marched to death — a misconception which had blown the marches, hideous as they were, out of all proportion. Simple mathematics, as well as the body count, showed that the majority had never left Sandakan.

Thoroughly engrossed in my research and living with the story on a day to day basis, I became so conversant with the intimate details of the camp and its inmates that Botterill, aware that his life was drawing to an end, decided that the time had come to tell me everything he knew. A casual remark to him one day, after I had read through the transcripts of the Cleary murder trial, that there was something horribly wrong with the evidence, led to his telling me how he and Moxham had framed Suzuki Saburo for the murder. While some may argue that, in the end, justice, in a rough sort of way had prevailed, my reaction was one of great disappointment. Apart from the moral question of sending someone, no matter how evil, to the gallows for a crime he did not commit, how could Botterill possibly expect me to believe any of his evidence when he and Moxham had lied under oath?

Yet I did, and do, believe him. He now had no reason to lie. Many more details came flooding out — the circumstances of Quailey's death, their perjury at the Arthur Bird murder trial, how he placed Lytton's wallet in his pocket as he buried him, in the hope that when and if he were found he would be identified, the murder of Ron Sullivan and Wal Alberts, and the reason why, at the place where Murray killed the goat, the five bodies were buried in two separate graves. He also set the record straight on rice-carrying, correcting the misconception that dozens died on these trips. But it was the death of Richie Murray, who had sacrificed his life to save the others, which preyed most on his mind. He spoke of his deep affection for Murray, the finest man he had ever met and the only real friend he had ever had, of his despair at never finding his body and giving it a decent burial, of his discovery, through the stoolpigeon in the cell at Rabaul, that it had been tossed into a bomb crater on the track leading back to the large cemetery at the Ranau 1 Camp. Little did either of us imagine that these fine, almost trivial details would lead to perhaps the most amazing discovery of all, the identification of a number of 'unknown' soldiers, including that of his friend, Richie Murray.

It had started out routinely enough. I had been examining diaries belonging to the war graves recovery units when, mixed up with the day to day trivia, such as complaints about the cost of postage, I came across a tatty piece of paper. It was a sketch map — a few simple lines drawn on cheap quality notepaper, giving the barest details of the recovery of a body. Recognising the layout as that of the Ranau camp I took a closer look. Pencilled against a square with a circle inside it were the words 'bamboo fence' and 'bomb crater'. The alarm bells went off. Could this be the bomb crater Botterill had spoken about? There was only one way to find out and that was to reproduce the map, minus the bomb crater, and ask him to mark the spot where he believed Murray had died.

Working on the assumption that the body found there could be that of Murray, I began an immediate search to find paperwork which would enable me to track this particular recovery from Ranau to the Sandakan cemetery and from that cemetery to Labuan. And so began possibly the most difficult and laborious task I had ever undertaken. The first break came when, having been handed a pile of records with which no one had ever bothered, as they were meaningless reference numbers, I located the place at Sandakan where the body exhumed from the Ranau crater had been buried. But the hardest part was yet to come. No one had any idea how to track the Sandakan exhumations to Labuan, the final burial place. Enquiries faxed to the War Graves' Commission in London by Air Vice-Marshal Alan Heggen, Director of the Office of Australian War Graves, drew a blank. It looked as if I had reached a brick wall. However, I refused to believe that such vital documentation no longer existed, a view also shared by Alan Heggen, who gave me written authorisation to access any files I might require to continue my search.

And so I began to sift through recovery records — tens of thousands of them. When the 22 000 or so I started with had been whittled down to about 4000, the search began in earnest. What I needed was to look at every single entry to find the piece of paper which matched the serial number I had found on the tatty archives' map and on the Sandakan cemetery records. Hours went by, but my concentration was such that neither my stomach nor my body noticed the time. When at long last I turned over the sheet whose reference number matched the one in my hand, I could scarcely believe it. However, caution prevailed. If Botterill could not show me the place where Murray had been killed, my efforts would have been wasted — well, not entirely. By this stage I realised that, provided I had enough information, I might be able to identify other 'unknown' soldiers.

A fortnight later, I am about to put my new-found knowledge to the test. A bistro at lunch hour is an unlikely place to finish the investigation, but, should my eyewitness blow my work out of the water, at least it will be on a full stomach. After wining and dining in leisurely style, I show Keith the map on which I have marked the main Ranau 1 Cemetery, the Japanese huts, the contour of the hill and the track linking the camp with the Number 1 Jungle Camp. The only thing missing is any reference to the bomb crater. Handing him a pen, I ask him to mark upon the map the place where he believes Murray was murdered. He looks at the sketch for some seconds. Then, with a shaky hand he draws a cross, to the north of the cemetery and the right of the track, in precisely the place where the bomb crater is marked on the archives' map.

All three — Keith, Frank and Maureen — are looking at me expectantly. What is this all about? Taking a large scale plan of Labuan War Cemetery from my attache case I point to a gravesite to the left of the entrance. 'This is Plot 21, Row E, Grave 7', I tell them. 'It is the place where Frank's father is buried.' No one says anything. The occasion is too momentous for mere words. But I know what it means to Frank. I can see it in his eyes. And I know what it means to Keith, a man who has always found it difficult to demonstrate affection and who recoils from being touched. He leans over and kisses me.

When the shock wears off it is down to business. The evidence will be forwarded to the Commonwealth War Graves Commission in London. If accepted, the 'unknown' plaque will be removed and a new headstone, bearing Richie Murray's details, erected. In due course, Alan Heggen will inform us that the Commission is satisfied that the body recovered from the bomb crater is that of Private Richard Murray.

Encouraged by the result I will begin to comb the files to see whether anyone else can be identified. During 1997, I will identify the general burial sites of all victims and the specific sites of another seventeen. By the end of the year the Commission will accept the evidence and begin organising new plaques. Some, such as the five officers massacred at Ranau, Neil Christie, Herb Lytton, Albert Sheard and Eddie McAppion, I know well. The rest I know very little about. Another 32, including Cleary, Crease, Keith's friend Quailey, John Nicholson and the last of the first march survivors, as well as the 21 Australians murdered with Tom Burns, will, in May 1998, be submitted for consideration.

Although Keith will live long enough to find I have located Lytton, he will not live to see the headstone. Becoming very ill in the latter half of 1996, he will die on the eve of Australia Day 1997. He will, however, hang on long enough to see proof positive that his mate, Richie Murray, has been buried properly, and that there is now a name to his grave. Just as Alan Heggen and the Commission promised, in late 1996 the old headstone to an 'unknown soldier' on Grave 7, Row E, Plot 21 will be replaced with a new one, the words inscribed beneath the Rising Sun badge of the Australian Imperial Forces reading:

NX 33361 Private
R Murray
2/19 Australian Infantry Battalion
20th May 1945. Age 28

Then will follow the epitaph, chosen by his son, Frank. It is only thirteen words in length, but it says it all.

He stepped forward to sacrifice his life for his mates. Lest we forget.

Chronological Sequence of Events

1942

08 Feb	Battle for Singapore Island begins
15 Feb	Allied forces surrender
07 July	B Force leaves Singapore
18 July	B Force arrives Sandakan
late July	Contact made with Sandakan Assistance group
	POWs engage in general camp maintenance, preliminary work at airfield
30 July	1st death at camp. Buried in Sandakan Civil Cemetery
31 July	11 POWs escape
08 Aug	4 escapees recaptured
mid Aug	Camp underground established by Matthews
	Parts for crystal set smuggled into camp
15 Aug	Hoshijima officially appointed camp commandant
25 Aug	2 escapees recaptured
late Aug	Proper airfield construction begins
02 Sep	'Signing Ze Oase' Day
mid Sep	Rails, skip arrive at airstrip
early Oct	Major Suga arrives to inspect camp
	Basher gangs arrive, work load increases
08 Oct	Officers stage 'Radio Rubbish'
09 Oct	British POWs leave Singapore for Borneo
13 Oct	Escapees sent to Kuching for trial
mid Oct	Locals allowed to trade food at airstrip
	Parts for wireless smuggled into camp
	Wells & Weynton begin work on wireless receiver
	Mu Sing contacts Tawi Tawi guerrillas with news of POWs
19 Oct	British POWs arrive Jesselton
25 Oct	Recaptured escapees sentenced to Outram Road Gaol
27 Oct	Walsh and other senior officers sent to Kuching
04 Nov	Radio picks up first transmission
mid Nov	Death toll reaches 14
	Esau constructed, first punishments
early Dec	Opening of 1st stage of airstrip
	Hospital/chapel opened. Art and craft show

1943

early Jan	Arms smuggled from Tawi Tawi secreted near camp
12 Jan	Women and children internees moved from Berhala Is to Kuching
mid Jan	Hoshijima becomes suspicious of Matthews' movements
27 Jan	Remaining 5 escapees arrested
17 Feb	Guards bash Darlington
20 Feb	Young and Brown try to escape
mid March	Male internees transferred from Berhala to Kuching
late March	Young, Brown, Darlington and 5 escapees sent to Kuching
28 March	E Force leaves Singapore
01 April	E Force arrives Kuching. Some senior officers, ORs remain there
08 April	200 British POWs arrive at Sandakan from Jesselton
09 April	Remainder of E Force leaves for Sandakan
14 April	E Force arrives Berhala Is
18 April	Rest of British (576) arrive from Jesselton. All British in camp near airstrip
20 April	Nagai and kitchi guards begin duties at Sandakan
in April	Wells rebuilds wireless, then builds transmitter
30 April	Wallace, Harvey, MacKay escape from main camp
01 May	Officers stage 'Let's Boong It On'.
01 May	New cemetery opened near 8 mile peg
04 May	Mo Davis hits Ali Asar
11 May	Harvey & MacKay recaptured, shot dead
in May	POWs permitted to send a postcard home
26 May	Hoshijima introduces 'Amusing Hours'
30 May	Wallace hides on Berhala
04 June	Dit Party escapes from Berhala compound. 3 flee to Tawi Tawi
05 June	Rest of E Force moves to Sandakan No 3 camp
07 June	Mo Davis, 17 officers and 4 ORs sent to Kuching
mid June	Security at Australian camp strengthened
14 June	3 Berhala escapees arrive Tawi Tawi

313

26 June	Wallace and rest of Dit Party leave Berhala Young, Brown, Darlington and escapees sentenced to Outram Road Gaol
27 June	British officers accept invitation to visit Japanese canteen
30 June	Wallace and rest of Dit Party arrive Tawi Tawi
17 July	Underground betrayed. Arrests begin
22 July	Australian camp raided. Matthews and others arrested
24 July	Wells arrested. Hands over transmitter
late July	Many other arrests. Radio discovered. POW rice ration cut as punishment
in Aug	Interrogations, arrests continue
16 Aug	All but 9 of 40 British officers transferred to Kuching
18 Aug	British POWs move from airstrip to No 2 Compound
Sep	Attempted uprising in Dutch Borneo
06 Oct	Python party arrives in Borneo
10 Oct	Double Tenth uprising in Jesselton
16 Oct	Fitzgerald beaten up. All but 8 Australian officers transferred to Kuching
17 Oct	E Force amalgamated with B Force
25 Oct	Those arrested over Sandakan Incident transferred to Kuching for trial
early Dec	Chester pledges help to Qwok and Kinabalu guerrillas
19 Dec	Qwok surrenders

1944

18 Jan	Sub arrives with Python's stores. Qwok's arms left behind
19 Jan	Brandis, of Python, goes missing
24 Jan	Qwok and his men executed
09 Feb	Brandis arrested by kempei-tai
15 Feb	SRD receives first report from Python regarding POW camp
16 Feb	Japanese discover that Python party is in Borneo
29 Feb	Main Sandakan conspirators tried at Kuching. Sentenced to death or imprisonment
02 Mar	Matthews and 8 local men executed by firing squad
March	Japanese step up search for Python
13 Mar	3 Berhala escapees return to Australia with report on POW situation.
24 Mar	Rudwick, McKenzie captured
April	Python still at large. Several rescue attempts bungled
05 May	1st proposal to rescue POWs floated at SRD
08 June	Python rescued
early June	Rice deliveries to Sandakan cease. POW rice ration cut to 275 grams 100 POWs from British camp transferred to Labuan with Nagai
16 June	Nagai's party arrives Labuan
June	Conditions at Sandakan begin to deteriorate
July	Cook requests Hoshijima to build another punishment cage
5 July	Plan for rescue of POWs submitted to SRD by Chester
01 Aug	Plans for Operation Agas and rescue drawn up
15 Aug	200 POWs arrive at Labuan from Kuching
18 Aug	Agas team begins training
22 Aug	Agas plans, not forwarded by AIB to MacArthur for approval, returned to SRD for amendment
Sep	Camp canteen closes and trading with local people ceases Third cage now in operation Air raids begin on Sandakan town and airstrip Large POW sign placed on ground at camp
25 Sep	Amended plans for Agas submitted
early Oct	Chester requests high priority reconnaissance photos of Borneo coast
11 Oct	Agas plans finally approved. Monsoon has begun. Deferred until January
20 Oct	Americans invade Philippines.
30 Oct	American aircraft strafe Sandakan camp. Three Australians killed
early Nov	Complex rescue plans drawn up
in Nov	Sick POWs moved from Number 3 Compound to main camp Cook confines 8 POWs to the cage 'for the duration'
06 Dec	Chester's request for photos finally forwarded but sent to wrong agency
14 Dec	American POWs murdered during US invasion of Palawan
15 Dec	All Sandakan rescue plans approved by MacArthur
December	POW deaths begin to escalate. Coffin-making ceases

CHRONOLOGICAL SEQUENCE OF EVENTS

25 Dec	Heavy air raid renders airstrip inoperable
26 Dec	POWs sent to clear unexploded bombs from airfield
28 Dec	Another heavy raid closes airstrip
30 Dec	3 captured Python men hanged at Jesselton

1945

early Jan	All work on airfield ceases
06 Jan	AIB realises Chester's photo request sent to wrong agency
07 Jan	Agas arrives Fremantle to leave for Borneo, but no submarine arranged
10 Jan	Rice ration to POWs ceases. Now reliant on accumulated stores. Quota set at 70 grams
16 Jan	Agas leaves for Borneo without photographic reconnaissance
17 Jan	Apple party inserted into Dutch Borneo
28 Jan	First of 455 POWs set out from Sandakan for Ranau in 9 groups
28 Jan	Agas arrives Borneo but believes insertion point under Japanese control. Agas returns to Australia
06 Feb	POWs in Philippines rescued by 'Flying Column' on MacArthur's orders
during Feb	Paul Muir monitors signals from secret agent re movement of POWs Owen Campbell has encounter with secret agent near Sandakan camp
mid Feb	Marchers from groups 1-5 arrive Ranau. 70 die on way
mid Feb	Groups 6-9 arrive at Paginatan. 44 die on way
22 Feb	Rice carrying between Ranau-Paginatan begins
24 Feb	Agas leaves Darwin for another attempt to enter Borneo
25 Feb	Nagai arrives at Ranau from Labuan
in Mar	Death toll escalates at Ranau, Paginatan, Sandakan.
01 Mar	Crease and Cleary escape from Ranau
03 Mar	Agas sets up base to north of Labuk River
4 Mar	Orr shot dead at Sandakan
06 Mar	112 survivors from 300 sent to Labuan move to Brunei.
12 Mar	Cleary recaptured
13 Mar	Crease recaptured
14 Mar	Crease shot dead at Ranau
17 Mar	Hoshijima receives orders that all POWs are to be eliminated
20 Mar	Cleary dies at Ranau
26 Mar	Survivors of groups 6-9 (50-60) leave Paginatan for Ranau
30 Mar	Groups 6-9 arrive at Ranau.
late Mar	Local Agas agents begin to gather information on POW camp at Sandakan
03 Apr	Agas signals SRD that all POWs have been moved from Sandakan
16 Apr	Movement of POWs 'confirmed'. Rescue mission cancelled.
mid Apr	At Sandakan, British moved to wired section of Australian camp. Reports of heavy Japanese build up at Ranau
25 Apr	Ranau airstrip bombed and strafed by Allied aircraft. 2 POWs killed
27 Apr	56 Ranau survivors move to jungle camp
late Apr	Nagai transferred from Ranau
01 May	Australians invade Tarakan
08 May	81 survivors from Labuan party moved from Brunei to Kuala Belait
17 May	Hoshijima relieved as camp commandant. Replaced by Takakuwa
20 May	Murray murdered at Ranau
21 May	Chester reports to SRD in Morotai that all POWs now at Ranau. Discovers MacArthur is to be made scapegoat for bungled rescue mission
23-26 May	Allied air force attacks 'empty' Sandakan camp. A number of POWs killed
27 May	Combined air-sea attack on Sandakan. 51 Kuala Belait survivors moved to Miri
29 May	536 POWs sent on 2nd march to Ranau. 288 sick left behind
07 June	Allied aircraft strafe marchers on track. Campbell and four others escape from march
08 June	Allied warships reported off west coast of North Borneo. Miri POWs moved to deeper into jungle
09 June	Braithwaite escapes from 2nd march.
10 June	Australian 9th Division lands on Labuan
10 June	Miri POWs massacred

315

10 June	10 'fit' Ranau POWs moved to new jungle camp, south of village. 8 too sick to move are massacred	01 Aug	10 POWs alive at Sandakan 17 ill POWs massacred at Ranau
14 June	Braithwaite rescued by American PT boat. Reports POWs still at camp.	07 Aug	Ripley finally arrives Lansat, N-E of Ranau, after six-week trek.
15 June	75 POWs leave Sandakan on 3rd march	09 Aug	Local SRD agents reach Sticpewich, but Reither died day before
21 June	SRD sends Ripley into Borneo to check on Ranau POWs	12 Aug	Ripley ordered to cease all activity
25 June	Chester and Sue see last 4 left alive from 3rd march at 40 mile peg.	14 Aug	2 POWs alive at Sandakan. One dies during night
28 June	183 survivors of 2nd march arrive at Ranau. Only 6 from 1st march left alive	15 Aug	Murozumi beheads last Sandakan POW Japan surrenders to the Allies Australian Army at Tarakan prepares plan to rescue Sandakan POWs
end June	Blow sent to check on Sandakan camp. Takes word of locals that all have left. Moritake crucifies British officer.	17 Aug	Surrender leaflets dropped at Sandakan, Ranau and along track
02 July	Attempted assassination of Japanese officers at Ranau	18 Aug	Agas reinforcements parachute into Lansat
07 July	Botterill, Short, Moxham, Anderson escape from Ranau. 100 left alive	20 Aug	Sandakan camp abandoned. Australian HQ learns all POWs there are dead and cancels rescue mission.
08 July	Ripley leaves Pitas to attempt rescue of Ranau POW		
13 July	23 POWs murdered at Sandakan	22 Aug	2nd set of surrender leaflets dropped at Ranau
17 July	Moritake dies		
24 July	Campbell rescued by flying boat. Confirms POWs left at Sandakan.	24 Aug	Agas party rescues Botterill, Short and Moxham.
26 July	RAAF finally learns POW may still be at Sandakan, on track. Attacks cease.	27 Aug	Massacre of rice carrying parties near Muanad Massacre of last 15 left alive at Ranau. Japanese abandon Ranau camp.
28 July	Sticpewich and Reither escape. 40 POW left alive at Ranau	20 Sep	4 Ranau survivors evacuated by air to Labuan
29 July	Anderson dies at jungle hide-out		

Appendix 1: Nominal Rolls

Sandakan, Ranau and Track Deaths

The Nominal Rolls of the 1787 Australians and 641 British known (or believed) to have died in Sandakan, Ranau or on the track, have been compiled from many primary sources, including translations of Japanese records. The records for the Australian POWs are quite extensive and consist of information collated from record cards held at Kuching, records found at various camps, death certificates, running sheets, and a death roll. Unfortunately, records relating to British POWs are not nearly as comprehensive.

Evidence from survivors and the identification of various remains show that the Australian records are generally reliable. However, some entries on the death roll (a document hastily compiled on the orders of 9th Division shortly after the Australians gained control of the west coast), are a complete fabrication. Translations show that, while death roll entries compiled from records held at POW headquarters or from information relayed directly from a POW camp, are accurate, all death roll dates relating to deaths at the Number 2 Compound for June and July, when communication to HQ was restricted, or for those who escaped or 'disappeared', are not. On the other hand, death roll dates (the only record available) for Ranau after Dr Jeffrey became ill, and before the arrival of the second march, appear to be accurate and agree with information provided by survivors. All Ranau death roll dates between 26 June and 29 July are accurate and agree with all other records. Those for August are false.

Records often include date of birth, as well as full name, rank, nationality, POW number, date of onset of illness, place and date of death. The format differs slightly, depending on whether the record is classified as a 'Diagnosis Sheet of Dead Person' or a 'Certificate of Identity'. An analysis of surviving paperwork shows that those signed by Captain Takakuwa relate to POWs on the second march despite the fact that, for many of them, the place of death is given as East Coast Residency and/or Sandakan.

Owing to the fragmented nature of British records some information is conflicting or uncorroborated. In these cases the data deemed to be the most accurate has been selected. *Note*: The British were moved from the airstrip on 18 August 1943, and to the Number 1 Camp in April 1945, about six weeks before the second march left. The date selected for this latter move for the purposes of this roll is 15 April. Note also that for a large number of British POWs there is no information other than the death roll.

An analysis of corroborated information (that is, any information not marked as being Death Roll only) shows that place of death and date fall into line with expected numbers. For example, it is known that there were 2428 who died at Sandakan, on the track or at Ranau. The number who left on the two marches was 455 (first) and 536 (second). As eight returned (three from first and five from second), another 75 left on a third march, at least ten died outside the camp (escaped or at the hands of the Kempei-tai) and one was cremated by the guards, the number of POWs who die at Sandakan should be in the vicinity of 1359 (NB: remains of 1358 have been recovered). If the questionable numbers are added to the firm Track/Ranau deaths, these totals also fall into line. Nevertheless, it is not possible to establish where these occurred nor determine how many of the dates are false. However, from the information available on the Australians, it appears that the majority of those who went on the third march were British.

As much of the information used to compile these rolls was not available in 1946, details may be different from the officially accepted records. Where additional details, provided by survivors or gathered from investigation documents, dovetail with other records, they have been included.

The Nominal Rolls for Sandakan, Ranau and the track have been compiled under the headings which follow.

Name: name of POW.

Force (Australian Roll): the force to which the POW was attached — B or E, from Singapore; J/E for those captured in Java and then sent to Kuching, where they joined E Force. 'Br' has been added to the two Australians who remained in the British camp. (The third was transferred to Labuan.)

— (British Roll): An 'A' or 'R' indicates whether the POW was British Army or RAF.

State (Australian Roll only): the state in which the POW enlisted (including one from New Guinea–NG), or, in the case of the sailors, RAN (Royal Australian Navy); and the lone airman, RAAF (Royal Australian Air Force).

Number: the POW number allotted to each prisoner by the Japanese. Some postcards sent by POWs bear this number on the top right hand corner.

Age: age at death.

Date: date of death, taken either from death certificates, POW record cards or, in a few cases, the death roll. The death roll alone is not reliable. Where no further corroborative evidence is available, all entries marked with 'DE' should be treated with caution.

Place: place of death. (See Key to Roll).

Buried: place where body would have been buried or recovered. (See key below to identify where body may have been recovered. To find where bodies are currently buried, see Burial Table.)

Key to Roll

Abbreviations used in several columns:
1M: first march
2M: second march
K: known to have been killed
DR: death roll. Only known record is death roll, which may be true, or a complete fabrication in one or more elements.

Abbreviations & place names, under heading 'Died': (refer to map and Burial Table for further details) NB: names are phonetic and may vary from current-day spelling. Alternate spellings appearing on documents are in brackets.
Boto: (Borto), 103 miles from Sandakan
B'uran: Beluran (Turn off at 42mile)
Celo: (Celio, Sesilo, Shiro Shiro), a tributary of Sapi River, about 85 miles from Sandakan
Dusan: (Duson), tributary of Labuk, 33 miles from Sandakan
ECR: East Coast Residency. This refers only to POWs who died on the second march. The place of death is somewhere on track between Sandakan and Ranau. To calculate approximate location, refer to the section dealing with the second march in the text, which gives a general idea of the progress of POWs along the route. However, as some POWs were made to labour along sections of the track, not all will have progressed with the main body.
K: known to have been killed
Kemansi: a village near Telupid (not to be confused with Kemansi Estate, on the lower reaches of the Labuk)
Kolapis: a tributary of the Labuk which crosses the track about 45 miles from Sandakan
m: miles (fr=from, e=east, w=west)
M'adai/M'ai: Mankadai, west of Milulu
M'atto: Murawatto, in vicinity of 42 mile peg, near the track to Beluran
Melio: (Malio, Mairu), a rest house on Melio River, west of Gumbaron and east of Telupid
M'kau: Murakau, about 2 miles east of Ranau
M'ngan: Maringan (Murikan), east of Tampias
M'rin: Mandorin (Mandoring, Mandrin, Mandarin), a tributary of the Labuk, about 60 miles from Sandakan
Muanad: (Moynard, Murnard, Munyed), a tributary of the Labuk, 49.5 miles from Sandakan. The place where track crosses river was known as Tangkul Crossing
M'ulu: Milulu, a high mountain range between Melio staging post and Tampias
Muruk: (Muraked, Muroko), 8 miles east of Ranau
N'pak: Nelapak (Nelapad, Narapa, Naraba, Neraba), 12 miles east of Ranau

nr: near
N'tan: Nebutan (Nopitan) approx 15 miles east of Ranau
Pag: Paginatan, 26 miles east of Ranau
Pag-Ran: died between Paginatan and Ranau while moving to Ranau 1 Camp with groups 6-9, first march
Papan: see Tapang
Pint'an: Pinintalangan (Pintadakan), about 80 miles west of Sandakan, to west of Tuanintin River
Ran: Ranau, 164 miles from Sandakan township, 156 miles from the Sandakan POW camps
Ran 1: Ranau 1 Camp (near the airstrip)
Ran1J: Ranau Number 1 Jungle Camp (near Sinarut)
Ran 2J: Ranau Number 2 Jungle Camp (near 110 mile peg, Tambunan track, about 5 miles south of Ranau)
RC: may have died during rice carrying from Ranau-Paginatan, as date of death coincides with one of the trips.
San 1: Sandakan Number 1 Camp
San 2: Sandakan Number 2 Camp *(Note:* The British moved from this camp to the Number 1 Camp on about 15 April 1945. All survivors left behind after the second march then moved back again, to a wired section of the Number 2 on 29 May)
San 2A: original Number 2 British Camp, at airstrip
San 3: Sandakan Number 3 Camp
Sandala E: Sandala Estate, 12 miles from Sandakan township
Segindai: (Segendai, Shigindai), about 18 miles from Ranau, between Nelapak and Paginatan
Tan'tin: Tuanintin (Tuaninting, Tuanting, Tanintin), a tributary of the Sapi River, approx 80 miles from Sandakan
Tapang: (Papan), a tributary of the Labuk between the Telupid and Baba Rivers
Telupid: (Telupit), a tributary of the Labuk River, west of Boto
T'ias: Tampias (Tampios, Tanipiyasu), on tributary of Labuk River, east of Paginatan
?: information (date and/or place) is suspect

Abbreviations under heading 'Buried':
died: according to Sticpewich, the POW died or was killed on track
d out: According to Sticpewich, the POW dropped out of the march. It is not possible to establish whether the POW subsequently died or was killed.
KG: known grave, (body recovered, identified and reburied in Labuan Cemetery). For grave location, see Labuan Burial Register, Office of Australian War Graves.
KG (New): body recovered and buried, but only

recently identified following research by author. For new grave locations, see Burial Table, this book.

Jungle: POWs known to have died in the jungle. No bodies, apart from a small group at Kemansi village, were recovered away from the track.

MS: massacre sites, Ranau Jungle Camp 2 (i.e: site of massacre of Other Ranks at the 111 mile or the sick at the Ranau Jungle 2B cemetery — see below).

ORs: Other Ranks' massacre

Pag Cem: Paginatan Cemetery. For deaths close to Paginatan, see Burial Table, 'Track, Paginatan'.

Presumed: for records purposes, based on last known information, the DOD has been presumed by Australian Army Records

Ran 1A: first cemetery at Ranau 1 Camp, used until about 15 March 1945.

Ran 1B: main cemetery Ranau 1 Camp, used from approximately 16 March 1945 — 29 April 1945.

Ran 1J: covers all burials at the Ranau 1 Jungle Camp (Sinarut).

Ran 2JA: first cemetery, near Japanese hut, at Ranau Number 2 Jungle Camp. In use from 11 June until approximately 9 July 1945

Ran 2JB: main cemetery, Ranau Number 2 Jungle Camp. In use from approx. 10 July 1945.

RC: may have died on one of rice-carrying trips. If so, any remains recovered will be under Track Recoveries, Paginatan-Ranau, in Burial Table.

San 1: Number 1 Cemetery Sandakan (on crest of hill, eastern side of track leading to Number 1 Compound, near 8 mile post). First Australian burial (cremated remains), May 1943. Prior to this date, all burials at Civil Cemetery in township. In use until about 23 March 1945.

San 2: Number 2 Cemetery, Sandakan (on eastern side of track, on hillside, just before boiler house). First known use 23 March 1945. In use until 29 May 1945.

San 3: slit trenches in Number 2 Compound. Burial site of all those who died after 29 May, with the exception of Captain Mills, those massacred near the airstrip, escapees and the 75 who went on the third march.

San 4: slit trenches near airfield where 23 were massacred. See note re massacre victims under Burial Table.

S3/Cpd: San 3 or slit trenches in Number 1 Compound, where some of those who died being moved to Number 2 on 29 May were buried.

TR: track recoveries along the Sandakan-Ranau route.

?: information (date and/or place) is suspect

Abbreviations under 'other details':

ae: cause of death given as acute enteritis

air raid: died as result of Allied air raid

appen: cause of death given as appendicitis

bb: cause of death given as beriberi

bay: bayonetted to death

bomb: died as a result of an Allied bomb

bro'itis: cause of death given as bronchitis

cbb: cause of death given as cardiac beriberi

cge: died after being put in cage

CI(British roll only): available information is conflicting

dys: cause of death given as dysentery

ewb: cause of death given as exhaustion of whole body, impossible to walk on foot, and although nursed by the member of medical department, not recovered and died

enc: cause of death given as encephalitis

false dod: false date of death (covers all deaths at Ranau after 29 July. Dates prior to this are correct)

esc: escaped

gas ulcer: cause of death given as gastric ulcer

heart f, h f: cause of death given as heart failure

jaund: cause of death given as jaundice

K: known to have been killed

m: cause of death given as malaria

m men: cause of death given as malarial meningitis

u/ulc/ulcer: cause of death given as tropical ulcers

No detail: no other information found

pneu'ia: cause of death given as pneumonia

RC: known to have died while rice-carrying

RO: relic found at other location (see Relics)

RR: relic found at Ranau

RS: relic found at Sandakan

RT: relic handed in by locals — may have been found anywhere from Sandakan to Ranau.

shot: known to have been shot dead

Australians (1787 names)

Note: aka= 'also known as', the name in which the POW enlisted

NAME	FCE	STATE	POW	AGE	DIED	PLACE	BURIED	EXTRA
ABBOTT, E.A.	B	NSW	390	24	21/01/43	SAN I	KG	RR/enc
ABFALTER, P.J.	B	VIC	378	26	26/03/45	SAN I	SAN 2	m
ADAIR, J.	B	NSW	395	24	22/02/45	SAN I	SAN I	ae
ADAM, J.C.	E	NSW	1567	28	26/05/45	SAN I	SAN 2	m
ADAMS, H.	B	NSW	401	43	14/06/45	ECR	TR	2M/ae
ADAMS, T.	B	NSW	385	40	19/06/45	M'NGAN	TR	2M/m
ADDISON, P.R.	B	NSW	405	26	15/05/45	RAN IJ	RAN IJ	RR/m
ADLINGTON, N.C.	B	VIC	408	26	12/02/45	4m N'PAK	TR	IM/cbb
AINSWORTH, T.L.	B	WA	404	24	09/06/45	ECR	TR	2M/m
ALBERTS, W.	B	VIC	379	26	31/03/45	20m RAN	TR/K/RC	IM/RC
ALBRESS, A.S.	B	QLD	376	41	19/06/45	37m RAN	TR-killed	2M/m
ALLAN, L.B.	B	NSW	384	24	21/02/45	SAN I	SAN I	m
ALLEN, J.M.	B	NSW	135	44	23/07/45	RAN 2J	RAN 2JB	2M/ae
ALLEN, S.J.	B	NSW	391	23	07/06/45	ECR (2)	TR	2M/m
ALEXANDER, E.C	E	NSW	1569	26	07/04/45	RANI	RAN IB	M
ALLIE, N.R.	E	NSW	1570	26	10/06/45	RAN IJ	RAN IJ	IM/K
ALLINGHAM, M.A.	B	VIC	403	31	08/04/45	SAN I	SAN 2	m
ALLNUTT, S.G.	B	VIC	136	40	20/05/45	SAN I	SAN 2	m
AMBROSE, G.	B	NSW	379	24	28/04/45	SAN I	SAN 2	m
ANDERSON, A.	B	NSW	402	39	11/05/45	SAN I	SAN 2	RS/m
ANDERSON, E.R.	B	VIC	377	25	09/02/45	SAN ?	SAN ?	DR/m
ANDERSON, F.D.	E	QLD	1571	25	28/07/45	RAN (esc)	KG	'ANDY'
ANDERSON, J.F.	B	NSW	386	39	10/06/45	SAN 2	SAN 3	m
ANDERSON, P.A.	B	VIC	282	35	25/02/45	RAN I/RC	R IA/TR	IM/ae
ANDERSON, W.O.	J/E	NSW	1568	23	25/12/44	SAN I	SAN I	mm
ANDREWS, S.	B	NSW	387	24	05/05/45	SAN I	SAN 2	m
ANNAND, D.	E	NSW	1566	35	14/04/45	SAN I	SAN 2	m
ANNEAR, L.J.	B	NSW	381	24	20/02/45	SAN I	SAN I	CAGE/m
ARCHARD, C.	E	NSW	1572	24	14/07/45	RAN 2J	RAN 2JB	2M/m
ARCHIBALD, G.R.	E	NSW	1573	37	31/03/45	SAN I	SAN 2	dys
ARGO, D.N.	B	VIC	398	24	25/05/45	SAN I	SAN 2	m
ARMSTRONG, F.	B	WA	1467	31	30/07/42	SAN I	KG	ulcer
ARMSTRONG, J.W.	B	NSW	407	24	12/07/45	RAN 2J	RAN 2JB	2M/m
ARMSTRONG, R.W.	B	NSW	406	26	07/05/45	SAN I	SAN 2	m
ARMSTRONG, T.E.	E	NSW	1574	23	13/05/45	RAN IJ	RAN 2J	IM/m
ARNOLD, J.H.	B	NSW	393	44	05/04/45	SAN I	SAN 2	m
ARNOLD, L.R.	B	VIC	380	22	04/06/45	ECR	TR	2M/m
ARTHUR, H.A.	B	QLD	399	28	11/06/45	SAN 2	SAN 3	m
ARTHUR, R.G.	B	QLD	400	28	05/06/45	46m SAN	TR	2M/ae
ASGILL, C.C.	B	NSW	383	25	17/07/45	SAN ?	SAN ?	DR/m
ASHBY, F.R.	B	VIC	394	38	15/03/45	SAN I	SAN I	m
ATTENBOROUGH, A.	B	WA	392	28	12/04/45	RAN I	RAN IB	RR/ae
AULD, R.J.	E	NSW	1575	30	05/06/45	42m SAN	TR	2M/ae
AVICE, S.	E	NSW	1576	25	21/01/45	SAN I	SAN I	m
AYRES, C.H.	B	NSW	396	31	10/04/45	SAN I	SAN 2	m
AYTON, A.C.	B	TAS	388	24	15/02/45	2m e T'IAS	TR	IM/cbb
BACCUS, A.A.	E	NSW	1579	28	23/05/45	SAN I	SAN 2	M
BACON, S.T.	B	VIC	389	31	20/06/45	SAN 2	SAN 3	RS/m
BADGERY, B.L.	B	NSW	156	30	30/03/45	SAN I	SAN 2	m
BAGNALL, N.W.	B	NSW	442	23	05/05/45	SAN ?	SAN ?	DR/m
BAGUST, R.H.	B	NSW	457	23	18/07/45	SAN 2	SAN 3	m
BAILEY, E.G.	B	NSW	140	32	05/06/45	42m SAN	TR	2M/ae
BAILEY, I.S.	B	NSW	445	23	04/12/44	SAN ?	SAN ?	DR/m
BAILEY, N.E.	B	WA	485	24	10/06/45	SAN 2	SAN 3	m
BALDING, H.M.	B	VIC	138	45	03/04/45	SAN I	SAN 2	m
BALGUE, D.N.	B	QLD	509	24	04/06/45	ECR	TR	2M/m
BALL, C.G.	B	QLD	505	24	04/06/45	ECR	TR	2M/m
BALLARD, G.M.	B	NSW	441	22	23/03/45	SAN I	SAN 2	-
BANCROFT, E.D.	B	QLD	148	25	10/06/45	SAN 2	SAN 3	m
BARAGWANATH, W.	B	VIC	474	25	19/03/45	PAG	PAG CEM	IM/ae
BARBER, G.K.	B	QLD	456	37	08/12/44	SAN I	SAN I	CGE/mm
BARKER, D.T.	B	QLD	496	25	07/06/45	SAN 2	SAN 3	m
BARKER, G.J.	B	SA	432	29	03/03/45	RAN I/RC	R IA/TR	IM/ae
BARKER, J.H.	B	QLD	507	28	15/02/45	2m e T'IAS	TR(IM)	RT/cbb
BARKLA, E.A.	B	SA	141	44	07/06/45	SAN 2	SAN 3	m
BARLOW, W.J.	B	VIC	498	28	07/06/45	ECR	TR - died	2M/m
BARNARD, L.G.	B	QLD	421	24	18/03/45	RAN I/RC	R IB/TR	IM/bb
BARNES, K.G.	B	VIC	431	37	01/05/45	SAN I	SAN 2	m
BARNES, Reginald	B	VIC	446	26	07/03/45	SAN I	SAN I	RR/m
BARNES, Ronald	B	QLD	146	25	14/02/45	SAN I	SAN I	m
BARNIER, J.N.	B	NSW	424	25	12/06/45	SAN 2	SAN 3	m
BARRATT, R.H.	B	VIC	499	35	10/12/44	SAN I	SAN I	mm

Name		State	No.	Age	Date	Loc1	Loc2	Notes
BARRIE, J.	B	NSW	?	56	15/06/45	ECR	TR - d out	2M/m
BARTILS, G.H.	B	VIC	447	31	21/06/45	ECR	TR	m
BASTIN, J.C.	E	NSW	1500	37	17/03/45	SAN I	SAN I	m
BATES, A.E.R.	E	NSW	1580	24	26/03/45	SAN I	SAN 2	CGE/m
BATESON, D.F.	B	VIC	576	23	26/12/44	SAN I	SAN I	ae
aka Chandler, R.W.								
BAXTER, M.P.	B	NSW	155	34	08/06/45	SAN 2	SAN 3	RS/ROm
BAYLEY, A.E.	B	NSW	458	43	10/02/45	SAN I	SAN I	RT/m
BEARD, W.H.	B	WA	470	34	10/07/45	SAN 2	SAN 3	m
BEASLEY, H.C.	B	NSW	440	26	22/03/45	SAN I	SAN I	ae
BEAUMONT, F.J.	B	NSW	430	37	10/03/45	SAN I	SAN I	m
BEAZLEY, J.D.	B	WA	429	31	07/07/45	SAN 2	SAN 3	m
BEDFORD, R.D.E.	E	NSW	1501	26	10/06/45	SAN 2	SAN 3	m
BEER, N.P.	B	NSW	463	27	09/06/45	SAN 2	SAN 3	m
BEER, W.H.	B	NSW	501	41	21/03/45	SAN I	SAN I	m
BEER, W.J.	E	WA	1581	28	14/06/45	4m e BOTO	TR	2M/m
BEETSON, G.J.	B	NSW	149	39	01/11/44	SAN I	KG	m
BEHRENDORFF, C.	E	QLD	1582	27	17/05/45	SAN I	SAN 2	m
BELFORD, N.T.	B	NSW	439	35	23/05/45	SAN I	SAN 2	bb
BELL, M.C.	E	NSW	1584	25	05/06/45	42m SAN	TR	2M/ae
BELL, R.M.	B	NSW	410	43	29/04/45	SAN I	SAN 2	m
BENDALL, B.A.	B	WA	482	30	12/02/45	4m N'PAK	TR	cbb
BENNETT, A.D.	B	VIC	464	29	22/03/45	SAN I	SAN I	m
BENNETT, H.C.	B	VIC	472	42	17/02/45	SAN I	SAN I	m
BENNETT, H.P.	E	WA	1585	30	15/02/45	5m w M'ngan	TR	1M/cbb
BENNETT, W.D.	E	NSW	1586	22	14/07/45	RAN 2J	RAN 2JB	m
BENNISON, R.J.	B	VIC	153	45	14/03/45	SAN I	SAN I	m
BENSON, G.E.	B	QLD	448	24	09/04/45	SAN I	SAN 2	m
BETTS, J.	B	NSW	144	30	15/02/45	SAN I	SAN I	RR/ae
BETTS, J.M.	B	NSW	158	30	12/04/45	SAN I	SAN 2	m
BEVES, E.M.	E	NSW	1587	21	13/07/45	SAN 2	SAN 4	K/m
BEXTON, S.O.	B	NSW	411	24	14/06/45	23m SAN	TR (RC)	2M/m
BEXTON, T.	B	NSW	412	25	25/07/45	RAN 2J	RAN 2JB	2M/m
last 2 are brothers								
BICE, C.J.	B	QLD	473	31	28/01/45	SAN I	SAN I	m
BIGGS, F.	E	NSW	1588	29	23/03/45	SAN I	SAN 2	m
BIGNELL, K.W.	B	QLD	413	34	11/06/45	TAN'TIN	TR- d out	2M/ae
BILLS, W.R.	B	VIC	414	27	28/02/43	SAN I	KG	cbb
BILLS, L.	B	NSW	459	31	14/02/45	PRESUMED	–	No detail
BINSTEAD, A.H.	B	QLD	449	23	28/05/45	SAN I	SAN 2	m
BIRD, A.W.	B	NSW	428	28	08/07/45	RAN 2J	RAN 2JA	1M/K/m
BIRD, B.S.	E	VIC	1502	25	22/06/45	SAN 2	SAN 3	m
BIRD, C.R.	B	WA	487	28	26/07/45	RAN 2J	RAN 2J	2M/ae
BIRD, J.E.	B	NSW	1416	41	10/10/42	SAN I	KG	dys
BIRD, J.K.	B	VIC	415	30	16/04/45	SAN I	SAN 2	RS/m
BLACK, J.	B	NSW	416	46	25/03/45	SAN I	SAN 2	m
BLACKIE, J.W.	B	NSW	1437	46	02/06/45	SAN 2	SAN 3	m
BLACKWOOD, L.C.	B	VIC	422	42	07/06/45	SAN 2	SAN 3	RS/m
BLAIR, W.F.	E	NSW	1590	40	14/05/45	SAN I	SAN 2	m
BLATCH, W.G.	E	NSW	1591	25	16/06/45	TAN'TIN	TR/RC	2M/ae
BLEWETT, C.B.	B	WA	151	43	23/03/45	SAN I	SAN 2	m
BLOOM, E.	B	VIC	418	42	08/02/45	SAN I	SAN I	m
BLUFORD, E.H.	B	NSW	423	37	02/06/45	SAN 2	SAN 3	m
BLUNDEN, A.J.	B	NSW	475	25	06/06/45	SAN 2	SAN 3	m
BOARD, W.E.	B	NSW	1464	44	11/09/42	SAN I	KG	dys
BOBBIN, R.J.	B	NSW	417	29	27/07/45	RAN 2J	RAN 2JB	2M/ae
BOCK, H.J.	B	QLD	510	25	07/03/45	PAG	PAG CEM	1M/m
BOESE, R.J.	E	QLD	1592	26	29/03/45	RAN/RC	RAN/TR	1M/ae
BOLLARD, J.T.	B	NSW	471	44	27/03/45	SAN I	SAN 2	m
BOLTON, E.D.	B	NSW	476	23	22/06/45	SAN 2	SAN 3	m
BOLTON, G.A.	B	NSW	438	33	29/07/45	RAN 2J	RAN 2JB	2M/ae
BOND, F.T.	B	VIC	466	27	07/12/43	SAN I	KG	Jaundice
BONIS, R.T.	B	NSW	468	41	03/05/45	SAN I	SAN 2	m
BOOTH, C.L.	B	NSW	150	26	24/11/44	SAN I	SAN I	TB
BOTT, J.E.	B	VIC	443	25	02/07/45	SAN 2	SAN 3	m
BOURGOURE, O.W.	B	QLD	503	43	21/05/45	SAN I	SAN 2	ae
BOURNE, P.J.	B	QLD	142	29	27/05/45	SAN I	SAN 2	m
BOUSIE, G.	B	NSW	145	38	26/01/45	SAN I	SAN I	m
BOUSTEAD, M.G.	B	NSW	461	31	21/02/45	SAN I	SAN I	m
BOVEY, A.R.	B	QLD	508	23	24/04/45	RAN I	RAN IB	ae
BOW, W.	E	NSW	1593	31	13/06/45	SAN 2	SAN 3	m
BOWE, J.M.	B/E	NSW	1568	21	12/05/45	SAN I	SAN 2	CGE/ae
aka Anderson, J M								
BOWE, W.J.	E	VIC	1594	28	26/07/45	RAN 2J	RAN 2JB	2M/ae
BOWERMAN, H.F.	E	NSW	1595	25	17/06/45	3m e MALIO	TR	2M/m
BOWMAN, H.R.	B	NSW	483	26	27/12/44	SAN ?	SAN ?	DR/m
BOXHORN, K.	B	WA	427	35	17/05/45	SAN I	SAN 2	dys
BOYCE, A.R.	E	NSW	1596	24	06/03/45	RAN I	RAN IA	1M/bb
BOYD, J.W.	B	NSW	478	31	16/05/45	SAN I	SAN 2	m

BOYD, J. W.	E	VIC	1597	26	23/06/45	SAN 2	SAN 3	m
BOYD, R.	B	QLD	497	44	23/05/45	SAN 1	SAN 2	m
BOYD, R.T.	E	NSW	1589	26	22/03/45	RAN 1/RC	R 1B/TR	1M/ae
BOYES, W.E.	B	VIC	460	25	13/07/45	SAN 2	SAN 4	K/m
BOYLE, C.R.	E	NSW	1599	28	07/02/45	2m e M'RIN	TR	1M/cbb
BOYLEY, W.A.	B	SA	450	34	17/06/45	ECR	TR	2M/m
BRABHAM, V.G.	E	NSW	1600	39	26/05/45	SAN 1	SAN 2	air raid
BRACK, D.	B	NSW	437	21	17/05/45	SAN 1	SAN 2	m
BRACKEN, C.N.	E	NSW	1601	23	13/04/45	SAN 1	SAN 2	ae
BRADY, C.	J/E	VIC	1583	35	22/02/45	RAN 1	RAN 1A	ae
BRADY, W.P.	E	NSW	1602	24	08/02/45	2m w M'RIN	TR	1M/dys
BRAY, E.W.	B	NSW	504	27	02/06/45	28 m SAN	KG	2M/m
BRAY, J.	B	VIC	159	43	07/06/45	ECR	TR	RS/m
BREDBURY, I.	B	NSW	479	36	23/05/45	SAN ?	SAN ?	DR/m
BRETT, N.F.	B	NSW	465	26	01/01/45	SAN 1	SAN 1	RS/m
BRIEN, D.H.	B	VIC	500	26	24/02/45	RAN 1	RAN 1A	1M/ae
BRINKMAN, J. H.	E	NSW	1503	27	07/03/45	PAG	PAG CEM	1M/ae
BRODY, L.	E	SA	1603	23	04/06/45	ECR	TR	2M/m
BROOKER, W.	B	NSW	480	41	27/05/45	SAN 1	SAN 2	m
BROOMHAM, C.F.	E	NSW	1604	26	27/05/45	SAN 1	SAN 2	m
BROUGHTON, W.E.	B	VIC	451	28	03/12/44	SAN 1	SAN 1	m
BROWN, A.A.	B	QLD	444	21	02/06/45	ECR	TR	2M/m
BROWN, C.	B	QLD	506	52	03/01/45	SAN 1	SAN 1	m
BROWN, E.G.	B	VIC	154	47	04/02/45	SAN 1	SAN 1	m
BROWN, F.	B	NSW	452	44	10/03/45	SAN 1	SAN 1	ae
BROWN, J.E.	B	NSW	502	24	07/02/45	SAN 1	SAN 1	m
BROWN, M.	B	NSW	436	31	20/06/45	T'IAS-PAG	KG	2M/ae
BROWN, N.N.	E	NSW	1504	31	31/03/45	RAN/RC	R 1B/TR	1M/m
BROWN, R.G.	B	NSW	160	31	11/07/45	RAN 2J (2M)	RAN 2JB	RR/m
BROWN, Samuel	B	NSW	435	32	15/07/45	RAN 2J	RAN 2JB	RR/m
BROWN, S.W.	E	NSW	1605	26	15/07/45	SAN 2	SAN 4	K/m
BROWN, V.M.	E	QLD	1606	28	21/05/45	SAN 1	SAN 2	m
BROWN, W.	E	NSW	1578	38	19/03/45	PAG	PAG CEM	1M/m
BROWN, W.F.	E	VIC	1607	26	22/03/45	SAN ?	SAN ?	DR/ae
BROWNING, J.H.	B	WA	489	25	16/07/45	SAN 2	SAN 4 ?	K?/m
BROWNLEE, G.F.	B	NSW	137	33	11/07/45	RAN 2J	RAN 2JB	2M/m
BRUCE, F.W.	E	VIC	1608	32	14/02/45	M'ngan	TR	1M/m
BRUCE, R.C.	B	NSW	434	36	31/03/45	SAN 1	SAN 2	m
BRYANT, F.L.	B	VIC	426	36	08/06/45	SAN 2	SAN 3	RS/ae
BRYANT, J.C.	B	NSW	484	25	29/03/45	SAN 1	SAN 2	m
BUCKLEY, H.W.	B	NSW	467	28	04/08/45	SAN ?	SAN ?	DR/ae
BUCKLEY, J.J.	E	NSW	1609	23	08/06/45	ECR	TR	2M/dys
BUCKLEY, L.F.	E	NSW	1610	32	11/02/45	SAN 1	SAN 1	RT/bb
BULLEN, E.F.	B	NSW	481	30	25/04/45	SAN 1	SAN 2	m
BUNCH, N.H.	E	QLD	1611	27	17/06/45	ECR (2M)	TR	RT/dys
BUNDEY, G.W.	B	NSW	157	28	29/04/45	SAN 1	SAN 2	RS/m
BURCHNALL, F.A.	B	VIC	453	23	04/06/45	ECR	TR	2M/m
BURCHNALL, F.R.	B	VIC	454	52	19/05/43	SAN 1	KG	m
(last two entries are son and father)								
BURGESS, J.	B	QLD	439	39	30/07/45	RAN 2J	RAN 2JB	2M/ae
BURGESS, L.	B	NSW	433	34	19/09/44	SAN 1	KG	mm
BURGUN, G.	B	NSW	492	40	06/03/45	SAN 1	SAN 1	m
BURKE, F.J.	B	SA	419	34	07/06/45	ECR	TR (died)	2M/m
BURKE, J.E.	E	QLD	1612	38	31/07/45	RAN 2J (2M)	RAN 2JB	RR/ae
BURKE, W.J.	E	VIC	1613	30	12/06/45	SAN 2	SAN 3	m
BURLEY, K.B.	B	WA	425	40	18/05/45	SAN 1	SAN 2	m
BURLING, J.H.	B	NSW	493	30	02/04/45	SAN 1	SAN 2	m
BURNELL, A.D.	B	VIC	139	30	17/07/45	RAN 2J	RAN 2JB	2M/ae
BURNES, F.C.	E	NSW	1505	37	23/05/45	SAN 1	SAN 2	m
BURNETT, E.R.	E	QLD	1614	29	30/03/45	RAN 1/RC	R 1B/TR	1M/ae
BURNS, C.E.	B	WA	490	28	04/02/45	1m M'ATTO	TR	cbb
BURNS, R.N.	E	VIC	1615	25	05/06/45	44.5m SAN	KG(New)	2M/mbb
BURNS, S.A.	E	NSW	1616	20	31/01/45	SAN ?	SAN ?	DR/m
BURNS, T.	B	NSW	462	37	13/07/45	SAN 2	KG	K/RS
BURRIDGE, F.R.	B	NSW	420	27	27/08/44	SAN ?	SAN ?	DR/m
BURROWS, J.	B	NSW	486	42	25/04/45	SAN 1	SAN 2	RS/m
BURTON, E.G.	E	WA	1506	24	21/02/45	SAN 1	SAN 1	m
BURTON, G.	B	NSW	143	42	07/05/45	SAN 1	SAN 2	m
BURZACOTT, M.	E	SA	1617	34	03/05/45	SAN 1	SAN 2	m
BUSHELL, R.F.	E	SA	1618	24	07/06/45	ECR	TR	2M/m
BUTHERWAY, J.H.	B	VIC	455	26	08/07/45	RAN 2J	RAN 2JA	2M/m
BUTLER, T.L.	E	NSW	1507	29	17/04/45	SAN 1	SAN 2	m
BYCROFT, A.B.	B	NSW	494	23	07/03/45	SAN 1	SAN 1	m
BYRNE, B.	E	NSW	1620	35	09/03/45	RAN1/RC	R 1A/TR	1M/ae
BYRNE, N.B.	B	NSW	495	36	12/01/45	SAN 1	SAN 1	m
CADWGAN, A.D.	B	WA	566	43	02/06/45	19m SAN	TR	2M/m
CAIN, C.J.	E/J	NSW	1661	39	17/05/45	SAN 1	SAN 2	m
CALLANDER, H.M.	E	VIC	1630	30	05/06/45	47m SAN	TR	m/cbb

APPENDIX1: NOMINAL ROLLS

Name		State	Num	Age	Date	Loc1	Loc2	Cause
CAMERON, C.M.	B	QLD	579	33	31/01/45	SAN 1	SAN 1	m
CAMERON, D.T.	E	NSW	1622	29	11/04/45	SAN 1	SAN 2	m
CAMERON, F.	B	QLD	571	42	07/06/45	SAN?	SAN?	RS/m
CAMERON, J.K.	B	VIC	565	23	13/05/45	SAN 1	SAN 2	m
CAMPBELL, C.	B	NSW	559	25	19/06/45	M'ngan	TR	ae
CAMPBELL, D.A.	B	NSW	178	44	11/05/45	SAN 1	SAN 2	m
CAMPBELL, D.S.	B	VIC	180	41	23/03/45	SAN 1	SAN 2	m
CAMPBELL, J.	B	QLD	-	26	08/06/45	(PRESUMED)		No detail
CAMPBELL, M.L.	E	SA	1623	29	03/06/45	SAN 2	SAN 3	m
CAMPBELL, R.	E	VIC	1625	23	05/07/45	SAN 2	SAN 3	RS/m
CAMPBELL, W.R.	B	NSW	181	26	03/06/45	SAN 2	SAN 3	m
CANDLISH, G.A.	B	QLD	524	44	04/12/44	SAN 1	KG	dys/bb
CANNING, B.C.	B	VIC	523	26	08/04/45	RAN 1	RAN 1B	1M/bb
CANTERBURY, L.C.	E	VIC	1626	25	07/05/45	RAN 1J	RAN 1J	1M/ae
CAPON, W.A.	B	NSW	560	22	03/03/45	PAG	PAG CEM	1M/ae
CAPPER, G.H.	B	VIC	560	22	21/03/45	SAN 1	SAN 1	m
CARLETON, R.V.	B	WA	531	29	09/06/45	SAN 2	SAN 3	RS/m
CARLEY, F.A.	B	NSW	564	28	13/06/45	SAN 2	SAN 3	m
CARLSON, A.R.	E	QLD	1508	27	23/05/45	SAN 1	SAN 2	m
CARLSON, R.D.	B	VIC	522	43	22/06/45	SAN 2	SAN 3	m
CARNIE, R.M.	E	VIC	1627	24	17/03/45	SAN 1	SAN 1	m
CARR, B.	B	NSW	521	32	06/06/45	SAN 2	SAN 3	m
CARROLL, M.	B	NSW	604	42	10/05/45	SAN 1	SAN 2	m
CARSON, W.J.	E	VIC	1627	22	28/02/45	(PRESUMED)		No detail
CARTER, G.C.	B	VIC	518	23	13/04/45	SAN 1	SAN 2	1M(ret)
CARTER, P.W.	B	QLD	578	26	02/03/45	RAN 1/RC	R 1A/TR	1M/ROm
CARTHEW, J.A.	B	NSW	182	37	12/02/45	SAN 1	SAN 1	ae
CARVETH, A.J.	E	NSW	1629	31	05/06/45	46m SAN	TR	M2/m
CASSIDY, L.A.	B	NSW	173	24	26/04/45	SAN ?	SAN ?	DR/m
CATERSON, K.R.	B	NSW	517	38	13/06/45	SAN 2	SAN 3	m
CAVENAGH, C.R.	B	NSW	177	26	20/06/45	ECR	TR	2M/m
CHAMBERLAIN, J.R.	B	VIC	532	43	08/10/44	SAN 1	KG	cbb
CHANDLER, M.A	B	VIC	516	34	28/03/45	SAN 1	SAN 2	m
CHANDLER, R.K.	E	SA	1631	26	22/03/45	RAN 1/RC	R 1B/TR	1M/bb
CHANT, J.R.	E	NSW	-	34	02/06/45	ECR	TR	2M/ae
CHAPMAN, A.W.	B	NSW	179	39	09/02/45	SAN 1	SAN 1	m
CHAPMAN, B.B.	B	NSW	561	20	25/04/45	SAN 1	SAN 2	ae
CHAPMAN, C.K.	E	NSW	1632	30	28/07/45	RAN 2J	RAN 2JB	2M/ae
CHAPMAN, E.F.	E	NSW	1509	28	29/03/45	SAN 1	SAN 2	m
CHAPMAN, J.J.	B/E	QLD	1438	38	05/07/45	RAN 2J	RAN 2JA	2M/m
CHAPMAN, S.	B	NSW	530	43	04/06/45	ECR	TR	2M/m
CHAPMAN, S.H.	B	NSW	562	31	03/05/45	RAN 1J	RAN 1J	RT/m
CHAPMAN, W.P.	B	TAS	515	40	10/02/45	SAN 1	SAN 1	m
CHARLES, G.F.	B	QLD	602	24	07/06/45	SAN 2	SAN 3	RS/m
CHARLTON, R.J.	B	QLD	166	42	18/07/45	RAN 2J	RAN 2JB	ae
CHENHALL, N.J.	E	NSW	1633	27	07/04/45	SAN 1	SAN 2	RS/m
CHILD, F.T.	B	NSW	584	40	19/10/44	SAN ?	SAN ?	DR/m
CHILVERS, H.A.	E	WA	1634	33	31/03/45	SAN 1	SAN 2	m
CHIPPERFIELD, R.	B	WA	591	28	11/02/45	5m S'DAI	KG	1M/cbb
CHISHOLM, H.F.	F	NSW	1635	25	09/02/45	PAPAN	TR	cbb
CHISOLM, R.S.	B	QLD	570	44	07/06/45	ECR	TR	2M/m
CHRISTENSEN, H.G.	B	NSW	608	29	28/02/45	PRESUMED		No detail
CHRISTIANSEN, W.	B	QLD	601	37	07/06/45	ECR	TR	2M/m
CHRISTIE, N.McN.	B	QLD	163	40	05/06/45	43.5m SAN	KG (New)	2M/mbb
CLACK, J.P.	E	NSW	1510	28	02/06/45	ECR	TR	2M/m
CLAIR, T.E.	B	NSW	537	39	02/06/45	ECR	TR	2M/m
CLARK, D.S.	E	NSW	1636	42	29/12/44	SAN ?	SAN ?	DR/m
CLARK, F.H.	E	NSW	1637	26	05/03/45	RAN 1	RAN 1A	1M/ae
CLARK, G.W.	B	NSW	575	29	08/06/45	SAN 2	SAN 3	m
CLARK, J.C.	B	NSW	175	43	15/04/45	RAN 1	RAN 1A	1M/m
CLARK, R.P.	B	VIC	538	42	24/02/45	SAN 1	SAN 1	m
CLARK, W.B.	E	NSW	1638	25	02/08/45	SAN 2	SAN 3	m
CLARKE, A.	E	WA	1639	27	04/06/45	SAN 2	SAN 3	RS/m
CLARKE, L.A.	B	NSW	563	26	14/06/45	SAN 2	SAN 3	m
CLARKE, L.B.	E	QLD	1640	24	05/06/45	44m SAN	KG	2M/m
CLARKSON, J.M.	B	VIC	594	24	14/02/45	9m e MILULU	TR	2M/cbb
CLAYTON, J.H.	B	VIC	583	40	07/02/45	SAN 1	SAN 1	m
CLEAR, J.P.	B	TAS	603	36	24/05/45	SAN 1	SAN 2	m
CLEARY, A.N.	B	VIC	593	22	20/03/45	RAN 1	KG (New)	1M/K
CLEMENT, A.W.	B	NSW	605	23	09/03/45	SAN 1	SAN 1	m
CLEMENTS, T.	E	QLD	1641	44	16/04/45	SAN 1	SAN 2	m
CLIFFORD, E.T.	E	NSW	1642	31	08/02/45	.5m PAPAN	TR	cbb
CLISSOLD, J.J.	E	NSW	1643	35	14/07/45	SAN 2	SAN 4	RS/K
CLUCAS, J.B.	E	SA	1644	26	19/05/45	SAN 1	SAN 2	m
CLYDESDALE, T.J.	E	NSW	1645	26	28/03/45	RAN 1/RC	R 1B/TR	RS?/1M ulcer/ae
CLYNE. E.F.	B	NSW	187	36	27/03/45	SAN 1	SAN 2	m
CLYNE, P.J.	B	NSW	554	30	10/02/45	SAN 1	SAN 1	m
COCHRANE, E.A.	B	QLD	539	40	06/10/44	SAN 1	KG	mm

Name								
CODE, L.J.	B	QLD	540	25	02/02/45	SAN I	SAN I	m
CODLIN, J.M.	B	NSW	184	36	06/08/45	RAN 2J	R2JB/MS	false dod
COFFEY, M.J.	B	NSW	529	32	18/04/45	SAN I	SAN 2	m
COGGINS, P.R.	B	NSW	183	27	07/06/45	ECR	TR	2M/bb
COGHLAN, R.V.	B	NSW	541	41	03/04/45	SAN I	SAN 2	m
COKER, R.H.	B	SA	167	45	07/05/45	SAN I	SAN 2	RS/ae
COLE, E.H.	E	SA	1646	35	18/05/45	SAN I	SAN 2	m
COLE, T.W.	B	NSW	585	23	09/05/45	SAN 2	SAN 3	m
COLEMAN, W.J.	B	NSW	552	35	02/03/45	SAN I	SAN I	m
COLLINS, A.C.	E	VIC	1647	21	12/06/45	SAN 2	SAN 3	m
COLLINS, C.R.	E	NSW	1648	36	08/06/45	SAN 2	SAN 3	m
COLLINS, H.W.	B	QLD	567	30	15/02/45	1m M'ngan	TR	bb
COLLINS, R.B.	E	QLD	1649	26	26/04/45	SAN I	SAN 2	m
COLLINS, S.G.	B	QLD	542	40	13/02/45	SAN ?	SAN ?	DR/m
COLLS, L.W.	E	QLD	1650	27	16/04/45	SAN I	SAN 2	m
COLUMBINE, R.E. aka Aylett, R.	E	VIC	1577	20	07/02/45	42m SAN	TR	1M/cbb
COLYER, G.W.	B	NSW	168	31	12/02/45	SAN I	SAN I	m
COMBER, C.O. aka Dempsey, P.	B	SA	649	39	28/03/45	SAN I	SAN 2	bb
COMMERFORD, G.F.	B	NSW	528	25	09/02/45	2 m MILULU	TR (1M)	RR/cbb
COMMINS, J.S.	B	QLD	162	33	08/05/45	SAN I	SAN 2	RS/m
CONDON, L.J.	B	NSW	527	30	16/05/45	SAN I	SAN 2	m
CONLEY, H.S.	B	TAS	548	39	06/04/45	SAN I	SAN 2	m
CONNELL, F.	B	VIC	600	32	08/04/45	SAN I	SAN 2	m
CONNELL, J.F.	B	NSW	590	42	28/04/45	SAN I	SAN I	m
CONNOLLY, T.W.	B	NSW	165	36	09/08/45	RAN 2J	R 2JB/MS	false dod
CONNOR, H.F.	B	VIC	513	30	15/03/45	SAN I	SAN I	m
CONNOR, J.C. (last two were brothers)	B	VIC	543	32	25/02/45	SAN I	SAN I	m
CONQUIT, G.D.	E	NSW	1651	24	02/06/45	ECR	TR	m
CONSTABLE, W.A.	B	VIC	592	29	18/05/45	SAN I	SAN 2	killed
COOK, A.J.	B	QLD	556	26	10/04/45	SAN I	SAN 2	m
COOK, G.R.	B	NSW	20	38	27/08/45	RAN 2J	KG(NEW)	killed/ae
COOK, J.T.	E	NSW	1652	24	19/04/45	SAN I	SAN 2	m
COOK, L.C.	B	VIC	544	38	22/03/45	SAN I	SAN I	m
COOKE, W.	B	QLD	669	34	10/06/45	SAN 2	SAN 3	m
COOLING, M.W.	B	SA	545	40	08/06/45	SAN 2	SAN 3	m
COOMBE, R.J.	B	SA	546	44	16/03/45	SAN I	SAN I	m
COONEY, J.	B	NSW	536	35	15/04/45	SAN ?	SAN ?	DR/m
COOPER, J.A.	B	NSW	599	23	05/04/45	RAN I	RAN IB	1M/ae
COOPER, T.S.	B	NSW	547	31	16/02/45	SAN I	SAN I	m
COPE, W.G.	B	NSW	588	32	27/03/45	SAN I	SAN 2	m
COPELIN, H.V.	B	QLD	577	29	27/05/45	SAN I	SAN 2	m
COPP, E.F.	B	NSW	171	26	12/05/45	SAN I	SAN 2	m
CORBETT, J.W.	B	NSW	549	25	04/03/45	SAN I	SAN I	m
CORCORAN, F.L.	E	NSW	1653	33	10/07/45	SAN 2	SAN 3	RS/m
CORDY, F.	B	VIC	598	23	15/03/45	SAN I	SAN I	m
CORE, S.R.	E	NSW	1654	19	20/06/45	ECR	TR	m
CORNEY, L.C.	B	QLD	569	24	25/02/45	RAN I	RAN IA	m
CORNISH, F.	B	VIC	520	42	21/05/45	SAN I	SAN 2	m
COSTELLO, J.	B	QLD	574	32	21/06/45	ECR	TR	m
COSTELLO, K.	E	VIC	1655	28	01/07/45	SAN 2	SAN 3	m
COSTIN, K.H.	B	QLD	526	24	21/06/45	nr MUANAD	JUNGLE	esc/m ae
COUGHLAN, T.	B	NSW	573	31	14/02/45	6m w CELO	TR	bb/m
COUGHLIN, C.J.	B	NSW	186	30	16/04/45	SAN I	SAN 2	m
COULTER, W.J.	E	SA	1511	27	03/06/45	nr DUSAN R	JUNGLE	esc 2M
COULTON, G.L.	B	NSW	525	38	14/04/45	SAN ?	SAN ?	DR/m
COUSINS, S.J.	B	QLD	550	24	20/06/45	SAN 2	SAN 3	RS/m
COWLEY, M.C.	B	QLD	607	27	17/05/45	SAN I	SAN 2	m
COX, A.H.	E	NSW	1656	25	07/05/45	SAN I	SAN 2	m
COX, G.K.	B	NSW	587	19	05/04/45	RAN I	RAN IB	1M/m
COX, L.	B	VIC	555	41	20/04/45	SAN I	SAN 2	m
COX, R.C.	E	NSW	1512	35	13/04/45	SAN 1?	SAN 1?	DR/m
COY, F.T.	B	NSW	524	27	20/06/45	ECR	TR died	2M/m
CRAGO, G.	B	NSW	606	42	29/11/44	SAN I	KG	mm
CRAIG, A.C.	B	VIC	519	39	26/03/45	SAN I	SAN 2	m
CRAIG, R.F.	E	VIC	1657	20	08/06/45	SAN 2	SAN 3	m
CRANE, A.B.	B	NSW	169	44	09/06/45	ECR	TR died	2M/m
CRANNEY, R.T.	B	NSW	551	24	21/04/45	SAN ?(DR)	SAN ?	RR/m
CRAPP, H.S.	B	NSW	589	43	23/04/45	SAN I	SAN 2	m
CRAWFORD, J.O.	B	NSW	535	25	11/07/45	RAN 2J	RAN 2JB	2M/m
CRAWFORD, V.O.	B	TAS	597	32	07/06/45	SAN 2	SAN 3	RS/m
CRAZE, R.	E	VIC	1658	25	02/04/45	RAN I	RAN IB	m
CREASE, W.	B	NSW	595	24	14/03/45	RAN I	KG(New)	Shot/m
CREES, R.J.	B	QLD	558	30	08/02/45	.5m PAPAN	TR	1M/RR RT/cbb
CREWSDEN, A.J.	B	QLD	125	26	27/04/45	SAN ?	SAN ?	DR/m
CRIBB, T.B.	B	QLD	572	23	19/02/45	SAN I	SAN I	m

APPENDIX 1: NOMINAL ROLLS

Name		State	No.	Age	Date	Loc1	Loc2	Notes
CRIGHTON, R.S.	E	NSW	1659	32	20/05/45	SAN 1	SAN 2	m
CRILLEY, R.J.	B	WA	557	44	06/04/45	SAN 1	SAN 2	m
CRIPPS, W.G.	B	VIC	-	34	04/07/45	SAN 2	SAN 3	m
CROCKETT, E.R.	B	NSW	-	32	07/06/45	ECR	TR	m
CROSS, A.H.	B	NSW	164	35	23/03/45	SAN 1	SAN 2	CGE/m
CROSS, J.R.	B	NSW	161	28	12/06/45	ECR	TR	m
CROSSMAN, E.R.	B	NSW	534	31	04/06/45	ECR	TR	m
CROUCH, A.G.	B	VIC	170	27	24/04/45	SAN 1	SAN 2	m
CROWTHER, G.G.	B	NSW	533	44	08/03/45	SAN 1	SAN 1	RT/m
CRUMPTON, R.F.	B	NSW	581	26	05/06/45	SAN 2	SAN 3	RS/m
CULL, A.	E	NSW	1660	38	17/06/45	ECR	TR	m
CUMMING, D.A.	B	QLD	553	29	21/01/45	SAN 1	SAN 1	m
CUMMINGS, A.L.	B	NSW	582	27	07/06/45	SAN 2	SAN 3	m
CUMMINGS, N.G.	E	VIC	1513	29	24/06/45	8m e RAN	TR	ae
CUNDY, M.H.	B	SA	1462	27	04/10/42	SAN 1	KG	m/bb
CUNNINGHAM, J.M.	B	QLD	568	32	22/02/45	SAN 1	SAN 1	m
CURREY, J.E.	E	QLD	1662	27	18/12/44	SAN 1	SAN 1	appendix
CURREY, W.J.	E	QLD	-	25	04/07/45	RAN 2J	RAN 2JA	RS/m
(last two entries were brothers)								
CURROW, R. W.	E	NSW	1514	23	28/03/45	SAN 1	SAN 2	m
DALE, A.	B	QLD	635	38	14/02/45	BOTO	KG	1M/b/ae
DALTON, W.J.	E	NSW	1666	35	16/11/44	SAN 1	KG	mm
DALTON-GOODWIN, C.R.	B	WA	658	40	01/05/43	SAN 1	KG	bb
DARRAGH, L.A.	E	NSW	1667	26	20/06/45	ECR	TR	2M
DAUGHTERS, J.S.	B	VIC	618	42	11/02/45	SAN 1	SAN 1	m
DAVEY, B.A.	E	SA	1668	38	09/02/45	2m MALIO	TR	1M/ewb
DAVEY, C.W.	B	WA	640	34	04/03/45	SAN 1	SAN 1	m
DAVIDSON, F.G.	E	NSW	1516	24	04/07/45	RAN 2J	RAN 2JA	2M/m
DAVIDSON, G.L.	E	VIC	1517	30	10/06/45	(PRESUMED-TR dropped out 2M)		
DAVIDSON, R.R.	B	VIC	195	40	06/03/45	SAN 1	SAN 1	RS/m
DAVIES, D.T.	B	WA	641	37	04/01/45	SAN 1	SAN 1	m
DAVIES, E.D.	B	NSW	629	25	16/06/45	RAN 2J	RAN 2JA	1M/m relic-S
DAVIS, H.R.	B	SA	191	40	23/02/45	SAN 1	SAN 1	m
DAVIS, J.A.	B	QLD	188	34	09/08/45	SAN 2	SAN 3	m
DAVIS, J.T.	B	NSW	655	41	05/01/45	SAN 1	SAN 1	m
DAVIS, R.	B	NSW	N/R	-	13/10/44	SAN 1	SAN 1	cbb
DAVIS R.J.	E	NSW	-	22	13/07/45	SAN 2	SAN 4	K/m
DAVIS, R.V.	E	NSW	1670	26	07/06/45	ECR	TR	2M/m
DAVISON, E.	B	NSW	657	32	13/07/45	RAN 2J	RAN 2JB	2M/m
DAVISON, J.	B	QLD	659	39	30/03/45	SAN 1	SAN 2	m
DAWES, L.A.	B	SA	189	28	13/01/45	SAN 1	SAN 1	m
DAWSON, A.B.G.	B	NSW	654	39	04/12/44	SAN 1	SAN 1	m
DAWSON, T.	B	VIC	194	39	29/04/45	SAN 1	SAN 2	m
DAY, A.T.	B	NSW	631	29	26/03/45	SAN 1	SAN 2	m
DAY, G.	E	VIC	1672	25	08/07/45	RAN 2J	RAN 2JA	2M/RS/RR/mal
DEAGAN, M.	E	NSW	1673	41	27/05/45	SAN 1	SAN 2	ae
DE COSTA, G.F.	B	QLD	656	26	04/06/45	ECR	TR	2M/m
DE FAYE, C.L.	B	VIC	644	25	04/02/45	SAN 1	SAN 1	m
DE FAYE, J.	B	VIC	645	28	03/01/45	SAN 1	SAN 1	m
(last two were brothers)								
DELAHUNT, C.W.	B	VIC	648	28	21/04/45	SAN 1	SAN 2	m
DELL, W.C.	E	VIC	1518	30	04/03/45	SAN 1	SAN 1	m
DEMAS, H.J.	E	NSW	1674	34	28/04/45	SAN 1	SAN 2	m
DEMPSTER, C.	E	NSW	1675	32	06/02/45	4m e Pint'an	TR	1M/cbb
DENGATE, A.J.	B	NSW	633	23	17/06/45	SAN 2	SAN 3	m
DENNEHY, A.C.	B	VIC	637	28	24/04/45	SAN 1	SAN 2	m
DESHON, F.H.	B	QLD	638	38	15/02/45	w of MILULU	TR	1M/m
DEZIUS, F.C.	E	NSW	1676	27	29/05/45	SAN ?	SAN?	DR/m
DICKIE, G.O.	B	QLD	650	28	12/04/45	SAN 1	SAN 2	m
DICKMAN, F.H.	E	NSW	1519	31	21/05/45	SAN 1	SAN 2	m
DICKSON, L.H.	B	VIC	651	32	26/05/45	SAN 1	SAN 2	m
DIGBY, G.H.	E	NSW	1677	29	30/03/45	RAN 1/RC	R1B/TR	1M
DIXON, J.	E	NSW	1439	44	09/06/45	ECR(Killed)	TR	2M/m
DIXON, K.A.	B	QLD	620	31	06/03/45	RAN 1	RAN 1A	1M/bb
DIXON, T.F.	B	NSW	628	31	24/01/45	SAN 1	SAN 1	m
DOBSON, T.R.	B	TAS	625	24	10/06/45	SAN 2	SAN 3	m
DOCWRA, G.A.	B	NSW	652	33	26/02/45	PAG	PAG	1M/ae
DOHERTY, L.L.	B	VIC	636	44	13/04/45	SAN 1	SAN 2	m
DONOHUE, J.A.	B	NSW	624	24	30/05/45	RAN 1J	RAN 1J	1M/m
DOOLEY, F.E.	B	NSW	621	38	30/01/45	SAN 1	SAN 1	m
DORAN, P.M.	B	NSW	197	40	13/02/45	1m T'IAS	TR (1M)	RR/bbm
DORIZZI, G.	B	WA	622	28	11/02/45	SAN 1	SAN 1	1M/m
DORIZZI, H.	B	WA	623	26	11/02/45	4m S'DAI	TR (1M)	RR/cbb
DORIZZI, T.H.	E	WA	1678	31	11/03/45	RAN 1	RAN 1A	bb
(last three were brothers, first two have relics, Ranau)								
DOUGLAS, W.E.	B	QLD	613	32	20/06/45	SAN 2	SAN 3	m

DOWLING, E.	B	NSW	612	27	06/03/45	RAN I	RAN IA	1M/bb
DOWN, T.H.	B	QLD	196	27	05/01/45	SAN I	SAN I	m
DOWNES, I.G.	B	VIC	653	22	12/04/45	RAN I	RAN IB	1M/RSm
DOWNEY, H.A.	E	NSW	1665	37	08/02/45	3m w M'RIN	TR	1M/m
DOWNARD, N.L.	B	VIC	643	28	23/05/45	SAN I	SAN 2	m
DOYLE, A.G.	B	NSW	611	27	09/08/45	RAN 2J	R2JB/MS	false dod
DOYLE, E.A.	E	NSW	1679	27	15/02/45	near M'ngan	TR	1M/bb
DOYLE, L.H.	B	NSW	198	37	02/08/45	RAN 2J	R2JB/MS	false dod RR
DOYLE, P.J.	B	NSW	639	25	12/06/45	ECR	TR	2M/m
DRINKWATER, J.R.	B	NSW	647	29	26/05/45	SAN I	SAN 2	Bomb
DUCKWORTH, S.	B	SA	646	46	10/03/45	SAN I	SAN I	m
DUDDINGTON, H.	B	WA	615	37	28/03/45	SAN I	SAN 2	m
DUFFY, L.J.	B	NSW	627	34	03/04/45	SAN I	SAN 2	m
DUFFY, S.D.	E	NSW	1520	28	19/03/45	PAG	PAG CEM	1M/ae
DUGGAN, S.J.	B	VIC	634	27	26/03/45	RAN I	RAN IB	RS/ae
DUNCALF, V.A.	E	NSW	1680	26	20/01/45	SAN I	SAN I	m
DUNCAN, J.W	B	VIC	614	25	15/03/45	SAN I	SAN I	M
DUNDAS, R.C.	E	NSW	1681	28	21/04/45	SAN I	SAN 2	m
DUNHILL, E.G.	B	NSW	632	24	04/06/45	ECR	TR	2M/m
DUNHILL, M.R.	B	SA	192	41	22/03/45	SAN I	SAN I	m
DUNKINSON, J.L.	B	NSW	193	36	12/06/45	RAN IJ	RAN IJ	1M/ae/
(from Japanese records, appears to have been one of those murdered with Allie. Relic also found)								
DUNN, C.H.	B	WA	190	44	21/03/45	SAN I	SAN I	m
DUNNE, J.J.	B	VIC	617	35	16/04/45	SAN I	SAN 2	m
DURAND, G.P.	B	VIC	616	24	04/02/45	SAN I	SAN I	m
DWYER, J.	E	VIC	1682	26	17/04/45	RAN I	RAN IB	1M/m
DYER, W.	B	NSW	610	26	24/06/45	ECR	TR	2M/ae
DYSON, F.A.	J/E	VIC	1528	27	09/04/45	SAN I	SAN 2	m
DYSON, R.R.	E	NSW	1521	31	09/03/45	SAN I	SAN I	m
EARLE, L.H.	B	QLD	664	44	12/06/45	SAN 2	SAN 3	m
EARNSHAW, W.H.	E	WA	1684	25	15/03/45	SAN I	SAN I	m
EASTON, H.	E	NSW	1685	22	20/04/45	SAN I	SAN 2	m
EASTWOOD, G.E.	B	QLD	662	33	21/02/45	SAN I	SAN I	m
EBZERY, T.	B	NSW	201	40	05/06/45	46m SAN	TR	2M/mbb
EDWARDS, G.E.	B	NSW	663	28	25/07/45	RAN 2J	RAN 2JB	2M/m
EDWARDS, G.H.	E	WA	1686	34	20/03/45	SAN I	SAN I	m
EDWARDS, H.J.	E	VIC	1688	36	27/04/45	SAN I	SAN 2	m
EGEL, R.C.	B	SA	675	25	06/02/45	8m e Pint'an	PAG	1M/cbb
ELDERTON, W.J.	E	NSW	1689	38	25/03/45	SAN I	SAN 2	m
ELLIOTT, S.	E	NSW	1690	33	21/02/45	RAN I	RAN IA	1M/ae
ELLIOTT, S.W.	B	VIC	674	27	15/06/45	SAN 2	SAN 3	m
ELLIOTT, T.A.	E	NSW	1522	31	08/03/45	RAN I	RAN IA	1M/m
ELLIOTT, W.G.	B	NSW	665	26	13/01/45	SAN I	SAN I	m
ELLIS, A.G.	E	NSW	1691	38	15/02/45	nr M'ngan	TR (1M)	RT/bb
ELLIS, K.E.	B	SA	667	42	21/01/45	SAN I	SAN I	m
ELSLEY, G.L.E.	B	NSW	670	42	01/04/45	SAN I	SAN 2	m
ELY, T.H.	E	VIC	1692	22	13/02/45	2m e N'TAN	TR	1M/cbb
EMMETT, E.V.	B	NSW	-	24	18/06/45	escaped/ shot/ fell into M'rin R		
EMMETT, G.	E	NSW	1693	42	31/03/45	SAN I	SAN 2	ae
ENGELHART, N.	E	SA	1694	25	21/06/45	10m e S'DAI	TR	2M/m
ERNST, J.A.	E	QLD	1695	43	08/06/45	SAN 2	SAN 3	m
ERWIN, L.R.	E	NSW	1757	35	02/06/45	ECR	TR	m
aka Irwin, R.G..								
ESSEX, R.F.	B	VIC	660	43	14/03/45	SAN I	SAN I	m
ETCHELL, A.E.	B	VIC	671	23	16/02/45	SAN I	SAN I	m
ETHERIDGE, J.O.	B	QLD	673	23	19/07/45	RAN 2J	RAN 2JB	2M/ae
EVANS, B.H.	B	WA	669	29	20/06/45	10.5m e PAG	TR-killed	2M/m
EVANS, E.C.	E	NSW	1696	24	11/06/45	SAN 2	SAN 3	ae
EVANS, G.J.	E	SA	1683	29	21/07/45	RAN 2J	RAN 2JB	ae
EVANS, J.W.	J/E	NSW	1664	26	16/06/45	1m MALIO	TR	m
EVANS, L.M.	B	SA	199	39	14/02/45	SAN I	SAN I	m
EVANS, O.R.	B	NSW	666	24	01/08/45	RAN 2J	R 2JB	2M/K
EVANS, R.B.	B	VIC	672	43	14/03/45	SAN I	SAN I	m
EVANS, W.C.	B/E	WA	1465	43	14/06/45	KOLAPIS	KG	esc San I
EVANS, W.G.	B	WA	1457	24	06/11/42	SAN I	KG	dys
EVANS, W.R.	B	VIC	1465	42	28/08/42	SAN I	KG	dys
EWERS, C.E.	B	QLD	661	22	17/05/45	SAN I	SAN 2	m
EWING, H.	B	VIC	676	38	11/02/45	3m S'DAI	TR	1M/cbb
EZZY, A.J.	B	NSW	668	38	05/03/45	SAN I	SAN I	RT/m
FAHEY, A.M.	B	NSW	678	33	10/08/45	RAN 2J	R 2JB/MS	2M/RT/ false dod
FALCO, J.	E	VIC	1698	26	26/02/45	SAN I	SAN I	m
FARRELL, A.R.	E	NSW	1699	44	26/01/45	SAN I	SAN I	m
FARRELL, V.H.	B	NSW	209	41	19/07/45	RAN 2J	RAN 2JB	RT/ae
FARREY, L.W.	E	NSW	1700	27	20/06/45	ECR	TR	m
FARROW, H.	B	QLD	695	34	30/05/45	ECR	TR	2M/m

FELDBAUER, T.A.		B	VIC	880	35	27/03/45	SAN 1	SAN 2	m
FERGUSON, A.J.		B	VIC	208	38	30/07/45	RAN 2J	RAN 2JB	2M/ae
FERGUSON, J.		B	NSW	691	28	17/02/45	SAN 1	SAN 1	m
FERGUSON, K.D.		E	NSW	1701	20	14/07/45	SAN 2	SAN 4	K/m
FERGUSON, N.J.		B	NSW	206	27	20/06/45	ECR	TR-d out	2M/m
FERGUSON, R.P.		B	WA	692	32	23/03/45	RAN 1/RC	R 1B/TR	1M/ae
FERGUSSON, N.W.		B	SA	709	31	14/06/45	SAN ?	SAN ?	DR/m
FERRIS, G.R.		B	TAS	710	48	22/03/45	SAN 1	SAN 1	bb
FEWER, J.R.		B	NSW	685	27	22/03/45	SAN 1	SAN 1	RS/m
FIELD, G.L.C.		B	WA	699	41	01/06/45	SAN 2	SAN 3	RS/m
FIELD, S.A.		B/E	VIC	1488	47	31/01/45	SAN 1	SAN 1	m
FILEWOOD, A.A.		E	NSW	1702	26	01/08/45	SAN 2	SAN 3	RS/m
FINCH, W.H.		B	NSW	698	25	07/06/45	ECR	TR	2M/m
FINDLAY, J.G.		B	NSW	687	24	12/06/45	SAN 2	SAN 3	m
FINGHER, R.E.		B	VIC	693	24	21/03/45	SAN 1	SAN 1	m
FINN, A.H.		B	NSW	684	36	20/07/45	RAN 2J	RAN 2JB	2M/ae
FINN, J.A.		B	NSW	688	24	09/08/45	RAN 2J	R 2JB/MS	false dod RR
FINN, W.M.		E	SA	1703	40	06/04/45	SAN 1	SAN 2	m
FISHER, P.L.		B	NSW	711	48	10/04/45	SAN 1	SAN 2	m
FISHER, R.J.		E	NSW	1704	23	16/04/45	SAN 1	SAN 2	m
FITZGERALD, G.S.		E	NSW	1522	37	02/06/45	ECR	TR	bb
FITZGERALD, H.R.		B	VIC	712	30	07/03/45	RAN 1/RC	R 1A/TR	1M/m
FITZGERALD, J.D.		B	NSW	205	37	22/03/45	SAN 1	SAN 1	m
FITZGERALD, L.N.		B	NSW	683	24	15/07/45	RAN 2J	RAN 2JB	2M/m
FITZPATRICK, D.A		B	NSW	700	28	10/06/45	RAN 1J	RAN 1J	K?/m
FITZPATRICK, F.J.		B	VIC	713	45	05/08/45	RAN 2	R 2JB/MS	2M/RR/ false dod
FLANAGAN, W.J.		B	NSW	686	27	09/06/45	TR (e Boto)	TR	2M/m
FLAVELLE, R.R.		E	NSW	1705	28	17/02/45	15m e RAN	TR	1M/cbb
FLEMMING, A.C.		E	NSW	1706	28	17/03/45	SAN 1	SAN 1	ae
FLETCHER, B.A.		B	NSW	202	32	11/06/45	SAN 2	SAN 3	RS/m
FLETCHER, F.G.		B	NSW	1458	37	11/10/42	SAN 1	KG	dys
FLETCHER, J.S.		E	VIC	-	28	10/06/45	(PRESUMED)	JUNGLE	esc 2M
FLINT, A.E.		B	NSW	-	28		June/July 45, reached Ranau, no other details		
FLOOD, L.A.		E	NSW	1708	32	03/07/45	RAN 2J	RAN 2JA	m
FLOYED, A.E.		E	WA	1709	26	12/03/45	SAN 1	SAN 1	m
FOGARTY, J.M.		B	NSW	701	43	03/03/45	SAN 1	SAN 1	m
FOGARTY, M.J.		B	NSW	706	43	15/11/44	SAN 1	KG	ae
FOLKARD, S.B.		B	NSW	-	27	10/06/45	(PRESUMED)	TR?	on 2M
FOOTE, P.N.		B	VIC	207	40	05/02/45	MANDORIN	TR	1M/bbm
FORRESTER, C.H.		B	NSW	687	26	15/06/45	SAN 2	SAN 3	escaped on 29 May while on march, recaptured/m
FORSTER, W.C.		B	NSW	679	44	08/03/45	SAN 1	SAN 1	m
FOSBURY, B.J.A.		B	VIC	681	25	14/02/45	7m e MILULU	TR	1M/cbb
FOSTER, D.		B	WA	703	40	07/06/45	M'ATTO	TR	2M/ae
FOTHERINGHAM,T.		B	WA	715	24	07/06/45	M'ATTO	TR	2M/bb
FOX, E.H.		B	NSW	707	27	10/02/45	SAN 1	SAN 1	m
FOXWELL, C.A.		B	QLD	689	27	08/05/45	RAN 1J	RAN 1J	1M/m
FRAME, C.W.		E	NSW	1710	35	19/05/45	SAN 1	SAN 2	m
FRANCIS, F.C.		B	NSW	698	29	24/04/45	RAN 1	RAN 1B	m
FRANKLIN, F.G.		B	NSW	694	38	14/02/45	5m T'IAS	TR	1M/mbb
FRASER, T.W.		B	VIC	682	39	25/02/45	RAN 1	RAN 1A	1M/m
FRAZIER, J.W.		E	VIC	-	25	03/06/45	nr DUSAN R	JUNGLE	esc 2M
FRENCH, R.F.		B	VIC	708	28	19/07/45	RAN 2J	RAN 2JB	2M/ae
FROST, E.I.		B	VIC	705	28	02/08/45	SAN 2	SAN 3	m
FROST, H.T.		B	VIC	204	25	24/07/45	RAN 2J	RAN 2JB	2M/RR/ ae
(last two were brothers)									
FRY, V.J.		B	VIC	716	38	01/07/45	MURAWATTO	TR(RC?)	2/3M/?
FULLER, E.J.		B	NSW	702	26	14/02/45	KEMANSI	KG	esc 1M/ RO/ae m
FULLGRABE, A.C.		B	SA	704	25	20/04/45	SAN 1	SAN 2	m
FUSS, C.R.		E	SA	1697	44	17/03/45	SAN 1	SAN 1	m
GAGAN, L.A.		E	NSW	1712	24	30/07/45	RAN 2J	RAN 2JB	2M/ae
GALE, P.R.		E	VIC	1525	25	16/04/45	SAN 1	SAN 2	RS/m
GALLARD, R.F.		E	NSW	1713	25	30/05/45	SAN 2	SAN 3	m
GALTON, D.		B	NSW	218	40	12/07/45	RAN 2J	RAN 2JB	2M/m
GANNON, W.J.		E	QLD	1711	26	17/06/45	TAMPIAS	KG	2M/m
GARDE, H.G.		B	NSW	760	24	12/03/45	SAN 1	SAN 1	m
GARDNER, A.W.		B	NSW	755	30	05/06/45	SAN 2	SAN 3	RS/m
GARDNER, C.A.		B	NSW	718	26	06/04/45	SAN 1	SAN 2	m
GARDNER, E.J.		B	WA	747	41	09/07/45	RAN 2J	RAN 2JB	2M/m
GARDNER, I.L.		B	NSW	216	27	28/03/43	SAN 1	KG	RS/ peritonitis
GARLAND, A.W.		E	VIC	1527	40	18/03/45	PAG	PAG CEM	1M/m
GARNER, G.C.		E	VIC	1714	27	05/04/45	SAN 1	SAN 2	bb
GARRARD, J.H.		B	NSW	750	30	07/06/45	ECR	TR	2M/m
GARVIN, J.T.		B	NSW	217	43	04/06/45	SAN 2	SAN 3	RS/m

GASKIN, J.	E	NSW	1715	35	20/07/45	SAN 2	SAN 3	RS/m
GAULD, G.T.	B	SA	749	43	10/02/45	SAN 1	SAN 1	m
GAULT, H.R.	B	NSW	748	30	27/04/45	SAN 1	SAN 2	m
GAVEN, J.	B	NSW	220	32	11/03/45	RAN 1	RAN 1A	1M/ae
GAY, A.P.R.L	B	VIC	210	41	14/06/45	SAN 2	SAN 3	RS/m
GAYNOR, B.G.	B	VIC	738	25	09/03/45	SAN 1	SAN 1	m
GELLATLY, R.A.	E	NSW	1526	25	09/07/45	RAN 2J	RAN 2JA	2M/RTm
GEMMILL, S.C.	B	NSW	725	29	02/06/45	ECR	TR	2M/m
GENTLE, T.R.	B	NSW	724	36	01/06/45	23m SAN	KG	2M/m
GHANANBURGH,C. aka Maurice, C.M.	B	NSW	1024	22	07/06/45	M'ATTO	TR	2M/ae
GIBBS, S.H.	E	WA	1717	41	24/02/45	SAN 1	SAN 1	ae
GIBSON, J.B.	B	NSW	742	24	28/02/45	(PRESUMED)		No detail
GIBSON, N.A.	B	WA	720	25	24/06/45	28m SAN	KG (RC?)	2M/ae
GILL, H.M.	E	VIC	1718	37	23/02/45	SAN 1	SAN 1	ae
GILLEN, P.P.M.	B	SA	773	47	08/01/45	SAN 1	SAN 1	m
GILLESPIE, W.G.	B	NSW	140	42	01/07/45	SAN 2	SAN 3	RS/m
GILLETT, K.B.	B	VIC	537	25	14/03/45	RAN 1	RAN 1A	1M/bb
GILLHAM, A.J.	E	NSW	1719	25	13/03/45	RAN 1/RC	R 1A/TR	ae
GILLIES, A.J.	B	NSW	754	37	20/06/45	SAN 2	SAN 3	m
GILLIGAN, C.A.	E	NSW	1720	34	22/05/45	SAN 1	SAN 2	m
GLADWIN, F.J.	B	QLD	731	43	22/01/45	SAN 1	SAN 1	m
GLENNIE, J.T.	B	NSW	773	34	15/03/45	SAN 1	SAN 1	m
GLOAG, D.	B	NSW	771	30	01/03/45	SAN 1	SAN 1	m
GLOVER, C.R.	B	NSW	219	27	24/05/45	SAN 1	SAN 2	bomb
GLOVER, F.M.	B	NSW	744	27	18/06/45	MILULU	TR	2M/m
(the above two entries were twins)								
GLOVER, S.	B	WA	763	36	05/06/45	44m SAN	KG (New)	2M/m
GODE, H.	B	QLD	729	39	24/12/44	SAN 1	SAN 1	RS/mm
GODSON, C.H.	B	NSW	761	38	06/06/45	SAN 2	SAN 3	RS/m
GOLDFINCH, S.C.	B	WA	774	44	13/07/45	SAN 2	SAN 4	K/m
GOLDIE, J.McL.	B	WA	739	26	04/06/45	38m SAN	TR	2M/ae
GOLDING, R.S.	B	NSW	722	25	10/03/45	SAN 1	SAN 1	CGE/m
GOLDSWORTHY,T.	B	VIC	732	38	20/04/45	SAN ?	SAN ?	DR/m
GOOD, G.	B	NSW	50	35	13/07/45	RAN 2J	RAN 2JB	2M/RS/RT/m RR
GOODEAR, N.F.	B	NSW	719	30	07/06/45	M'ATTO	TR	2M/ae
GOOUD, L.	B	NSW	709	42	18/06/45	MILULU	TR	2M/m
GORDON, T.	B	VIC	737	39	15/07/45	RAN 2J	RAN 2JB	2M/m
GOULD, A.R.	B	QLD	-	38	16/03/45	SAN 1	SAN 1	m
GOULD, R.G.	B	WA	214	39	03/03/45	SAN 1	SAN 1	m
GOW, A.W.	B	NSW	759	40	25/06/45	SAN 2	SAN 3	m
GOWER, E.H.	B	QLD	1463	41	15/09/42	SAN 1	KG	dys
GRAF, P.F.	B	NSW	768	37	01/07/45	SAN 2	SAN 3	m
GRAHAM, G.A.	B	NSW	753	33	21/02/45	SAN 1	SAN 1	m
GRAHAM, J.L.	B	VIC	736	33	24/04/45	SAN 1	SAN 2	m
GRAHAM, R.	B	NSW	726	26	04/06/45	ECR	TR	2M/m
GRAHAM, R.J.	E	NSW	1722	26	05/06/45	42 m SAN	TR	2M/m
GRAHAM, W.H.	B	VIC	752	24	09/04/45	RAN 1	RAN 1B	1M/m
GRANT, E.T.	E	NSW	1723	23	21/06/45	PAG	PAG-TR	2M/m
GRANT, F.M.	B	NSW	762	38	14/02/45	3m M'ADAI	TR	1M/dys
GRANT, J.J.	E	NSW	1724	20	07/06/45	ECR	TR	2M/m
GRAVE, R.L.	B	NSW	717	40	07/06/45	M'ATTO	TR	2M/m
GRAY, R.S.	B	NSW	727	24	12/03/45	PAG	PAG CEM	1M/ae
GREEN,A.A.	B	NSW	723	38	13/06/45	ECR	TR	2M/m
GREEN, E.A.	B	QLD	211	30	12/04/45	SAN 1	SAN 2	m
GREEN, T.W.	J/E	WA	1716	24	22/01/45	SAN 1	SAN 1	m
GREENFELD, F.R.	B	NSW	721	26	24/04/45	SAN 1	SAN 2	m
GREENUP, C.R.	B	QLD	762	32	12/03/43	SAN 1	SAN 1	TB
GREENWAY, A.C.	B	NSW	733	39	05/06/45	46m SAN	TR	2M/m
GREENWOOD, R.J.	B	NSW	213	27	24/06/45	5m M'KAU	TR	2M/aem
GREGORY, G.E.	B	QLD	725	37	06/05/45	SAN 1	SAN 2	m
GRIFFIN, K.C.	E	NSW	1725	30	07/06/45	ECR	TR	2M/m
GRIFFIN, T.M.	B	VIC	734	39	06/02/45	SAN 1	SAN 1	m
GRIFFITHS, E.R.	B	QLD	728	25	20/03/45	SAN 1	SAN 1	m
GRIGSON, A.G.	B	WA	766	28	09/06/45	MANDORIN	TR	2M/m
GRILLS, V.E.	B	NSW	751	25	03/07/45	SAN 2	SAN 3	m
GRIMWOOD, H.	B	NSW	215	33	17/07/45	RAN 2J	RAN2JB	2M/ae
GRIMWOOD, J.R.	B	NSW	743	28	02/07/45	SAN 2	SAN 3	m
GRINTER, C.A.	B	VIC	730	42	28/03/45	SAN 1	SAN 2	m
GRIST, N.S.	B	NSW	756	24	10/07/45	RAN 2J	RAN 2JB	1M/m
GRONO, P.R.	B	NSW	764	25	01/05/45	SAN 1	SAN 2	RT/m
GROSVENOR, L.L.	B	NSW	746	24	06/03/45	RAN 1	RAN 1A	1m/ae
GROSVENOR, R.J.	B	NSW	745	27	30/04/45	SAN 1	SAN 2	m
(last two entries were brothers)								
GRUBB, D.	B	VIC	741	40	02/04/45	SAN 1	SAN 2	RS/m
GUINEA, J.D.	B	NSW	758	44	09/04/45	SAN 1	SAN 2	m
GULLIDGE, H.E.	B	NSW	765	26	28/05/45	SAN 1	SAN 2	m

APPENDIX1: NOMINAL ROLLS

HACK, A.M.	B	WA	779	38	04/02/45	1m M'RIN	TR	1M/cbb
HACKLAND, E.C.C. aka Toohey, C.J.	E	NSW	1940	38	27/01/45	SAN 1	SAN 1	m
HADDON, T.	B	NSW	240	38	13/07/45	SAN 2	SAN 4	K/m
HAGSTON, G.	B	VIC	244	26	30/06/45	SAN 2	SAN 3	RS/m
HALDEN, W.J.	B	NSW	850	39	23/06/45	SAN 2	SAN 3	m
HALES, L.J.	B	NSW	775	28	05/04/45	RAN 1	RAN 1B	1M/RO/ bbm
HALES, R.A.	B	SA	828	44	04/12/44	SAN 1	SAN 1	m
HALL, R.W.	E	NSW	1528	34	10/07/45	RAN 2J	RAN 2JB	m
HALL, T.B.	E	NSW	1726	40	12/04/45	SAN 1	SAN 2	m
HALLFORD, M.E.	B	NSW	809	25	29/03/45	SAN 1	SAN 2	m
HALLIGAN, J.	B	WA	781	25	04/02/45	1m M'ATTO	TR	1M/m
HALLS, R.S.	B	NSW	227	37	14/10/43	SAN 1	SAN 1	gas ulcer
HALY, S.O'G.	B	WA	800	29	15/06/45	SANDALA	KG	esc/m
HAMALAINEN, F.E.	E	QLD	1727	43	17/03/45	SAN 1	SAN 1	m
HAMILTON, H.	E	NSW	1728	36	29/05/45	SAN 1	S 3/CPD	m
HAMILTON, J. aka Colville, J.H.	B	VIC	512	40	30/03/45	SAN 1	SAN 2	m
HAMS, N.T.	B	NSW	801	24	25/03/45	SAN 1	SAN 2	m
HANCOCK, M.J.	B	NSW	786	47	23/04/45	SAN 1	SAN 2	m
HANCOCK, W.J.	B	QLD	238	42	15/08/45	SAN 2	SAN 3	m
HANKIN, P.E.	B	QLD	223	42	15/06/45	SAN 2	SAN 3	RS/m
HANKINSON, R.F.	B	VIC	827	41	07/06/45	ECR	TR	2M/m
HANNAN, M.E.	B	NSW	776	31	05/02/45	SAN 1	SAN 1	m
HANSELL, H.N.	B	NSW	849	43	27/02/45	SAN 1	SAN 1	m
HANSON, K.D.	B	QLD	808	27	15/05/45	6m w M'ngan	TR (1M)	RS/bb
HARCOURT, R.B.	B	NSW	848	48	03/05/45	SAN 1	SAN 2	m
HARDING, L.C.	B	NSW	850	30	28/02/45	(PRESUMED)		No detail
HARDSTAFF, R.A.	B	TAS	812	22	14/04/45	RAN 1(1M)	RAN 1B	RR/m
HARDY, A.A.	E	NSW	1530	32	18/04/45	SAN 1	SAN 2	m
HARDY, G.R.	B	TAS	791	27	31/05/45	RAN 1J	RAN 1J	1M/m
HARDY, L.E.	B	NSW	841	41	19/05/45	SAN 1	SAN 2	m
HARGRAVE, C.H.	B	NSW	224	38	03/03/45	SAN 1	SAN 1	RS/RRm
HARGRAVES, J.V.	B	NSW	819	33	06/06/45	SAN 2	SAN 3	RS/m
HARPER, B.G.	B	NSW	777	41	30/03/45	SAN 1	SAN 2	m
HARPER, H.C.	E	NSW	1729	41	13/05/45	SAN 1	SAN 2	m
HARPLEY, J.C.	E	NSW	1531	28	20/07/45	RAN 2J	RAN 2JB	ae
HARRINGTON, R.E.	E	VIC	1730	43	29/05/45	SAN 1	S 3/CPD	m
HARRIS, C.	B	WA	797	31	27/05/45	SAN 1	SAN 2	m
HARRIS, C.H.	B	QLD	820	27	18/06/45	ECR	TR	2M/m
HARRIS, C.M.	E	NSW	1713	37	20/04/45	RAN 1	RAN 1B	1M/m
HARRIS, J.O.	B	NSW	846	44	02/06/45	SAN 2	SAN 3	RS/m
HARRIS, L.A.	E	NSW	1732	25	04/06/45	ECR	TR	m
HARRIS, R.C.	B	NSW	845	44	19/06/45	ECR	TR	2M/m
HARRIS, S.N.	E	VIC	1733	24	05/06/45	44.5m SAN	KG(New)	2M/m
HARRIS, W.L.	E	VIC	1734	23	26/02/45	RAN 1	RAN 1A	1M/ae
HARRISON, W.R.	B	VIC	787	24	16/03/45	SAN 1	SAN 1	m
HARSTORFF, D.P.	B	QLD	813	25	05/06/45	SAN 2	SAN 3	m
HARVEY, G.E.	B	WA	790	43	08/03/45	SAN 1	SAN 1	ae
HARVEY, H.F.	B	NSW	806	21	11/05/43	SAN 1	SAN 1	esc/shot
HARWOOD, F.	E	NSW	1735	24	31/03/45	RAN1/RC	R1B/TR	1M/bb
HASLUCK, L.N.	B	WA	792	42	06/04/44	SAN 1	KG	RT/h f
HASTED, J.J.	B	QLD	221	37	29/01/45	SAN 1	SAN 1	m
HASTIE, L.J.	B	VIC	844	21	11/03/45	RAN 1	RAN 1A	1M/bb u
HAWKINS, C.A.	E	VIC	1736	42	04/06/45	ECR	TR	2M/m
HAY, C.G.	B	SA	235	38	18/02/45	SAN 1	SAN 1	m
HAYE, L.J.	B	WA	793	39	08/02/45	.5m MUANAD	TR	killed/m
HAYES, J.W.	B	NSW	831	35	13/05/45	SAN 1	SAN 2	bb
HAYES, W.C.	B	QLD	234	25	12/05/45	SAN 1	SAN 2	m
HAZLEGROVE, M.B.	B	NSW	826	25	27/01/45	SAN 1	SAN 1	RS/m
HEADFORD, F.W.	B	NSW	843	34	10/04/45	RAN 1	RAN 1B	1M/m
HEASLOP, J.E.	B	QLD	56	30	19/07/45	RAN 2J	RAN 2JB	2M/ae/RR
HEDLEY, G.W.	B	NSW	833	31	28/04/45	SAN ?	SAN ?	DR/m
HELLIWELL, K.J.	E	NSW	1737	30	19/05/45	SAN 1	SAN 2	m
HENLEY, J.B.	B	VIC	243	42	06/06/45	SAN 2	SAN 3	RS?/m
HENLEY, K.H.	B	VIC	782	26	24/04/45	SAN 1	SAN 2	RS?/m
HENSBY, H.	B	NSW	822	30	27/03/45	SAN 1	SAN 2	m
HENWOOD, E.J.	B	NSW	231	37	20/03/45	SAN 1	SAN 1	m
HERD, B.	B	NSW	804	23	12/07/45	RAN 2J	RAN 2JB	2M/m
HEWITT, H.	B	NSW	242	42	04/06/45	37m SAN	TR - d out	2M/m
HEWITT, H.F.(Turk)	E	VIC	1738	26	28/07/45	SAN 2	SAN 3	m
HEWITT, N.L.	B	VIC	805	26	05/03/45	SAN 1	SAN 1	CGE/m
HEYWOOD, A.McC.	E	VIC	1739	24	19/05/45	SAN 1	SAN 2	m
HEYWORTH, W.	B	NSW	785	36	19/04/45	SAN 1	SAN 2	m
HIBBERT, S.E.	E	VIC	1740	42	21/11/44	SAN 1	KG	m men
HICKMAN, C.	B	NSW	802	34	20/04/45	RAN 1	RAN 1B	m
HICKS, H.R.	B	NSW	816	30	01/07/45	RAN 2J	RAN 2JA	2M/ae
HICKS, V.O.	B	NSW	815	28	11/02/45	2m MALIO	TR	1M/bbm

HIGGISON, F.M.	B	NSW	817	36	12/06/45	SAN 2	SAN 3	m
HIGGS, J.A.	B	NSW	832	48	12/04/45	SAN 1	SAN 2	m
HIGHAM, G.E.	B	NSW	818	37	02/02/45	SAN 1	SAN 1	m
HILL, C.S.	B	VIC	825	36	02/06/45	ECR	TR	2M/m
HILL, E.T.	B	WA	830	27	28/05/45	SAN ?	SAN ?	m
HILL, W.	B	VIC	842	27	04/04/45	SAN 1	SAN 2	m
HINCHCLIFF, W.H.	B	NSW	794	27	10/04/45	SAN 1	SAN 2	m
HINE, V.M.	E	NSW	1755	24	10/02/45	SAN 1	SAN 1	m
HITCHENS, R.	J/E	VIC	1905	37	19/04/45	SAN 1	SAN 2	m
HOBBS, J.S.	B	NSW	801	25	04/03/45	SAN 1	SAN 1	m
HODDER, W.J.	B	NSW	222	52	31/01/45	SAN 1	SAN 1	m
HODGES, D.	B	NSW	780	24	07/06/45	ECR	TR	2M/m
HODGES, G.H. aka McIntosh, G.H.	E	NSW	1804	22	11/02/45	1m fr PAG	TR(PAG)	1M/cbb
HODGES, J.D.G.	B	NSW	230	44	01/07/45	RAN 2J	RAN 2JA	RS/ae
HODGES, R.E.	B	QLD	789	26	09/06/45	MANDORIN	TR	killed/m
HOGAN, D.	B	QLD	1459	21	17/10/42	SAN 1	KG	insane
HOGBIN, C.W.	B	NSW	798	40	24/03/45	SAN 1	SAN 2	RS/m
HOGG, W.	B	VIC	823	39	03/03/45	SAN 1	SAN 1	m
HOLDAWAY, L.J.	E	NSW	1536	41	01/01/44	SAN 1	KG	ulcers— died after leg amputated — cremated
HOLDEN, N.N.	E	NSW	1714	40	21/03/45	SAN 1	SAN 1	RS/m
HOLLAND, H.W.	E	WA	1742	30	15/06/45	ECR	TR	m
HOLLAND, J.	B	NSW	807	29	02/05/45	SAN 1	SAN 2	m
HOLLAND, L.U.	E	NSW	1743	26	06/07/45	RAN 2J	RAN 2JA	2M/m
HOLLIER, H.F.	B	VIC	811	21	12/05/45	SAN 1	SAN 2	m
HOLME, C.	E	WA	1744	22	07/06/45	ECR	TR	2M/m
HOLMES, R.F.	B	VIC	236	25	12/06/45	SAN 2	SAN 3	RS/m
HOLST, E.J.	E	WA	1745	31	20/03/45	SAN 1	SAN 1	m
HONOR, B.	B	QLD	788	36	08/04/45	SAN 1	SAN 2	m
HOOD, R.J.	B	QLD	841	39	05/12/44	SAN 1	SAN 1	m
HOOPER, W.R.	B	WA	226	41	21/05/45	SAN 1	SAN 2	m
HOPKINS, A.G.	E	NSW	1746	33	10/04/45	SAN 1	SAN 2	m
HOPKINS, W.R.	B	NSW	778	31	25/07/45	RAN 2J	RAN 2JB	ae
HORDER, R.J.	B	NSW	241	48	09/07/45	RAN 2J	RAN 2JA	killed/m
HORNE, G.D.	B	TAS	795	22	05/11/44	SAN 1	KG	m men
HORNE, N.	E	NSW	1747	25	01/04/45	RAN 1	RAN 1B	ulcer
HOTCHIN, D.P	B	VIC	840	53	07/03/45	SAN 1	SAN 1	ae
HOTSTON, L.	B	NSW	784	27	06/06/45	SAN 2	SAN 3	m
HOW, V.K.	E	SA	1748	28	03/06/45	SAN 2	SAN 3	RS/m
HOWARD, E.	B	VIC	232	25	18/11/44	SAN 1	KG	m
HOWELL, D.W.	B	WA	798	28	11/06/45	ECR	TR	2M/m
HOWSON, H.R.	B	NSW	799	36	18/03/45	SAN 1	SAN 1	ae
HUBBARD, E.A.F	E	NSW	1746	42	24/06/45	SAN 2	SAN 3	m
HUCKLE, R.A.	B	NSW	810	41	24/03/44	SAN 1	KG	heart f
HUGHES, A.P.	B	NSW	237	38	11/05/45	SAN 1	SAN 2	ae
HUGHES, K.G.	E	NSW	1750	24	15/07/45	SAN 2	SAN 4	K/m
HUGHES, R.	E	WA	1751	38	04/06/45	36.5m SAN	TR	2M/m
HUGHES, R.R.	B	NSW	245	33	20/03/45	SAN 1	SAN 1	m
HUMBLER, B.P.	B	QLD	783	32	05/12/44	SAN 1	SAN 1	m
HUMFREY, P.C.	B	NSW	228	43	23/05/45	SAN 1	SAN 2	bb/m
HUMPHREYS, P.G.	B	NSW	-	41	26/05/45	SAN 1	SAN 2	air raid/Relic-R
HUMPHRIES, D.	E	NSW	1752	27	13/02/45	1m MALIO	TR	1M/shot
HUNT, N.F.	B	VIC	838	40	29/05/45	SAN 1	S3/ CPD	m
HUNT, R.P.	B	SA	837	42	13/02/45	3m M'NGUN	TR	1M/cbb
HUNTER, A.C.	B	NSW	246	23	12/07/45	RAN 2J	RAN 2JB	2M/m
HUNTER, H.D.	B	NSW	851	42	04/12/44	SAN 1	SAN 1	m
HURLEY, E.T.	B	NSW	834	24	10/12/44	SAN 1	SAN 1	m men
HURST, R.E.	B	NSW	809	29	02/04/45	SAN 1	SAN 2	m
HUSTLER, F.E.	B	WA	835	36	05/06/45	ECR	TR	2M/m
HUTCHINSON, J.N.	B	NSW	-	35	04/02/45	SAN 1	SAN 1	m
HUTCHINSON, V.	B	NSW	233	39	02/06/45	ECR	TR	2M/m
HUTCHISON, C.E.	B	QLD	836	36	19/04/45	SAN 1	SAN 2	m
HUTCHISON, G.E.	B	QLD	814	27	26/04/45	SAN 1	SAN 2	m
HUTTON, A.C.	B	QLD	1440	42	30/03/45	SAN 1	SAN 2	m
HUTTON, J.K.	B	NSW	229	30	22/04/45	SAN 1	SAN 2	m
HYETT, R.G.	B	QLD	804	40	10/04/45	SAN 1	SAN 2	m
I'ANSON, W.L.	B	VIC	248	44	01/05/45	SAN 1	SAN 2	m
ILES, C.	B	QLD	855	43	21/05/45	SAN 1	SAN 2	m
INCE, J.W.	E	NSW	1754	26	04/06/45	37m SAN	TR	2M/RSm
INGHAM, A.E.	B	NSW	850	25	29/04/45	RAN 1	RAN 1B	m
INGRAM, C.E.	E	NSW	1755	31	05/06/45	SAN 2	SAN 3	m
INGS, E.H.	E	NSW	1756	41	24/02/45	SAN 1	SAN 1	m
INGS, J.	B	NSW	856	24	30/05/45	ECR	TR	RS/2Mm
IRELAND, G.A.	B	NSW	857	26	15/03/45	RAN 1/RC	R 1B/TR	1M/bb
IRVING, R.F.	B	VIC	858	41	02/06/45	SAN 2	SAN 3	RS/m
ISBEL, C.E.	B	QLD	854	26	25/03/45	RAN 1	RAN 1B	1M/m

APPENDIX 1: NOMINAL ROLLS

Name		State	No.	Age	Date	Place	Cemetery	Notes
IZZARD, C.H.M	B	QLD	853	24	19/03/45	PAG	PAG CEM	IM/bb
JACKAMAN, G.E.	E	QLD	1759	24	02/06/45	ECR	TR	2M/m
JACKES, W.K	B	NSW	250	32	15/03/45	SAN I	SAN I	m
JACKS, R.J.	B	VIC	869	36	11/04/45	SAN I	SAN 2	m
JACKSON, F.P.	B	NSW	859	27	02/07/45	SAN 2	SAN 3	RT/m
JACKSON, J.	B	NSW	249	29	29/04/45	SAN I	SAN 2	m
JACKSON, L.W.	B	NSW	867	27	16/04/45	RAN I	RAN IB	IM/m
JACKSON, L.E.	B	NSW	868	38	08/07/45	SAN 2	SAN 3	m
JACOBS, C.J.	B	NSW	885	44	22/06/45	ECR	TR	2M/m
JACOBS, F.W.	E	VIC	1790	22	06/07/45	SAN 2	SAN 3	m
JACOBS, G.W.	J/E	NSW	1589	38	09/04/45	RAN I	RAN IB	IM/m
JACOBSON, A.	B	WA	883	40	24/12/44	SAN I	SAN I	bro'itis
JAMES, G.L.	B	NSW	866	26	12/02/45	SAN I	SAN I	RS/m
JAMES, J.R.	E	NSW	1758	25	06/07/45	SAN 2	SAN 3	m
JAMES, R.W.	B	NSW	251	44	02/04/45	SAN I	SAN 2	m
JANTKE, R.J.	B	SA	881	42	21/03/45	SAN I	SAN I	m
JARRETT, P.	B	VIC	880	28	20/04/45	SAN I	SAN 2	m
JEAVONS, J.A.	B	QLD	253	37	14/07/45	RAN 2J (2M)	RAN 2JB	RT/ae
JEFFREY, R.L.	B	NSW	61	35	06/05/45	RAN IJ	RAN IJ	IM/m
JEFFREY, V.A.	B	TAS	885	25	13/02/45	9m e M'ULU	TR	IM/cbb
JENYNS, N.W.	B	QLD	875	27	12/06/45	SAN 2	SAN 3	OR/m
JESPERSON, T.F.	E	NSW	1762	28	01/03/45	SAN I	SAN I	m
JEWISS, A.C.	E	NSW	1763	27	13/07/45	RAN 2J	RAN 2JB	2M/m
JILLETT, R.E.	E	QLD	1764	25	05/06/45	ECR	TR	2M/m
JOHNSON, A.E.	B	VIC	873	43	16/02/45	SAN I	SAN I	m
JOHNSON, C.G.	B	QLD	863	32	11/02/45	rest h M'RIN	TR	IM/bb
JOHNSON, H.L.	B	NSW	876	47	14/03/45	SAN I	SAN I	RS/m
JOHNSON, H.V.	E	NSW	1765	31	29/06/45	SAN 2	SAN 3	ae
JOHNSON, S.H.	B	NSW	870	27	22/06/45	SAN 2	SAN 3	RS/bb
JOHNSON, S.R.	B	NSW	878	28	11/02/45	M'ORIN	TR	1M/mbb
		(official date is 28/02/45 (PRESUMED). New information obtained from 'corrupted names' list						
JOHNSTON, A.B.	E	NSW	1766	38	10/05/45	SAN I	SAN 2	m
JOHNSTON, C.(Vic)	B	NSW	866	29	04/06/45	37m SAN	TR	2M/m
JOHNSTON, C.S.	B	NSW	875	30	14/07/45	SAN 2	SAN 4	K/appen
JOHNSTON, S.	B	VIC	862	21	21/04/45	SAN I	SAN 2	ae
JONES, A.F.	B	NSW	877	41	02/06/45	ECR	TR	2M/m
JONES, D.H.	B	NSW	248	42	13/07/45	SAN 2	SAN 4	K/m
JONES, F.J.	B	QLD	871	35	23/05/45	SAN I	SAN 2	m
JONES, H.B.	B	NSW	884	28	05/06/45	44.5m SAN	KG(New)	2M/bb
JONES, J W	B	VIC	255	35	18/03/45	PAG	PAG CEM	IM/ae
JONES, K.	E	VIC	1765	27	17/05/45	SAN I	SAN 2	m
JONES, V.	B	WA	874	43	05/04/45	RAN I(IM)	RAN IB	RR/bb
JONES, W.N.	B	NSW	864	25	26/02/45	RAN I	RAN IA	IM/ae
JORDAN, W.A.	B	NSW	861	29	26/05/45	SAN I	SAN 2	m
JOSELAND, K.A.	B	NSW	256	44	01/11/44	SAN I	KG	m
JOYNES, C.	B	WA	860	31	07/06/45	SAN 2	SAN 3	RS/m
JUBELSKI, C.W.M.	B	WA	389	31	16/06/45	SAN 2	SAN 3	m
aka Anderson, C.W.M.								
JUCHAU, R.F.	B	NSW	252	27	23/07/45	RAN 2J	RAN 2JB	2M/ae
JUKES, C.G.H.	B	QLD	254	39	23/07/45	RAN 2J	RAN 2JB	2M/ae
JURY, S.H.	B	VIC	872	36	15/03/45	SAN I	SAN I	m
JUSTICE, A.J.	E	NSW	1768	26	21/03/45	SAN I	SAN I	m
KANE, G.F.	E	NSW	1769	25	12/01/45	SAN I	SAN I	appendix
KAVANAGH, L.M.	E	SA	1770	42	15/02/45	RAN I	RAN IA	m
KEALEY, J.V.	B	QLD	888	35	30/07/45	RAN 2J	RAN 2JB	2M/ae m
KEARNEY, J.	B	NSW	898	29	24/05/45	SAN I	SAN 2	RO/m
KEATING, P.M.	B	NSW	889	49	05/02/45	SAN I	SAN I	m
KEATING, W.M.	B	NSW	897	36	03/02/45	SAN I	SAN I	m
KEAY, V.A.	B	WA	258	39	15/01/45	SAN I	SAN 2	m
KEAYS, D.C.	E	VIC	1772	22	19/03/45	RAN I	RAN IB	bb
KELLY, B.H.	B	VIC	-	27	08/05/45	SAN I	SAN 2	-
KELLY, F.W.	B	NSW	891	28	21/06/45	ECR	TR	2M/m
KELLY, H.A.	J/E	RAN	1775	-	20/01/45	SAN I	SAN I	m
KELLY, S.J.	B	NSW	899	37	07/06/45	ECR	TR	2M/ae
KEMP, H.A.	J/E	NSW	1721	43	05/04/45	SAN I	SAN 2	bb
KEMP, M.W.	B	VIC	890	48	04/04/45	SAN I	SAN 2	M
KENT, E.J.	B	NSW	902	27	24/04/45	RAN I	RAN IB	IM/m
KERR, J.R.	B	NSW	900	23	15/02/45	nr M'ngan	TR	IM/BB
KERRIS, J.L.	B	VIC	904	30	26/06/45	SAN 2	SAN 3	m
KILMINSTER, E.G.	B	WA	907	32	04/12/44	SAN I	SAN I	m
KILPATRICK, C.H.	B	VIC	906	43	22/03/45	SAN I	SAN I	m
KILPATRICK, J.	B	NSW	910	40	03/04/45	SAN I	SAN 2	m
KINDER, J.W.	B	RAAF	1441	28	10/06/45	RAN IJ	KG	IM/dys
KING, C.H.	B	VIC	903	41	18/07/45	RAN 2J	RAN 2JB	2M/ae
KING, E.	B	VIC	896	48	10/06/45	ECR	TR	2M/m
KING, J.S.	B	WA	908	35	13/06/45	ECR	TR	2M/m
KING, P.C.	B	QLD	895	36	17/06/45	ECR	TR	2M/m

KING, R.A.	E	NSW	1776	40	12/05/45	SAN I	SAN 2	m
KINGSLEY, C.M.	B	VIC	259	39	02/06/45	ECR	TR	2M/m
KINNON, V.R.	B	QLD	886	28	07/06/45	ECR	TR	2M/m
KIRBY, E.A.	E	NSW	1777	32	19/04/45	SAN I	SAN 2	m
KLINE, J.	B	NSW	901	32	16/02/45	SAN I	SAN I	m
KNAPP, W.G.	B	SA	894	30	15/06/45	SAN 2	SAN 3	m
KNIGHT, H.E.	B	NSW	260	39	01/05/45	SAN I	SAN 2	m
KNIGHT, H.R.	B	VIC	911	42	30/01/45	SAN I	SAN I	RS/m
KNIGHT, V.	B	VIC	893	45	16/02/45	SAN I	SAN I	bb
KNOWLES, J.	B	NSW	905	49	20/02/45	SAN I	SAN I	m
KNOX, E.G.	E	VIC	1778	39	19/04/45	SAN I	SAN 2	bb
KNOX, J.W.	E	NSW	1534	31	22/03/45	SAN I	SAN I	m
KOHLER, L.G.	E	SA	1779	34	27/03/45	SAN I	SAN 2	m
KOPANICA, J.F.	E	VIC	1780	25	05/08/45	RAN 2J(2M)	R 2JB/MS	false dod
KREIGER, L.C.	B	NSW	909	35	24/02/45	SAN I	SAN I	m
KROSCHEL, E.M.	B	VIC	887	24	18/01/45	SAN I	SAN I	m
KYTE, H.G.	B	QLD	892	25	18/06/45	SAN 2	SAN 3	m
LAIDLAW, A.J.	B	QLD	942	30	10/04/45	SAN I	SAN 2	m
LAKE, G.	E	WA	1782	23	08/04/45	SAN I	SAN 2	m
LAKE, W.T.	B	NSW	-	34	25/05/45	SAN I	SAN 2	m
LAMBERT, G.	J/E	VIC	1774	42	08/03/45	SAN I	SAN I	ae
LANCASTER, W.J.	B	VIC	262	46	07/06/45	ECR	TR	2M/bb
LANE, DR	E	WA	1783	24	16/01/45	SAN I	SAN I	bb
LANE, T.H.	B	NSW	938	40	18/04/45	SAN I	SAN 2	m
LANG, J.A.	B	QLD	939	36	07/02/45	SAN I	SAN I	m
LANGTON, C.G.	B	QLD	943	35	25/05/45	SAN I	SAN 2	m
LARCOMBE, C.T.	B	NSW	948	26	28/02/45	(PRESUMED)		No detail
LARKINS, M.J.	B	VIC	945	35	22/06/45	ECR	TR	2M/m
LARNER, V.G.	B	SA	266	31	03/03/45	SAN I	SAN I	appendix
LAST, A.B.	B	NSW	927	29	10/07/45	RAN 2J(2M)	RAN 2JB	RR/m
LAUNDER, F.A.	B	NSW	952	41	24/05/45	SAN I	SAN 2	air raid
LAW, A.W.	B	NSW	918	25	21/03/45	SAN I	SAN I	m
LAWRENCE, A.S.	B	NSW	268	27	18/06/45	ECR	TR-d out	2M/m
LEA, R.	E	NSW	1784	34	22/03/45	SAN I	SAN I	m
LEADBEATTER, W.	B	NSW	928	24	15/05/45	RAN IJ	RAN IJ	RR/m
LEAR, H.B.	E	WA	1785	25	17/03/45	SAN I	SAN I	m
LEAR, J.	B	NSW	917	43	17/06/45	ECR	TR	2M/m
LEARMONTH, R.G.	B	VIC	936	26	06/03/45	SAN I	SAN I	m
LEBEAU, W.H.	E	NSW	1786	22	24/01/45	SAN I	SAN I	m
LE CLERCQ, A.E.	B	NSW	944	21	04/03/45	SAN ?	SAN ?	DR/m
LE CUSSAN, E.W.	B	NSW	947	32	08/03/45	RAN I	RAN IA	IM/ae
LEDWIDGE, F.B.	E	NSW	1781	43	12/03/45	23m SAN	KG	esc/m
LEE, D.H.	B	NSW	932	28	04/06/45	SAN 2	SAN 3	m
LEEDHAM, C.A.	B	SA	924	43	18/02/45	SAN I	SAN I	RS/m
LE FEVRE, R.	J/E	NSW	1781	34	06/05/45	SAN I	SAN 2	m
LEINSTER, V.P.	B	QLD	925	26	22/02/45	PAG (IM)	PAG CEM	RT/ae
LEITH, F.A.	B	VIC	950	25	22/05/45	SAN ?	SAN ?	DR/m
LENNON, V.J.	E	NSW	1788	26	07/02/45	SAN I	SAN I	m
LESTER, J.B.	B	SA	394	38	30/03/45	SAN ?(DR)	SAN ?	RS/bb
LETHBRIDGE, T.C.	B	NSW	916	38	15/07/45	RAN 2J	RAN 2JB	2M/m
LEVER, A.L.	E	NSW	1789	26	02/06/45	SAN 2	SAN 3	RS/RO m
LEVEY, R.E.	B	NSW	915	31	14/06/45	ECR	TR-d out	2M/m
LEVIS, H.	E	NSW	1536	43	16/06/45	MALIO	KG	2M/m
LEWIS, C.W.	B	NSW	933	39	17/01/45	SAN I	SAN I	m
LEWIS, F.A.	B	NSW	927	23	24/03/45	SAN I	SAN 2	m
LEWIS, J.	B	VIC	937	33	19/04/45	SAN I	SAN 2	m
LEY, P.	B	NSW	931	42	28/04/45	SAN I	SAN 2	m
LIGHT, J.W.	E	QLD	1790	24	15/02/45	SAN ?	SAN ?	DR/m
LILLYMAN, J.A.	B	NSW	261	37	17/06/45	SAN 2	SAN 3	m
LINDQVIST, L.R.	E	SA	1791	32	29/05/45	SAN I	S3 /CPD	RS/m
LINDSAY, R.L.	B	NSW	930	42	18/06/45	SAN 2	SAN 3	m
LISTER, A.W.	B	NSW	929	23	15/06/45	SAN 2	SAN 3	RS/m
LIVET, V.L.	B	NSW	922	22	07/04/45	RAN I	RAN IB	IM/ae
LIVINGSTONE, H.H.	B	QLD	926	32	28/03/45	SAN I	SAN 2	RT/ae
LLOYD, H.G.	B	NSW	265	42	05/06/45	ECR (2M)	TR-d out	RS/m
LOADER, K.M.	B	SA	267	33	13/05/45	SAN I	SAN 2	m
LOAN, J.B.	E	NSW	1792	38	19/01/45	SAN I	SAN I	m
LOBEGEIGER, J. aka Randoll, J.	B	NSW	1203	23	14/03/45	RAN I	RAN IA	IM/ ae ulcer
LOCK, B.C.	B	VIC	923	26	18/02/45	RAN I(IM)	RAN IA	RR/ae
LOCKE, J.	B	NSW	263	30	20/03/45	SAN I	SAN I	m
LOGAN, R.W.B.	B	NSW	935	41	26/03/45	RAN I/RC	R IB/TR	u/bb
LONGBOTTOM, H.	B	NSW	941	28	11/02/45	SAN I	SAN I	bb
LONGLEY, H.	B	NSW	946	22	05/07/45	RAN 2J	RAN 2JA	2M/m
LOURAY, F.L.	B	VIC	949	43	03/06/45	SAN 2	SAN 3	m
LOVE, W.H.	E	VIC	1794	44	18/11/44	SAN I	KG	m
LOVERIDGE, A.A.	E	NSW	1793	42	09/01/45	SAN I	SAN I	m
LOWE, A.J.	B	VIC	951	31	17/03/45	SAN I	SAN I	m

APPENDIX 1: NOMINAL ROLLS

Name								
LOWE, J.T.	B	NSW	920	25	15/06/45	SAN 2	SAN 3	m
LUDBEY, R.B.	B	TAS	912	48	05/11/43	SAN 1	KG	jaundice
LUMBY, V.A.	B	NSW	919	31	04/03/45	SAN 1	SAN 1	m
LUPTON, L.	J/E	NSW	1863	30	08/04/45	SAN 1	SAN 2	m
LUPTON, S.J.	E	QLD	1795	31	05/06/45	SAN 2	SAN 3	RS/m
LUTON, H.W. aka McCormack, H.W.	E	NSW	1800	22	04/07/45	RAN 2J	RAN 2JA	2M/m
LYNCH, J.J.	B	WA	269	44	20/06/45	ECR	TR	2M/m
LYNE, G.N.	B	NSW	914	25	04/06/45	SAN 2	SAN 3	m
LYNTON, R.L.M.	B	QLD	270	45	06/06/45	SAN 2	SAN 3	m
LYSAGHT, H.W.	B	NSW	913	36	04/07/45	RAN 2J	RAN 2JA	RR/ae
LYTTON, H.	B	QLD	940	25	15/05/45	RAN 1J	KG (New)	2M/RR
MABEN, R.R.	B	NSW	940	34	31/05/45	ECR	TR	2M/m
MABIN, D.W.	B	QLD	970	22	14/02/45	4m e MALIO	TR	1M/cbb
MACADAM, S.J.	B	NSW	1066	44	03/04/45	SAN 1	SAN 2	dys
McAPPION, H.E.	B	WA	1013	26	04/04/45	26m SAN	KG (New)	RS/m
MACAULAY, W.A.	B	VIC	1034	45	29/04/45	SAN 1	SAN 2	dys
McCALL, K.B.	B	NSW	987	24	12/04/45	SAN 1	SAN 2	m
McCALLUM, H.D.	B	QLD	998	34	17/04/45	SAN 1	SAN 2	m
McCARDLE, P.E.	B	NSW	1060	43	20/04/45	SAN 1	SAN 2	m
McCARTHY, J.F.	B	QLD	983	36	09/04/45	SAN 1	SAN 2	ae
McCARTHY, J.F.	B	SA	273	42	01/06/45	ECR	TR	2M/ae
McCARTHY, L.	B	NSW	1039	44	02/03/45	PAG (1M)	PAG CEM	RT/ae
McCLINTOCK, W.A.	B	NSW	1059	36	22/03/45	SAN 1	SAN 1	m
McCLOUNAN, R.L.	B	SA	1058	25	09/06/45	29m e BOTO	TR	2M/m
McCONNELL, A.	B	WA	1065	42	09/06/45	28m e BOTO	TR	2M/m
McCONVILLE, J.H.	E	NSW	1799	35	16/04/45	SAN 1	SAN 2	m
McCORLEY, K.	E	QLD	1538	33	22/07/45	RAN 2J	RAN 2JB	2M/ae
McCORMACK, R.A.	B	NSW	988	41	15/04/45	SAN 1	SAN 2	m
McCRACKEN, W.E.	B	VIC	1016	35	10/06/45	SAN 2	SAN 3	RS/m
McCRUM, A.	E	NSW	1801	43	25/03/45	RAN 1/RC	R 1B/TR	1M/bb
McCULLOCH, C.R.	B	VIC	1053	20	01/03/45	SAN 1	SAN 1	m
McCULLOUGH, W.	J/E	WA	1964	40	20/04/45	SAN 1	SAN 2	m
McDONALD, A.	B	SA	274	40	05/02/43	SAN 1	KG	m
McDONALD, C.H.	J/E	NSW	1958	32	03/06/45	SAN 2	SAN 3	m
McDONALD, F.R.	B	NSW	997	24	30/03/45	SAN 1	SAN 2	m
McDONALD, G.A.	B	VIC	959	57+	26/12/44	SAN 1	SAN 1	m men
MacDONALD, L.	B	NSW	1062	25	30/05/45	ECR	TR	2M/m
MacDONALD, R.H.	B	QLD	278	39	21/02/45	SAN 1	SAN 1	m
McDONALD, W.B.	E	NSW	1539	44	13/08/45	RAN 2J(2M)	R 2JB/MS	false dod
McDONOUGH, J.B.	B	WA	1012	41	15/03/45	SAN 1	SAN 1	m
McEWAN, R.I.	B	NSW	275	29	08/07/45	RAN 2J	RAN 2JA	2M/M
McEWEN, G.A.	B	NSW	1019	38	01/06/45	SAN 2	SAN 3	m
McFARLANE, J.	B	WA	1054	37	20/06/45	ECR	TR	2M/M
McGEARY, E.D.	B	VIC	994	25	21/06/45	SAN 2	SAN 3	m
McGEE, H.A.	E	NSW	1802	24	25/02/45	RAN 1	RAN 1A	1M/m
McGEE, W A	E	NSW	1540	28	14/04/45	RAN 1	RAN 1B	RR/m
McGILL, L.	B	NSW	985	27	11/04/45	SAN 1	SAN 2	m
McGLINN, A.J.	B	NSW	287	41	09/07/45	RAN 2J	RAN 2JA	2M/m
McGOWAN, W.J.	B	NSW	989	43	03/04/45	RAN 1(1M)	RAN 1B	RR/bb
McGRATH, P.J.	B	NSW	285	44	25/04/45	SAN 1	SAN 2	m
McGREGOR, J.A.	E	NSW	1796	36	03/05/45	SAN 1	SAN 2	m
McGREGOR, R.	E	NSW	1541	25	05/04/45	SAN 1	SAN 2	m
McGUIRE, A.D.	E	NSW	1803	34	14/07/45	RAN 2J	RAN 2JB	2M/m
McHENERY, L.G.	B	NSW	1055	41	07/05/45	SAN ?	SAN ?	DR/m
McILLHAGGA,W.J.	B	NSW	1063	44	19/06/45	1m w M'GAN	TR	2M/ae
McILROY, K.A.	B	NSW	1033	25	05/07/45	RAN 2J	RAN 2JA	2M/m
McIVER, C.A.	B	QLD	1015	39	19/08/44	SAN 1	KG	m
McIVER, D.	E	QLD	1805	31	26/02/45	RAN 1	RAN 1A	RS/ae
MACKAY, F.J.	B	QLD	1454	35	08/11/42	SAN 1	KG	dys
MACKAY, T.	B	NSW	995	40	02/06/45	32m SAN	TR	2M/m
MACKAY,T.R.B. aka McKenzie, D.H.	B	QLD	975	32	11/05/43	SAN 1	KG	esc/shot
McKEAN, I.	B	VIC	1014	30	14/06/45	SAN 2	SAN 3	m
McKELVIE, M.	B	VIC	1057	48	24/04/45	SAN 1	SAN 2	m
McKENNA, C.R.	B	WA	1036	34	01/02/45	SAN 1	SAN 1	m
MacKENZIE, C.	B	VIC	980	21	20/04/45	SAN 1	SAN 2	m
MacKENZIE, D.H.	B	QLD	1020	44	24/06/45	8m e RAN	TR-d out	2M/m
MacKENZIE, D.	B	NSW	298	40	26/02/45	SAN 1	SAN 1	m
McKENZIE, W.J.	B	NSW	990	27	07/04/45	RAN 1	RAN 1B	1M/ae
McKERROW, E.A.	E	QLD	1806	26	28/06/45	RAN 2J	RAN 2JA	2M/m
MACKIE, A.G.	B	NSW	979	26	13/05/45	SAN 1	SAN 2	m
MacKINNON, D.C.	E	NSW	1798	29	01/07/45	SAN 2	SAN 3	m
McKINNON, V.H.	B	SA	1037	29	14/04/45	RAN 1	RAN 1B	1M/m
MACKLIN, K.G.	B	NSW	1061	22	17/05/45	SAN 1	SAN 2	m
McLACHLAN, K.J.	E	NSW	1807	30	20/06/45	ECR	TR	2M/M
McLAGHLAN, T.D.	B	NSW	991	29	31/05/45	ECR	TR	m
McLAUGHLIN, B.L.	E	NSW	1809	28	18/03/45	RAN 1	RAN 1B	1M/m

Name		State	No.	Age	Date	Place 1	Place 2	Cause
McLAUGHLIN, R.G.	B	NSW	984	20	31/03/45	RAN I/RC	R 1B/TR	1M/m
McLEENAN, L.A.	E	NSW	1810	21	13/02/45	3m MILULU	TR	1M/bbm
McLELLAN, A.P.	B	QLD	958	26	02/06/45	9m SAN	TR	2M/m
McLENNAN, L.H.	E	VIC	1811	34	22/05/45	SAN 1	SAN 2	M
McLEOD, C.J.	B	VIC	271	30	14/05/45	SAN 1	SAN 2	m
McLEOD, J.R.	B	VIC	1017	24	09/03/45	SAN 1	SAN 1	ae
McLEOD, N.P.	E	VIC	1812	32	13/02/45	3m MILULU	TR	1M/bbm
McLEOD, W.	B	NSW	986	25	14/04/45	RAN 1	RAN 1B	1M/m
McMAHON, J.	B	VIC	1038	26	10/07/45	SAN 2	SAN 3	m
McMANUS, S.J.	B	VIC	289	28	27/03/45	SAN 1	SAN 2	m
McMARTIN, J.	B	VIC	1018	23	07/08/45	RAN 2J	R 2JB/MS	false dod
MACMEIKAN, D.J.	B	VIC	288	30	18/07/45	SAN 2	SAN 3	m
McNAUGHTON, D.	B	NSW	1056	43	28/06/45	SAN 2	SAN 3	RS/m
MACONACHIE, R.D.	B	WA	1067	25	03/06/45	26m SAN	TR	2M/ae
McPHERSON, S.D.	E	NSW	1813	23	19/03/45	PAG	PAG CEM	1M/ae
McSWEENEY, J.M.	B	VIC	903	28	29/12/44	SAN 1	SAN 1	m men
MADDEN, W.	E	NSW	1815	34	13/07/45	SAN 2	SAN 4	K/RO/m
MADDISON, J.W.	B	NSW	957	27	07/03/45	SAN ?	SAN ?	m
MADDOCK, N.L.	B	VIC	1442	25	24/07/45	RAN 2J	RAN 2JB	2M/ae
MAGUIRE, J.	B	NSW	1004	45	07/06/45	8m fr B'URAN	TR	RS/2Mm
MAHONEY, G. aka 'gut', 1M	B	NSW	1006	33	14/02/45	3m fr M'ADAI	TR	'blind-
MAHONEY, K.P.	B	QLD	-	34	24/01/45	SAN ?	SAN ?	DR/m
MAIN, C.D.	B	VIC	1002	22	05/06/45	35m SAN	TR	2M/ae
MAINSTONE, C.D.	B	NSW	1009	20	17/03/45	PAG	PAG CEM	1M/m
MAIZEY, C.W.	B	VIC	276	26	18/07/45	RAN 2J	RAN 2JB	RS/ae
MAKIM, G.J.	E	NSW	1814	23	17/06/45	ECR	TR	2M/ewb
MALIN, W.M.	E	QLD	1816	29	07/06/45	M'ATTO	TR	2M/m
MANKS, E.F.	B	NSW	1044	37	01/06/45	ECR	TR	2M/m
MANN, C.N.	B	QLD	279	37	02/03/45	PAG	PAG CEM	1M/ae
MANN, W.R.	B	NSW	295	31	06/07/45	RAN 2J(2M)	RAN 2JA	RR/m
MANTON, L.C.	E	SA	1816	27	22/07/45	SAN ? (DR)	SAN ?	RT/m
MARR, S.	B	VIC	978	40	28/03/45	SAN 1	SAN 2	m
MARSH, C.K.	E	NSW	1810	29	08/11/44	SAN 1	KG	pneu'ia
MARSH, H.A.	B	WA	972	40	08/06/45	SAN 2	SAN 3	RS/m
MARSH, W.R.	B	QLD	1023	27	16/03/45	PAG	PAG CEM	1M/ROm
MARSHALL, A.	B	NSW	962	34	07/06/45	SAN 2	SAN 3	m
MARSHALL, J.L.	E	VIC	1819	26	02/06/45	SAN 2	SAN 3	m
MARSHALL, L.F.	B	VIC	1455	27	05/11/42	SAN 1	KG	dys
MARSHALL, P.O.	B	NSW	1010	22	03/04/45	RAN 1	RAN 1B	1M/men
MARTIN, F.J.	B	NSW	995	43	04/12/44	SAN ?	SAN ?	DR/m
MARTIN, J.T.	E	NSW	1821	25	18/03/45	PAG	PAG CEM	1M/bb
MARTIN, J.W.	B	NSW	1064	27	13/02/45	4m e S'DAI	TR	1M/cbb
MARTIN, M.F.	E	SA	1537	29	04/10/43	SAN 3	KG	l'tning
MASKEY, L.W.	B	NSW	1045	27	01/08/45	RAN 2J	RAN 2JB	2M/bb/ killed at cemetery with the 17 ill
MATCHETT, H.D.	B	NSW	1046	43	22/07/45	RAN 2J	RAN 2JB	2M/ae
MATHEW, A.W.	B	NSW	954	36	02/06/45	ECR	TR	RS/m
MAUNSELL, J.F.	B	VIC	1001	20	19/03/45	RAN 1	RAN 1B	1M/bb u
MAWHINNEY, G.B.	B	NSW	283	35	20/01/45	SAN 1	SAN 1	m
MAY, D.J.	B	VIC	1080	28	03/08/45	RAN 2J	R 2JB/MS	false dod
MEAGHER, G.F.	B	QLD	956	32	29/05/45	SAN ? (DR)	SAN ?	RS /m
MEEK, D.R.	E	NSW	1543	26	18/03/45	RAN I/RC	R 1B/TR	1M/m
MEEK, E.L.	E	NSW	1542	40	14/07/45	SAN 2	SAN 4	K/m
MENZIES, H.W.	B	NSW	960	39	28/05/45	SAN 1	SAN 2	m
MERCER, R.L.	B	VIC	1011	25	04/05/45	SAN 1	SAN 2	RS/m
MEREDITH, D.H.	B	NSW	1028	23	15/04/45	SAN 1	SAN 2	m
MERRITT, R.L.	B	VIC	999	32	07/06/45	nr BELURAN	TR	2m/ae
MIDGLEY, J.J.	B	NSW	1047	44	16/03/45	SAN1	SAN 1	RS/m
MIDLANE, D.L.	B	NSW	291	28	05/06/45	ECR	TR	2M/m
MILDENHALL, J.S	B	NSW	1048	36	09/06/45	MANDORIN	TR	2M/shot
MILLER, A.M.	B	NSW	1031	24	26/03/45	SAN 1	SAN 2	m
MILLER, S.B.	B	VIC	1040	24	29/04/45	SAN 1	SAN 2	M
MILLIKEN, W.E.	B	VIC	961	38	12/02/45	SAN 1	SAN 1	m
MILLS, J.K.	B	NSW	280	35	18/05/45	SAN 1	SAN 2	m
MILNE, G.W.H	B	WA	1027	41	14/02/45	SAN 1	SAN 1	m
MILNE, R.A.	B	NSW	1029	23	13/04/45	SAN ?	SAN ?	m
MITCHELL, A.L.	E	NSW	1822	43	22/06/45	ECR	TR	2M/m
MITCHELL, E.E.	B	NSW	284	39	28/03/45	SAN 1	SAN 2	m
MITCHELL, J.W.	E	NSW	1544	31	20/02/45	RAN 1	RAN 1A	1M/ae
MITCHELL, R.J.	E	SA	1825	29	22/06/45	ECR	TR	2M/m
MITCHELL, W.E.	B	NSW	297	45	10/05/45	SAN 1	SAN 2	m
MITCHELL, W.G.	B	QLD	982	43	05/02/45	SAN 1	SAN 1	m
MOLAN, D.T.	B	NSW	1049	37	20/05/45	SAN 1	SAN 2	m
MOLDE, K.C. aka Dawson, L.K.	B	NSW	619	28	late May 45	KEMANSI	KG	esc1M RS/RO
MOLLOY, J.	B	NSW	1050	41	03/05/45	RAN 1J	RAN 1J	1M/m
MOLONEY, S.W.	B	NSW	1041	26	13/01/45	SAN 1	SAN 1	m
MONAGHAN, H.J.	B	NSW	971	33	29/03/45	SAN 1	SAN 2	m

APPENDIX 1: NOMINAL ROLLS

Name								
MONGAN, D.	B	NSW	1032	45	30/10/44	SAN 1	KG	air raid
MONLEY, F.J.	E	QLD	1545	26	22/02/45	RAN 1	RAN 1A	1M/ae
MONRO, W.	B	VIC	277	42	27/05/45	SAN 1	SAN 2	
MOORE, A.C.	E	NSW	1824	43	10/04/45	SAN 1	SAN 2	m
MOORE, A.W.	B	WA	974	40	29/03/45	SAN 1	SAN 2	RS/m
MOORE, C.G.	B	NSW	963	24	27/05/45	SAN 1	SAN 2	m
MOORE, E.G.	B	NSW	281	24	04/06/45	SAN 2	SAN 3	m
MOORE, E.J.	B	VIC	953	32	01/07/45	SAN 2	SAN 3	m
MOORE, J.E.	E	NSW	1825	29	20/03/45	SAN 1	SAN 1	
MOORE, L.C.	B	VIC	1007	27	28/04/45	SAN 1	SAN 2	ae
MOORE, M.F.	B	NSW	964	31	13/02/45	SAN 1	SAN 1	bb
MOORE, S.L.	B	NSW	929	46	03/01/45	SAN 1	SAN 1	
MOORE, T.A.	J/E	VIC	1877	24	31/03/45	RAN 1/RC	R 1B/TR	1M/m
MORAN, J.P.	E	NSW	1826	27	07/04/45	SAN 1	SAN 2	m
MORAN, R.K.	E	WA	1827	21	28/06/45	SAN 2	SAN 3	RS/m
MORGAN, E.	B	NSW	1042	25	22/03/45	PAG	PAG CEM	1M/m
MORGAN, H.A.	B	VIC	1053	31	26/03/45	SAN 1	SAN 2	RS/m
MORGAN, H.C.	E	SA	1828	27	10/04/45	RAN 1	RAN 1B	1M/ae
MORGAN, L.C.	B	SA	278	34	21/02/45	SAN 1	SAN 1	m
MORGAN, L.G.	B	VIC	996	22	05/04/45	RAN 1	RAN 1B	2M/bb
MORGAN, N.L.	B	VIC	1025	29	09/06/45	SAN 2	SAN 3	m
MORLAND, R.G.	B	VIC	1015	28	20/03/45	RAN 1	RAN 1B	1M/bb u
MORRISS, G.J.	J/E	RAN	1858	-	29/05/45	SAN 1	CPD 1	m
MORRIS, H.	B	NSW	1008	23	18/02/45	6mw N'PAK	TR	1M/bb
MORRIS, R.W.	B	VIC	1052	24	23/06/45	SAN 2	SAN 3	m
MORTIMER, C.H.	B	QLD	1026	33	23/03/45	SAN 1	SAN 2	m
MORTIMER, H.W.	B	NSW	296	47	17/02/45	SAN 1	SAN 1	
MORTON, H.A.	B	NSW	1005	35	31/03/45	SAN 1	SAN 2	m
MOTLEY, L.	B	NSW	973	35	05/06/45	SAN 2	SAN 3	m
Moule-Probert, J.	B	NSW	1003	48	10/05/45	SAN 1	SAN 2	m
MULLIGAN, R.P.	B	NSW	966	24	21/02/45	SAN 1	SAN 1	m
MULRAY, W.P.	B	NSW	967	32	06/04/45	RAN 1	RAN 1B	1M/ae
MULVOGUE, R.H.	B	VIC	1021	31	05/03/45	RAN 1	RAN 1A	1M/ae
MUMME, L.W.	E	SA	1797	26	02/03/45	PAG	PAG CEM	1M/ae
MUNFORD, F.A.	B	NSW	968	24	06/02/45	SAN 1	SAN 1	
MUNRO, E.L.	E	VIC	1546	34	03/08/45	RAN 2J (M)	R 2JB/MS	false dod
MUNRO, J.F.	B	QLD	294	29	28/05/45	SAN 1	SAN 2	air raid
MUNRO, L.A.	B	NSW	1043	23	01/06/45	RAN 1J	RAN 1J	1M/m
MURNANE, W.J.	B	VIC	1022	37	26/01/43	SAN 1	KG	pneu/bb
MURRAY, D.A.	B	NSW	293	40	25/03/45	RAN 1	RAN 1B	1M/ae
MURRAY, G.B.	B	NSW	297	44	21/04/45	SAN 1	SAN 2	m
MURRAY, L.W.	B	QLD	1460	35	18/10/42	SAN 1	KG	dementia
MURRAY, R.	B	NSW	969	30	20/05/45	RAN 1J	KG(New)	1M/K
MURRAY, R.J.	E	VIC	1829	26	10/03/45	SAN 1	SAN 1	m
MYERS, C.D.	E	NSW	1830	32	29/04/45	SAN 1	SAN 2	
NAGLE, M.J.	B	VIC	1070	30	15/06/45	SAN 2	SAN 3	m
NASH, C.O.	E	WA	1831	26	23/03/45	RAN 1(1M)	RAN 1B	RR/ae u
NAZZARI, F.	E	WA	1832	29	24/04/45	SAN 1	SAN 2	ae
NEAL, C.S.	B	NSW	1068	37	02/10/44	SAN 1	KG	m men
NEAL, F.W.	B	NSW	1073	42	05/06/45	SAN 2	SAN 3	RS/m
NEAL, K.T.	B	QLD	1077	25	14/04/45	SAN 1	SAN 2	RS/m
NEAL, R.	E	VIC	1833	23	25/05/45	SAN 1	SAN 2	m
NEALE, D.M.	E	NSW	1834	26	09/03/45	SAN 1	SAN 1	m
NEALE, S.E.	B	WA	835	30	28/02/45	(PRESUMED)		No detail
NEALE, T.S.	B	NSW	1466	43	14/09/42	SAN 1	KG	fever
NEAVES, G.M.	B	NSW	300	39	07/06/45	BELURAN	TR (2R)	RR/ae
NEGRI, P.J.	E	WA	1836	25	21/01/45	SAN 1	SAN 1	m
NEILSON, R.R.	B	NSW	1074	31	18/11/44	SAN 1	KG	m men
NEWHOUSE, F.	B	NSW	1444	51	12/07/45	SAN 2	SAN 3	bb
NEWLANDS, T.S.	B	QLD	1072	44	05/03/45	SAN 1	SAN 1	m
NEWLING, R.W.	B	WA	1071	33	13/06/45	RAN 2J	RAN 2JA	1M/m
NEWMAN, C.W.	E	NSW	1837	24	11/03/45	SAN 1	SAN 1	m
NEWSON, J.A.	E	NSW	1838	29	06/06/45	SAN 2	SAN 3	m
NEY, W.C.	B	NSW	1080	28	02/05/45	SAN 1	SAN 2	m
NICHOLS, S.T.	B	NSW	1069	24	01/02/45	SAN 1	SAN 1	m
NICHOLSON, E.C.	E	NSW	1839	44	11/06/45	SAN 2	SAN 3	RS/m
NICHOLSON, G.	E	NSW	1840	26	26/01/45	SAN 1	SAN 1	m
NICHOLSON, J.F.	E	NSW	1841	25	15/02/45	AT T'IAS	TR	1M/cbb
(last two entries were brothers)								
NINK, L.	B	NSW	301	32	14/07/45	SAN 2	SAN 4	K/m
NIXON, J.H.	B	VIC	1076	28	01/02/45	SAN 1	SAN 1	m
NOAKES, A.H.	B	NSW	1075	32	13/02/45	1m MILULU	TR	1M/bbm
NOAKES, A.W.	E	NSW	1842	30	27/03/45	RAN 1	RAN 1B	1M/bb
NOBLE, F.R.	E	WA	1843	25	26/05/45	SAN 1	SAN 2	m
NOLAN, G.N.	E	SA	1844	26	18/06/45	ECR	TR	2M/m
NOON, J.T.	E	NSW	1845	25	15/03/45	SAN 1	SAN 1	m
NOONAN, E.G.	B	NSW	1079	28	31/07/45	RAN 2J (2M)	R2JB	RR/m
NOONAN, W.A.	B	NSW	1078	25	23/07/45	RAN 2J	R2JB	2M/ae

SANDAKAN — A CONSPIRACY OF SILENCE

Name								
NUNN, J.O.	E	NSW	1846	32	09/02/45	PAPAN	TR	1M/ae m
OAKESHOTT, J.B.	E	NSW	1493	44	27/08/45	RAN 2J	KG (New)	2M/K
OAKLEY, J.H.	B	VIC	1097	33	23/05/45	SAN 1	SAN 2	m
OBEE, A.L.	B	VIC	1104	37	23/04/45	SAN 1	SAN 2	m
O'BRIEN, F.	B	NSW	304	34	23/05/45	SAN 1	SAN 2	m
O'BRIEN, M.V.	B	NSW	1094	36	22/06/45	ECR	TR	2M/m
O'BRIEN, W.M.	B	QLD	1090	35	01/04/45	SAN 1	SAN 2	m
O'CONNELL, J.T.	B	VIC	1083	37	14/01/45	SAN 1	SAN 1	m
O'CONNOR, A.H.	E	NSW	1847	25	26/02/45	SAN 1	SAN 1	m
O'CONNOR, G.	B	QLD	1085	27	07/03/45	RAN 1/RC	R1A/TR	1M/m
O'CONNOR, H.B.	B	VIC	302	29	27/07/45	RAN 2J	RAN 2JB	2M/ae
O'CONNOR, J.H.	J/E	VIC	1687	40	11/04/45	SAN 1	SAN 2	m
O'CONNOR, R.M.	E	NSW	1848	22	15/06/45	2m MALIO	KG	2M/
O'DONNELL, T.E.	B	NSW	1089	30	28/05/45	SAN 1	SAN 2	m
O'DONOHUE, E.J.	B	NSW	1101	24	11/08/45	RAN 2J (M)	R 2JB/MS	false dod
OGILVIE, D.J.	B	QLD	1084	32	30/06/45	SAN 2	SAN 3	m
O'HARA, M.T.	B	NSW	1093	34	29/05/45	(PRESUMED)		No detail
O'HARA, R.T.	B	NSW	1098	24	25/05/45	SAN 1	SAN 2	m
OHLSON, F.J.	E	VIC	1849	25	02/02/45	SAN 1	SAN 1	m
O'KEEFE, H.J.	B	NSW	1081	25	25/07/45	RAN 2J	RAN 2JB	2M/ae
OLIVE, E.R.	E	NSW	1850	30	17/05/45	SAN 1	SAN 2	m
OLIVER, J.	E	QLD	1851	30	16/03/45	SAN 1	SAN 1	m
OLLIS, J.N.	B	VIC	1099	28	16/02/45	SAN 1	SAN 1	m
O'LOUGHLIN, G.J.	B	NSW	1100	37	04/06/45	SAN 2	SAN 3	M
OLVER, K.F.	B	QLD	1098	34	17/02/45	SAN 1	SAN 1	m
O'MALLEY, G.F.	B	VIC	1096	25	17/02/45	nr M'ADAI	TR	1M/ae
O'MEARA, J.J.	B	VIC	1095	25	09/06/45	SAN 2	SAN 3	m
O'NEALE, J.T.	B	NSW	1088	28	03/06/45	SAN 2	SAN 3	m
O'NEIL, L.	E	WA	1852	36	16/12/44	SAN 1	SAN 1	appendix
O'NEILL, C.F.	B	QLD	303	41	19/03/45	SAN 1	SAN 1	m
O'ROURKE, T.J.	B	VIC	1087	26	31/05/45	23m SAN	TR	2M/m
ORR, E.J.K.	E	SA	1853	23	20/03/45	RAN 1	RAN 1B	1M/ae
ORR, J.S.	B	NSW	1091	22	04/03/45	SAN 1	SAN 1	shot/m
ORTLOFF, F.C.	B	SA	1086	35	18/02/45	SAN 1	SAN 1	RS/m
OSBORNE, S.A.	B	WA	1105	31	21/06/45	SAN 2	KG	RS/m
OSGOOD, A.	B	NSW	1445	43	07/03/45	SAN 1	SAN 1	m
OTTER, L.T.	E	VIC	1854	23	02/04/45	SAN 1	SAN 2	m
OVENS, H.	B	QLD	1082	26	05/06/45	44.5m SAN	KG(New)	2M/ae
OWER, W.J.	B	NSW	1102	44	18/07/45	RAN 2J	RAN 2JB	2M/ae
PAGE, R.A.	B	WA	1127	26	17/02/45	RAN 1	RAN 1A	1M/ae
PALLISTER, R.	B	NSW	1162	42	05/06/45	44.5m SAN	KG(New)	2M/ae
PALMER, A.	B	NSW	309	44	11/06/45	SAN 2	SAN 3	RS/m
PALMER D.	B	VIC	307	38	13/02/45	1m MILULU	TR (1M)	RR/bbm
PALMER, H.W.	B	NSW	1144	25	27/03/45	SAN 1	SAN 2	m
PALMER, N.W.	E	NSW	1856	32	07/06/45	M'ATTO	TR	2M/ae
PALMER, S.J.	B	NSW	315	26	19/04/45	SAN 1	SAN 2	m
PANTON, O.W.	B	TAS	1142	24	20/06/45	SAN 2	SAN 3	m
PARFREY, T.H.	E	NSW	1857	36	10/06/45	SAN ?	SAN ?	DR/m
PARHAM, A.G.	B	SA	1137	27	29/06/45	SAN 2	SAN 3	RO/m
PARKER, N.L.	B	NSW	1118	24	29/03/45	nr MURUK	TR	1M/K
PARKINSON, D.S.	B	QLD	312	34	19/02/45	RAN 1	RAN 1A	1M/ae
PARNELL, R.J.	B	VIC	1113	28	29/05/45	(PRESUMED)		No detail
PARSONS, J.W.	B	NSW	1147	49	12/07/45	RAN 2J (2M)	KG	RR/m
PARTRIDGE, N.E.	B	NSW	1117	32	04/07/45	SAN 2	SAN 3	m
PASHEN, J.W.	B	QLD	1135	34	03/02/45	SAN 1	SAN 1	m
PASSMORE, E.W.	B	WA	1145	41	13/02/45	SAN 1	SAN 1	m
PATERSON, S.	E	SA	1855	25	16/03/45	SAN 1	SAN 1	m
PATTEN, C.E.	B	NSW	1143	22	04/03/45	PAG	PAG CEM	1M/ae
PATTERSON, H.A.	B	QLD	1149	28	21/06/45	SEGINDAI	TR	2M/ae
PATTERSON, R.A.	B	NSW	1116	30	29/05/45	SAN 1	S3/ CPD	RS/m
PATTERSON, T.B.	B	NSW	1119	33	18/06/45	SAN 2	SAN 3	RO/m
PATTESON, E.	B	NSW	1148	43	22/02/45	SAN 1	SAN 1	m
PAULETT, L.	B	QLD	317	33	29/07/45	RAN 2J	RAN 2JB	2M/ae
PAWSON, C.	B	NSW	1150	56	19/04/45	SAN 1	SAN 2	m
PAXMAN, C.	E	VIC	1859	42	10/06/45	SAN 2	SAN 3	RS/m
PAYNE, H.J.	E	QLD	1860	25	04/06/45	36m SAN	TR	2M/m
PEACH, J.T.	B	VIC	308	27	16/07/45	RAN 2J	RAN 2JB	2M/m
PEACOCK, C.K.	B	VIC	318	28	15/03/45	SAN 1	SAN 1	m
PEARCE, J.S.	B	NSW	1120	27	07/06/45	M'ATTO	TR	2M/ae
PEARCE, K.J.	B	NSW	1163	43	08/06/45	nr BELURAN	TR	2M/bb
PEARCE, W.H.	B	VIC	1151	30	01/04/45	RAN 1	RAN 1B	1M/ulc
PECK, F.	B	VIC	306	35	16/03/45	SAN 1	SAN 1	RS/m
PEDERSON, P.M.	B	SA	319	47	21/01/45	SAN 1	SAN 1	m
PEGNALL, C.W.	B	QLD	311	27	02/05/45	SAN 1	SAN 2	m
PEOPLES, D.J.	B	VIC	1146	28	09/02/45	SAN 1	SAN 1	m
PEPPER, C.D.	B	NSW	1124	21	30/05/45	RAN 1J	RAN 1J	1M/m
PEPPER, G.D.	E	NSW	1548	30	10/03/45	RAN 1/RC	R 1A/TR	1M/bb

APPENDIX 1: NOMINAL ROLLS

Name								
PERCIVAL, E.J.	B	QLD	1161	39	25/02/45	SAN 1	SAN 1	m
PERROTT, C.E.	B	NSW	1160	33	15/02/45	SAN 1	SAN 1	m
PERRY, J.C.	E	NSW	1862	28	28/05/45	SAN 1	SAN 2	m
PERRY, K.G.	E	NSW	1861	25	18/02/45	6m w N'PAK	TR	1M/bb
PERRY, W.G.	B	VIC	1114	24	05/06/45	RAN 1J	RAN 1J	1M/m
Perry-Circuitt,E.	B	NSW	1140	40	17/04/45	SAN 1	SAN 2	m
PETERS, C.J.	B	QLD	1141	42	07/06/45	ECR?	TR?	2M
PETERS, K.A.	E	NSW	1547	40	07/06/45	RAN 1J	RAN 1J	RT/ae

(Information on last two is confused. C.J. Peters believed to have dropped out on 2M. K.A. Peters believed to have died at Ranau, but actual date of death, given as above, believed to be incorrect)

PETERSON, J.W.	B	QLD	313	26	08/07/45	SAN 2	SAN 3	m
PHELAN, M.J.	B	VIC	1112	36	27/06/45	SAN 2	SAN 3	RS/m
PHELPS, R.L.	B	NSW	1159	41	12/04/45	RAN 1	RAN 1B	1M/dys
PHILLIPS, B.	B	NSW	305	28	03/06/45	SAN 2	SAN 3	m
PHILLIPS, E.J.	B	VIC	1158	40	27/06/45	RAN 1	RAN 1B	1M/m
PHILLIPS, R.	B	VIC	1157	27	26/07/45	RAN 2J	RAN 2JB	2M/ae
PHILLIPS, W.A.	B	NSW	1156	43	22/01/45	SAN 1	SAN 1	m
PICKERING, J.A.	B	NSW	1121	43	27/03/45	SAN 1	SAN 2	m
PICONE, D.G.	B	QLD	96	36	27/08/45	RAN 2J	KG (New)	2M/K
PILE, E.N.	E	QLD	1864	23	13/06/45	SAN 2	SAN 3	m
PIPER, R.	B	QLD	1129	38	21/05/45	SAN 1	SAN 2	m
PLATFORD, J.	B	NSW	1126	45	23/05/45	SAN 1	SAN 2	RS/RR/RT/m
PLATT, S.H.	B	NSW	1125	30	26/05/45	SAN 1	SAN 2	bomb/m
PLAYER, G.C.	B	SA	1155	35	07/06/45	RAN 1J	RAN 1J	1M/m
PLEWES, K.A.	B	NSW	1107	40	15/03/45	SAN 1	SAN 1	m
PLUNKETT, G.W.	B	NSW	1128	26	14/06/45	SAN 2	SAN 3	ae
PLUNKETT, J.	B	NSW	1130	42	03/04/45	SAN 1	SAN 2	bb
POGSON, C.R.	E	NSW	1865	40	15/06/45	ECR	TR	2M/bb
PONTIN, R.W.	B	VIC	1111	23	26/06/45	SAN 2	SAN 3	m
POPE, J.G.	B	NSW	1134	37	02/03/45	SAN 1	SAN 1	dys
PORRITT, N.A.	B	VIC	1115	27	20/05/45	SAN 1	KG	m
PORTEOUS, A.A.	B	WA	1154	39	03/11/44	SAN 1	KG	bb
POTTER, N.	B	VIC	1153	44	25/03/45	SAN 1	SAN 2	m
POWELL, C.A.	E	NSW	1863	34	03/09/44	SAN ?	SAN ?	DR/m

(as relics found San 2 Camp, dod probably June-Aug 1945)

POWELL, K.N.	B	VIC	1110	22	17/06/45	ECR	TR	2M/m
POWELL, L.V.	B	QLD	310	25	29/07/45	RAN 2J	RAN 2JB	2M/ae
POWER, C.G.R.	B	NSW	1122	32	20/07/45	RAN 2J	RAN 2JB	2M/ae
POWER, R.G.	B	QLD	1131	29	08/05/45	SAN 1	SAN 2	m
PRAETZ, N.H.	B	SA	1152	36	07/06/45	SAN 2	SAN 3	RS/m
PRENDERGAST,J.J.	B	NSW	1106	23	18/06/45	ECR	TR	appendix
PRIDE, V.H.	B	NSW	1164	24	27/05/45	SAN 1	SAN 2	appendix
PRIEST, H.E.	B	NSW	316	37	06/04/45	SAN 1	SAN 2	m
PRIESTER, F.	B	SA	1136	44	22/03/45	RAN 1/RC	R 1B/TR	1M/bb
PRINGLE, F.W.R.	B	QLD	1138	42	14/02/45	SAN 1	SAN 1	m
PRIOR, L.	B	WA	1109	40	18/04/45	SAN ?	SAN?	m
PROSSER, W.R.	B	VIC	1108	24	15/02/45	6mw M'ngan	TR	1M/hf
PRYOR, D.R.	B	NSW	1123	23	16/04/45	RAN 1(1M)	RAN 1B	RR/ROm
PURCELL, J.S.	E	NSW	1867	24	17/06/45	SAN 2	SAN 3	RS/m
PURDON, T.	B	NSW	314	44	18/03/45	SAN 1	SAN 1	ae
PURSELL, A.L.	B	VIC	1139	38	06/04/45	SAN 1	SAN 2	m
PURTILL, J.F.	B	QLD	1132	28	20/04/45	RAN 1	RAN 1B	1M/m
PURVIS, R.C.	B	QLD	1133	31	04/06/45	36.5m SAN	TR	2M/m
QUAILEY, A.C.	B	NSW	1166	24	16/02/45	m N'PAK	TR	1m/bay
QUINTAL, E.A.	B	NSW	1165	42	02/02/45	SAN 1	SAN 1	m
RADFORD, C.	B	VIC	1214	35	26/02/45	SAN 1	SAN 1	m
RADNEDGE, G.	B	NSW	1194	23	20/06/45	23 m SAN	KG	esc San
RAE, J.	B	NSW	1215	33	13/07/45	SAN 2	SAN 4	K/m
RAISON, V.R.	E	NSW	1869	29	02/06/45	ECR	TR	2M/m
RALEIGH, J.	E	VIC	1870	24	23/07/45	RAN 2J	RAN 2JB	2M/RS ae
RALPH, B.D.	B	VIC	1205	35	18/02/45	SAN 1	SAN 1	m
RALPH, W.D.	B	VIC	1206	33	12/01/45	SAN 1	SAN 1	m
RAMSAY, G.A.	B	VIC	1207	28	21/07/45	SAN 2	SAN 3	m
RANKIN, C.F.	B	NSW	1202	23	18/04/45	SAN 1	SAN 2	m
RANKIN, C.W.	B	NSW	1235	22	16/02/45	SAN 1	SAN 1	RT
RANKIN, G.H.	B	NSW	1201	25	28/04/45	SAN 1	SAN 2	m
RANKIN, J.R.	B	NSW	1226	33	15/03/45	SAN 1	SAN 1	m
RAPHAEL, H.N.	E	NSW	1872	23	02/06/45	ECR	TR	2M/m
RATCLIFF, R.B.	B	NSW	1177	39	08/05/45	RAN 1J	RAN 1J	1M/bb
RAWLINGS, B.A.	B	NSW	1200	39	15/04/45	SAN 1	SAN 2	m
RAYMOND, K.M.	E	QLD	1871	24	10/02/45	SAN 1	SAN 1	m
REA, E.H.	B	VIC	1193	35	01/06/45	ECR	TR	2M/m
READ, W.G.	B	NSW	1199	25	15/07/45	RAN 2J (2M)	RAN 2JB	RT/m
READING, T.A.	B	NSW	1174	33	11/08/45	RAN 2J (2M)	R 2JB/MS	false dod
REARDON, F.W.	B	NSW	1225	32	09/06/45	SAN ?	SAN ?	DR/ROm

REAY, S.V.	E	NSW	1873	23	08/02/45	3m w M'RIN	TR	1M/m
REDMAN, W.H.	B	NSW	1469	31	12/08/42	SAN I	KG	dys
REED, E.A.	B	VIC	1172	33	19/09/43	SAN I	SAN I	m
REID, D.A.	B	QLD	1179	41	29/06/45	SAN 2	SAN 3	m
REID, F.C.	E	SA	1549	27	20/06/45	ECR	TR	2M/m
REID, R.D.	B	VIC	325	44	27/02/45	RAN I	RAN IA	1M/ae
REID, W.	B	VIC	1181	39	27/12/44	SAN I	SAN I	heart f
REILLEY, V.A.	E	NSW	1874	30	02/06/45	ECR	TR	2M/m
REITHER, H.	B	VIC	1192	38	08/08/45	w of RAN	KG	esc/dys
REITZE, H.	B	VIC	1208	27	30/05/45	RAN IJ	RAN IJ	1M/m
RENAUD, E.C.	B	NSW	1227	32	14/03/45	SAN I	SAN I	m
RENDALL, D.	E	NSW	1875	36	09/06/45	ECR	TR	2M/m
RENNIE, O.A.	E	NSW	1876	28	07/06/45	ECR	TR	2M/m
REYNOLDS, C.	B	NSW	1181	42	05/06/45	44 m SAN	KG (New)	2M/m
RICHARDS, E.M.	B	SA	1209	44	18/03/45	SAN I	SAN I	m
RICHARDS, E.R.	B	NSW	1167	32	20/07/45	RAN 2JB	KG	2M/ae m
RICHARDS, Evan	B	NSW	1222	31	07/06/45	ECR	TR	2M/m
RICHARDS, R.M.	B	NSW	1198	23	11/02/45	e TAMPIAS	KG (K)	1M/cbb
RICHARDSON, J.	B	NSW	1197	32	06/04/45	SAN I	SAN 2	m
RICHARDSON, J.G.	B	NSW	324	32	23/05/45	SAN I	SAN 2	m
RICHARDSON, J.L.	B	NSW	1176	25	04/06/45	37m SAN	TR	2M/m
RICHARDSON, L.W	B	NSW	1182	25	18/06/45	ECR	TR	2M/m
RICHMILLER, K.J.	B	VIC	1190	27	30/04/45	SAN I	SAN 2	m
RICKERBY, K.W.	B	QLD	1175	28	19/06/45	ECR	TR	2M/ROm
RIDLER, C.J.	B	QLD	1171	44	05/03/45	RAN I	RAN IA	1M/ae
RIGHETTI, L.J.	B	NSW	1228	28	17/02/45	RAN I	RAN IA	1M/m
RING, R.	B	NSW	1183	40	29/06/45	SAN ?	SAN ?	m
ROBBINS, T.H.	B	SA	1185	43	04/06/45	SAN 2	SAN 3	RS/m
ROBERTS, F.	E	NSW	1878	35	23/06/45	SAN 2	SAN 3	RS/m
ROBERTS, H.A.	B	NSW	1196	21	05/03/45	PAG	PAG CEM	1M/ae
ROBERTS, H.E.	E	NSW	1879	25	26/03/45	SAN I	SAN 2	m
ROBERTS, L.J.	E	VIC	1879	31	13/02/45	SAN I	SAN I	m
ROBERTS, Stanley	E	NSW	1880	28	19/06/45	RAN 2J	RAN 2JA	1M/ m
ROBERTS, Sydney	B	QLD	1204	42	21/05/45	SAN I	SAN 2	m
ROBERTS, W.F.	B	VIC	1210	31	30/03/45	SAN I	SAN 2	m
ROBERTSON, E.E.	B	SA	1211	44	23/05/45	SAN I	KG	m
ROBERTSON, F.H.	E	NSW	1881	26	11/07/45	RAN 2J	RAN 2JB	2M/m
ROBERTSON, G.C.	B	VIC	1223	28	23/05/45	RAN I	RAN IB	1M/ae
ROBERTSON, R.J.	E	NSW	1882	39	02/06/45	ECR	TR	2M/m
ROBINS, C.W.	B	QLD	1178	36	09/02/45	SAN I	SAN I	m
ROBINSON, B.A.	B	NSW	1195	23	23/05/45	SAN I	SAN 2	m
ROBINSON, F.	B	NSW	1229	31	10/04/45	RAN I	RAN IB	1M/bb
ROBINSON, F.G.B	B	VIC	323	25	14/02/45	SAN I	SAN I	m
ROBINSON, G.B.	B	NSW	1234	26	08/03/45	PAG	PAG CEM	1M/ae
ROBINSON, H.	B	NSW	1186	27	04/06/45	SAN 2	SAN 3	m
ROBINSON, J.F	E	VIC	1883	24	29/06/45	RAN 2J	RAN 2JA	2M/ae
ROCHFORD, F.	B	VIC	1217	31	30/03/45	SAN I	SAN 2	m
RODGERS, E.A.	B	NSW	1187	41	07/06/45	ECR	TR	2M/m
RODRIQUEZ, J.F.	B	VIC	1213	34	04/02/45	1m M'RIN	TR	1M/cbb
ROEBUCK, J.T.	B	NSW	1230	28	16/05/45	RAN IJ (1M)	RAN IJ	RT/m
ROGERS, J.S.	B	NSW	1232	41	17/06/45	ECR	TR	2M/ewb
ROLLS, W.F.	B	NSW	1188	27	09/04/45	SAN I	SAN 2	m
ROOKE, D.R.	B	NSW	1168	27	06/04/45	RAN I	RAN IB	1M/bb
ROOKE, R.G.	B	NSW	322	40	19/06/45	ECR	TR-d out	2M/m
ROSS, D.	E	WA	1885	32	23/05/45	SAN I	SAN 2	m
ROSS, J.H.	E	VIC	1868	29	10/02/45	7m w M'ULU	TR	1M/m/colitis
ROSS, W.	B	VIC	1216	44	12/02/45	SAN I	SAN I	m
ROUSE, J.F.	E	NSW	1884	36	02/06/45	ECR	TR	2M/bb
ROUSE, M.H.	B	SA	321	32	17/03/45	SAN I	SAN I	m
ROWAN, H.J.	B	NSW	1184	24	24/05/45	SAN I	SAN 2	m
ROWE, C.H.	B	QLD	1220	25	05/06/45	ECR	TR	2M/m
ROWLEY, B.	B	WA	1173	43	16/03/45	PAG (1M)	PAG CEM	RO/ae
RUANE, R.M.	E	NSW	1886	24	25/06/45	RAN	TR	2M/m
RUDD, W.T.	B	VIC	1169	40	13/07/45	SAN 2	SAN 4	K/RS/m
RUMMELL, V.C.	B	QLD	1224	38	18/03/45	SAN I	SAN I	m
RUNDLE, C.A.	B	NSW	1221	25	05/07/45	SAN 2	SAN 3	m
RUSCOE, G.	B	QLD	1212	34	02/06/45	ECR	TR	2M/m
RUSH, M.J.	B	QLD	1180	24	08/02/45	3m w M'RIN	TR	1M/m
RUSSELL, A.W.	B	NSW	1231	26	23/05/45	SAN I	SAN 2	m
RYAN, J.G.	B	NSW	1888	29	18/04/45	SAN I	SAN 2	m
RYAN, J.J.	B	VIC	1189	25	05/04/45	SAN I	SAN 2	m
RYAN, R.T.	B	NSW	1219	30	07/06/45	ECR	TR	2M/m
RYAN, W.A.	E	QLD	1889	27	04/06/45	37m SAN	TR	2M/m
SADLER, R.E.	B	NSW	1446	26	01/06/45	ECR	TR (K)	2M/m
SALTER, P.J.	B	QLD	350	33	14/02/45	2m e N'TAN	TR	1M/cbb
SAMPSON, H.R.	B	VIC	1278	24	23/03/45	SAN I	SAN 2	m
SANDERCOCK, H.A.	B	SA	1245	40	03/04/45	SAN I	SAN 2	RS/m

Name								
SANKOWSKY, R.H.	B	QLD	1289	25	15/02/45	SAN 1	SAN 1	m
SAVAGE, E.C.	E	WA	1891	34	10/06/45	(PRESUMED)		No detail
SAVAGE, T.	E	WA	1892	40	30/01/45	SAN ?	SAN ?	DR/m
(last two entries were brothers)								
SAWFORD, B.G.	B	VIC	1296	30	11/04/45	SAN 1	SAN 2	m
SCAMBREY, W.E.	B	NSW	331	37	20/03/45	SAN 1	SAN 1	m
SCHIBECI, D.	E	NSW	1893	28	13/06/45	ECR	TR	2M/m
SCHIPHORST, A,.	B	SA	1277	41	17/03/45	SAN 1	SAN 1	m
SCHMUTTER, W.J	B	NSW	1292	24	18/07/45	SAN ?	SAN ?	DR/m
SCHOLEFIELD, R.	B	VIC	-	36	18/07/45	RAN 2J	RAN 2JB	2M/ae
SCHUTT, L.V.	B	VIC	1276	26	02/04/45	RAN 1	RAN 1B	1M/ulc
SCOLLEN, T.P.	E	NSW	1980	28	07/05/45	SAN ?	SAN ?	DR/ae m
SCOTT, C.	B	QLD	1246	43	14/04/45	SAN 1	SAN 2	m
SCOTT, J.	B	WA	1257	43	19/01/45	SAN 1	SAN 1	m
SCOTT, J.M.	B	NSW	-	33	28/02/45	(PRESUMED)		No detail
SCULLY, J.S.	B	NSW	1256	26	20/03/45	SAN 1	SAN 1	m
SEARLE, L.E.	B	VIC	344	49	07/06/45	ECR	TR-d out	2M/m
SEELEY, J.W.	B	QLD	326	25	05/06/45	ECR (2M)	TR	RR/aem
SEFTON, B.L.	B	NSW	1263	44	01/03/45	SAN 1	SAN 1	m
SEFTON, I.G.	E	NSW	1894	42	04/04/45	RAN 1	RAN 1B	1M/bb
SEVIER, J.	E	WA	1895	38	07/06/45	ECR	TR	2M/M
SEWELL, A.E.	B	VIC	1275	41	05/03/45	RAN 1	RAN 1A	1M/ae
SHACKELL, J.H.	B	NSW	341	30	14/04/45	RAN 1	RAN 1B	1M/m
SHARP, W.	E	NSW	1896	22	01/04/45	RAN 1	RAN 1B	1M/m
SHAW, A.D.	B	NSW	1251	25	10/06/45	SAN 2	SAN 3	m
SHAW, D.R.	B	QLD	1249	31	17/03/45	RAN 1	RAN 1B	1M/ae
SHAW, G.	B	NSW	1249	33	19/04/45	SAN 1	SAN 2	m
SHAW, R.	E	NSW	1978	36	19/07/44	SAN 1	KG	m
SHEARD, W.A.	E	QLD	1899	36	15/03/45	9m e RAN	KG (New)	RC/shot
SHEARMAN, S.G.	B	NSW	1299	20	31/03/45	RAN /RC	R 1B/TR	1M/m
SHEEDY, R.H.	B	VIC	1300	31	27/03/45	SAN 1	SAN 2	m
SHELVOCK, C.B.	E	WA	1900	38	17/04/45	SAN 1	SAN 2	bb
SHEPHERD, G.A.	B	NSW	1236	25	02/08/45	RAN 2J (2M)	R 2JB/MS	false dod
SHEPHERD, W.P	B	VIC	1274	29	05/06/45	ECR	TR	2M/m
SHERMAN, M.O.	E	SA	1901	26	16/03/45	SAN 1	SAN 1	m
SHERRING, F.	B	NSW	337	29	12/02/45	MALIO	TR	1M/cbb
SHERWOOD, S.	E	NSW	1902	25	22/04/45	RAN 1	RAN 1B	1M/m
SHIELDS, E.J.	B	QLD	339	43	07/06/45	SAN 2	SAN 3	m
SHIELDS, R.	B	NSW	1314	52	21/11/44	SAN 1	KG	m men
SHIPSIDES, R.A.	B	VIC	338	32	03/04/45	SAN 1	SAN 2	m
SHIRLEY, A.F.	B	WA	1298	36	10/05/45	SAN 1	SAN 2	RS/m
SHORT, E.R.	B	VIC	1248	32	26/04/45	SAN 1	SAN 2	m
SHORT, M.N.	B	NSW	1266	25	13/07/45	SAN 2	SAN 4	K/m
SIMPSON, Henry	B	VIC	1267	33	02/06/45	ECR	JUNGLE	esc/m
SIMPSON, Herbert	E	NSW	1904	32	10/02/45	SAN 1	SAN 1	m
SIMPSON, L.P.	B	VIC	328	23	June 1945	ECR	TR-d out	false date/ place on DR
SIMPSON, S.A	B	QLD	1273	25	24/03/45	SAN 1	SAN 2	m
SINCLAIR, I.A	B	NSW	332	36	05/08/45	SAN 2	SAN 3	m
SINCLAIR, I.McD	B	NSW	1240	32	09/03/45	SAN 1	SAN 1	m
SINCLAIR, W.	B	QLD	1283	31	13/04/45	RAN 1	RAN 1B	1M/m
SINNAMON, F.	B	QLD	1252	28	07/06/45	ECR	TR	2M/ae
SKEWS, R.	B	VIC	1304	42	07/06/45	ECR	TR	2M/m
SKINNER, E.K.	B	NSW	-	27	16/06/45	nr MUANAD	JUNGLE	esc 2M/ committed suicide/brother of J.F. Skinner
SKINNER, G.T.	B	VIC	1255	44	17/01/45	SAN 1	SAN 1	m
SKINNER, J.F.	B	NSW	1239	31	15/08/45	SAN 2	KG (New)	RS/K
SKINNER, T.R.	E	SA	1906	31	17/04/45	RAN 1(1M)	RAN 1B	RR/m
SLATTER, A.J.	B	QLD	1250	24	23/03/45	RAN 1	RAN 1B	1M/ae
SLEEP, J.	B	VIC	1265	22	06/07/45	RAN 2J	RAN 2JA	2M/m
SLIGAR, G.W.	B	QLD	1272	43	05/02/45	2m M'ATTO	TR	1M/cbb
SLIGO, N.K.	B	RAN	1751	-	31/08/42	SAN 1	KG	dys
SLIP, E.C.	B	NSW	1284	23	17/03/45	SAN 1	SAN 1	m
SMALL, R.D.	B	NSW	1262	27	23/06/45	SAN 2	SAN 3	RS/m
SMALL, R.P.	B	WA	1258	43	08/04/45	SAN 1	SAN 2	m
SMALLDON, H.J.	B	NSW	1241	26	04/07/45	SAN 2	SAN 3	m
SMEETON, B.L.	E	NG	1287	27	15/02/45	bet. Malio & Mankadai/		TR/bb
SMITH, A.A.	B	NSW	1290	34	25/03/45	SAN 1	SAN 2	m
SMITH, A.J.	B	VIC	1271	26	14/04/45	SAN 1	SAN 2	m
SMITH, A.W.L.	B	NSW	1264	27	29/01/45	SAN ?	SAN ?	DR/m
SMITH, C.T.	B	NSW	1280	30	24/03/45	RAN 1	RAN 1B	1M/ae
SMITH, E.I	B	QLD	1279	25	15/03/45	SAN 1	SAN 1	m
SMITH, Ernest	B	WA	1297	34	08/03/43	SAN 1	KG	m
SMITH, E.S.	B	QLD	1303	24	14/07/45	RAN 2J	RAN 2JB	2M/m
SMITH, F.A.O	B	NSW	1305	36	07/06/45	SAN 2	SAN 3	RS/m
SMITH, F.S.	B	VIC	1306	40	17/05/45	SAN 1	SAN 2	m
SMITH, G.	E	WA	1550	42	07/06/45	ECR	TR	2M/m
SMITH, G.A.	E	NSW	1908	43	08/03/45	SAN 1	SAN 1	m
SMITH, G.J.	B	WA	1259	40	04/06/45	SAN 2	SAN 3	m

SMITH, H.V.	E	NSW	1909	29	01/06/45	ECR	TR	m
SMITH, J.B.I.	E	NSW	1551	25	13/02/45	2m e T'PIAS	TR	1M/aem
SMITH, J.D.	E	NSW	1910	38	16/03/45	PAG	PAG CEM	1M/m
SMITH, J.S.	B	NSW	1285	45	13/03/45	RAN 1	RAN 1A	1M/ae
SMITH, M.H.	B	VIC	1301	43	01/12/44	SAN ?	SAN ?	DR/m
SMITH, O.	B	NSW	1297	25	27/06/45	RAN 2J	RAN 2JA	2M/m
SMITH, R.E.	B	NSW	1288	36	31/03/45	SAN 1	SAN 2	m
SMITH, R.J.V.	B	VIC	1456	50	10/11/42	SAN 1	KG	dys
SMITH, T.E.	E	WA	1911	32	18/12/44	SAN 1	SAN 1	-
SMITH, W.H.	B	NSW	1261	42	05/03/45	SAN 1	SAN 1	m
SMITH, W.J.	E	NSW	1552	34	14/04/45	RAN 1(1M)	RAN 1B	RR/m
SMITH, W.S.	E	NSW	1912	33	07/06/45	ECR	TR	2M/m
SMYTH, C.G.	E	NSW	1553	36	07/05/45	RAN 1J	RAN 1J	1M/m
SOLOMON, J.H.	B	NSW	1284	36	11/02/45	2m e M'ULU	TR	1M/cbb
SOMMERVILLE, A.C.	J/Br	VIC	2660	44	14/04/45	SAN 1	KG	m
SORBY, W.T.	B	QLD	1291	34	20/01/45	SAN 1	SAN 1	m
SOTHERON, B.E.	E	NSW	1913	35	03/04/45	SAN 1	SAN 2	m
SOUTER, G.A.	E	NSW	1914	30	02/06/45	SAN 2	SAN 3	RS/m
SPEAKE, C.R.	B	SA	1307	41	25/05/45	SAN 1	SAN 2	air raid
SPEARS, N.	B	NSW	1281	39	13/11/42	SAN 1	KG	ae
SPENCE, R.H.	B	WA	1237	40	31/05/45	ECR	TR	m
SPENCER, H.F.	E	NSW	1915	34	27/03/45	RAN 1	RAN 1B	1M/bb
SPROUL, L.J.	B	VIC	333	37	03/05/45	SAN ?	SAN ?	DR/m
SPURLING, T.	B	WA	1448	42	11/03/45	SAN 1	SAN 1	m
SPURWAY, R.S.	E	NSW	1554	23	21/04/45	RAN 1	RAN 1B	1M/m
STACE, R.A.	E	NSW	1916	26	07/06/45	ECR	TR	2M/m
STACY, R.L.	E	NSW	1555	27	25/07/45	RAN 2J	RAN 2JB	1M/ae Relic-R
STAGGS, F.L.	B	NSW	346	52	31/03/45	SAN 1	SAN 2	m
STANDRING, H.C.	E	NSW	1917	25	08/04/45	SAN ?	SAN ?	DR/m
STANLEY, J.R.	E	NSW	1918	31	25/05/45	RAN 1J	RAN 1J	1M/m
STANLEY, R.	B	NSW	1242	29	08/02/45	SAN 1	SAN 1	bb
STANTON, A.J.	B	NSW	348	25	16/07/45	RAN 2J	RAN 2JB	2M/m
STANTON, E.	E	NSW	1919	28	18/03/45	SAN 1	SAN 1	m
STANWELL, O.M.	E	WA	1556	39	12/03/45	SAN 1	SAN 1	m
STAPLETON, T.N.	B	NSW	343	36	18/12/44	SAN 1	SAN 1	bb
STARKIE, J.D.	B	VIC	1270	24	10/05/45	SAN 1	SAN 2	m
STARKY, C.B.	E	QLD	1890	38	17/01/45	SAN 1	SAN 1	m
STEEL, J.A	E	NSW	1920	31	25/06/45	RAN 2J	RAN 2JA	2M/m
STEELE, A.R.	B	NSW	1293	41	10/05/45	SAN 1	SAN 2	m
STEEN, W.S.	B	QLD	1308	22	13/07/45	SAN 2	KG	killed
STEINBECK, W.J.	B	NSW	1449	39	15/07/45	RAN 2J	RAN 2JB	2M/m
STEVENS, Charles	E	NSW	1922	24	03/12/44	SAN ?	SAN ?	DR/m
STEVENS, C.C.	B	NSW	536	30	18/04/45	SAN ?	SAN ?	m
STEVENS, J.J.	B	NSW	1309	44	19/04/45	SAN 1	SAN 2	m
STEVENSON, T.S.	B	QLD	1310	42	11/02/45	SAN 1	SAN 1	m
STEWART, A.B.	B	QLD	1302	31	04/02/45	1 m M'RIN	TR	1M/cbb
STEWART, B.P. aka McNab, R	B	NSW	879	21	29/01/45	SAN 1	SAN 1	ae
STEWART, H.J.	B	VIC	1369	42	25/05/45	SAN 1	SAN 2	m
STEWART, H.T.	E	NSW	1557	24	21/06/45	SAN 2	SAN 3	m
STEWART, S.K.	B	VIC	1311	36	25/12/44	SAN 1	SAN 1	ulcer
STEWART, W.	B	VIC	1268	29	14/05/45	SAN 1	SAN 2	m
STIRLING, C.	B	QLD	1287	31	16/06/45	1 m MALIO	TR(2M)	RR/m
STIRLING, D.H. aka Matson-Stirling	E	VIC	-	19	15/07/45	SAN 2	SAN 4	K/m
STIRLING, G.McB.	B	VIC	1312	24	23/05/45	SAN 1	SAN 2	m
ST LEON, G.	B	NSW	327	28	03/06/45	SAN 2	SAN 3	ae
STOCKLEY, R.R.	B	NSW	1294	23	01/03/45	SAN 1	SAN 1	m
STOLARSKI, C.	B	VIC	1260	25	24/03/45	PAG	PAG CEM	1M/ae
STONE, H.D.	B	NSW	1243	32	12/05/45	SAN 1	SAN 2	m
STONE, R.D.	B	NSW	1282	24	17/02/45	RAN 1	RAN 1A	1M/bbm
STOREY, G.J.	B	NSW	1295	29	08/04/45	RAN 1	RAN 1B	1M/m
STRACHAN, G.	B	QLD	1254	45	06/04/45	SAN 1	SAN 2	m
STRANG, P.	B	SA	345	41	20/02/45	SAN 1	SAN 1	m
STROUT, E.A.	E	QLD	1558	35	28/03/45	SAN 1	SAN 2	m
STUCHBURY, I.	B	WA	349	42	17/11/44	SAN 1	KG	M
SULLIVAN, D.	E	NSW	1923	32	18/01/45	SAN 1	SAN 1	m
SULLIVAN Ronald	B	NSW	330	30	31/03/45	6m w PAG	TR (RC)	1M/bay
SULLIVAN, Roy H.	B	NSW	1253	26	17/06/45	ECR	TR	2M/bb
SUTTON, J.E.	E	QLD	1924	28	23/03/45	RAN 1	RAN 1B	1M/ae
SWAN, C.W.	B	VIC	1313	33	05/03/45	RAN 1	RAN 1A	1M/jaun
SWAN, W.A.	B	WA	336	42	01/02/45	SAN 1	SAN 1	RS/m
SWIFT, D.S.	E	NSW	1925	31	30/06/45	SAN 2	SAN 3	RS/m
SYKES, R W	B	NSW	1450	34	11/07/45	RAN 2J	RAN 2JB	2M/m
SYME, A J	B	NSW	1244	24	04/06/45	38m	SAN	TR2M/m
SYMES, A V	E	NSW	1926	25	11/04/45	SAN 1	SAN 2	RS/m
SYMONS, G H	B	NSW	342	26	10/04/45	RAN 1	RAN 1B	1M/m

APPENDIX1: NOMINAL ROLLS

Name								
TAIT, R.	B	VIC	1325	42	16/03/45	SAN I	SAN I	m
TANKO, V.K.	B	NSW	1317	32	07/02/45	10m e Pint'an	TR	1M/cbb
TANNER, V.G.	B	VIC	1335	28	21/02/45	SAN I	SAN I	m
TANZER, H.J.	B	QLD	355	32	02/06/45	ECR	TR	2M/m
TAPPER, S.(James)	E	NSW	1929	24	06/03/45	RAN I	RAN 1A	1M/bb
TAYLOR, A.A.	E	NSW	1930	36	13/03/45	PAG	PAG CEM	1M/ae
TAYLOR, D.	E	NSW	1559	23	01/04/45	RAN 1/RC	R1B/TR	1M/m
TAYLOR, G.L.	B	WA	1344	25	07/06/45	ECR	TR	2M/m
TAYLOR, G.C.	B	VIC	1321	29	14/04/45	SAN I	SAN 2	ae
TAYLOR, G.J.	B	NSW	1327	27	12/04/45	SAN ?	SAN ?	DR/m
TAYLOR, G.W.	E	WA	1560	43	02/03/45	SAN I	SAN I	RS/m
TAYLOR, H.B.	E	VIC	1931	27	14/06/45	SAN 2	SAN 3	RS/m
TAYLOR, H.T.	B	QLD	352	38	05/06/45	ECR	TR-d out	2M/m
TAYLOR, I.	B	NSW	1341	33	03/05/45	SAN I	SAN 2	bb
TAYLOR, J.A.	B	NSW	1351	27	05/05/45	rest h M'RIN	TR	1M/cbb
TAYLOR, N.H.	E	NSW	1927	32	05/06/45	BELURAN	TR	2M/m
TAYLOR, T.C.	B	NSW	1451	43	26/07/45	RAN 2J (2M)	RAN 2JB	RR/ae
TAYLOR, W.C.	B	NSW	1328	40	08/05/45	SAN ?	SAN ?	DR/m
TELFORD, G.F.	B	VIC	1329	21	12/12/44	SAN I	SAN I	m/bb
TEMPLE, R.J. aka Moore, R.J.	B	NSW	965	23	03/04/45	SAN I	SAN 2	RS/m
TENNYSON, B.G.	E	VIC	1932	22	07/05/45	SAN I	SAN 2	m
TERRETT, E.	B	NSW	1337	25	07/08/45	RAN 2J (2M)	R 2JB/MS	false dod
THISTLEWAITE,V.	B	NSW	1319	34	15/07/45	RAN 2J	RAN 2JB	m
THOMAS, A.D.	B	NSW	1349	25	10/08/44	SAN ?	SAN ?	DR/m
THOMAS, E.	B	WA	1352	38	21/03/45	PAG	PAG CEM	1M/ae
THOMAS, J.O.	E	SA	1933	26	15/05/45	SAN I	SAN 2	m
THOMAS, M.G.	B	NSW	1348	25	26/05/45	SAN I	SAN 2	m
THOMPSON, A.H.	B	TAS	117	42	19/06/45	2m e T'IAS	KG-d out	2M/ae
THOMPSON, F.	E	NSW	1934	25	10/06/45	SAN 2	SAN 3	m
THOMPSON, R.J.	B	NSW	1340	33	30/03/45	SAN I	SAN 2	m
THOMPSON, V.R.	B	QLD	1339	26	23/05/45	SAN I	SAN 2	m
THOMPSON, W.	E	NSW	1935	24	04/03/45	SAN I	SAN I	m
THOMSON, A.	B	NSW	1324	36	13/01/45	SAN I	SAN I	m
THOMSON, E.F.	B	NSW	1347	33	01/04/45	SAN I	SAN 2	m
THONDER, W.C.	B	VIC	1330	27	19/06/45	SAN ?	SAN ?	DR/m
THORLEY, I.E.	B	WA	351	43	04/03/45	SAN I	SAN I	m
THORNEYCROFT,C.	B	VIC	1315	32	30/10/44	SAN I	KG	air raid
THORNS, A.S.	E	WA	1936	27	08/08/45	RAN 2J	R 2JB/MS	2M/RR/ false dod
THOROUGHGOOD, H.	E	NSW	1937	26	10/02/45	1m w M'RIN	TR	1M/bb
THORPE, H.	E	NSW	1938	28	08/04/45	SAN I	SAN 2	m
THURSTON, H.W.	B	WA	1323	37	11/03/45	SAN I	SAN I	m
TICKLE, W.	B	NSW	1336	27	24/02/45	SAN I	SAN I	bb
TIERNEY, J.E.	E	QLD	1928	24	17/06/45	ECR	TR	2M/m
TIERNEY, M.J.	B	QLD	1331	34	02/06/45	ECR	TR	2M/m
TINNING, R.J.	E	NSW	1561	36	23/05/45	SAN I	SAN 2	bomb
TIPPING, N.A.	B	NSW	1345	22	04/07/45	RAN 2J	RAN 2JA	2M/m
TOLLIDAY, A.S.	B	VIC	1322	37	18/02/45	SAN I	SAN I	m
TOMKYNS, E.A.	E	NSW	1939	31	25/06/45	SAN 2	SAN 3	m
TOMS, H.	B	NSW	1332	48	02/04/45	SAN I	SAN 2	m
TOOMBS, R.E.	B	SA	1333	51	23/05/45	SAN I	SAN 2	air raid
TRESEDER, H.A.	B	QLD	354	48	12/05/45	SANDALA E	KG	esc, RS
TRAVIS, J.H.	B	NSW	1338	29	07/06/45	SAN 2	SAN 3	m
TREVILLIEN, R.G.	B	NSW	353	47	25/01/45	SAN I	SAN I	m
TRIGWELL, A.G.	E	WA	1941	23	04/05/45	SAN I	SAN 2	m
TRINDER, L.G.	B	NSW	1342	23	05/06/45	ECR	TR	2M/m
TRODD, R.J.	B	VIC	1320	41	22/10/44	SAN I	KG	g.ulcer
TUCKERMAN, J.H.	E	NSW	1942	27	18/06/45	SAN 2	SAN 3	m
TULLY, N.McK.	B	VIC	1334	50	01/07/45	RAN 2J	RAN 2JA	2M/m
TURNER, A.J.	B	NSW	1318	37	10/06/45	ECR	TR	2M/m
TURNER, E.H.	B	WA	356	27	18/06/45	ECR (2M)	TR	RR/m
TURNER, H.Ray	E	WA	1944	25	08/05/45	SAN I	SAN 2	m
TURNER, H.Robert	E	SA	1943	25	18/02/45	rest h MALIO	TR	1M/m
TURNER, K.M. aka Maitland-Turner	B	NSW	1443	25	15/07/45	SAN 2	SAN 4	K/m
TURNER, N.	B	NSW	1316	28	23/03/45	PAG	PAG CEM	1M/m
TURNER, R.E.	B	NSW	1346	26	25/01/45	SAN I	SAN I	m
TWISS, R.T.	B	NSW	1326	23	15/10/44	SAN ?(DR)	SAN ?	RR/m
TYRES, K.H.	B	VIC	1343	27	05/02/45	SAN I	SAN I	bb
TYRRELL, A.R.	J/Br	WA	2350	40	24/06/45	ECR	TR (2M)	RS?/m
TYRRELL, Ronald	B	QLD	1350	22	07/02/45	SAN I	SAN I	RS?/m
TYRRELL, Reginald	E	NSW	1945	25	23/07/45	RAN 2J	RAN 2JB	2M/ae
VARRIE, G.B.	B	NSW	1353	31	07/06/45	M'ATTO	TR-d out	2M/m
VAUGHAN, W.J.	E	VIC	1562	26	30/07/45	RAN 2J	RAN 2JB	2M/ae
VEAL, R.J.	B	VIC	1335	23	08/03/45	SAN I	SAN I	m
VICTORSEN, L.M.	E	QLD	1563	23	18/03/45	RAN 1/RC	R 1B/TR	1M/m
VOGELE, G.L.	B	VIC	1354	26	14/02/45	SAN I	SAN I	m

Name								
VOLLHEIM, E.C.		B	NSW	1356	45	12/02/45	SAN 1	SAN 1	m
WACHNER, E.C.		E	SA	1948	26	24/03/45	RAN 1/RC	R 1B/TR	1M/m
WADDINGTON, G.		B	NSW	369	42	10/06/44	SAN 1	KG	dys/men
WALKER, E.T.		B	SA	1429	43	09/06/45	SAN 2	SAN 3	RS/m
WALKER, J.S.		E	NSW	1564	24	19/02/45	RAN 1(1M)	RAN 1A	RT/m
WALKER, N.G.		B	NSW	1384	23	11/02/45	3m e MALIO	TR	1M/cbb
WALKER, R.G.		E	QLD	1949	28	02/07/45	RAN 2J	RAN 2JA	2M/ae
WALL, R.H.		B	NSW	364	28	01/03/45	SAN 1	SAN 1	m
WALLACE, H.W.		B	NSW	1405	23	10/04/45	SAN 1	SAN 2	m
WALLER, T.		B	NSW	1365	21	05/06/45	SAN 2	SAN 3	RS/m
WALSH, F.V.		B	VIC	1395	34	04/03/45	SAN 1	SAN 1	ae
WALSH, L.J.		B	NSW	1394	42	22/01/45	SAN 1	SAN 1	m
WALTER, R.W.		B	QLD	1383	30	24/06/45	7m e RANAU	TR (2M)	RR/m
WALTERS, A.F.		B	QLD	1362	28	18/02/45	RAN 1	RAN 1A	1M/ae
WALTERS, L.E.		B	VIC	1369	37	04/03/45	SAN 1	SAN 1	bb
WALTON, D.R.		E	NSW	1950	38	07/06/45	MURAWATTO	TR	2M/m
WAPLING, J.H.		B	VIC	358	25	22/05/45	SAN 1	SAN 2	RR/m
WARD, J.A.		E	NSW	1951	23	10/06/45	ECR	TR	2M/M
WARD, R.		B	VIC	1416	42	22/04/45	SAN 1	SAN 2	m
WARD, S.W.		B	VIC	1415	22	02/04/45	RAN 1	RAN 1B	1M/ae
WARDALE-GREENWOOD, H.		B	VIC	47	36	18/07/45	RAN 2J	RAN 2JB	2M/
WARDMAN, J.		B	NSW	1423	27	10/06/44	SAN ?	SAN ?	DR/m
WARNER, Bertie		E	VIC	1952	34	15/06/45	DUSAN	KG	DR date
WARREN, H.J.		B	VIC	1369	42	22/03/45	SAN 1	SAN 1	m
WARREN, J.McK.		B	QLD	1431	39	14/06/45	MALIO	TR	2M/bb
WARRINGTON, C.W.		B	NSW	1452	32	14/05/45	RAN 1J	RAN 1J	1M/m
WASTNIDGE, R.		B	VIC	367	44	13/02/45	SAN 1	KG	m
WATERHOUSE, A.		E	NSW	1953	27	30/01/45	SAN 1	SAN 1	m
WATERS, A.J.		B	NSW	373	44	09/06/45	SAN 2	SAN 3	m
WATSON, Clarence		B	QLD	1361	30	14/03/45	SAN 1	SAN 1	m
WATSON, C.Y.		B	QLD	1453	45	06/03/45	RAN 1	RAN 1A	RR/bb
WATSON, F.W.		B	VIC	362	33	04/07/45	SAN 2	SAN 3	m
WATSON, T.N.		B	NSW	1380	42	15/12/44	SAN 1	KG	bb/m
WATSON, W.J.H.		E	NSW	1954	33	23/03/45	SAN 1	SAN 2	m
WATTERS, L.L.		B	SA	1345	38	22/12/44	SAN 1	SAN 1	bb/m
WATTS, D.L.		B	NSW	1422	23	30/07/45	SAN 2	SAN 3	m
WATTS, E.R.		E	NSW	1955	24	17/06/45	ECR	TR	2M/ewb
WATTS, T.J.		E	VIC	1956	32	15/03/45	RAN 1/RC	R 1A/TR	1M/m
WEATHERBY, W.S.		B	NSW	359	34	15/07/45	RAN 2J	RAN 2JB	2M/m
WEBBER, S.A.		B	NSW	1386	28	18/06/45	escaped/shot/fell into M'rin R		
WEBSTER, A.G.		B	TAS	1370	28	02/06/45	ECR	TR-died	2M/bbm
WEEKS, F.N.		E	NSW	1957	34	04/02/45	SAN 1	SAN 1	m
WEHL, F.G.		B	QLD	1377	39	02/08/45	SAN 2	SAN 3	RS/m
WEIR, S.J.		B	VIC	1372	52	15/07/45	SAN 2	SAN 4	K/RS/m
WEISSEL, G.		B	NSW	1371	35	23/05/45	SAN 1	SAN 2	bomb
WELCH, W.A.		B	NSW	1406	44	09/06/45	SAN 2	SAN 3	RS/m
WELLARD, C.J.		B	NSW	1368	28	08/06/45	SAN 2	SAN 3	m
WELLS, G.D.		B	NSW	1387	43	05/07/45	RAN 2J	RAN 2JA	2M/m
WELLS, H.G.		B	NSW	1367	33	04/03/45	SAN 1	SAN 1	m
WEST, J.S.		B	NSW	1424	28	08/06/45	MANDORIN	drowned	2M/m
WESTON, W.E.		E	NSW	1959	27	14/03/45	RAN 1	RAN 1A	1M/ae u
WESTWOOD, Bert		B	NSW	1403	30	01/07/45	SAN 2	SAN 3	m
WHEELER, J.E.		B	NSW	360	40	28/06/45	SAN 2	SAN 3	m
WHEREAT, M.C.		B	NSW	370	40	22/03/45	SAN 1	SAN 1	m
WHITE, Bernard		B	VIC	1373	32	06/04/45	SAN 1	SAN 2	m
WHITE, C.H.		B	NSW	1397	38	06/04/45	SAN 1	SAN 2	m
WHITE J.A.		B	QLD	1404	30	05/06/45	43m SAN	TR	2M/m
WHITE, L.A.		B	QLD	1427	27	10/06/45	SAN 2	SAN 3	m
WHITE, S.H.		B	VIC	1388	25	06/02/45	SAN 1	SAN 1	m
WHITEHEAD, B.C.		B	NSW	368	39	13/07/45	RAN 2J	RAN 2JB	2M/m
WHITEHEAD, W.		E	NSW	1960	21	15/02/45	6m w M'DAI	TR	1M/m
WHITELAW, J.R.		B	NSW	1389	31	26/07/45	RAN 2J	RAN 2JB	2M/ae
WHITING, W.G.		E	NSW	1961	25	17/07/45	RAN 2J	RAN 2JB	2M/ae
WHYBIRD, J.A.		B	NSW	372	28	14/07/45	RAN 2J	RAN 2JB	2M/m
WHYMAN, H.A.		B	TAS	1398	25	24/03/45	SAN 1	SAN 2	m
WHYTE, R.J.		B	VIC	1414	28	05/06/45	ECR	TR	2M/m
WILKES, H.R.		B	NSW	1402	27	04/06/45	38m SAN	TR	2M/ae
WILKIE, J.		E	WA	1962	36	17/05/45	SAN 1	SAN 2	m
WILKINS, G.H.		B	NSW	1399	54	09/04/45	SAN 1	SAN 1	m
WILKINS, K.		B	NSW	1401	25	03/02/45	SAN 1	SAN 1	m
WILKINSON, D.L.		B	NSW	361	25	08/08/45	RAN 2J (2M)	R 2JB/MS	false dod
WILLIAMS, A.T.		E	NSW	1963	39	05/07/45	RAN 2J	RAN 2JA	2M/m
WILLIAMS, G.E.		B	QLD	1374	35	15/02/45	nr M'ngan	TR	1M/m
WILLIAMS, H.P.		B	NSW	1381	26	14/04/45	RAN 1(1M)	RAN 1B	RR/m
WILLIAMS, J.C.		E	QLD	1947	30	03/05/45	SAN 1	SAN 2	m
WILLIAMSON, L.R.		E	NSW	1965	25	04/06/45	SAN 2	SAN 3	m
WILLMOTT, A.C.		B	WA	1390	40	29/06/45	RAN 2J	RAN 2JA	2M/ae
WILLMOTT, K.W.		B	VIC	1359	33	15/05/45	SAN 1	SAN 2	m

APPENDIX 1: NOMINAL ROLLS

NAME	FORCE	POW	AGE	DIED	PLACE	BURIED	EXTRA
WILMOTT, A.J.	B	NSW	-	26 JUNE 45	ECR	JUNGLE	esc 2M
WILSON, A.	B	NSW	1421	32 02/07/45	SAN 2	SAN 3	RS/m
WILSON, A.E.	B	VIC	1430	44 29/11/44	SAN 1	KG	m
WILSON, C.B.	B	NSW	1417	40 23/05/45	SAN 1	SAN 2	m
WILSON, C.W.	E	NSW	1966	43 23/05/45	SAN 1	SAN 2	m
(Wilson,C.W. believed incorrect date; confused with Wilson,C.B. Said to have died Feb 45, at SAN)							
WILSON, D.G.	B	NSW	1409	24 21/03/45	RAN 1	RAN 1B	1M/ae
WILSON, E.	B	NSW	1408	34 27/03/45	RAN 1	RAN 1B	1M/m
WILSON, E.W.	B	VIC	1364	33 09/02/45	6m w PAPAN	TR	1M/cbb
WILSON, G.	B	VIC	1426	24 20/01/45	SAN ?	SAN ?	DR/m
WILSON, G.E.	B	VIC	1407	24 13/05/45	SAN 1	SAN 2	m
WILSON, H.	E	QLD	1946	30 16/03/45	PAG	PAG CEM	1M/ae
WILSON, L.A.	E	SA	1967	33 30/12/44	SAN 1	SAN 1	RS/m
WILSON, R.J.	B	VIC	366	42 24/07/45	RAN 2J	RAN 2JB	2M/m
WILSON, R.M.	B	WA	374	35 25/12/44	SAN 1	SAN 1	m men
WILSON, R.S.	B	QLD	1413	29 13/05/45	SAN ?	SAN ?	DR/m
WILSON, S.C.	B	QLD	1420	26 16/06/45	MILULU	TR	2M/m
WINKS, A.K.	B	QLD	1379	41 07/07/45	SAN 2	SAN 3	m
WINNING, H.	B	QLD	1376	31 07/02/45	2m PINT'AN	TR	1M/hf
WINTER, S.C.	B	VIC	1418	31 02/03/45	SAN 1	SAN 1	m
WINTERBOTTOM,A	B	QLD	1419	28 05/06/45	ECR	TR	2M/m
WISEMAN, E.W.	E	QLD	1968	24 10/06/45	SAN 2	SAN 3	RS/m
WISEMAN, R.H.	E	QLD	1969	25 30/07/45	RAN 2J	RAN 2JB	2M/ae m
WITT, K.C.	B	NSW	371	27 20/04/45	SAN 1	SAN 2	m
WOLFE, E.J.	B	QLD	1393	26 02/07/45	RAN 2J	RAN 2JA	RS/2M u
WOLFE, G.	B	NSW	1358	45 07/06/45	M'ATTO	TR	2M/m
WOLTER, G.J.	B	QLD	1378	32 03/02/45	SAN 1	SAN 1	m
WOOD, R.B.	B	WA	1362	32 02/11/44	SAN 1	KG	m
WOODALL, J.	B	NSW	363	34 07/06/45	ECR	TR	2M/m
WOODCROFT, K.R.	E	NSW	1970	23 10/12/44	SAN 1	KG	appen hf
WOODFORD, C.A.	E	VIC	1971	23 30/05/45	RAN 1J	RAN 1J	1M/m
WOODLEY, E.G.	B	NSW	1360	26 05/08/45	SAN 2	SAN 3	m
WOODLEY, F.E.	B	VIC	357	39 06/02/45	SAN 1	SAN 1	m
WOODS, C.J.	B	VIC	1366	36 08/02/45	.5m PAPAN	TR	1M/cbb
WOODS, F.H.	B	NSW	1412	32 06/07/45	SAN 2	SAN 3	RS/m
WOODS, M.P.	B	VIC	1410	34 10/03/45	RAN 1	RAN 1A	1M/ae
WOOLARD, A.I.	B	VIC	1357	41 06/03/45	SAN 1	SAN 1	m
WOOLNOUGH, A.W.	B	NSW	1363	30 15/02/45	6m w M'DAI	TR	1M/bbm
WORBY, R.P.	E	SA	1972	26 19/06/45	ECR	TR	2M/ae
WORLAND, N.C.	E	NSW	1973	29 15/02/45	5m w M'ngan	TR	1M/bb
WRAIGHT, D.C.	B	VIC	1411	43 11/02/45	5m e T'IAS	TR	1M/cbb
WREN, C.R.	E	VIC	1974	23 13/05/45	RAN 1J	RAN 1J	1M/m
WRIGHT, C.	E	NSW	1976	39 08/06/45	SAN 2	SAN 3	m
WRIGHT, C.L.	E	SA	1975	30 13/06/45	RAN 2J	RAN 2JA	1M/app
WRIGHT, F.P.	B	QLD	488	25 12/06/45	ECR	TR	2M/m
WRIGHT, T.J.	E	NSW	1978	25 16/01/45	SAN 1	SAN 1	m
WRIGLEY, K.G.	E	QLD	1977	24 26/02/45	SAN 1	SAN 1	m
WRIGLEY, K.H.	B	NSW	1400	25 25/07/45	RAN 2J	RAN 2JB	2M/m
WYE, F.R.C.	B	NSW	1392	22 21/03/45	PAG	PAG CEM	1M/m
WYNN, W.E.	B	NSW	1419	27 21/03/45	SAN 1	SAN 1	RS/m
YATES, G.	B	SA	1432	31 09/03/45	RAN 1	RAN 1A	1M/ae u
YOUNG, A.D.	B	VIC	1435	23 16/03/45	SAN 1	SAN 1	m
YOUNG, D.	E	VIC	1979	25 26/05/45	SAN 1	SAN 2	RS/m
YOUNG, D.G.	B	NSW	1433	34 21/06/45	ECR	TR-died	2M/m
YOUNG, J.S.	B	WA	1436	37 04/04/45	SAN 1	SAN 2	RS/m
YOUNG, T.O.	B	NSW	375	35 10/06/45	SAN 2	SAN 3	m

British (641 names)

NAME	FORCE	POW	AGE	DIED	PLACE	BURIED	EXTRA
ALLEN, J.	A	2377	24	20/06/45	TR	TR	2M/RS/m
ALLSON, K.G.	R	2376	30	07/01/45	SAN 2	SAN 1	m
ALLSOP, K.H.	R	2220	-	24/07/45	RAN 2J	RAN 2JB	mRR
AMOSS, A.C.	A	2379	39	19/05/45	SAN 1	SAN 2	m
ANDERTON, W.C.	A	2375	23	16/05/45	SAN 1	SAN 2	m
ANDREWS, H.	A	2381	34	22/03/45	SAN ?	SAN ?	DR/m
APLIN, C.E.	A	2384	31	29/03/45	PG-RAN	TR	1M/m
ARCHIBALD, T.M.	A	2373	37	22/02/45	SAN ?	SAN ?	DR/m
ASHLIN, B.	R	2218	-	04/02/45	SAN 2	KG	m
ASHMORE, H.	A	2383	42	29/05/45	SAN 1	S3/ CPD 1	m
AUSTIN, T.H.	R	2374	-	17/02/45	nr PAG	TR	1M/m
AYNSLEY, F.A.	R	2221	26	16/04/45	SAN 1	KG	m
BAGULEY, L.	R	2420	35	12/06/45	SAN 2	SAN 3	RS/m
BAGWELL, A.A.	A	2390	36	27/02/45	PAG	PAG CEM	1M/m

Name							
BAKER, K.W.G.	A	2292	-	31/03/45	SAN 2	SAN 2	m
BAKER, T.G.	A	2401	35	21/03/45	PAG	PAG CEM	1M/m
BAREHAM, W.J.	A	2399	30	19/02/45	TR	TR	m
BARKER, M.	A	2392	34	16/04/45	SAN ?	SAN ?	DR/m
BARNES, F.W.	A	2405	35	22/05/45	SAN 1	SAN 2	RS/m
BARNES, L.S.	R	2434	24	12/06/45	RAN 1J	RAN 1J	1M/K?
BARTLETT, A.E.	A	2437	34	22/05/45	SAN 1	SAN 2	m
BASSETT, E.R.	R	2419	-	23/03/45	SAN 2	KG	
BATES, E.C.	R	2421	27	06/07/45	TAN'TIN	TR	2M/m
BATTY, L.G.	A	2425	24	27/04/45	SAN 1	KG	m
BAULCOMBE, H.J.	A	2441	36	20/02/45	PAG	PAG CEM	1M/m
BAYER, J.H.	A	2471	26	29/03/45	PAG-RAN	TR	1M/bb
BEALE, E.P.	R	2438	26	04/04/45	SAN 2	KG	m
BEARDSHAW, H.	R	2415	39	MAY 45	KEMANSI	KG	esc 1M/ae
BEARDSLEY, J.	R	2414	24	29/03/45	PAG-RAN	TR	1M/m
BECK, J.	A	2235	47	21/03/45	PAG	PAG CEM	1M/m
BEEVER, E.	R	2412	25	10/02/45	SAN 2	KG	m
BELL, A.	R	2417	27	29/03/45	PAG-RAN	TR	1M/ae
BELLAMY, H.	A	2427	-	20/04/45	SAN 1	KG	m
BENN, E.T.	A	2404	29	15/07/45	SAN 2	SAN 3	
BENNETT, R.J.	A	2393	-	01/05/45	SAN 1	KG	ae
BENTLEY, W.	A	2436	34	17/02/45	SAN 2	SAN 1	m
BESSANT, J.W.	R	2236	45	04/04/45	SAN 2	KG	m
BIRD, C.G.	A	2388	33	26/12/44	SAN 2	KG	m
BIRD, F.L.	A	2426	28	12/06/45	SAN 2	SAN 3	m
BIRD, M.C.	A	2406	34	22/05/45	SAN 1	KG	m
BISHOP, E.G.	R	2415	26	14/04/45	SAN 2	KG	m
BLACK, L.W.	A	2433	38	13/02/45	1m BOTO	TR	1M/m
BLAZELEY, T.W.	R	2411	22	04/06/45	ECR	TR	2M/m
BLUCK, H.G.M.	R	2395	-	13/03/45	PAG	PAG CEM	1M/ae
BLYTH, W.	R	2409	24	15/06/45	SAN ?	SAN ?	DR/m
BOOTH, F.	R	2408	30	04/03/45	SAN ?	SAN ?	DR/bb
BOURNE, R.	A	2400	36	12/02/45	?	?	CI/m
BOUTCHER, D.G.	R	2223	-	15/04/45	RAN 1	RAN 1B	1M/m
BOWDEN, J.A.	R	2224	-	04/07/45	RAN 2J	RAN 2JA	2M/m
BOYD, J.	A	2430	29	04/05/45	SAN ?	SAN ?	DR/m
BRACKENBURY, R.	A	2422	-	26/03/45	SAN ?	SAN ?	DR/m
BRAMLEY, C.B.	A	2440	29	24/03/45	SAN ?	SAN ?	DR/m
BRATT, F.	A	2402	40	08/07/45	RAN 2J	RAN 2JA	2M/m
BRETT, P.J.	R	2226	31	19/03/45	PAG	PAG CEM	1M/m
BROADBENT, F.	A	2428	34	13/03/45	SAN ?	SAN ?	DR/bb
BROOM, C.L.	A	2234	34	16/02/45	SAN 2	KG	m
BROWN, A.E.	R	2423	39	16/03/45	SAN ?	SAN ?	DR/m
BROWN, L.D.	R	2398	28	04/12/44	SAN 2	KG	m
BROWN, R.H.	A	2229	23	14/04/45	RAN 1	RAN 1B	1M/m
BROWN, W.	A	2432	34	08/02/45	SAN 2	KG	m
BUCKINGHAM, H.F	A	2435	31	05/06/45	ECR	TR	2M/m
BUCKLE, H.	A	2407	32	29/04/45	SAN 1	KG	m
BULL, W.	R	2397	33	25/09/44	SAN 2	KG	m
BUNDOCK, G.E.	A	2391	41	21/04/45	SAN 1	KG	m
BURDETT, N.	A	2429	36	10/03/45	SAN 2	SAN 1	m
BURGESS, H.	R	2181	41	27/08/45	RAN 2J	KG (new)	2M/RR/K
BURGESS, Richard	A	2403	33	21/02/45	SAN 2	SAN 1	m
BURGESS, R..R	R	2410	36	07/01/45	SAN 2	KG	m
BURKE, G.H.	A	2233	28	23/03/45	PAG	PAG CEM	1M/m
BURROUGHS, J.G.	R	2396	25	06/07/45	ECR	TR	2M/m
BUTT, H.J.	A	2230	26	24/03/45	PAG	PAG CEM	1M/m
CAMBERG, D.	R	2449	25	28/04/45	SAN 1	KG	
CAMPBELL,T. McG.	A	2465	23	08/03/45	SAN 2	SAN 1	m
CAMPLING, F.	R	2445	-	21/03/45	PAG	PAG CEM	1M/ae
CANN, W.G.	A	2457	34	28/03/45	SAN 2	SAN 2	m
CARSON, C.	A	2470	28	06/06/45	SAN 2	SAN 3	m
CARTWRIGHT, E.	R	2242	33	15/02/45	SAN ?	SAN ?	DR/m
CARVER, P.	A	2490	38	06/03/45	SAN 2	SAN 1	m
CASTLE, S.	R	2482	24	25/02/45	SAN 2	SAN 1	m
CHALLIS, G.	A	2455	35	01/04/45	SAN 2	KG	m
CHAPPLES, I.	R	2486	26	05/04/45	RAN 1	RAN 1B	1M/bb
CHARLES, J.	A	2479	23	25/07/45	RAN 2J	RAN 2JB	2M/m
CHARLESWORTH, R.S.	A	2478	37	18/02/45	SAN 2	SAN 1	m
CHERRY, F.A.	A	2468	-	02/04/45	SAN 2	KG	m
CHINCHEN, H.J.	R	2237	29	14/04/45	SAN 2	KG	m
CHOPPING, G.	A	2185	26	12/08/45	RAN 2J (2M)	R 2JB/MS	false dod
CLARK, Charles	R	2238	26	22/02/45	?	?	CI/m
CLARK, Hugh E.	R	2244	24	23/04/45	SAN 1	KG	m
CLARK, R.W.J.	R	2487	40	21/12/44	SAN 2	KG	m
CLARKE, Horace B.	R	2488	-	28/02/45	PAG	PAG CEM	1M/ae
CLAYTON, J.	R	2245	28	02/03/45	SAN 2	SAN 1	ae
CLIFF, R.	R	2483	25	09/06/45	SAN 2	SAN 3	m

APPENDIX 1: NOMINAL ROLLS

Name							
CLIFF, S.	A	2448	-	20/01/45	SAN 2	KG	m
CLOUTER, F.J.	A	2476	-	22/10/44	SAN 2	KG	m
COFFIN, E.G.	A	2458	24	19/06/45	SAN 2	SAN 3	m
COGGON, H.	R	2447	22	24/06/45	SAN ?	SAN ?	DR/m
COGHLAN, N.	R	2243	-	19/03/45	SAN ?	SAN ?	DR/m
COLE, E.	R	2484	-	19/01/44	SAN 2	KG	m
COLE, F.G.H.	A	2469	29	10/04/45	SAN 2	KG	m
COLE, P.	R	2480	23	09/06/45	SAN 2	SAN 3	m
COLLINS, A.E.	R	2481	37	26/03/45	SAN ?	SAN ?	DR/m
COLLINS, D.G.	A	2459	35	14/07/45	RAN 2J	RAN 2JB	DR/m
COOMBS, J.	R	2451	31	07/07/45	SAN 2	SAN 3	m
COPPIN, E.	A	2452	35	13/06/45	SAN 2	SAN 3	m
COSHAM, F.	R	2450	-	08/03/45	PAG	PAG CEM	1M/ae
COSSENS, R.E.	R	2444	-	05/07/45	SAN 2	SAN 3	m
COSSEY, C.E.	R	2473	-	24/02/45	SAN 2	SAN 1	RS/m
COSTELLO, M.	A	2467	33	12/06/45	SAN 2	SAN 3	m
COX, A.	A	2491	-	01/04/45	SAN 2	KG	m
COX, J.W.	A	2475	37	18/03/45	SAN ?	SAN ?	DR/m
CRESSEY, S.W.	R	2186	47	09/07/45	RAN 2J	RAN 2JA	2M/m
CROMBIE, R.	A	2461	23	10/02/45	SAN 2	KG	m
CRONE, J.K.	R	2443	23	05/04/45	SAN 2	SAN 2	ae
CROOK, A.	R	2472	-	12/06/45	8m e Boto	TR	2M/m
CROW, W.S.	A	2456	28	11/03/45	SAN 2	SAN 1	m
CRYER, E.	A	2463	39	01/03/45	PAG	PAG CEM	1M/m
CUNNINGHAM, E.	A	2241	38	21/03/45	SAN ?	SAN ?	DR/m
CURTIS, R.S.	R	2466	35	16/01/45	SAN 2	KG	m
DARBY, P.E.	R	2508	22	26/11/44	SAN 2	KG	m
DANIELS, F.K.	A	2190	28	27/08/45	RAN 2J	KG (New)	2M/killed
DAVEY, W.	R	2510	-	16/09/44	SAN 2	SAN 1	m
DAVIES, C.A.C	A	2499	35	16/06/45	SAN ?	SAN ?	DR/m
DAVIES, J.	R	2511	-	08/03/45	PAG	PAG CEM	1M/m ae
DAVIES, L.	R	2479	26	30/04/45	SAN 1	KG	m
DAVIES, T.B.	R	2496	24	19/05/45	RAN 1J	RAN 1J	1M/RR/m
DAVIS, E.	A	2503	33	25/07/45	RAN 2J	RAN 2JB	m
DAVISON, G.M	A	2506	38	09/02/45	SAN 2	KG	m
DEACON, W.J	R	2493	25	11/03/45	PAG	PAG CEM	1M/ae
DENNISON, C.	A	2502	23	02/06/45	29m SAN	TR	2M/m
DOE, J.H	R	2516	-	27/03/45	SAN 2	SAN 2	m
DREW, J.H.	R	2515	22	21/03/45	SAN 2	SAN 1	bb
DREW, R.E.	R	2514	23	25/04/45	RAN 1	RAN 1B	1M/RR/m
DUNNETT, J.	A	2513	31	07/06/45	49m SAN	TR	2M/m
DURHAM, J.A.	R	2246	31	21/03/45	PAG	PAG CEM	1M/m
DURRANT, R.	A	2492	28	28/02/45	SAN 2	SAN 1	m
DYER, W.V.	R	2512	26	05/06/45	SAN 2	SAN 3	RS/m
EADEN, R.S.	A	2252	39	10/03/45	PAG	PAG CEM	1M/RR/m
EAST, E.J.	A	2520	34	02/05/45	SAN ?	SAN ?	DR/m
EDDEN, S.V.	R	2528	31	19/03/45	SAN 2	SAN 1	m
EDWARDS, J.	A	2250	27	05/08/45	SAN ?	SAN ?	DR/m
EDWARDS, S.E.	A	2251	28	14/03/45	PAG	PAG CEM	1M/ae
EFFORD, P.H.	A	2525	-	08/02/45	SAN 2	KG	ae
ELDER, A.H.	R	2527	38	22/04/45	SAN 1	KG	m
ELLIOTT, D.	R	2526	23	17/03/45	PAG	PAG CEM	1M/RR/ae
ENDERSBY, R.W.	R	2517	24	16/01/45	SAN 2	KG	m
ENGSTROM, R.C.B.	A	2249	24	11/06/45	SAN 2	SAN 3	m
EPSTINE, A.	A	2523	23	27/02/45	SAN ?	SAN ?	DR/m
EVANS, F.G.	A	2522	29	18/03/45	SAN ?	SAN ?	DR/m
EVANS, T.F.	A	2521	30	14/07/45	SAN 2	SAN 3	m
EYLES, W.A.R.	R	2518	31	12/03/45	SAN ?	SAN ?	DR/m
FAILES, C.E.	R	2530	32	05/04/45	SAN 2	KG	m
FAIRGRAY, N.	R	2253	-	28/02/45	SAN 2	SAN 1	m
FAULKES, C.H.	A	2540	27	16/02/45	SAN 2	SAN 1	ae
FELTHAM, M.R.	R	2529	24	02/07/45	RAN 2J	RAN 2JA	2M/RT/m
FENN, N.	R	2254	-	14/06/45	SAN 2	SAN 3	m
FENNER, R.A.	A	2260	30	17/02/45	?	?	Cl/m
FIELDING, T.O.	A	2544	36	20/06/45	w of PAG	TR	2M/m
FILBEY, C.H.	A	2546	23	14/03/45	?	?	Cl/m
FILLINGHAM, W.	A	2545	36	12/06/45	SAN 2	SAN 3	m
FINCH, R.F.	A	2547	24	14/02/45	SAN 2	KG	m
FINNIGAN, W.	A	2537	24	27/03/45	SAN 2	SAN 2	m
FISHER, E.	R	2536	-	09/02/45	SAN 2	KG	m
FISHER, T.W.S	R	2253	23	23/03/45	SAN 2	SAN 2	m
FISHWICK, W.	A	2531	30	01/03/45	SAN ?	SAN ?	DR/m
FITZGERALD, H.J.	A	2257	33	27/01/45	SAN 2	KG	m
FLETCHER, J.	R	2535	-	29/03/45	PAG-RAN	TR	1M/m
FLETCHER, S.N.	R	2552	25	03/03/45	SAN 2	SAN 1	m
FLINN, M.M.	R	2551	-	04/10/44	SAN 2	KG	ae

SANDAKAN — A CONSPIRACY OF SILENCE

FOLEY, M.J.	R	2259	35	21/07/45	RAN 2J	RAN 2JB	2M/m
FORD, E.	R	2532	24	24/02/45	SAN 2	SAN 1	m
FORSTER, J.J.	A	2256	34	08/07/45	RAN 2J	RAN 2JA	2M/m
FOSTER, E.	R	2533	27	07/06/45	SAN 2	SAN 3	m
FOSTER, L.	A	2542	23	26/03/45	SAN ?	SAN ?	DR/m
FRAMPTON, E.J.	A	2550	-	15/02/45	SAN 2	KG	m
FRATER, A.	A	2548	22	12/03/45	SAN ?	SAN ?	DR/m
FREEMAN, P.R.C.	R	2255	29	03/04/45	SAN 2	KG	m
FROST, D.A.	A	2538	23	05/03/45	SAN ?	SAN ?	DR/m
FROST, N.	A	2541	30	15/07/45	RAN 2J	RAN 2JB	1M/ae
GALLAGHER, J.	A	2474	24	25/01/45	SAN 2	KG	m
GANE, J.	A	2263	31	22/02/45	SAN 2	SAN 1	m
GARDINER, A.L.	A	2569	24	02/12/44	SAN 2	KG	m
GARDNER, H.D.	A	2571	28	08/12/44	SAN 2	KG	m
GARMAN, H.	A	3015	23	27/04/45	SAN 1	KG	m
GARRARD, E.R.	R	2562	23	08/04/45	RAN 1	RAN 1B	1M/ae
GATES, A.	R	2561	34	11/03/45	SAN 2	SAN 1	m
GAVIGAN, E.P.	R	2563	35	14/01/45	SAN 2	KG	m
GEDDES, W.	A	2564	24	02/04/45	SAN 2	KG	m
GIBBS, C.F.	R	2559	21	23/02/45	SAN ?	SAN ?	DR/m
GIFFEN, W.	R	2560	-	17/03/45	SAN 2	SAN 1	m
GILDER, A.J.	R	2581	-	13/03/45	SAN 2	SAN 1	m
GLOVER, J.B.	R	2556	28	02/04/45	SAN 2	KG	m
GODLONTON, A.G.	R	2570	-	06/04/45	SAN 2	KG	ae
GOLLOP, W.D.	R	2557	24	30/06/45	SAN 2	SAN 3	m
GOODWIN, F.R.	R	2578	-	08/03/45	SAN ?	SAN ?	DR/m
GORDON, H.C.	R	2575	32	12/05/45	SAN 1	SAN 2	m
GOULD, W.J.	A	2582	-	22/01/45	SAN 2	KG	m
GRAHAM, A.S.	A	2264	31	15/06/45	SAN ?	SAN ?	DR/ae
GRANGER, H.P.	R	2554	-	22/06/45	30m RAN	TR	2M/m
GRAY, J.D.	R	2583	-	31/12/44	SAN 2	KG	m
GREEN, Henry	R	2555	24	17/06/45	SAN 2	SAN 3	m
GREEN, Horace	A	2553	34	22/01/45	SAN 2	SAN 1	m
GREGSON, A.	A	2580	23	16/03/45	PAG	PAG CEM	1M/m
GREWCOCK, L.H.	A	2262	29	13/02/45	?	?	Cl/m
GRICE, R.W.	R	2568	24	30/03/45	RAN 1	RAN 1B	1M/ae
GRIFFITHS, D.	A	2267	27	22/07/45	RAN 2J	RAN 2JB	2M/m
GRIFFITHS, E.S.	R	2577	25	03/03/45	SAN ?	SAN ?	DR/m
GRIFFITHS, I.	R	2576	25	29/12/44	SAN 2	KG	m
GROUNDON, S.E.	R	2566	24	22/03/45	SAN 2	SAN 1	m
GROVES, F.	A	2574	28	07/03/45	SAN ?	SAN ?	DM/m
GUERIN, D.L.	R	2265	37	25/04/45	SAN 1	KG	ae
GUY, G.	R	2565	27	27/02/45	SAN 2	SAN 1	m
GWILLIAM, F.H.	A	2572	-	19/01/45	SAN 2	KG	m
HALL, J.E.W.	A	2273	45	09/05/45	RAN 1J	RAN 1J	1M/m
HALL, L.	R	2586	39	01/03/45	SAN 2	SAN 1	m
HALL, Robert	A	2611	29	09/04/45	SAN 2	KG	m
HALL, Robert Joseph	R	2593	26	20/06/45	ECR	TR	2M/m
HALLSEY, G.	A	2606	29	14/03/45	SAN ?	SAN ?	DR/m
HAMMOND, B.I.	A	2619	29	11/05/43	SAN 2A	KG	m
HANLEY, J.B.	A	2276	-	31/03/45	SAN 2	KG	m
HANNANT, N.J.	A	2653	24	13/02/45	SAN 2	KG	m
HARDACRE, G.	A	2627	23	10/03/45	PAG	PAG CEM	1M/m
HARDMAN, J.	A	2631	-	22/04/45	SAN 1	KG	m
HAROLD, R.R.	A	2634	29	11/12/44	SAN 2	KG	m
HARRINGTON, D.	A	2278	29	31/03/45	SAN 2	KG	m
HARRIS, Bert	R.	2594	28	22/03/45	SAN 2	SAN 1	m
HARRIS, C.	R	2603	22	30/04/45	SAN 1	KG	m
HARRIS, J.	R	2602	-	15/06/45	SAN 2	SAN 3	m
HARRISON, H	R	2280	31	03/04/45	SAN 2	KG	m
HARROLD, J.G.	A	2279	36	21/03/45	SAN ?	SAN ?	DR/m
HART, M.	A	2610	32	16/04/45	SAN 1	KG	m
HASLAM, S.J.	R	2595	27	21/06/45	nr PAG	TR	2M/m
HAWKINS, C.	R	2597	-	15/06/45	SAN 2	SAN 3	ae
HAWKINS, E.R.	A	2640	-	31/03/45	SAN 2	KG	RS?/m
HAYWARD, S.A.	A	2272	31	07/07/45	SAN 2	SAN 3	ae
HAZELTINE, J	A	2605	24	07/06/45	SAN ?	SAN ?	m
HAZZARD, E.	A	2626	36	22/02/45	SAN 2	SAN 1	m
HENSHALL, N.H.	A	2275	28	06/03/45	PAG	PAG CEM	1M/m
HESTER, W.V.	R	2590	-	14/03/45	SAN 2	SAN 1	m
HEYWOOD, C.	A	2600	38	06/05/45	SAN 1	SAN 2	m
HICKSON, F.	R	2591	39	01/12/44	SAN 2	KG	m
HILL, J.	A	2604	33	27/05/45	SAN 1	SAN 2	m
HILL, W.R.	A	2601	24	17/02/45	?	?	Cl/m
HIRSTLE, L.	A	2636	32	27/03/45	SAN 2	SAN 2	m
HOBBS, F.W.	R	2270	25	23/05/45	SAN 1	SAN 2	RS/m
HODGES, T.	R	2585	-	05/02/45	SAN 2	KG	m

APPENDIX1: NOMINAL ROLLS

Name							
HODGKINSON, F.	R	2624	23	16/10/44	SAN 2	KG	m
HODGKINSON, J.E.	R	2598	30	21/04/45?	?	?	Cl/m
HODGKINSON, Derek	A	2607	24	21/03/45	PAG	PAG CEM	1M/m
HODGSON, R.	A	2616	24	02/08/45	RAN 2J (2M)	R 2JB/MS	false dod Relic R
HOGGETT, W.V.	A	2618	34	02/04/45	SAN 2	KG	m
HOLBEN, R.J.	R	2599	35	05/04/45	SAN 2	KG	ae
HOLDER, C.J.	A	2632	27	14/06/45	14m Boto	TR	2M/RS/m
HOLDER, H.J.	A	2277	32	06/03/45	SAN ?	SAN ?	DR/m
HOLMAN, R.	R	2838	31	13/05/45	RAN 1J	RAN 1J	1M/m
HOOF, A.	A	2638	24	08/01/45	SAN 2	KG	m
HOPKINSON, H.	A	2615	29	11/03/45	SAN ?	SAN ?	DR/m
HORRELL, F.	A	2628	-	30/03/45	SAN 2	KG	m
HUDGELL, H.E.	R	2623	33	14/07/45	SAN 2	SAN 3	m
HUGHES, A.J.	R	2588	-	28/03/45	SAN ?	SAN ?	DR/ae
HUGHES, B.F.	R	2587	-	09/07/45	RAN 2J	RAN 2JA	2M/m
HUGHES, D.J.	A	2612	28	17/06/45	w of Boto	TR	2M/m
HUMPHRIES, W.G.	R	2592	23	24/05/45	SAN 1	SAN 2	RS/m
HUMPHRIES, J.H.	A	2625	38	20/06/45	ECR	TR	RS/ae
HUTCHINSON, J.	A	2274	23	04/02/45	SAN 2	KG	ae
ILES, R.J.	A	2642	41	30/06/45	SAN 2	SAN 3	ae
INGHAM, H.	R	2641	29	23/03/45	SAN ?	SAN ?	DR/bb
IRELAND, H.S.	A	2281	31	13/02/45	SAN 2	SAN 1	ae
JACOBI, H.C.	A	2287	38	26/03/45	PAG	PAG CEM	1M/m
JACOBS, A.	R	2644	23	01/06/45	SAN 2	SAN 3	ae
JAMES, H.O.	R	2645	40	25/01/45	SAN 2	KG	m
JAMIESON, J.	R	2665	40	23/03/45	SAN 2	SAN 2	m
JARDINE, A	A	2655	23	15/02/45	6mw M'dai	TR	1M/bb
JAZEWCIS, W	R	2662	30	23/02/45	SAN 2	SAN 1	m
JEFFERIES, J.P.	R	2663	-	21/02/45	SAN 2	SAN 1	m/bb
JEFFERSON, H.T.	R	2284	-	05/04/45	SAN 2	KG	m/bb
JEWELL, W.J.	R	2648	33	03/04/45	SAN 2	KG	ae
JOHNSON, E.G.	R	2661	-	14/02/45?	?	?	Cl/m
JOHNSON, J.E.	A	2650	36	30/03/45	SAN 2	KG	m
JOHNSON, K.A.	A	2286	28	30/06/45	SAN 2	SAN 3	bb
JONES, B.P.	R	2283	24	15/04/45	SAN 2	KG	m
JONES, C.	A	2682	24	20/04/45	SAN 1	SAN 2	-
JONES, E.B.	A	2643	30	08/03/45	SAN 2	SAN 1	m
JONES, J.H.	A	2664	28	09/06/45	RAN 1J	RAN 1J	1M/m
JONES, M.P.	R	2660	-	13/07/45	SAN 2	SAN 3	m
JONES, Thomas	A	2649	23	07/02/45	SAN 2	KG	m
JONES, Thomas	R	2658	27	27/03/45	SAN ?	SAN ?	DR/m
JONES, Tivy	R	2659	23	20/07/45	SAN 2	SAN 3	RS/m
JONES, W .	R	2646	-	01/04/45	RAN 1	RAN 1B	RR/m
JORDAN, F.J.	R	2654	31	12/06/45	SANDALA	KG	RS/esc San
KEABLE, A.	A	2670	24	14/06/45	BOTO	TR	2M/bb
KEARNEY, F.W.	R	2677	32	21/02/45	2mw M'lu	TR	1M/bb ae
KEAVENEY, P.E.	A	2678	23	12/05/45	SAN 1	SAN 2	m
KEEBLE, N.	A	2676	33	05/06/45	SAN 2	SAN 3	m
KENNERLEY, K.	R	2675	-	25/04/45	SAN 1	KG	m
KENT, G.H.	R	2674	-	19/06/45	SAN 2	SAN 3	m
KIBBLE, E.	A	2672	26	15/12/44	SAN 2	KG	m
KIDBY, H.G.	A	2290	38	21/03/45	SAN ?	SAN ?	DR/m
KITCHINGHAM, T.	R	2673	23	26/03/45	SAN 2	SAN 2	RS/m
KLEISER, E.L.	R	2293	-	28/03/45	SAN ?	SAN ?	DR/m
KNAPPER, G.W.	R	2671	24	15/06/45	SAN ?	SAN ?	DR/m
KNOWLES, J.H.	A	2291	24	01/02/45	?	?	Cl/m
KNUTTON, H.	A	2667	33	21/04/43	SAN 2A	KG	m
LAIN G, R.	A	2294	28	19/03/45	PAG	PAG CEM	1M/m
LANE, A.	R	2679	-	14/02/45	SAN 2	KG	m
LANHAM, H.	A	2695	27	28/04/45	SAN 1	KG	m
LARTER, G.R.	R	2684	39	21/02/45	M'GAN	TR	1M/bb ae
LATHAM, R.	A	2699	26	26/12/44	SAN 2	KG	bb
LAW, D.R.	A	2296	38	07/06/45	TR	TR	m
LAWRENCE, E.G.	R	2681	38	06/02/45	SAN 2	KG	m
LEALAND, J	R	2682	-	23/04/45	SAN 1	KG	m
LE CLERQ, R.R.	A	2297	35	03/06/45	SAN 2	SAN 3	ae
LEE, R.	R	2691	24	30/03/45	SAN 2	KG	m
LESLIE, G.	R	2690	33	31/12/44	SAN 2	KG	m
LESTER, C.F.	A	2698	37	01/07/44	SAN 2	KG	bb
LEVINS, P.	A	2685	-	04/04/45	SAN 2	KG	m
LEWIS, V.F.	A	2696	23	22/05/45	SAN 1	SAN 2	m
LINGE, A.J.	R	2202	53	27/06/45	RAN 2J	RAN 2JA	2M/ae
LITTEN, A.J.E.	A	2298	40	13/03/45	SAN 2	SAN 1	m
LITTLEWOOD, E.L.	R	2295	28	17/03/45	PAG	PAG CEM	1M/m ae

LOCKHART, J.	A	2679	41	04/05/45	SAN 1	SAN 2	m	
LOMAS, G.T.	A	2692	31	01/07/45	RAN 2J	RAN 2JA	2M/ae	
LONG, G.	A	2688	29	21/02/45	SAN 2	SAN 1	m	
LONGHURST, L.	A	2686	24	22/06/45	SAN 2	SAN 3	m	
LONGWORTH, T.	A	2687	24	17/03/45	SAN 2	SAN 1	m	
LUCAS, C.R.	R	2680	25	31/03/45	SAN 2	KG	ae	
LUSCOTT, T.	A	2693	23	02/03/45	PAG	PAG CEM	1M/ae	
McARTHUR, P.	A	2750	24	08/04/45	SAN 2	SAN 2	m	
McCANDLESS, J.R.	R	2731	28	11/08/45	RAN 2J (2M)	R 2J/MS	false dod	
McCOMISKY, H.	A	2310	27	20/12/44	SAN 2	KG	m	
McCONNELL, W.	A	2730	25	13/03/45	SAN 2	SAN 1	m	
McCULLOCH, W.	A	2709	22	16/02/45	?	?	Cl/ae	
McDERMOTT, T.H.	R	2314	40	27/07/45	RAN 2J	RAN 2JB	2M/m	
McDONALD, J.A.	A	2710	33	03/07/45	SAN 2	SAN 3	m	
MACE, F.	A	2717	35	19/03/45	SAN 2	SAN 1	ae	
McGOUGH, M.	A	2742	25	30/03/45	SAN 2	KG	m	
McGREGOR, N.E.	R	2740	32	25/11/44	SAN 2	KG	m	
McKEON, L.	R	2300	26	27/03/45	SAN 2	SAN 2	m	
McLELLAN, R.	R	2707	39	03/01/45?	?	?	Cl/ae	
McMEECHAN, C.	A	2746	35	18/05/45	SAN 1	SAN 2	m	
McMENEMY, D.	A	2718	37	16/02/45	SAN 2	SAN 1	m	
McNAB, C.P.	A	2703	35	15/03/45	SAN 2	SAN 1	m	
McNEE, S.R.		-	26	23/01/45	SAN 2	KG	-	
MADELEY, J.W.	A	2721	31	12/04/45	RAN 1	RAN 1B	1M/RR/bb	
MAHON, E.	R	2309	37	30/06/45	RAN 2J	RAN 2JA	2M/ae	
MAGUIRE, C.	A	2747	43	28/04/45	SAN 1	KG	-	
MAGUIRE, J.	A	2743	35	03/04/45	SAN 2	SAN 1	m	
MAITLAND, T.	R	2734	31	03/02/45	SAN 2	KG	ae	
MANNIX, J.	A	2706	23	10/05/45	SAN 1	SAN 2	m	
MARRIOTT, P.C.	R	2301	26	18/02/45	PAPAN	TR	1M/m	
MARSDEN, J.	A	2712	23	07/06/45	43m San	TR	2M/m	
MARSH, E.	R	2299	23	05/06/45	SAN 2	SAN 3	m	
MARTIN, J.R.	A	2711	31	14/02/45	?	?	Cl/m	
MASON, W.	A	2716	34	05/03/45	SAN ?	SAN ?	DR/bb	
MATTHEWS, T.	A	2308	23	27/11/44	SAN 2	KG	m	
MATTHEWS, T.R.	R	2729	23	14/07/45	SAN 2	SAN 3	m	
MAYLAM, H.E.	R	2719	32	10/05/45	SAN 1	SAN 2	m	
MEARS, R.	A	2715	22	08/11/43	SAN 2	KG	-	
MELLOR, E.	A	2702	36	16/02/45	SAN 2	SAN 2	m	
MELLOR, S.	A	2700	35	15/06/45	SAN 2	SAN 3	m	
MERCHANT, A.H.	R	2303	38	18/07/45	RAN 2J	RAN 2JB	2M/ae	
MIDDLETON, N.	R	2724	33	30/03/45	SAN 2	KG	m	
MILEMAN, A.E.	A	2749	-	16/02/45	SAN 2	KG	ae	
MILES, G.A.	A	2704	29	07/06/45	SAN ?	SAN ?	m	
MILLAR, P.R.	R	2302	31	21/07/45	RAN 2J	RAN 2JB	2M/m	
MILLARD, W.E.	R	2725	40	28/01/45	SAN 2	SAN 1	RS/m	
MILLER, D.C.	R	2726	23	07/06/45	ECR	TR	2M/m	
MILLER, H.L.	A	2313	35	18/02/45	?	?	Cl/m	
MILLS, J.F.D.	A	2203	30	03/07/45	SAN 2	believed executed, no grave		
MILTON, H.E.	R	2305	29	30/04/45	SAN 1	KG	m	
MITCHELL, A.W.	R	2307	31	03/06/45	SAN 2	SAN 3	m	
MOORE, D.	R	2736	-	27/02/45	PAG	PAG CEM	1M/m	
MOORE, F.W.	R	2737	25	11/02/45	5mw M'ai	TR	1M/m	
MOORE, J.E.	A	2311	33	08/04/45	RAN 1	RAN 1B	1M/AE	
MORRIS, L.	R	2733	24	28/03/45	PAG-RAN	TR	1M/m	
MORRIS, Reginald	A	2744	29	05/03/45	SAN 2	SAN 1	m	
MORRIS, Ronald	A	2312	31	06/03/45	SAN 2	SAN 1	m	
MORRISON, H.	A	2713	36	10/03/45	SAN 2	SAN 1	-	
MORTON, F.	A	2745	27	13/05/45	SAN 1	SAN 2	m	
MYERS, S.	A	2705	27	01/03/45	SAN ?	SAN ?	DR/m	
NATHAN, G.	R	2754	28	14/02/45	nr B'uran	TR	1M/m	
NEWALL, J.E.	A	2762	35	25/03/45	SAN 2	SAN 2	m	
NEWMAN, F.K.	R	2753	23	07/03/45	PAG	PAG CEM	1M/RR/ae	
NEWMAN, F.R.	R	2752	-	21/03/45	PAG	PAG CEM	1M/ae	
NEWTON, A.	A	2758	27	14/04/45	SAN 2	KG	m	
NICHOLAS, J.L.	A	2756	28	16/06/45	PAPAN	TR	2M/ae	
NICKSON, S.D.	A	2763	32	15/02/45	SAN 2	KG	bb	
NOBLE, J.	A	2761	28	04/04/45	SAN 2	KG	bb	
NORTHFIELD, A.	A	2755	23	14/04/45	RAN 1	RAN 1B	1M/ae	
NORTON, B.J.	A	2759	23	19/05/45	SAN 1	SAN 2	m	
OAKHAM, G.	A	2767	31	13/03/45	SAN 2	SAN 1	-	
OLDING, A.E.	A	2764	27	29/01/45	SAN 2	KG	ae	
OLDROYD, H.G.	R	2770	27	16/04/45	RAN 1	RAN 1B	1M/m	
OLIVER, H.S.	A	2766	34	12/03/45	SAN ?	SAN ?	DR/m	
ORMOND, W.J.	R	2772	34	04/09/44	SAN 2	SAN 1	m	
ORR, H.	R	2768	24	09/01/45	SAN 2	KG	m	

APPENDIX1: NOMINAL ROLLS

Name		No.	Age	Date	Col1	Col2	Notes
O'SHEA, D.M.P.	A	2773	24	20/05/45	SAN 1	SAN 2	m
PALMER, H.J.	A	2319	24	17/03/45	PAG	PAG CEM	1M/ae
PARFITT, A.W.C	R	2791	25	07/03/45	PAG	PAG CEM	1M/ae
PARKER, F.H.	R	2322	-	12/03/45	SAN ?	SAN ?	DR/m
PARKER, L.N.J.	A	2776	28	22/03/45	PAG	PAG CEM	1M/ -
PARKER, R.C.	R	2792	30	14/03/45	PAG	PAG CEM	1M/m
PARSONS, F.J.H.	A	2818	33	14/03/45	PAG	PAG CEM	1M/m
PASK, J.K.	R	2793	21	15/06/45	SAN 2	SAN 3	m
PASSEY, F.M.	R	2774	25	13/05/45	SAN ?	SAN ?	DR/bb
PATCHESA, H.	R	2794	24	02/06/45	ECR	TR	2M/bb
PATERSON, L.	R	2797	-	14/06/45	ECR	TR	2M/m bb
PATERSON, R.	A	2777	34	18/05/43	SAN 2A	KG	m
PATRICK, F.W.	A	2802	23	28/03/45	SAN ?	SAN ?	m
PAYNE, B.G.	A	2814	29	06/03/45	PAG	PAG CEM	1M/m
PAYNE, W.E.	R	2796	30	07/06/45	54m San	TR	2M/m
PEARCE, C.	R	2812	23	05/03/45	PAG	PAG CEM	1M/ae
PEARSON, C.B.	R	2318	30	02/06/45	ECR	TR	2M/m
PEAT, J.H.	A	2805	32	15/04/45	SAN 2	SAN 2	m
PEEL, J.	A	2804	23	09/05/45	SAN ?	SAN ?	DR/m
PELAN, H.G.	R	2325	25	25/02/45	SAN ?	SAN ?	DR/m
PENNELL, R.W.	R	2811	30	23/01/45	SAN 2	KG	ae
PENROSE, S.H.	A	2317	33	21/04/45	RAN 1	RAN 1B	1M/m
PERKINS, J.W.F.	R	2810	-	07/04/45	SAN 2	KG	m
PERRY, G.H.	A	2324	-	24/03/45	SAN ?	SAN ?	DR/m
PERRY, H.S.	R	2320	40	15/05/45	SAN ?	SAN ?	DR/m
PETHERAM, K.G.	R	2785	24	20/03/45	SAN 2	SAN 1	m
PETHERWICK, N.G.	A	2799	-	14/04/45	SAN 2	KG	m
PHILLIPS, D.G.	R	2798	36	13/03/45	SAN 2	SAN 1	m
PHILLIPS, J.W.	R	2795	37	04/10/44	SAN 2	SAN 1	m
PICOT, E.J.	A	2783	32	30/07/45	SAN ?	SAN ?	m
PIMBLETT, E.	R	2321	24	01/07/45	SAN 2	SAN 3	-
PITTENDREIGH, W.	R	2816	26	12/03/45	SAN ?	SAN ?	DR
PLATT, J.S.	A	2781	24	12/03/45	SAN ?	SAN ?	DR/m
PLUMMER, H.W.	R	2808	30	15/07/44	SAN 2	KG	m
POLDEN, L.W.	R	2809	30	07/03/45	SAN 2	SAN 1	m
PORTSMOUTH, R.A.	A	2780	25	09/07/45	SAN 2	SAN 3	m
POTTER, A.A.	R	2316	27	21/02/45	SAN 2	SAN 1	m
POTTER, A.H.	A	2860	-	26/05/43	SAN 2A	KG	m
POTTS, L.G.	R	2807	21	19/05/45	SAN 1	SAN 2	m
POWELL, J.F.	R	2786	22	26/11/44	SAN 2	KG	m
PRATT, J.C.	A	2803	24	06/02/45	SAN 2	KG	m
PRENTICE, D.E.	A	2775	29	06/05/45	SAN 1	SAN 2	m
PRESLAND, R.A.	A	2817	40	12/06/43	SAN 2A	KG	m
PRICE, D.J.	R	2806	38	21/02/45	PAG	PAG CEM	1M/m
PRICE, G.	R	2789	32	03/04/45	SAN 2	KG	m
PRIDDLE, G.F.	R	2788	-	12/06/45	RAN 1J	RAN 1J	1M/m
					(believed kiled with Allie and the sick)		
PRIVETT, D.E.	A	2782	24	30/03/45	SAN 2	KG	m
PROUTEN, G.	A	2315	54	14/06/45	ECR	TR	2M/m
RAMSAY, H.J.	R	2821	25	30/06/45	SAN 2	SAN 3	m
RAMSAY, J.O.	R	2828	35	29/01/45	SAN 2	KG	m
RANSOME, H.	R	2327	25	23/03/45	SAN 2	SAN 2	m
RATCLIFFE, W.W.	R	2843	-	23/03/45	SAN ?	SAN ?	DR/m
READ, J.	A	2848	24	02/07/45	SAN 2	SAN 3	m
REDMAN, C.	A	2850	34	04/01/45	SAN 2	KG	m
REEVES, G.F.	R	2842	24	02/03/45	SAN ?	SAN ?	DR/m
REID, K.W.	A	2847	23	28/01/45	?	?	CI/m
RENNIE, G.	R	2830	-	15/07/45	SAN 2	SAN 3	m
RICHARDS, L.	R	2841	23	30/03/45	SAN 2	KG	m
RICHARDS, T.H.I.	A	2331	35	22/03/45	SAN ?	SAN ?	DR/m
RICKARD, T.	R	2831	27	08/06/45	SAN 2	SAN 3	m
ROBB, H.S.	R	2835	-	20/02/45	SAN 2	SAN 1	m
ROBERTS, Bois	A	2822	28	MARCH 45	KEMANSI	KG	esc 1M/ae
ROBERTS, O.G.	R	2834	30	12/12/44	SAN 2	KG	m
ROBERTS, R.	A	2328	38	06/03/45	PAG	PAG CEM	1M/RR/m
ROBERTS, W.L.	R	2855	23	18/07/45	SAN 2	SAN 3	m
ROBINSON, A.W.	A	2827	31	17/03/45	PAG	PAG CEM	1M/m
ROBSON, J.R.	R	2832	27	13/07/45	SAN 2	SAN 3	m
ROCKER, S.S.	A	2844	24	14/03/45	SAN ?	SAN ?	DR/m
RODDEN, M.J.	A	2823	36	28/02/45	SAN ?	SAN ?	DR/m
ROLFE, I.D.	A	2211	25	27/06/45	SAN 2	SAN 3	RS/m
ROGERS, E.R.	A	2851	30	30/06/45	SAN 2	SAN 3	m
ROGERS, J.W.	A	2329	28	13/03/45	PAG	PAG CEM	1M/m
ROOKER, H.	A	2326	31	09/08/45	SAN 2	SAN 3	m
ROOKWOOD, L.J.	A	2330	29	27/02/45	PAG	PAG CEM	1M/m
ROSS, J.G.	A	2849	32	20/02/45	SAN ?	SAN ?	DR/m
ROUCHY, J.F.	R	2846	-	26/03/45	SAN ?	SAN ?	DR/m

Name		No.	Age	Date	Location 1	Location 2	Code
ROWARTH, J.	R	2836	26	27/03/45	SAN 2	SAN 3	m
ROWLAND, J.	R	2852	-	08/06/44	SAN 2	KG	m
RUSSELL, H.G.	A	2826	30	08/03/45	SAN ?	SAN ?	DR/m
RUSSELL, J.S.	A	2856	38	22/04/45	SAN 1	KG	m
SADLER, F.E.	A	2858	36	22/07/45	RAN 2J	RAN 2JB	2M/m
SAID, A.	A	2884	23	06/03/45	PAG	PAG CEM	1M/m
SALTER, A.H.	A	2338	38	19/03/45	SAN ?	SAN ?	DR/m
SAMPSON, F.S.	R	2862	24	05/02/45	SAN 2	KG	m
SANDERS, T.W.	R	2332	-	27/12/44	SAN 2	KG	m
SANDS, A.	R	2861	-	03/08/45	RAN 2J (2M)	R 2JB/MS	false dod
SARGINSON, J.	R	2868	26	09/02/45	3me M'rin	TR	1M/bb
SAUNDERS, R.	R	2865	26	24/04/45	SAN 1	KG	m
SAVILLE, W.	A	2889	24	01/03/45	SAN ?	SAN ?	DR/m
SCOTT, J.G.	A	2888	39	03/01/45	SAN 2	KG	m
SCOTT, R.C.	A	2857	27	13/04/45	SAN 2	KG	ae
SCOTT, T.	A	2899	23	01/09/44	SAN 2	KG	ae
SEAL, C.A.	R	2867	39	02/03/45	PAG	PAG CEM	1M/mm
SECKINGTON, E.	R	2341	23	18/04/45	RAN 1	RAN 1B	1M/RR/m
SHACKLETON, N.	R	2874	26	25/02/45	SAN 2	SAN 1	m
SHARP, H.	A	2335	26	28/03/45	SAN ?	SAN ?	DR/m
SHATWELL, C.	R	2880	-	30/11/44	SAN 2	KG	m
SHAW, A.W.	A	2885	32	05/02/45	SAN 2	KG	bb
SHAW, G.P.	R	2918	23	08/12/44	SAN 2	KG	m men
SHAW, R.	R	2917	29	21/06/45	SAN 2	SAN 3	m men
SHEARSMITH, D.	A	2898	23	14/06/45	SAN 2	SAN 3	m men
SHERRIFF, F.C.	R	2866	40	05/06/45	ECR	TR	2M/m
SHIPLEY, G.	A	2336	31	17/03/45	PAG	PAG CEM	1M/m
SHIPPEN, J.W.	A	2882	34	15/03/45	PAG	PAG CEM	1M/m
SHRUBSHALL, W.F.	A	2909	35	18/03/45	SAN ?	SAN ?	DR/m
SHUFFLETON, J.A.	A	2875	-	24/03/45	SAN ?	SAN ?	DR/m
SIME, J.R.	A	2334	-	28/05/45	SAN 1	SAN 2	m
SIMMONDS, T.J.N.	A	2896	27	23/07/45	SAN 2	SAN 3	m
SIMPSON, B.	A	2901	32	25/03/45	SAN ?	SAN ?	DR/m
SIMPSON, G.A.	R	2916	-	27/03/45	SAN 2	SAN 2	m
SIMPSON, G.W.	R	2915	25	11/06/45	SAN 2	SAN 3	m
SIMMS, E.	R	2914	24	29/05/45	SAN 1	S3/ CPD	m
SLADE, A.E.	A	2897	35	17/02/45	TR	TR	m
SLATER, J.E.	R	2876	-	02/06/45	SAN ?	SAN ?	DR/m
SMALL, J.N.	A	2343	29	14/03/45	PAG	PAG CEM	1M/m
SMITH, A. Cyril	A	2904	32	04/02/45	SAN 2	KG	m
SMITH, A. Edward	A	2881	28	21/02/45	SAN 2	SAN 1	m men
SMITH, G.	A	2344	-	12/01/45	SAN 2	KG	m men
SMITH, G. Bernard	R	2877	-	15/03/45	SAN ?	SAN ?	DR/RS/ae
SMITH, John	R	2870	29	08/07/45	RAN 2J	RAN 2JA	2M/m
SMITH, Joseph H.	R	2872	33	09/03/45	SAN 2	SAN 1	m
SMITH, S.J.	R	2864	38	01/08/45	RAN 2J (2M)	R 2J/MS	false dod
SMITH, T.D.	R	2871	39	30/04/43	SAN 2A	TR	m
SOORIER, M.K.	R	2869	-	03/04/45	Kempei-tai HQ San		m (K?)
SNEDDEN, T.	A	2883	33	11/06/45	SAN 2	SAN 3	m men
SOUTHWELL, J.R.	R	2910	-	03/05/45	SAN 1	SAN 2	-
SPENCER, F.	R	2873	40	14/02/45	SAN 2	KG	m
SPERRING, A.J.	R	2337	38	18/03/45	SAN ?	SAN ?	DR/m
STAMMERS, A.G.	R	2333	28	05/06/45	SAN 2	SAN 3	m
STAPELEY, O.W.	R	2890	22	16/07/45	RAN 2J	RAN 2JB	2M/m
STARMER, W.C.	A	2907	-	09/05/43	SAN 2A	KG	m/bb
STEPHENS, J.C.	R	2342	25	14/04/45	RAN 1	RAN 1B	1M/m bb
STEPHENS, Joseph	A	2911	24	05/04/45	SAN 2	KG	m bb
STEPHENSON, A.	A	2892	31	14/06/45	SAN 2	SAN 3	m
STEVENSON, A.B.	A	2339	36	07/06/45	RAN 1J	RAN 1J	1M/m
STICKLEE, H.S.	A	2879	44	01/12/44	SAN 2	KG	m
STOCKWELL, W.J.	A	2902	34	30/07/45	RAN 2J	RAN 2JB	2M/m
STREET, A.	R	2345	-	16/02/45	BOTO	TR	1M/m
SUMMERFIELD, V.	R	2912	27	03/03/45	SAN 2	SAN 1	m
SWEENEY, E.	A	2900	31	12/04/45	SAN 2	KG	m
SWEENEY, M.	A	2903	33	07/05/45	SAN ?	SAN ?	DR/m
SWEETING, A.J.	A	2906	41	29/03/45	RAN 1	RAN 1B	1M/m
SWINDELL, G.	R	2893	32	13/03/45	SAN 2	SAN 1	m
SYMONDS, A.G.	R	2894	32	15/03/45	SAN ?	SAN ?	DR/m
TABBERER, J.H.	A	2353	31	27/03/45	SAN ?	SAN ?	DR/m
TAMPIN, G.W.	A	2942	39	11/02/45	SAN 2	KG	m
TANT, F.C.	A	2930	29	23/04/45	RAN 1	RAN 1B	1M/m
TASKER, E.L.	A	2352	41	15/02/45	SAN 2	SAN 2	m
TAYLOR, A.	R	2935	28	28/03/45	SAN ?	SAN ?	DR/m
TAYLOR, C.	A	2939	28	28/02/45	SAN ?	SAN ?	DR/m
TAYLOR, E.W.	R	2933	-	20/03/45	SAN ?	SAN ?	DR/m
TAYLOR, J.C.	A	2946	-	29/09/43	SAN 2	KG	m
TAYLOR, W.	A	2947	-	16/02/45	SAN 2	KG	m

APPENDIX 1: NOMINAL ROLLS

Name		No.	Age	Date			
TEASDALE, W.J.	A	2346	41	21/02/45	SAN 2	SAN 1	RS/m
TENNENT, B.G.	R	2351	35	21/07/45	RAN 2J	RAN 2JB	2M/m
TESTER, E.J.	A	2931	32	11/06/45	SAN 2	SAN 3	m
THOMAS, B.	R	2356	-	02/04/45	SAN 2	KG	m
THOMAS, H.J.	A	2348	36	12/07/45	RAN 2J	RAN 2JB	2M/m
THOMPSON, E.H.	R	2355	-	23/04/45	SAN ?	SAN ?	DR/m
THOMPSON, R.	R	2932	21	15/06/45	ECR	TR	2M/m
THOMPSON, S.	R	2934	-	26/03/45	PAG	PAG CEM	1M/m
THORNETT, W.J.	A	2926	34	14/06/45	TR ?	TR?	CI/2M/m
THOROUGHGOOD, C.R.	A	2347	24	14/03/45	PAG	PAG CEM	1M/m
THORPE, A.G.	A	2940	28	14/02/45	?	?	CI/m
THURSTON, R.G.	A	2941	28	28/03/45	SAN ?	SAN ?	DR/m
TITLEY, J.	A	2919	37	04/02/45	SAN 2	KG	m
TOMKINSON, D.L.	A	2921	25	02/03/45	PAG	PAG CEM	1M/m
TONKIN, J.	A	2944	23	17/04/45	RAN 1	RAN 1B	1M/m
TONKINSON, J.S.	A	2923	27	23/05/45	SAN 1	SAN 2	RS/m
TOVEY, G.H.	A	2938	25	27/03/45	SAN 2	SAN 2	ae
TOYE, J.W.A.	R	2920	29	27/02/45	PAG	PAG CEM	1M/m
TRICKETT, E.S.	R	2943	-	01/06/45	SAN 2	SAN 3	m
TRITTON, V.J.	A	2936	33	28/07/45	RAN 2J	RAN 2JB	2M/m
TUGWELL, W.P.	R	2349	26	21/03/45	PAG	PAG CEM	1M/ae
TURLAND, P.C.	R	2927	23	02/05/45	SAN 1	KG	m
TURNBULL, E.D.	R	2928	-	03/04/45	SAN 2	KG	m
TUTTY, J.G.	A	2924	-	09/06/45	SAN 2	SAN 3	ae
UMPLEY, E.	R	2948	27	20/03/45	SAN 2	SAN 1	m
URRY, F.	R	2952	27	17/03/45	SAN 2	SAN 1	m
VARNEY, H.L.	A	2950	29	22/04/45	SAN 1	KG	m
VENTON, C.L.	A	2951	-	06/02/45	SAN 2	KG	RS/m
VICKERMAN, H.	R	2372	31	07/06/45	ECR	TR	2M/m
WAIDSON, F.	A	2367	32	24/07/45	RAN 2J	RAN 2JB	2M/m
WAITE, S.A.	A	2992	32	01/06/43	SAN 2A	KG	m
WAKEFIELD, A.L.B.	A	2983	38	30/12/44	SAN 2	KG	m
WALKER, J.S.	R	2974	24	24/02/45	SAN 2	SAN 1	m
WALKER, N.G.	A	2358	35	29/03/45	RAN 1	RAN 1B	1M/m
WALLACE, R.A.	R	2975	-	06/04/45	SAN 2	SAN 2	m
WALMSLEY, M.W.	R	2365	-	12/07/45	RAN 2J	RAN 2JB	2M/ae
WANLESS, J.T.	R	2973	-	30/06/45	RAN 2J	RAN 2JA	2M/ae
WARE, J.	R	2999	24	03/04/45	SAN 2	KG	m
WARNER, S.	R	2364	36	21/04/45	SAN 1	KG	m
WATERHOUSE, C.	R	2972	36	08/02/45	SAN 2	KG	m
WATKINS, K.O.	R	3000	28	24/02/45	PAG	PAG CEM	1M/m
WATSON, A.J.	R	2366	24	09/07/45	RAN 2J	RAN 2JA	2M/m
WATSON, W.T.	R	3001	22	05/05/45	SAN ?	SAN ?	DR/m
WATTS, J.T.	A	2956	-	15/01/45	SAN 2	KG	m
WATTS, R.	R	2981	29	29/07/45	SAN 2	SAN 3	m
WAUD, K.J.	R	2362	26	08/03/45	SAN 2	SAN 1	m
WEBB, D.T.	A	3006	24	02/04/45	SAN 2	SAN 2	m
WEBB, H.L.	A	2991	36	13/02/45	SAN 2	KG	m
WEBSTER, W.	R	2363	40	11/06/45	SAN ?	SAN ?	m
WEBSTER, W.B.	A	2993	-	11/12/44	SAN 2	KG	M
WELLER, E.H.	A	2964	41	18/02/45	SAN 2	SAN 1	m
WELLS, E.W.	R	2982	35	19/02/45	SAN 2	SAN 1	m
WELLS, F.	R	2980	23	29/05/45	SAN 1	SAN 2	m
WESTON, S.	A	2994	37	07/05/45	SAN 1	SAN 2	m
WHITE, C.E.	A	2959	35	23/06/43	SAN 2A	KG	m
WHITE, S.J.	A	2985	28	08/12/44	SAN 2	KG	m
WHITEHEAD, R.M.	R	2967	23	14/02/45	nr PAG	TR	1M/m
WHITESIDE, R.McD.	R	2371	29	14/06/45	SAN 2	SAN 3	m
WHITTLE, T.C.	A	2954	31	28/02/45	SAN 2	SAN 1	m
WHITTLE, William T.	A	2957	37	08/03/45	SAN ?	SAN ?	DR/m
WILKIE, J.	R	2997	19	22/02/45	SAN ?	SAN ?	DR/m
WILKINSON, J.	A	2963	-	21/12/44	SAN 2	SAN 1	m
WILKINSON, W.A.	A	2958	24	03/01/45	SAN 2	KG	m
WILLIAMS, A.E.	R	2977	40	05/01/45	SAN 2	KG	m
WILLIAMS, C.E.	A	3009	-	06/01/45	SAN 2	KG	m
WILLIAMS, C.R.	R	2978	33	10/03/45	SAN 2	KG	m
WILLIAMS, J.L.	R	2976	26	17/03/45	PAG	PAG CEM	1M/ae
WILLIAMS, R.H.	R	2979	25	19/02/45	SAN ?	SAN ?	DR/m
WILLIAMS, S.	R	2970	32	28/04/45	SAN ?	SAN ?	m
WILLIAMS, T.H.	R	2968	35	18/06/45	SAN 2	SAN 3	m
WILLIAMSON, J.	A	2960	36	04/03/45	SAN ?	SAN ?	DR/m
WILLIS, E.R.	A	2368	34	30/03/45	SAN 2	KG	m
WILLIS, F.A.J.	A	2248	32	19/02/45	SAN 2	SAN 1	m
WILMOTH, A.W.	R	2966	29	27/06/45	SAN 2	SAN 3	m
WILSON, C.J.	A	2984	30	28/03/45	SAN 2	SAN 2	m
WILSON, George	R	2361	26	14/06/45	SAN 2	SAN 3	m

WILSON, G. Edward	A	2357	28	21/03/45	PAG	PAG CEM	1M/m
WILSON, J.	A	2359	38	17/03/45	SAN ?	SAN ?	DR/m
WILSON, L.	R	3002	24	22/06/45	8m e N'pak	TR	2M/m
WINDER, C.	R	3003	25	16/04/45	SAN 1	SAN 2	ae
WIPER, T.	R	3004	27	28/04/45	SAN 1	KG	ae
WOODS, A.A.	A	2990	28	12/03/45	SAN ?	SAN ?	DR/ae
WOODS, E.A.	A	2369	32	18/06/45	SAN 2	SAN 3	m
WOOLBAR, R.C.	A	2370	33	28/02/45	SAN 2	SAN 1	m
WOOLF, W.H.	A	3005	32	10/03/45	SAN 2	SAN 1	m
WRAGG, E.	R	3007	24	13/03/45	SAN 2	SAN 1	m
WRIGHT, A.	A	2996	33	17/03/45	SAN 2	SAN 1	m
WRIGHT, K.	R	2988	24	19/06/45	4m w Boto	TR	2M/ae
WRIGHT, S.W.	A	2965	24	10/04/45	SAN 2	SAN 2	m
YORK, Reginald	R	3010	26	05/04/45	SAN 2	KG	m
YORK, Richard	A	3011	30	16/06/45	SAN ?	SAN ?	m
YOUNG, P. H.	A	2217	27	26/07/45	RAN 2J	RAN 2JB	2M/RS/m bb

Jesselton Deaths

Fifty-one British POWs died at Jesselton before the camp was moved to Sandakan. All were recovered from their marked graves by 23 Australian War Graves Unit and reburied at Labuan War Cemetery. *Note:* RAF personnel are marked with an *.

Auerbach, H.A., 36, 16/4/43; Bareham, G.A., 39, 14/1/43; Bentley, D.H., 31, 12/2/43; Blackburn, J., 36, 28/3/43; Bond, A.G., 37, 2/2/43; Booth, J. B., 28,12/2/43, chronic colitis; Brennan, D.G., 21, 20/1/43; Butterfield, A.W., 11/2/43; Chadburn, E.F.*, 24, 23/4/43, amoebic dysentery and beriberi; Cousins, T., 26, 6/2/43; Crossley, S., 24,15/12/44; Daynes, E,W.C., 33, 10/4/43; Draper, R.C., 31,15/1/43; Druce, E.V., 33,13/1/43; Durnford, R.G.G., 33,18/12/42; Eastwood, W.L., 21,13/2/43; Field, R.J, 33,2/1/43; Fox,I.E, 20, 21/3/43, amoebic dysentery; Green, H., 33, 5/4/43; Griffiths, C., 22/1/43; Harvey, T.H., 36, 21,1,43; Hellewell, G.W., 31, 23/1/43; Henderson, E.C., 33, 21/2/43; Hick, H., 28/12/42; Hill, F.L., 32, 14/12/42; Hitchings, A.L., 31,12/3/43; Hood, G., 21, 29/12/42, amoebic dysentery; Howard, J.R., 33, 27/11/42; Jones, R., 27, 4/1/43; Keaney, J.R., 26, 4/1/43; Kerslake, W. P.*, 24, 1/12/42, appendicitis and peritonitis; Lawrence, A.E., 29, 14/12/42; McLeod, J.B.*, 35, 2/1/43, amoebic dysentery; Mendy, H.J.*, 29, 28/12/42, amoebic dysentery; Morgan, R.H.*, 23, 18/3/43, acute enteritis; Myers, J.G.*, 27, 2/1/43, diphtheria; Nash, E., 29, 17/1/43; Needham, J.B., 21, 25/10/42; O'Brien, F.W., 22, 15/12/42; Potter, C.A, 28, 21/2/43; Robertson, J.D.*, 40, 14/3/43; Scullion, J., 22, 11/1/42; Smith, S.*, 14/4/43, acute enteritis; Speed, A.D.*, 36, 17/1/43, amoebic dysentery; Stirzaker, J., 32, 14/2/43; Thomasson, J.H., 34, 10/4/43; Venables, S.L., 21, 7/2/43; Watson, W.A., 26, 21/1/43; Wood, H., 35, 13/10/43; Wright, J.W., 22, 28/1/43; Young, R.G., 31,17/4/43.

Labuan Island, Brunei, Kuala Belai, Tanjong Lobang and Miri Deaths

Records relating to the six Australians (five AIF from Kuching and one AIF from the British Camp at Sandakan) and 284 British known to have died at these locations are very poor (death roll, paybooks, some tattered lists and occasional running sheets). However, of the 100 prisoners said to have been sent from Sandakan, the names of 97 have been verified. The other three are believed to be Arthur Weller, Ernest Weller and William Young, all of whom (in common with those known to have died at Labuan) have been omitted from the master Sandakan/Ranau Japanese Death Roll. In the absence of further firm information they have been included with the Labuan and Brunei casualties. Two POWs, whose names appear on a list compiled by Flight-Lieutenant Peter Lee, RAF, who was not at Sandakan when the transfers took place, have not been included. The body of one, Andrew Sommerville, was recovered from Number 2 Cemetery, Sandakan; the other, Albert Tyrrell, has a full set of paperwork, including running sheets, showing that he died on the second march. Details for Labuan-Miri vary, but, where available, ages, dates of death and cause of death have been included. The place of death has been based on the death date and, other recovered records. Where there is no other information other than part of a name, it has not been possible to reach a conclusion as to the identity of the other ten POWs said to have been transferred from Kuching.

Labuan (16 June 1944 — 6 March 1945):

Note: According to the following list, 226 POW died at Labuan. As the maximum the Japanese admitted to was 188 out of 300, at least 38 of these dates are false and they are believed to be the missing Riam Road massacre victims. Unfortunately, it is not possible to determine which of the dates are false. The death tally between 23 January and 7 March appears to be correct — the officer in charge stated there were 45 deaths, a figure which tallies. For abbreviations see 'Key to Roll — other details'.

From Sandakan (76 British and one AIF, a total of 77):

50 Army: Adrian, W., 32, 31/12/44; Barber, A.T., 28, 1/11/44; Bexfield, F.G., 30, 27/11/44; Blake, T.J., POW 2442,13/2/45; Bristow, A.J., 31, 5/12/44; Britten, E.D.G., 28, 20/1/45; Clarke, C.B., 32, 7/10/44; Copley, A., 35, 1/10/44; Cox, A.J., 23, 9/11/44; Cretton, W., 34, 18/12/44, m bb; Daniels, P., 28, 28/10/44; Dobson, E.A., 30, 18/10/44; Everett, H., 34, 25/11/44; Feast, A.H.,27, 6/1/45; Hastie, J., 36, 13/2/45; Hessey, S, 23, 15/2/45, m bb; Hewitt, H.W., 38, 30/12/44; Hood, G., 36, 29/9/44; Hopkins, A.H., 28, 27/11/44; Hynes, C.A., 31, 6/3/45; Jenkins, A.W.E, 29, 20/1/45; Johnston, J., 37, 28/11/44, m bb; Kaeo, C.R.V.,25, 31/12/44; Lee, J.A., 44, 24/12/44; Mansi, L.L., 33, 1/1/45; Mayhew, H.J., 39, 14/12/44; Metcalfe, A., 30, 11/12/44; Miles, C.F., 38, 5/12/44; Parks, K., 23, 7/3/45 (identity disk found); Penn, E.W., 27, 1/10/44; Pope, C.E., 31, 30/12/44; Potter, E.R., 28, 1/1/45; Powell, S.G.T., 32, 23/9/44; Pretlove, J., 35, 17/2/45; Rafferty, J., 24, 19/2/45; Rawlings, D., 29, 20/1/45; Relf, A.T.R., 30, 7/12/44; Rudling, J.W.P., 32, 24/10/44; Seamarks, W.H., 21, 6/2/45; Skilbeck, E., 40, 8/11/44; Snell, C., 23,14/9/44, KG; Taylor, A.L., 29, 9/12/44; Thompson, A., POW 2929, 23, 18/12/44; Tominey, T., 39, 17/2/45; Trevorrow, H.D., 31, 4/1/45; Warwick, A.W., 14/11/44; Weller, A.L., 24, 15/02/45; Weller, E.H., 41, 18/2/45;

Wessendorf, J.G., 23, 18/1/45; Young, W., 33, 01/11/44; Zinn, Aubrey, C. (AIF, ex Java, in British Camp at Sandakan), 37, 20/11/44, bb m.
27 RAF: Beavis, V.F., 25, 5/2/45; Bell, G., 23, 19/12/44, m bb; Cawsey, A.R., 24, 5/12/44; Clavery, R.B., 5/2/45, m bb; Davis, C., 22, 5/1/45, m bb; Garner, J.H., 30,15/12/44, m bb; Greenfield, A., 28, 3/1/45, m bb; Hill, L.W., 27, 4/12/44, m bb; Holdsworth, J.V., 26, 7/1/45, m bb; Hornsby, A.E., 30, 7/2/45, m bb; Hynes, C.A., 31, 6/3/45, m bb; Joy, R.L.T., 26, 2/12/44; Kay, R., 13/12/44, m bb; Lewis, A., 39, 5/1/45, m bb; Marks, R.G., 8/11/44, m bb; Morton, G.S., 27, 27/12/44; O'Keefe, A.J., 26, 26/1/45, m bb (identity disk found); Orange, T., 5/3/45, m bb; Palmer, E.A., 29, 13/12/44, m bb; Pepper, W.J., 22, 17/2/45; Preston, A.A., 32, 7/3/45, m bb; Quy E.C., 32, 1/3/45, m bb; Read, L.W., 23, 30/11/44, m bb; Rowley, A., 33, 2/12/44, m bb; Soutar, D.C., 33, 1/11/44, m bb; Spuffard, E.N., 24, 17/12/44, m bb; Tout, R., 26, 11/12/44, bb.

From Kuching: (144 British and 5 Australians, a total of 149)

5 Australians: Adams, A.M.(enlisted as White), B Force, POW 1428, 22, 26/1/45, m bb; Crome, J., B Force, 20, 28/2/45; Ford, W.D., B Force, 23, 3/12/44, m bb; Geelan, W., E Force, POW 3084 Kuching, 24, 4/1/45, m bb; Radcliffe, K.E., ex-Java, 25, 28/9/44, m bb.

136 from various Army units: Allen, W.J., 28, 30/10/44; Anderson, F., 20/1/45; Bartley, R., 25, 20/1/45; Barton, G.F.T., 34, 13/1/45; Bell, A.H., 30, 30/10/44; Bell, J.J., 32, 22/9/44; Bennett, J., 32, 23/9/44; Bird, G.L., 17/1/45; Blackburn, W.S., 23, 21/11/44; Blair, D.D., 28/1/45; Blakeley, R.F., 27, 29/10/44; Bridgewater, A.E., 24, 30/9/34; Bridgman, J.H., 32, 25/10/44; Brown, R.B., 10/12/44; Brown, J. (RAOC), 28, 4/12/44; Brown, J. (RASC), 25, 23/11/44; Caddick, R., 23, 20/1/45; Champ, J., 40, 11/11/44; Codd, J., 27, 16/10/44, m bb; Collins, R.G., 28, 3/1/45; Daisley, H. 30, 26/12/44; Dawson, J.(Australian serving with British), 28, 29/1/45; Deacon, H.J., 24, 20/1/45; Deans, A.G., 37, 17/1/45; Dobson, E.A., 30, 18/10/45; Donaldson, C.A., 27, 24/2/45; Eckford, E.F., 28, 13/11/45; Edge, F., 41, 20/1/45; Edridge, S.R., 27, 28/9/44; Edwards, T.K., 38, 5/12/44; Elliott, K.I., 29, 1/2/45; Ellwood, W.J., 42, 1/12/44; Elsworth, A., 42, 12/2/45; Fennell, R.R., 13/2/45; Ferguson, J. G.R., 27, 20/1/45; Fraser, H., 34, 17/11/44; Ghey, G.O., 33, 5/12/44; Gibb, A., 31, 29/9/44; Glover, V.T., 31, 6/2/45; Hampson, H., 26, 16/2/45; Hastings, W., 30, 9/1/45; Hawkins, J.J., 30, 24/12/44; Hay, J., 32, 17/12/45; Hayes, W., 36, 4/11/44; Hedgington, A.V., 26, 26/1/45; Hill, L.W., 27, 4/12/44; Hirst, G., 27/11/44, m bb; Hitchen, T., 26, 23/11/44; Hogan, G.L., 25, 6/8/44; Hooper, R.A., 31, 6/8/44; Hopkins, A.H., 28, 27/11/44; Hubble, P.W., 30/11/44; Hutchings, N.W., 23, 6/8/44; Imray, J., 30, 23/10/44; Janacek, R., 13/2/45; Jenkins, H., 32, 8/10/44; Kendall, S.D., 28, 1/10/44; Kendrey, D.W., 25, 28/11/44; Kenneison, A.R., 11/10/44; Laing, D., 28, 18/12/44; Lambert, H., 26, 4/12/44; Laurie, W. T., 40, 4/3/45; Lawcock, C.E., 28, 23/2/45; Lennane, W., 34, 15/9/44; Leslie, J., 32, 8/2/45; London, H.W., 23, 12/10/44; Lord, A.O., 26, March 45; Loveday, J.A., 28, 6/8/44; McCallan, J., 29, 20/1/45; McCarthy, F.W., 33, 28/2/45; McClardie, R., 24, 20/1/45; McConingley, J., 13/11/44; MacDonald, D., 29, 25/12/44; McGurk, B.D., 22, 23/2/45, m bb; McLean, C.G., 27, 26/11/44; Macleod, A., 26, 8/11/44; McMeekin, W., 25, 30/11/44, m bb; Major, J.S., 25/1/45; Malcolm, J.A., 25, 25/11/44; Maplebrook, J., 24, 11/12/44; Mason, J.H., 30, 21/11/44; Maxwell, R., 29, 25/2/45; Millar, R.D., 27, 5/1/45; Mennie, J., 31, 19/12/44; Millard R, 29, 11/11/44; Milne H, 27, 20/11/44; Mitchell A.J.M, 21, 29/11/44; Moran, F., 35, 7/2/45; Moreton, G., 23, 30/1/45, m bb; Moyes, A.D., 25, 13/1/45; Murray, H.J., 26, 19/11/44; Musgrave, A., 27, 20/1/45; Oppenheim, L.A. (Australian serving with British Unit), 15/2/45; Osborne, W., 33, 6/8/44; Padfield, R.F., 33, 21/11/44; Parker, J.J., 33, 28/12/44; Petrie, W.McG., 26, 23/11/44; Philpots, J.H., 10/2/45; Porter, A.S., 36, 9/12/44; Reid, G., 26, 4/12/44; Richardson, E.M., 34, 6/8/44; Ritchie, G.O., 36, 19/2/45; Richie, R., 31,17/11/44; Rowland, F.E., 39, 21/12/44; Russell, J.W., 1/10/44; Russell, W.H., 39, 4/10/44; Shanks, W.P., 27, 11/12/44; Shepherd, J.F., 29, 9/2/45; Sherriff, A.G.(NZ), 31/10/44; Shun, C.W.A., 25, 5/11/44; Simms, A., 6/10/44; Smith, C., 36, 28/10/44; Smith, D., 27, 7/11/44; Smith, F.N.J.*, 32, 20/12/44; Smith, J., 27, 26/9/44; Sowden, G.C., 30, 31/10/44; Spare, G.H., 7/2/45; Staplehurst, A., 29, 19/11/44; Stewart, J., 28, 21/12/44; Stokes, W., 34, 6/8/44; Storch, A.G., 27, 22/1/45; Sullivan, L.K., 19/11/44; Tennant, C., 33, 10/9/44; Thornton, A.K., 24, 20/1/45; Trench, J.P., 30, 13/02/45; Turcan, J.P., 35, 1944; Usher, G.J.D., 25, 16/1/45; Vasey, D., 32, 4/12/44; Van Cuylenburg, R.,19, 29/11/44; Wain, F., 25, 20/2/45; Wales, H.P., 29, 6/8/44; Walker, S.E., 5/3/45; Wark, D., 24/11/44; Wickstead, P.H. (Australian), 32, 6/8/44; Will, R.C., 26, 5/12/44; Wiseman, R., 32, 19/6/44.

4 RAF: Burridge, E.T., 29, 18/11/44; Holdsworth, J.V., 26, 7/1/45; Hynes, C.A., 31, 6/3/45; Lewis, A., 39, 5/1/45.

4 British POW, origins unknown: Burnett, E., (Leading Seaman RN), 16/2/45, m bb; Griffiths, G., RAF, 22/9/44, KG, m bb; Howlett, C., 26/2/45, m bb; Lumb, J.C. (RAF 90564), 6/9/44.

Brunei: (March 8-May 3)

Note: According to the Japanese, 30 died here (plus another, identity and date unknown, at Kempei-tai HQ). As 48 names (17 too many) appear on the following list, it is possible that the date of the transfer to Kuala Belait was about 16 April, not 3 May as stated in the intelligence summary. If the cut off date for Brunei is taken as 16 March, the figures for Kuala Belait (one POW only out of 37 identified), begin to fall into line. The remainder of the missing are believed to be among the 18 'unidentified' names which appear at the end of the Miri roll.

Ex Sandakan: (total of 13)
6 Army: Avenell, J.B., 24, 14/3/45; Day, F.A., POW 2500, 40, 9/3/45; Forster, J.W., 40, 14/3/45; Mason, E.J., POW 2751, 27, 17/3/45; Wix, D.J., 29, 24/4/45; Wright, G., 23, 5/4/45.

7 RAF: Balls, A.J., POW 2222, 27, 19/4/45; Collins, A.E., 37, 26/03/45; Davey, R.T., 24, 21/4/45; Hayward, G.L., 24, 19/3/45; Mullaney, J., POW 2735, 24, 11/3/45; Rigby, W., 26, 12/3/45, m bb; Scotcher, F.R., 24, 21/4/45.

Ex Kuching: (total of 35)
34 Army: Allen, G.P., 28, 15/3/45; Allen, W., 25/4/45; Brown, C.H., 29, 28/3/45; Cartwright, S.A., 31, 8/3/45; Chambers, W.H., 31, 26/3/45; Davis, W.R., (NZ) 33, 1/4/45; Day, F.A., 40, 9/3/45; Finley, W., 31, 27/4/45; Godber, J.G., 30, 27/4/45; Haddock, A., 29, 18/4/45; Hall, F.W., 35, 18/4/45; Holmes, A., 29, 10/4/45; Hutchings, B.L., 21, 25/4/45; Innes, A., 25, 17/4/45; Jackson, A., 34, 23/3/45; Kennedy, L.H., 33, 27/4/45; Leijssius, I., 28, 26/3/45; McCutcheon, A.Q. (Australian), 2/4/45; McDougall, G.H., 34, 16/3/45; Montigney, L.M., 40, 5/4/45 (bag found); Mulvey, W.T., 31, 12/4/45; Newton, H.O., 26, 18/4/45; O'Brien, F.W., 31, 3/4/45; Penman, T., 26, 31/3/45; Phillips, W.A., 34, 15/4/45; Pothan, R.F., 29, 16/4/45; Purdey, T.H., 29, 16/4/45; Redfern, F.A., 23, 10/4/45; Ryan, R.W., 1/4/45; Tadman, T.W., 25, 3/4/45; Thompson, J., 29, 19/4/45; Vitek, K., 18/3/45; Wharf, T.A., 27, 31/3/45; Wilson, C.G., 24, 27/4/45; Wilkinson, T.W., 27, 29/4/45;

1 RAF: Collins, A.E., 37, 26/3/45.

Kuala Belait (May 3–May 26)
Note: According to the Japanese 37 POW died here. Some (a maximum of seven) may have been Indian POWs. There is no explanation for the 36 missing names, other than the date given for the transfer from Brunei is incorrect. However, if the eighteen listed as dying after 16 April are removed from the Brunei list, there is still a deficit of eighteen. It is possible that these missing Kuala Belait POWs are the eighteen unidentified POWs whose names appear at the end of the Miri roll.

1 Army from Kuching: Weir, E.D., 28, 20/5/45.

Tanjong Lobang, Miri (May 26—June 8):
3 Army: Munro, J., 29, 28/5/45 and Watson, P., POW 2962, 29, 7/6/45 (both from Sandakan), and De Souza, J.F., 31/5/45 (from Kuching).

These three bodies were recovered, but at the time not identified.

Riam Road, Miri:
Although forty-six bodies were recovered from the 3, 6 and 5 mile pegs (2, 29 and 15 respectively), there are only eight POW with death dates fitting into this time frame. According to the dates, all eight died during the massacre on 10 June. It is believed that the other thirty-nine POW have been given false dates to make the massacres less obvious. It is not possible to determine their identities.

Massacres at 6 and 5 mile (10 June)
5 Army: Ackland, G.J., 32, (from Sandakan, official date of death 1/10/44, known to be false; Ackland named by Japanese as dying at 6 mile massacre); Bretherton, G., 28; Campbell, C.F. (died 5 mile); Mitchell, F., POW 2304, 28 (from Sandakan, official date of death 13/6/45, but 10/6/45 presumed correct); and Ward, C.V. (from Kuching).

4 RAF from Sandakan: Barclay, G., 29; Blackledge, R.D. (died 6 mile); Joshua, J.M. and Wigglesworth, L.H., 24.

Note: The following eighteen names, or corruptions of names, also appear on various items found at Labuan and Brunei. They may be the 'missing' POWs from Kuching (the Japanese state 300 were sent but only 290 have been accounted for). However as there is no other supporting evidence, the information should be treated with great caution as items may belong to POWs who were never in Borneo: Burrell, Dunne, H. (Pte), Gary, Hampson (Cpl), Hume (Sgt), Harper (Pte), Jones (Pte), Jeffra (Pte), Primm, Pemmell, Reynolds (Pte), Scott (Pte), Szthkeitwtz (Pte), Simpson (Stoker RN, probably died Labuan), Summers (RN marine, probably died Labuan), Tonks, Tindale, Young, J.A. (Pte).

Kuching
Australians:
Six officers and three ORs died at Kuching. The officers were: Campbell, Maj. George, POW 30186, 49, 2/9/45, malaria and heart attack; Flett, Lt. Frederick, 29, 18/8/45, tuberculosis; Matthews, Capt. Lionel (executed), 31, 2/3/44; Pascoe-Pearce, Lt. Bradford, 36, 15/8/45, dysentery; Stewart, Lt. Peter, 30, 8/7/45, beriberi; and Young, Capt. Cyril, 27, 27/7/45, malaria. The three ORs were Harrington, Driver Thomas, 30, 15/12/42 (died in Gaol); Keating, L.Cpl Edward, 36, 11/2/44 (died in Gaol) and Picken, Pte. James, 23, 3/4/43 (electrocuted). All are buried in Labuan War Cemetery.

The 144 officers (* denotes E Force officers) who were recovered were: Andrews, F., Armstrong, G., Arvier, A., Blanksby, L., Baker, G., Batros, G., Bayliss, C., Bathgate, A., Bell, J., Bennett, W., Brown, L.*, Brown, R., Boundy, A.,

Bowden, L.*, Boscolo, E., Brennan, M.*, Britz, J., Carment, D., Carter, W., Chandler, J., Clarke, B., Clayton, H., Cowden, A., Crabbe, G., Craig, R., Crawford, K., Crozier, J., Davidson, N.*, Day, A., Dengate, E., Dick, N., Doswell, J., Draney, L., Dunsdon, F., Durrant, R., Eddey, H.*, Eden, J., Earley, T., Ellice-Flint, R., Elliott, F., Esler, E., Ewin, R., Fairley, J.*, Filmer, C., Fleming, F., Fleming, T. (YMCA), Forbes, G., Forsyth, C., Foster, R., Fox, H., Fraser, J., Fraser, W., Garland, D., Gaven, F.*, Gettens, G., Glover, L., Gollan, A., Gray, A., Grenfell, R., Hains, I., Heintz, I., Hollway, F., Hosford, J., Howlett, R., Hufer, D., Hunter, J., Jackson, L., Johnston, D, Johnstone, C., Kelleher, J., Kelly, L., Lambe, M., Lawler, J., Lewis, T., Loxton, A., McIver, R., McLean, J., MacLean, R., McLeod, G., McMillan, A., Madin, K., Maffey, R., Maxwell, G., May, R., Meagher, B.*, Miller, J., Millner, J., Mills, F., Minto, W., Missingham, W., Moore, K., Morrison, J., Mosher, K., Moss, P., Nicholson, V., O'Donovan, A., Ollis, R., Owen, A., Owen, C., Owen, G., Peck, W., Phillips, M., Pickford, C., Pool, J., Potter, M., Price, J., Rae, V., Rayson, H., Reid, F., Richardson, R.*, Robin, R., Rogers, J.*, Rowell, J., Ryan, L., St John, H., Scrivener, J., Shand, S., Sheppard, C., Sheppard, E., Simpson, E., Sinfield, V., Sleeman, G., Smith, I., Solomon, G., Speirs, R., Stanistreet, R., Thom, J., Thomas, H., Thompson, K., Throssell, J., Topham, R., Waddle, B., Walker, A., Walsh, A., Walton, A.*, Waring, R., Washington, F., Watson, C., Watson, P., While, A., White, K., Woods, S., Workman, J., Wilson,.R (Red Cross).

34 ORs were also recovered, with one other, presumed to have been recovered from Kuching.

5 B Force, sent from Sandakan: Cheel, A., Constant, F., Davis, E. (Mo), Outram, S. and Watson, F.

14 E Force, left behind at Kuching: Albretch, E., Bell, J., Bindon, F., Currey, J., Edwards, H., Gordon, R., Kent, R., Kent, W., Lothian, J., Patis, F., Rixon, D., Simpson, J., Weekes, N. and Williams, F.

3 E Force sent from Sandakan following 'Sandakan Incident': Davies, L., Lander, C., and Weston, A.

12 from Java (never at Sandakan): Cure, W., Daly, T., Fraser, R., Free, H., Geissman, W., Goodwin, K., Gunning, G., Horskins, W., McLachlan, J., Stephenson, V., Tomlin, G. and Welfare, A. And also possibly Ellis, A.J., NX 57069, 2/19th Battalion, who appears on the Master Roll for B Force with the notation 'recovered', but whose name does not appear on the Nominal Roll of Internees and POWs recovered from Kuching.

British and Civilians:
See Chapter 15.

Outram Road Gaol
Australians:
A total of thirty POWs (including escapees), were sent to Outram Road Gaol. Those who died while in prison were Pte E. Allen on 10/7/43, Sapper R. Davis, 13/10/44, Sapper D. Marshall. 11/8/44, and Cpl A. Small, 9/11/44. Fairey (5/4/44) &Shelley (29/10/44) died after being transferred to the POW hospital at Changi Gaol.

The other 24, Macalister Blain, M.P. Brown, Matt Carr, Jimmy Darlington, Stan Davis, Tommy Graham, Sgt Holly, Driver M. Jacka, Sgt James, Sapper Jensen, Mac McDonough, Bruce McWilliams, Allan Minty, Frank Martin, Cpl Mills, Norm Morris, Fred New, J. Rickards, Pte E Rumble, Alf Stevens, Herb Trackson, Rod Wells, Gordon Weynton and Billy Young, all survived.

Civilians: All survived except Gerald Mavor.

Summary
Australians:

Total number B Force, E Force, ex-Java, and with British at Sandakan:	2025
Died Sandakan, Ranau, track:	1787
Died Labuan ex Kuching:	5
Died Labuan, ex Sandakan:	1
Died Kuching:	9
Died Outram Road:	6
Died Tawi Tawi:	2
TOTAL DEAD:	**1810**
Survived Sandakan/Ranau:	6
Removed to Kuching, survived (officers):	144
Removed to Kuching, survived (ORs):	22
At Kuching, survived:	13
Sent to Outram Road, survived:	24
Escaped to Tawi Tawi, survived:	6
TOTAL SURVIVED:	**215**

British:

Total British Jesselton, Sandakan, Kuching (ex Sandakan) and Labuan (ex San, excluding 1 AIF assigned to British camp)	824
Died Jesselton:	51
Died Sandakan, Ranau, Track (all):	641
Died Labuan, ex Sandakan (all):	99
Died Kuching, ex Sandakan:	1
TOTAL DEAD:	**792**
Officers removed to Kuching, survived:	30
ORs removed Kuching, survived:	2
TOTAL SURVIVED:	**32**
To Labuan from Kuching (known):	185
(unknown):	2

There were no survivors

Of the 1793 Australian and 641 British POWs left at the Sandakan Camps (2434), 6 survived, a death rate of 99.75%.

Appendix 2: Burial Table

The burial places in Labuan War Cemetery of those who died at Sandakan, Ranau or along the track have been compiled from almost 4000 separate recovery documents from the three Australian War Graves Units working in the area. The first figure refers to the plot, the second to the row and the third to the grave number. To determine where the recovered remains of POWs have been reburied, refer to the 'burial' entry on the Nominal Roll before consulting the burial table. For example, since John Barnier died at location 'SAN 2' (the number 2 compound) he was buried in 'SAN 3', the slit trenches, shown in the next column. The burial table for 'SAN 3' shows that he is one of 198 unidentified bodies recovered from the slit-trenches. *Note:* The changeover dates from one cemetery to another are not absolute. For deaths occurring on or near the changeover date, it may be necessary to consider more than one cemetery site. An * denotes recent identification.

SANDAKAN:

(a total of 1358 remains including 6 who escaped and were buried at Sandala Estate)

Sandakan Civil Cemetery:

23 Identified Australians (for individual locations, see Commonwealth War Graves Burial Registers)

Sandakan Number 1 Cemetery (SAN 1): 147 identified and 529 unidentified remains. In use from May 1943 (earliest known burial) —22/3/45.

39 identified Australians, 108 identified British. (For individual locations, see Commonwealth War Graves Commission Burial Registers.)

34 unidentified Australians: 14 E–16; 16 E 1–2; 19 E 1–16

90 unidentified British: 2 A 1–16; 2 B 1–16; 2 C 1–16; 2 D 1–16; 26 A 1–16; 26 B 1–10.

405 unidentified POWs (Australian and British): 1 A 1–8; 1 B 1–8; 1 C 1–8; 1 D 1–8; 1 E 1–8; 3 A 1–2; 3 A 3–8; 3 B 1–8; 3 C 1–8; 4 A 1–16; 4 B 1–16; 4 C 1–16; 4 D 1–16; 5 E 1–16; 6 E 1–16; 7 E 3–16; 8 E 1–15; 9 A 14–16; 9 B 1–16; 9 C 1–3; 9 C 8; 9 C 10–16; 9 D 1–2; 11 A 1–16; 11 B 1–14; 11 B 16; 11 C 1–16; 11 D 1–16; 24 E 1–16; 26 B 11–16; 26 C 1–16; 26 D1–16; 27 E 1–2; G E 1–16; H E 1–16; J E 1–16; K E 1–16; R AA 14

Sandakan Number 2 Cemetery (SAN 2): 82 identified and 345 unidentified remains. In use from 23/3/45 —29/5/45.

Note: Australian Andrew Sommerville, whose body was recovered, was at the British Camp.

3 identified Australians, 79 identified British (For individual locations, see Commonwealth War Graves Burial Register.)

252 unidentified Australians: 3 D 1–8; 3 E 1–8; 11 E 8–16; 12 E 1–16; 13 E 1–16; 15 E 1–2; 18 E 1–16; 22 A 1–16; 22 B 1–16; 22 C 1–16; 22 D 1–16; 22 E 1–16; 23 E 1–4; 25 A 7–16; 25 B 1–10; 25 B 12–15; 25 C 1–12; 27 E 2–16; 28 A 1–2; 30 A 1–16; 30 B 1–16; V E 9–16.

93 unidentified POWs (British and Australian): 15 E 3–16; 20 D 4–16; 25 A 1–6; 25 C 13–16; 25 D 1–16; A E 1; V C 1–16; V D 2–16; V E 1–8.

Sandakan Number 1 Compound slit trenches, containing 3 remains:

1 unidentified Australian * (Morriss, G. J.) & 2 unidentified POWS (Australian and British): 20, C 16; 20 D 1–2.

Sandakan Number 3 Cemetery (SAN 3) slit trenches in Number 2 Compound: 2 identified and 198 unidentified remains

2 identified Australians: Skinner, J. (new), 20 C 12; Osborne, S., A 20 C 13.

198 unidentified POWs (Australian and British): A E 2–16; B E 1–16; L E 1–16; M E 1–16; 7 A 1–2; 7 B 1–16; 7 C 1–16; 7 D 1–16; 9 D 3–16; 10 D 1–6; 20 A 1–16; 20 B 1–16; 20 C 1–12; 20 C 14–15; 20 D 3; 23 A 1–11; 23 D 8–15.

Sandakan Number 4 Cemetery (SAN 4 airport massacre): 2 identified and 21 unidentified remains

2 identified Australians: Burns, T., 10 C 3; Steen, W.S., 10 C 5.

21 other Australians*: 10 B 10–16; 10 C 1–2; 10 C 4; 10 C 6–16, believed to be the 20 who died between 13–15 July (the dates given for Burns and Steen), and one possible other, who died on 16 July. (Beves, E.M., Brown, S.W., Boyes, W.E., Clissold, J.J., Davis, R.J., Ferguson, K.D., Goldfinch, C., Haddon, T., Hughes, K.G., Johnston, C.S., Jones, D.H., Madden, W., Meek, E.K., Nink, L., Rae, J., Rudd, W.T., Short, M.N., Stirling, D.H., Turner, K.M. and possibly Browning, J.H.)

Sandala Estate: 3 identified and 3 unidentified remains

2 identified Australians: Treseder, H.A. and Haly, S.O., 16 E 4 & 5

1 identified British: Jordan, F.J., 16 E 6

3 unidentified Australians: 16 E 7–9

RANAU: (a total of 395 remains recovered)

Ranau Number 1 Camp: 2 identified and 172 unidentified remains:

2 identified Australians*: Cleary, A. 21 E 6; Crease, W. 10 D 13.

Cemetery A (RAN 1A), in use prior to 15/3/45:

48 identified POWs* (Australian): 10 A 1–16; 10 B 1–9; 19 C 10–16; 19 D 1–16.

Cemetery B (RAN 1B), in use from 16/3/45—28/4/45:

124 unidentified POWs (Australian and British): 17 E 1–16; 21 E 1–5; 28 A 3–16; 28 B 1–16; 28 C 1–5; 28 C 13–16; C E 1–16; D E 1–16; E E 1–16; F E 1–16

Ranau Number 1 Jungle Camp (RAN 1J), in use from 29/4/45—10/6/45: 46 remains:

3 identified Australians: Kinder, J., 19 B 16; Lytton, H., 21 E 9 (new); Murray, R., 21 E 7 (new). 31 identified and 12 unidentified POWs (Australian and British); 11 E 4-6 & 19 C 4-5 (where the goat was killed); 19 A 6-16; 19 B 1-15; 19 C 1-3; 21 E 8, 10-16; 25 E 1.

Ranau Number 2 Jungle Camp (RAN 2J), containing 175 remains:

Cemetery A (RAN 2JA), in use from 10/6/45 until approximately 9/7/45: 45 identified* remains:

12 A 15–16; 12 B 1–16; 12 C 1–16; 12 D 1–7, and. 19 C 6-9 (Davies, E.,* Newling, R.,* Roberts, S.,* Wright, C. L. *, from swamp).

Cemetery B (RAN 2JB), in use after approximately 10/7/45, containing 3 identified and 104 unidentified remains:

3 identified Australians: Evans, O.,* Maskey, L. & Richards, E.R., 25 E 16; 104 unidentified POWs (Australian and British): 2 E 1–16; 4 E 1–16; 9 E 1–16; 12 A 1–14; 10 D 14–15; 10 E 1–16; 25 E 6–15; 29 E 1–16.

Massacre Sites (MS):

Officers, near 111 mile peg:

5 identified Australians and 2 identified British (new): Captains G. Cook, R. Oakeshott, D. Picone of the AIF; Flying Officer H. Burgess, RAF and Captain F. Daniels, R.A. are in a mass grave, 12 D 8-12.

ORs, between 109–110 mile peg:

8 unidentified POWs (Australian and British):11 E 1–3; 10 D 15; 12 D 13–16.

Also 2 skull-less remains, reburied at massacre site in bag with other scattered bones.

Miscellaneous Locations near Ranau (8 remains):

1 identified Australian: Reither, H., (reburied at Ranau 1 by locals):16 E 11.

1 identified Australian: Anderson, F., (died 5m Tuaran Track): 16 E 12.

1 unidentified POW, near track leading to 110 mile camp:11 E 7.

4 unidentified POW, believed to have escaped from 2 Jungle Camp:10 D 9–12.

1 unidentified POW, believed to have escaped from 2 Jungle Camp, found to west of the camp:20 E 15.

PAGINATAN AND THE TRACK: (a total of 410 recoveries)
Paginatan:

Main cemetery, containing 95 unidentified remains

94 unidentified POWs (Australian and British): 14 A 1–16; 14 B 1–14; 15 D 1–3; 15 D 13–16; 17 A 1–16; 17 B 1–13; 21 C 7–16; 21 D 1–16; 27 D 2; 27 D 15–16.

Track:

Moving from east to west, a total of 315 remains recovered:

Note: I A = identified Australian (for names of previously identified Australians, see Nominal Roll)

I B = identified British

UA = unidentified Australian

UPOW = unidentified POW

Section 1: Sandakan to Muanad River (194 remains):

11–15 mile (Sandala): 4UPW, 19 A 1–2; 23 D 16; 9 C 9

16 ½ mile: 1 UPW, 10 D 8

17 mile: 2 UPW, 23 D 6-7

18 mile: 2 UPW, 20 E 14; 23 D 5

19 mile: 3 UPW, 9 A 10-12

20 mile: 1UPW, 23 D 4

23 mile: 3 IA & 6 UPW, 20 E 10-13; 23 C 15-16; 23 D 1-3

23 ½ mile: 1 UPW, 9 A 9

24 mile: 3 UPW, 23 C 12-14

25 ½ mile: 1 UPW, 9 A 8

26 mile: 1 (new) IA (McAppion, E.) 9 A 7

27 mile: 1UPW, 23 C 8

28 mile: 7 UPW, 20 E 5-9; 23 C 3-4

29 mile: 9 UPW, 23 B 10-16; 23 C 1-2

30 mile: 2 UPW, 20 E 3-4

Tindok River (25-30 mile):10 UPW, 9A 5-6; 17 D 15-16; 23 C 5-7,9-11

Samawang (about 31 mile): 3 UPW, 9 A 1-2; 17 D 14

Dusan River (near 33 mile): 4 UPW, 9 A 3-4; 20 E 2; 23 B 9

Kolapis River area (approx 35 mile to 45 mile, includes Manjang, Beluran, Murawatto):

8 (new) identified Australians (Burns, R.N., Harris, S.N., Jones, H.B. & Ovens, R.A. in 16 D 4-7; Christie, N.McN, 16 D 10; Pallister, R. & Reynolds, C. in 17 D 9 & 10; Glover, S. in T D 14) 2 IA, 16 E 14;16 D 9

APPENDIX 2: BURIAL TABLE

32 UPW, 9 C 4; 16 E 13, 15-16; 17 C 15; 17 D 1-8, 11-13; RA A 16; 20 E 1; 23 A 12-16; 23 B 1-8

Muanad River (at or near 49.5 mile, including Tangkul Crossing massacre): 1 IA & 88 UPW, 14 D 6-16; 16 A 1-16; 16 B 1-16; 16 C 1-16; 16 D 1-3; 17 C 16; 23 E 5; 23 E 10 -16; 26 E 1-16; RA A 14-15

Section 2: Muanad to Boto (42 remains):

Bineowang river (approx. 60 mile): 4 UPW, 14 D 3-5; 23 E 6

Mandorin River (62 mile): 3 UPW, 14 D 1-2; 23 E 9

Muanad-Sapi (65 mile): 3 UPW, 17 C 12-14

Sapapiyu River (approx. 70 mile): 11 UPW, 14 C 7-16; 23 E 7

Sapi River/ Batas village (approx 80 miles, between Sapapiyu and Tuantin): 6 UPW, 7 A 15-16; 14 C 5-6; 17 C 11; 23 E 8

Tuaninitin River (approx. 80 miles): 1 IB & 2 IA*, (Bignell, K.W., Blatch, W.) 14 C 2-4

Pinintalangan: 1UPW, 14 C 1

Celo River (approx. 85 miles): 1 UPW,14 B 16

Bongkud River: 1 UPW, 14 B 15

Boto: 9 UPW, 7 A 13-14; 17 C 7-10; 21 A 1-3

Section 3: Boto to Tampias (50 remains):

Gumbaron River (near Boto): 3 UPW, 7A 12; 9 C 6; 21 B 9

Malio: 2 IA & 9 UPW, 9 C 7; 21 A 10-11 & 13-16; 21 B 1-4

Telupid River: 2 IA, 2 IE & 9 UPW, 21 A 4-8; 21 B 5-8, 10-13

Tapang River (Papan): 2 UPW, 17 C 4-5

Baba River: 1 IA & 2UPW, 7 A 11; 17 C 2-3

Milulu area (includes Tara Rangang, Taguk, Mankadai, Maringun, Mosomban, Lolosing): 2 IA & 10 UPW, 7 A 3-10; 21 C 2; 21 B 14; 21 B 15-16

Tampias: 2 IA east of Tampias, 7 A 3 (Richards R), 21 C 1 (Thompson, A); 3 UPW, east of Tampias, 21 C 1,3 4; 1 IA* (Nicholson, J., at Tampias), 21 C 6. For explanation regarding mix-up in identity between Thompson and Nicholson, see Ch 16, end note 2.

Section 4: Tampias to Ranau, excluding Paginatan Cemetery (29 remains):

Near Paginatan: 1 IA (Brown M, 21 D 16) & 11 UPW, 9 C 5; 16 D 12-15; 17 B 14-16; 17 C 1; 27 D 2; 27 D 14

19½ miles from Ranau: 1 UPW, 27 D 1

18 miles from Ranau (Segindai): 5 UPW, 5 D 12-16

11½ miles from Ranau: 2 UPW, 5 D 11; 9 A 13

11 miles east of Ranau, 1 mile west of Nelapak: 1 IA*, Quailey, A., 25 E 3

9 miles east of Ranau, 3 miles west of Nelapak: 1 IA*, Sheard, W.A., 25 E 4

8 miles east of Ranau (Muruk): 4 IA* (Adlington, N.C., Bendall, B.A., Cummings, N.G., Mc Kenzie, D.H) 5 B 1-4

7½ miles east of Ranau: 1 IA* (Walter, R.W), 25 E 5

7¼ miles east of Ranau: 1 UA

6¼ miles east of Ranau: 1 UPW, 25 E 2

Summary:

Number of Australians on Nominal Roll:	1787
Number of British on Nominal Roll:	641
Number who survive:	6

Total POWs at camp:	**2434**
Number who left on first march:	455
Number sent back, escaped from march or escaped from Ranau :	10
Total who died track, Paginatan or Ranau on first march:	**445**
Number who left on second march:	536
Number sent back, escaped from march or escaped from Ranau:	9
Total who died track or Ranau on second march:	**527**
Number who died on third march:	75
Number who left Sandakan:	1066
Number who left marches/survived:	19
Total who died on all marches:	**1047**
Number at Sandakan after marches:	1368
Number who returned first march:	3
Number who returned second march:	5
Number who escaped, recaptured:	5
Number dying at Sandakan:	1381
Number dying on marches:	1047
TOTAL DEAD:	**2428**

Recoveries:

Sandakan:

Number at Sandakan:	1381
Recoveries from Sandakan :	1358
Number not recovered:	23

(includes 18 cremations and 5 who died in Kempei-tai custody)

Ranau/Paginatan and Track:

Number on marches:	1047
Recoveries from Ranau:	395
Recoveries from Paginatan and Track:	410
Number not recovered:	242
Total recoveries:	**2163**
Total not recovered:	**265**

This includes 23 from Sandakan (Soorier and 4 others who were tortured to death at Kempei-tai HQ, plus Mills and another 17 cremated/ incompletely recovered), 6 from Ranau and 236 from the marches, rice carrying and Paginatan)

LABUAN/BRUNEI/KUALA BELAIT/MIRI:

In June 1944, 100 British POWs (including one

AIF) were moved from Sandakan to Labuan, where they were joined by another 190 (known) and 10 (unknown) POWs, five of whom were Australian, transferred from a camp just outside Kuching.

Labuan *(total of 152 recovered):*
Note: Of the 188 believed to have died here, it appears that 36 were cremated.

Number 1 Compound Cemetery, near harbour in grounds of Victoria Golf Club, (total of 43 recovered):
6 identified POW: D A 6-10; R D 5
37 unidentified POW: DC 3-16; CC 8-16

Number 2 Compound Cemeteries (compound on a spur at the 3 mile peg on Macarthur Road. Main cemetery sited 270 metres away to the north, at the foot of a hill. Another burial site was nearby, in a Chinese cemetery):
107 unidentified POW in main cemetery: E C 2-E D 16; G A 1-G D 16; H C 1-12.
2 unidentified POW in Chinese cemetery: H D 16; T A 16

Brunei *(total of 24 recovered):*
POW Cemetery was 225 metres up steep path to north of compound. 30 POWs said to have died here, and another at Kempei-tai HQ:
24 unidentified POW: D A 1-5; D A 11-D B 13

Kuala Belait, *where they were joined by 7 Indian troops (total of 11+/37 recovered):*
Near Tutong Ferry (1 set remains):
1 unidentified POW: E B 15

Near picture theatre (4 bodies + approximately 26 cremated remains in three separate graves):
4 unidentified POW and cremated remains: D C 1-2 (cremated); D C 6; D C 15; E B 16; E C 1.

Other locations (6 remains):
2 identified POW: L C 15; M A 8
4 unidentified POW: C C 4-7

Miri *(total of 49 recovered):*
Residency Road compound (3 remains):
3 POW (previously unidentified): 969870, Corporal John Munro, RAFVR, aged 29, 28/5/45 and 1826753 Gunner Peter Watson, 95 Battery, 48 Light Anti-Aircraft, British Army, POW 2962, aged 29, 7/6/45 (both from Sandakan), and Private J.F. De Souza, SSVF, 31/6/45 (from Kuching). They are buried in graves E A 11-13.

Riam Road, 3 mile peg (2 remains):
2 unidentified POW: E A 14-15

Riam Road, in swamp near 6 mile peg (29 remains):
Sergeant C. Ackland, Flight-Lieutenant Blackledge and 27 unidentified POWs: C C 1-3; C D 1-16; E A 1-10

Riam Road, 5 mile peg (15 remains last to be murdered):
Captain C.F.Campbell and 14 unidentified POW: E A 16-E B 14

Summary:

Number of British known transferred to Labuan:	284
Number of Australians known transferred to Labuan:	6
Number of Indians joining them at Kuala Belait:	7
Additional POWs said to have been transferred:	10
Total:	**307**
Recoveries from Labuan including cremated remains:	152 +
Recoveries from Brunei:	24
Recoveries from Kuala Belait including cremated remains:	11+
Recoveries from Miri	49
Total recoveries for Labuan-Miri:	**236 +**

JESSELTON:
POW Cemetery:
Remains of 51 British POW recovered (see Commonwealth War graves registers for locations)

Appendix 3: Recovery of Relics

Not all relics recovered from the various camps belonged to prisoners interned there, and, because of a paucity of information, not all are identifiable. Articles which the author is able to identify as belonging to Borneo POWs have been listed alphabetically, according to the name of the owner.

Miscellaneous Items (RS on nominal roll) found at Sandakan Number 2 Compound

Australians:

Note: Check also paybook list.

Name	Article
Anderson, A.	metal disc
Bacon, S.	fork
Baxter, M	two holdalls, sergeant's chevron
Bird, J.K.	tin mug
Blackwood, L.G.	kit bag
Braithwaite, R. (escaped)	jacket
Bray, J.	identity disc
Bundey, G.W.	slip of paper
Burns, T.	identity disc, haversack, diary, miscellaneous papers, Christmas 1943 menu (same as listed below, except for R. Davidson)
Burrows, J.	POW tag
Campbell, R.	groundsheet
Clydesdale, T.J.	cigarette case?
Coker, R.	two pairs shorts, identity disc
Commins, J.S.	kitbag
Corcoran, F.L.	identity disc
Cousins, S.J.	identity disc
Currey, W.J.	fork
Davies, E.D.	jacket
Day, G.	kitbag
Field, G.L.	letter to
Filewood, A.A.	POW tag
Gale, P.	name on hut floor
Garvin, L.	paybook
Gillespie, W.G.	web equipment
Gode, H.	watch
Good, G.	yoke of shirt
Grubb, D.	respirator
Hankin, P.E.	paybook
Hanson, K.D.	identity disc
Hargrave, C.	haversack, web equipment
Harris, J.O.	identity disc
Hazelgrove, B.F.	leave pass
Henley, J.B.	letter to?
Hodges, J.D.	piece of metal
Hogbin, C.W.	identity disc
Holden, N.	web pack, piece of fabric
Holmes, R.F.	felt hat
Ings, J.	cigarette case
Irving, R.F.	identity disc, driver's licence
Johnson, S.	dixie lid
Joynes, C.	identification disc
Knight, H.R.	photo wallet
Leedham, C.A.	match box holder
Lever, L.	canteen order, 2 identity discs
Lindqvist, L.R.	identity disc, POW tag
Lister, A.W.	web pack
Lloyd, H.G.	Red Cross envelope
McAppion, E.	piece of aluminium
McIver, G.D.	cloth gaiter
Maguire, H.J.	match box holder, cigarette lighter
Maizey, C.W.	identity disc
Marsh, H.A.	two identity discs
Mathew, A.W.	match box holder
Meagher, G.F.	paybook
Mercer, S.	spoon
Midgley, J.	respirator
Moore, A.W.	POW tag
Morgan, H.A.	watch
Neal, K.T.	piece of paper
Ortloff, F.C.	watch
Osborne, S.A.	haversack, tin mug, web equipment
Paxman, C.	two mess tins
Peck, F.	web equipment
Platford, J.	kitbag
Robbins, T.H.	plate from *Yubi Maru* life raft
Sandercock, H.A.	two haversacks
Shirley, A.F.	paybook
Skinner, J.	piece of aluminium
Small, R.D.	paybook
Soutar, G.A.J.	paybook
Swan, W.A.	aluminium plate
Steen, W.S.	identity disc
Swift, S.D.	identity disc
Symes, A.V.J.	identity disc
Taylor, H.B.	wallet, paybook
Temple (Moore), R.J.	identity disc
Treseder, H.A.	identity disc
Tyrrell, A.R. or R.C.	felt hat
Walker, E.T.	identity disc
Waller, T.	POW tag
Wehl, F.	piece of aluminium, fork
Weir, S.J.	identity disc
Wilson, A.	heart-shaped disc
Wiseman, E.W.	POW tag
Wolfe, E.J.	kitbag
Woods, F.H.	POW tag

Wynn, W.E.   kitbag
Young, David   POW tag
Young, J.   web equipment

Christmas Menu 1943 [not 1942, as stated by Australian Archives], signed by Brett, J., Burns, T., Chenhall, S.J., Davidson, R., Dawson, L., Downes, I.G., Duggan, S.J., Gloag, D., Grosvenor, L., Ince, J.W., Molloy, J., Raleigh, J., Roberts, F., Roberts, D., Short, N.A.E., Solomon, J.H., Stanley, J.

Wooden bucket, with initials C.H. carved on it — seven possible owners.

Paybooks found under groundsheets, Number 2 Compound: Bryant, F.L., Carleton, R.V., Charles, G.F., Clarke, A., Clissold, J.J., Corcoran, J.J., Crawford, V.O., Crumpton, R.F., Field, G.L.C., Fletcher, B.A., Gardner, A.W., Gardner, I.L.G., Gaskin, J., Gay, A.P.R., Godson, C.H., Hagston, G., Harris, J.O., How, V.K., Johnson, S.H., Lester, J., Lindqvist, L.R., Lupton, S.J., McCracken, W.E., McNaughton, D., Moran, R., Neal, F.W., Nicholson, E.C., Osborne, S.A., Palmer, A., Patterson, R.A., Paxman, C., Phelan, M.J., Powell, C.A., Praetz, N.H., Purcell, J.S., Roberts, F., Rudd, W.T., Smith, F.A.O., Taylor, G.W., Welch, W.A., Wheeler, J.E., Wiseman, E.W., Woods, F.H., Walker, E.T. (also paybook of Wood, F.A., who died 25/04/42 in Malaya and whose book, it appears, was taken to Borneo by one of his 2/19th batallion mates).

British:

Allen, J.   jacket
Baguley, L.   kitbag
Barnes, F.W.   identity disc
Cossey, C.E.   wrist identity tag
Dyer, W.V.   identity disc
Fitzgerald, H.J.   paybook
Hawkins, E.R.   probable owner of holdall
Hobbs, F.W.   diary
Holder, C.   identity disc, metal disc
Humphreys, J.A.   kitbag, piece of metal
Humphreys, W.G.   mess tin, money pouch, hair brush
Jones, Tivy   RAF dental card
Jordan, F.J.   identity disc
Kitchingham, T.   haversack
Millard, W.E.   respirator
Rolfe, I.D.   haversack, web equipment
Smith, G.B.   identity disc
Teasedale, W.J.   wallet
Tonkinson, J.S.   identity disc
Venton, C.L.   identity disc
Watson, P.   identity disc (died at Brunei)
Woods, E.   identity disc
Young, P.H.   haversack

Miscellaneous Items (RR on nominal roll) found at Ranau

Ranau Number1 Camp I

Australians:

Abbott, E.   POW tag
Addison, P.R.   souvenir plate
Attenborough, A.R.   identity disc
Betts, Jack   POW tag
Brown, Samuel   POW tag
Dorizzi, G.   POW tag
Dorizzi, H.   identity disc
Hardstaff, R.A.   POW tag
Jones, V.   souvenir plate
Leadbeater, W.C.   identity disc
McGee, W.A.   identity disc
McGowen, J.   POW tag
Macmeiken, D.J.   POW tag
Pryor, D.R.   POW tag
Skinner, T.R.   identity disc
Smith, W.J.   identity disc
Wapling, J.H.   POW tag
Watson, C.   two identity discs
Williams, H.P.   POW tag

British:

Drew, R.E.   POW tag
Hodgson, R.   POW tag
Jones, W.J.   POW tag
Madeley, J.W.   identity disc
Newman, K.F.   POW tag

Number 1 Jungle Camp, Sinarut (under POW hut)

Australians:

Barnes, R.   POW tag
Comerford, G.   groundsheet
Crees, R.J.   photo insert from paybook
Dunkinson, J.L.   identity disc
Lock, B.C.   identity disc
Stirling, C.   kitbag
Twiss, R.T.   part of paybook

British:

Davies, T.B.   POW tag
Eaden, R.S.   sweat band from beret

Also, Herb Lytton's wallet, photo, etc. and Will belonging to Englishmen Donald Elliott and Robert Roberts, as well as various badges in or near grave area.

Number 2 Jungle Camp, 110 $1/4$ mile

Australians:

Brown, R.G.   paybook, souvenir metal disc
Burke, J.E.   two identity discs
Cranney, R.T.   POW tag
Day, G.   paybook cover
Doyle, L.H.   identity disc
Finn, J.A.   paybook

APPENDIX 3: RECOVERY OF RELICS

Fitzpatrick, F.J.	POW tag
Frost, H.T.	identity disc
Good, G.	POW tag
Hargrave, C.H.	hat
Heaslop, J.	POW tag
Humphries, P.G.	haversack
Last, A.B.	paybook
Lysaght, H.W.	groundsheet
Mann, W.R.	identity disc
Nash, C.O.	POW tag
Neaves, G.M.	identity disc
Noonan, E.C.	identity disc
Palmer, D.	clothing
Parsons, J.W.	housewife
Platford, J.	greatcoat
Seeley, J.W.	will
Stacy, R.	POW tag
Taylor, T.C.	identity disc
Thorns, A.S.	POW tag
Turner, H.E.	paybook
Walter, R.W.	identity disc

British:

Allsop, K.	POW tag
Seckington, E.	POW tag

At site of Officers Massacre, 111 mile

Sam Browne belt; khaki drill shirt with epaulettes to fit badges of rank for Captain, with thermometer in pocket (belongs to Daniels, Picone or Oakeshott); three British army pattern web belts; two expended .25 calibre cartridge cases; one RAF officer's cap and badge (Flight-Lieutenant Burgess).

Items (RT on nominal roll) brought in by local people

Australians:

Barker, J.H.	pack
Bayley, A.E.	pack
Buckley, L.F.	wallet with photo
Bunch, N.	jacket
Chapman, S.H.	jacket
Crees, R.J.	rest of paybook
Crowther, G.G.	shorts
Ellis, A.G.	jacket
Ezzy, A.J.C.	pack
Fahey, A.M.	pack
Farrell, A.R.	dixie
Gellatly, R.A.	dixie
Good, G.	haversack, officer's cap
Grono, P.R.	pack
Hasluck, L.N.	shorts
Jackson, F.	pack
Jeavons, J.A.(?)	jacket
Leinster, V.P.	jacket
Livingstone, H.H.	pack
McCarthy, L.	haversack
Manton, L.G.	jacket
Peters, K.A.	pack
Platford, J.	greatcoat
Read, W.G.	wallet
Roebuck, J.T.	jacket (British army)
Taylor, G. (one of four)	blanket
Walker, J.	Japanese haversack

British:

Feltham, M.R.	pack webbing

Other recoveries (RO on nominal roll)

Kudat: watch belonging to W Madden, removed from body of Japanese officer by SRD patrol in August 1945. Inscribed 'To Bub from Mum, 20/8/40. NX35726'.

Muanad: photo belonging to Percivalle W.F. Carter, handed to Captain Sutcliffe by Kulang, inscribed 'Dear Perc, All here except Dad. Will try to get one of him for next letter. Love Mum'. Added in purple ink, in block capitals, is 'L. Haye 9/2/20 d - T.M. , WX 7247', the POW who was shot at Tangkul Crossing, Muanad River.

Paginatan-Sapi: mess tin belonging to Alf Leaver.

Ranau: watches inscribed with the names of Michael Baxter, Norman Jenyns (both of whom died at Sandakan) and Bernard Rowley (died Paginatan) confiscated from Japanese garrison by Flight-Lieutenant Ripley, along with a huge heap of unidentifed property.

Telupid: Radio Rubbish concert programme, on the back of which were the names of Privates Bill Marsh, Tom Patterson, Keith Rickerby, Jack Kearney, Darcy Pryor, Gene Parham, Frank Reardon and Sergeant Les Hales. Statement signed by E Fuller, K Molde(Dawson), and Englishmen Roberts and Beardshaw.

23 mile peg: mug belonging to Wilfred Bennett

Appendix 4: Corrupted/Incomplete Names

Although quite explicit details of the fate of POWs who died on the march were noted by the Japanese, some of the names became very corrupted during translation and retranslation, or were simply surnames. Confronted with an investigation involving thousands of missing prisoners, these records were put aside in 1945, considered too difficult to decipher. However, while researching this book, the author realised their value and, by cross referencing data, was able to decipher all the previously unintelligible material. The following is a list of these names, and the real identity of POWs concerned.

Real Name	Corrupted/Incomplete name
Adlington, Norman Charles	Adringthorn, Norman Charles
Aylett, Ray	Islet, Lay
Ayton, Arthur Clement Ivan	Aiton, Alsaclement Tweeban
Bendall, Bertram	Endal, Bart
Bennett, Henry	Venett
Burns, Clifford Edward	Browns, Surford Edward
Chipperfield, Robert William	Shiperfield, Robert Billien
Chisholm, Henry Frank	Naciolm, Henry Frank
Commerford, Gerald	Carmerford, Gerald
Coughlan, Thomas	Cogran
Crees, Randle John	Krees, Randal John
Davey, Bernard Alfred	Derby, Bernard Alfred
Dempster, Cyril	Lampster, Cycle
Deshon, Frank	Deacon
Downey, Harold	Dawny
Egel, Raymond Claude	Agel, Raymond Cloud
Ewing, Herbert	Iving, Herbert
Fosbury, Bertie James Arthur	Favowy, Beetom Arthur
Grant, Francis	Grand
Hack, Alexander Meora	Huck, Alexander Mayler
Halligan, Jack	Hargen, John
Hicks, Vernon Owen	Hicoks, Barnon Owen
Humphries, David	Hampaless, David
Jeffrey, Vincent Alexander	Pyphlis, Vincent Alexander
Kerr, James	Keller
Larter, George Robert (RAF)	Loster, George Robert,
Mabin, Robert	Marvin, Rabbit
McLeod, Norman Pope	McRoad, Norman Pope
Moore, F W A (RAF)	Moore
Morris, Henry	Maurice
Nicholson, John Francis	Neulson, John
Noakes, Arthur Henry	Knox, Albert Harley
Nunn, John Oswald	Narne, John Oswald
O'Malley, George	Olmerley
Reay, Stanley	Hay
Ross, James Henry	Roth, James Henry
Sherring, Frank	Sharlink, Frank
Sligar, George William	Sligger, George William
Smeeton, Basil	Smeaton
Thoroughgood, Henry	Taragood
Turner, Harold	Turner
Winning, Harry	Waning, Harley

Appendix 5: Wanted or Convicted War Criminals

The following is a list of some of those who were wanted or brought to trial and convicted. In 1954, all those serving gaol sentences were transferred to Sugamao prison, Japan. Despite the sentences handed down, not a single war criminal served any longer than thirteen years.

Key: San=Sandakan; Ran=Ranau; 1M=first march (/numeral=group); 2M=second march; KS=killing squad; CO = Commanding Officer

Note: some of those involved in murder were charged with, or found guilty of, a lesser crime. Spellings of names may also differ from document to document.

Name	Nickname	Crime	Where	Sentence
Abe, Lt Kasuo		murder	1M/KS	hanged
Not known	Adorma	brutality	San	wanted
Baba, Gen Maseo		murder	Borneo	hanged
Beppu, Sgt Yoichi		murder	Ran	15 years
not known	Boy Bastard	brutality	San	wanted
not known	Charlie	brutality	San	wanted
not known	Coffee King	brutality	San	wanted
Ehara, Sgt-Maj.	Bulldog	brutality	San	wanted
Ekeda Yoshio		murder	San	15 years
Endo, Hiraki Pte		murder	1M/ 9	wanted
Fujita, Hiroshi Sgt-Maj.		murder	Ran	wanted
Fujita, Maseo W.O.		brutality	1M/6, Ran	wanted
Fujiwara		brutality	San	wanted
Fukishima, Maseo	Black Bastard,	murder	2M/Ran	15 years
"	Private Detective,			
"	Black Prince			
Fukuda, Nobuo		brutality	San	not guilty
Fukuda, Seiichi Lt		murder	1M	wanted
Not known	Georgie	brutality	San	wanted
Gotunda, Kireku W.O.		brutality	1M/3	not guilty
Gotunda, Mitsugo W.O.		brutality	1M/ 7	wanted
Goto, Tsuneyoshi		murder	2M	12 years
"		murder	Ran	15 years
Goto, Yoshitaro		murder	San	15 years
Hashimoto, Maseo		murder	Ran	15 years
Hayashi, Lt		murder	M	wanted
Hayashi, Yoshinori	Ming the Merciless	brutality	San	15 year
"		and also murder Noel Parker		hanged
Hayashida, Kiyoshi		murder	Ran	15 years
Hayashida, Mitsujiro		murder	1M	10 years
Hinata, Genzo	Sourpuss	murder	San	wanted
Hirano, Yukihiko Lt		murder	1M	10 years
Hirochi, Jiro		murder	2M	12 years
"		murder	Ran	15 years
Hirota, Ginjiro		murder	2M	15 years
"		murder	Ran	life
Hirota, Nebuo		murder	San	Not guilty
Horikawa, Koichi Lt		murder	1M/ 8	10 years
Hoshijima, Susumi Capt		murder	CO PW Camp	hanged
Hosotani, Naoji Sgt (K-tai)		murder	15 mile	hanged
Ichikawa, Sgt (believed dead)		murder	Ran	wanted
Iino, Shigero Capt		murder	1M/1	10 years
Ikeda, Yoshio		brutality	San	15 years
Not known	The Indian	brutality	San	wanted
Ishii, Fujio		brutality	San	10 years
Ito, Lt		murder	M	wanted
Ito, Takeo	Stutterer	murder	1M/4	wanted
Iwabe, Shigaru Sgt		murder	Ran	14 years

Name	Alias	Charge	Camp	Sentence
Iwashita, Lt (believed dead)		murder	3rd M	wanted
Janeda, Miyoshi		brutality	Ran	wanted
Kada, Civilian	Black Prince, Black Mick, Mad Mick	murder	San	wanted
Kamimura, Shoichi		murder	2M	10 years
Kaneshige, Yoshio		murder	Ran1	12 years, but died accidentally while in custody at Rabaul
Kato, Chuichiro		brutality	San	15 years
Kawakami, Kiyoshi	Gold-Toothed-RuntShin	murder	Ran	15 years
"	Gold-Toothed-Kicking-Bastard	murder	Ran	hanged
"	Duck's Arse			
Kawashigi, Masakichi		murder	Miri	10 years
Kitamura, Kotaro		murder	1M	15 years
"		murder	Ran	hanged
Kiyoshima, Tadeo	Panther Tooth, Black Panther	brutality	San	15 years
Kobayashi, Titsuo/Shizuo		murder	2M	10 years
Kochi (believed dead)		murder	Ran	wanted
Kono, Kinzaburo (K-tai)		torture	San	wanted
Kosaka, W O (K-Tai)		murder	San	20 years
Kunosawa (believed dead)	Euclid	brutality	San	wanted
Matsuba, Shokichi		murder	2M	12 years
"		murder	Ran	20 years
Matsuda, Kenji	Gentleman Jim, Top Hat	murder	2M	20 years
Matsuda, Nobunaga		murder	2M	not guilty
Matsuda, Takeo		murder	San	15 years
Matsumoto Harukichi		murder	Miri	10 years
Matsumura, Yoshio		brutality	1M/1	wanted
Memora (Japanese)		brutality	San	wanted
Miajima, Hikozabuo	English-speaking-Bastard	murder	1M/6	wanted
Miyake, Tadeo		murder	2M	12 years
"		murder	Ran	life
Mitzua, Kyuchi Capt.		murder	1M/4	10 years
Moriata, Maseo		murder	Ran/Jess	wanted
Morioka, Teichichi		murder	1M/6	10 years
"		murder	Ran	10 years
Moritake Lt		murder	San	dead
Motoki, Hirochi (K-tai)		torture	San	life
Murakami, Seisaku Lt		murder	SAN	death
Murozumi, Hisao		murder	San	life
Nagahiro, Maseo		murder	2M	12 years
"		murder	Ran	15 years
Nagata, Shinichi		brutality	San	12 years
Nakamura, Koji (believed dead)		murder	Ran	wanted
Nakano, Ryoichi		brutality	San	wanted
Nakao, Ijiro (believed dead)		murder	San	wanted
Nakayama Tamao		murder	2M	12 years
Nishikawa, Moriji		murder	2M	15 years
Nishikawa, Yoshinori		murder	San	12 years
Ohara, Nobura		brutality	San	wanted
Ohashi, Kiichi Sgt		brutality	1M/8	wanted
Okada, Toshiharu Sgt		murder	Ran	life
Okahara, lt		brutality	San	wanted
Osawa, K-Tai (believed dead)		brutality	San	wanted
Oshima, Hidekichi		murder	1M/9	wanted
Oyama, Tatsuo	Potato Jones	murder	2M	not guilty
Not known	Pimple face	brutality	San	wanted

APPENDIX 5: WNTED OR CONVICTED WAR CRIMINALS

Not known	Ramona	brutality	San	wanted
Sanada, Shigenori	Dumbbell	murder	2M	14 years
Sato, Hideo (believed dead)		murder	1M/9	wanted
Sato, Shinichi Sgt (died)		murder	1M/9	not guilty
Sato, Tatsuo Lt		murder	1M/1	10 years
Shoiji, Shinsuka	Sparkles	murder	2M	8 years
"		murder	Ran	8 years
Sigimura, Shinichi Lt		murder	1M/7	10 years
Sone, Takeyashi	Shin Kicker	murder	2M	15 years
Not known	Speedo	brutality	San	wanted
Sugino, Tsuruo	The Jersey Bull	murder	Miri	shot
Suzuki Lt		brutality	Ran	dead
Suzuki, Saburo		murder	Ran	15 years
"		murder	Ran	hanged
Takakuwa, Takuo Capt		murder	San/Ran CO	hanged
Takada, Sgt-Maj.		murder	1M/1	wanted
Takata, Kunio		murder	1M/4	5 years
Takeda, Kuzahiro W.O.		murder	1M/2	wanted
Takemoto, Taseo		murder	2M	9 years
Takeuchi, Yoshimitsu		murder	2M	10 years
"		murder	Ran	20 years
Tanaka, Shojiro Lt		murder	1M/6	10 years
Tomiyama, Shintaro		murder	2M	not guilty
Tornika		brutality	San	wanted
Toya, Yasuo		murder	1M/8	wanted
Toyahara, Lt (believed dead)		murder	2M	wanted
Toyanaga, Shizemori		murder	2M	wanted
Toyoda, Kokichi		murder	San	2 years mitigated
Toyoka, Eijiro		murder	2M	15 years
Tsuji, Sgt-Maj (believed dead)		murder	2M/KS	wanted
Tsukamoto, Shineji		brutality	San/Ran	wanted
Umehara, Katsuyoshi		murder	2M	wanted
Umemura, Kenburi		murder	2M	not guilty
Umemura, Kiyoshi		brutality	Ran	wanted
Utsonomiya, Seiichi		brutality	San	not guilty
Watanabe, Genzo Lt		murder	2M/KS	hanged
Watanabe, Sgt		brutality	San	wanted
Watanabe, Yoshio Maj		murder	OC Ran	wanted
Yamaguchi, Yasutaro		murder	1M	wanted
Yamamoto, Jiro		murder	2M	10 years
Yamamoto, Soichi Capt		murder	1M/CO	hanged
Yamasaki, Lt		murder	1M/1	wanted
Yanagawa, Hideo		brutality	San	15 years
Yanagawa, Shigemori		brutality	San	not guilty
Yanai, Kenji		brutality	Ran	not guilty
Yasuyama, Eikichi		murder	Ran	15 year
Yokoto, Hideo/Kenzo Sgt		murder	2M	9 years
Yoshikawa, Tatsuhiko	Masturbation	murder	2M	15 years
"		murder	Ran	20 years
Yoshimura, Hideo		murder	2M	12 years
Yoshioka, Shigeo		murder	Ran	15 years
Yoshiya, Kinjo (died before trial)		murder	Ran	not tried
Yuwabe, Sgt		murder	Ran	wanted

Four more Japanese officers were executed for crimes at Kuching, and another 42 sentenced to various terms of imprisonment, ranging from 1-20 years.

Appendix 6: Bibliography and Subject References

Printed books

Allen, Louis, *The Politics and Strategy of the Second World War*, Singapore 1941-1942, London 1977.

Barber, Noel, *Sinister Twilight*, London 1958.

Bennett, Lieut-Gen. H Gordon, *Why Singapore Fell*, Sydney 1944.

Braddon, Russell, *The Naked Island*, London 1952.

Burfitt, James, *Against All Odds, The History of the 2/18 Battalion A.I.F.*, Sydney 1991.

Callahan, Raymond, *The Worst Disaster*, London 1977.

Churchill, Winston S., *The Second World War Volume IV The Hinge of Fate*, London 1951.

— *The Second World War Vol 7, The Onslaught of Japan*, London 1951.

Cody, Les, *Ghosts in Khaki: The History of the 2/4 Machine Gun Battalion, 8th Division AIF*, Perth 1997.

Daws, Gavin, *Prisoners of the Japanese*, New York 1994.

Day, David, *The Great Betrayal*, Sydney 1988.

Evans, Stephen R., *Sabah (North Borneo) Under the Rising Sun Government*, Singapore 1990.

Falk, Stanley L., *Seventy Days to Singapore*, London 1975.

Firkins, Peter, *Borneo Surgeon, The Story of Dr James P Taylor*, Perth 1995.

Goodwin, Dr Bob, *Mates and Memories, Recollections of the 2/10 Field Regiment*, Brisbane 1995.

Griffiths-Marsh, Rowland, *The Sixpenny Soldier*, Sydney, 1990.

Hall, Timothy, *The Fall of Singapore*, 1983.

Heatherington, John, *Blamey Controversial Soldier*, Canberra 1973.

Horner, D.M. (ed) *The Commanders*, Sydney 1984.

Howard, Frederick, *Kent Hughes*, Melbourne 1972

Imperial War Graves Commission, *The War Dead of the British Commonwealth and Empire*, Labuan Memorial and War Cemetery Registers, London 1960.

Keith, Agnes, *Three Came Home*, London 1948.

Kirby, Major-General S.Woodburn, *Singapore: The Chain of Disaster*, London 1971.

— *The War Against Japan*, London 1957.

Leasor James, *Singapore*, London 1968.

McGregor, John, *Blood on the Rising Sun*, Perth n.d.

Moffitt, Athol, *Project Kingfisher*, Sydney 1989.

Odgers, George, *Air War Against Japan*, Canberra 1957.

Owen, Frank, *The Fall of Singapore*, London 1960.

Penfold, A.W., Bayliss, W.C., Crispin, K.E, *Galleghan's Greyhounds* [2/30th Battalion history], Sydney 1979.

Percival, Lt.Col. A.E., *The War in Malaya*, London 1949.

Richardson, H., *One Man War: the Jock McLaren Story*, Sydney 1957.

Rolfe, P., *The Journalistic Javelin: An Illustrated History of the Bulletin*, Sydney 1979

2/19th Battalion Association, *The Grim Glory of the 2/19 Battalion A.I.F.*, Sydney 1975.

2/10 Australian Field Ambulance Association (Connolly, R. & Wilson, R., ed.), *Medical Soldiers, 2/10 Australian Field Ambulance 8 Div 1940–45*, Kingsgrove 1985.

2/12 Field Regiment Association, *Gunfire: History of 2/12 Australian Field Regiment, 1940-46*, Chiltern, Victoria 1991

2/29th Battalion Association (Christie, R.W.,ed), *A History of the 2/29 Battalion – 8th Australian Division AIF*, Stratford Victoria 1985.

Silver, Lynette Ramsay, *The Heroes of Rimau*, Sydney 1990.

—, *Krait: The Fishing Boat That Went to War*, Sydney 1992.

Simson, Ivan, *Singapore: Too Little, Too Late*, London 1970.

Smyth, Sir John, *Percival and the Tragedy of Singapore*, London 1971.

Swinson, Arthur, *Defeat in Malaya: the Fall of Singapore*, London 1970.

United States Army Services, SWPA, *A Pocket Vocabulary of Malay, Pidgin English and Japanese Phrases For the Use of US Troops in the Southwest Pacific Area*, 15 September 1942.

Tanaka, Yuki, *Hidden Horrors: Japanese War Crimes in WWII*, Boulder, Colorado 1996.

Wall, Don, *Singapore and Beyond*, [2/20th Battalion history] Sydney 1985.

Wallace, Walter, *Escape from Hell*, London 1958.

Walsh, Verdun, *Cry Crucify*, Sydney 1991.

Whitelocke, Cliff, *Gunners in the Jungle*, [2/15 Field Regiment History], Eastwood 1983.

Wigmore, Lionel, *Australia in the War of 1939-1945: The Japanese Thrust*, Canberra 1957.

Wyett, John, *Staff Wallah at The Fall of Singapore*, Sydney 1996.

Young, Bill, *Return to a Dark Age*, Sydney 1991.

Newspapers, Journals, Documentaries etc

Many of the articles cited in newspapers below contain inaccuracies, and should not be used as

APPENDIX 6: BIBLIOGRAPHY AND SUBJECT REFERENCES

source material without further checking.

Argus, 17 Sept 45, 21 July 47.
Australian, 15-16 June, 25-26 July 92.
Australasian Post, 6 Oct 83; 1 April 89
Borneo Bulletin, 10 Aug 85
Bulletin, The,16 Jan,13 March 46; 26 Nov, 17, 31 Dec 47.
Canberra Times, 6 Feb 95
Daily Express, 8 May 1982
Herald (Melbourne), 7 July, 22 Aug,11 Sept, 13 Oct, 17 Nov 45; 19, 20 Nov, 4 Dec 47.
Return To Sandakan, Film Australia, 1995
Stand-To, Journal of ACT Branch, RSS &AILA, Vol 8, No 5, Sept-Oct 1963 (Article by Rex Blow)
Sun (Melbourne), 11 Sept 45; 20 Nov, 4 Dec 47.
Sunday Mirror, 23 Aug 59
Sunday Telegraph, 9 July 95.
Sun Herald, 17 April, 88;25 July 93; 9 July 95.
Sydney Morning Herald, 11 Oct 45; 3, 4 Jan, 6 Feb,12,15 March, 6,8 April 46; 21 Nov 47; 7 July,14 Aug 95.
Table Tops, [AMF Troop Newspaper], 18,22 Sep 45.
Time-Life, After the Battle (Singapore), periodical publication, 1981.
Vic Eddy, Journal of Eighth Division Signals Association, Vol 65, March 1996 (article by Rus Ewin).
West Australian, 10, 12,14 July 1995
University of Queensland Law Journal, The Tokyo War Crimes Trial, A.J. Mansfield.

Documents in the Public Record
Abbreviations:

AA ACT: Australian Archives, Canberra, ACT.
AA VIC: Australian Archives, Melbourne, Victoria.
AWM: Australian War Memorial, Canberra, ACT.
SP: Silver Papers
Note: Some of the names against file numbers have been changed to give a clearer indication of the contents.

Australian Archives, ACT

Bennet's [sic], Major General Gordon, Report on Malayan Campaign, March 1942, A5954 Item 264/3
Defence Security, D Notices, A816/59 10/301/130; A5954 1956/6
D Notices, Correspondence, A5954 1956/2
Natives, Compensation to, A 1838/1 1464/1/4
Percival, Maj.Gen. A.E., Despatch on Operations in Malaya 8/12/41 to 15/2/42, A816 Item 37/301/330
Plan for Relief of PW, PM's Reply, A 663/10148/2/470
Plan, Operational, Relief of POWs, A5954 265/6
POW Borneo, Information on, A 1067 IC46/12/1
POW Borneo, Information on, CP78/24 1914/16/89/271
POW, Relief of Australian, A5954 676/9
RAAF, Co-operation with SRD, 1 TAF, A 1969/100
Silver, Lynette Ramsay, *Report on Special Operations Australia and the Fraser Island Commando School*, Australian Archives Magazine and Library.
Special Operations Australia (SOA), Operational Files, A 3269 Items:
A1 Agas 1
A2 Agas II
A3 Agas III
A4 Agas IV
A5 Agas V
A5a Agas Intelligence Reports
A7 Python
A10 Stallion II
A12a Stallion Intelligence Reports
A20 Summary of SRD Operations in support of Oboe
A20a Oboe II Planning (Allied invasion of Borneo)
A21 Oboe IV (Allied invasion of Borneo)
22 Kingfisher
A28 Operations, BNB
A31 Geographical Information, Static report BNB
A32 Special Report Lae–Labuan
A37 K Mission
C17 Falcon
D3 Cobra messages
D4 Lagarto messages
D5 Lagarto, Cobra
H1 SRD Intelligence reports, Correspondence AIB
H4 SRD organisation
H9 Intelligence Summaries
H13 SRD Projects
J1 Intelligence Reports Group A
J2 Progress Reports Group A
J3 Progress Reports, Group A
J26 Progress Reports
J31 Sectional Reports
K3 Group B progress report
M1 Planning
M3 AIB Monthly Status Reports
N1 Correspondence AIB
O2 History Correspondence
07 History 0f SOA–Organisation
O8 History of SOA–Operations
012/13/14 Operations of AIB GHQ SWPA
V5 Reorganisation and Disbandment, Special

Intelligence organisation
V9, V10 Consolidated Status reports
V16 32 2nd Echelon Missing personnel
V17 Tracing and Recovery of SRD POWs
V18 Rescue of Allied POWs
V19 Report on Investigations Australian and Allied POW–9 Aust Div Area
War Graves Registration Sheets, A8234
War Crimes Trials:
Hayashi Yoshinori and others, Trial of, A 471/1/80779
Murozumi H, and others, Trial of, A 471/1/80776
Yamawaki and others, Trial of, A 471/1 81956.
Webb Report, Publication of, A 1067/1 UN 46/WC/17

Australian Archives, Victoria:

Army minister, Statement by, regarding BNB POWs MP 742 255/15/1291
Bodies, Recovery of 109, MP 742/1 132/1/529
Casualty Reports (of other POW), by Campbell, B 3856 144/1/244
Casualty Reports, (of other POW) by Braithwaite, Campbell, B 3856 144/1/246
Censorship of Press, B 3856/O 146/1/16
Documents, Mass Grave, Sandakan B 3856/0 Item 144/14/140
Department of War Graves Services (ie body recoveries), Reports MP 742/1 132/1/529
Japanese Policy re wounded, MP 1582/7 Item 144
Jackson, Lt.-Col H, Awards to helpers, MP 742 328/1/32
Laband, Statement by Dr, MP 749/1 44/431/101
9 Div Report on Investigations BNB, B 3856 145/4/147; B3856/0 144/1/255
Nominal Rolls, Internees and POW, B 3856 140/1/41
Nominal Rolls, Items Recovered, B 3856 144/1/255
POWs, Borneo, B3856 144/1/372
POW Casualties, B3856 145/4/137
POW, Contact Inquiry Unit 3, MP 729/8/0 44/431/101
POWs, Died Borneo, B3856 144/4/84
POW, Information on, MP 729/8 44/431/101
POWs, Loss of, MP 742 51/1/269
POWs, Missing, Borneo, B 3856 144/1/235
Rayson, Statement by, MP 742 336/1/153
Red Cross, Lists Malai [sic] to Borneo since 1/4/44, B 3856 144/1/21
Red Cross Cables re above, B 3856 144/1/22,26,27
Red Cross transfers, B 3856 144/1/30,32,113,115
Taylor, Dr, Statement by MP 897/1 156/19/152

War Crimes Investigations, 1945–1949, MP 375/14
War Crimes Investigations/Trials Series MP 742 File 336/1/–includes a number of statements by POWs:
153: Sandakan, Ranau (incl. statements by POWs)
252: Kempei-tai Sandakan
258: Sandakan Death march, Trial of Nagahiro Maseo and Others
268: Massacre at Ranau, Goto and others
314: Trial of Hayashi, Y and others
343: Affidavits, from Members of AMF (parts 1 & 2)
606: 2nd Death March, Takakuwa, Watanabe
614: War criminals, nominal rolls
636: Affidavits (parts 1 & 2)
707: Hoshijima, Susumi
786: War Crimes Act 1945
838: Trials, Rabaul
1113: Trials of Major War Criminals, Tokyo
1016: Diary, 1 Australian War crimes Section
1180: Baba, Lt-Gen and others
1182: Last PW/Crucifixion, Sandakan
1319: Baba, Lt-Gen Masao
1416: Sandakan, 1st March
1470: War Crimes, Borneo, General (incl. additional Sticpewich Statement)
1548: Rudwick and others, Execution of
1697: Hosotani, Trial of (murders at 15 mile)
1698: Ikada and others (cemetery massacre)
1715: Murozumi and others (incl. statement by Botterill re Toyoda)
1731: Beppu and others (Ranau massacres)
1806: Yamamoto and others (first march)
1811: Civilians Yamamoto and Katayama
1816: Civilian Hayashi (Parker)
1830: Suzuki, Cpl
1840: Ueno, Cpl
1846: Yunome, Civilian
1854: Matthews, Wells and others, Torture of; Matthews murder, Kuching.
1943: Ill-treatment, Kempei-tai
2121: Yamawaki and others
2044: Publication of names of victims
2054: Prevention of Press Publication re atrocities
2093: Yamamoto Shoichi and others (first march)
B 5569/1: Hayashi Yoshinori and others
5569/1 NN: Hoshijima
MP 742/1 132/1/465: Massacre of 23 POW (Sandakan)
MP 375/14 WC 18,19: Murder of Unknown PW (Sandakan)
MP 375/14 WC 20: Murder, Crucifixion
War Criminals, 1945-47 MP 1395/2

APPENDIX 6: BIBLIOGRAPHY AND SUBJECT REFERENCES

War Criminals, Personal Dossiers, MP 375/15
War Graves Recovery, B3856/0 114/1/235
Wells, Report dated 16/5/49, MP 897/1/0 156/19/152
Wells, Weynton, Affidavits, MP 897/1 156/19/152
Wilson, R.H., Report by, B3856 399

Australian War Memorial Collection, ACT

Abe Soichi and others, trial of (first march), AWM54 1010/3/116
Agas Patrol report, AWM54 779/3/82
Allen, Driver, report of Death (Outram Road), AWM54 554/11/1
AWGU 8, AWM52 21/2/9
AWGU 23, AWM52 21/2/24
AWGU 31, AWM52 21/2/32
Baba, Gen, Trial of, AWM54 1010/3/88
B Force Activities (Wells), AWM54 554/3/1
B Force, Nominal Roll, AWM92 NN
Blow and McClaren, PR story, AWM54 779/10/1
Bombing restrictions, AWM54 779/13/12
Borneo, General Report 1945–46, AWM54 1010/1/5
Borneo Mission, Report by Lt.-Col H. Jackson, AWM 84/231 Item 21
Braithwaite, Richard, Death March from Sandakan, AWM76 15434
Campbell, Owen, Interrogation, AWM54 1010/1/2
Campbell, Owen, Statements, AWM54 1010/4/27
Chalmers, Hec, Diary of, PR 84/252
Chan, Chi To, ex-Sandakan, Preliminary Interrogation, AWM54 779/3/8
Official Historian, Comments re interviews with Thyer and Kappe, AWM 54 554/11/38.
Darling, Captain, Report on Investigations by, AWM54 779/4/5
Darling, Captain, Report on Investigations by, AWM54 1010/9/111
Death Certificates, Borneo AWM127 70
E Force, Report on, by Major Fairley, AWM54 554/6/1
Funk, Paddy Account of Experiences, 3DRL 7408
Fukushima, Maseo, Trial of, AWM54 1010/6/5
Hammer's Report, re Guerrillas at Sulu, AWM54 519/2/8M
Hayashi, Noshinori, Trial of, AWM54 1010/6/89
Hoshijima, Trial of AWM54 1010/3/46
Hoshijima, Pencil Sketch of, 3DRL 7914
Intelligence Reports, AWM54 779/3/97
Investigation Report, AWM54 1010/9/12
Iwakiri, Maj-Gen, Report of Death, Death Certificate, 20/10/46, AWM54 779/1/6

Jackson, Harry, statement, Private Records
Japanese IDs of Officers, NCOs on first march, AWM54 779/3/5
Japanese, Interrogations of (various), AWM54 1010/4/134
Japanese Interrogations, conducted by Capt. Brereton, AWM54 779/3/4
Japanese Interrogations, by 163 Language Detachment, HQ I Aust Corps, AWM 54 779/3/38
Japanese Interrogations, Kuala Belait, AWM54 779/3/80
Japanese POW Interrogation reports, 24 Corps, ATIS, AWM54 779/3/39
Japanese, outline of plan re release of POWs (August 1945), AWM54 555/2/3
Japanese, statements by, AWM54 1010/4/158
Japanese, statements by, relating to first march, AWM54 779/3/5 and AWM 54 1010/6/59
Japanese, statements by, relating to Massacres and other murders and Ranau, AWM54 1010/4/174
Japanese Sworn Statements, AWM54 1010/4/158 Pts. 1-18
Kitamura, Kawakami, Suzuki, Trial of, AWM54 1010/6/105
Maffey, Dr, Report by, MS S051
Maps, Borneo Camps, AWM54 779/13/5
Massacre, Sandakan AWM54 1010/9/99
Mort, Capt., Report by, AWM54 779/3/82
Moxham, William, Statement, AWM54 1010/4/107
Medical Reports, General, AWM54 481/12/174
Murozumi, Hiseo, Interrogation of AWM54 1010/9/99
Nagai, petition on behalf of 37th Army personnel for clemency, AWM54 1010/7/3
Natives, Special Reports and Interrogations of, AWM54 424/4/7
9th Division Area, Report on Investigation, Allied and Australian POW, Aug–Nov 1945, AWM54 779/1/25
9th Division Report, AWM 54 1010/9/111
Official History Files, Sandakan (including Braithwaite article), AWM76 B434
Parker, Pte Noel, Murder of AWM54 1010/6/89
Press Censorship, AWM127 25
Photographic Collection, Sandakan
Photographic Reports, AWM54 621/2/15
POW, Allied, Borneo, Collated Information, AWM54 779/3/81, 779/3/97
POW, Allied, Kuching, report by Lt Abbott, AWM54 779/3/103
POW & Internees, Report of Investigation, AWM54 779/1/25
POW Camps, Far East, Locations of AWM54 779/13/13

POW Camps, Messages, Reconnaissance and Photographic Interpretation Reports, AWM54 424/4/15
POW Contact and Inquiry Unit, Report by Captain Mort, AWM 54 554/3/2
POW, Labuan, AWM54 1010/9/22
POW Liaison Office, Report by Captain McKinnon, attached to 9 Div, AWM54 779/1/16
POWs, Recovered, Interrogation of, AWM54 779/3/8
POW, Recovery Plan, 26 Infantry Brigade, AWM54 779/2/12
POW, Report of, at Brunei, Miri, Kuching, AWM54 779/1/17
POW, Outline of Plan for release of, (if recovered) AWM54 555/2/3
Rabaul Trials, AWM54 1010/6/59
Sandakan Force, AEME Activity Report, October 1945 AWM54 314/2/7
Sandakan, Massacre at AWM54 1010/9/99
Short, Nelson, Statement, AWM54 1010/4/129
Simpson's Report, AWM54, 773/4/11
SRD Intelligence Reports, XIII-28, Sandakan, AWM54 627/4/16 Part 18
Steele, Captain Ray, Report by, AWM54 627/4/16
Sticpewich, Affidavits, Statutory Declarations, by, AWM54 1010/4/174; 134
Sticpewich, Collected information, AWM54 779/2/16
Sticpewich, Private papers of, PR 00637
Surrender Instructions, AWM54 554/1/15
3 Aust PW&I Unit, AWM54 554/3/2
26 Australian Infantry Brigade, Yamamoto, trial of, AWM54 1010/3/116 and AWM54 1010/6/59
Troop Dispositions, AIF, AWM54 554/11/29
War Criminals, Sentence Register, AWM26 15
War Diary, 8th Division HQ Branch, AWM52 1/5/17
War Diary, 27th Infantry Brigade, AWM52 8/2/27
Watanabe and Takakua, Trial of, AWM54 1010/3/94; 1010/6/59
Watanabe Genzo, Interrogation, AWM54 779/3/14
Webb, Sir William, Report by, AWM226 8A
Wong, Memoirs of Mr, MSS 1492
Wootten, Gen., Message from re Surrender (FELO leaflet) AWM27 118/4

Australian Broadcasting Commission Archives
Six From Borneo, transcript of Radio Documentary, and Tapes, 1947. Unedited tape transcripts *Australia Under Nippon*, including interviews with K. Botterill, J. Braithwaite, R. Braithwaite, O. Campbell, S. Davis, J. Hodges, K. Mosher, N. Short, R. Steele, J. Sue and H. Trackson, recorded by Tim Bowden, 1983

RAAF Museum and Library, Point Cook
Report on Data Extraction of EE88–RAAF Aircraft History Sheets for C37 Aircraft, (Maintenance records), mid-April to mid-May 1945

State Library, NSW
Transcripts, International Military Tribunal For the Far East, (Tokyo War Crimes Trials), including Evidence of Botterill, Moxham, Sticpewich, Wells, Weynton; Statements by Japanese officers and guards; Japanese Policy, Jesselton Revolt, Kuching Camp, Labuan Camp

Private Collections, Correspondence
Apostol, Lamberto, Statement by, (original copy in SP, formerly property of F. Murray)
Birkett, Bill, ex 2/13, 2/15 Btn
Blow, Rex
Brown, Pte. R.J.T., NX29116, 2/30th Battalion, Wartime Experiences (Brown Papers)
Ewin, Rus (Ewin Papers)
Funk, John, Obituaries, printed in *Time & Tide* and *Sydney Morning Herald* (SP)
Johnstone, Charlie, Diary of, (copy in SP)
Commonwealth War Graves Commission, London (Private Correspondence, SP)
Hooley, Ray, Ruston-Bucyrus Expert, Machinery and Engine Collector (Private Correspondence, SP)
Hywood, Skeet, Statements relating to Agas I, Stallion IV, Agas III (Hywood Papers, copy in SP)
Kappe, Lt.-Col, Lecture notes on the Malayan Campaign, delivered in Selarang barracks, 1942, (Les Hartshorne Private Papers)
Korum, Cpl, Statement by, (copy in SP)
Lee, Peter, Diary (copy SP)
Marshall, Ron, Obituary, 2/18th Btn Association Newsletter, No 106, July 1996.
Mosher, Imelda, copy of Address by Major F.A. Fleming, Christmas 1942 (Mosher Papers)
Muir, Paul, notes re Death March and Service record (Muir Papers, copy in SP)
Ollis, Ronald Nesbitt, Memoirs (Ollis Papers)
POWs, letters to families from Albert Anderson, John Barnier, Ray Carlson, George Plunkett, Bill MacDonald
Privilege in the Prisoner-of-War Camp, Paper delivered at AWM Seminar by Joan Beaumont, 12 February 1981 (Brown Papers)
Robinson, Graeme, Photographs, Memorabilia from 31 AWGU (Robinson Papers)
Shaw, Maj. J.A.L., Diary of, (Verdun Walsh Private Papers)
Short, Nelson, Diary of, and Statement of Experiences (Short Papers)
Steele, Report by Capt. Ray, (Steele Private Papers, copy in SP)
Taylor, Brigadier H., Lecture on the Campaign

of Singapore Island, delivered at Selerang 1942, (Les Harshorne Private Papers)
2/3 MAC, Unit Notes, (Shoebridge Papers)
27th Brigade War Diary (copy), (Verdun Walsh Private Papers)
Wells, Rod (extensive correspondence, SP)
Wilkins, Tony (various memorabilia, Wilkins Papers)
Young, Bill (paintings, sketches of Sandakan Camp, Outram Road Gaol), (Young Papers)

Interviews

Ex-Military Personnel/Experts in Various Fields:

8th Division veterans, including Keith Botterill, Ray Brown, Stan Bryant-Smith, Ted Burrey, Owen Campbell, D Carment, Roy Cornford, Alec Dandy, Eric Davis, Rus Ewin, Frank Gaven, Bob Goodwin, Athol Hill, Charlie Gersting, Jim Millner, Arch Mitchell, Ken Mosher, Neville Milston, Stan O'Grady, Ginty Pearson, Reg Piper, Rus Savage, Nelson Short, Ray Steele, Rod Wells, Roy Whitecross, Bill Young.

Ray Battram (War Graves Recovery), Ted Boyd (9th Division, Sandakan Force), Brian Burke (water, boiler engineer), Air Commodore W. 'Bull' Garing (ex-RAAF, WWII), Cyril Hutchings (steam expert), Skeet Hywood (ex-SRD), J. 'Lofty' Hodges (ex-SRD), Bruce McDonald (machinery expert) Paul Muir (AIF, AIB Signals Monitoring), Eric Pierce (water, boiler engineer), Tony Ramsay (wireless expert), Graeme Robinson (photographer, War Graves Recovery), Wing Commander Rowan Sharples (RAAF), Jack Sue (ex-SRD), Yoshi Tosa (all Japanese translations), David Wilson (RAAF Historical Branch)

Relatives of Borneo POW:

Various interviews with/papers, memorabilia of: Joyce Braithwaite, Richard Braithwaite Jnr, Ray Brown, David Bundey, Fay Corbert, Maureen Devereaux, Helen Evans, Joy Farnham, Jimmy Higgins, Marie McCarthy, Enid Maskey, Rod Moran, Bob Oakeshott, Eva Shepherd, Colleen Short, Mary Stanwell, Helen Sullivan, Judy Tomkyns and Toni Trotter.

Subject References

Owing to the complex nature of this book, for which hundreds of references were used, a departure has been made from the usual form of referencing. The text has been split into main subject areas, with full referencing for each subject covered, while the Endnotes, flagged in the text, refer only to additional or explanatory information. For locations of main references used, please consult the archival lists. Wherever possible, the subjects have been placed chronologically, as the action unfolds.

Note: Each of the Sandakan survivors, including those removed from the camp, has made a number of general statements. These statements include various testimony at the trials of Hoshijima, Yamamoto, Baba, Watanabe, Takakua as well as ABC radio interviews. The reference 'statement of' in the following notes, includes all statements made by the deponent.

The Singapore Campaign:

Printed books/periodicals: Allen, Barber, Bennett, Braddon, Burfitt, Callahan, Churchill, Cody, Day, Falk, Goodwin, Hall, Kirby, Leasor, Owen, Penfold, Percival, Silver, Simson, Smyth, Swinson, 2/19th Btn, 2/10 Fld Amb, 2/29th Btn, Time-Life, Wall, Walsh, Whitelocke, Wigmore, Young,.

Documents: Bennett Report, Burns Diary, Chalmers Diary, Kappe Lecture, Percival Despatches, Taylor Lecture, Troop Dispositions AIF, War Diary 8th Div., War Diary 27th Bde.

Private Papers: Brown Wartime Experiences; Letters of Barnier, Anderson, Carlson, Plunkett, MacDonald; Shaw Diary; Johnstone Diary, Marshall Obituary, 2/3 MAC Notes.

Interviews: Botterill, Brown, Bryant-Smith, Burrey, Campbell, Cornford, Davis E, Gersting, Hill, Mitchell, Mosher, O'Grady, Pearson, Piper, Short, Steele, Whitecross, Young.

Memorabilia etc: Braithwaite, J.&R., Brown, Corbett, Devereaux, Evans, Farnham, Higgins, McCarthy, Moran, Moxham, Oakeshott, Ollis, Short, C., Stanwell, Sullivan, Tomkyns, Trotter, Wells, Young.

Conditions, Singapore Camps, and AIF Morale:

Printed Books/Periodicals: Braddon, Burfitt, Goodwin, Howard, Penfold, Time-life, Wall, Wigmore, Wyett, Young.

Documents/Statements: Blow, Braithwaite, Brown Experiences, Burns' Diary, Campbell Comments by Official Historian, Short memoirs, Sticpewich.

Interviews, papers of: Blow, Botterill, Brown, Bryant-Smith, Carment, Davis E., Millner, Short, Wells, Whitecross, Young.

Personal Details of AIF members:

See 'Relatives of Borneo POW' in Bibliography.

Composition of B Force:

Documents: B Force Roll.
Interviews: Botterill, Davis, E., Ewin, Millner, Wells, Young.

Voyage on Yubi Maru:

Books: Connolly & Wilson, Hanada, Young.
Statements/Documents: Botterill, Braithwaite, Burns Diary, Carment, Davis, S., Jackson Rpt., Maffey, Sticpewich.

Interviews: Botterill, Davis, E., Davis, S., Wells, Young.

Description Sandakan/Movement to The Eight Mile Camp:

Books: Evans, Firkins, Keith, Wallace, Young.

Documents/Statements: B Rpt, Burns Diary, Jackson Rpt, SRD files, A22, A31; Sticpewich, Wells, photographs, maps.

Statements/Interviews: Botterill, Wells, Young.

Civilian Life under Japanese Administration:

Books: Evans, Firkins, Keith.

Documents: Steele Rpt.

The Sandakan POW Camps, July 1942— September 1943:

Books: *Borneo Burlesque*, Connolly & Wilson, Goodwin, Wallace, Young.

Documents: B Rpt, B Roll, Burns Diary; Death Records, Jackson Rpt, Johnstone, Lee, SRD/ Intelligence Reports, Maps (see A22 and Hoshijima trial also), aerial photographs; Nagai (re rice rations), sketches of Compound by Unknown Artist and Young, Steele Rpt, War Crimes files re treatment at Sandakan, 23/31 WGU records, Webb Rpt, Wilson (re food purchases).

Statements: Botterill, Braithwaite, Campbell, Davis, S., Fleming, Maffey, Nagai, Rayson, *Six from Borneo*, Sticpewich, Trackson, Wagner, Wells.

Memorabilia: Carlson, Barnier

Interviews: Botterill, Davis, E., Davis, S., Ewin, Millner, Wells, Young.

The Camp Water and Electricity Supply:

Davis, E. and Wells, technical advice from Burke and Pearce.

Airfield Construction/Treatment:

Books: Connolly & Wilson, Goodwin, Tanaka (Yamada interview p.16), Wallace, Wigmore, Young.

Documents/Statements: B Rpt, Botterill, Braithwaite, Campbell, Fleming, Hirota Nobuo (AWM 54 1010/4/174), Maffey, Moxham, *Six from Borneo*, Sticpewich, War Crimes Trials re treatment at Sandakan, Yamawaki (papers relating to, MP 742 336/ 1/1416)

Interviews: Botterill, Davis, E., Young.

The Sandakan Underground:

Books: Evans, Firkins, Keith, Tanaka (re uprising in Dutch Borneo), Wallace, Wigmore.

Documents/Statements: Apostel, B Rpt, Carment, Funk J, Funk P, Jackson Rpt, Jackson statement, Koram, Laband, *Six from Borneo*, Sticpewich, Taylor, War Crimes Trials re Sandakan & Matthews, Wells, Weynton, Wong.

Interviews: Davis, E., Ewin, Milston (re Matthews biog), Mosher, K., Wells.

Early Escapes:

Books: Wigmore.

Documents/Statements: B Roll (notations), B Rpt, Burns Diary, Jackson Rpt, Laband, Sticpewich, Trackson, SRD file V17, War crimes File MP742 336/1/1740

Outram Road Gaol:

Books: McGregor, Silver (*Heroes*), Young.

Statements: Trackson, Wells.

Interviews: Wells, Young.

Signing Ze Oase:

Books: Goodwin, Wallace, Young.

Statements/Documents: B Rpt, Braithwaite, Burns Diary, Ewin, Hoshijima statement, Hoshijima trial, Jackson Rpt, Wells, Young.

Camp Morale:

Interviews: Botterill, Davis, E., Davis, S., Ewin, Millner, Wells, Young.

The Wireless and Transmitter:

Books: Wallace

Documents/Statements: Apostol, B Rpt, Funk, J., Jackson Rpt, Wells, Wong.

Interviews: Ramsay, Wells.

British Experiences:

Documents: Burial records, Nominal rolls, Johnstone, Lee, War Crimes File MP 742 336/1/1470.

Movement of POWs to Kuching:

Annotations, B Force Roll

E Force to Sandakan Camp:

Books: Goodwin, Keith, Richardson, Wallace, Wigmore.

Documents/Statements: Blow, B Rpt, Campbell, E Rpt, Jackson Rpt, Koram, POWs Borneo (AA VIC), Steele Rpt, Short Diary.

Interviews: Campbell, Gaven, Short, Steele.

E Force & Wallace Escapes/Shooting of McKenzie and Harvey:

Books: Richardson, Wallace.

Documents/Statements: Blow, B Rpt, Funk P, Jackson Rpt, Koram, Lee Diary, Steele Rpt, War Crimes MP742 336/1/153, AWM54 1010/4/174; War Graves Records.

The Sandakan Incident, Trials, Execution:

Books: Evans, Firkins, Goodwin, Wallace.

Documents/Statements: see Sandakan Underground refs and War Crimes trials.

APPENDIX 6: BIBLIOGRAPHY AND SUBJECT REFERENCES

Interviews: see Sandakan Underground refs, also Botterill re Graham's pistol.

Double Tenth Uprising:
Books: Evans.
Documents: SOA Files A7, O8, O10.
Interviews: Sue.

Operation Python/Fate of Brandis, Rudwick, Mckenzie:
Documents: SOA Files A7, O8, O12, O13, O14, V7, V16; War Crimes Files 1470,1548 (AA VIC).
Interviews: Sue.

Background to Special Operations/Falcon, Rimau, Timor Projects:
Books: Silver (*Heroes, Krait*).
Documents: SOA Files C17, O7, O8, O9, O12, O13, O14; Silver (*Report on Special Operations Australia*).

SRD Operations in BNB (All Agas Missions, incl. Kingfisher):
Documents/Statements: SOA Files, A1, A2, A3, A4, A5, A5a, A22, A28, A31, A32, 37, H1, H9, H10, H13, J1, J2, J3, J26, J31, K3, M1, M3, N1, V9, V10, V16, V17, V18, V19.
Interviews: Hodges, Hywood, Sue.

In the Sandakan Camps, September 1943–August 1945:
Documents/Statements: Botterill, Braithwaite, Campbell, Moxham, Short, Sticpewich, Death Certificates, various POW and Investigation Reports, Nominal Rolls, SRD Intelligence Reports, Maps, War Crimes Files re Sandakan.
Interviews: Botterill, Campbell, Short.

Behaviour of Camp Staff:
Documents: Botterill, Hoshijima statements (Hoshijima Trial); Short diary.
Interviews: Botterill, Campbell, Short.

The First March:
Documents/Statements: Botterill, Jackson Rpt, Moxham, Sticpewich (NB: some is hearsay), Webb Rpt, Investigation Files, SRD A1, A5a, H1, J1, J2, J3, J26, M3, V9, V10, V16, V17, V19 and War Crimes Files relating to march.
Interviews: Botterill.

Events Leading to Collapse of Rescue Mission:
Documents: SOA File A1, reports, signals etc, 8A, 15, 22, 29-32, 34, 35 (A, F, G, L, M), 37 (A-C, H, M, N); File A5a, reports of 4, 16, 30 April 45 & 11, 20, 21, 22, May; File H1, reports of 4, 15, 24 April & 10, 21, 24, May; File V5 Schedule of Current Operations.

Statements/Interviews: Sue, John Overall (Canberra Times 6/2/95); J Chapman 16/10/45 (SP).

The Labuan Parties:
Documents: Information on Labuan, Brunei, Miri in MP 729/8 44/431/101, AWM54 779/3/82, AWM54 1010/4134, Nominal Rolls, WGU Registrations.

Paginatan and Ranau Camps:
Documents/Statements: Botterill, Moxham, Short, Sticpewich, Intelligence information in SRD Files A1, A5a, various POW and Investigation Reports, Webb Rpt, WGU Records, War Crimes Files relating to Ranau Camps.
Interviews: Botterill, Short.

The Second March:
Documents/Statements: Braithwaite, Campbell, various POW and Investigation Reports, Jackson Rpt, Short, SRD files (see previous entry, first march), Sticpewich, War Crimes Trials relating to march, Webb Rpt.

Sandakan Massacres:
Documents: War Crimes Files re Last POW, Crucifixion, Massacre 23.

War Crimes Trials Documents:
See various crimes in AA VIC, AA ACT and AWM.

Post-War Investigations:
Documents: See various files relating to investigations, Borneo Mission, War Graves Units, Missing POW, etc.

Press Coverage/Censorship:
Newspaper items: See main list, 1945–46.
Documents: AWM127 Item 25, and MP742/1/0 255/15/1291, B3856 146/1/16 (AA VIC) and Files relating to D Notices.

'No Planes' Announcement:
Newspapers: Various — see November/December 1947.
Documents: A663/1 O148/2/470, A5954 256/6, A5954 676/9, data extraction re C47 maintenance sheets.
Interviews: Sue.

Kingfisher Cover-up:
Documents: For evidence of, see SOA File A22 (all 'working' paperwork, signals, RAAF & RAN instructions, memos etc missing); Official History File O8 (no reference to Agas problems Oct 44-Mar 45; vital material in SOA Files A1, 5a, 7, H1 omitted).
Statements/Interviews: Sue, John Overall (Canberra Times 6/2/95).

Endnotes

Chapter 2: Selarang

1. His brothers were Henry (Harry) and Tom. Harry drowned on 12 September 1943 when *Rokuyu Maru*, was torpedoed in the South China Sea en route to Japan by an American submarine. Tom, who survived the sinking by gaining control of a rowing boat after drowning the craft's only occupant, the ship's captain, was rescued and taken to Japan. He died in Tamworth, NSW on 21 December 1997.

Chapter 3: To Sandakan

1. In an interview fifty years later POW escort Masharu Yamada 'recalled' the name of the ship as *Umi Maru* — 'Ship of the Ocean'. However, the name etched on a metal plate, 'souvenired' from the vessel by one of the POWs and found post war was *Yubi Maru*.

2. Harrington died in Kuching Gaol on 12 December, a day or so after the others sailed. The two officers remained in Kuching.

Chapter 4: White Coolies

1. The date of the opening is not clear, but Young says it was before Christmas and at the height of the monsoon.

Chapter 6: Comings and Goings

1. According to Japanese records, 641 officers and men and two Australians (Andrew Sommerville and Albert Tyrrell) remained in the British Camp (dead or alive) after the transfer of 31 officers and two ORs to Kuching, and another 100 (including one Australian, Sapper Aubrey Zinn) to Labuan. The number which arrived initially at Sandakan therefore must have been 776. Another 51 died at Jesselton and 10 on the voyage from Singapore, bringing the number which left Roberts Barracks to 837.

2. His mates were Ptes E.R. Burnett, E.L.G. Wilkie and K.P. Kelly, all of Queensland.

3. McLaren's story, as told to Hal Richardson in *One Man War*, contains a number of inaccuracies, including the name of the officer, which is given as Evans.

4. For list of 14 who stayed behind, see Nominal Roll, Kuching. The 15th was Geelan, who died at Labuan.

5. The 16 extras were Anderson, W.O., Brady, C.P., Cain, C.J., Dyson, F., Evans, J.W., Green, T.W, Hitchins, R., Jacob, G.W., Kemp, H., Lambert, G., Le Fevre, R., Lupton, L., McCullough, W.N., McDonald, C.H., Moore, T.A., O'Connor, J.H.

6. Steele says 1800 tonnes, Fairley 1300, McClaren says 900.

7. Gavan confirms the guards were 6 feet away, not 6 feet tall as was claimed by one writer.

8. Another statement by Morioka Teichichi, File 416, AWM 54 1010/4/174 gives name of executioner as Nagura.

9. The first known remains buried at the new cemetery were those of Private Dalton-Goodwin of Western Australia, who died on 1 May 1943. A small number of Australians were cremated.

Chapter 11: To Ranau

1. In Botterill's transcribed statement, this incident took place at the 16 mile, but, in 1996, Botterill stated that no one died until the fourth day, when the NCO was shot, by which time his group was between the Kolapis and Muanad Rivers. It appears, that 16 was typed instead of 46.

2. Haye's mess tin was also found at the site post-war.

3. The others were Jimmy Darlington, James Perry, Colin Ball and Jacky Jackson.

4. The Japanese figure of 455, the number given by Hoshijima and supported by figures supplied by over 40 Japanese on this march, has been taken as correct, (the group figures being 55, 50, 50, 55, 55, 40, 50, 50, 50). In a post-war statement Sticpewich, who was not on this march, gives the number as 470. However, in the same statement he gives the breakdown of the groups (55, 55, 55, 50, 50, 40, 50, 50, 55), which only totals 460. He claims that group 3 had 55 POWs and that 22 died, a statement refuted by Botterill, who says there were 50 in his group and 10 died, figures also given by the Japanese officer in charge of this group. Sticpewich's claim that group 7 was entirely English is not correct as this is the group to which Moxham belonged. He also claims 9 died, while Moxham gives the figure as seven. At the trial of Yamamoto, although prosecutor Athol Moffitt cited Sticpewich's incorrect tally of 470, the court concluded that the figure was 'approximately 450'.

5. The numbers given by Moxham in his debriefing post-war are ambiguous. The bodies of 220 were recovered from Ranau 1 and Number 1 Jungle Camps. Since no more than 174 bodies from groups 1–5 are buried there (195 Australians, less thirteen rice-carrying less eight, who, with two Englishmen from groups 6-9 moved to Jungle Camp 2), another 46 must have come from Paginatan with groups 6-9.

Chapter 12: Annihilate them all

1. The number of POWs known to have been transferred to Labuan is 290 — 99 British and one AIF from Sandakan and 185 British and five AIF from Kuching. According to the Japanese another ten were sent from Kuching, but who they were is not known. The figures quoted have been derived from Japanese statements and recovery records. From the nominal roll it appears that, in order to minimise the number massacred (29 at the 6 mile and fifteen at the 5 mile), the dates of 39 POW deaths have been falsified.

2. No names on the flag tally with those

known to have been sent to Labuan. They may belong to British personnel who died at some other camp.

3. Cook is described by Botterill as being 'fat as a pig'.

4. 15 other Australians known to have died on 23 May were Arthur Baccus, 28, Fred Burnes, 37, Arthur Carlson, 27, Patrick Humfrey, 43, Francis Joseph Jones, 35, Cecil Mortimer, 33, James Oakley 33, Francis O'Brien, 34, Joseph Platford, 45, John Gordon Richardson, 32, Edward Robertson, 44, Bryan Robinson, 23, Albert Russell, 26, Vincent Thompson, 26, and Charles Wilson, 43. Two British POWs known to have died on 23 May were the RAF's Frederick Hobbs and Gunner Tonkinson, both aged 25.

5. The names of 4 other Australians and two Englishmen known to have died that day are: Hector Hamilton, 36; Redclyffe Harrington, 43; Norris Hunt, 40; Leonard Lindqvist, 32; Harold Ashmore, 42 of the British Army and Frederick Wells, 35, RAF.

6. Campbell gives the name of the fifth man as Jack Austen. No person by this name appears on any records or nominal roll as being a POW in Borneo. There was an Air-Craftsman Thomas Holister Austin, RAF, at Sandakan. However, even assuming that his date of death (17 February 1945) is incorrect, T.H. Austin is a most unlikely candidate since all British personnel were in Party 3, Groups 9, 10 and 11, while Campbell was in Party 2, Group 5. Gunner Leslie Hotston, is also eliminated as the records confirm that he died at Sandakan on 6 June 1945. There was, however the AAMC's Keith Hamilton Costin who, along with escapees Skinner, Webber and Emmett, has no proper record of death. While it is not known whether Costin was known as 'Jack' or if Campbell had the Christian name, as well as the surname, wrong, it is believed that the army stenographer taking down Campbell's deposition transcribed 'Jack Costin' as 'Jack Austen'. Such mistakes were not unknown. Private Orr (shot dead in March 1945) appears in war crimes paperwork as Private Hall.

7. Blatch was with Braithwaite at the 60 mile staging camp on 9 June. Tuanintin River is another 20 miles further west. It does not seem possible that Blatch could have taken, or be permitted to take, seven days to travel this distance, which the column reached sometime during 11 June. If the date, 16/6/45 given on the running sheet is accurate, the most likely explanation for his being in the area is that he, being somewhat stronger than many of the others, was kept behind to carry rice.

Chapter 13: As the situation dictates

1. The number said to have been sent on a third march is 75. The total claimed to have been left behind is 288. According to statements by the Japanese and Sticpewich, another 5 returned to the camp, bringing the total to 293. If 75 left the camp, 218 bodies should have been found. However 223 were recovered (200 in the compound, another 23 at the airstrip), which appears to be an excess body count of five, or six if Captain Mills's body, which was cremated (see Ch. 13) is taken into consideration. However, it appears that at least five of the eight who died on the day of transfer were buried in the compound. The other three were recovered from the slit trenches in the Number 1 camp. If these bodies are included in the tally, the Japanese claim that 75 went on the third march appears correct.

2. The total number of soldiers is given as 57. Since 37 were said to have come from the Okuyama Btn, it is assumed, since Corporal Katayama was with the Okumura Btn, that the rest were also from this unit. Although the date of departure of this march is given variously as 9, 12 and 15 June, it is believed the latter date is correct since (a) other evidence puts the POWs in the vicinity of the 15 mile in mid-June and (b) Chester's and Sue's observations, made on about 25 June in the vicinity of the 40 mile peg, is in keeping with the calculated progress of the column.

3. The only British officer whose name was difficult to pronounce and who answers Wong's description — senior officer, receding hair, moustache, hooked nose and quite tall, (5'10") is Captain Mills. Because Wong's description of the officer's headgear matched that of a naval captain, it was assumed that the victim was from the RN. However, no naval officers, apart from Sligo, who died in 1943, were imprisoned at Sandakan. If the cap was a naval cap, Mills may have taken it from a clothing pool. Mills' date of death is given as 3 July, which is in keeping with the movements of POWs at the camp and of Hinata and Moritake, who became ill shortly afterwards. The only other officer at Sandakan whose name was difficult to pronounce was Lieutenant Rolfe, who died on 26 June and who, besides being 2 inches shorter and fair-haired, was junior to Mills. It seems that the crucifixion victim was Captain Mills. *Note:* Although Wong has given descriptions of at least three separate POWs in his statements (one being Chipperfield of the AIF) it seems that the British officer was definitely crucified after the third group of prisoners had left for Ranau, when the Number 2 Compound was again in use. Had his crime occurred while the British were still in exclusive residence (that is, before April 1945), Sticpewich and Short would most certainly have learned of it when the British and Australian camps were amalgamated.

4. According to Japanese confessions, two POWs only were alive on the evening of 14–15 August. According to Japanese records, both Skinner and Hancock died on 15 August. According to Wong, the last POW left alive was tall, had black hair and, before the rations were cut, was well-built. Central Army Records show that

Skinner (aged 31) was 5'10" (178cm) tall, heavily built and with dark hair, while Hancock (aged 42) was 5' 5" (165 cm) tall, of slight build, with dark hair and glasses. The skeleton exhumed from the slit trench was estimated by Sticpewich as being 6' 2" (188 cm). While forensic experts advise that estimation of the height of a person from decapitated skeletal remains laid out on the ground is difficult, they agree that Hancock's short stature precludes any possibility of his being the victim. While a 4" (10 cm) error in the estimation of the height is understandable, not even a layman would make an error of 9" (23 cm). *Note:* This evidence, presented by the author to the Commonwealth War Crimes Commission in 1997 was accepted as sufficient to identify the remains found in the slit trench as those of Skinner.

Chapter 14: And then there were six

1. Sticpewich identifies the man as 'Sapper Moore'. However, there is no trace of any engineer by that name dying at Ranau.

2. According to the death certificate, Bird died on 9 July. According to Sticpewich he died on 8 July. It seems likely, as was known to be the case in other death dates, that the date on the official record is the date on which the death was reported or the date of burial. That Bird did not die on 7 July, was confirmed by Botterill in 1996, when he told the author the truth about what had really happened — see Chapt.15.

3. In some other statements, Sticpewich says that 32 were alive. However, his statement to War Graves, citing 40 as the number, confirms the figure gleaned from death records. It appears that the figure of 32 refers to the number of Australian ORs alive including himself and Reither on 28 July. For a full list of those still alive on this date, see note 4, Chapt.15.

4. It appears that Zimban and Gimbahan, the name given by Ripley as Sticpewich's messenger, are one and the same person.

5. Decades later, Short stated that the gunfire must have been the sound of the Ranau POWs being murdered. However, this assertion is discounted as (a) owing to the density of the foliage and the heavy humid atmosphere, the sound of rifle fire travels only a few hundred metres in the jungle. At this point the escapees were twenty kilometres away from the camp; and (b) the dates do not coincide. The murders at Ranau took place on 1 and 27 August. On 1 August Moxham, Short and Botterill were still with Baragah. On 27 August they had been evacuated to Labuan.

6. At 5pm on 15 July Cooper strafed possible Japanese concentrations N-W of Ranau. Turning sharply into the valley he came back for a second pass when, trying to avoid high ground, the aircraft flicked, hit a tree, flipped over and crashed in flames to the east of the track. He was posted missing in action.

7. This figure of 2434 includes the survivors themselves. The figures for Sandakan were 1787 Australians and 641 British left after the removal of the others to Kuching and Labuan.

Chapter 15: And not leave any traces

1. The names of the guards assigned to Okada Toshiharu were Hirioto Ginjiro, Hirouchi Jiro, Matsuda Nobunaga, Miake Tadeo, Morikoa Teikichi, Shoji Shinsuke, Yoshikawa Tatsuhiko, Yoshioka Shigeo and Yasuyama Eikichi.

2. The Japanese stated that one grave was for the murdered and the other for those who had died of natural causes. A total of 40 POWs were alive on 28 July. As there were only 32 left on 1 August, eight must have died in the interim period. As Sticpewich stated that those who died on 27 and 28 July were not buried (three on 27 July, one on 28 July), twelve who had died of natural causes since 27 July must have been buried on 1 August. The three who died on 27 July were: Sgt Tom McDermott (40, RAF); Pte Reginald Bobbin (29, AASC); Cpl Hurtle O'Connor (29, AAMC). Pte Colin Chapman (30, 2/20 Btn) died on 28 July. Lt Chopping, whom the Japanese claim died before the massacre of the officers, must have either been among the sick or have died prior to the cemetery murders, as he was still alive when Sticpewich left.

3. The guards assigned to Tsuji were Fukushima Maseo, Goto Tsuneyoshi, Hayashida Kiyoshi, Kaneshige Yoshio, Matsuba Shokichi, Moriata Maseo (a Kempei-tai corporal), Takeuchi Yoshinitsu, Nishikawa Moriji, Suzuki Saburo and Toyoka Ekjiro. Tomiyama was also in attendance but was not required to take any part in the killing.

4. The thirty Australian ORs still alive on 28 July who subsequently died or were murdered were: Jim Burgess, 39*; John Burke, 38*; George Bolton, 33; John Codlin, 36; Thomas Connolly, 36; Albert Doyle, 27; Len Doyle, 37; Owen Evans, 24; Andrew Ferguson, 38*; Jimmy Finn, 24**; Frank Fitzpatrick, 45; Len Gagan, 24; John Kealey, 36*; Joe Kopanica, 25; Bill McDonald, 44*; Jack McMartin, 23*; Lance Maskey, 27; Douglas May, 28**; Ernest Munro, 34*; Edmund Noonan, 28*; Johnny O'Donohue, 24*; Lawrence Paulett, 33*; Lyall Powell, 25*; Thomas Reading, 33; George Shepherd, 25*; Edward Terrett, 25**; Arthur Thorns, 27*; William Vaughan, 26; Don Wilkinson, 25*; and Ray Wiseman, 25*. (Names marked with * came from the country, those without, from the city. For those with ** there is no information.) The three Australian officers were George Cook, 38; John Oakeshott, 44; Domenic Picone, 36.

The four British ORs were: Roy Hodgson, 24, RA; Joe McClandless, 28, RAF; Albert Sands, —, RAF and Samuel Smith, 38, RAF. The three officers were Humphrey Burgess, 41, RAF; Geoffrey Chopping, 26, RA, and Frank Daniels, 39, RA.

5. For full list of tags, identified by author, see *Relics*.

Chapter 16: 'A most regrettable business'

1. The ORs were two Australian soldiers named Hanley and Thornley. The overseers were Sompik (a Javanese), two Dusans named Ayuh and Gileh, and Adamat, who had previously acted as an interpreter.

2. It does not seem possible that this body, buried in Plot 21, Row C, Grave 6, which co-ordinates show was recovered at Tampias itself, is that of Thompson. According to Sticpewich, he died $1^{1}/_{4}$ miles east of Tampias, and to Japanese records, 2 miles. As identification was based on Sticpewich's statement, it seems that Thompson's identity was given to the wrong set of remains. From available evidence, it appears that the body buried in Grave 6 is actually that of NX 10233, Gunner John Nicholson, the only prisoner recorded as dying at the river. It is believed Thompson's body, one of three recovered in the same area and the last before the river, is currently buried in Labuan in Plot 21, Row C, Grave 1.

3. It seems certain that these remains, buried away from the others, are those of Albert Cleary. According to Botterill, the body was buried, but not with the others, an edict perfectly in keeping with Japanese who wanted to impose an additional 'punishment' on an already 'disgraced' corpse. The half-pair of glasses provides no clue. One of the most valuable items a POW could acquire was a spectacle lens to concentrate the rays of the sun and so provide the means for making a flame.

4. They were Sergeant Roberts, Corporal McManus, Private Reading, an interpreter and coolies.

5. This figure includes two skeletons from the ORs' massacre site, whose skulls were not found, and so were not officially counted as 'bodies'.

6. The figures for the three camps during this search were 170 dead (169 recovered) at 1 Ranau, 46 dead (46 recovered) at Number 1 Jungle, and 187 (167 recovered, including sole body to west, and two skull-less remains) at Number 2 Jungle. (Number 2 Jungle: 183 arrive on second march, joined by 6 from first=189, plus four bodies already buried=193, less six escape=187). The bodies of Anderson and Reither, which were also recovered, are not included in the tally. NB: This final tally was 170 recovered Ranau 1, 46 at Jungle 1 and 181 (6 missing) at or from Jungle 2.

7. For list of victims, see *Burial Table*.

8. According to Davis, Sticpewich claimed he was 'promoted in the field' by Lord Mountbatten, who had visited Labuan shortly after the Japanese surrender.

9. The most likely person to be the owner of this watch is Sergeant-Major John Stanton, aged 25, of the Dental Unit, who died in the Number 2 Jungle Compound on 16 July. As far as can be ascertained, he is the only POW who can be associated with Concord, a western suburb of Sydney.

10. These figures were extracted from the EE88–RAAF Aircraft History Sheets maintained for each aircraft, by staff at the RAAF Museum, Point Cook.

Index

Note: This index has been restricted to key figures and multiple entry names. Names appearing in Appendices, with the exception of Endnotes, have not been repeated in the index.

Abe, Lt K 188, 202, 204, 270, 274
Abin, Sgt 54, 58, 86, 88, 91, 102, 108, 126, 127, 133,134, 153
Adzcona, Felix 53, 109, 134, 153
Agas missions, personnel 174-6, 178-84, 207, 231, 232, 240-2, 248-9, 251-8, 260-1, 265-7, 274, 299
AIB, agencies, personnel 138, 172-3, 175, 238,
AIF, Singapore
    Changi camps 21, 22, 27, 28
    discipline 23, 24, 28
    hospitals 16, 17, 18, 20, 21, 24, 25
    positions of 7, 9, 17
    working parties 24, 25, 26, 27, 30
air raids 164-5, 168-70, 185, 207-8, 220-1, 223, 226, 249
Alberts, Gnr Wally 201,294,309
Ali Asar 86, 111-2, 234, 237
Allen, Dvr E.A. 54-7, 256
Allie, Cpl Norm 209-10, 212
Anderson, Pte Albert 12, 6, 33, 34, 222, 263
Anderson, Dot 34, 281
Anderson, Gnr F (Andy) 245, 246-8, 269, 291, ch16 n6
Annear, Pte Len 32, 162, 167, 216
Apostol, Lamberto 53, 58, 64, 86, 90, 106, 111, 124, 125, 133, 134, 153
Apple party 172-4, 180, 216
Armstrong, Cpl J 285-6
Aruliah, Samuel 126, 135

Baba, Gen 270, 287
Bancroft, Sgt Errol 167
Baragah, Katus 247-54, 291, 297, ch14 n5
Barber, Pte Gordon 166,167
Barnier, Pte John 11-13, 32, 34-5, 112-3, 118, 158, 194, 222, 234, 281, 307
Barnier family 11,34-5, 281, 284, 307, 311
Beale, Maj 17, 24, 126
Beardshaw, A-C Herbert 203, 262, 289
Bennett, Gen H. Gordon 12, 20, 31
Beppu, Yoichi 208, 258, 259, 260
Berhala Camp 107-8
B Force,
    composition of 31-4
    to Sandakan 36-43
Bird, Spr Arthur (Dickie) 215, 245, 259, 275, 311, ch14 n2
Blackledge, F-L t R 120, 142, 214
Blain, Sgt A. Macalister 97, 122, 133, 151, 304, 305, 307
Blamey, Gen Thomas 138, 174, 184, 231, 282, 301-7

Blatch, Gnr Wally 10, 14, 47, 226, 228, 308, ch12 n7
Blow, Lt Rex 104, 115, 184, 233 (also, Dit Party)
Bostock, AVM William 177, 304, 307
Botterill, Pte Keith 9-10,17-8, 24, 26-7, 33-4, 36, 46, 49, 52, 60, 68-9, 78, 85, 126, 141-3, 161-5, 167, 169-70, 189-93, 185, 197, 199, 201-2, 205-12, 215-6, 245-8, 250, 252, 254-6, 269, 271, 274-6, 280, 282, 286-7, 292, 294-5, 297, 307-11, ch11 n1, n4; ch14 n2,n3; ch16 n3
Boundy, Lt 51
Bowe, Pte Jim 32, 107, 119, 162, 167, 217
Braithwaite, Bdr Richard 10, 14, 32, 38, 47, 161, 164-66, 169-71, 220, 225-31, 263, 280, 307-8, ch12 n7
Brazier, Lt L 288-90, 293, 294
British POWs 99-101, 120-1, 131, 142-3, 157, 165, 213, 216-7, 223, 251, 257, 292, ch6 n1
Brown, Mr G 54, 58, 90, 106, 123
Brown, Pte M.P. 78, 92, 94-6, 118, 256
Brown, Capt R. H. (Pom) 128, 144
Bryant, Pte John (Snowy) 81-2, 216
Bundey, Sgt George (Bill) 82, 216
Burgess, F-Lt Harry 99, 222, 259-60, ch15 n4
Burns, Pte Tom 5, 6, 9, 13, 18, 19, 21, 27, 32, 36, 38, 46, 55, 63, 72, 73, 120, 143, 158, 171, 189, 223, 236, 263, 293,311
Butler, Pte Rex 113-6, 147 (also, Dit Party)

Callaghan, Lt-Gen (Boots) 31, 34,103
Campbell, Capt C. F. 214-5
Campbell, Maj George 56, 257
Campbell, Lt-Col H.A. 175, 231
Campbell, Gnr Owen 142, 160, 166, 173, 225-6, 239-41, 280, 308, ch12 n6
cannibalism, 265, 266, 278
Carlson Pte Ray 12,32,112-3, 158, 223, 234
Carr, Pte Matt 54-7
Carter, Dvr George 204, 216, 223
Carter, Gnr Perc 197-8
censorship 276-8, 283-6
Chan (Ah) Ping 48, 58-9, 64, 86-7, 102, 111, 127-8, 153
Chapman-Walker, Lt-Col John 174,175,177
Chester, Maj F. 'Gort' 137-9, 145-9, 173-6, 178, 180-3, 185, 207, 220, 230-3, 260-1, 300, 302, 307, 309, ch13 n2
Chifley, Ben 303-7
Chipperfield, Gnr Bob 189, 194, 196, 235, ch13 n3
Chopping, Lt Geoffrey 142, 217, 222, ch15 n2, n4
Christie, Admiral 175, 178

INDEX

Christie, Cpl Neil 12, 13, 28, 32, 104, 118, 216, 224, 311
Cleary, Gnr Albert 198, 199-201, 213, 245, 275-6, 292, 309, 311, ch16 n3
Clement, Pte Arthur 166, 167, 217
Codlin, Sgt John (Mort) 121, 259, ch15 n4
Cohen, Mrs Moselle, 53-4, 73, 115, 133-4, 257
compensation, post-war 297, 298, 299
Constable, Sig Bill 87, 219
Cook, Capt George 112, 118-20, 141, 161-2, 166-7, 169, 171, 189, 216-9, 222, 244, 246, 251, 259, 270, 273, ch12 n3, ch15, n4
Cooper, F-Lt Harold 256, 269, ch14 n6
Costin, Pte Keith 226, 239-40, ch12 n6
Cox, Pte Keith 162
Crease, Gnr Wally 197-200, 245, 292, 294, 311
Crome, Pte Joey 32, 39, 76, 78-80, 118-9, 213
Cross, Cpl Arthur 167, 216
Cull, Pte Arthur 167-8

Daniels, Capt F 120, 142, 163, 222, 259, 260, ch15 n4
Darlington, Pte Jimmy 81, 93-6, 118, 272, ch11 n3
Davis, Pte Eric (Mo) 9, 15, 20, 26, 32, 39-40, 60, 64, 71, 80, 84, 94, 103, 111-2, 117-9, 128,152, 155-6, 257, 293, ch16 n8
Davis, Pte Stan 123, 15
Davis, Spr Roy 124, 129, 256
death march 1,
 conditions etc 189-95, 197,202
 death toll 196, 202, 203, 205, 206
 route of 187-8, 193-5
 selection for 189, 202, ch11 n4
death march 2,
 conditions etc 215, 222-8
 death toll 288
 escapes from 225, 226-7, 229-30, 239-41
death march 3 232-3, ch13 n1, n2
de Klerk 104-5
Devereaux, Maureen (see Barnier family)
Dihil bin Ambilid (Godohil) 251, 291, 297
Dit Party 104,109,113-116,146
Dixon, WO Jonathan 222, 227-8
Dobson, Pte Trevor 78, 234
Dohohue, Pte James (Punchy) 32, 79-82, 162, 167, 189, 211
Dorizzi brothers 120, 189, 194, 196, 199, 269
Double Tenth Uprising 136-7, 140, 144, 145, 156

Eager, war correspondent 276-7, 278
Eddey, Maj H 103, 121, 122
E Force 102-8, 117, 142
Ehara, Sgt-Maj (Bulldog) 132-5, 245, 270
Eight Mile Camp,
 airfield 49-51, 60-1, 63-4, 66, 69, 70-2, 160
 airfield opening 76-7, ch4 n1

amalgamation of 142
arms at 89-90
arrests at 124, 126-31
burials at 122, 165-6, 169, ch6 n9
cages at 75, 111, 161-2, 164, 166, 167
conditions-description 46-9, 56-7, 66-70, 73-4, 92, 122, 131, 140, 142-3, 156-8, 163-8, 170-1, 216-21, 233-7
crucifixion at 234-5
death toll 57, 121, 142-3, 165, 169, 216-7, 235
discipline at 52, 160, 161-2, 166, 167
entertainment, morale at 78-85, 111, 120, 158-60, 168
escapes from 54-6, 90-1, 109-10, 113, 156-7, 166, 296
health/medicine at 73, 82-3, 122, 142-3, 157-8, 165, 170, 219, 234, 272
murders at 236-7,
officers, NCOs at 52-3, 60, 69, 141, 144, 160-2, 218
punishments at 66, 67-8, 129 (also, cages)
radio/transmitter 86-9, 101-2,
sabotage at 65, 71,72
tortures at 131-5
underground 53,54, 58-9, 64, 86-90, 97, 122-35, 144, 150-6

Ellis, Malcolm (Ek Dum) 284, 299, 304-5
Emmett, Cpl Ted 226, 239-40, ch12 n6
Evans, Dvr Owen 249, 250, 258, ch15 n4
Ewin, Lt Rus 56, 58, 69, 88, 126, 127, 129,155, 297

Fairley, Maj John 103, 105, 106
Fairy, Cpl W.F. (escape of) 91, 96
Filmer, Capt Charles 128
Fitzgerald, Cpl Gerald 141, 160, 224
Fitzgerald, Pte Les 246, 250
Fleming, Mr H J 33
Fleming, Maj E. 85, 87, 88, 89, 92, 97, 102, 108, 132
Ford, Pte W (Henry) 118, 119, 166
Forde, Frank 97, 166, 277, 278, 297, 305
Formosan guards (various) 67-8, 70, 93, 95, 97, 121, 164, 208, 210-12, 217, 227, 232, 235-7, 244-5, 250, 258-60, 270, ch15 n1,n3
Forster, Maj J. 253-5, 257
Frost, Gnr Norm 215, 245-6
Fugita Sgt-Maj 158, 199, 244-5, 258
Fukishima, Maseo (The Black Bastard) 76, 79-80, 92, 160, 224, 245, 259, 270, 275, ch15 n2
Fuller, Gnr Eric 203, 262, 289
Funk family 53, 58, 106, 118, 123, 125-6, 134-5, 153, 299

Gallagher, Lt-Col Fred (Black Jack) 30, 32, 103
Garland, Cpl Alan 103, 141, 160, 165, 199, 205, 291
Gaven, Capt Frank 105, 120
Gaven, Sgt Jack 83, 107, 120, 199

Gillett, Pte Keith (The Shearer) 81-2, 201, 216
Gillon, Lt Miles 104 (see Dit Party)
Glover, Cec and Fred 220, 228
Golding, Pte Ray 167, 216
Good, Lt Gordon 141, 170, 218, 222, 224, 250, 260, 270
Gotunda, Sgt-Maj 190, 192, 193, 274, 276
Graham, Cpl Tommy 17, 24, 32, 47, 124, 126, 129, 151
Grinham, Cpl L (Blue) 253, 255, 256
Grist, Pte Norm 209-10, 215, 245, 250
guerrillas 89, 116, 123-5, 135-7, 140, 144-7, 149, 184
Gundi, O.T. 261-2, 265

Hamner, Capt J. 139, 140, 146
Hancock, Sgt Walter 237, ch13 n4
Hardie, Sqn-Ldr E. 99-100, 120
Harrington, Dvr T I 54-7, ch3 n2
Harvey, Pte Howard 97, 109-10, 121
Hayashi, Yoshinori (Ming the Merciless) 163, 197, 205, 276
Haydon, Pte 'Bluey' 30
Heaslop, Capt Jim 57, 89, 141, 143, 222, 250, 260
Haye, Spr Len 197, 266, ch11 n2
Heggen, AVM Alan 310-11
Heng, Joo Ming 69, 84, 86-7, 90, 101, 109, 113, 124-6, 153
Hewitt, Pte Howard (The Turk) 103, 106, 108, 237, 293
Hewitt, Sgt Harry 161, 162, 224
Hewitt, Pte Norm 167, 216
Hodge, Pte J (Lofty')253-5
Hodges, Pte Rex 226, 227, 229
Hollingworth, Lt H 231, 241
Holly, Sgt R 123, 133
Horder, Sgt Robert 250
Hoshijima, Capt Susumi 42, 52, 59, 60, 62-3, 68-9. 74-5, 77, 84, 91-3, 95, 107-8, 111-2, 114, 117-20, 126-7, 130-1, 135,140, 142-3, 156, 160-2, 164-71, 188-9, 202, 216-9, 222, 225, 270-3, 283, 285-6, ch11 n4
Hosotani, Sgt Naoji 233, 265, 283
Humphries, Pte David 189, 193, 194
Hywood, Cpl Amos (Skeet) 182, 231, 241-2

Ings, Pte Jacky 17, 25, 32, 222, 223

Jacka, Dvr M.E. 54-7
Jackson, Col Harry & Borneo Mission 297-9
Jackson, Pte John (Jacky) 11, 223, ch11 n3
Japanese atrocities 20, 21, 24-5, 33, 36, 55-57, 89, 93-5, 125-35, 149-50, 169-70, 200, 221, 225, 265, 267, 285
Jeffrey, Capt Rod 31, 89, 141, 189, 199, 206-7, 209, 276
Jensen, Spr C 106, 108, 114, 133
Johnston, Pte C.A. (Vic) 32, 38, 47, 224
Jones, AM George 304, 307

Kada (Mad Mick) 67, 93, 270

Kawakami, Kyoshi (Gold-Toothed-Shin-Kicking-Bastard) 121, 163, 189, 197, 199-200, 208, 210-12, 259, 275-6
Keating, Spr Edward 106, 108, 114, 122, 133, 151
Keith family 54, 73-4, 77, 106,111,140
Kelly, Able Seaman H 107
Kennedy, Spr Jim 113-5, 147 (see Dit Party)
Kenny, General G 177, 304, 307
Kent brothers, 103, 106, 155-6
Kinder, WO John 160, 166, 205, 208, 211, 292
Kingfisher project
  cover-up 300-7
  project and personnel 176-7, 180-1, 184, ch16 n10
  questions in parliament 304-7
Kitamara, Kotaro 121, 160, 163, 167-8, 197, 270, 275-6
Kiyoshima, Tadeo (The Black Panther) 121, 163, 170
Kulang, O.T. 187, 196-7, 240-1, 265-7, 288-9
Kunizowa (Euclid) 163, 167-8, 169
Koram, Cpl 53, 64, 73, 108, 113, 115, 125, 129 298-9
Kuching Camp 44, 56, 168, 257

Labuan party 157, 166, 213-5, ch12 n1
Lagan, Ernesto 53, 89, 109, 113, 115, 125-7, 129, 134, 153, 299
Lander, Sgt Colin 123, 133, 150
Lim, Teng Fatt 123, 137,147,149
Lo, Jackie Ah Fok 92, 124
Longley, Pte Harry 12, 26, 30-2, 78, 93,250
Lytton, Pte Herb 32, 189, 209, 292, 309, 311

McAppion, Pte Eddie 32, 158, 224, 311
MacArthur, Gen Douglas 138, 175, 177, 181, 278, 301, 304, 305, 307
McDonald, S-Sgt Bill 13, 121, 168, 246, 251, 259, ch15 n4
McDonough. Sgt W. (Mac) 87, 93-4, 133
MacKay, Pte Theodore 97, 109-10, 121
McLaren, Pte R.(Jock) 104, 106, 107, 113-6, 184, ch6 n3
McMillan, Cpl 128,152
McWilliam, Pte Bruce (escape by) 91, 96
Maddock, WO Laurie 66, 120, 160-2, 222, 225
Maffey, Maj Errol 36, 118
Majinal, Dick 53, 54, 59, 86, 125, 133, 153
Malau, Cpl 213-4, 268
Manaki, Gen Takanobu 188, 219
Marshall, Spr Don 106, 108, 114, 133, 256
Martin, Pte Frank 97, 109, 110,133, 151
Maskey, Pte Lance 66, 161, 245, 258, ch15 n4
Matsuda, Kenji (Top Hat) 227-8
Matthews, Capt Lionel 53, 57-9, 64, 73, 87-9, 99, 113, 117, 124, 126-9, 132-3, 135, 150-6, 169, 219, 298, 309
Matusup bin Gangau 53, 92, 126, 143, 153, 298

Mavor, Gerald 53, 58, 86, 102, 125, 127, 133, 151
Mildenhall, Pte Jake 226, 227, 229
Mills, Capt J 142, 218, 223, 235, 272, 296, ch13 n1,3
Mills, Cpl C. 87 133, 151
Minty, Pte Allan (escape by) 91,96
Miura, Isamu 130
Moffitt, Capt Athol 271-2, 274, 284, ch11 n4
Molde, Pte Ken (Dawson) 143, 203, 262, 289
Mongan, Gnr Daniel 164
Moran, Pte Ron 14, 103, 223, 234, 263
Moritake, Lt 66-7, 95, 110, 122, 128, 158, 161-2, 202, 217-9, 232-7, ch13 n3
Morris, Pte Norm (escape by) 91, 96
Morriss, Seaman G 107, 221
Mosher, Capt Ken 33, 44, 65, 89, 94, 102, 174
Mosher, Imelda 174
Moule-Probert, Pte Johnny 38-9
Moxham, L-Bdr Bill 28-30, 32, 161, 165, 202, 203, 204, 208, 211, 212, 216, 245-8, 252, 254-6, 269, 271, 274-6, 282, 190, 297, 307, 309, ch11 n4, 5; ch 14 n5
Muir, Cpl Paul 171, 172-4, 216
Murozumi, WO Hisao 170-1, 189, 234-9, 295
Murray, Frank 307, 311
Murray, Pte Richard 9, 10, 17, 18, 24, 26, 33, 34, 36, 46, 49, 52, 60, 81, 142, 143, 161,163, 170, 189, 192-3, 195, 197, 201, 206-11, 275, 280-2, 292, 307-10

Nagai, Capt Hirawa 97-8, 101, 120, 122, 157-8, 197, 199, 200-1, 206, 208-9, 213, 268, 270, 286-7
Nakamura Koji 244
New, L-Cpl Fred (escape by) 91, 96
newspaper reporting 277-9, 281-2, 283-5, 299, 302, 304-5
Ney, Pte Bill 33, 216
Nicholson, John & Gerard 189, 194, 289, 311, ch16 n2

Oakeshott, Capt John 103, 141, 217, 222, 243, 245-6, 251, 259, ch15 n4
O'Donohue, Pte Johnny 11, 222, ch15 n4
Okada, Toshiharu 208, 276, 258
Okahara, Lt 38, 61, 65, 66, 68, 69
Okamura, Lt 146
Ollis, John & Ron 33, 141, 168
O'Loan, Maj Roderick 172-4
Orr, Pte Jack 217, 272, ch12 n6
O'Toole, Paddy 12, 15, 16, 257
Otsuka, Col 221
Outram, Pte Sid 39, 96, 118, 155
Outram Road Gaol 57, 256-7
Ozawa, Interpreter 56, 59, 62, 66, 79-80, 107, 118, 135, 151, 226

Parker, Pte Noel 202, 205, 275, 276
Percival, Gen Arthur 19, 20, 24
Phillips, Mr 53, 55, 102, 133

Picone, Capt Dominic 58, 94, 141, 170, 173, 216-7, 219, 222, 243, 245-6, 250-1, 259, 275, ch15 n4
Picken, Pte Jim 105-6, 142
Pickering, Pte Jim 128
Plunkett, Pte George 16, 17, 25, 32, 78, 222, 234
police constabulary 53-4, 64, 89, 109,134,153
post-war investigations 262-9, 280
POW records, 194, 224, 280
POWs, disposal of 180
POWs, final rescue plan 238-9
POWs, Japanese policy 188, 214, 218
POWs, massacre of American 181
POWs, rescue of American 181
Python, mission & personnel 137-40, 144-50, 156, 169, 173-4, 179, 232

Quadra, Alberto 108, 109, 115-16, 126
Quadra, Bernard 126
Quailley, Pte Allan (Sticky) 162, 163, 189, 194-5, 289, 309, 311
Qwok, Albert 123-4, 135-7, 140, 144-5, 147

Rae, Capt Vern 78, 124, 129,144
Ranau 1 Camp,
    conditions at 195-7, 201, 206-7
    escapes from 198
Ranau 1 Jungle Camp,
    conditions at 208-12
    massacre 212
rice carrying 197-8, 199, 200, 201, 202, 205, 206
Ranau 2 Jungle Camp,
    burials at 243
    conditions at 212, 215, 243-6, 249-50
    death toll at 243, 249, 250, 251, ch14 n3
    escapes from 246-8, 251-2
    massacres at 258-60
Read, Pte Wally 249, 297
Reither, Pte Herman 128, 251-2, 268, 291, 292, ch16 n6
Rice-Oxley, Police Chief 54, 64, 89, 106, 124,151
Richards, Pte Rod 203-4, 290
Richardson, Capt Rod 15, 17, 104, 114, 141
Rickards, Cpl J 87-8, 102, 133,151
Ripley, F-Lt, G.C. 231, 241-3, 248-9, 251-2, 255, 257-8, 260-2, ch14 n4
Risley, Pte Hilton (Terry) 118, 155
Roberts, Gnr Bois 203, 262, 289
Roberts, Cpl Fred F (Nutsy) 103, 117, 234
Roffey, Cpl 128, 152
Rogers, Fr John 103, 104, 142
Rolfe, Lt Ian 142, 263, ch13 n3
Rowell, Capt John 126, 128, 155
Rumble, Pte T 122, 133

Sachs, Lt John 179, 284-5
Salleh, Mohamet 54, 64, 108, 113-5, 126
Sandakan assistance group 53-5, 58-9, 90-1
    arrests, trial of 124-35, 144, 151-3, 155-6
    fate of 257

Sandakan town 40-42
Saurez, Lt-Col 89, 115, 123, 136, 140, 147, 149, 299
Shaw, Gnr Allan 220
Sheard, Gnr Wright 200, 311
Shelley, Dvr J.N. 54-7, 256
Sheppard, Col 48, 54, 58, 69
Scrivener, Capt Doug 56
Shipsides, Cpl Bob 12, 15, 30-2, 62, 81, 95, 118, 216
Short, Pte Nelson 20, 28-30, 103, 105, 142-3, 157-61, 168, 216, 222, 225, 245-8, 250, 252, 254-6, 271, 299, 307, ch13 n3, ch14, n5
Simpson, Cpl Henry (Gunboat) 80-1, 160, 224
Singapore campaign, 7, 8, 13,-15, 17-19
Sini (Chin Piang Syn) 90, 96, 113, 125, 153
Skinner, Pte Ted 120, 222, 226, 239, ch12 n6
Skinner, Pte John 120, 222, 237, 295, ch13 n4
Sligo, Lt Norman 53, 54, 55, 57
Small, Cpl Arnold 87, 133, 151, 256
Smith, Pte James 32-3, 210
Smyth, Sgt Colin 18, 120, 143, 189, 209
Sommerville, Pte Andrew 99
Soorier, A-C M. 217, 296
SRD, admin & personnel 138, 145, 149, 174-5, 178, 18-5, 207, 230-1, 239-40, 260, 270, 282, 285, 299, 300, 302, 304, 307
SRD missions (various) 178, 285, 302
Stacy, Sgt Richard 215, 245, 250, 260
Steele, Capt Ray 104-5, 147, 174, 280, 307
Stevens, Sgt Alf 71, 86, 111, 128, 152-4
Sticpewich, WO Bill 54, 68, 128, 156, 160-1, 166-7, 169, 216-7, 222-4, 226, 243-4, 249-52, 255, 268, 271-2, 274-5, 280-7, 290-2, 296-7, 307-8, ch11 n4; ch13 n1, n3, n4; ch14 n1, n2, n3, n4; ch15 n1; ch16 n6
St John, Capt Harold 128, 129, 141, 144
Stookes, Dr J 53, 91, 257
Sue, Sgt Jack Wong 179, 182-3, 231-33, 302, 307, 309, ch13 n2
Suga, Col Tatsuji 56, 65-6, 72, 100, 111-2, 152-3, 155, 164, 216, 219, 257, 270-1
Sugino, Sgt-Maj Tsuruo 213-5, 268, 270
Sullivan, Cpl Ron 198, 201-2, 281, 294, 309
Sullivan family, 202, 281
Sutherland, Gen R 176, 177
Suzuki, Lt 197, 199-200, 208-10, 212, 214-5, 244, 245, 258, 275
Suzuki, Saburo 197, 205, 208, 212, 216, 259, 270, 275-6, 309, ch15 n2

Takahara, 243, 250, 208
Takakuwa, Capt Takuo 91-2, 218, 220, 222-3, 225, 233, 235, 243-4, 250-1, 258-60, 270, 272-4, 285
Taka Maru 105-7
Tanaka, Capt Shojiro 203,204,274
Tanuke, Gov Kumabe 82-3, 263
Taylor, Pte Alan 160
Taylor, Brig Harold 9, 15, 34, 35, 82

Taylor, Dr Jim 53-4, 58, 64, 73, 88-90, 97, 113, 115, 125, 129, 132, 135, 151, 154, 257, 272
Temple, Pte Reg 167, 217
Thompson, Padre Albert 141, 228, 289, ch16 n2
Thompson, Gnr Bill 172, 216
Tomkyns, Gnr Eric 10, 14, 223, 234
Toyoda, Kokishi 68, 276
Toyohara, Lt 190, 191
Trackson, L-Cpl Herb 54-7
trials, POW 96, 150-4
Tsuji, Sgt-Maj 224, 228, 258, 259

Wagner, Lt Charlie 105, 108, 114
Wallace, Sgt Walter 42-3, 46, 69, 84, 86-7, 90, 96-7, 109-10, 113-4, 116, 124-6, 147, 174
Walsh, Lt-Col Alf 34, 46, 52, 59, 62-3, 68-9, 106-7, 155, 280
Wanless, Padre John 120, 142, 250
war crimes policy 271
war crimes trials & investigations 271-6, 278, 282-7
Wardale-Greenwood, Padre Harold 14, 97, 141, 222, 224, 228, 250
War Graves Units & recovery 263, 269, 287-97, 299, ch11 n5; ch13 n1; ch16 n2, 3, 5, 6
Warrington, WO Clive 190-1, 209
Watanabe, Sgt 143, 160, 169, 202
Watanabe, Lt Genzo 221, 223, 224, 228, 245, 249, 258, 260, 270, 273
Watson, WO Charles, 189, 198
Webb, Sir William 278, 286
Webber, Pte Sid 226, 239-40, ch12 b6
Weeks, Sig Fred 166, 167, 217
Wells, Lt Rod 33, 56, 58, 59, 68, 71, 86-9, 99, 101-2, 118, 124, 126-8, 130-1, 151-4, 156, 256, 308-9
Wells, Mrs 132
Weston,Sgt Joe 106, 108, 114, 133, 144
Weynton, Lt A. Gordon 69, 86-9, 101-2, 111-2, 126, 128, 130-3, 150-1
Willie, Mr B.S. (Sandshoe) 173, 183, 184, 187, 196, 229, 232, 240
Wilson, Mr Ronald 33, 69, 70, 213
Wong, Hiong 234-7, 295, ch13 n3
Wong, Mu Sing 89-90, 96, 109, 113, 123-5, 153, 298
Wong, Yun Siow (Pop) 52, 59, 72, 84, 86, 111, 133-4, 170
Workman, Maj 29, 59, 63, 69

Yamamoto, Capt Shoichi 186-8, 195, 270, 274, 284, ch11 n4
Yamawaki, Lt-Gen Masataka 77, 156, 186, 219
Young, Lt Philip 142, 223, 237, 263
Young, Pte Billy 11, 12, 15, 16, 24-6, 31-2, 36, 39, 49-52, 54, 60-1, 63-4, 69-70, 74, 76, 78-83, 85, 92, 94-6, 118-9, 165-6, 216, 250, 256-7, 272
Yubi Maru 36-41, 60, 78, 263, ch3 n1